Modern
WOODWORKING
TOOLS, MATERIALS AND PROCEDURES

by
WILLIS H. WAGNER
Professor, Industrial Arts, Technology
University of Northern Iowa, Cedar Falls

South Holland, Illinois
THE GOODHEART-WILLCOX COMPANY, INC.
Publishers

Library of Congress Cataloging in Publication Data

Wagner, Willis H
    Modern Woodworking.

    Bibliography: p.
    1.   Woodwork   I.   Title.
TT185.W32   1974   684'.08   74–8878
ISBN 0–87006–180–1

INTRODUCTION

Wood is one of our greatest natural resources. As a construction and building material, it continues to grow in importance and in popularity.

MODERN WOODWORKING provides up-to-date information about wood and wood products, and instruction in the use of hand and power tools in the woodworking field. It provides exploratory experiences which give the student an insight into the major areas of woodworking. The practical approach to design supplies guidelines which the student may apply to his construction activities. There is a section on mass production in the school shop. Good performance in this area is assured by the use of the many special setups, jigs and devices described.

MODERN WOODWORKING provides basic instruction and information in the areas of furniture construction, upholstery, cabinetmaking, patternmaking, and boatbuilding. Also included is an important unit on modern finishing materials and their application; those that are most practical for the school shop and those that are used in industry.

MODERN WOODWORKING illustrates and describes numerous industrial methods and processes. Procedures adaptable to the school shop are related to those in modern industrial plants. The importance of developing safe work habits is stressed throughout the text.

MODERN WOODWORKING covers the technical aspects of wood structure, growth, and physical properties of wood with which the student should become familiar. It includes also, sections on job opportunities, and establishing a home workshop.

MODERN WOODWORKING is intended to reflect the growing, expanding interest in wood and woodworking skills, and to help maintain woodworking as an important subject in the fields of Industrial Arts and Technical Education.

CONTENTS

Unit 1

PLANNING AND DESIGNING

Planning is a general term and may be as simple as determining activities for a day or as complicated as planning a house, a school building, or even a space capsule. It means thinking through an activity before it is performed. In modern industry, planning is one of the chief functions of the engineering department and includes such divisions as product selection and design, methods of fabrication, time schedules, plant layout, and equipment selection, Fig. 1-1.

terials, and methods of construction. If you are in a beginning class your instructor will very likely provide specific directions and rather complete planning materials for your first construction activities. After you complete several projects and/or exercises, you will then be able to prepare some of your own plans and designs.

As you gain more "know-how" and experience in woodwork, you will be expected to build more difficult and complicated projects. These will

Fig. 1-1. Planning and designing in a modern industrial plant.
(Charles Bruning Co.)

Great emphasis is placed on this activity because careful planning can save time, materials, and energy and insure a good product and a profitable operation.

In the school shop, you will find that careful planning will help you avoid mistakes, get more work done, and do better work. A complete planning operation in woodwork will include the following activities; project selection, developing or refining the design, preparing presentation drawings and working drawings; developing procedures, listing materials, and estimating costs.

In order to do a good job of planning in woodwork, you must have some knowledge of tools, ma-

intensify your interest and you will secure greater pleasure and satisfaction from the work. Give careful attention to directions and demonstrations presented by your instructors. Study your textbook and other reference material, and prepare and organize your planning materials so that you can make the best use of your class time.

Wood As A Construction Material

Wood is one of our most popular and versatile raw materials. It can be easily formed, shaped, and smoothed, and offers a variety of tones, grain patterns, and surface textures. In products where the visual aspects (appearance) are of major importance, the designer makes full use of these characteristics, Fig. 1-2.

The porosity or cellular structure of wood provides a material that is light in weight, relatively strong, and makes possible the driving and fitting of nails, screws and other metal fasteners. This porosity also accounts for its high insulating value (thermo resistivity) which causes it to seem warmer to the touch than a piece of metal. For example: touch a wooden bench top and then the metal jaw of the vise and note that the metal seems cooler than the wood even though they are the same temperature. This is one of the reasons many people prefer furniture and cabinets made of wood instead of metal or plastics.

Fig. 1-2. Well-proportioned chest cabinet with carefully selected walnut grain patterns. (Herman Miller, Inc.)

Designing Wood Products

Designing is a complex activity that includes creating, inventing, searching, and developing. It is a selective process where ideas are studied, tried-out, analyzed, and then either discarded or incorporated into the design. These ideas are recorded in words, drawings, or models.

At the outset, you should formulate a clear, concise statement of the problem, whether it be an original design or a modification and improvement of an existing design. This statement should include a description of the purpose and use of the product and any specific requirements concerning materials, size and shape. Thorough study should then be given to the problem. Information is gathered and decisions are made concerning the kind of material and methods of fabrication. Other products of similar design are studied. As possible solutions are visualized, they should be recorded in sketch form. At times it may be help-

ful to experiment with a few pieces of the kind of wood that has been selected. Test its workability and cut sample joints. A model or mock-up, built of a soft, inexpensive wood, may provide a worthwhile check on certain designs. These activities will require considerable time but are fully justified when a major project is undertaken.

Fig. 1-3 shows the three chief considerations in design and how they are interrelated. FUNCTIONAL requirements grow out of the use and purpose of the product. It must serve the purpose for which it is designed. A chair must provide comfortable support for the human anatomy. A chest should hold the articles for which it was designed. A tool holder must support the tool securely, protect its cutting edge, and permit easy removal. The function of a folding screen may be to separate space while the main purpose of a wood carving or wall plaque is simply to provide interest and beauty. When the function of a product has been clearly defined, certain guide lines will have been established concerning its form and other design requirements.

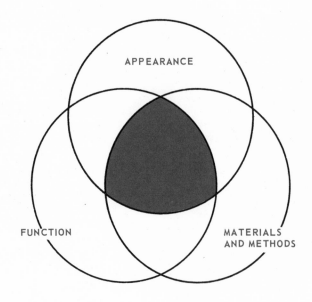

Fig. 1-3. Interrelationship of important design factors.

MATERIAL requirements are developed through a study of those that will be most suitable and appropriate. Consideration must be given to strength, beauty, durability and economy. Softwoods may be perfectly satisfactory for one structure and unsatisfactory for another. For example: red cedar, which has many appropriate uses, has color, grain, and structural qualities that are unsatisfactory for furniture construction. Select a wood that has the qualities and characteristics required. If a dark tone is desired, it is desirable to use a dark wood. Staining one wood to imitate another tends to destroy the feeling of genuineness that is essential in good design.

Other materials can often be effectively combined with wood. Metal legs may provide the best solution in a table design. Be cautious of extreme

Fig. 1-4. *This comfortable and attractive chair is made of appropriate materials, using practical construction methods. (Herman Miller, Inc.)*

contrasts. One material or kind of wood should dominate. Combinations of light and dark wood, sometimes used for turnings may detract from the basic form and result in a "flashy" or "gaudy" product that is soon discarded.

METHODS of construction must be given consideration as materials are selected. The size of structural parts and types of joints or fasteners will not be the same for weak, soft-textured woods as for those that are strong and hard. Some experimentation with the material may result in improved joinery methods or a reduction in the size of the parts. Make use of new glues and bonding methods, plywood and hardboard, laminated construction, special metal fasteners, and other new methods and products that extend the design potential of wood.

The APPEARANCE (visual aspect) of the design is the most difficult to handle, especially for the beginner. In good design you must recognize such principles as proper balance; correct proportion; unity and harmony among the various elements; points of emphasis and interest; compatible colors; and interesting textures. There are no firmly established rules or standards that can be applied to appearance, and learning to recognize good design will take time and effort. Simply memorizing a list of principles will be of slight

value. Your ability in this area will grow through experience, practice, and reflection. Study articles that are well designed. Analyze them with respect to their function, materials used, construction features, and how an attractive and pleasing appearance was obtained.

Today, designers of wood products place great emphasis on function. They then build the design through the use of smooth, trim lines; simple shapes and forms; and interesting grain patterns, colors, and textures. They are cautious about using extra shapes, carvings, and inlays just to add to the appearance. Their purpose is to create pleasing visual aspects that seem to grow from and blend with the function, the materials, and practical construction techniques, Fig. 1-4.

Before preparing working drawings or starting the construction of a project, ask yourself some of these questions about your design: Will the article serve the function for which it was designed? Have the most appropriate kind of wood and other materials been selected? Does the design make economical use of the material? Will construction methods be simple and practical to perform? Has proper attention been given to proportion and balance? Will it be durable and easy to maintain? Is the design free of superficial ornamentation? Will the product fit or blend into the surroundings in which it will be used?

Furniture Styles

Furniture designs have evolved through the years. Newer styles are often adaptations of those developed in an earlier period. Many of the period styles of furniture were developed in Europe during the eighteenth century. Kings and queens of the various countries employed skilled cabinetmakers who worked full time over a period of many years to produce elaborate and often overdecorated furniture to match their luxurious surroundings. Some of the designs produced were named for the ruler; some carried the name of the cabinetmaker. Space permits only a brief description of a few of todays most popular styles. Most design textbooks will include detailed information about these and many others.

TRADITIONAL furniture can be described by such words as formal, elegant and gracious, Fig. 1-5. Sometimes it is named for its original eighteenth century English designer which would include such craftsmen as the Adams brothers, Sheraton, Chippendale and Hepplewhite. Also included would be Duncan Phyfe, the only American cabinetmaker to have a period furniture design named for him. The work of these designer-

Fig. 1-5. Traditional furniture.
(Drexel Furniture Co.)

Fig. 1-6. French Provincial styling.

craftsmen was influenced by the earlier Queen Anne period and that of the French King, Louis XV.

Typical decorations include gilt, fretwork, carvings, claw-and-ball feet, and extravagant fabrics. Chairs and tables often feature the graceful cabriole leg that is one of the familiar trademarks of traditional styling.

FRENCH PROVINCIAL (made in the provinces of France) is keynoted by its grace and charm. It was adapted and developed from the elaborate court furniture of Louis XV and is an outgrowth of an era when rich families employed artists and craftsmen on a full time basis to construct furniture for their homes.

It is a beautiful style of furniture with fine proportions and graceful contours. A characteristic feature is the curved leg and scroll foot. The darker hardwoods, especially cherry and walnut are used in its construction. French Provincial, especially in bedrooms, quite often is finished with beautiful painted surfaces. See Fig. 1-6.

EARLY AMERICAN styling traces its origin to our Colonial artisans. Even though these men probably would have liked to build furniture similar to that which they had known in England, the limitation of time, tools, and talent made this impractical. They developed a simple and practical type of furniture that was rugged in construction and free of excess decorations.

Through the years it has been refined and today it offers a casual style that appeals to a great many Americans, Fig. 1-7. Predominate characteristics are the turned legs, rails, and spindles. Ladder-back chairs and gateleg tables are also an identifying feature. The Federal Eagle is often

used as an accent point and indicates the high level of Nationalism that prevailed in the early years of our Country.

Originally a great deal of pine was used in its construction because it was readily available and easy to work. Today, quality furniture of this style is made of beech, birch, hard maple and cherry; usually finished in warm tones of tan and brown.

CONTEMPORARY DESIGN, or design for today, places great emphasis on functional consider-

Fig. 1-7. Early American

ations. It attempts to provide grace and charm through the use of interesting forms and shapes; constructed out of modern materials with the newest methods and procedures. Beautiful grained hardwoods, especially walnut, are often used, Fig. 1-8. Plastics and lighter weight metals are sometimes utilized. This design reflects the modern trend in architecture and undoubtly will receive even greater acceptance in the future, especially in public and institutional buildings.

To be acceptable, contemporary design must be carefully based on accepted principles; lines and forms must be attractive and provide the ut-

are also excellent for showing your instructor what you have in mind as you secure his approval and suggestions.

There are several methods of making a sketch. A beginner should experience early success through the procedure shown in Fig. 1-9. First, with the pencil held several inches from the point, make light block-in lines. Use sweeping strokes with the forearm pivoting at the elbow. It will be easiest to make a series of long dashes, aimed at a predetermined point. For vertical or diagonal lines that are long, revolve the paper and use the same stroking position. A finger movement can

Fig. 1-8. Contemporary furniture design.
(Drexel Furniture Co.)

most in function; construction must be simple and light but still provide adequate strength. The development of the design for a piece of contemporary furniture will generally require a great deal more thought, study, and experimentation, than the design for other styles.

The Scandinavian countries of Europe have long been noted for their craftsmanship. Their influence in recent years has been seen in contemporary furniture styles called Danish Modern and Swedish Modern.

Sketching

The ability to develop your ideas through freehand sketches is desirable. The sketches can be made quickly, using a pencil and paper and are a good way to record your ideas. Freehand sketches

be used for short lines. The position, size, and overall proportion of your sketch will be determined by these block-in lines so try to apply good "eye" judgment to their spacing.

After major block-in lines are complete, darken the lines you want to show. Grip the pencil near the point and press down firmly. Follow along the block-in lines with a series of strokes formed by a wrist movement. Move your hand to a new position after several strokes are made. Vertical or diagonal lines may be made by shifting the paper or using a finger movement.

Details are sketched in about the same way. Sometimes it may be helpful to use a ruler to lay out a few sizes of a detail as shown. After the measurements are made, continue to draw the lines freehand. The keynote of the sketch is speed. If you take time to draw too many mechani-

Fig. 1-9. Making a freehand sketch. A-Blocking-in. B-Dark-
ening outlines. C-Adding details.

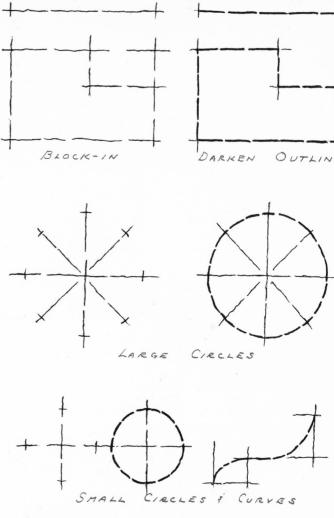

Fig. 1-10. Sketching procedure.

cal lines you will defeat this purpose. Procedures for making circles and curves are shown in Fig. 1-10.

The degree of refinement in a sketch is determined by its use. Sketches, hurriedly made to supplement an oral description can be rough and incomplete. As you think through a problem, quick sketches will help you record your ideas so they will not be forgotten. Accurate and more complete sketches can be made of final solutions.

The beginner may become discouraged with his first attempts at sketching because he sets too high a standard in line quality. A great deal of practice is required before "snappy looking" drawings can be produced by this method. In freehand sketching, give most of your attention to approximate proportions and try to keep the lines

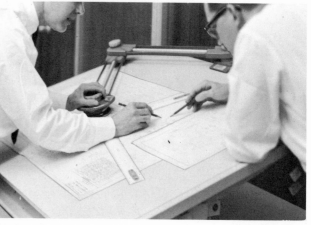

Fig. 1-11. Drawing is the language of design. Here designers discuss design problem. (Charles Bruning Co.)

running in about the correct direction. Do not attempt to produce perfectly straight and accurate lines. Drawings requiring this level of line quality should be made with instruments.

Fig. 1-12 shows freehand sketching applied to the development of a design for a portable house-

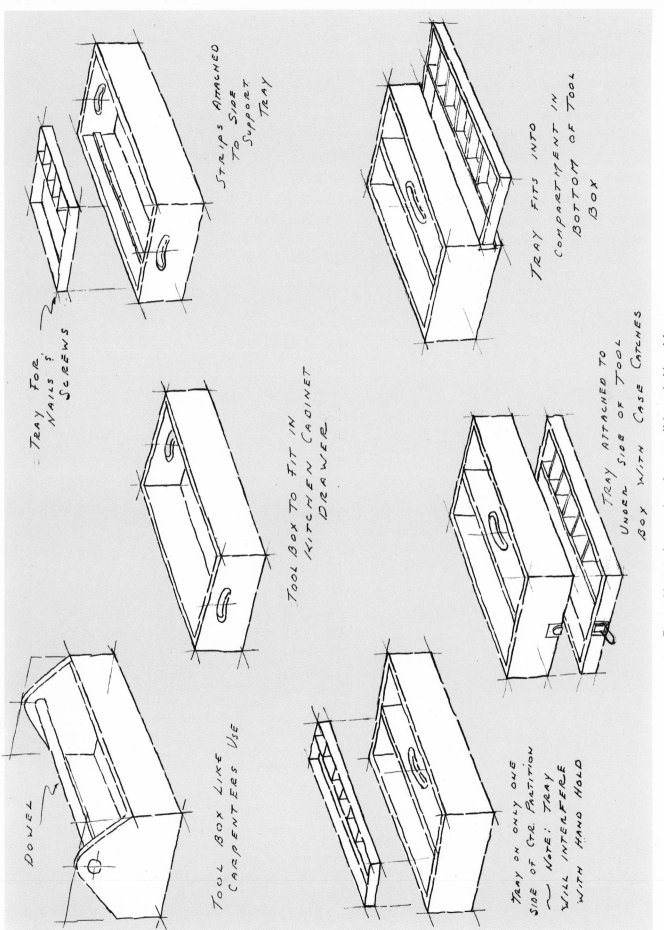

STRIPS ATTACHED
TO SIDE
TO SUPPORT
TRAY

TRAY FOR
NAILS &
SCREWS

TRAY FITS INTO
COMPARTMENT IN
BOTTOM OF TOOL
BOX

TOOL BOX TO FIT IN
KITCHEN CABINET
DRAWER

TRAY ATTACHED TO
UNDER SIDE OF TOOL
BOX WITH CASE CATCHES

DOWEL

TOOL BOX LIKE
CARPENTERS USE

TRAY ON ONLY ONE
SIDE OF CTR. PARTITION
— NOTE: TRAY
WILL INTERFERE
WITH HAND HOLD

Fig. 1-12. Developing ideas for a small household tool box.

hold tool box. The design problem included the following specifications:

1. Box must include space for common tools used in minor household repairs, and for such jobs as hanging a picture or installing a towel bar.

Presentation Drawings

After your design is refined and fairly well developed you should prepare a presentation drawing similar to the one shown in Fig. 1-13. It will serve to further organize your ideas and will pro-

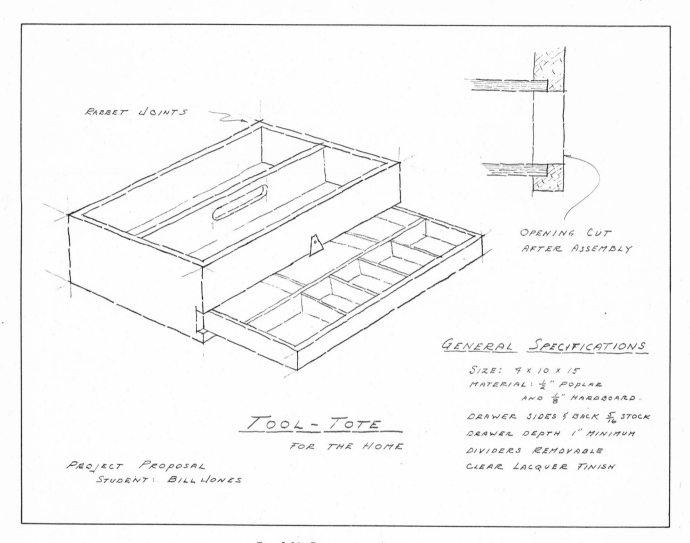

Fig. 1-13. Presentation drawing.

2. Include some kind of a compartment for nails, screws, plumbing washers, and similar items.
3. Design the box so that it will be compact and can be easily stored in a kitchen cabinet drawer.
4. Include some kind of a handle so it can be easily carried.

As ideas were stabilized, a list of tools, complete with size descriptions was prepaired. Also a listing of the most likely supply items was needed to establish the size requirements for the tray. The kitchen cabinet drawer in which the tool box would be stored was measured.

vide a drawing that you can use to present your project purposal to your instructor. Presentation drawings will be especially helpful in the preparation of working drawings.

Presentation drawings are usually freehand sketches. Various types of pictorial drawing can be used. Isometric and cabinet, Fig. 1-14, are the easiest and most commonly used. In isometric drawings, first block in cubes and rectangles that hold the shapes and then locate finished outlines from the edges and surfaces of the blocked-in form.

For a cabinet drawing make a profile or front view, and then secure the third dimension (picture effect) by drawing back at an angle. Make the lines drawn at an angle only about one-half their actual length.

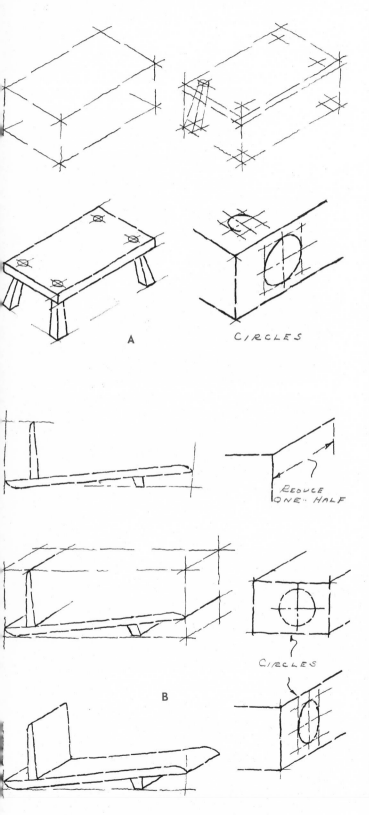

Fig. 1-14. Making pictorial sketches.
A-Isometric. B-Cabinet.

Show only visible outlines and keep the drawing as simple as possible. Only overall dimensions should be included and may be given in note form. Include any key details that will be helpful in describing the methods and details of construction and list general specifications concerning materials and finish. Sometimes it may be desirable to add shading or color to the drawing to give a clearer picture of the finished product. Study a drafting textbook for suggestions and procedures in this technique.

Multiview projection (orthographic views) can also be used for presentation drawings, Fig. 1-15. When used for this purpose, only visible outlines are shown. Sometimes they are drawn to an accurate scale with mechanically made lines. When made in this way they are especially valuable for checking the proportion, balance and other visual aspects of the design. Multiview projections are commonly used in the preparation of working drawings.

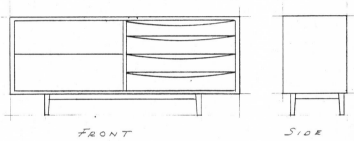

Fig. 1-15. Multiview drawing.

Working Drawings

After you have secured approval of your project ideas through the use of presentation drawings, you are ready to prepare a working drawing, Fig. 1-16. This drawing will provide complete shape and size description of the product and its various parts. The goal of the working drawing is to provide such a complete description that the product could be constructed by someone else without further explanations or information.

Working drawings must include assembled views of the product, complete with overall sizes. Most wood construction will be of such a size that these views will need to be drawn to a smaller scale. Multiview projections are commonly used, however, various pictorial types of drawings may be satisfactory. In addition to assembled views, detailed views will be required to show the exact size and shape of parts, and the joints and fasteners used to assemble them. In woodworking drawings these details are often drawn full size and

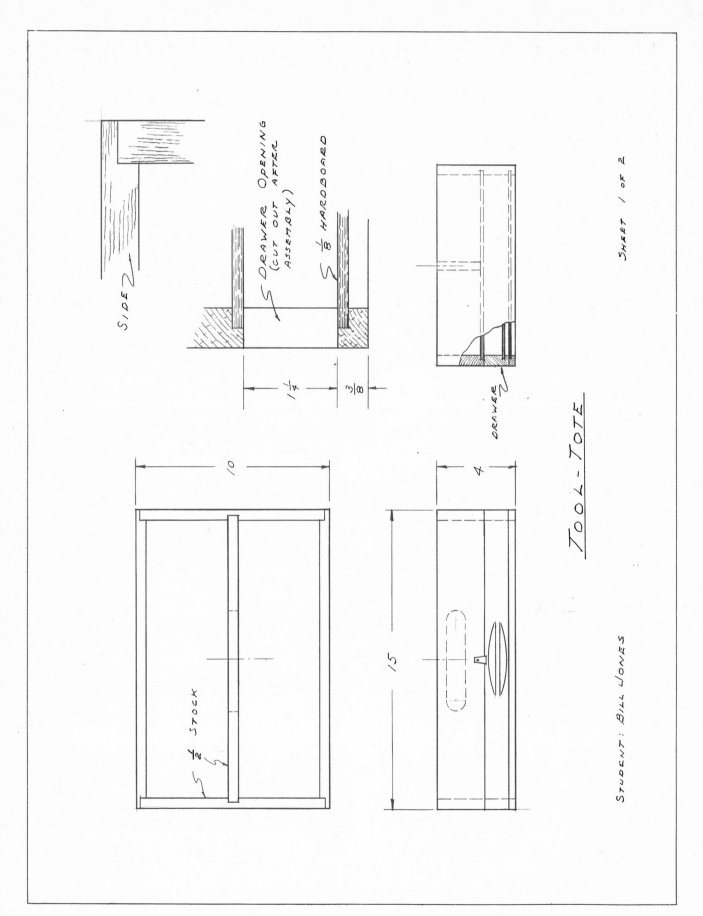

SIDE

DRAWER OPENING
(CUT OUT AFTER
ASSEMBLY)

$\frac{1}{8}$ HARDBOARD

$1\frac{1}{4}$

$\frac{3}{8}$

SHEET 1 OF 2

DRAWER

10

$\frac{1}{2}$ STOCK

15

4

TOOL-TOTE

STUDENT: BILL WONES

Fig. 1-16. Working drawings.

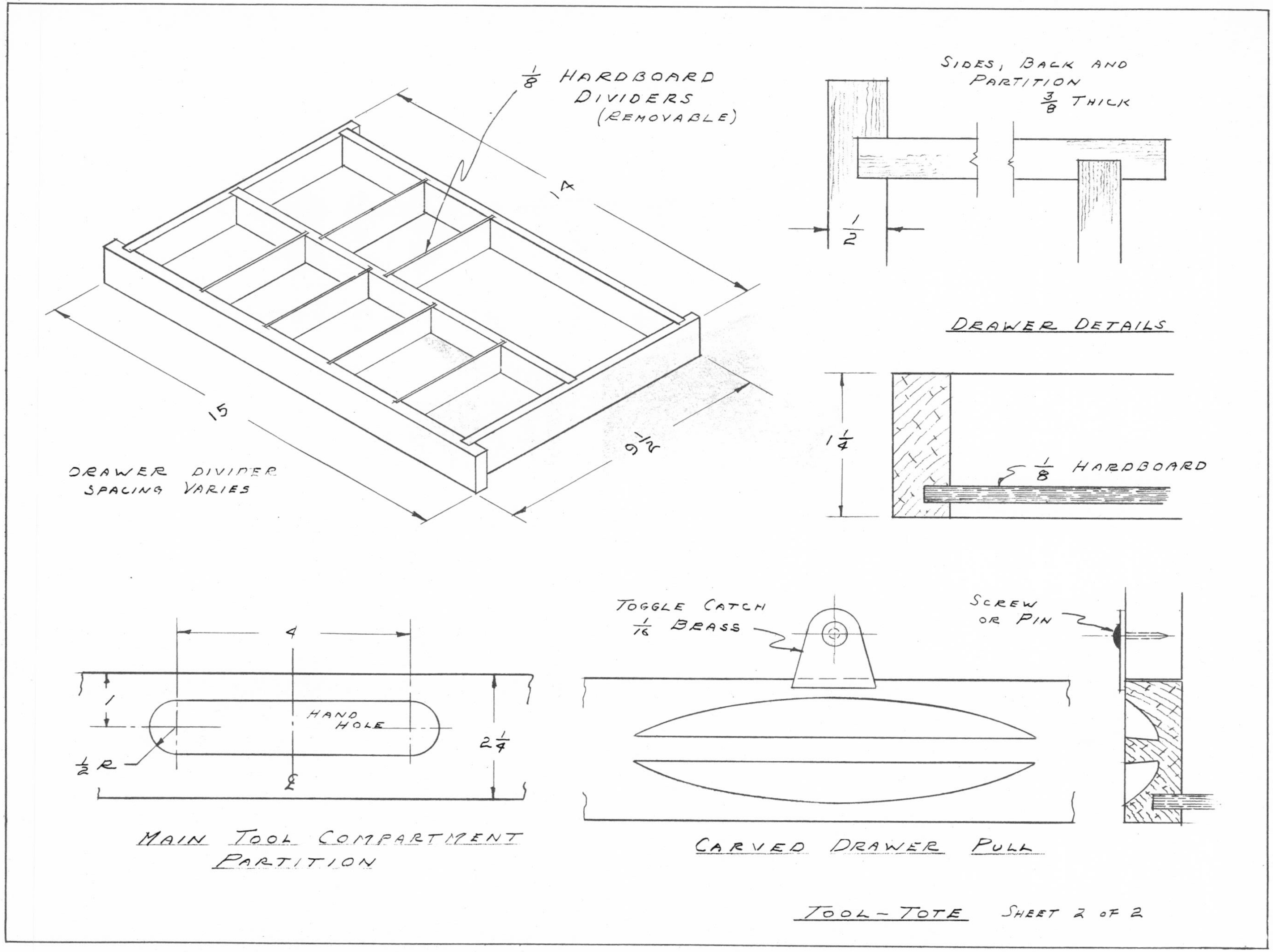

1/8 HARDBOARD
DIVIDERS
(REMOVABLE)
14
15
9 1/2
DRAWER DIVIDER
SPACING VARIES
SIDES, BACK AND
PARTITION
3/8 THICK
1/2
DRAWER DETAILS
1 1/4
1/8 HARDBOARD
4
1
HAND
HOLE
2 1/4
1/2 R
MAIN TOOL COMPARTMENT
PARTITION
TOGGLE CATCH
1/16 BRASS
SCREW
OR PIN
CARVED DRAWER PULL
TOOL-TOTE SHEET 2 OF 2

Fig. 1-16 Continued.

dimensions are not included. The builder simply scales (measures) the drawing to determine the size. Large pieces with an irregular contour are carefully drawn to scale and then a grid of squares is superimposed on the contour lines so that accurate patterns can be developed in the shop. In complicated assemblies, exploded pictorial drawings are often used to provide clear descriptions.

As you prepare a working drawing, decisions with respect to the methods and details of construction must be made. You must select the type and size of fasteners (nails and screws), proportion wood joints for the greatest strength, and determine the exact size of various parts. Study appropriate sections of this book and also reference books including a drafting textbook, for information and standards. A working drawing for a wooden product might also include a suggested design for a jig or fixture that could be used to insure accuracy in some important step of the fabrication processes.

Making a Plan of Procedure

A plan of procedure is a carefully prepared list of the steps you propose to follow in the construction of your project. It will require a careful study of your drawings to recognize the various operations and work required. This is one of the very important parts of your project plans as it will help you organize your work and prevent mistakes.

Steps should be listed in outline form. The list should not be too brief; neither should it be too long and detailed. Usually listing the exact operations and defining the part involved will be sufficient. Some special or unusual process might be described in detail. It is not necessary to list the

Fig. 1-17. Photograph of completed Tool-Tote.

size of parts since the working drawing will supply this information. Listed below is a plan of procedure that could be used to construct the "Tool-Tote."

1. From a study of the working drawings, prepare a bill of material and a stock cutting list. See Fig. 1-18.
2. Select and cut out the stock.
3. Prepare the stock for the sides, ends and center partition of the main box.
   a. Surface to finished thickness.
   b. Rip to width and cut to length.
   c. Lay out and cut hand hold in center partition.
4. Cut joints for main box.
   a. Grooves for hardboard panels.
   b. Dados for center partition.
   c. Rabbets for corners.
5. Cut hardboard panels to size and make a trial assembly of the main box.
6. Disassemble and sand all inside surfaces.
7. Glue up the box.
8. Trim outside surfaces and edges.
9. Cut the opening for the drawer. Use a dado head or make multicuts with a single blade. Have your instructor check this setup.
10. Prepare the stock for drawer front, sides, back and partition.
    a. Surface to finish thickness.
    b. Rip to width and cut to length.
11. Cut joints of drawer.
    a. Groove front and sides for bottom panel.
    b. Cut dado joints in front and side pieces.
    c. Lay out and cut dados in front, back, and partition for hardboard dividers.
12. Prepare bottom panel and hardboard dividers.
13. Make a trial assembly of the drawer. Check its fit in drawer opening.
14. Disassemble and sand solid stock parts. Carve finger pull in the drawer front.
15. Glue up the drawer.
16. Fit drawer to opening. Make and prefit drawer catch.
17. Prepare for finish.
18. Apply a sealer coat of finish to all surfaces.
19. Rub down sealer and apply a coat of paste wax.
20. Attach drawer catch.

Making a Bill of Material

A bill of material is a detailed list of the items you need to build the project. This includes: number of pieces, exact size (including allowance for joints), kind of wood, and name of the part. List the dimensions of your stock in this order: thickness x width x length. The width is the dimension across the grain, the length is along the grain. A piece of stock could be wider than it is long. A complete bill of material includes hardware and finishing materials.

No.	Size	Kind	Part
(Main Box)			
2 pcs.	1/2 x 4 x 15	Poplar	Sides
2 pcs.	1/2 x 4 x 9-5/8	Poplar	Ends
1 pc.	1/2 x 2-1/4 x 14-1/2	Poplar	Partition
2 pcs.	1/8 x 9-1/2 x 14-1/2	Hardboard	Bottoms
(Drawer)			
1 pc.	1/2 x 1-1/4 x 15	Poplar	Front
2 pcs.	3/8 x 1-1/4 x 9-1/4	Poplar	Sides
2 pcs.	3/8 x 1 x 13-5/8	Poplar	Partition and Back
1 pc.	1/8 x 9-1/4 x 13-5/8	Hardboard	Bottom
6 pcs.	1/8 x 1 x 4-3/8	Hardboard	Dividers
(Hardware)			
1 pc.	1/16 x 3/4 x 3/4	Brass	Drawer Catch
1 pc.	1/2 x No. 4	Oval headed brass screw	
(Finish)			
Sanding Sealer and Wax			

Fig. 1-18. Bill of material for Tool-Tote.

A stock-cutting list can be developed from the bill of material. It is useful for estimating costs and checking out your lumber. Add about 1/16 in. to the thickness dimension if the stock must be planed. The width of each piece should be increased from 1/4 to 1/2 in. and the length about 1/2 to 1 in. A bill of material will list the actual size of the finished pieces, while a stock-cutting list should give the nominal (name) size of the lumber required. Try to group the parts together

as much as possible. Stock-cutting lists may vary for a given bill of material depending on the sizes of lumber that are available. A stock-cutting list for the Tool-Tote is listed below:

STOCK-CUTTING LIST FOR TOOL-TOTE

No.	Size	Kind	Parts
1 pc.	*3/4 x 4-1/2 x 68	Poplar	Main box and Drawer front
1 pc.	*1-1/4 x 1-1/2 x 24	Poplar	Resaw to make sides, partition, and back of drawer.
1 pc.	1/8 x 16 x 30	Hardboard	Box and drawer bottoms and dividers

*Nominal size

You must use good judgment in selecting stock; allowing sufficient material for milling and trimming operations but still not incurring unnecessary waste. The sizes given in the stock-cutting list can be used to estimate the cost of the wood however, the actual cost may be somewhat more, depending on the sizes available in the stock room. For example, it may be necessary for you to purchase 1 in. (nominal size) stock for the first items in the above list if no 3/4 in. is available. Also you may need to purchase a 6 foot piece to secure the 68 in. rough cutting.

Test Your Knowledge

1. When planning a woodworking project you must have some knowledge of tools, _____, and construction methods.
2. The first step in designing a wood product consists of making sketches of your ideas. True or False?
3. When designing a wood product you should

Fig. 1-19. Wood in the space age. Construction of a wooden mock-up of the Apollo spacecraft. (National Aeronautics and Space Admin.)

Fig. 1-20. Completed mock-up of command module which is shown in Fig. 1-19. This is instrumented with displays of guidance and navigation gear and used for crew training.

give attention to its use and purpose, materials and methods, and _____.

4. A period style of furniture that makes extensive use of turned parts is called _____.

5. The kind of wood most often used in contemporary furniture is _____.

6. Freehand sketches that are used to supplement an oral description may be rough and incomplete. True or False?

7. When making an isometric drawing, first draw a profile or front view of the object. True or False?

8. Orthographic views are better than pictorial views for checking the proportion and balance of a design. True or False?

9. A typical item in a plan of procedure includes the name of the part and the _____ to be performed.

10. A bill of material should list the size, number of pieces, name of the part and the _____.

Outside Assignments

1. Select a wood product that you believe is well designed. Prepare a written report or make an oral report to the class in which you analyze its function, the materials and methods used in fabrication and its appearance.

2. Prepare sketches and/or mechanical drawings that will describe some of the elements and principles of the visual aspects of design. Include line, shape and mass; formal and informal balance, proportion, harmony, repetition, gradation, texture and color. Secure information from reference books and magazines.

Technician performs final inspection of 5/8 in. plywood panels. Conveyor line mechanism turns panel over so both sides can be checked. Panels are then automatically stacked by equipment shown in foreground. (Weyerhaeuser Co.)

Unit 2
SELECTING AND
ROUGHING OUT MATERIALS

Kinds of Wood

Lumber may be classified as either softwood or hardwood. Softwood comes from the evergreen or needle bearing trees. These are called "conifers" because many of them bear cones. See Fig. 2-1. Hardwood comes from broadleafed (deciduous) trees that shed their leaves at the end of the growing season. This classification is somewhat confusing, however, because many of the hardwood trees produce a softer wood than some of the so-called softwood trees.

Some of the more common kinds of softwoods and hardwoods are listed below. They are grouped according to the ACTUAL hardness of the wood rather than the classification just described.

SOFT	MED HARD	HARD
Balsa	CYPRESS	*Ash, White
Basswood	*Butternut	Beech
Cottonwood	DOUGLAS FIR	Birch
FIR, WHITE	Elm, American	Cherry, Black
PINE, PONDEROSA	HEMLOCK	*Hickory
PINE, WHITE-WESTERN	*Limba (Korina)	Maple, Sugar
PINE, SUGAR	Magnolia	*Oak, Red
Poplar, Yellow	*Mahogany (Honduras)	*Oak, White
SPRUCE	*Mahogany (Philippine)	*Walnut, Black
REDWOOD	*Prima Vera	*Teak
REDCEDAR, WESTERN	REDCEDAR, EASTERN	
Willow, Black	Sweet Gum	
	Sycamore	
	Tupelo	

*Open grained wood.
Note: Softwoods are set in caps; the others are classified as Hardwoods.

Some hardwoods have large pores in their cellular structure and are called OPEN GRAIN woods. They usually require special or additional operations in the finishing procedure.

In addition to hardness or softness, different kinds of wood will vary in weight, strength, color, texture, grain pattern and odor. You should become familiar with these characteristics for the common woods pictured in this section. To further develop your ability to identify various woods you will need to study actual specimens of the wood.

In wood identification it is often helpful to use a magnifying glass (about 10X) to study the cellular structure. For example: a sure way to

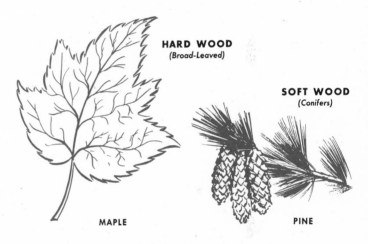

HARD WOOD
(Broad-Leaved)

SOFT WOOD
(Conifers)

MAPLE   PINE

Fig. 2-1. General classification of wood.
(Paxton Lumber Co.)

distinguish White Oak from Red Oak is to magnify the end grain and observe the tyloses (frothy growth) in the cells of the White Oak.

Most of the samples shown in the color section, following page 2-12, were cut from plain-sawed or flat-grain boards. A view of the edge grain would look considerably different. The weight of the wood is given for one cubic foot which would be equal to a board 1 in. thick, 12 in. wide and 12 ft. long.

Selecting Wood

As you become acquainted with the characteristics of various woods you will be able to determine those that will be best suited for your work. For some of your first projects where you may be doing considerable work with hand tools, you will very likely want to select such woods as basswood, pine, poplar or willow. These woods are easily worked and are fine for boxes, small cases, frames, toys, models and similar items.

After you have gained some experience, you will probably want to select from the list of medium-hard woods that work well with both hand and power tools. They can be used in the construction of wall shelves, small radio cabinets, chests, lamps, trays and many other household accessories.

When your project requires wide widths of stock you probably will want to consider using plywood. It takes time to glue up widths of solid stock. Plywood provides a saving in time and also greater dimensional stability and resistance to warpage. It is good practice to combine solid stock and plywood of the same species. Furniture manufacturers quite often do this and refer to the materials as "solids and veneers."

Advanced projects will usually be constructed with the aid of power machines. This will make it possible for you to use hardwoods. You should give careful attention to the selection of the kind of wood that will be appropriate for your design. Remember that the very best design along with fine workmanship cannot result in a satisfactory project if the kind and quality of the wood was not properly selected.

Grades of Lumber

The quality or grade of lumber depends on the size of the pieces and the amount of clear cuttings that they contain. Standards are established by associations of lumber producers and may vary somewhat, especially in the softwood classification.

In general, softwoods are divided into a select and common classification. The select grades range from A to D with B AND BETTER (sometimes called No. 1 and No. 2 clear) the highest grade usually available. The C SELECT grade must be clear on one side while the D SELECT grade may contain pin knots and other slight defects. Common grades of softwood range from No. 1 COMMON to No. 5 COMMON with the three top grades most often available in local lumber yards. These grades apply mainly to structural lumber such as used in house framing.

Softwoods (especially pine) that are used for millwork such as window frames, door frames and trim are often classified as FACTORY AND SHOP LUMBER with grades of third clear, No. 1 shop, No. 2 shop, and No. 3 shop.

In hardwood lumber the best grade is Firsts and the next is Seconds. These grades are nearly always combined into one grade called FIRST

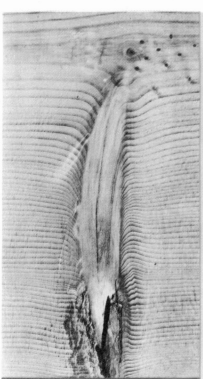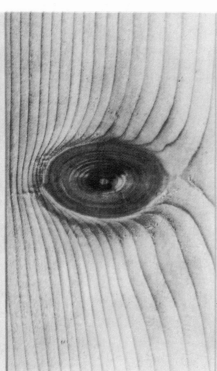

Fig. 2-2. Common kinds of knots. Left. Spike. Center. Intergrown. Right. Encased.
Note: The encased knot will probably loosen and fall out.
(Forest Products Lab.)

AND SECONDS (FAS) and require that pieces be not less than 6 in. wide by 8 ft. long and yield at least 83-1/3 percent clear cuttings. The next lower grade is SELECTS (sometimes called FAS 1 face) and permits pieces 4 in. wide by 6 ft. long with more defects on the second or back face (surface).

A still lower grade of hardwood is called No. 1 COMMON and is usually available and acceptable for school shop work. It permits smaller pieces and yields 66-2/3 percent clear cuttings. No. 2 COMMON and No.3 COMMON require 50 percent and 33-1/3 percent of clear cuttings but are not often listed in hardwood catalogues. Retailers usually cut out the defects in these grades and sell them as SHORTS (short lengths and narrow widths).

Defects

Defects in lumber usually lower the strength, durability and appearance. Some of the more common ones include:

KNOTS: an embedded limb or branch of the tree. It reduces the strength but in some cases may add to the appearance. See Fig. 2-2.

SPLITS and CHECKS: a separation of the wood along the grain and across the annual growth rings. See Fig. 2-3.

Fig. 2-3. Splits and checks.

SHAKE: a separation along the grain and between the annual growth rings. See Fig. 2-4.

PITCH POCKET: internal cavities that contain resinous material and sometimes bark.

HONEYCOMBING: separation of the wood fibers in the interior of wood, usually along the wood rays. May not be visible at the surface.

WANE: is the presence of bark or the absence

Fig. 2-4. Shake. (Forest Products Lab.)

of wood along the edge of a board. It forms a bevel and reduces the useable width.

WARP: is any variation from a true or plain surface and may include any one or combination of the following; cup, bow, crook and twist (also called wind). See Fig. 2-5.

Seasoning

The quality of lumber is also indicated by the method of drying. Green lumber from a freshly cut log will have an excessive amount of moisture (sap) most of which must be removed before it can be used. AIR DRIED (AD) lumber is simply exposed to the air over a period of time. By this method the moisture content is reduced to 12 to 18 percent.

KILN DRIED (KD) lumber is dried in huge ovens where temperature and humidity is carefully controlled. It will have a lower moisture content (7 to 10 percent) and will be free of internal stresses that are often present in air dried lumber. Also there usually will be fewer seasoning defects such as splits, checks and warp. Lumber that is to be used for furniture, cabinetmaking and other fine woodwork should be kiln dried.

Cutting Methods

Most lumber is cut in such a way that the annular rings form an angle less than 45 degrees with the surface of the board. This method produces lumber that is called FLAT-GRAINED if it is softwood or PLAIN-SAWED if it is hardwood.

Lumber can also be cut so that the annular rings form an angle of more than 45 degrees with the surface of the board. This method produces lumber that is called EDGE-GRAINED if it is softwood, and QUARTER-SAWED if it is hardwood. It is more difficult and expensive to use this method but it does result in lumber that is less likely to warp, and may produce a more attractive grain pattern. The edge-grain of some softwoods such as Douglas Fir, wears better than flat-grained surfaces.

Fig. 2-6. Rough and surfaced lumber.

(RGH) or surfaced on both sides (S2S), Fig. 2-6. Surfaced thicknesses are somewhat different from those for softwoods, as shown in the following table. To avoid waste, hardwoods are usually not cut to any standard width or length. They are cut and sold in what is called RANDOM WIDTHS and LENGTHS (RW & L).

ROUGH AND FINISHED SIZES

SOFTWOODS		HARDWOODS	
Rgh	S4S	Rgh	S2S
1 x 2	3/4 x 1-1/2	3/8	3/16
1 x 4	3/4 x 3-1/2	1/2	5/16
1 x 6	3/4 x 5-1/2	5/8	7/16
1 x 8	3/4 x 7-1/4	3/4	9/16
1 x 10	3/4 x 9-1/4	1 (4/4)	13/16
1 x 12	3/4 x 11-1/4	1-1/4 (5/4)	1-1/16
2 x 2	1-1/2 x 1-1/2	1-1/2 (6/4)	1-5/16
2 x 4	1-1/2 x 3-1/2	2 (8/4)	1-3/4
2 x 6	1-1/2 x 5-1/2	2-1/2	2-1/4
2 x 8	1-1/2 x 7-1/4	3	2-3/4
2 x 10	1-1/2 x 9-1/4	3-1/2	3-1/4
4 x 4	3-1/2 x 3-1/2	4	3-3/4

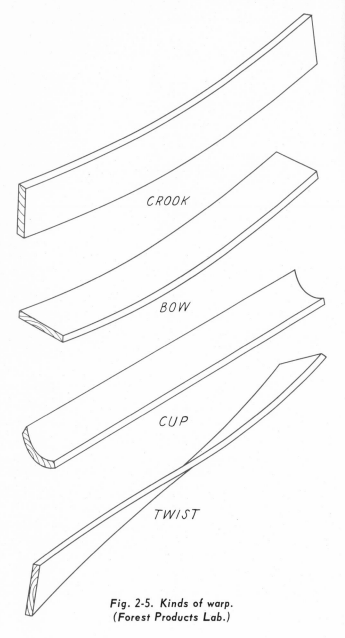

CROOK

BOW

CUP

TWIST

Fig. 2-5. Kinds of warp.
(Forest Products Lab.)

Surface and Size

Softwoods are surfaced (planed) on all faces and edges (S4S). See Fig. 2-6. They are sold in specified widths from 2 in. to 12 in. by 2 in. intervals and in lengths of 8 ft. to 20 ft. by 2 ft. intervals. Because the surfacing removes some of the wood, the thickness and width will actually measure less than the sizes listed. For example, a 2 x 4 will be reduced to 1-1/2 x 3-1/2 in.

Hardwoods can be purchased either rough

WOODY SAYS:

"Lumber is always listed and sold according to its rough or nominal (name) size even though it has been surfaced. You should follow the same practice as you refer to, or list stock in the shop."

Standard thickness of hardwoods of one inch and over are sometimes designated in quarters of an inch and often referred to as four-quarter, five-quarter, etc. This also applies to White Pine and a few of the other softwoods.

Plywood

Plywood is constructed by gluing together a number of layers (plies) of wood with the grain direction turned at right angles in each successive layer. An odd number (3, 5, 7, --) of plies are used so that they will be balanced on either side of a center core and so that the grain of the outside layers will run in the same direction. The outer plies are called FACES or face and back. The next layers under these are called CROSS-BANDS and the other inside layer or layers are called the CORE. See Fig. 2-7. A thin plywood panel made of three layers would consist of just faces and a core.

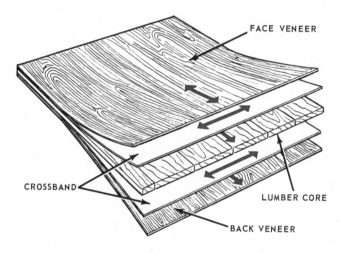

Fig. 2-7. *Plywood construction. Top layer, face veneer; Second, crossband; Third, lumber core; Fourth, crossband; Bottom, back veneer. (Fine Hardwoods Assoc.)*

Plywood is classified as either hardwood or softwood depending upon the kind of wood used in the face veneers. It is available in nearly all of the fine hardwoods and many of the softwoods. The softwoods most generally available are Douglas Fir and Ponderosa Pine. In the last section of this book you will find information about the manufacturing of plywood.

There are two basic types of plywood; exterior and interior. EXTERIOR PLYWOOD is bonded with waterproof glues and can be used for boats, siding, concrete forms and other construction that will be exposed to the weather or excessive moisture. INTERIOR PLYWOOD is bonded with glues that are not waterproof and is used for

cabinets, furniture and inside construction where the moisture content of the panels will not exceed 20 percent.

Plywood can be secured in thicknesses of 1/8 in. to more than 1 in. with the common sizes being 1/4, 3/8, 1/2, 5/8, and 3/4 in. A standard panel size is 4 ft. wide by 8 ft. long. Smaller size panels are available in the hardwoods.

The grade of a plywood panel depends on the quality of the face and back veneers. In softwood the highest grade is designated by the letter N and then ranges down through A, B, C and D. For example, a grade A-A panel would have a good grade of veneer on each side while a A-D grade would specify a panel that was good on one side and that had a back with knots, splits and other defects.

Hardwood plywood faces and backs are graded 1, 2, 3, 4. A grading specification of 1-2 would require a good face with grain carefully matched and a good back but without careful grain matching. A number 3 back would permit noticeably defects and patching but would be generally sound. A special or PREMIUM grade of hardwood is known as "architectural" or "sequence-matched." This requires an order to a plywood mill for a series of matched plywood panels that result in a dramatic and beautiful effect when installed. It is quite expensive and usually limited to public or institutional buildings.

For either softwood or hardwood plywood it is common practice to designate in a general way the grade by G2S (good two sides) or G1S (good one side).

In addition to the various kinds, types and grades, hardwood plywood is made with different core constructions. The two most common are the veneer core and the lumber core, as shown in Fig. 2-8. VENEER CORES are the least ex-

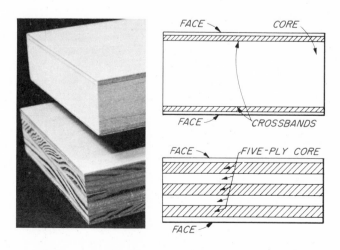

Fig. 2-8. *Plywood: Above. Lumber core. Below. Veneer core.*

Fig. 2-9. Manufactured materials for woodwork. Left. Hardboard. Right. Particle board.
(Weyerhaeuser Co.)

pensive and are stable and warp resistant. LUMBER CORES are easier to cut, the edges are better for shaping and finishing and they hold nails and screws better. Plywood is also manufactured with a particle board core. It is made by gluing 1/28 in. veneers directly to the particle board surface. Nail and screw holding power is low but it does provide a very stable panel.

Hardboard and Particle Board

Hardboard and particle board is used in all the woodworking industries. In house construction, it can be used for siding, interior walls and ceilings, partitions, built-ins and cabinetwork. In furniture manufacturing these materials are often used for drawer bottoms, concealed panels and backs for cases, cabinets and chests. Fig. 2-9, shows some of the various types of hardboard and particle board that are available. They are manufactured by many different companies and sold under their own trade names. Your lumber dealer can supply you with the names of the products available locally.

Hardboard is made of refined wood fibers, pressed together to form a hard, dense material (50 - 80 lbs. per cu. ft.). There are two types: STANDARD and TEMPERED. Tempered hardboard is impregnated with oils and resins that makes it harder, slightly heavier, more water resistant and darker in appearance. Hardboard is manufactured with one side smooth (S1S) or both sides smooth (S2S). S1S has a reverse impression of a screen on the back side. Hardboard is available in thicknesses from 1/12 in. to 5/16 in. with the most common thickness being 1/8,

3/16 and 1/4 in. Panels are 4 ft. wide and come in standard lengths of 8, 10, 12 and 16 ft.

Particle board is made of wood flakes, chips and shavings bonded together with resins or adhesives. It is not as heavy as hardboard (about 40 lbs. per cu. ft.) and is available in thicker pieces. Particle board may be constructed of layers made of different size wood particles; large ones in the center to provide strength and fine ones at the surface to provide smoothness. Extensive use is made of particle board as a base or core for plastic laminates and veneers. It is available in a wide range of thicknesses from 1/4 in. to 1-7/16 in. The most common panel size is 4 x 8 ft.

Particle board and hardboard can be worked with regular woodworking machines and hand tools, using standard blades and knives. Hardboard is dense and does wear cutting edges more rapidly than wood. Hard-tipped or carbide-tipped blades should be used if there is a large amount of cutting to be done.

Handling and Storing

Lumber that will be used for cabinetmaking and finished woodwork should be handled carefully, especially if it is surfaced. It should be protected from excessive moisture, dust and dirt, and dents and scars. Whether rough or surfaced it must be kept carefully stacked to minimize warpage.

A carefully laid stack of RW & L lumber is shown in Fig. 2-10. Long boards are placed in the bottom tiers (layers) and shorter ones on top so that each board is completely supported. Wide and narrow boards are laid so that "joints are broken" in each successive tier. One end of the stack is dressed (aligned) so that it will be easy to count the number of pieces and figure the footage. If the lumber is delivered with a considerably higher or lower moisture content than it will attain in the storage area, it should be open stacked with stickers (see glossary) so that air can circulate freely around each piece.

Plywood, especially the fine hardwoods, must be handled with great care. The faces are sanded and they can easily become soiled and scarred. The best method of storing is to lay the panels flat. If they are stored in a vertical position, then pressure should be applied to the sides to keep them in a true plane.

Fig. 2-10. A carefully built stack of RW & L lumber.

Figuring Board Footage

The unit of measure for lumber is the board foot. This is a piece 1 in. thick and 12 in. square or its equivalent (144 cu. in.). You can figure the board feet in some pieces very easily. For example, a board 1 x 12 and 10 ft. long will contain 10 bd. ft. If it were only 6 in. wide it would be 5 bd. ft. If the original board had been 2 in. thick it would have contained 20 bd. ft. For most pieces of stock however, you will need to use the following formula: (all of the sizes must be in inches).

$$\text{Bd. ft.} = \frac{\text{No. pcs. } \times T \times W \times L}{1 \times 12 \times 12}$$

For an example: Find the number of board feet in 2 pieces of stock that are 1 x 9 x 36.

$$\text{Bd. ft.} = \frac{2 \times 1 \times \overset{3}{\cancel{9}} \times \overset{3}{\cancel{36}}}{1 \times \underset{4}{\cancel{12}} \times \underset{1}{\cancel{12}}} = \frac{18}{4} = 4\ 1/2$$

Stock that is less than 1 in. thick is figured as though it were 1 in. When the stock is thicker than 1 in. the nominal size is used. When this size contains a fraction such as 1 1/2, change it

to an improper fraction (3/2) and place the numerator above the formula line and the denominator below. For example: find the board footage in 3 pieces of stock 1 1/2 x 10 x 56.

$$\text{Bd. ft.} = \frac{\overset{3\searrow}{\cancel{3}\text{ pcs.}} \times \overset{1}{\cancel{3}} \times \overset{5}{\cancel{10}} \times \overset{\overset{7}{\cancel{14}}}{\cancel{56}}}{\underset{1}{\cancel{2}} \times \underset{1}{\cancel{12}} \times \underset{2}{\cancel{12}}} = \frac{35}{2} = 17\ 1/2$$

Always USE THE NOMINAL SIZE of lumber to figure the board footage. If the stock is long and the length is given in feet then one of the twelves (12s) can be dropped from the lower half of the formula. In random width lumber it is good practice to "round off" to the nearest inch. For example: if the board were anywhere between 7 1/2 to 8 1/2 in., figure it as 8 inches.

When working with large quantities of RW & L lumber the use of the formula would be impractical and a BOARD RULE should be used. See Fig. 2-11. On the metal head and also at the handle, are numbers for various lengths of boards. Running along the body from these numbers are tables that read in surface feet.

To use the board rule, first determine the length of the board and then place the rule across the surface with the head against one edge. Select the line that corresponds to the length and follow across to the other edge. Here you can read the board footage if the piece is 1 in. thick. If the nominal size of the board were 1 1/2 in., add 50 percent to the reading; for 2 in. stock double the reading.

Fig. 2-11. Board rule.
(Lufkin Rule Co.)

Boards of the same length can be placed side by side and their total footage found in one reading. Board rules are available with various combinations of tables. A good one for hardwoods has five tables on each side, running in odd and even feet from 7 through 16.

The unit of measure for plywood, hardboard and particle board is the SQUARE FOOT (sq. ft.). A standard 4 ft. x 8 ft. panel contains 32 sq. ft. Prices are quoted per square foot on the basis of full panel purchase, and vary widely depending on the kind, thickness and grade.

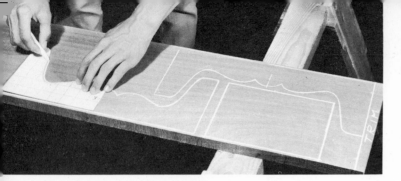

Fig. 2-12. Using a template to determine size of rough cutting.

Fig. 2-13. Marking a cutting line along the tongue of the framing square. The blade is held against the edge of the stock.

Selecting and Laying Out

After you have made a stock cutting list you are ready to look over the lumber racks and select the items of stock best suited for your project. This requires lots of good judgment. If you have not had much experience in woodwork, you should ask your instructor for help.

After you have selected a piece that appears to offer economical cuttings, look it over carefully on both sides for defects. Make a rough layout of the parts of the project using a bench ruler and/or a template. See Fig. 2-12. White chalk works fine for this since it can be easily wiped off if you want to try other arrangements. These lines will not be used for finished cutting but only to help you see how the piece will cut after it has been planed.

Be sure to look at the end of the stock. If it is rough, as it came from the sawmill, it will have small splits and checks that must be trimmed. You must allow for this in your rough layout. You will need to make your layout "around" other defects, however some of them may be covered or placed on the back of your project. Very tight knots may even be desirable because of the interesting grain patterns around them.

In a rough layout 1/16 in. extra thickness should be allowed for planing; about 1/4 in. for each width you will cut and about 1/2 to 1 in. for each length. Check over your layout and be sure the grain is running in the right direction in each piece. Use the framing square to make a cutting line across the stock as shown in Fig. 2-13.

Cutting Stock to Rough Length

Select a crosscut saw with 8 or 10 points to the inch. Fig. 2-15, shows the shape of crosscut teeth. They are beveled on each side to form a series of knife points that cut smoothly across the fibers of the wood. Note that the teeth are set (bent) out on alternate sides so that they will cut a kerf (groove) wider than the thickness of the blade, thus permitting it to move freely through the work, Fig. 2-16.

Place the board on sawhorses so that the position of the cut will be well supported. One knee can be placed on the board to hold it firmly. Hold the saw in your right hand (if you are right handed) and grasp the board in your left hand. Use your thumb as a guide, raising it well above the board so there is no danger of it being cut. Study

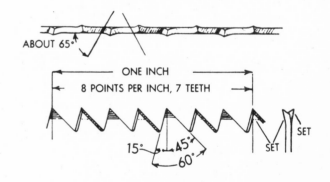

Fig. 2-14. Parts of a hand saw.
(H. K. Porter Co.)

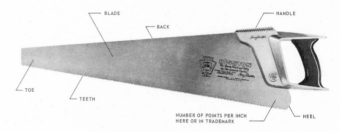

Fig. 2-15. Crosscut saw teeth.
(Stanley Tools)

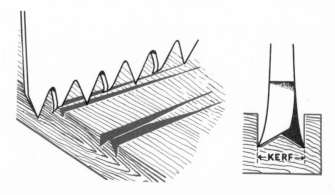

Fig. 2-16. How crosscut teeth cut.

Fig. 2-17. A block of wood, held in position at the cutting line could be used. Start the cut on the waste side of the line by pulling the saw toward you several times until you have cut a kerf 1/4 to 1/2 in. deep.

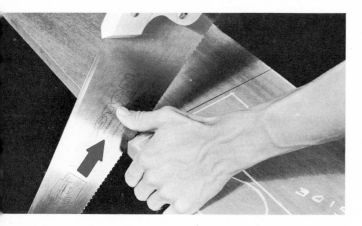

Fig. 2-17. *Starting the cut.*

As soon as the saw is started, move your left hand away from the blade. With the saw held at about a 45 degree angle, take long, even strokes, using nearly the entire length of the saw. Apply just enough pressure so it cuts smoothly. See Fig. 2-18. If the saw starts to cut away from the line, you can bring it back by twisting it slightly.

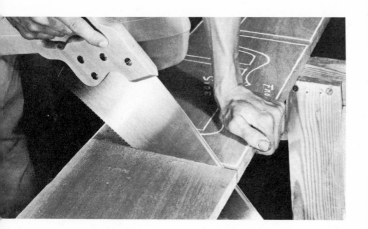

Fig. 2-18. *Making the cut with full, smooth strokes.*

WOODY SAYS:

"When roughing out stock, be careful that the saw does not cut into the sawhorses or bench."

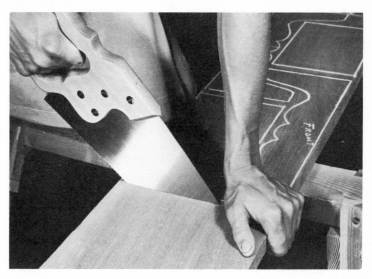

Fig. 2-19. *Finishing the cut.*

Slow down as you near the end of the cut. Be sure both pieces are well supported. You may need to add another sawhorse or have someone assist you. If the board is wide you may be able to grasp both pieces as shown in Fig. 2-19.

Short pieces of stock are difficult to support and hold on sawhorses. It is better to clamp them in a vise as shown in Fig. 2-20.

Fig. 2-20. *Crosscutting with stock held in vise.*

Ripping Stock to Rough Width

Select a rip saw with about 5 1/2 points to the inch. Fig. 2-21, shows the shape of rip teeth. They are filed approximately straight across and look like a series of narrow chisels.

Follow about the same procedure for ripping as crosscutting. The rip saw is held at about a 60 degree angle. Start the cut with the board extended out over the sawhorse and then move the

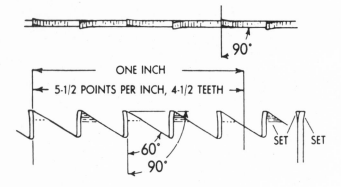

Fig. 2-21. Rip saw teeth. The 90 deg. angle is often increased to give the tooth a negative rake.
(Stanley Tools)

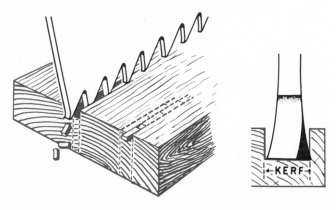

Fig. 2-22. How rip saw teeth cut.

sawhorse back as the cut is advanced. After cutting some distance, the sawhorse can then be moved to a position in front of the saw as shown in Fig. 2-23. If the saw tends to bind in the kerf, a wedge can be inserted to hold it open.

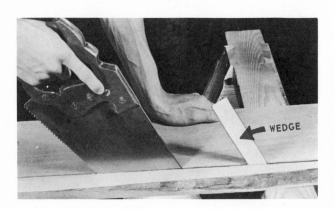

Fig. 2-23. Ripping stock to width. Note the defect called "wane" along the edge of the board.

The crosscut saw can be used for ripping but it will cut much slower. The rip saw, however should not be used for crosscutting as it will not cut through cross grain fibers easily and leaves a very rough cut.

Laying Out and Cutting Plywood

Since plywood has a finished (sanded) surface and is expensive, especially in hardwood, it must be cut out carefully. If there are many pieces, or the parts are complicated, it will be best to make a scaled drawing on paper before making the layout on the panel. This will insure the most economical layout and prevent errors such as cutting pieces with the grain running in the wrong direction.

Since you will be cutting almost to finished size, it is good practice to use a DOUBLE LINE layout as shown in Fig. 2-24. The width of the cut-

Fig. 2-24. Laying out plywood cuttings.

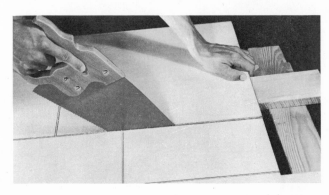

Fig. 2-25. Cutting plywood with a 10 pt. crosscut saw. Note the "stringers" placed on sawhorses to support the panel.

ting space will vary with the kind of plywood, type of saw, and the method that will be used to smooth the edge. Use a 10 point or finer toothed CROSS-CUT SAW for cutting plywood. See Fig. 2-25. Work carefully and try to avoid excessive splintering on the under side. Always be sure the panel is well supported and try to prevent any damage to the surface.

The portable sabre saw is a good tool to use for cutting plywood, Fig. 2-26. It cuts on the up-stroke and this will tend to splinter the top surface. Directions for using this tool are included in Unit 13.

Use the same general procedures for cutting hardboard and particle board.

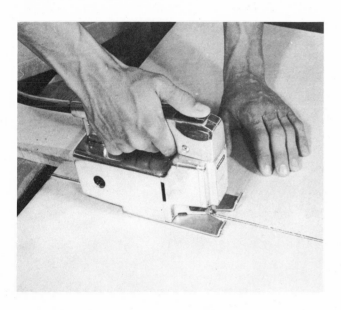

Fig. 2-26. Cutting plywood with a sabre saw.

Sharpening a Hand Saw

Sharpening or refitting a hand saw is one of the more difficult processes in hand tool maintenance. However, as you gain skill and experience in wood-working you should not hesitate to undertake this task. Start with a saw that has become dull but still has well shaped teeth. Sharpening a saw that is in poor condition with teeth out of shape is a challenge for even the experienced craftsman. Such saws should be sent to a local saw shop or to the factory where they can be machine filed and refitted by an expert.

The process of sharpening a saw includes three basic operations: JOINTING, SETTING and FIL-ING. They are usually performed in this order, however a heavy jointing operation will reduce the size of the teeth and they will need to be filed and reshaped before setting is possible. Since a

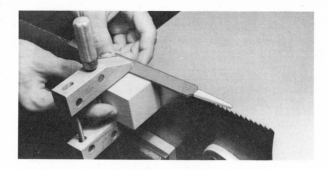

Fig. 2-27. Jointing a hand saw using an 8 in. smooth mill file clamped to a square block of wood.

saw can be lightly jointed and filed several times before additional set is required, these operations will be described first.

JOINTING is the operation of lightly filing off the points of the teeth so that they are all the same height. Clamp the saw in a vise and run a smooth mill file along the teeth. Clamping the file to a square block of wood as shown in Fig. 2-27, will keep it in a horizontal position and guide it along the blade.

Move the file lightly over the teeth several times until tiny "flats" or "brights" are visible on the points of the teeth. The jointing process for the instructional pictures that follow was con-siderably "overdone" so that the flats could be easily seen. In actual practice, the jointing should be as light as possible and stopped just as soon as flats appear on nearly all of the teeth.

Patented saw jointing devices are available that have a built-in file or abrasive stone, or hold a standard mill file.

FILING a hand saw is done with a triangular saw file like the one shown in Fig. 2-28. They are available in lengths from 4 to 8 in. and widths or

Fig. 2-28. Triangular taper saw file.
(Nicholson File Co.)

cross sections designated as regular taper, slim taper, extra slim taper and double extra slim taper. For a 5 or 6 point rip saw use a 7 in. slim taper. For a 10 point crosscut a 5 in. extra slim taper is usually recommended. Be sure the file is equipped with a tight fitting handle.

Mount the saw in a regular saw-filing vise with the handle to your right. If one is not avail-able, it can be mounted between two strips of wood in a regular woodworking vise. The teeth should project above the strips about 1/4 in. Start at the heel of the blade and work toward the toe. Place the file in the first gullet where it will contact the back of a tooth set away from you. Position the file to fit the bevel of the teeth so that you will file the front of a tooth and the back of an adjacent tooth in a single stroke.

Rip saw teeth are filed almost straight across with the handle end of the file just a few degrees below a horizontal line. See Fig. 2-29. Crosscut teeth are filed at an angle of about 65 degrees with the handle end of the file about 10 degrees below the horizontal as shown in Fig. 2-30.

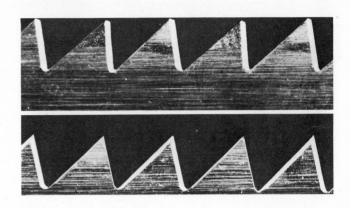

Fig. 2-31. Correctly filed saw teeth. Above. Rip teeth. Below. Crosscut teeth. (Nicholson File Co.)

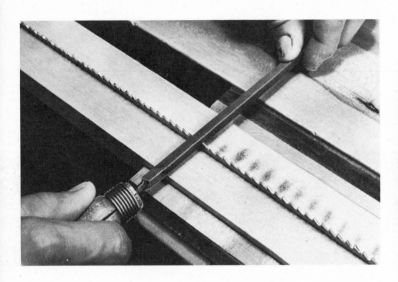

Fig. 2-29: Filing rip saw teeth. Filing nearly straight across with the file handle down about 2 deg.

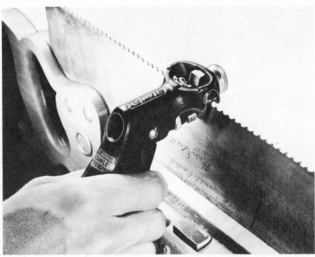

Fig. 2-32. Setting the teeth. In this position the saw set will bend the teeth away from you.

Fig. 2-30. Filing a crosscut saw. Above. Filing at about a 65 deg. angle with the handle down about 10 deg. Below. Close-up view.

Use long full strokes, with just enough pressure to make the file cut easily. Raise the file out of the gullet on the return stroke so that you can observe the work. Continue to file until you have removed about one-half of the "flat" of the teeth on each side. File every other gullet until you reach the toe of the blade. Reverse the saw in the clamp and file the other gullets, stopping just as soon as the flats disappear. This is very important for when the "flats" are gone you will lose your reference point and may file some teeth shorter than others. Fig. 2-31, shows correctly filed crosscut and rip teeth.

SETTING is the operation of bending the teeth slightly outward. The amount of set is determined by the points per inch and most SAW SETS are calibrated on this basis. The proper amount of set should produce a saw kerf that is a little less than 1 1/2 times the thickness of the blade. This will require that each tooth be bent out slightly less than one-fourth of the blade thickness.

ASH, WHITE. Strong, stiff, and fairly heavy (42 lbs. to cu. ft.). Works fairly well with hand tools but splits easily. Heartwood is a pale tan with a texture similar to Oak. Used for millwork, cabinets, furniture, upholstered frames, boxes and crates. Used extensively for baseball bats, tennis rackets, and other sporting equipment.

WOOD
IDENTIFICATION

A key element in woodworking and in carpentry is the proper identification of the wood.

This insert, which is intended as a guide and an aid to the student in learning to identify various woods, shows typical color and grain characteristics of 71 different species.

ASPEN. Soft, light, close-grained, and easy to work. White sapwood with light tan and brown streaked heartwood. Source: Europe, Western Asia and Middle Atlantic States. Used for furniture, and interior paneling.

AVODIRE. Has a distinctive odor and lustrous appearance. Medium hard, open-grain, and about the same weight and working characteristics as Mahogany. Source: Ivory Coast of West Africa. Used for fine furniture, fixtures and wall paneling.

AYOUS. Also called African Whitewood. Fairly soft, lightweight, even textured and open-grained. Source: West Africa, mainly Ivory Coast and Nigeria. Used mainly for plywood, solid stock is available.

BALSA. The lightest wood available (12 lbs. to cu. ft.). Very soft and easily cut with knives. Best known for its use in model aircraft construction. Also used for life rafts, duck decoys, hat blocks, and other lightweight items. Chief source is Ecuador.

BASSWOOD. The softest and lightest (26 lbs. to cu. ft.) hardwood in commercial use. Fine, even texture with straight grain. Especially easy to work with hand tools and highly resistant to warpage. Heartwood is a light yellowish-brown. Used for drawing boards, food containers, moldings, woodenware and core stock for plywood.

BEECH. Heavy, hard and strong. (44 lbs. to cu. ft.) A good substitute for Sugar Maple but somewhat darker in color, with a slightly coarser texture. Used for flooring, furniture, brush handles, food containers, and boxes and crates.

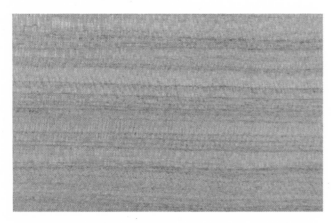

BELLA ROSA. Moderately hard, heavy and coarse textured. Striped and mottled grain patterns. Source: Philippine Islands. Available in veneer and lumber. Sample shows quartered veneer.

BENGE. A medium hard and dense wood with open grain. Heartwood is light brown with dark brown or reddish brown stripes. Source: West Africa. Used mainly for veneer in fabricating plywood. Solid stock is seldom available.

BIRCH. A hard, strong, wood (47 lbs. to cu. ft.). Works well with machines and has excellent finishing characteristics. Heartwood, reddish-brown with white sapwood. Fine grain and texture. Used extensively for quality furniture, cabinetwork, doors, interior trim, and plywood. Also used for dowels, spools, toothpicks, and clothespins.

BIRCH, WHITE. Selected sapwood rotary-cuttings of regular birch veneer. Same characteristics as birch except nearly white in color. Used to make plywood for installations requiring a very light, fine textured material.

BOXWOOD. Hard, close, and smooth grained. A very indistinct grain pattern with a light yellow color. Source: Europe, Asia, and West Indies. Used for inlays, marquetry, and instruments, especially fine rulers and scales.

BUBINGA. Also called African Rosewood. A hard, heavy wood with open grain. The reddish brown color is often streaked with lines of dark purple. Source: West Africa. Used for fine cabinetwork in both solids and veneers.

BUCKEYE. A soft, close-grained wood that is not very strong. Nearly white in color, often blemished with dark stained lines. Source: Eastern United States. Rather scarce and usually available only in veneers.

BUTTERNUT. Fairly soft, weak, light in weight (27 lbs. to cu. ft.), with a coarse texture. Grain patterns resemble walnut. Large open pores require a paste filler. Works easily with hand or machine tools. Sometimes used for interior trim, cabinetwork, and wall paneling.

CANALLETTA. A very hard, medium textured wood. Dark brown to purplish color with very dark stripes that form interesting patterns. Source: Northern South America. Used for tool and knife handles, turnings, and walking sticks.

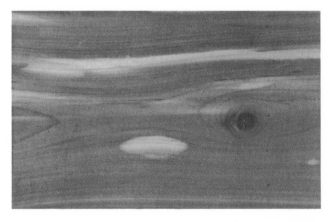

CEDAR, RED, EASTERN. Medium dense softwood, (34 lbs. to cu. ft.). Close grained and durable. Heartwood is red; sapwood is white. It has an aroma that inhibits the growth of moths. Knotty wood is available only in narrow widths. Used mostly for chests and novelty items.

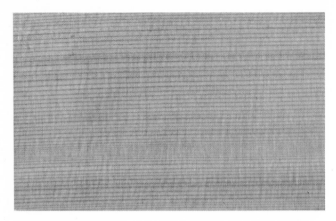

CEDAR, RED, WESTERN. A soft wood, light in weight (23 lbs. per cu. ft.). Similar to redwood except for cedar-like odor. Pronounced transition from spring to summer growth (see edge-grain sample). Source: Western coast of North America, especially Washington. Used for shingles, siding, structural timbers and utility poles.

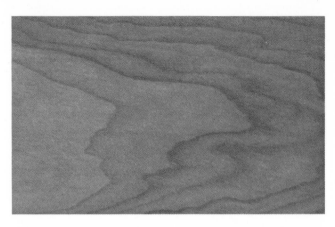

CHERRY, BLACK. Moderately hard, strong and heavy (36 lbs. to cu. ft.). A fine, close-grained wood that machines easily and can be sanded to a very smooth finish. Heartwood is a reddish-brown with beautiful grain patterns. One of the fine furniture woods, however, there is a scarcity of good grades of lumber.

CHESTNUT. Coarse textured, open grain, and very durable. Reddish brown heartwood. Easily worked with hand or machine tools. Source: Eastern United States. Available only in a wormy grade due to the "chestnut blight."

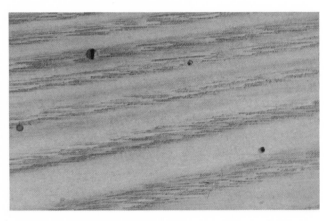

COCOBOLA. Dense, hard and oily. A difficult wood to work because of an interwoven grain. Bright red when freshly cut, but soon darkens. Source: Central America. Used for fancy cabinetwork and knife handles.

CYPRESS. Light in weight, soft and easily worked. Fairly coarse texture with annual growth rings clearly defined (sample shows edge grain). Source: Southeastern Coast of the United States. Noted for its durability against decay. Used for exterior construction and interior wall paneling.

EBONY. Extremely hard and so dense that it will not float in water. Difficult to work. Source: Ceylon, Africa and East Indies. The true black ebony comes from Ceylon and is expensive. Suitable for inlays, marquetry and small decorative articles.

ELM, AMERICAN. Strong and tough for its weight (36 lbs. to cu. ft.). Fairly coarse texture with open pores. Annular ring growth is clearly defined. Bends without breaking and machines well. Used for barrel staves, bent handles, baskets, and special types of furniture.

EMERI. Also called Ireme. A medium-hard, open-grained wood with a texture and grain pattern similar to African mahogany. Good working and finishing qualities. Source: West Africa. Used for wall panels and cabinetwork. Moderately priced. Solid stock is available.

FIR, DOUGLAS. A strong, moderately heavy (34 lbs. to cu. ft.) softwood. Straight close grain with heavy contrast between spring and summer growth. Splinters easily. Used for wall and roof framing and other structural work. Vast amounts are used for plywood. Machines and sands poorly. Seldom used for finish.

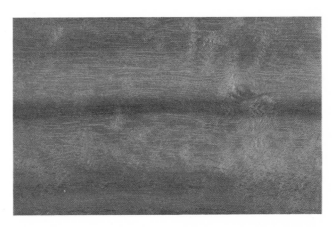

GONCALO ALVES. Strong and durable. Small open pores with a texture that varies. Fairly easy to work however, and very smooth surfaces can be produced. Source: Mexico and tropical South America. Used for furniture and cabinetwork.

GREENHEART. Extreme hardness, weight, and strength. Open pores. Light olive green to nearly black in color. Source: British Guiana and West Indies. Used for the construction of ships, docks and piling. Available only in solid stock.

GUM, SWEET. Also called Red Gum. Fairly hard and strong (36 lbs. to cu. ft.). A close grained wood that machines well but has a tendency to warp. Heartwood is reddish-brown and may be highly figured. Used extensively in furniture and cabinetmaking. Stains well, often used in combination with more expensive woods.

HAREWOOD. A close-grained wood nearly white in color. Grain pattern is often highly figured. Sometimes dyed to a gray color and called Silver Harewood. Source: England. Used for marquetry, inlay and paneling.

HEMLOCK. A softwood. Light in weight and moderately hard. Light reddish brown in color with a slight purplish cast. (Sample shows edge grain.) Source: Pacific Coast and Western States. Used for construction lumber and pulpwood; also for containers and plywood core stock.

HOLLY. Light, tough and very close-grained. Nearly white when cut but turns slightly brown with age and exposure. Source: South Central and Southern States. Used for inlays and marquetry and to a limited extent in cabinetwork.

IMBUYA. Also called Brazilian Walnut. Moderately hard and heavy with an open-grain and fine texture. Source: Brazil. Used for high grade furniture, cabinetwork and paneling.

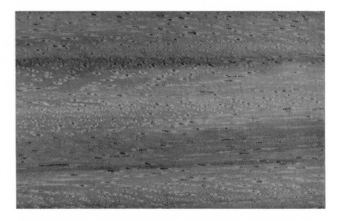

KELOBRA. Coarse texture with very large pores. Pronounced grain patterns are large and often have wavy lines. Source: Mexico, Guatemala and British Honduras. Used for furniture and cabinetry mainly in the form of veneers.

KOA. Medium hard with a texture similar to walnut. Open-grained. Color is golden to dark brown, often with dark streaks. Polishes to a lustrous sheen. The best known hardwood of the Hawaiian Islands. Used for fine furniture, art objects, and musical instruments.

LACEWOOD. Medium hard with flaky grain formed by wood rays. Usually quartered to produce small uniform flakes (as shown). Source: Australia. Occasionally used for decorative overlays on furniture and for wall paneling.

LIGNUM VITAE. Very hard and heavy (specific gravity 1.20). Oily and mildly scented, with a fine interwoven grain texture that makes it hard to work. Source: Central America, West Indies, and Northern South America. Used for bearings, pulleys, brush backs, and similar items.

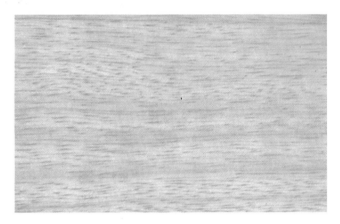

LIMBA. A light blond wood from the Congo, often sold under the trade name Korina. It has an open grain with about the same texture and hardness of Mahogany. Works easily with either hand or machine tools. Used for furniture and fixtures, especially where light tones are required.

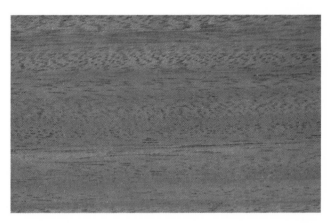

MAHOGANY, AFRICAN. Characteristics are similar to American varieties. Slightly coarser texture and more pronounced grain patterns. Quarter sawing or slicing produces a ribbon grain effect (as shown). Source: Ivory Coast, Ghana and Nigeria. Used for fine furniture, interior finish, art objects and boats.

MAHOGANY, HONDURAS. Medium hard and dense (32 lbs. to cu. ft.). Excellent working and machining qualities. A very stable wood, with even texture, open pores, and beautiful grain patterns. Used for high grade foundry patterns and quality furniture. It turns and carves especially well.

MAHOGANY, PHILIPPINE. Medium density and hardness (37 lbs. to cu. ft.). Open grain and coarse texture. Works fairly well with hand or machine tools. Varies in color from dark red (Tanguile) to light tan (Lauan). Used for medium price furniture, fixtures, trim, wall paneling. Also, boat building and core stock in plywood.

MAKORE. Also called African Cherry and Cherry Mahogany. Somewhat like mahogany but with a finer texture and also harder and heavier. May often have a more pronounced grain pattern than sample shown. Source: West Africa, especially Nigeria. Used for furniture and cabinetry.

MAPLE, BIRDSEYE. Hard or Sugar Maple with tiny spots of curly grain that look like bird's eyes. The cause of this figure is not known. It may be distributed throughout the tree or located only in irregular stripes or patches. Used for highly decorative inlays and overlays.

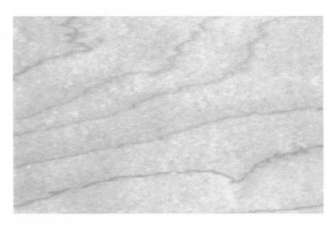

MAPLE, SUGAR. Also called Hard Maple. It is hard, strong, and heavy (44 lbs. to cu. ft.). Fine texture and grain pattern. Light tan color, with occasional dark streaks. Hard to work with hand tools but machines easily. Is an excellent turning wood. Used for floors, bowling alleys, woodenware, handles, and quality furniture.

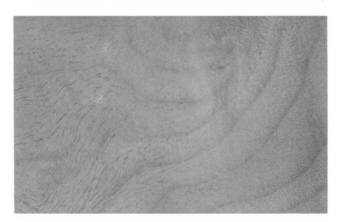

MYRTLE. Hard and strong with pore size and distribution about the same as walnut. Golden brown color with an olive green cast. Machines easily and can be polished to a high luster. Source: Southwestern Oregon. Used for decorative panels in furniture and architectural woodwork; also for art objects and novelties.

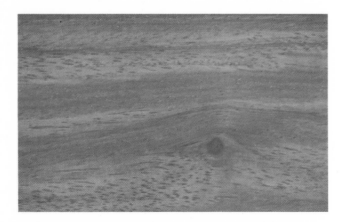

NARRA. Heavy, hard, and durable. Has a distinct grain pattern and open pores. Generally a golden yellow brown but may be found in a rose or deep red color. Source: Philippines and Malaysia. Used for high grade furniture and interior finish of ships.

OAK, ENGLISH. Open-grained with a texture similar to regular oak. Light tan to deep brown color with dark spots that create an unusual figure and grain character. Source: England. Used for fine furniture and special architectural woodwork.

OAK, QUARTERED. Sawing or slicing oak in a radial direction results in a striking pattern as shown. The "flakes" are formed by large wood rays that reflect light. Used where dramatic wood grain effects are desired.

OAK, RED. Heavy (45 lbs. to cu. ft.) and hard with the same general characteristics as White Oak. Heartwood is reddish-brown in color. No tyloses in wood pores. Used for flooring, millwork and inside trim. Difficult to work with hand tools.

OAK, WHITE. Heavy (47 lbs. to cu. ft.), very hard, durable, and strong. Works best with power tools. Heartwood is greyish-brown with open pores that are distinct and plugged with a hairlike growth called tyloses. Used for high quality millwork, interior finish, furniture, carvings, boat structures, barrels and kegs.

ORIENTALWOOD. Also called Australian Laurel. Medium weight with wood characteristics similar to walnut. Color is pinkish gray to brown with dark stripes as shown. Source: Australia. Used for highest quality furniture and cabinetwork.

PADOUK. Also called Vermillion. Hard firm texture with some interlocked grain that makes it difficult to work. Large open pores. Red color, may have streaks of yellow or brown. Source: Burma and West Africa. Used for art objects and novelties.

PALDAO. A fairly hard wood with large pores that are partially plugged. Grain patterns are striking and beautiful and provide an excellent example of an "exotic" wood. Source: Philippine Islands. Sometimes selected by architects for special fixtures or built-ins for public or institutional buildings.

PEARWOOD. A very fine textured, close-grained wood with pores that are indistinct. Subdued grain pattern, sometimes with mottled figure. Source: United States and Europe. Used for fine furniture, marquetry, saw handles and rulers.

PINE, PONDEROSA. Lightweight (28 lbs. to cu. ft.) and soft. Straight grained and uniform texture. Not a strong wood but works easily and has little tendency to warp. Heartwood is a light reddish-brown. Change from springwood to summerwood is abrupt. Used for window and door frames, moldings, and other millwork; toys, models.

PINE, SUGAR. Lightweight, (26 lbs. to cu. ft.) soft, and uniform texture. Heartwood, light brown with many tiny resin canals that appear as brown flecks. Straight grained and warp resistant. Cuts and works very easily with hand tools. Used for foundry patterns, sash and door construction, and quality millwork.

PINE, WHITE. Soft, light (28 lbs. to cu. ft.) and even texture. Cream colored with some resin canals but not as prevalent as in Sugar Pine. Used for interior and exterior trim and millwork items. Knotty grades often used for wall paneling. Works easily with hand or machine tools.

POPLAR, YELLOW. Moderately soft, light in weight (34 lbs. to cu. ft.), and even textured. Heartwood is a pale olive-brown and sapwood is greyish-white. Works well with hand or machine tools and resists warping. Used in a wide variety of products including inexpensive furniture, trunks, toys, and core stock for plywood.

PRIMAVERA. Sometimes called white or golden mahogany. Medium to coarse texture with straight and somewhat striped grain. Very similar to mahogany except for the color which is a light straw to golden yellow. Source: Southern Mexico, Guatemala, Honduras, and Salvador. One of the fine cabinet woods of the world.

REDWOOD. Soft and light in weight (28 lbs. to cu. ft.). Texture varies but is usually fine and even grained. Easy to work and durable. Heartwood is reddish-brown. Used for structures, outside finish and sometimes for interior paneling. Its durability makes it especially valuable for products exposed to water and moisture.

ROSEWOOD, BRAZILIAN. A very hard wood with large irregular pores. Various shades of dark brown with conspicuous black streaks. Rosewood with different colors and characteristics also comes from India, Ceylon, Madagascar and Central America. A beautiful wood used for art objects, levels, tool handles and musical instruments.

SAPELE. Grain, color, and figure are typical of African Mahogany but somewhat heavier and harder. Also not as dimensionally stable. Source: Ivory Coast and Nigeria. Used extensively in veneer and solid form for furniture, fixtures, cabinets, and boats.

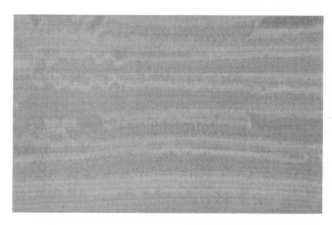

SATINWOOD. Fine grain texture, hard and heavy, with a slight oiliness. Golden yellow in color with beautiful wavy grain patterns that often give a mottled effect. Source: Puerto Rico. Honduras, Ceylon and East Indies. Used for inlays, marquetry, fine brush handles and similar items.

SPRUCE. A soft wood, light in weight (24 lbs. per cu. ft.). Transition from spring to summer growth is gradual (see edge grain sample). There are several species; Sitka, Englemen, and a general classification called Eastern. Source: various parts of the United States and Canada. Used for pulpwood, light construction and carpentry.

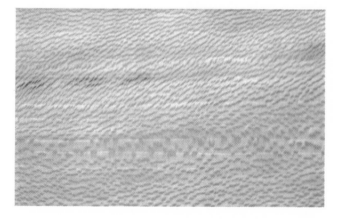

SYCAMORE. Medium density, hardness, and strength. A close-grained wood with a rather coarse texture. Easily identified by the flaky pattern of wood rays observed best in quartered stock. Source: Eastern half of United States. Used for drawer sides and lower priced furniture. Veneers are used for berry and fruit boxes.

TAMO. Also called Japanese Ash. The physical characteristics of the wood resembles American Ash. Grain patterns are extremely pronounced. Figures may consist of swirl, fiddleback or blister types. Source: Japan. Used for inlays and overlays where a highly decorative surface is required.

TEAK. Strong and quite hard. Resembles walnut except for a lighter tawny yellow color. Silicates and minerals in the wood give it an oily feel and dulls regular tools more quickly. Source: Burma, India, Thailand and Java. Used for fine furniture and paneling. Also used for ship building because of its great durability.

TULIPWOOD. Hard, medium textured, open-grained wood, with small pores that vary in size. Red and yellow color streaked with dark lines. Source: Northeastern Brazil. A highly decorative wood used for inlays, turnings, and novelties.

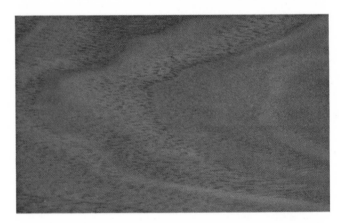

WALNUT, BLACK. Fairly dense and hard. Very strong in comparison to its weight (38 lbs. to cu. ft.). Excellent machining and finishing properties. A fine textured open grain wood with beautiful grain patterns. Heartwood is a chocolate brown with sapwood near white. Used on quality furniture, gun stocks, fine cabinetwork, etc.

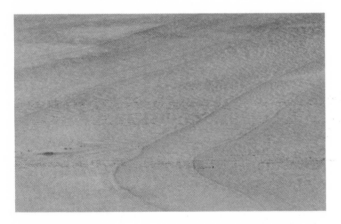

WILLOW, BLACK. Very soft and light in weight (27 lbs. to cu. ft.). Resembles basswood in workability, although there is some tendency for the machined surface to be fuzzy. Heartwood varies from light gray to dark brown. Used for some inexpensive furniture, core stock for plywood, wall paneling, toys, and novelty products.

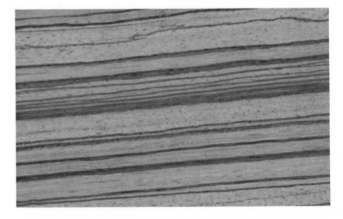

ZEBRAWOOD. Also called Zebrano. Heavy, hard, open-grained wood with a medium texture. Light gold in color with narrow streaks of dark brown in quartered stock (see sample). A highly decorative wood from Central and West Africa. Made into quartered veneer and used where a spectacular effect is desired.

Study the manufacturer's directions and adjust the saw set. Clamp the saw in the vise and set the teeth bent away from you. See Fig. 2-32. Only about the upper half of the tooth should be set. Reverse the saw in the vise and set the remaining teeth.

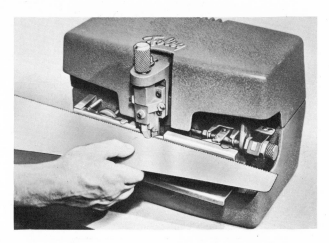

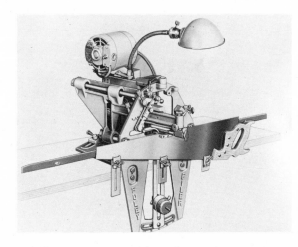

Fig. 2-33. *Automatic saw filer. This machine can be set up to file circular saws as well as hand saws.*

An automatic filing machine and setting machine is shown in Figs. 2-33, and 2-34. After these machines are set up and adjusted they can do a perfect job of filing and setting in just a few minutes.

Fig. 2-34. *Automatic power setting machine. After it is set up it takes less than one minute to set a hand saw. It can also be used to set band saw blades.*
(Foley Mfg. Co.)

Take good care of your hand saws. Be sure the lumber you cut with them is clean, dry and free of nails. When not in use they should be kept in a tool rack or holder that will protect them from damage. Keep the screws in the handle tight and wipe the blade frequently with a cloth lightly saturated with oil. Some craftsmen use a lemon oil furniture polish instead of machine oil since it has a slight cleaning action and also leaves a light oily film that protects the metal surface from rust.

Grading hardwood plywood at a large plywood manufacturing plant.
(United States Plywood Corp.)

Test Your Knowledge

1. Softwood comes from the evergreen or needle bearing trees that are called _____ .
2. Which one of the following kinds of wood is classified as softwood: basswood, cottonwood, redwood or willow?
3. Which one of the following kinds of wood is the heaviest: white ash, cherry, walnut or white oak?
4. In general the softwoods are graded under a _____ and common classification.
5. The best grade of hardwood lumber that is generally available is _____ .
6. One grade of hardwood lumber is called No. 1 common and contains _____ percent clear cuttings.
7. A defect caused by a separation between the annual growth rings is called a _____ .
8. The warp in a board can be more clearly defined by stating that it is cupped, bowed, _____ , or twisted.
9. Quarter-sawed hardwood lumber is cut by the same method used to produce _____ softwood lumber.
10. One item on a hardwood purchase order reads: 200 bd. ft. - 4/4 walnut, FAS, KD, RW & L, Rgh. or S2S to 13/16. Define each of the abbreviations used.
11. A plywood panel that was listed as G2S would be _____ _____ _____ .
12. Hardboard is _____ (lighter, heavier) than particle board.
13. If 6/4 ponderosa pine is selling for 36 cents a board foot, a piece 10 in. by 24 in. would cost _____ .
14. It is good practice to use a rip saw for cutting plywood along the grain. True or False?
15. The three basic operations for sharpening a hand saw are _____ , setting and filing.

Outside Assignments

1. Plan and construct an electrically operated wood identification panel. It might operate in such a way that when the correct name is matched with the sample a light will glow or a buzzer sound. You might prefabricate the parts in the shop and do the assembling and wiring at home. Wood sample kits can be secured from hardwood lumber dealers.
2. On a strip of heavy cardboard, develop the tables for a board rule that would measure stock 2, 3, 4, 5 and 6 ft. long. Try it out in the shop and check your readings with the board foot formula.
3. Study the catalogue of a supplier or manufacturer and develop a complete description (kind, length, points per inch, etc.) of a number of hand saws. Include current retail prices for each. Star the ones you would select for a home workshop.
4. From a study of reference materials, develop a list of saw file sizes that should be used for sharpening saws ranging from 5 to 16 points per inch.

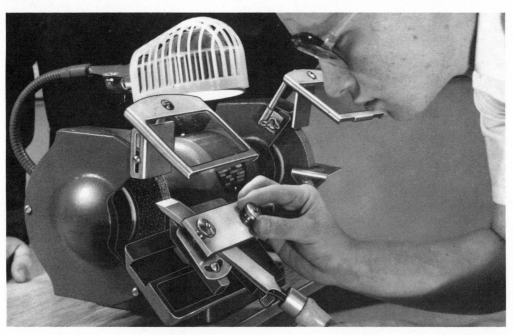

Total eye protection includes the use of safety glasses and shields along with enough good light to see what you are doing without straining your eyes.

GENERAL SAFETY RULES

WOODY SAYS:

"An important part of your experience in woodwork will be learning to follow safe practices and procedures that will prevent injuries to YOURSELF AND OTHERS. Give close attention to the instructions and demonstrations given by your instructor and study the directions for using tools and machines listed in this book. As you learn to use them the correct way you are also learning to use them the safe way.

Develop a good attitude toward safety. This means that you have a strong feeling toward the importance of safety and are willing to give time and attention to learning the safest way to perform your work. It means that you will be certain to work carefully and follow the rules -- even when no one is watching you. A safe attitude will protect you and others, not only in the shop but also in activities outside of school.

Carefully study the safety rules which follow. Your instructor may also recommend some additional rules. If you follow the rules and directions carefully, many of them will soon become safety habits that you will perform almost automatically.

SECURE APPROVAL: Secure your instructor's approval for all work you plan to do in the shop. He is the one to decide if the work can and should be done and will be able to suggest the best, easiest, and safest way to do it.

CLOTHING: Dress properly for your work. Remove coats, and jackets; tuck in your tie and roll up loose sleeves. It is advisable to wear a shop apron that is snugly tied.

EYE PROTECTION: Wear safety glasses or a face shield when doing any operation that may endanger your eyes. Be sure you have enough good light to see what you are doing without straining your eyes.

CLEAN HANDS: Keep your hands clean and free of oil or grease. You will do better and safer work, and the tools and your project work will stay in good condition.

CONSIDERATION OF OTHERS: Be thoughtful and helpful toward other students in the class. Be sure that the work you are doing does not endanger someone else. Caution other students if they are violating a safety rule.

TOOL SELECTION: Select the proper size and type of tool for your work. An expert never uses a tool unless it is sharp and in good condition. Inform your instructor if tools are broken, have loose handles, or need adjustments.

CARRYING TOOLS: Keep edged and pointed tools turned down and do not swing your arms or raise them over your head while carrying them. Carry only a few tools at one time unless they are in a special holder. Do not carry sharp tools in your pockets.

CLAMPING STOCK: Whenever possible, mount the work in a vise, clamp, or special holder. This is especially important when using chisels, gouges or portable electric tools.

USING TOOLS: Hold a tool in the correct position while using it. Most edged tools should be held in both hands with the cutting motion away from yourself and other students. Be careful when using your hand or fingers as a guide to start a cut. Test the sharpness of a tool with a strip of paper or a scrap of wood. Do not use your fingers.

WORKING SPEED: Do not "rush and tear" through your work. The good craftsman knows that a steady, unhurried pace is safest and will produce the best work.

BENCH ORGANIZATION: Keep your project materials carefully organized on your bench with tools located near the center. Do not "pile" tools on top of each other. Never allow edged or pointed tools to extend out over the edge of the bench. Close your vise when it is not in use and see that the handle is turned down. Keep drawers and cabinet doors closed.

FLOOR SAFETY: The floor should be clear of scrap blocks and excessive litter. Keep projects, sawhorses and other equipment and materials you are using out of traffic lanes. Wipe up immediately any liquids spilled on the floor.

MATERIAL AND PROJECT STORAGE: Store and stack your project work carefully in assigned areas. If the storage is overhead, be sure the material will not fall off. Straighten the lumber rack when you remove a board. Do not leave narrow strips protruding from the end of the storage rack, especially at or near eye level.

LIFTING: Protect your back muscles when lifting heavy objects. Have someone help you and lift with your arm and leg muscles. Secure help with long boards, even though they are not heavy.

FIRE PROTECTION: Apply and handle finishing materials only in approved areas. Close cans of finishing materials and thinners immediately after use. Use flammable liquids in very small quantities. Be sure the container is labeled. Dispose of oily rags and other combustible materials immediately or store them in an approved container. Secure the instructor's approval before you bring any flammable liquids into the shop.

INJURIES: Report all injuries, even though slight, to your instructor."

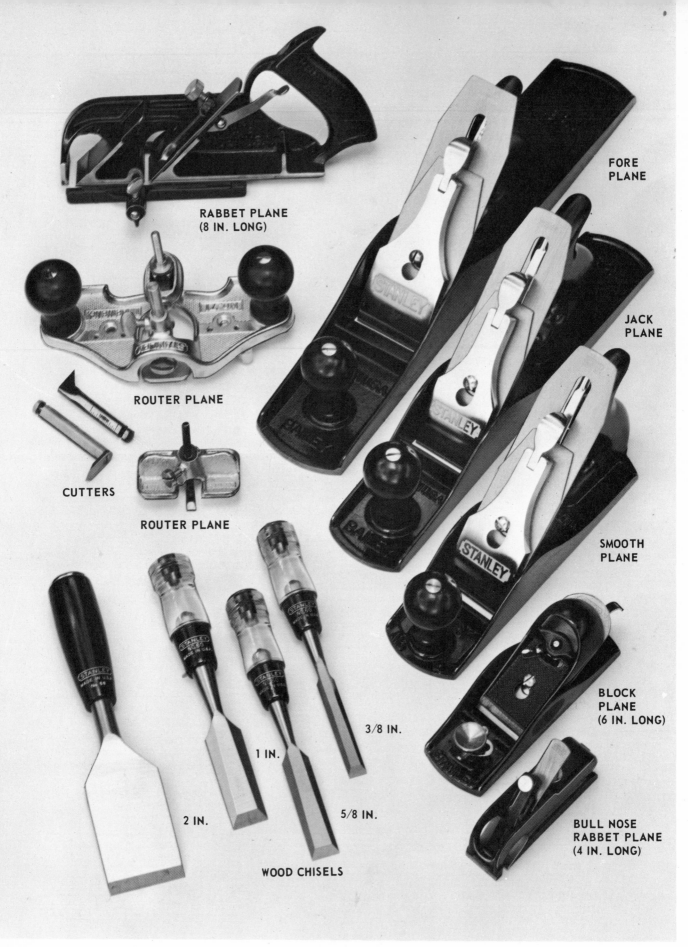

RABBET PLANE
(8 IN. LONG)

ROUTER PLANE

CUTTERS

ROUTER PLANE

FORE
PLANE

JACK
PLANE

SMOOTH
PLANE

BLOCK
PLANE
(6 IN. LONG)

BULL NOSE
RABBET PLANE
(4 IN. LONG)

3/8 IN.

1 IN.

5/8 IN.

2 IN.

WOOD CHISELS

Fig. 3-1. Planes and chisels.
(Stanley Tools)

Unit 3

PLANING AND SAWING STOCK
TO FINISHED DIMENSIONS

This Unit, and several that follow, deal with hand tool operations. They include basic skills that apply to a wide range of construction problems. As you gain experience in woodworking you will of course, want to take advantage of the efficiency and time saving factors that power machines provide. If you have a good understanding of the correct procedures in using hand tools, you will develop skills in the use of the machines more rapidly.

As you undertake advanced projects, involving the use of power machines, you will find that the need for hand tools continues to exist. The expert craftsman knows how to use both hand tools and machine tools.

Kinds and Sizes of Planes

The standard hand plane is used to make a wood surface smooth and flat. Some of the common kinds of planes are shown in Fig. 3-1. Three of the planes are constructed in the same way and vary only in size. The SMOOTH PLANE is 9 in. long with a 2 in. cutter and is used on uneven surfaces and small pieces. The FORE PLANE is 18 in. long with a 2-3/8 in. cutter and is used to plane large surfaces and especially the edges of long boards. The JACK PLANE is 14 in. long with a 2 in. cutter and is a general purpose plane that can be used for many planing operations. The sizes listed are the most common, however other sizes are available. For example: the jack plane is available in lengths from 11-1/2 to 15 in. with a cutter width of 1-3/4 to 2-1/4 in.

You should become thoroughly acquainted with the standard plane and how it is assembled and adjusted. Study your plane and refer to Fig. 3-2, to learn the name of the parts and how they fit together. To remove the plane iron (also called the cutter or blade) raise the lever on the lever cap and remove. The double plane iron (plane iron and plane iron cap) can now be lifted from the plane. To disassemble the double plane iron, loosen the cap screw, pull the cap iron back from

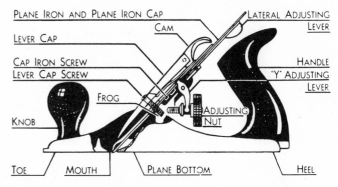

Fig. 3-2. Parts of a plane.

the plane iron edge, turn it sideways and then slide it toward the edge until the cap screw clears the hole in the plane iron.

Sharpening Plane Iron

Sharpening a plane iron includes operations of grinding and honing (also called whetting). GRINDING is the shaping and forming of the cutting edge and bevel. HONING involves work on only the tip of the cutting edge to make it sharp. A plane iron that is in good condition can be honed a number of times before it will require grinding.

Oilstones used for honing are either natural or manufactured materials. One of the well-known NATURAL oilstones is the Arkansas, which is white to light gray in color and sometimes has darker streaks showing in the surface. It is made of natural novaculite stone, has a fine cutting surface and is used as the "final touch" for a razor-sharp edge. The ARTIFICIAL (manufactured) oilstones are made from aluminum-oxide (reddish-brown color) and silicon-carbide (dark gray color). They are available in a large variety of shapes and sizes and are graded as coarse, medium, and fine. Aluminum-oxide stone is often referred to as an India oilstone while silicon-carbide stones are sold under such trade names as Crestolon and Carborundum.

HONING: Apply a small amount of thin oil to the face of a medium grade oilstone and place the bevel of the plane iron flat on the surface. Now

3-1

raise the other end a few degrees so that just the cutting edge rests on the stone. Maintain this angle and move the plane iron forward and backward over the entire surface as shown in Fig. 3-3(A). Continue these strokes until you can feel

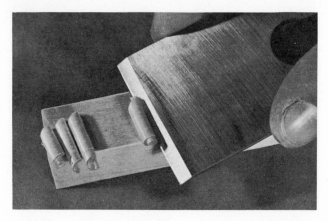

Fig. 3-4. Testing the sharpness of a plane iron. The iron should cut a fine, "silky" shaving with only slight pressure applied.

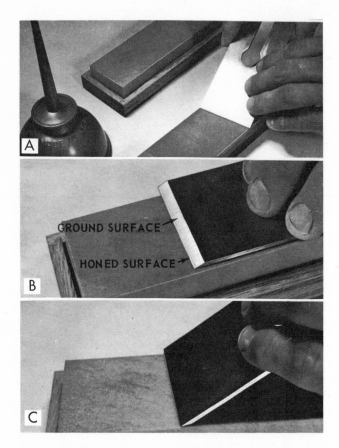

GROUND SURFACE

HONED SURFACE

Fig. 3-3. Honing a plane iron. Above. Honing beveled side until a slight wire edge is formed. Center. Plane iron turned over and honed lightly while held **FLAT** on the stone. Below. Final honing on a fine oilstone.

a fine wire edge when you pull your finger out over the edge. This fine wire edge should exist all the way across the plane iron. Now turn the plane iron over, LAY IT FLAT on a fine oilstone and stroke it a few times as shown in Fig. 3-3(B).

Turn the plane iron back to the bevel side on the fine stone for a few light strokes, then again stroke the top of the iron held flat on the oilstone. Repeat this procedure several times until the wire edge has disappeared. The edge should now be sharp and "keen" and should cut a smooth, silky shaving when tested on a piece of wood as shown in Fig. 3-4.

Be sure to use sufficient oil on the surface of the oilstone. The oil will carry the fine steel cuttings and prevent them from becoming embedded in the pores of the stone and glazing the surface. When you finish using the oilstone, wipe off the surface and replace the cover.

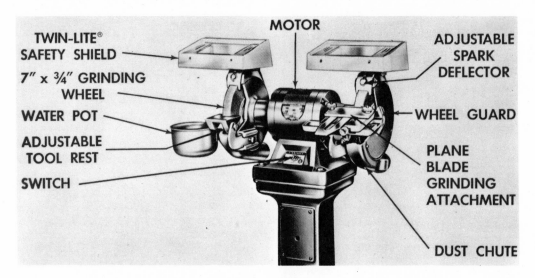

TWIN-LITE® SAFETY SHIELD

7" x ¾" GRINDING WHEEL

WATER POT

ADJUSTABLE TOOL REST

SWITCH

MOTOR

ADJUSTABLE SPARK DEFLECTOR

WHEEL GUARD

PLANE BLADE GRINDING ATTACHMENT

DUST CHUTE

Fig. 3-5. Parts of a tool grinder. A medium-fine (60 grain size) aluminum-oxide grinding wheel will be satisfactory for most woodworking tools. (Delta Power Tools)

GRINDING: Forming an accurate bevel on a plane iron requires the use of a guide or grinding attachment. Sometimes the cap iron can be turned crosswise and tightened to the plane iron so that

When using a grinding attachment, first place the plane iron in the carrier with the bevel against the grinding wheel. Then adjust the angle of the attachment so that the surface of the bevel ground

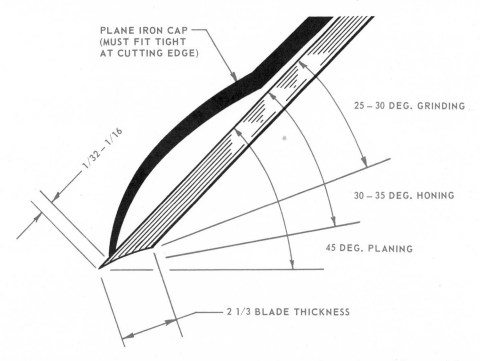

PLANE IRON CAP
(MUST FIT TIGHT
AT CUTTING EDGE)

1/32 – 1/16

25 – 30 DEG. GRINDING

30 – 35 DEG. HONING

45 DEG. PLANING

2 1/3 BLADE THICKNESS

Fig. 3-6. A double plane iron assembly showing the grinding and honing angles.

it serves as a guide along the tool rest of the grinder. Fig. 3-7, shows a plane iron clamped in a grinding attachment that makes it easy to form a bevel that is properly shaped.

will be about two and one-third times the thickness of the plane iron. Tighten the clamp that holds the plane iron, turn on the grinder, take a light cut and check the grinding angle. If it is correct, grind the bevel by moving it back and forth across the wheel. Do not let the edge go beyond the center of the wheel face in either direction. Continue grinding until the edge is thin and a slight burr starts to form. Grind slightly more on the outside corners so they will be about 1/32 in. lower than the main part of the edge. Some woodworkers prefer to form this slight crown on the oilstone. Remove any burr that was formed in the grinding operation on a coarse or medium oilstone and then proceed to hone the plane iron as previously described.

Fig. 3-7. Attachment for grinding plane irons, chisels and
other beveled edge tools.
(Delta Power Tools)

WOODY SAYS:

"During the grinding operation, KEEP THE PLANE IRON COOL by dipping it in water. If the grinder does not have an approved eye shield, YOU SHOULD WEAR GOGGLES."

Adjusting Plane

Position the plane iron cap on the plane iron as shown in Fig. 3-8, and tighten the cap iron screw. The edge of the plane iron cap must fit

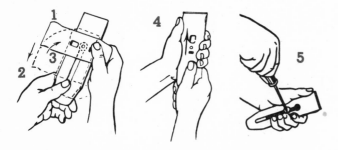

Fig. 3-8. Assembly of double plane iron. 1-Lay the plane iron cap on the plane iron with cap screw in slot. 2-Draw the cap back. 3-Turn it straight with the plane iron. 4-Advance the plane iron cap until it is within 1/16 to 1/32 in. of the cutting edge. 5-Tighten the cap screw.

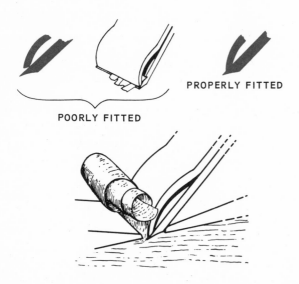

PROPERLY FITTED

POORLY FITTED

Fig. 3-9. The plane iron cap must fit tight to the plane iron. Its purpose is to break and curl the shavings and prevent the wood from splitting ahead of the cutting edge. On cross-grained or curly-grained woods it should be close to the cutting edge. (Stanley Tools)

tight against the top of the plane iron; otherwise, shavings will feed under it and prevent the plane from cutting properly. See Fig. 3-9.

Carefully place the double plane iron into the plane and secure its position with the lever cap. If necessary, adjust the setting of the lever cap screw so that the cam of the lever cap locks in place with smooth, firm pressure.

Turn the plane upside down and sight across the bottom. Look toward a window or other source of light. Turn the adjustment nut clockwise until

the blade projects above the plane bottom about 1/16 in. Now move the lateral adjustment lever from side to side until the cutting edge is parallel to the bottom of the plane. Turn the adjustment nut counterclockwise until the cutting edge is withdrawn below the surface of the plane bottom. Place the plane on the surface of the stock and turn the adjustment nut clockwise until the plane edge just begins to cut.

Planing a Surface

If you will look closely at lumber that has been surfaced you will find there are very small "waves" (called mill marks) which were formed by the rotating knives of a power planer. See Fig. 3-10. These should be removed with a hand

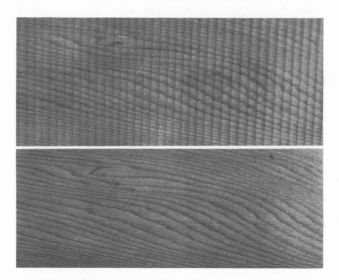

Fig. 3-10. Above. Millmarks on stock surfaced with a power planer. Below. Surface after hand planing.

plane. It takes a great amount of hand sanding to remove such marks, and since they are slightly compressed into the wood by the machine, there is a tendency for them to reappear when finish is applied. Hand planing may also be used to remove warp and other imperfections.

Plane the best face of the stock first. By examining the edge of the board try to determine the direction of the grain and clamp the stock in position so you will be planing WITH the grain. Most stock can be laid flat on a bench and clamped between a bench stop and vise dog as shown in Fig. 3-11.

Place the plane on the stock and move it over the surface, gradually turning the adjustment nut until a fine shaving is cut. You may find that the plane cuts in some spots and not in others. This indicates high places in the surface. Continue to

Fig. 3-11. Planing a surface.

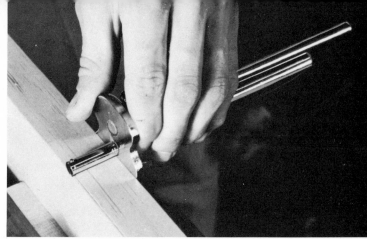

Fig. 3-13. Using a mortise gauge to lay out stock thickness.

Fig. 3-12. Checking the surface. The rule or straightedge must be placed diagonally across the stock to reveal twist (wind).

Fig. 3-14. Clamping thin pieces for planing. Keep the vise dog below the surface of the stock so it will not damage the plane.

plane these high spots until they disappear and the plane "takes" a shaving across the entire surface. Keep the plane set for a very fine cut. THE SHAVINGS SHOULD BE LIGHT AND FEATHERY and should seem to almost float when you drop a handful to the floor. Try to produce a smooth, true surface with as little planing as possible. Check the surface with a rule as shown in Fig. 3-12.

WOODY SAYS:

"Take good care of your plane. In addition to sharpening the plane iron, keep the knob, handle, and frog tightened. Keep the plane clean by wiping it with a slightly oiled cloth. Some craftsmen apply a little paste wax to the bottom and sides to reduce friction and also to protect against rust."

Generally, it is considered best to plane the surface of your stock while it is in one piece and before it is cut into smaller parts. If, however, there is much warpage present, it may be best to cut the stock into smaller pieces before hand planing. Warped stock can be straightened by planing across the grain or diagonally with the grain.

TURN THE STOCK END OVER END and plane the other side. Measure the stock at several points to determine finished thickness. A marking gauge can be used for this or to lay out a thickness measurement all the way around the edge as shown in Fig. 3-13.

On some work, the hand surfacing operation should be done later. If it is necessary to make edge joints to secure the required width of stock, then the hand surfacing operation should be left until after these joints have been made.

Small thin pieces are hard to clamp and hold while they are being planed. A board with a strip of hardboard glued to one end can be used as shown in Fig. 3-14.

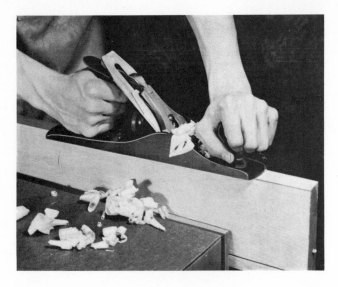

Fig. 3-15. Planing an edge.

Planing an Edge

After both surfaces have been planed, clamp the stock in the vise with the best edge up and the grain running in the right direction. The best edge is planed first since defects on the second edge will likely be removed when the stock is reduced to the required width.

Start the cut with most of the pressure on the plane knob and continue this pressure until the plane is well supported by the stock. Finish the cut with extra pressure on the plane handle. Fig. 3-15 shows a jack plane being used. A smooth plane will also work but may not produce as straight an edge.

In planing an edge, use the same general procedure as in planing a surface. Continue to plane until you can produce one continuous cut the entire length of the board. Use the try square to check the edge for squareness with the face, Fig. 3-16.

From the finished edge, lay out the required width and draw a line down the length of the stock. Turning the stock end over end from the position used to plane the first edge should place the grain

Fig. 3-16. Checking the edge to see that it is square with the face.

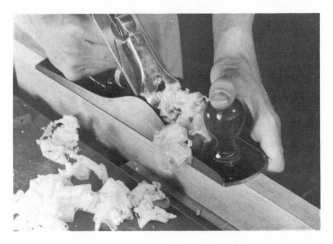

Fig. 3-17. Guiding the toe of the plane with fingers held on the plane bottom. Used for a fine and accurate cut.

Fig. 3-18. Clamping methods. Left. A long strip needs the support of the bench top. Right. Large panel supported with the vise and a hand screw.

in the right direction. Some woodworkers prefer to square the ends to finished length before planing the second edge.

For very accurate planing it is sometimes helpful to hold the plane as shown in Fig. 3-17. The fingers under the plane serve as a guide to hold it in proper alignment throughout the cut. This will result in the shaving being cut by the same section of the plane iron.

Stock should always be held securely for planing operations. Fig. 3-18 shows some clamping setups. A long strip cannot be held in the vise because it will bend under the weight of the plane and prevent accurate work. In the same figure, note that the good face of the plywood panel is being protected with a block of wood. Use great care in handling stock that has been planed and smoothed so you will not need to remove nicks, dents, and soiled spots when you prepare your project for finish.

When the pieces of stock are very small it may be more practical to clamp or secure the tool and move the wood. Such a setup is shown in Fig. 3-19, for planing the edge of small pieces of walnut. A carefully made straightedge is glued to a piece of flat stock and this unit and a jack plane are clamped in the vise.

Fig. 3-19. Special set-up for planing small pieces. The jack plane being used has a corrugated bottom, preferred by some workers because they feel it reduces friction.

Squaring Stock to Length with Backsaw

Lay out the position of the cut and then mark a line across the surface using a try square and sharp pencil. Hold the handle of the try square

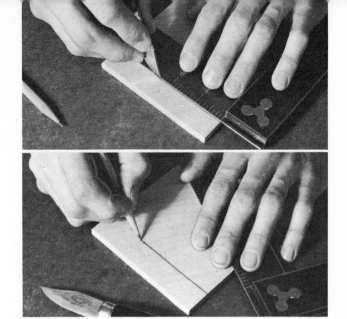

Fig. 3-20. Precision layout. Above. Knife drawn along the blade of a try square. Below. Sharp pencil drawn in the knife cut to make it easier to see.

against the edge of the stock and draw the line along the blade. For precision work use a knife as shown in Fig. 3-20.

The backsaw is used for making fine, accurate cuts. It has teeth similar to the crosscut saw but much finer (14 points). The blade is thin and is reinforced with a heavy metal strip.

When cutting with a backsaw, the stock is held in a horizontal position, in a vise, on a bench hook, or by other means. The saw cut is started in about the same manner as a regular handsaw but at a lower angle. After the cut is started, slowly lower the handle as you continue sawing and follow the cutting line across the surface of the stock. See Fig. 3-21. Use horizontal strokes to finish the cut.

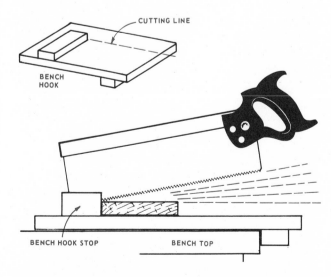

Fig. 3-21. A backsaw cut with the stock held on a bench hook. The bench hook stop serves as a guide for the saw when starting the cut.

For a precision cut with the backsaw, you may want to use the procedure shown in Fig. 3-22. It takes a little longer to set up; but since you are assured of a square cut that will require little or no planing, you may actually save time. An important part of this setup is an accurate "straightedge." This is a straight piece of stock with faces and edges perfectly square. Clamp the straightedge firmly along the cutting line. Tighten the outside spindle of the handscrew last since it provides the greatest leverage.

Place the blade of the backsaw against the straightedge and start the cut. With the left hand, apply pressure to the side of the saw so the blade will be held snugly against the straightedge throughout the cut. A block of wood can be held against the blade as shown in Fig. 3-22(A). The teeth of a backsaw are small and will not cut fast, so use long steady strokes. Sawdust cut near the center of the board must be moved to the edge of the stock, before it can be cleared from the saw kerf. Short strokes will not clear the sawdust and it will work up along the sides of the saw and cause the blade to bind. Notice that the stock is clamped to a scrap piece that protects the saw from the vise and supports the wood fibers on the underside of the cut.

From the squared end lay out the finished length. Use the same procedure to cut off the second end. Whenever possible, clamp the straightedge on the stock so that the saw kerf will be on the "waste" side of the line. If you cannot do this, you will need to make an allowance for the width of the saw kerf.

Planing End Grain

End grain is hard to plane. Although a jack plane or smooth plane can be used, a BLOCK PLANE will do the best work. The blade of the block plane is positioned at a very low angle, with the BEVELED SIDE TURNED UP. It is designed to be held in one hand, leaving the other hand free to hold the work.

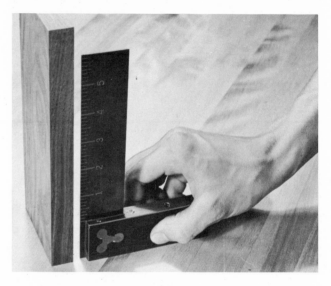

Fig. 3-23. Precision check for squareness.

When planing end grain the cut should not continue over an edge or end unless the wood fibers are supported as shown in Fig. 3-24. When the board is wide, plane in from each edge, toward the center. Always adjust the plane for a very light cut.

Fig. 3-22. Using straightedge to guide backsaw. A-Holding saw against straightedge with block of wood. B-Completed cut. C-Setting straightedge for second cut. D-Making second cut.

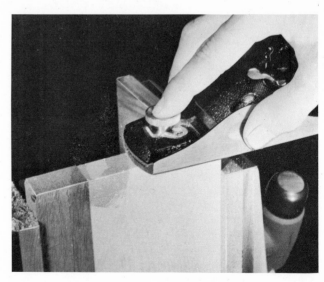

Fig. 3-24. Planing end grain. The edge is supported with scrap stock.

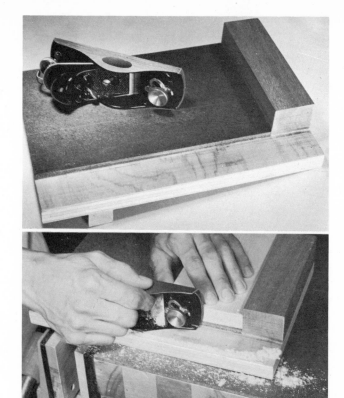

Fig. 3-25. *Above. Block plane and shooting-board. Below.*
Planing end grain.

A good way to plane end grain is with a device called a "shooting-board" as shown in Fig. 3-25. It is constructed somewhat similar to a bench hook with the addition of a guide for the plane bottom. When using the shooting-board, the stock should be held firmly against the stop and fed into the cut after each stroke.

When planing the edge of plywood you will always be cutting some end grain. The block plane is a good tool to use for this operation, Fig. 3-26.

STOP CLAMPED
IN VISE

Fig. 3-26. *Using block plane to smooth edge of plywood.*

Squaring Small Pieces of Stock

Small pieces and parts are difficult to plane and saw. They are hard to clamp and hold and the regular tools seem large and "clumsy." A sawing jig that works well is shown in Fig. 3-27. It

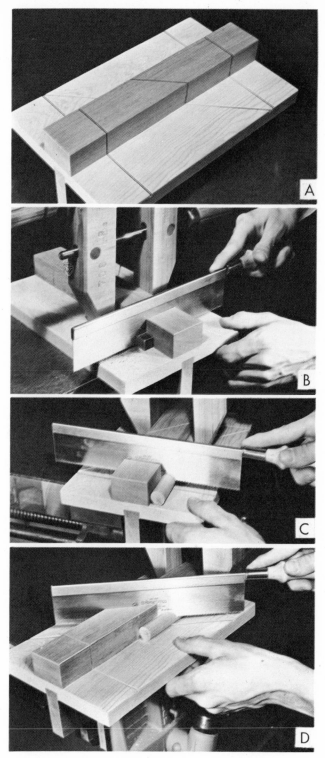

Fig. 3-27. *A-Sawing jig for small parts. B-Cutting a small square block. C-Squaring-off piece of dowel. D-Cutting dowel at an angle.*

clamps into the vise and operates about like a miter box. The DOVETAIL SAW being used has fine teeth, a thin blade and makes a smooth and accurate cut.

When constructing the jig, square the main center piece and then cut it into parts with the miter box. These pieces are then carefully glued

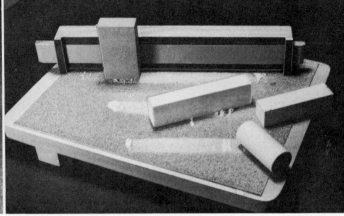

Fig. 3-28. Left. Squaring small parts on a sanding board using a sliding carrier. Right. View of the sliding carrier and finished pieces.

in place on the baseboard, using spacers equal to the saw blade thickness. Apply some paste wax to the slot to make the saw run smoothly.

Jigs like this are not hard to build and will help you do better work in less time. Some jigs may be specialized and designed to perform just one operation on a given part. They are used on mass production projects where many identical parts are produced.

Sanding should usually not be started until all edge tool operations are complete. Small parts, however, can be squared easily and quickly on a sanding board. They can be held perpendicular to the surface with a straightedge or a sliding carrier shown in Fig. 3-28. This carrier eliminates the tendency for the part to tip over as it is moved along the straightedge.

Test Your Knowledge

1. The smallest type of plane that uses a double plane iron assembly is called _____ plane.
2. The front end of the plane bottom is called the _____.
3. To remove the double plane iron from the jack plane you must first loosen and remove the _____.
4. An oilstone that is reddish-brown in color is made of a manufactured abrasive called _____.
5. Why is oil applied to the surface of the oilstone when honing an edge?
6. The bevel of a plane iron should be ground so that the included angle is from _____ to _____ degrees.

7. To increase the depth of cut of the jack plane the adjusting nut is turned _____ (clockwise, counterclockwise).
8. If the plane is not "taking" a shaving over the entire surface then the depth of cut should be increased. True or False?
9. To align the plane iron edge with the plane bottom the _____ adjustment lever is moved.
10. If the stock is to be edge-glued to form wider widths, then the surfacing operation is performed later. True or False?
11. The backsaw has "crosscut" shaped teeth that are small and number about _____ points per inch.
12. The blade of the block plane sets at a low angle with the beveled side turned _____.

Outside Assignments

1. Make a design sketch of a shooting-board that can be adjusted to plane the ends of pieces at a 45, 60, and 90 degree angle.
2. Make a design sketch of a sawing jig that could be used to cut 100 pieces, exactly 2 in. long from strips of stock 3/4 in. square.
3. From the catalog of a supplier or manufacturer, develop a list of the various kinds of oilstones with a description that includes sizes, grades, materials and current retail prices.
4. Visit a local hardware store and make a list of the types of hand planes on display. Include a complete size description and current prices.

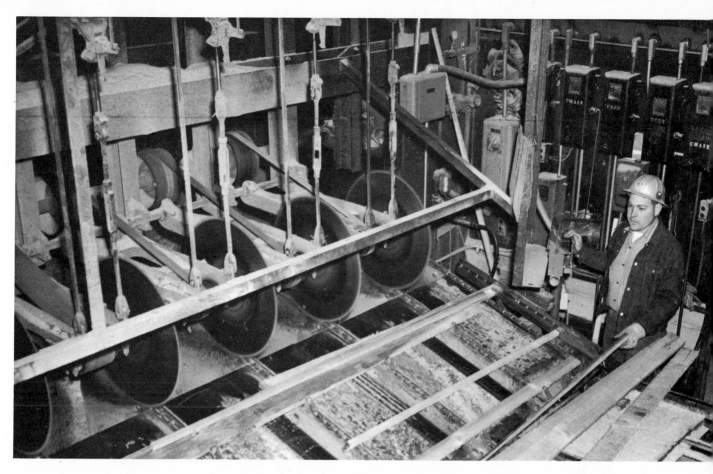

Industry photos. Above. Multiple trimmer saw cuts rough boards to length. By simply pressing buttons, operator can lower any of the blades to make desired cuts as boards pass underneath. Note feed chains located in table. (Weyerhaeuser Co.) Below. Skilled operator using a modern saw grinder to sharpen a large circular saw blade. Special controls provide uniform tooth height, depth, and shape. The machine can be set up to sharpen any type of blade. (Foley Mfg. Co.)

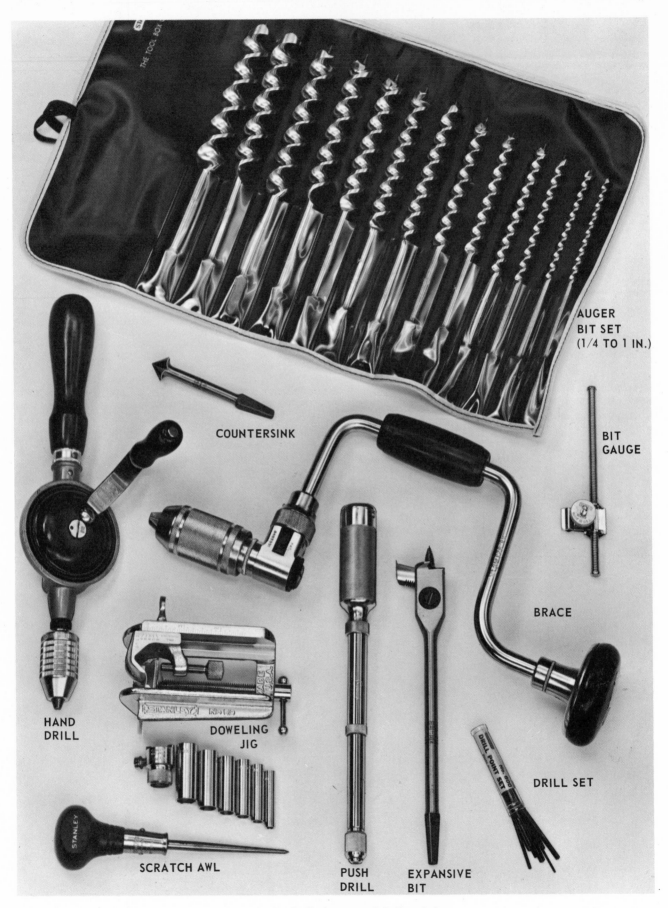

AUGER
BIT SET
(1/4 TO 1 IN.)

COUNTERSINK

BIT
GAUGE

BRACE

HAND
DRILL

DOWELING
JIG

DRILL SET

SCRATCH AWL

PUSH
DRILL

EXPANSIVE
BIT

Fig. 4-1. Tools for boring and drilling holes.
(Stanley Tools)

Unit 4

DRILLING AND BORING HOLES

Braces and Auger Bits

In working with hand tools, holes larger than one-quarter inch in diameter are bored with auger bits, Forstner bits and expansion bits. These tools are mounted in a brace that holds them in position and provides the leverage to turn the bits into the wood. Holes 1/4 in. and smaller are usually drilled with a hand drill.

The parts of a standard ratchet brace are shown in Fig. 4-2. The shell and jaws form a chuck that is designed to hold the square shank of the various bits. The size of the brace is determined by its "sweep" which is the diameter of the circle the handle forms as it is turned. Braces are available in sizes from 8 to 14 in. A good size for the school shop is 8 or 10 in. Most braces are equipped with a ratchet that permits boring in a corner even though a full revolution of the handle cannot be made. In heavy boring, the ratchet is helpful since the handle can be positioned for the greatest leverage.

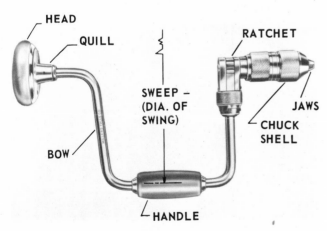

Fig. 4-2. Parts of a standard ratchet brace. (Millers Falls Co.)

The brace requires little maintenance other than a few drops of fine oil on the threads of the chuck, and on the ratchet, handle, and head bearing, from time to time.

Auger bits will vary in the shape and design of the twist but all of them will have about the same parts as shown in Fig. 4-3. The FEED SCREW centers the bit and draws it into the wood. The pitch of the feed screw determines the rate of feed. Bits are available for fast, medium, and slow boring. The SPURS (also called nibs) score the perimeter of the hole as the LIPS (also called cutters) cut the shavings from the inside. After the shavings are cut, the TWIST moves them out of the hole.

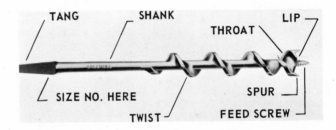

Fig. 4-3. Parts of an auger bit (solid center type).

The size (diameter) of standard bits range from 3/16 in. to as large as 2 in. The more common sizes are from 1/4 to 1 in. The size is stamped on the tang in sixteenths of an inch so that a 1/2 in. bit would carry a No. 8 (for 8/16 or 1/2 in.). For a 3/4 in. hole a No. 12 would be used. The length of auger bits range from 7 to 10 in. with the exception of dowel bits that are about 5 1/2 in.

Sharpening an Auger Bit

Sharpening an auger bit requires considerable skill and careful work. Check with your instructor before attempting this operation.

A special auger bit file is available for sharpening auger bits, however, other small, fine files can be used. Sharpen the lips or cutters first by stroking upward through the throat as shown in Fig. 4-4. Use medium pressure. Stop as soon as the cutters are sharp. Try to maintain the original

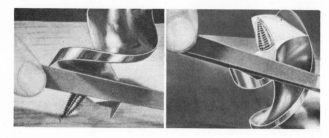

Fig. 4-4. Left. Filing the cutting lip. Right. Filing the spur. Try to maintain original bevel and do not file the outside.

bevel. Do not file the underside (side next to the screw). Turn the bit over, rest it on the edge of the bench and file the INSIDE OF THE SPURS. Try to keep the bit balanced by filing about the same amount on each side.

Layout and Marking

Holes are usually bored and drilled after the stock has been surfaced and squared to finished size. Study your working drawings and then with a ruler, square, and sharp pencil, lay out the center lines that will locate the exact position of

WOODY SAYS:

"The edges of auger bits will stay sharp a long time if they are carefully handled. When not in use, keep them in special boxes or holders or in fabric rolls. They will stay bright and "shiny" if you wipe them with a cloth lightly saturated with oil."

also provides material for the feed screw to enter and "pull" the bit through to complete the hole.

Select the correct size bit and insert it well into the chuck of the brace with the corners of the tang held in the V of the jaws. Tighten the jaws on the bit by holding the chuck shell and turning the brace, as shown in Fig. 4-6.

Guide the bit with your left hand and set it into the hole marked with the awl. Turn the brace clockwise and keep the bit perpendicular to the surface of the stock. Have another student help

Fig. 4-5. Left. Laying out center lines to locate the position of holes. Right. Making a hole for the feed screw of the bit.

the holes. See Fig. 4-5. Draw these lines lightly so that those remaining after the holes are bored, can be easily erased. Use a scratch awl to punch a hole where the center lines intersect. This hole will make it easy to start the feed screw of the bit in the correct location.

Boring a Hole

The stock should be securely held, either in the vise, or clamped to the bench. If the hole is to be bored all the way through, it should be firmly clamped to a piece of waste stock that will support the wood around the edges of the hole when the bit cuts through the opposite side. The waste stock

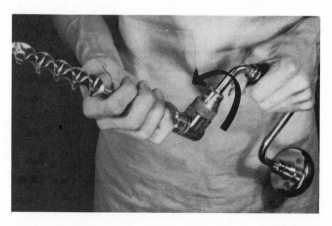

Fig. 4-6. Tightening the chuck of the brace by holding the shell and turning the handle.

you "sight" this angle or keep the bit aligned with try squares as shown in Fig. 4-7.

It is usually easier to keep the bit perpendicular to the surface when boring in a vertical position, but on large holes you may not be able to exert

Fig. 4-8. Above. Boring from the front side until the feed screw just starts to come through the back surface. Below. Stock is reversed and the holes finished from back surface. (A double twist type of bit is being used.)

Fig. 4-7. Boring a hole in a vertical position using try squares to align the bit. Note the waste stock under the work. Be careful not to bore on through the waste stock and into the the vise or bench.

enough pressure. This is especially true when boring holes into the end of stock because the feed screw will not "hold" in the end grain and you will need to apply extra pressure.

If it is not convenient to "back up" the work with waste stock the hole should be bored from both sides. Bore from one side until the feed screw just begins to come through, then reverse the stock and complete the hole as shown in Fig. 4-8. When boring a deep hole, withdraw the bit several times to cool it and clear the shavings. Lay out and bore the hole half way in from each end when boring lamp stems and similar pieces.

Use extra care when starting a hole in plywood or you may splinter the veneer around the edge of the hole. Start the feed screw and turn the bit until the spurs just begin to score the outside of the hole. Turn the bit about a half turn backward, and then forward, several times until the surface veneer is completely cut, before continuing to bore the hole. When boring a large hole in a small piece, especially near the end, you can help prevent splitting by applying pressure to the sides with a hand screw. See Fig. 4-9.

Fig. 4-9. Clamping the sides of a narrow piece to help prevent splitting.

Boring a Hole to Specified Depth

There are several patented bit gauges available that will control the depth of the bored hole. They are usually clamped to the twist or shank of the bit and adjusted to provide the required depth. One type of gauge is shown in Fig. 4-10.

You can make a simple depth gauge by boring through a block of wood, cutting it to length and then slipping it over the bit so the bit extends an amount equal to the hole depth required.

If you have just a few holes to bore, you can wrap a small strip of masking tape around the twist at a position that will provide the required depth.

Doweling Jigs

Doweling jigs are specially designed for making dowel joints, however they can also be used to insure straight holes in edges and ends of pieces.

Fig. 4-10. A bit gauge is used to control the depth of the hole. This one is a spring type that will not mar the surface. (Stanley Tools)

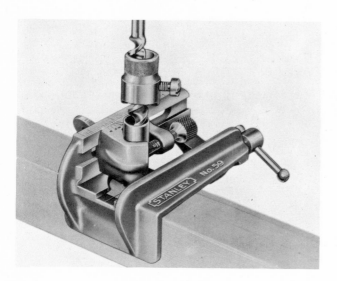

Fig. 4-11. Doweling jig with removable bit guides and adjustable guide carrier.

Figs. 4-11 and 4-12 show two types of jigs. One has a set of guides (sleeves) that matches auger bit Nos. 3 to 8. These guides are clamped in a carrier that can be set in various positions across the edge of the stock. The other doweling jig has a center guide block that always remains centered between the two outside jaws. Holes 1/2 in. and under can be bored.

Fig. 4-12. Doweling jig with a self-centering guide block. (Dowl-it Co.)

Counterboring

Sometimes it is necessary to have a hole of two different diameters. For example, you might want to place a screw or bolt head below the surface of the work. First bore the hole for the head to the required depth and then, make the hole that will match the shank of the bolt or screw. See Fig. 4-13. It is important that you bore the holes in this order. If the small hole is bored first there will be no way to center the larger bit.

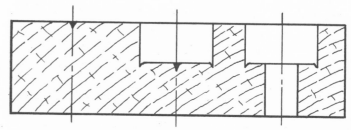

Fig. 4-13. Counterboring. Left. Position marked. Center. Large hole bored. Right. Smaller hole bored.

Fig. 4-14. Boring a hole at an angle.

Boring Holes at an Angle

To bore a hole at an angle, set a T-bevel square at the required angle (use a protractor or the miter gauge of a table saw) and place it on the surface to be bored. Start the feed screw in the marked hole with the bit vertical and then tilt it to the required angle. Bring the blade of the T-bevel close to the bit and use it to align the hole as shown in Fig. 4-14.

If you have a number of holes to bore at the same angle you can do more accurate work if you make a boring jig. There are many ways to make such a jig and the design and procedure will vary depending on the requirements of the work. Fig. 4-15 shows a jig that was designed to make a series of closely spaced holes on a wide board.

Fig. 4-16. *Boring a large hole with an expansive bit.*

Instead of boring the hole at an angle in the jig block, the hole was first bored square to the edge and then the block was cut at the required angle.

Using an Expansive Bit

An expansive bit is used to bore holes from about 7/8 to 3 in. in diameter. It has adjustable cutters (usually two).

Adjust the cutter so the distance from the spur to the feed screw is equal to the radius of the hole. Some bits have a scale that will help you make this setting. After the setting is made lock the cutter securely. Start a test hole in a scrap block and check the size before using it on your project.

In using an expansive bit to bore all the way through the stock, it is best to back-up the work with a scrap piece as shown in Fig. 4-16. Large holes will require lots of "power" so it is advisable to use a large brace (10-12 in.) to give you extra leverage.

Using a Forstner Bit

A Forstner bit does not have a feed screw. It is used for boring holes that go only part way through the stock and require a smooth flat bottom. It can be used to enlarge holes or bore holes in thin stock where the feed screw of a regular bit might cause the stock to split. A sharp Forstner bit works well for end grain boring. These bits are available in the same range of sizes as standard bits.

Locate the position of holes to be bored with a Forstner bit by drawing a circle or square the size of the bit. Another method that works well is shown in Fig. 4-17. The hole is started with a standard bit and then completed with a Forstner bit.

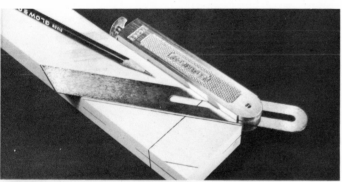

Fig. 4-15. *Making and using a boring jig. Above. Laying out required angles. Center. Boring a perfectly straight hole. Below. Using the jig after it has been cut out. Note how it is aligned with the center lines.*

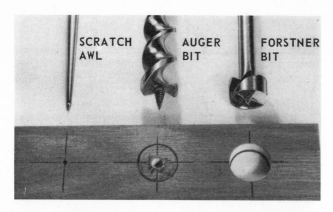

Fig. 4-17. Boring with a Forstner bit. Left. Standard layout procedure. Center. Score the hole with a regular bit. Right. Complete the hole with a Forstner bit.

Drilling Holes

As mentioned before, holes 1/4 in. and smaller are usually drilled with a hand drill, using straight shank drills. Study the parts of the standard model shown in Fig. 4-18. Apply a few drops of fine oil on the bearings of the gear and pinions when they need lubrication.

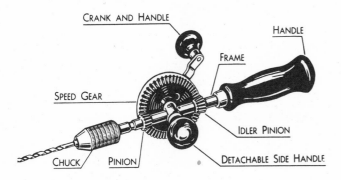

Fig. 4-18. Parts of a hand drill.

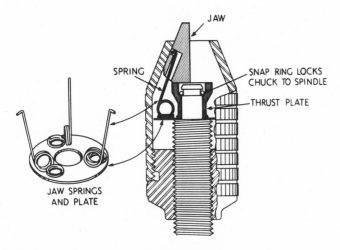

Fig. 4-19. Parts of a chuck. As the shell of the chuck is turned the jaws are moved in or out along the inside rim of the shell. The springs hold the jaws in position.

The size of a hand drill is determined by the capacity of its chuck. The most common size is 1/4 in. however a 3/8 in. size is also available. Fig. 4-19, shows the parts of a three-jaw chuck and how it works. Twist drills are made in a wide range of sizes. A good set for use in the hand drill should range from 1/16 to 1/4 in. by thirty-seconds or sixty-fourths.

In drilling holes, use the same procedure as suggested for boring holes. It is important that the hole be started with an awl since the twist drill has a blunt point. Place a twist drill all the way into the drill chuck and tighten the jaws. You can open and close the jaws by holding the chuck and turning the crank.

Hold the handle in one hand and keep the drill perpendicular to the surface, while turning the crank with your other hand. See Fig. 4-20. Small drills will break if you do not work carefully.

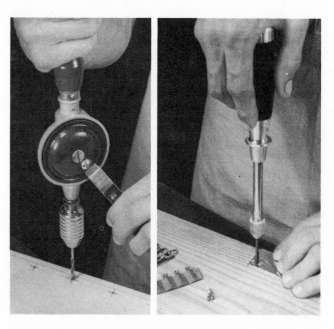

Fig. 4-20. Left. Drilling holes with a hand drill. Fig. 4-21. Right. Using an automatic drill to install a hinge.

Since there is no feed screw on a drill bit, you will control the feed by the pressure you apply. The amount of pressure to apply varies with the size of bit and the kind of wood. Drill to the required depth and continue to turn the drill while pulling it out of the hole. If the hole is deep, pull the drill out several times to clear the cuttings. Remove the drill from the chuck as soon as you have finished using it.

Automatic drills (also called push drills) are designed to drill small holes rapidly. When the handle is pushed down the drill revolves. A spring inside the handle forces it back to its original position when pressure is released. Automatic drills use a fluted bit (drill point) that fits into a special chuck. Sizes range from 1/16 to about 3/16 in. Carpenters quite often use this type of

3. The number size of the auger bit is stamped on the _____.
4. What size hole will bits with the following numbers bore? No. 4, No. 7, No. 14.

A well organized tool cabinet.
(Brodhead-Garrett)

drill to make holes for nails and screws. The main advantage of the automatic drill is that it can be operated with one hand as shown in Fig. 4-21.

Test Your Knowledge

1. A brace that is equipped with a _____ can be used to bore holes even though a complete revolution of the handle cannot be made.
2. The spur of the auger bit acts as a center and draws it into the wood. True or False?

5. The feed screw of the bit is easily started if a _____ _____ has been used to mark the center of the hole.
6. The threads in the chuck of the brace are right handed. True or False?
7. End grain is usually easier to bore than side grain. True or False?
8. When making a counterbored hole the _____ (largest, smallest) hole is bored first.
9. A boring tool that can be adjusted to make various sized holes is called an _____ bit.
10. The size of a hand drill is determined by the size of its _____.

Outside Assignments

1. Make a selected list of the boring and drilling hand tools for a home workshop. Include the size, description and cost for each item. Refer to suppliers' and manufacturers' catalogs for information.
2. Develop a presentation sketch and a working drawing of a tool holder for a complete set of standard auger bits. Design the holder so that it can be mounted on a vertical tool panel. A good tool holder will have many of the following features:
   (1) Holds the tool securely.
   (2) Holds the tool in correct position.
   (3) Protects the tool from damage.
   (4) Protects the worker from injury.
   (5) Includes name and size.
   (6) Easily cleaned and maintained.
   (7) Attractive in appearance.

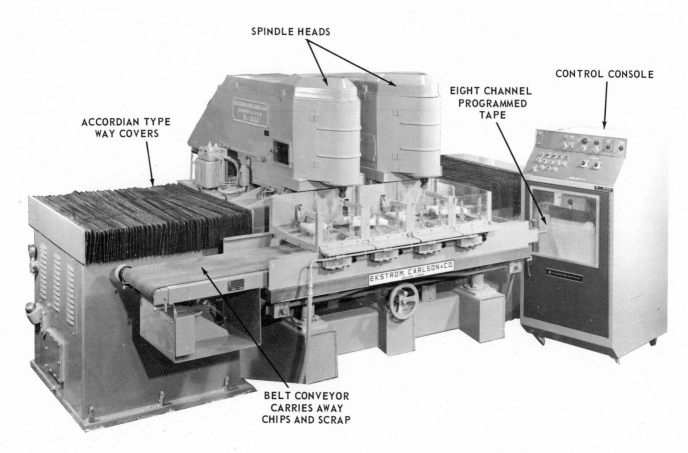

SPINDLE HEADS

CONTROL CONSOLE

EIGHT CHANNEL PROGRAMMED TAPE

ACCORDIAN TYPE WAY COVERS

BELT CONVEYOR CARRIES AWAY CHIPS AND SCRAP

Automatic tape controlled router and shaper (double headed). All machine movements are punched on tape for complete automatic operation, including contour and straight line cuts, spindle up and down, and spindle start and stop. Flat belt drives from 15 hp motors provide spindle speeds of 23,000 rpm. Longitudinal and transverse feeds are activated by high performance hydraulic-servo mechanisms at speeds that can be varied from 0 to 400 ft. per minute.
(Ekstrom, Carlson and Co.)

Routing gun stocks with single head machine. Note the complex fixture design required to hold and support work in exact position.

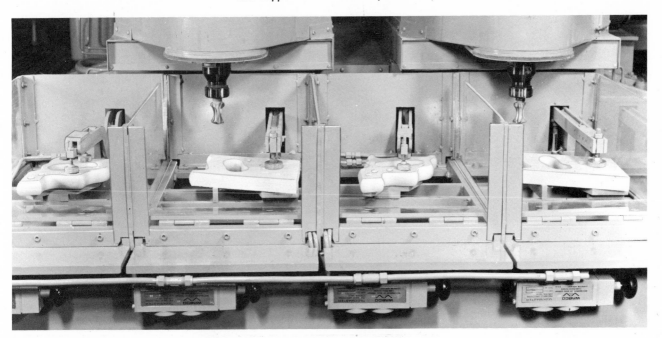

Close-up view shows two stations and spindles. Saw handle blank is first placed in a right-hand fixture where shaper bit cuts hand hole and about half of the outside edge. This partially completed work is then clamped in the left-hand fixture where contour and edge shaping is completed. Clamps holding the work in the fixtures are operated by air. Each operation is set up on a 30 sec. cycle which results in a production rate of about 180 saw handles per hour.

18 IN. LEVEL

BENCH RULE

CARPENTERS FRAMING SQUARE

STEEL SQUARE

6 IN. TRY SQUARE

COMBINATION SQUARE

TAPE RULE

10 IN. TRY SQUARE

T-BEVEL SQUARE

MARKING GAUGE

SCRATCH AWL

FOLDING RULE

MORTISE GAUGE

PLUMB BOB

Fig. 5-1. Layout tools for woodwork.
(Stanley Tools)

Unit 5
WOOD JOINTS

There are many kinds of wood joints used in building construction, cabinetmaking, pattern-making and boatbuilding. Most of them can be classified under the basic groups included in this Unit. Some wood joints are simple and easily recognized while others are complicated and may be a combination of several of the basic types.

Although many new and efficient metal fasteners have been designed, most fine furniture and cabinetwork is still assembled with glue. The strength of glued joints depends to a large extent on the contact area (the surface of one piece touching the other piece) and the quality of the fit. Some joints have interlocking features that may minimize the importance of the adhesive. Manufacturers of wood products often develop interlocking joints, held together with metal fasteners, that permit the article to be easily disassembled and reassembled. Such a feature helps to reduce storage space and simplify shipping problems.

When selecting wood joints for your project, you will need to give consideration to their strength, appearance, and difficulty of fabrication. This selection must also be based on the kind of wood you will use and the direction of the grain in the parts. In some projects the strength will be of primary importance while in others appearance must be the major concern. For example, when building a tote tray for carpentry tools the strength of the corner joints will be of primary importance while the appearance of the corner joints for a fine silverware tray or chest will be of greater importance. A desirable appearance does not necessarily mean that the joint must be invisible. Carefully proportioned and fitted visible joints may often add to the character and attractiveness of the design.

A good rule to follow is to select the simplest joint that will satisfy the needs of the construction.

The pieces to be joined should first be cut and squared to size. For some joints you will need to allow extra stock to form the joint. Lay out the cuts carefully, using a sharp pencil or knife.

When possible, it is good practice to mark one piece by holding the mating piece against it and in the correct position. Lay out all the same kind of joints at one time. Usually this is done by clamping identical pieces together. Identify the members of each joint with a number or letter so that they can be easily matched during assembly.

Illustrations and instructions in this chapter are for making most of the common joints with hand tools. See Fig. 5-1. The design, layout, and general procedures, however, will be about the same when they are constructed with the aid of power equipment.

Butt and Edge Joints

A butt joint is easy to make but is not as strong as many other joints. It is used extensively in house framing where overlays of additional material add to its strength. Simple boxes and frames are made with butt joints that are reinforced with nails, screws and other metal fasteners. When the butt joint is reinforced with dowels it is usually referred to as a dowel joint. Fig. 5-2 shows some typical butt joints, formed when the square end of one piece fits against the surface or edge of another piece.

The edge joint has many applications in buildint construction. In cabinetwork it is used to join narrow widths to form wider widths for table and desk tops, and other parts. There are many adaptations of the edge joint, a few of which are shown in Fig. 5-2.

The edge joint holds securely with glue and will be strong enough for most of your work if it is carefully made. A large piece, such as a table leaf, that will not be held by a frame or otherwise supported, should be reinforced with dowels or splines. Splines provide the greatest strength when they are cut so the grain will be across the joint. Dowels do not add a great amount of strength to the edge joint but help align the pieces when they are glued together.

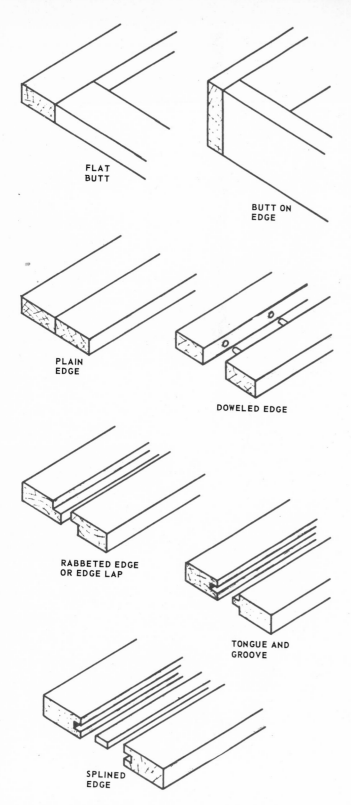

FLAT
BUTT

BUTT ON
EDGE

PLAIN
EDGE

DOWELED EDGE

RABBETED EDGE
OR EDGE LAP

TONGUE AND
GROOVE

SPLINED
EDGE

Fig. 5-2. Butt and edge joints.

To make a plain edge joint, position the pieces to be joined so the grain is matched and runs in the same direction. The annular rings should be reversed in every other piece as shown in Fig. 5-3. After the correct arrangement has been determined, make reference marks on the top surface at each joint.

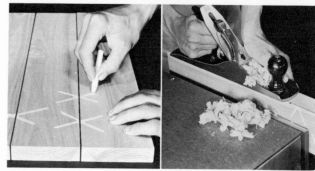

Fig. 5-3. Making an edge joint. Left. Selecting the position of the stock and marking. Right. Planing the joint. Note how the toe of the plane is guided along the edge of stock.

Clamp two adjacent pieces together in the vise with the top surfaces turned to the outside, Fig. 5-4. Plane the edges until you are able to take a light, thin shaving along the entire length. To do this you will need to apply extra pressure to the toe of the plane at the beginning of the cut and extra pressure to the heel as the cut is finished. Remove the pieces from the vise and place them together to check the fit. Slight variations in the joint can now be corrected by planing each piece separately. Instructions for gluing edge joints are included in Unit 7.

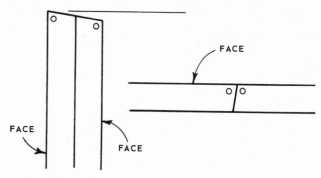

FACE

FACE

FACE

Fig. 5-4. How to clamp stock when planing an edge joint so an error in the angle will not result in a poor fit.

To install dowels in the edge joint, again clamp the pieces in the vise with the top surfaces outside, and the ends and edges even. Square lines across the edge where each dowel will be located, Fig. 5-5, above. Dowels should be spaced from 4 to 6 in. apart. A marking gauge is used to locate the center of each hole, from the top surface of each piece. If a doweling jig is used, this layout with the marking gauge is not necessary.

Boring the holes with a doweling jig as shown in Fig. 5-5, below, saves time and insures accurate work. Mount a bit guide of the correct diameter in the jig and position the carrier so the guide is located in the center of the stock. Place a depth gauge on the bit to provide a hole 1/16 in. deeper than half the dowel length. In a dowel joint the dowels should enter each piece of wood a distance equal to about two and one-half times their diameter. The diameter of the dowels should be equal to one-half the thickness of the stock.

Fig. 5-5. Installing dowels in an edge joint. Above. Making the layout. Below. Boring the holes with a doweling jig.

Line up the jig with the layout mark, clamp it securely and bore the hole. Turn the jig around so the fence is on the other side, align it with the mark and bore the matching hole. Follow the same procedure and bore all the other holes before re-moving the pieces from the vise. Make a trial assembly of the joint before gluing it together.

The edges of flooring and siding are joined with a tongue and groove or lap joint. In production woodwork, edges that will be glued together are often cut with a multiple tongue and groove.

Dados and Grooves

A dado joint is a rectangular recess, which is cut in the wood and runs across the wood grain. A groove is the same type of cut but runs along the grain. Both the dado and groove, Fig. 5-6, are usually cut to a depth equal to one-half the thick-

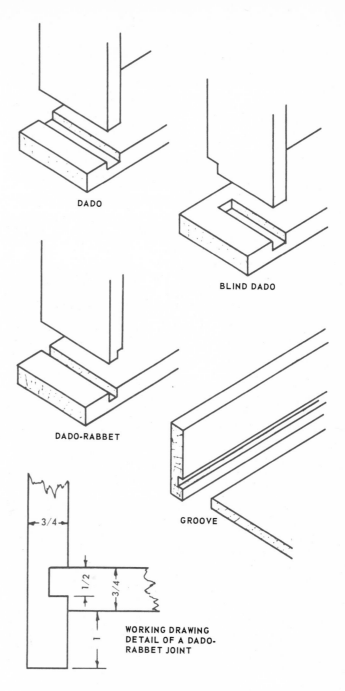

Fig. 5-6. Dado joints and grooves.

ness of the stock. In some construction it should be less, especially when working with veneer core plywood or particle board.

The dado joint is used for such jobs as in-stalling shelves, frames and partitions in book-cases, chests and cabinets. When carefully fitted and glued it makes a strong joint. When dados are used to carry shelves or similar parts, the up-rights should be clamped together and the position of the joints laid out along the edge, as shown in Fig. 5-7, above. Lines are then drawn across the surface, Fig. 5-7, below.

You can do a precision job of cutting a dado by following the procedure shown in Fig. 5-8. Clamp

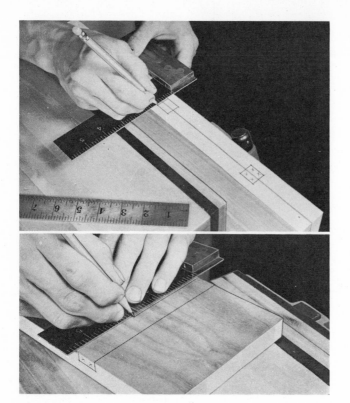

Fig. 5-7. *Laying out a dado joint. Above.* On the *edge. Below. Extending lines across the face.*

Use a chisel to remove the waste wood between the saw kerfs. The straightedge should be left in place, since it will serve as a guide for the chisel. Rough cuts should be made with the bevel of the chisel turned down or against the wood. For fine, finished cuts this position is reversed.

The dado can be finished with router plane as shown in Fig. 5-9. This will make the bottom of the dado level and true. Cut in from each side toward the center to prevent splitting the edges of the joint.

Grooves are used in drawer construction and panel work. They are usually cut on power machines but they can be cut by hand in about the same way as dados. The marking gauge can be used to lay out the groove and is especially helpful when working with long pieces. Use a straightedge to guide the saw when cutting the sides of the groove. The panel or mating part will help to position the straightedge for the second cut. Use a chisel to remove the wood from between the saw kerfs. A router plane can be used to finish the bottom of the groove.

The final trimming and fitting of grooves and dados can be done with a chisel. Lay the chisel

Fig. 5-8. *Cutting a dado joint. Left. Aligning the straightedge for the second cut. Center. Making the saw cut. Right. Removing waste stock with a wood chisel. Cut in from each side.*

a straightedge along one of the lines so that the kerf will be on the waste side and then make a cut to the proper depth with a backsaw. Move the straightedge to the other line and clamp it lightly. Place the part that will fit into the dado (mating part) against the straightedge and align its surface with the outside edge of the first saw cut. IF YOU MAKE THIS ADJUSTMENT CAREFULLY YOU WILL SECURE A PERFECT FIT. Clamp the straightedge securely, remove the mating part and make the second cut. When sawing wide boards, use long strokes, so the sawdust that is cut in the center of the piece, will be carried to the edge and removed from the saw kerf.

Fig. 5-9. *Using a router plane to smooth the bottom of a dado joint.*

flat on the work with the bevel turned out when making light, paring cuts. If the joint is too tight it is easier to plane off the thickness of the mating piece, (not recommended for plywood) than to enlarge the width of the dado or groove.

Rabbet Joints

The rabbet joint is made by cutting a recess in one or both of the pieces to be joined, Fig. 5-10. The recess may be cut on the end or along the edge. Rabbet joints are easy to make and can be

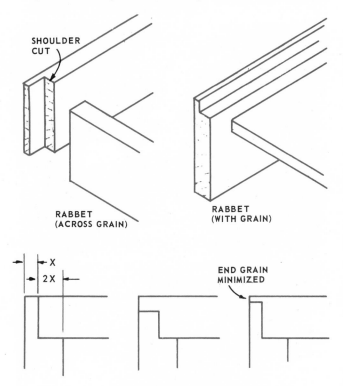

Fig. 5-10. Rabbet joints.

used for the corners of simple boxes, cases, and drawers. This type joint is commonly used to install the back panel in a cabinet. If the joint will be assembled with glue, the depth of the shoulder cut should be equal to two-thirds of the thickness of the stock; however, when nails or screws are used, the depth is usually reduced to one-half. Fig. 5-11 shows the layout of a rabbet joint.

The end grain cut is difficult to make unless you use a simple jig like the one in Fig. 5-12. The jig is constructed by gluing a thin strip (thickness determined by the size of the joint) to a flat piece of stock.

Fig. 5-13 shows a rabbet joint being cut with the aid of the jig and a straightedge. After the setup is made, place the mating part in position to check the accuracy. Be sure the clamp is tight. The cross grain or shoulder cut is made by the

same method used to square stock to length, except that the cut does not go all the way through. Hold the backsaw flat on the jig when making the end-grain cut. If there are any irregularities in the saw cuts, use a chisel to smooth them before removing the stock from the jig.

Fig. 5-11. Rabbet joint layout.

Fig. 5-12. A jig for making the end-grain cut of a rabbet joint.

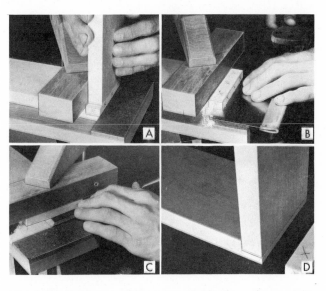

Fig. 5-13. Cutting a rabbet joint. A-Checking the straight-edge setting. B-Making the end-grain cut after completing the cross grain cut along the straightedge. C-Trimming the cut with a wood chisel. D-Completed joint.

When cutting a rabbet along the edge of stock it is best to use the rabbet plane. This type plane, shown in Fig. 5-14, has an adjustable fence and depth gauge that control the width and depth of the cut. The plane blade is sharpened in the same way as a regular plane iron.

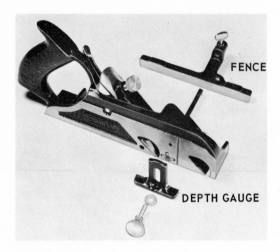

Fig. 5-14. Rabbet plane.

After adjusting the fence and depth gauge, Fig. 5-15, set the blade for a fine cut. This is somewhat difficult to do because the plane has no adjustment screw or lateral adjustment lever. It is best to place the plane bottom on a flat surface, set the blade in position, and tighten the clamp.

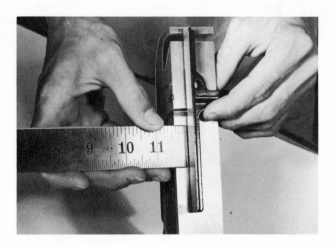

Fig. 5-15. Adjusting the fence of the rabbet plane.

Check the cut on a scrap piece of stock before working on your project. You may need to adjust the position of the blade several times before you secure a satisfactory cut. Fig. 5-16 shows the plane being used to cut a rabbet for a back panel. Fig. 5-17 shows an assembly made with dado and rabbet joints.

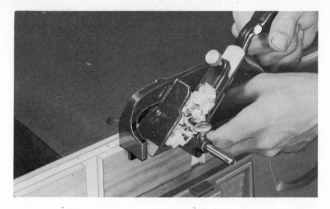

Fig. 5-16. Cutting a rabbet along the grain using a rabbet plane.

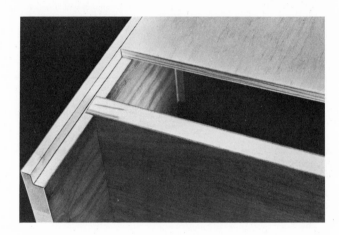

Fig. 5-17. An assembly made with dado and rabbet joints.

Lap Joints

In a lap joint an equal amount of wood is cut from each piece so that when the pieces are assembled their surfaces are flush. There are a number of forms of this type of joint as shown in Fig. 5-18. The HALF-LAP is used to splice two pieces of wood together, and the END-LAP is used as the corner joint for a simple frame. The CROSS-LAP is often used where the crossrails or braces of a table or bench join together. It is also used for grill work where parts running at different angles must form a flat plane. The MIDDLE-LAP provides a method of joining a brace to crossrails or midsections of a frame.

The same general procedure is used to lay out all of the lap joints. Fig. 5-19, Left, shows both parts of a cross-lap placed side by side with their ends even while a center line and cutting lines are laid out. The edges of each piece are laid out from the lines on the faces and a marking gauge (set at one-half the stock thickness) is then used to mark the depth of the cut. For accurate work the two pieces should be clamped together in exactly the correct position and a knife used to mark the cutting line. See Fig. 5-19, Right.

Use the same methods for sawing and removing the waste stock as described for cutting rabbet and dado joints. If the stock is very wide, it may be helpful to make several saw cuts in the waste stock before removing it with a chisel. When the joints fit too tightly, it will usually be easier to reduce the width of the pieces than to trim the shoulder cuts.

Mortise-and-Tenon

A well-made mortise-and-tenon joint is one of the strongest wood joints. It is used to join legs and rails of tables, benches, and chairs. It is also used in the best quality frame and panel construction. The mortise-and-tenon is made in a wide variety of forms, the most common of which are shown in Fig. 5-20.

The BLIND mortise-and-tenon provides a completely concealed joint. The thickness of the tenon should be not less than one-half the thickness of the stock. It usually has shoulder cuts on all sides so the mortise will be completely covered. The OPEN mortise-and-tenon (sometimes called a slip joint) makes a strong corner joint for a frame. It is somewhat easier to cut than the blind joint and is used extensively in cabinetwork. The HAUNCHED joint is used for the corners of a frame that is grooved to carry a panel. The tenon is cut with a "haunch" or extension that fills the panel groove. When the design requires that the legs and rails be flush, the mortise for a regular tenon may be too close to the surface. For a joint of this kind, the tenon is cut with a shoulder only on the front side and referred to as a BAREFACED mortise-and-tenon.

To secure the full strength from a mortise-and-tenon joint, its parts must be carefully proportioned. This is especially true of the blind joint. You should keep the following in mind when designing and laying out such a joint:

1. Keep the cross section of the tenon large. It should be no less than one-half of the thickness of the stock.
2. The length of the tenon should be at least two and one-half times its thickness.
3. The position and size of the mortise should not reduce the strength of the part.
4. When the mortise is cut at the end of a member, it should not be closer than 1/2 in., or the end will break out.

When making a mortise-and-tenon joint, the mortise is made first since it is easier to adjust the size of the tenon than it is to change the mortise for a good fit. This joint is usually used in assemblies that require a number of joints of equal size, and therefore should be laid out at the same time. Fig. 5-21 shows the layout of a set of table legs. After the outside (best) sides have

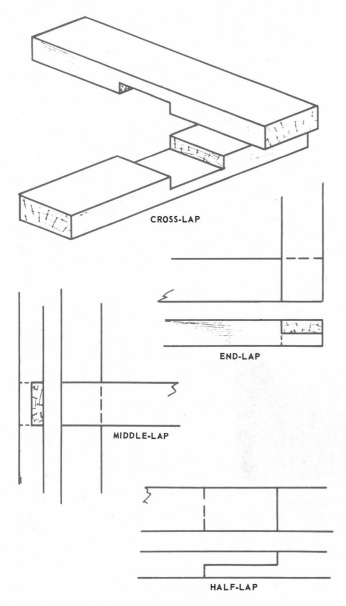

CROSS-LAP

END-LAP

MIDDLE-LAP

HALF-LAP

Fig. 5-18. Lap joints.

Fig. 5-19. Laying out a lap joint. Left. Marking the position on both parts. Right. Laying out the exact cutting line with a knife.

been selected, the legs are clamped together and lines squared across all of them at once. A marking gauge or mortise-gauge can be used to lay out the sides.

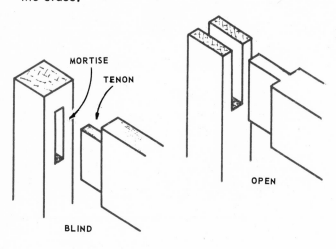

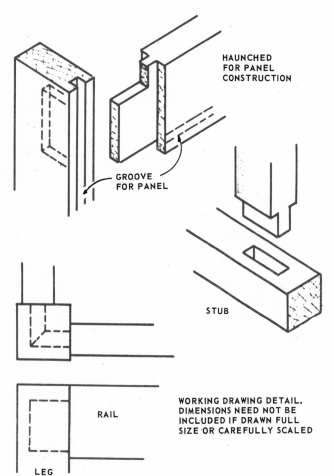

Fig. 5-20. Mortise-and-tenon joints.

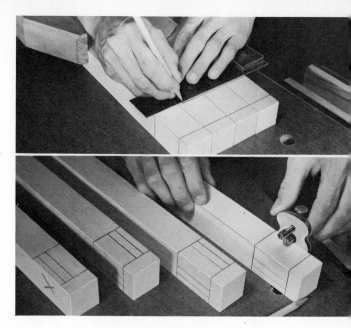

Fig. 5-21. Laying out mortises. Above. Length of mortise is marked on inside faces of legs. Below. A mortise gauge is used to layout width.

Fig. 5-22. Cutting the mortise. Above. Boring the mortise with the aid of a doweling jig. Below. Trimming with a chisel.

The mortise can be made either by boring a series of adjoining holes and cleaning the opening with a chisel or by cutting the entire opening with a chisel. Fig. 5-22 shows the first method. A doweling jig will insure an accurate boring job. However, if a center line is laid out and the centers of the holes are carefully marked with the scratch awl, good results can be secured without the use of the jig.

Fig. 5-23. Laying out tenons. Above. Shoulder cuts. Below. Using the mortise gauge to lay out cheek cuts.

Fig. 5-24. Cutting the tenon. A-Using a sawing jig to make the shoulder cut. B-Making the cheek cut. C-Trimming the cheek with a chisel. D-Completed joint.

Stock for the members (rails, stretchers) on which the tenons will be cut, must be squared to finished size with extra length allowed for the tenons. The tenons are carefully aligned and clamped together for the layout in about the same manner as the legs. See Fig. 5-23. Notice that a shoulder for the bottom edge is not included, since it would have reduced the width of the tenon too much to secure the required strength.

Make the SHOULDER CUTS first. These cuts are made with the backsaw, using either a bench hook, straightedge, or a sawing jig as shown in in Fig. 5-24(A). Make these cuts carefully and to the exact depth required. If you cut too deep you will greatly reduce the strength of the tenon. The CHEEK CUTS are hard to make and you should use some kind of a sawing guide or jig. The one used in Fig. 5-24(B) is similar to the jig used for cutting rabbet joints.

After all of the joints are cut they should be trimmed and fitted. This is usually done by working with each joint individually (selective fitting). Mark each member of the joint with a number or letter, so they can be easily and properly mated for final assembly.

WOODY SAYS:

"Be especially careful when making the shoulder cuts on rabbets and tenons. If you cut below the required depth you will greatly reduce the strength of the joint."

Mortises, especially those made by a machine, can be square, rectangular, or rectangular with rounded ends. A round mortise would simply be a hole. Tenons can be of the same shapes as mortises and also be round. The ROUND TENON is distinguished from the dowel by the fact that it is formed on the part and can therefore be much larger and stronger than an inserted dowel. The round tenon is used extensively in chair construction to join turned legs to the seat and to join rungs and legs. In industry, these round tenons are made on a CHUCKING MACHINE, which consists of a hollow cutter head with knives on the inside surface that cut the shape in a moment. Fig. 5-25 shows a procedure to follow in forming a round tenon by hand.

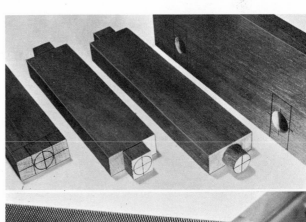

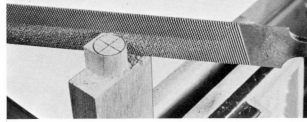

Fig. 5-25. Above. Steps in making a round tenon. Below. Forming a round tenon with a wood file.

Dowel Joints

A carefully designed and fitted dowel joint is very strong. It is easier to make than the mortise-and-tenon; and when carefully glued with one of the excellent adhesives now available, it can often be substituted for this joint.

Dowel joints are made in a wide variety of forms, Fig. 5-26. Some of the butt and edge joints previously described are often reinforced with dowels and called dowel joints. Dowels that are used for woodwork are round pieces of birch or maple, available either in the form of rods or pins. Dowel rods usually come in 3 ft. lengths in a diameter range of 1/8 in. to more than 1 in. Dowel pins are small pieces that are spiral grooved with rounded ends and ready to use. These are available in several sizes. The spiral groove permits air

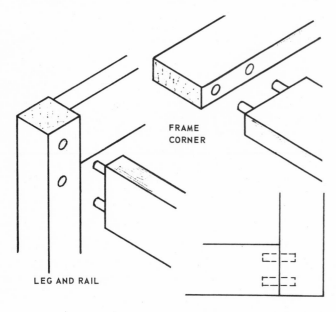

FRAME CORNER

LEG AND RAIL

Fig. 5-26. Dowel joints.

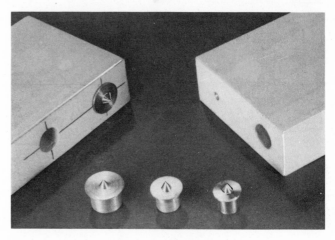

Fig. 5-27. Dowel centers.

Fig. 5-28. Application of a doweling jig to various dowel joints.
(Dowl-it Co.)

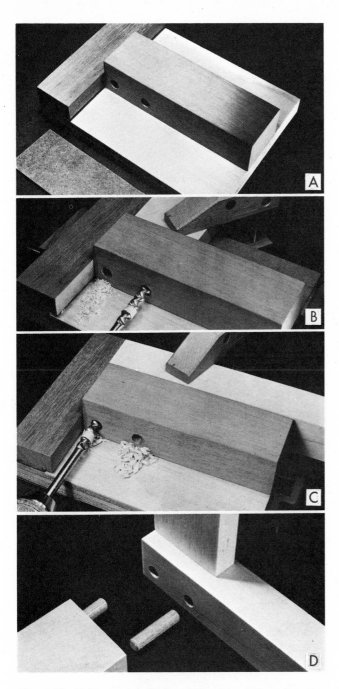

The layout of a dowel joint for leg and rail construction can be done in about the same manner as the mortises previously described. When possible, clamp the mating parts together so the center lines for the holes can be laid out at one time. Dowel centers as shown in Fig. 5-27, may be used to locate exact positions of the dowels in the mating parts. Instead of dowel centers you may use small brads. After making the layout on one part drive small brads into the center points. Cut off the heads of the brads, align the pieces and press them firmly together so the center points will be marked in the other piece.

Patented doweling jigs such as the one shown in Fig. 5-28 will save some layout time and help you do accurate work. If you have a number of joints to make that are all alike you may want to make a jig somewhat like the one shown in Fig. 5-29. The parts do not need to be laid out but are simply clamped in place and bored. A piece of hardboard is clamped under the rail to provide a 1/8 in. setback. The leg is clamped first on one side and then the other side. Fig. 5-30 shows a stool base assembled with dowels. Included in the view is the jig used to bore all the holes in the legs and rails.

Fig. 5-30. Stool base assembled with dowel joints. Note the boring jig.

Fig. 5-29. Making a dowel joint with a jig. A-Doweling jig. B-Boring the rail. C-Boring the leg. D-Completed joint.

Miter Joints

The miter joint is formed by cutting an equal angle (usually 45 deg.) on each of the mating parts. In this type of joint there is no end grain visible. The plain miter joint does not have much strength and is often reinforced with wood splines, dowels, or metal fasteners.

and excess glue to escape when the dowel pin is inserted into a hole during the gluing operation.

Use good judgment in spacing the dowels in a joint. Along an edge they may be 4 to 6 in. apart while in leg and rail assemblies, 3/8 in. dowels might be placed as close as 3/4 in. on center (OC). The diameter of the dowel should equal about one-half the thickness of the smallest member of the joint. The dowel should enter each piece of wood a distance equal to two and a half times its diameter. The depth of the hole will need to provide from 1/16 to 1/8 clearance.

The miter joint is used for picture frames and also for moldings on all kinds of furniture and cabinetwork. It is often selected for corner joints of boxes, cases, and cabinets. In house construction it is used extensively for door and window casings and other interior and exterior trim members. Fig. 5-31 shows a plain miter joint and some of the ways it can be cut and reinforced to provide added strength. Metal fasteners for miter joints are included in Unit 8.

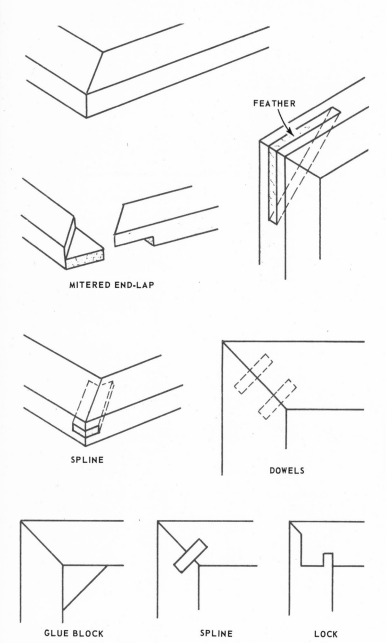

Fig. 5-31. Miter joints.

A plain miter joint can easily be cut with hand tools. The stock should be surfaced and planed to finished thickness and width. Lay out the length to the outside corner of the miter. When making a frame, always be sure to use the outside measure-

ments. Use a combination square to lay out the 45 deg. angle or, if the piece is wide or the angle is different, use a T-bevel square. Fig. 5-32 shows two methods of setting the T-bevel.

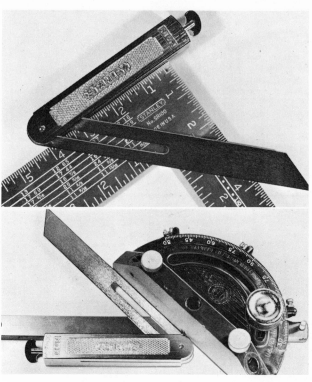

Fig. 5-32. Setting the T-bevel square. Above. With the framing square. Below. Using the miter gauge of a table saw.

Fig. 5-33. Setting a straightedge for a miter cut.

The cut can be made with a backsaw and straightedge in about the same way as squaring stock to length. Fig. 5-33 shows the straightedge being accurately set. Wood is slightly more difficult to cut at an angle with the grain so give extra attention to keeping the saw blade firmly against the straightedge during the cut. Use long, full strokes and feed the saw into the cut slowly.

5-12

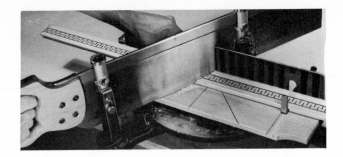

Fig. 5-34. Using the miter box to cut an angle.

The miter box shown in Fig. 5-34 is designed especially for cutting angles. Swing the saw carrier to the required angle and hold the stock firmly on the bed and against the back. For accurate work, the stock should be clamped in position, either with a hand screw or special clamps provided on some miter boxes. Use long steady strokes while making the cut. The weight of the saw will be sufficient to feed it into the work. On small pieces it may be necessary to "hold up" on the saw so it will not cut too fast. To cut the miter on the other end of a piece that will be used in a frame, the carrier is moved to the opposite side.

After the miter joint is cut, hold the two pieces together against the inside or outside edge of a square to check the fit. Slight adjustments can be made by taking a few light cuts with the block plane.

Fig. 5-35 shows a WOOD TRIMMER being used to make a finished cut on a miter joint. This tool is often used by the carpenter for inside trim work. The patternmaker also uses it for fine, accurate cutting of end grain and various angle

cuts. It consists of a table, guides, and a knife carriage, and is operated with a hand lever. The guides are adjustable so the stock can be securely held for the desired angle of cut. The wood trimmer is designed to make light shearing cuts so it is best to first rough out the angle with a saw.

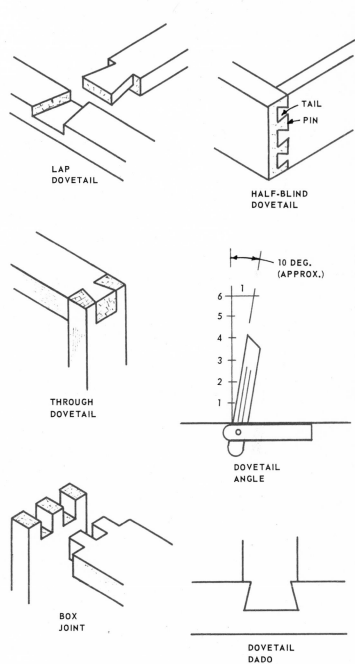

Fig. 5-36. Dovetail and box joints.

Generally, cuts of 1/16 to 1/8 in. can be easily made in softwood. Use finer cuts for hardwood. The knives are sharp and the edges should always be kept covered with a wooden guard block when not in use, to protect the edge and the worker.

Fig. 5-35. Using a wood trimmer to finish a miter cut. Above. View showing table and guides. Below. Shearing cut 1/16 in. thick.

Dovetail and Box Joints

The dovetail joint is used in high quality furniture for drawer construction and other corner joints. In furniture factories it is easily cut with specialized machines and can be rapidly assembled without the use of clamping devices. The multiple pin joint is difficult to cut with hand tools, and in the school shop it is usually made with a router and dovetailing fixture.

Several other forms of a dovetail joint are shown in Fig. 5-36. Joints like the THROUGH DOVETAIL and the LAP DOVETAIL are excellent joints for some structures and can be made with hand tools. Their interlocking feature makes them strong and easy to assemble. They might be an excellent solution for a rack or stand that could be easily assembled and held together with metal fasteners and then disassembled when not in use.

The box joint is strong and also easily assembled. It is often used in making high quality wooden shipping boxes. Like the multiple pin dovetail, it is hard to cut by hand. In Unit 12 you will find an explanation of how it is cut on the table saw.

Fig. 5-37 shows a pair of sawing jigs used to cut a simple two-tail joint. The "tail" part is clamped in position and two cuts made. It is then reversed for the other pair of cuts. After the end-grain cuts are made in each piece, waste stock is removed with a coping saw and chisel.

Fig. 5-37. Above. Jigs for cutting dovetail joints. Below. Completed joint.

The jigs must be laid out accurately and it will take time and careful work to produce the joints. The time and effort might be justified if you were building a fancy jewelry chest of such woods as Teak, Rosewood or Prima Vera.

Building Jigs

Building and working with jigs can provide interesting experiences. Their design and construction will test your creative and inventive ability and they should help you improve the quality of your project work. Quite often you may be able to save time by using a jig, especially when there are a number of similar parts to produce.

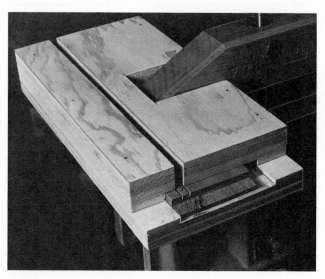

Jig to make the saw cuts for a groove.

Jigs can be classified as specialized or general purpose. The boring jig for the stool, Fig. 5-30, is a good example of a specialized jig. It was designed to position and guide the bit at a specific place and angle. A general purpose jig and its operation are shown in Fig. 5-38. Such a jig will guide the saw for a precision job of squaring stock (3/8 in. and less in thickness) to length. It can be used to make both the shoulder cut and end-grain cut of a rabbet joint in stock 5/16 in. thick. A miter joint can be cut in stock under 3/8 in.

You might want to construct a jig like this to use in your home workshop. Even though you may have a power saw, there will be times when you will need to cut small parts that are dangerous to cut on a power saw.

When building a jig, you must maintain a high level of accuracy in its construction otherwise it

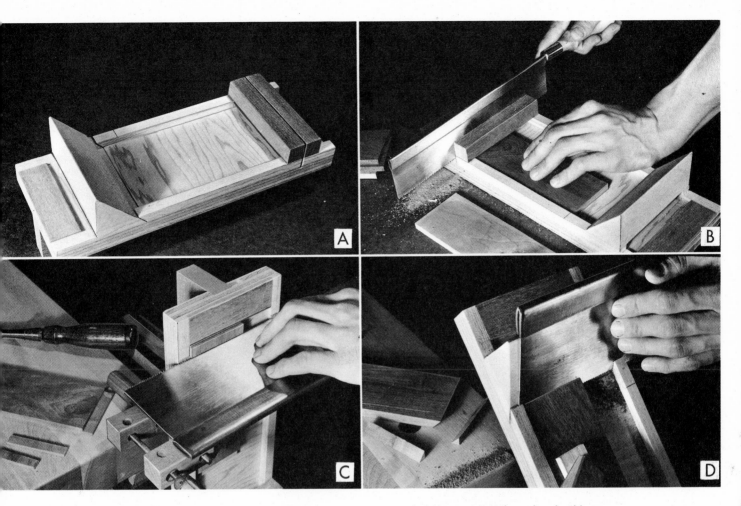

Fig. 5-38. A-General purpose sawing jig. B-Squaring stock to length. C-Making the shoulder cut for a rabbet joint. D-Cutting a miter joint.

will not be of much value. Some jigs may be quite complicated and/or may employ a new idea that will make it necessary to build and rework them several times before a satisfactory model is completed.

Test Your Knowledge

1. When selecting joints for your projects, you must consider the difficulty of fabrication, the strength, and the _____ .
2. Joints should be laid out and cut before the pieces are squared and cut to size. True or False?
3. When reinforcing an edge joint, a spline will provide greater strength than dowels. True or False?
4. In a dowel joint, the dowels should enter each member a distance equal to_____times the diameter of the dowel.
5. A groove and dado are the same kind of joint except that the groove is cut across the grain of the wood. True or False?
6. To install a back panel in a cabinet it is usually best to use a _____ joint.
7. The blade of a carpenter's framing square is 24 in. long and the tongue is _____in. long.
8. The combination square can be used to lay out a 45 deg. angle. True or False?
9. The lap-joint that would be used for the corner of a frame is called a _____ .
10. The open mortise-and-tenon is sometimes called a _____joint.
11. When a shoulder is cut on only one side of a tenon the joint is called a _____ mortise-and-tenon.
12. When making a mortise-and-tenon joint it is best to cut the tenon before cutting the mortise. True or False?
13. The cross section of a tenon can be rectangular, square, or round. True or False?
14. Plain miter joints can be reinforced with various metal fasteners, feathers, glue blocks, dowels, or _____ .
15. The included angle of a tail of a dovetail joint is about _____ degrees.

Outside Assignments

1. Make a list of the common woodworking tools that are used for measuring and layout work. Include a brief description of each tool and a brief explanation of how it is used.
2. Develop a table or chart that shows the measurement readings along the tongue and blade of a framing square, that can be used to set the T-bevel square at angles of 5, 10, 15, 22-1/2, 30 and 45 degrees.
3. Make a study of the various forms and adaptations of the mortise-and-tenon joint. Select a number of them you feel are practical, and prepare carefully proportioned detail drawings. If you do not draw them to scale, include dimensions.
4. Develop a working drawing sketch of a sawing jig to produce a MITERED HALF-LAP joint. Try to design a jig that will control the position of the cuts and also the depth. Plan for it to be used to cut stock of a specific size. Write an explanation of how it works or include adequate notations on the drawings.

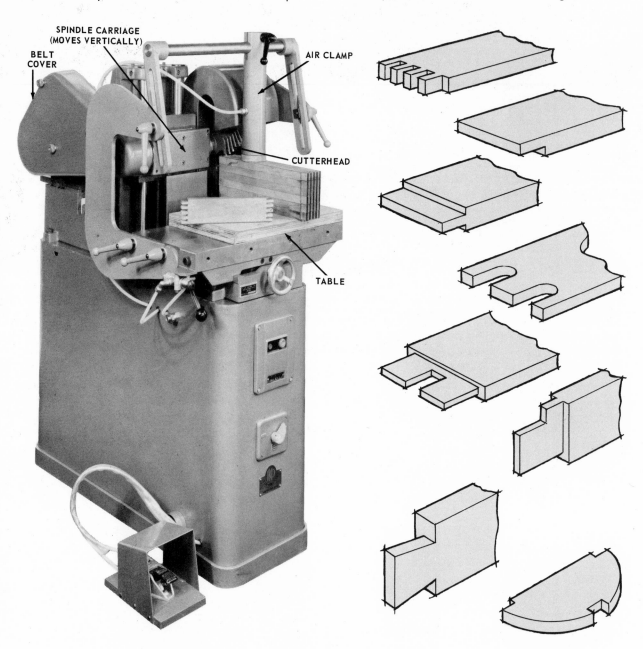

Left. Single End Notching Machine. Especially designed to form various joints on the ends of parts. Work is securely clamped to the table and remains stationary while the cutter moves downward, activated by a hydropneumatic cylinder. The feed speed and length of stroke is adjustable. Cutter spindle is belt driven from a 3 hp motor at a speed of 5600 rpm. (Forest City Tool Co.) Right. Typical joints and parts that can be fabricated.

Unit 6

FORMING IRREGULAR SHAPES, CHAMFERS AND BEVELS

As you progress in woodworking some of your projects will very likely contain curves and other irregular shapes. The cutting and forming operations for parts with irregular shapes are usually performed near the end of the fabrication se-

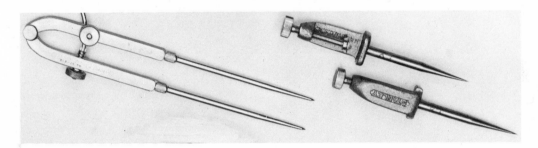

Fig. 6-1. Left. Wing dividers. Right. Trammel points.

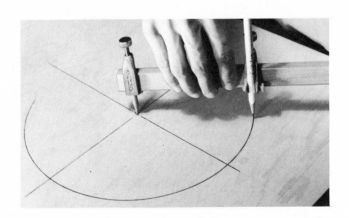

Fig. 6-2. Laying out a large circle with the trammel points.

quence. Stock should be surfaced, squared to size, and the joints made and fitted before contours are cut and formed. There will be exceptions to this when the design is such that considerable stock can be saved by roughing out the shape in advance of squaring operations.

Drawing Geometric Shapes

Circles and arcs can be laid out directly on the work, using dividers or a pencil compass,

Fig. 6-1. Set the dividers at one-half the diameter (radius) of the required circle, and place one leg at the center point. Tilt the dividers slightly in the direction of movement as you draw the circle. When using the dividers, apply enough pressure to score a fine sharp line in the surface of the wood. For large circles you can use the trammel points or a piece of string. Fig. 6-2 shows how trammel points are used.

The dividers or compass can also be used to lay out triangles, hexagons, octagons, and other figures. See Fig. 6-3. A good drawing textbook will include many other geometric constructions.

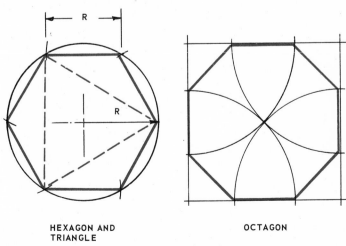

HEXAGON AND TRIANGLE

OCTAGON

Fig. 6-3. Geometric constructions.

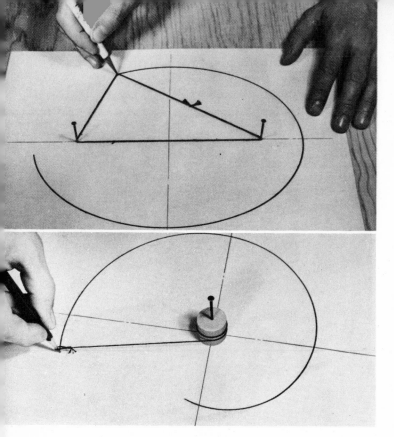

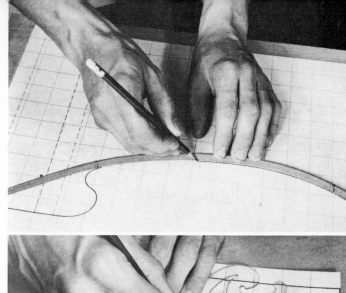

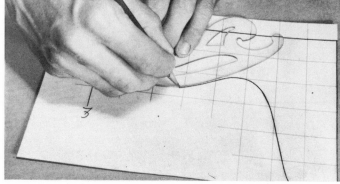

Fig. 6-4. Above. Using a string loop to draw an ellipse. Below. Drawing a spiral.

Fig. 6-5. Above. Laying out a smooth curve with a thin strip of wood. Below. Using an irregular curve.

Fig. 6-4 shows a practical way to lay out an ellipse and a spiral. You will need to experiment with the size of the string loop and the spacing of the nails to secure the desired shape and size of the ellipse. The spiral is formed as the string is unwrapped from a center post. The increase in the radius during a 360 deg. turn will be approximately equal to the circumference of the center post ($2\pi R$).

Curves

In designing a project a smooth flowing curve is usually more interesting than a perfect circle or arc. These are the curves you see in the contour of automobiles, boats, and airplanes. They are applied to furniture designs with interesting and attractive results. The engineer or draftsman call them "faired" lines. They may be produced by drawing a smooth curve through a number of previously established points using a long plastic spline, held in place with special lead weights.

In the shop you can lay out a large smooth curve in about the same way the draftsman uses a spline. For a single layout, bend a thin strip of wood into the curve you desire, clamp or hold it in place, and draw a line directly onto the wood. To develop a pattern, fasten a sheet of paper to a piece of cork board or soft wood, and set large pins or small nails at the points you want the curve to pass through. The wood strip is then "threaded"

through these points and the line drawn as shown in Fig. 6-5. Small curves are laid out with an irregular curve. You probably have had experience with this operation in a drafting class.

Patterns and Templates

A pattern is a full-sized outline of an object drawn on paper. Some patterns can be developed from dimensions given on a drawing. Complicated curves and outlines are included in working drawings but are usually not full-size and need to be enlarged. This can be done easily by a method called "enlarging with squares." It is accomplished by laying out small squares (if not included on the drawing) over the contour to be enlarged. On a sheet of paper lay out larger squares (size depends on the scale or ratio), and number them to correspond with the squares on the drawing. Work with one square at a time and draw a line through the large square in the same way it goes through the corresponding small square.

When a design is the same on both ends, you need only a half pattern. This is laid out on one side of a center line, and then turned over and laid out on the other side as shown in Fig. 6-6. Some designs require only a quarter pattern.

You can transfer a pattern to wood by cutting it out and drawing around the edge, or by placing a piece of carbon paper between the pattern and the wood surface and tracing over the lines. Secure the pattern to the work with drafting tape or thumb tacks so it will not slip. When tracing a pattern onto the wood, use a straightedge and irregular curve to produce smooth lines on your work.

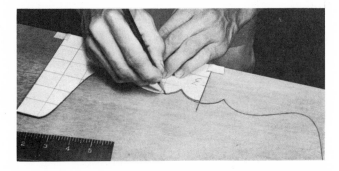

Fig. 6-6. Making a layout with a half-pattern.

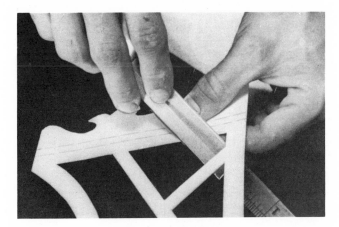

Fig. 6-7. Smoothing the edges of a template with sandpaper wrapped around a steel rule.

When you have a number of identical pieces to lay out, it is usually best to make a template. Glue your paper pattern (use rubber cement) onto a heavy piece of cardboard or a thin piece of ply-wood or hardboard. Cut out the contour carefully, and then smooth the edge with a fine file and sand-paper. See Fig. 6-7.

Cutting Out Curves

The coping saw, compass saw, and keyhole saw are hand tools used to cut curves, Fig. 6-8. The COPING SAW carries a blade that is easily replaced when it becomes dull or is broken. The blade has fine teeth, usually about 16 points per inch.

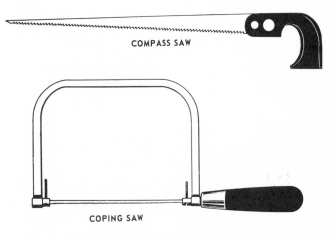

Fig. 6-8. Saws designed to cut curves.

Coping saw work can be clamped in the vise, or supported on a sawing bracket as shown in Fig. 6-9. When the work is held in a vise, the blade should be mounted in the saw frame with the teeth pointing away from the handle. When using the sawing bracket the teeth should point down-ward or toward the handle.

Fig. 6-9. Cutting with the coping saw. Left. Work held on a sawing bracket. Right. Work clamped in a vise. (Note that the joints for the wall shelf have already been cut.)

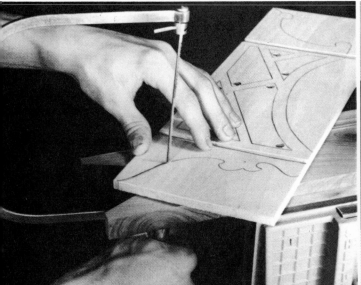
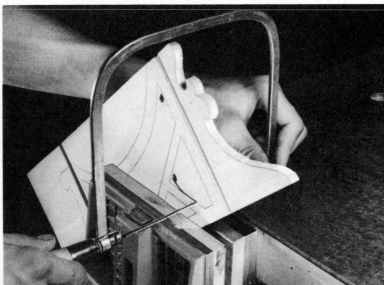

Start the cut in the waste stock and then guide the saw to the edge of the cutting line. Use full, uniform strokes, keeping the blade perpendicular to the surface. Give the blade plenty of time to cut its way. Use extra strokes as you go around corners. Reposition the work as you progress, so the cutting will take place near the point of the V of the sawing bracket, or close to the jaws of the vise. Working slowly and carefully will actually save time because you will not need to do as much filing or sanding to finish the edges.

The blade of the COMPASS SAW runs to a point; it is 10 to 14 in. long and has about 8 points to the inch. It is used for cutting large curves and circles. The keyhole saw is similar except that it has a smaller blade and finer teeth. The pointed blade of these saws makes it possible to start the saw in a small hole and cut sharp curves.

Fig. 6-10 shows a compass saw being used to cut out a speaker opening in a panel for a hi-fi cabinet. A hole was bored in the waste stock to start the saw. When using this type saw the length of the stroke will vary with the sharpness of the curve. Sharp curves must be cut with the point of the blade while the entire blade can be used for curves with a large radius. The compass saw leaves a fairly rough edge, so keep the cut well into the waste stock to allow sufficient material for smoothing and finishing. The compass and keyhole saw can be sharpened by the same method used for regular hand saws.

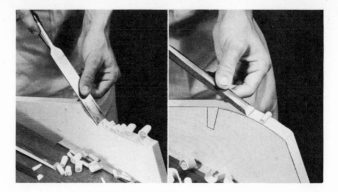
Fig. 6-11. Cutting curves with a chisel. Left. Inside or concave curves. Right. Outside or convex curves.

cuts should be made by hand, using very fine cuts as the layout line is reached. Outside (convex) curves are cut with the bevel turned up. Make a series of straight cuts, tangent to the curve, and then take a thin shaving along the layout line to finish the work. A shearing type of cut is usually made on end grain and hard woods.

The two general types of chisels are the SOCKET and the TANG. The handle of the socket chisel fits into a hollow cone and is the type that should be used for heavy work, when the chisel is driven with a mallet. See Fig. 6-12. The tang

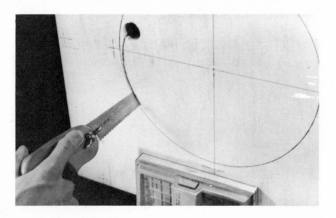
Fig. 6-10. Using compass saw to cut large circular opening.

Curves that are formed by removing only a small amount of stock can be cut and smoothed with a chisel as shown in Fig. 6-11. Inside (concave) curves are cut with the bevel held against the work so that the depth of cut can be somewhat controlled by the angle of the chisel. The first heavy roughing cuts can be made by driving the chisel (use a socket type) with a mallet. Finished

Fig. 6-12. Driving the chisel with a mallet. Always use a socket chisel for this operation.

chisel has a lighter handle attachment, a thinner blade, and is used for light shaping and paring cuts. The size of a chisel is determined by the width of the blade. Chisels are sharpened (ground and honed), using the same method that was described for the plane blade. See Fig. 6-13.

Smoothing Curves and Edges

The spokeshave is a tool used for smoothing and shaping curved surfaces and edges. Fig. 6-14 shows a typical model with depth adjustment nuts and a blade that is 2 1/8 in. wide. The blade of the spokeshave is ground at the same angle and honed in the same manner as a regular plane iron.

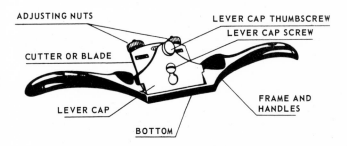

Fig. 6-14. Parts of the spokeshave.
(Stanley Tools)

The spokeshave can be used for both concave and convex curves. It is usually held and used as shown in Fig. 6-15, however, it can be reversed and pushed instead of being pulled. The setting for a fine shaving will vary with different shapes and sizes of curves. Hold the tool at an angle so it will make a shearing cut on end grain or hard wood.

Fig. 6-15. Using a spokeshave
to shape and smooth a contour.

A wood file is used for smoothing small pieces or those that have sharp curves. The most common files for woodworking are the round, half-round, and flat, Fig. 6-16. They are available in lengths of 8, 10, and 12 in. Small metal files are

A master craftsman using a chisel to form the outside contour of a valve housing pattern.
(Fisher Controls Co.)

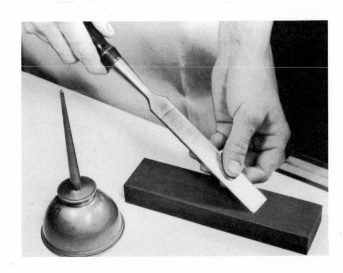

Fig. 6-13. Honing a chisel.

6-5

Fig. 6-16. Standard wood files. Above. Flat. Below. Half-round. (Nicholson File Co.)

Fig. 6-20. Multi-blade forming tool.
(Stanley Tools)

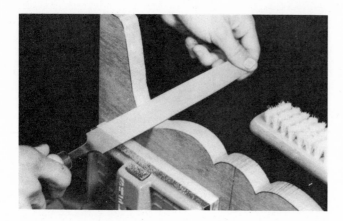

Fig. 6-17. Using the half-round wood file.

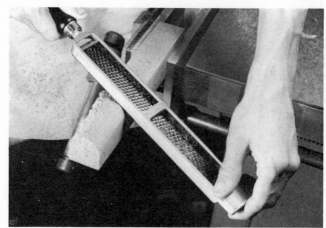

Fig. 6-21. Using the multi-blade tool to form a leg.

Fig. 6-18. File card and brush.

Fig. 6-19. Tungsten carbide coated file.
(Skil Corp.)

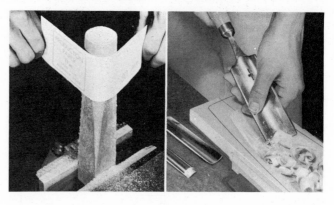

Fig. 6-22. Left. Shaping and smoothing with coarse sandpaper. Fig. 6-23. Right. Shaping an inside contour with an outside ground gouge.

sometimes helpful in smoothing intricate work. The file should be fitted with a handle and held as shown in Fig. 6-17. When possible, use a stroking action rather than filing straight across an edge. Try to file in from each edge to prevent splitting the opposite side; this is especially important in working with plywood. Use a file card or file cleaner to keep the teeth clean, Fig. 6-18.

Two other shaping and rough smoothing tools are the tungsten carbide coated file, Fig. 6-19, and the multi-blade forming tool, Fig. 6-20. Each of these tools cut rapidly and will do a considerable amount of work before they become dull. Fig. 6-21 shows the multi-blade tool being used to round the corners of a stool leg. This tool is available in various shapes and sizes.

Sandpaper can be used for smoothing curves and rounding edges. It can be wrapped around various forms to fit the contour of the work. Coarse sandpaper will cut away the wood fibers rapidly when used across the grain. See Fig. 6-22.

Carving and Shaping

Gouges, chisels, and knives of various shapes and sizes are used for carving wood. Carving tools are usually sold in a set that consists of such items as chisels, veiners, fluters, and gouges. They should be kept in a box or special holder when not in use to protect the worker from injury, and also the fine cutting edges of the tools.

It takes a lot of skill and patience to do fine wood carving. Always clamp the work securely, either in the vise or some special holder. Hold the tool in both hands and make the cuts by moving the cutting edge away from you. The angle of

out a chamfer with a sharp pencil held so the fingers serve as a guide along the edge of the stock, as shown in Fig. 6-27. A marking gauge cannot be used, since it will leave a groove.

Fig. 6-24. A finished tray that required the use of many forming and shaping tools.

ing the cutting edge away from you. The angle of the tool edges will vary; however, most of them can be held at about a 30 deg. angle. Cut with the grain wherever possible.

An outside ground gouge, Fig. 6-23, is used to form the inside contour of trays and bowls. Start in the center and gradually enlarge the area. Cut long, thin shavings with the tool moving toward the center. Guide the blade with one hand and use the other hand to force it through the wood. Rolling the edge slightly back and forth will help it cut, especially on end grain. Fig. 6-24 shows a finished candy tray that required the use of a gouge on the inside contour.

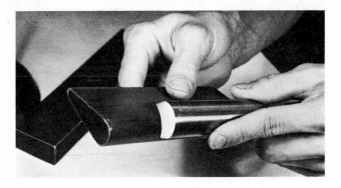

Fig. 6-25. Using a slip stone to hone a gouge.

WOODY SAYS:

"When using chisels and gouges always keep both hands behind the cutting edge, with the cutting motion away from you."

Gouges and carving chisels require very sharp edges. They can be honed many times before grinding is required. When grinding, try to maintain the original shape of the tool. Fig. 6-25 shows an outside ground gouge being honed with a slip stone after the beveled side was honed on a regular oilstone.

Chamfers, Bevels and Tapers

A CHAMFER removes the sharp corner from an edge and improves the appearance of some work. See Fig. 6-26. It is usually made at a 45 deg. angle with the surface or edge of the stock. Lay

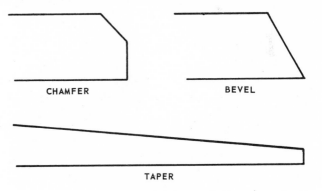

Fig. 6-26. Forms for wooden parts.

Clamp the stock in a hand screw and clamp the hand screw in a vise, so the work will be held at an angle. Plane the edges first, and then the ends with the plane held at an angle to make a shearing cut. Use the block plane to chamfer small pieces.

A BEVEL, Fig. 6-26, is a sloping edge that connects the two surfaces of the stock. It is planed in about the same manner as a chamfer. To lay out a bevel, the sliding T-bevel square is set at the required angle. It is then used to mark the

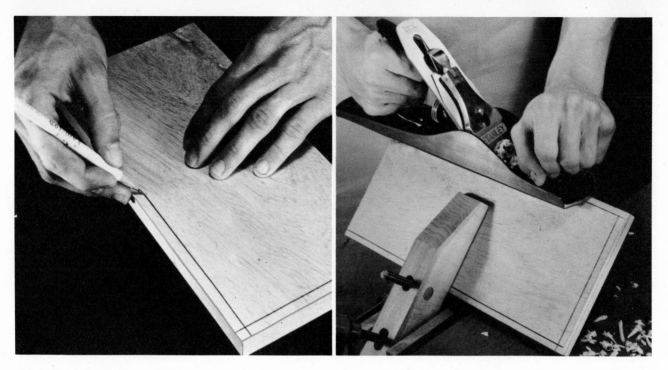

Fig. 6-27. Left. Laying out a chamfer. Right. Planing a chamfer.

angle on both ends of the stock. When possible, clamp the work so that the plane can be operated in a horizontal position. As the bevel nears completion, check it with the T-bevel square.

A TAPER, also shown in Fig. 6-26, runs along the length of the stock, making it smaller at one end. The legs of stools, chairs, and tables are often tapered to make them look lighter and more attractive. As in the forming of most irregular

shapes, the tapering operation is performed after the work has been squared to size, the joints cut, and a trial assembly made.

Lay out the length of the section to be tapered. When there are a number of similar pieces, clamp them together to make this layout. Mark the size on the small end and then draw the line of the taper on each surface. See Fig. 6-28. Clamp the work securely and plane toward the smaller end. Start with the short strokes at the small end and gradually increase their length as you progress with the work, as described in Fig. 6-29. When tapering adjacent surfaces, you will remove the layout line on the surface being planed and it will need to be replaced. Note that the legs shown in the figures are tapered on only the inside surfaces. Tapers are sometimes hard to clamp in a vise. You may need to work out some special clamping arrangement.

FIRST STROKE

LAST STROKE

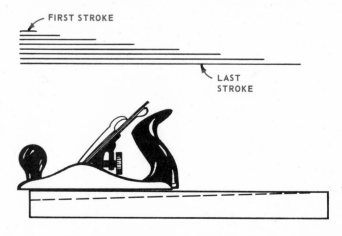

Fig. 6-28. Above. Laying out a taper. Below. Planing a taper.

Fig. 6-29. Procedure for planing a taper.

Test Your Knowledge

1. To lay out a large circle it is best to use a set of _____ _____.
2. What size of center post would you use to develop a spiral in which the radius increased approximately 1 1/2 in. in one revolution?
3. It is best to use a template to lay out many parts that have the same curved outline. True or False?
4. If a curved part is symmetrical, (the same on either side of a center line) it will save time to develop and use a _____ pattern.
5. When using a coping saw with the work supported on a sawing bracket, the teeth should point away from the handle. True or False?
6. What hand tool would you use to cut a 12 in. hole in the center of a piece of plywood that is 2 ft. square?
7. When smoothing a convex curve with a chisel the bevel should be held against the work. True or False?
8. The most common shapes of woodworking files are round, flat, and _____.
9. When using gouges or chisels the work should be held in one hand and the tool in the other. True or False?
10. When planing a taper, the cut should usually be made toward the _____. (Larger end, smaller end.)

Outside Assignments

1. Develop a selected list of hand forming tools (other than planes and chisels) that would be practical for use in a home workshop. Include a description of the shape and size of each item and also current prices.
2. Select or design a small article such as an Early American wall shelf that includes some curved parts. Prepare a scaled working drawing and then by using the enlarging with squares method, make full-size patterns of the curved parts.

Multiple-spindle carving machine. The operator moves the tracer over a master pattern and cutter bits mounted in each spindle produces an exact duplicate. Machines with as many as 32 spindles are available. Round and odd shaped workpieces are held between live centers that are connected by gears and can be turned simultaneously by the operator. Flat work is clamped to table.
(Thomasville Furniture Industries Inc.)

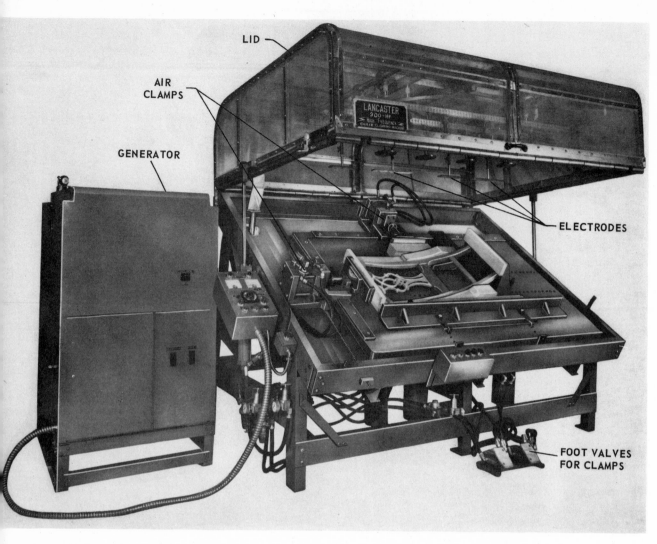

LID

AIR CLAMPS

GENERATOR

ELECTRODES

FOOT VALVES FOR CLAMPS

Modern high frequency gluing machine set up for chair backs. Electrodes are adjustable so they can be located directly over the glue lines. The lid which carries the electrodes is automatically raised and lowered by air power. See page 7-12 for information on high frequency gluing.
(J. M. Lancaster, Inc.)

Operator feeds particle board core stock (for cabinet woods) into double roll glue spreader. As stock emerges from back of spreader, veneer sheets are applied to both sides. Also see Fig. 7-29.   (Black Bros.)

Unit 7
GLUING AND CLAMPING

Gluing and clamping are important operations that are performed at various times during the total construction activity. At the outset, you may need to make edge or face joints to secure the wider widths or thicker pieces that your project requires. After parts are fabricated, there will be subassemblies and final assemblies to make. As the work nears completion, gluing operations may be included in the veneering of edges and the attachment of moldings and trim.

Gluing operations may involve the use of a number of different kinds of adhesive material. The term "adhesive" is defined as a substance that is capable of holding objects together by surface attachment. It is a general term that includes glue, paste, cement, and mucilage.

The research laboratories of our chemical industries have developed many new and wonderful plastic materials from such raw materials as coal, air, water, petroleum, and natural gas. Among these have been a wide range of synthetic-resin adhesives that have revolutionized the methods and procedures in wood fabrication.

Kinds of Glue

POLYVINYL RESIN EMULSION GLUE (generally called polyvinyl or white glue) is excellent for interior construction. It comes ready to use in plastic squeeze bottles, Fig. 7-1, and is easily applied. This glue sets up rapidly, does not stain the wood or dull tools, and holds wood parts securely.

Polyvinyl glue hardens when its moisture content is removed through absorption into the wood or through evaporation. It is not waterproof and should not be used in assemblies that will be subjected to high humidities or moisture. The vinyl-acetate materials used in the glue are thermoplastic, which means that under heat they will soften; therefore it should not be used in the construction of such articles as radios or TV cabinets where the temperature may rise above 165 deg.

The glue film remains elastic and the joint may tend to "creep" under prolonged heavy stress. This elasticity may be beneficial in some joints that undergo dimensional change with the expansion and contraction of the wood. Since the glue never gets "brittle" hard and tends to soften under

Fig. 7-1. Polyvinyl resin emulsion glue.

heat, it fouls sandpaper quickly. You should not attempt to sand it from a surface especially with power equipment. Polyvinyl glue has a corrosive effect on iron and steel and should never be allowed to remain on the metal surfaces of tools.

UREA-FORMALDEHYDE RESIN GLUE (usually called urea resin) is available in a dry powder form which contains the hardening agent, or catalyst. See Fig. 7-2. It is mixed with water to a creamy consistency for use. Urea resin is moisture resistant, dries to a light brown color and holds wood surfaces securely. It hardens through chemical action when water is added and sets at room temperatures in from 4 to 8 hours. Elevated temperatures greatly reduce the setting time. This kind of glue is often used for gluing plywood which is bonded in hot presses (240-260 deg.) in from 3 to 5 minutes.

Fig. 7-2. Urea-formaldehyde resin glue. Above. Catalyst incorporated type mixed with water. Below. Liquid resin and powdered catalyst mixed for use.

Urea resin is also available in liquid form. A powdered catalyst is added when it is prepared for use. This is the type generally used in production work where mixes, temperatures, and other conditions can be carefully controlled. Industry uses several other thermosetting resin glues similar to urea resin. They are better adapted to hot press work, and have more resistance to moisture and heat. Two of the more common ones are PHENOL RESIN and MELAMINE RESIN.

Powdered urea resin is a good glue to use for cutting boards, salad bowls, and other articles that may be subjected to moisture for a short

Fig. 7-3. Resorcinol-formaldehyde resin glue.

period of time. It has a much longer assembly time than polyvinyl and you may want to use it for a complicated assembly where you need extra time to get the pieces together. Be sure to keep the container tightly closed when not in use or the glue will absorb moisture from the air and deteriorate. Even under the best storage conditions, it has a "shelf-life" of only one year.

RESORCINOL-FORMALDEHYDE RESIN GLUE (called resorcinol glue) is available only in a two-part form; a dark reddish liquid resin, and a powdered or liquid hardener or catalyst. See Fig. 7-3. It is strong, durable, and waterproof. Its chief disadvantages are that it is quite expensive and leaves a dark glue line. It sets up at room temperatures in 8 to 10 hours. This glue is well suited for water skis, boats, and other structures that will be exposed for long periods to high humidities or water. Carefully follow the directions on the container for mixing and application.

EPOXY RESIN GLUE is a relatively new adhesive that is so strong it takes the place of rivets in many aircraft assemblies. Like resorcinol glue, it comes in two components; a white epoxy resin and a catalyst. Small amounts are available in a pair of tubes as shown in Fig. 7-4. Equal amounts

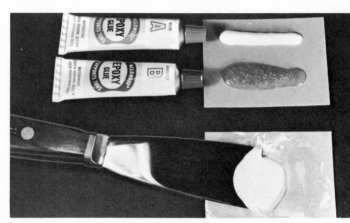

Fig. 7-4. Epoxy resin glue.

of the resin and hardener are squeezed out and blended together for use. Epoxy resin will bond all sorts of porous and nonporous surfaces, but it works best on rigid materials. In woodworking, it is ideal to use for attaching a metal bracket or some other nonwood fitting to a wood surface or assembly. Follow the directions on the containers. Do not interchange the caps on the tubes, and avoid contact with the skin.

CONTACT CEMENT is applied to each surface and allowed to dry until a piece of paper will not stick to the film. The surfaces are then pressed firmly together and bonding takes place im-

Fig. 7-5. Contact cement. Wood and other porous surfaces should be double-coated. Stir thoroughly.

mediately. The pieces must be carefully aligned for the initial contact because they cannot be changed after they touch. The bonding time is not critical and can be performed within a 1 to 2 hour period.

Contact cement comes in the form of a light tan liquid, Fig. 7-5. It is made with a neoprene rubber base. It is an excellent adhesive for applying plastic laminates or joining parts that cannot be clamped together easily. It works well for applying thin veneer strips to plywood edges (not true of the nonflammable type) because there is no water content to curl the veneer. It can be used to join any combinations of wood, cloth, leather, rubber, plastics, thin metal sheets. The regular type of contact cement contains volatile, flammable solvents and the work area where it is applied must be well-ventilated with no open

WOODY SAYS:

"When using any of the synthetic resin glues with which you are not thoroughly familiar; always read, study, and follow the directions listed on the label of the container."

flames or pilot lights. You should avoid prolonged inhalation (breathing) of the vapors.

CASEIN GLUE is made from milk curd, hydrated lime, and sodium hydroxide. It is supplied in powder form and is mixed with cold water for use. See Fig. 7-6. After mixing, it should set for about 15 minutes before it is applied. It is classified as a water resistant glue.

Casein glue is used for interior structural laminating and works well where the moisture content of the wood is high. It has good joint filling

qualities and is therefore often used on materials that have not been carefully surfaced. Casein is used for gluing oily woods like teak, padouk, and lemon wood. Its main disadvantages are that it stains the wood, especially such species as oak, maple, and redwood, and has an abrasive effect on tool edges.

ANIMAL GLUE (also called hide glue) is made from hides, tenons, and bones of cattle. Through the years and until the advent of the synthetic resin glues it was the glue used most by the woodworking industries. It is still available today but not widely used. Animal glue is sold in sheet, flake, pearl and ground forms. The dry forms of the glue are soaked in water for several hours and are then melted and used at temperatures of

Fig. 7-6. Casein glue. Mix the powder with cold water.

not over 150 deg. Animal glue is also available in liquid form and is packaged in plastic squeeze bottles as shown in Fig. 7-7. This form holds wood parts securely and is easy to handle. It is not waterproof.

Fig. 7-7. Animal glue. The flakes are prepared by soaking in water and then heating.

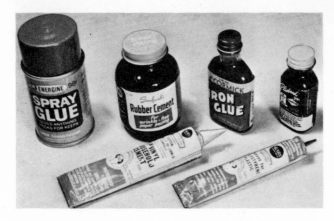

Fig. 7-8. Additional adhesives that may be helpful for woodworking.

Fig. 7-9. Parts ready for gluing. They are dry, clean, and fit together smoothly. Inside surfaces have been sanded.

PLASTIC CEMENT (often called airplane cement) comes in a tube as shown in Fig. 7-8. It is used for household repairs and is an excellent glue for model building. It sets up fast so it can be handled in about 10 minutes.

RUBBER CEMENT is valuable for the woodworker in gluing paper and cardboard patterns. Since there is no moisture present, the material remains wrinkle free. It can also be used to attach sandpaper to boards or special forms.

Preparing Wood for Gluing

Wood pieces that are to be assembled with glue should all have the same moisture content. This will take place automatically if all pieces of the wood are stored in the same area for a period of time. The moisture content at the time of gluing should be about equal to that which the glued article will attain when it is placed in service. The average moisture content for interior woodwork in the United States is about 8 percent but varies widely for different parts of the country. Exterior woodwork varies from 12 to 18 percent. High moisture contents (15 percent and above), will retard the curing time and may require the use of special glues.

The wood surfaces that will form the glue line should be dry, clean, and smooth, and make good contact with each other, Fig. 7-9. This kind of surface is prepared with hand planes, chisels and machines with sharp knives. Tests have proved that striating the surfaces with a sharp knife or scratch awl does not improve the strength of the joint and may actually reduce the strength if loose wood fibers prevent the surfaces from making good contact.

For many years it was felt that glue held wood together through MECHANICAL ATTACHMENT. This concept proposed that the liquid glue flowed into the pores and cavities of the wood and then hardened to form an interlocking solid material. Today the more acceptable explanation is called

SPECIFIC ADHESION. Briefly, this theory states that the molecular forces that cause certain molecules of different materials to be attracted to each other are the ones that operate in the gluing process. It is also believed that in some cases a kind of chemical reaction takes place that forms different molecules that add to these adhesive forces.

Trial Assemblies

Before applying any kind of glue you should first place all of the parts together and check the fit. See Fig. 7-10. Check the squareness of individual parts and also assembled parts. Check the clearance of interlocking joints so you can be sure they will slip together easily after the glue

Fig. 7-10. Checking trial assembly.

is applied. All joints and parts should fit together without excessive pressure from clamps. If you force an assembly together you will be gluing stresses into your project that may eventually cause the joints or structural members to fail.

When working with assemblies that are large and complicated, study and practice the sequence you will follow. If you are working with fast setting glue it is best to make several subassemblies rather than do all of the gluing at one time. Be certain that all parts are properly identified so you will not get them mixed or reversed during the gluing operation.

Adjust all the clamps and other gluing devices. Use small blocks of wood under the jaws of bar clamps to protect the smooth surfaces of final assemblies.

Preparing Glue

Polyvinyl, liquid hide, and contact cement are ready to use when purchased, while many of the other glues will need to be mixed and prepared. When preparing powdered glues, mix just the amount you will need for each job. These glues have a working life (pot life) of only a few hours and then must be discarded. A paper cup makes a good small quantity mixing container.

Pour the dry powder into the cup and add a small amount of water. Stir with a stiff brush or stick until it forms a heavy "gooey" mass, then add a few drops of water at a time until you have reduced it to a smooth creamy consistency. Manufacturers of urea resin glue usually recommend a proportion (by measure) of eight parts of powder to three parts of water. Casein glue is usually mixed in a proportion of one part of glue to two parts of water. If you use a brush to mix and apply the glue it can be cleaned with warm water and soap.

WOODY SAYS:

"Be sure to close the powdered glue container tightly, otherwise the glue will gather moisture from the air and harden."

Study and follow the manufacturer's recommendation on the label of the container when working with glue, particularly resorcinol and epoxy glues. It is best to use sticks or a putty knife to mix and apply these glues, since they are difficult to remove from a brush.

Making Glue Spread

Applying the glue to the wood surface is called "spreading." When the glue is applied to both wood surfaces to be joined it is called a "double spread" and when it is applied to only one surface it is called a "single spread." Glue can be spread with a stick, brush, knife, roller, or a mechanical spreader. On production work glue is sometimes applied with a spray gun. Woodworking industries often use a single spread since they have machinery that carefully controls the amount of glue applied. Fig. 7-11 shows a small single roll glue spreader and how it works.

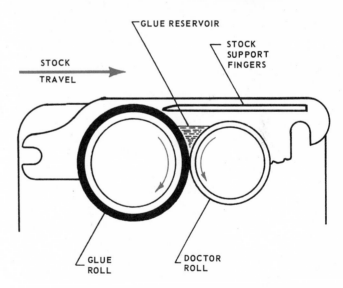

Fig. 7-11. A single roll glue spreader. Both rolls are powered. Adjustment between the glue roll and the doctor roll accurately controls the amount of glue spread. Coating speed is 100 lineal ft. per minute. Above. Spreader being used to coat a surface. Below. Section view showing roll arrangement.

For your work in the shop you should make a double spread. Use good judgment as to how much glue to apply. The surface should be thoroughly coated, yet not so heavy that you will have excessive "squeeze-out" for this will make the work messy and be wasteful of glue. Fig. 7-12 shows urea resin glue being spread on the faces of stock

Fig. 7-12. Left. Spreading urea resin glue with a brush. Right. Clamping the stock together. More pressure is applied by turning the assembly over and setting two more hand screws on the other side.

that is being used to form a larger blank. Note the approximately correct amount of squeeze-out on the assembled pieces. A good glue film is about .005 in. (5 mils) thick, however the thickness will vary with the material and the kind of glue being used.

The ASSEMBLY TIME refers to the total time between the spreading of the glue and the application of pressure. OPEN ASSEMBLY TIME is the period between glue spreading and the moment when the two surfaces are placed together. CLOSED ASSEMBLY TIME is the time the pieces remain in contact before pressure is applied. Open assembly time should usually be as short as possible, however if the parts are immediately brought together and excessive pressure applied, too much glue may be squeezed out resulting in a "starved" joint. This is most likely to happen when gluing a hard, dense wood with urea resin.

You will need to know the assembly time of the glue you are using. For example; the blank of wood, Fig. 7-12, could not have been glued with polyvinyl by the method shown, for the assembly time would have been too long. Polyvinyl glues have an assembly time of only about five minutes. The urea resin being used has an assembly time of 15 minutes at room temperature. To glue the blank successfully with polyvinyl, the pieces should be glued in pairs and then the two pairs glued together later. This would slow down the operation very little since polyvinyl work can be removed from the clamp in about 30 minutes.

Casein glue has an assembly time of about 20 minutes. Hide, resorcinol and epoxy glues all have relatively long assembly times and seldom present any problem in this respect. Glues with long assembly times also require long clamping periods. For example, resorcinol glued joints should be kept clamped for about 10 hours.

Gluing an Edge Joint

Fig. 7-13 shows a suggested procedure to follow when gluing an edge joint. The work is first assembled dry (without glue) and the clamps are adjusted. For joints of this kind the clamps are usually spaced about 12 to 16 in. apart. A rack or holder that will keep the bottom clamps on edge is helpful. Apply a bead of polyvinyl glue to one edge and then make the spread on both pieces by rubbing them together. Check the spread and apply additional glue to any areas that are not coated. After the spread is made on both joints the pieces are carefully aligned and the clamps underneath are tightened. A third clamp is placed across the top surface and tightened. Note the paper towel laid between the clamp and the glue line so the corrosive action of the polyvinyl glue on the metal clamp will not stain the wood. This protection is not necessary if the clamps are removed within 1 hour.

Joints like this and others that are used to build up the required dimensions of the stock are usually not cleaned immediately. The squeeze-out line of glue is easily removed with a hand or cabinet scraper after the joint has set up.

Even though polyvinyl glue will set up so that most assemblies can be removed from the clamps in about 30 minutes, the joint will not gain its full strength for several hours. Edge joints for high quality work should have several days to cure so that the extra moisture at the glue line can dry out. If the joint is machined and planed too soon, extra wood (expanded by moisture) will be removed and this will form a depression after it dries. This is true of all glues that have a high moisture content.

The clamps used in Fig. 7-13 are called BAR CLAMPS. They are available in various lengths (maximum opening) from 2 to 8 ft. When tightened firmly with one hand they will exert about 600 lbs. of pressure. When tightened with both hands on the crank you can apply pressure of well over 1200 lbs. Manufacturers of adhesives generally recommend 100 to 150 psi (pounds per square inch) for soft wood and 150 to 200 psi for hard wood. If one hand is used to tighten the clamps, Fig. 7-13 (C), then the three clamps will exert a total of about 1800 pounds of pressure. The stock

Fig. 7-14. Above. Bar clamp carrier. Sixty units mounted on an endless chain. Motor driven. Below. Clamp carrier in operation. Glue sets so that stock can be removed by the time it returns to the loading station.
(Billstrom Inc., & Black Bros. Co.)

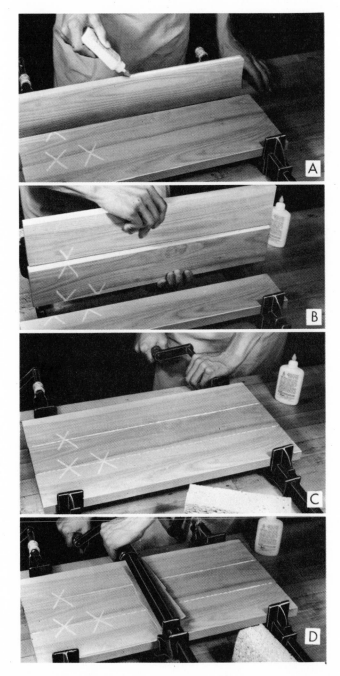

Fig. 7-13. Gluing and clamping edge joints. A-Applying a bead of glue on one edge. B-Rubbing the edges together to make a double spread. C-Tightening the bottom clamps. D-Applying a third clamp to the top surface.

is 3/4 in. thick and 24 in. long, making the area of the joint 18 sq. in. The psi of the joint is therefore about 100 lbs. which is satisfactory for soft wood.

Two types of bar clamp carriers are shown in Fig. 7-14.

HAND SCREWS are ideal clamps for woodwork because the jaws are broad and distribute the pressure over a wide area. The greatest pressure can be attained by tightening the outside or "end" spindle as it provides greater leverage than the "middle" spindle. Hand screws are available in sizes (total length of jaws) from 4 to 24 in. Sizes most commonly used in the school shop are 4, 6, 8, and 12 in.

C-CLAMPS provide a compact clamping device and are sometimes helpful in gluing operations. See Fig. 7-15. In woodwork they are often used to clamp parts to machines and make special setups. They are available in sizes (largest opening) from 1 in. to 12 in. with the smaller sizes of 2, 3, and 4 in. most often being used in woodwork.

Gluing Frames and Finished Assemblies

Before making the final glued assembly of paneled frames, legs and rails, and other structures, the parts should be sanded. This is especially important on inside surfaces. Always make a trial assembly, and determine the best and most efficient procedure to follow.

Fig. 7-15. C-clamps in use. This type clamp is also called a carriage clamp.

Fig. 7-16. A-Subassembly. Note the spacer strip used to hold the bottom of the legs the correct distance apart. B-Final assembly. Here a spacer strip is used to hold the frame square.

Fig. 7-16 shows the clamping of legs and rails. A subassembly of two legs and a rail are first made for each end of the table and then the final assembly is made. Note the blocks between the clamp jaws and the work; they protect the sanded wood surfaces. By shifting their position you can apply the pressure at the right point to obtain correct alignment. Also note the "spacer" strips; one is used to hold the legs the correct distance apart in the subassembly and the other keeps the frame square in the final assembly.

It is important to work on a good, flat surface for assemblies like this because the parts of a structure must not only be square with each other but also lie in the correct plane. In frame assemblies the contact area of the joints is usually small so even a light pressure from the clamp will provide the required psi.

In Fig. 7-17 a large frame is being assembled. If the frame is not square you can shift one or two of the bar clamps to a slight angle with the work

Fig. 7-17. Clamping arrangement for a large frame. (Adjustable Clamp Co.)

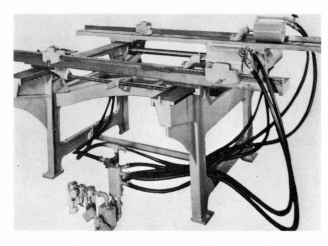

Fig. 7-18. Sash clamp. Designed to clamp window sash, screen doors, shutters and similar frame assemblies. Clamping pressure is supplied by compressed air. Note the foot pedal control. (Bell Woodworking Machinery)

Fig. 7-19. Setting glue blocks. Above. Applying a bead of glue. Below. Setting the block with firm pressure and a slight back and forth movement.

blemish in the finish. When the surface is bare of finish, glue "spots" may be hard to detect, but when finish is applied (especially stained work) they become noticeable.

Fig. 7-20. Cleaning a glue joint with a sponge moistened with hot water.

Fig. 7-21. Left. Miter clamp especially designed for picture frames. Center. Frame clamp. Right. Miter clamps that require a hole on the back side of the frame.

and use this diagonal force to pull it into the correct position. From a point level with the frame, sight across the horizontal plane that it forms to be sure it is not twisted.

After frame and panel or other assemblies are glued, it may be necessary to reinforce them with GLUE BLOCKS. A carefully squared piece of stock is ripped across corners and then cut to 1 or 2 in. lengths. These blocks are coated with glue and set in position as shown in Fig. 7-19. Press firmly on the block and move it back and forth a few times to spread the glue and "set" it in place. It will stay in position and does not need to be clamped.

See also Fig. 7-18 which shows a power clamp for sash assembly.

Cleaning Glued Joints

On final assemblies, where the wood surfaces have been sanded, extra precautions should be taken to keep them clean and free of glue. Even the slightest amount will seal the surface and cause a

Apply the glue carefully so there will be a minimum of squeeze-out. That which does appear around the joint (on front and top surfaces, and edges) should be removed. Use a sharp stick or wood chisel to remove as much as possible, then wipe the surface thoroughly with a sponge or cloth, moistened with hot water. See Fig. 7-20.

For extremely fine work, with joints that are hard to clean, you may want to apply masking tape around the edges of the joint to protect the surface from glue.

Gluing Miter Joints

Miter joints are more difficult to clamp and glue. Fig. 7-21 shows some clamping devices that are designed for this purpose. The miter clamp, Fig. 7-21, left, is especially helpful for assembling picture frames. Glue can be applied to the joint and then it can be firmly held in the clamp for nailing. The miter clamps shown in Fig. 7-21, right, fit into 5/8 in. blind holes bored in the back of the frame.

If there are no special miter clamps available, you can assemble miter joints as shown in Fig. 7-22. Small blocks of wood are temporarily glued to the sides of the frame and then split off after the glue has set.

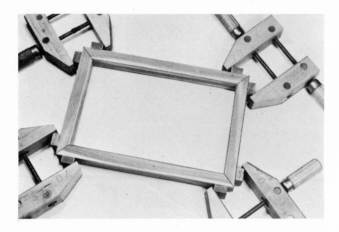

Fig. 7-22. Miter joints clamped by gluing small blocks on the frame.

WOODY SAYS:

"When applying glue to miter or butt joints, the end grain will absorb extra glue. You can insure a good joint if you apply a second coat after the first coat has had a few moments to soak into the wood."

Fig. 7-23. Band clamp.

Fig. 7-23 shows a band clamp being used to glue a cube table together. It has many applications in gluing irregularly shaped objects. The canvas band is 2 in. wide and available in several differ-

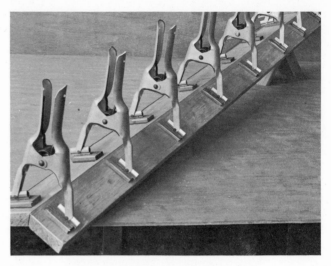

Fig. 7-24. Patented spring clamps. (Arvids Iraids)

ent lengths. A patented spring clamp Fig. 7-24, has pivoting jaws with serrated teeth along the edge. These teeth grip the surface of miter joints and other irregular shaped parts.

Shop Built Clamping Devices

You may wish to build a clamping device that you can use in the school shop or your home workshop. The press, Fig. 7-25, can be used to veneer panels, apply plastic laminates, clamp inlaid panels, and other similar operations. You

Fig. 7-25. Veneer Press. (Adjustable Clamp Co.)

will need to purchase four press screws which are available at hardware stores or industrial arts supply firms.

Figs. 7-26 and 7-27 show frame clamping jigs. One utilizes a standard hand screw to supply the

shown in Fig. 7-28. Yokes, similar to the ones used on the lamp, can be applied to other irregular shaped objects to simplify the assembly operations.

Fig. 7-26. Adjustable frame clamp.

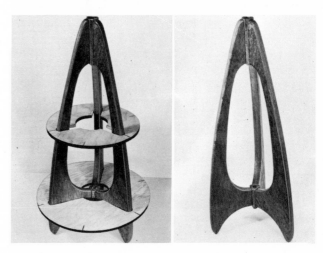

Fig. 7-28. Plywood yokes used to assemble a tripod lamp.

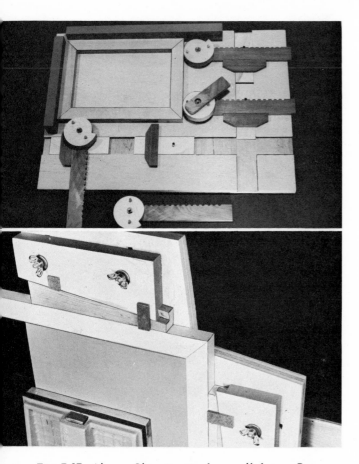

Fig. 7-27. Above. Clamping jig for small frame. Pressure is supplied by eccentrics. Below. Jig for assembling miter joints.

Fig. 7-29. Production glue spreader. Two neoprene covered rolls coat both the top and bottom surface of the work at speeds of 50 to 200 fpm.

Fig. 7-30. Electrically powered cold press. The retaining clamps are being applied after which the "package" is removed for setting and curing.
(Black Bros. Co.)

pressure and can be adjusted to fit any size of frame. The other jig uses eccentrics to supply pressure and is adjustable for various sizes of small frames. Dovetail slots in the baseboard carry the eccentric units. Jigs may be simple and designed for a single purpose like the one

Fig. 7-31. Air hose presses on either side of a lay-up table. Spreader is in center background. Pressure for the presses is secured by inflating heavy rubber hose with compressed air.

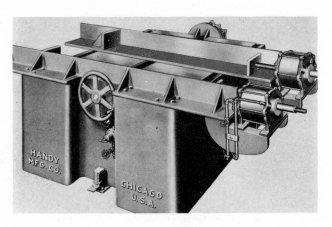

Fig. 7-32. Assembly machine for clamping square and rectangular frames as well as table tops. Pressure cylinders operate with compressed air.
(Handy Mfg. Co.)

Fig. 7-33. Sofa sectional assembly machine. Two workmen can assemble 100 units per day. Operates with compressed air.

Fig. 7-34. Automatic gluing machine. Platens are heated with electricity and clamping pressure cylinders are operated by compressed air. Stock is coated as it passes over rollers. (James L. Taylor Mfg. Co.)

Fig. 7-35. Automatic gluing machine. Stock travels across conveyor and through glue spreader. Worker at right loads table which then is moved to the left and into the press. Platens are heated with steam.

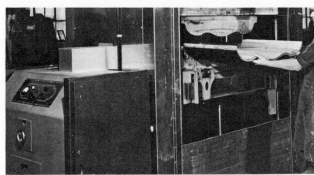

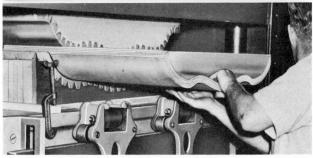

Fig. 7-36. Above. High frequency press with 30 KW generator. Dies are made of wood with a metal face that serves as the electrode. Press is closed and pressure applied by hydraulic power. Below. Removing finished panel, which will be used for serpentine drawer fronts.
(Lodge and Shipley Co.)

Production Methods and Equipment

Today, clamping and gluing operations in industry are carefully planned and controlled. A high level of efficiency is secured through the use of modern adhesives and the wide range of gluing equipment and machinery now available. See Figs. 7-29 to 7-34.

Production spreaders can apply a precisely controlled film of glue to thousands of square feet of surface per hour. Pneumatic and hydraulic cylinders operate clamping devices and press platens, smoothly and rapidly and provide the right amount of pressure, Fig. 7-35.

Thermosetting resin glues used with steam, hot water or electrically heated platens, reduce the setting and curing time to just a few minutes. This feature combined with automatic controls and equipment, permits a single worker to glue edge joints in several thousand board feet of stock per day.

High frequency gluing has greatly reduced the setting and curing time for certain assemblies. In this type of gluing, high frequency (2 to 30 megacycles) radio waves are used to supply the heat. With heating methods commonly used (steam, hot water, and electricity) to apply the heat to the surface of the wood, some time is required for it to "soak in" to the glue line. With high frequency gluing the radio waves penetrate to the glue line immediately and the glue is set and cured in less than a minute even though the stock or lay-up is several inches thick. Fig. 7-36 shows a high frequency press and how it operates.

Test Your Knowledge

1. Polyvinyl glue is a thermoplastic resin that hardens when its _____ content is removed.
2. The greatest disadvantages of polyvinyl glue are that it softens under high temperatures and is not _____.
3. Urea resin glue will set rapidly if the _____ of the glue line is _____.
4. Urea resin glue has a limited shelf-life and should not be stored over a long period of time. True or False?
5. Why is it recommended that the tube caps of epoxy glue not be interchanged?
6. Contact cement could be used to assemble a mortise-and-tenon joint. True or False?
7. A powdered glue that tends to stain certain wood is _____.
8. The moisture content of the wood at the time of gluing should be equal to that which the glued product will attain in use. True or False?
9. When gluing a complicated structure it is best to make _____ rather than glue all of it at once.
10. The operation of applying glue to the surface of the joint is called _____.
11. The assembly time is defined as the total elapsed time between applying the glue and removing the work from the clamps. True or False?
12. The greatest pressure can be applied by tightening the _____ (middle, end) spindle of the hand screw.
13. An extra coat of glue should be applied to butt and _____ joints.
14. Excess glue or squeeze-out on edge joints should be removed after it has hardened by using a _____.
15. A thermosetting type of glue is used in high frequency gluing. True or False?

Outside Assignments

1. Prepare a chart that will provide information on adhesives commonly used in woodwork. List the kinds of glue along the left side of the chart and use such headings as preparation, assembly time, application instructions, and disadvantages across the top. Secure data from container labels, manufacturer's booklets, and reference books.
2. Conduct an experiment in curing thermosetting adhesives with heat. Use several kinds of joints and apply heat with such items as a discarded electric iron, heating pad or infrared heat lamp. Prepare a written report of the results and include practical suggestions on how heat may be used to cure glue joints in the school shop.
3. Select or develop a working drawing for a small article, such as a book rack, wall shelf, box, toy, or model that includes some special gluing and assembly problem. Make design sketches of an assembly jig that would simplify and/or insure accurate construction. Include a written description of how it would be used.

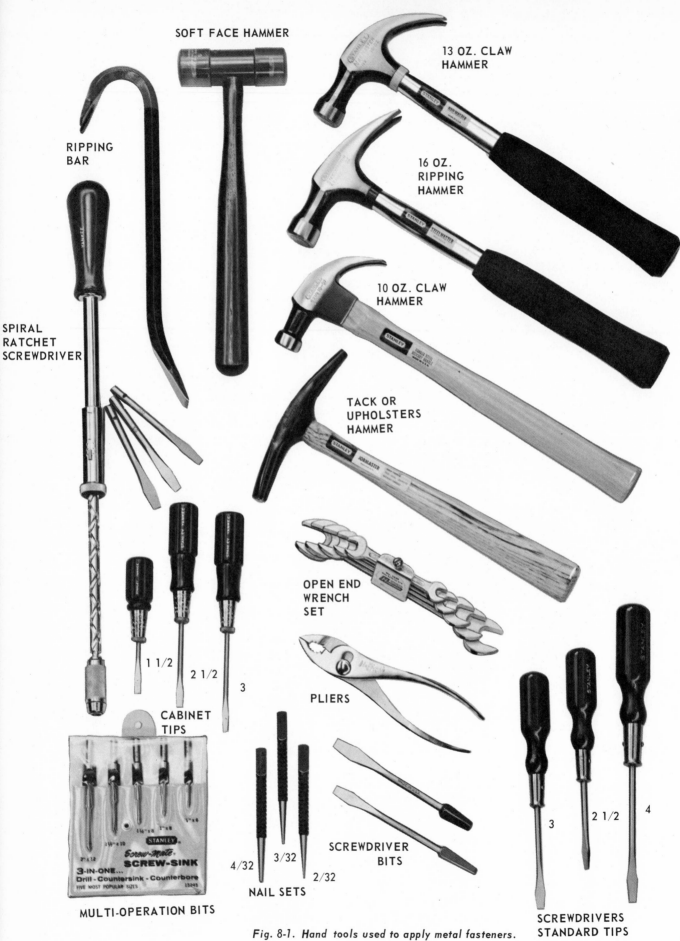

SOFT FACE HAMMER

13 OZ. CLAW HAMMER

16 OZ. RIPPING HAMMER

10 OZ. CLAW HAMMER

RIPPING BAR

SPIRAL RATCHET SCREWDRIVER

TACK OR UPHOLSTERS HAMMER

OPEN END WRENCH SET

1 1/2

2 1/2

3

PLIERS

CABINET TIPS

3 2 1/2 4

SCREW-SINK
3-IN-ONE...
Drill - Countersink - Counterbore
FIVE MOST POPULAR SIZES

4/32 3/32 2/32

SCREWDRIVER BITS

MULTI-OPERATION BITS

NAIL SETS

SCREWDRIVERS STANDARD TIPS

Fig. 8-1. Hand tools used to apply metal fasteners.
(Stanley Tools)

7-14

Unit 8
METAL FASTENERS

Metal fasteners for woodwork include nails, screws, staples, bolts, splines, and many special items. Fasteners are used in nearly every type and kind of construction. Nails and screws are still the most common. However, in industrial production where the work is done with power drivers, staples and patented fasteners are used extensively.

Fig. 8-1 includes a selection of hammers, screwdrivers, and other hand tools used to apply the more common wood fasteners.

Hammers

Two shapes of nail hammer heads are in common use: the curved claw and the ripping (straight) claw. The curved claw is the most common and more suitable for pulling nails. The ripping claw can be driven between fastened pieces and works somewhat like a chisel in prying them apart.

The parts of a standard hammer are shown in Fig. 8-2. The face can be either flat or have a slightly rounded convex surface (bell face). The bell face is most often used since it will drive nails flush with the surface without leaving ham-

mer marks on the wood. The hammer head is forged of high quality steel and heat-treated to give the poll and face extra hardness. The size of a claw hammer is determined by the weight of its head. It is available in a range from 7 oz. to 20 oz. The 10 oz. and 13 oz. are good sizes for work in the school shop. Carpenters usually select the 16 oz. or 20 oz. size for rough framing.

The hammer should be given good care. It is especially important to keep the handle tight and the face clean. If the handle becomes slightly loose it can be tightened by immersing the head in linseed oil and leaving it for several days. It can also be tightened by driving the wedges deeper or installing new ones.

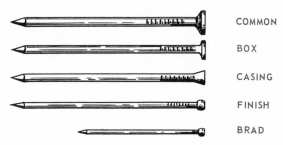

COMMON

BOX

CASING

FINISH

BRAD

Fig. 8-3. Kinds of common nails.

Nails

One of the easiest ways to fasten wood together is with nails. Nailed joints are not as attractive or strong as those that are glued but they are practical for packing boxes, crates, house framing, or in finish work where they will provide sufficient strength and the nail heads can be covered.

There are many kinds and sizes of nails. Those shown in Fig. 8-3 are standard types that you should be able to readily identify. Nails are usually made of mild steel; however, some are made of aluminum; others of mild steel with a galvanized coating for exterior work. The common nail has a heavy cross section and is used

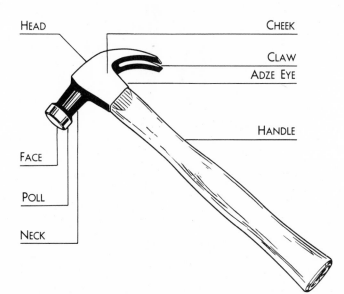

HEAD

CHEEK

CLAW

ADZE EYE

HANDLE

FACE

POLL

NECK

Fig. 8-2. Parts of a standard claw hammer.

for rough carpentry work. The lighter box nail is used for light construction, crating and boxes. The casing nail is the same weight as the box nail, but has a small conical head. It is used in finished carpentry work to attach door and window casings, and other interior woodworking trim. Finishing nails and brads are quite similar, and have the thinnest cross section and the smallest head. They are used for a great variety of small construction work.

The nail size unit is called a "penny" and is abbreviated with the lower case letter d. It indicates the length of the nail. A 2d (2 penny) nail is 1 in. long. A 6d (6 penny) nail is 2 in. long. See Fig. 8-4. This measurement applies to common, box, casing and finish nails. Brads and very small box nails are specified by their actual length and gauge number. The gauge number varies from 12 to 20 with the higher number being the smaller diameter. Nails are priced and sold by the pound.

Fig. 8-5 shows a few of the many specialized nails available today. Each is designed for a special purpose with either annular or spiral threads that greatly increase their holding power. Some nails have special coatings of zinc, cement or resin. Coating or threading a nail will increase its holding power to three or four times that of a smooth nail. These and various other forms of nails are made of such material as iron, steel, copper, bronze, aluminum, and stainless steel.

Driving Nails

Select an appropriate size hammer: a light one for light work and a heavier one for heavy work. Choose the nail with the smallest diameter

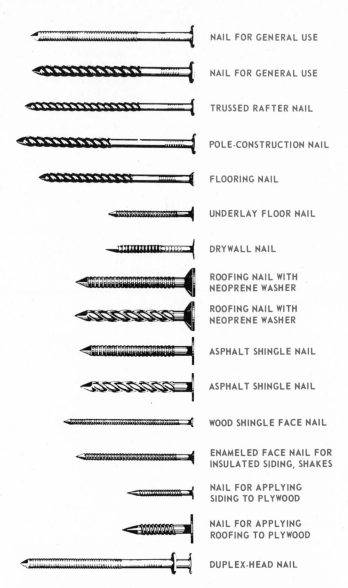

NAIL FOR GENERAL USE

NAIL FOR GENERAL USE

TRUSSED RAFTER NAIL

POLE-CONSTRUCTION NAIL

FLOORING NAIL

UNDERLAY FLOOR NAIL

DRYWALL NAIL

ROOFING NAIL WITH NEOPRENE WASHER

ROOFING NAIL WITH NEOPRENE WASHER

ASPHALT SHINGLE NAIL

ASPHALT SHINGLE NAIL

WOOD SHINGLE FACE NAIL

ENAMELED FACE NAIL FOR INSULATED SIDING, SHAKES

NAIL FOR APPLYING SIDING TO PLYWOOD

NAIL FOR APPLYING ROOFING TO PLYWOOD

DUPLEX-HEAD NAIL

Fig. 8-5. Annular or spiral threads on nails designed for special purposes. (Independent Nail and Packing Co.)

that will provide the necessary holding power. On precise work you may need to lay out the nailing pattern or mark the position of the bottom member so that you can easily locate the proper position for each nail. Always nail through the thin piece into the thicker piece. When possible, drive the nails into cross grain rather than end grain so they will have maximum holding power.

Grip the hammer well back on the handle and use a wrist movement to start the nail as shown in Fig. 8-6. Now move the hand that held the nail well out of the way and use a full swing (arm and wrist) to get power in the stroke. Keep your eyes firmly fixed on the nail head, just like you do when hitting a baseball or tennis ball. Ease up on the power of your strokes when the head gets close to the surface of the wood and stop when the head is flush. Try to avoid denting the wood

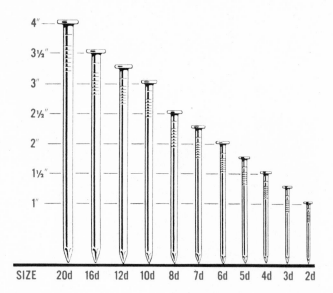

SIZE   20d 16d 12d 10d 8d 7d 6d 5d 4d 3d 2d

Fig. 8-4. Nail sizes. (United States Steel)

with marks from the hammer. If the nail begins to bend it is best to remove it and start with a new one.

Nails are easy to drive in soft wood but are difficult to drive in hard wood. When driving nails in hard wood a little wax or soap on the point will help. Be sure to keep the face of the hammer

WOODY SAYS:

"Use care when driving nails so that the hammer does not strike the surface of the wood. Hammer marks indicate the job was done by an amateur."

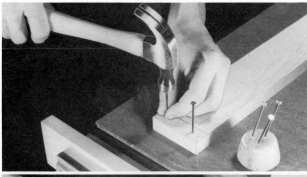

Fig. 8-6. Above. Starting nail with light strokes. Below. Driving nail with wrist and arm movement.

clean. For wood that is real hard, it is best to drill a pilot hole for the nail. When nailing at the end of a board, space the nail in from the end as far as possible while still retaining a good hold on the other member. Stagger the nailing pattern, Fig. 8-7, and avoid placing two nails close together along the same grain line. When there is danger of splitting the wood, blunt the sharp point of the nail with a hammer or cut it off with nippers. When the nail is slightly long for the work or you want to increase the holding power, drive

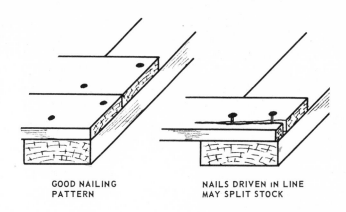

GOOD NAILING PATTERN

NAILS DRIVEN IN LINE MAY SPLIT STOCK

Fig. 8-7. Use a good nailing pattern.

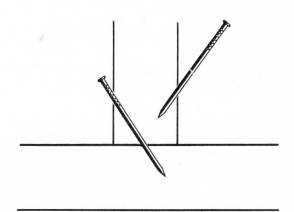

Fig. 8-8. Toenailing.

it at an angle. In toenailing, Fig. 8-8, select the position and angle carefully, and stagger the nails so they will not intersect.

When driving casing nails or finish nails, leave the head slightly above the surface and then use a nail set slightly smaller than the nail head to bring the head flush with the surface or about 1/16 in. below. See Fig. 8-9. The size of the nail

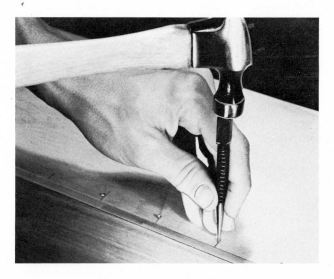

Fig. 8-9. Setting a nail.

set is determined by the size of its tip. Sizes range from 1/32 to 5/32 in. by thirty-seconds. Using a brad pusher or driver is shown in Fig. 8-10.

Fig. 8-11 shows correct procedures in pulling a nail. Force the claw under the nail head and start the removal. On some work you should protect the surface with a putty knife (as shown) or scraper blade. After the nail is withdrawn part way, use a block of wood under the head to protect the surface of the work and increase the leverage.

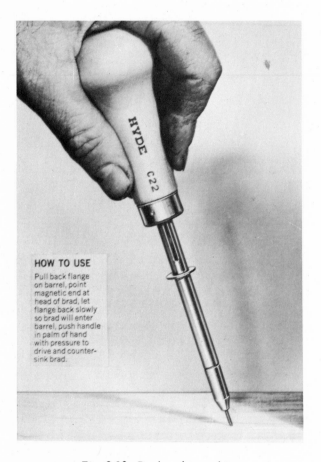

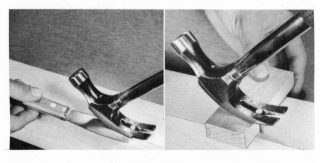

Fig. 8-10. Brad pusher or driver.
(Hyde Tools)

Fig. 8-11. Pulling a nail. Left. Using a putty knife to protect the surface. Right. Using a block of wood to protect the surface and increase leverage.

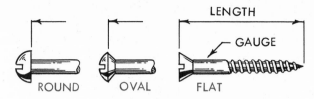

Fig. 8-12. Kinds of wood screws.

Wood Screws

Screws provide greater holding power than nails and offer the further advantage of easy disassembly and reassembly of parts. They require more time to install for which reason they are used chiefly in high grade cabinetwork and furniture construction.

Wood screw size is determined by the length and diameter (gauge number). Screws are classified according to the shape of head, surface finish, and the material from which they are made. See Figs. 8-12 and 8-13. Wood screws are available in lengths from 1/4 to 6 in. and in gauge numbers from 0 to 24. The gauge number can vary for a given length of screw. For example a 3/4 in. screw is available in gauge numbers of 4 through 12. The No. 4 would be a thin screw while the No. 12 would have a large diameter. From one gauge number to the next the size of the wood screw changes by 13 thousandths (.013) of an inch.

	0	1	2	3	4	5	6	7	8	9	10	11	12	14	16	18	20
DIAMETER DIMENSIONS IN INCHES AT BODY	.060	.073	.086	.099	.112	.125	.138	.151	.164	.177	.190	.203	.216	.242	.268	.294	.320
TWIST BIT SIZES For Round, Flat and Oval Head Screws in Drilling Shank and Pilot Holes.																	
SHANK HOLE HARD & SOFT WOOD	1/16	5/64	3/32	7/64	7/64	1/8	9/64	5/32	11/64	3/16	3/16	13/64	7/32	1/4	17/64	19/64	21/64
PILOT HOLE SOFT WOOD	1/64	1/32	1/32	3/64	3/64	1/16	1/16	1/16	5/64	5/64	3/32	3/32	7/64	7/64	9/64	9/64	11/64
PILOT HOLE HARD WOOD	1/32	1/32	3/64	1/16	1/16	5/64	5/64	3/32	3/32	7/64	7/64	1/8	1/8	9/64	5/32	3/16	13/64
AUGER BIT SIZES FOR COUNTERSUNK HEADS			3	4	4	4	5	5	6	6	6	7	7	8	9	10	11

Fig. 8-13. Wood screw sizes.

Most wood screws are made of mild steel with no special surface finish. They are usually concealed in the cabinet or furniture structure. Such screws are labeled as F.H.B., which stands for flat head bright. When screws will be visible, in high quality work, they should be nickel or chromium plated or made of brass. The heads should be round or oval. Wood screws are priced and sold by the box which contains one hundred (100). To completely specify wood screws they should be listed like this:

10 - 1-1/2 x No. 10 - Oval Head - Nickel.

Give careful consideration to the selection of the kind and size of screw that will be best suited for your work. To secure the maximum holding power the screw should enter the base piece of wood the entire length of the threads. This is about two-thirds of its length. This may not be possible in thin stock. Where the screw will be anchored in end grain you will need to use extra length since end grain does not hold screws well. It is good practice to use the smallest screw diameter that will provide the required holding power.

Drilling Holes for Wood Screws

When fastening wood with screws, two different size holes should be drilled. One should be the size of the screw shank, and the second a little smaller than the root diameter of the screw thread. See Fig. 8-14.

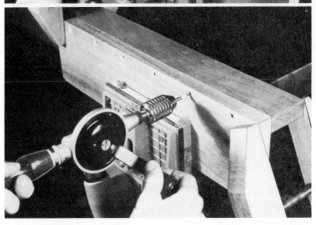

Fig. 8-15. Drilling holes for screws. Above. Shank hole. Center. Countersinking. Below. Pilot hole. Note masking tape wrapped around drill to mark hole depth.

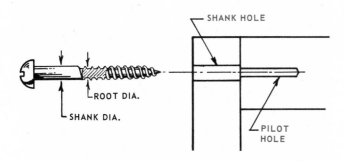

Fig. 8-14. Holes for wood screws.

Use good judgment in selecting the size of the drill bits. The size of the shank hole should be just large enough that the screw can be pushed in with the fingers. The size of the pilot hole (also called an anchor hole) for a given screw will vary depending on the hardness of the wood. For soft wood use a hole that is about equal to 70 percent of the root diameter and for hard wood about 90 percent. When working with hard wood, the pilot hole should be drilled almost as deep as the screw will go, while for soft wood it is drilled to about one-half of this depth. If you are using a large number of screws of equal size in an assembly, it will be worthwhile to experiment with scrap wood to determine just the right pilot hole for the size of screw and kind of wood you are using.

Use center lines to mark the position of the screws. Make this layout carefully so the screws will be properly spaced, especially if the screw heads will be visible. Fig. 8-15 shows a sequence of operations for drilling the holes. After the center of the screw hole is marked with a scratch awl, the shank hole is drilled. A countersink bit mounted in the brace is then used to countersink the hole to a size that will exactly match the screw head. The second piece of stock is then clamped in position and the pilot holes are drilled.

Both flat and oval head screws need to be countersunk. Use care in doing the countersinking so the head will fit correctly as shown in Fig. 8-16. Flat headed screws look especially bad if not perfectly aligned with the surface. Your work may require that the screw head be recessed and the hole plugged. For this the shank hole will need to be counterbored. Remember to bore the large hole (size of the screw head) first and then drill the shank hole.

Fig. 8-16. Drilling and countersinking for a flat head screw.

Setting Screws

The parts of a standard screwdriver are shown in Fig. 8-17. A number of sizes and styles are available. The size is specified by giving the length of the blade, measuring from the ferrule to the tip. The most common sizes for woodwork range from 1 1/2 to 6 in.

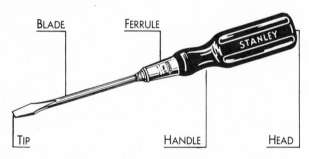

Fig. 8-17. Parts of a standard screwdriver.

The size of a Phillips screwdriver is given in a point size that ranges from a No. 0, the smallest, to a No. 4. Size numbers 1, 2 and 3, will fit most of the screws used in the school shop.

Tips of screwdrivers must be carefully shaped, and should look somewhat like those shown in Fig. 8-18. For a slotted screw they must be square, the correct width and fit snugly into the screw. The width of the tip should be equal to the length of the bottom of the screw slot. The

Fig. 8-18. Screwdriver tips. Left. Phillips. Center. Standard. Right. Cabinet.

sides of the screwdriver tip should be carefully ground to an included angle of not more than 8 deg. and to a thickness that will fit the screw slot. Use the side of the grinding wheel to form a flat surface. If the grinding is done across the sides, the tip will hold in the screw slot better. See Fig. 8-19.

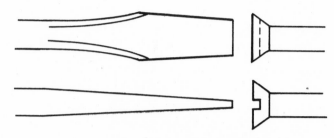

Fig. 8-19. The screwdriver must fit the screw.

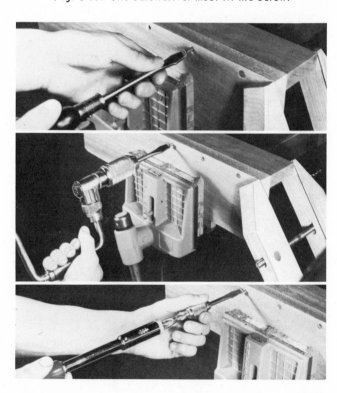

Fig. 8-20. Setting wood screws. Above. Screwdriver. Center. Screwdriver bit mounted in brace. Below. Spiral ratchet screwdriver.

If you have properly drilled holes for the screw, it is an easy matter to insert the screw in the shank hole and drive it "home" with the screwdriver, see Fig. 8-20. Use care that the screwdriver does not slip out of the slot and dent the surface of your work. Using Phillips type screws helps eliminate this problem because the tip cannot easily slip out of the screw slot. A screwdriver bit mounted in a brace is a good way to set large screws. The brace provides lots of leverage so be careful that you do not twist off the screw or damage the head. A spiral ratchet (automatic) screwdriver, will save time when you have a large number of screws to set.

A little wax or soap on the threads will make it easier to drive screws in hard wood. Do not apply too much force or the screw will twist off in the wood. They usually break just where the threads start, and the part embedded in the wood is very difficult to remove. If the screw turns too hard, it indicates that the holes were not properly drilled so you should remove the screw and make them larger.

WOODY SAYS:

"When setting screws, if you use too much force or a poorly shaped screwdriver tip, you will damage the slot in the screw heads and make your work appear shoddy."

Brass screws are much softer than steel screws and are easily twisted off or otherwise damaged. On very fine work it is often worthwhile to first drive a steel screw of the same size (this will cut the threads in the pilot hole), then remove it and set the brass screw.

When drilling holes for a large number of screws a great amount of time can be saved by using a special multi-operation bit like the one shown in Fig. 8-21. In a single stroke it will drill

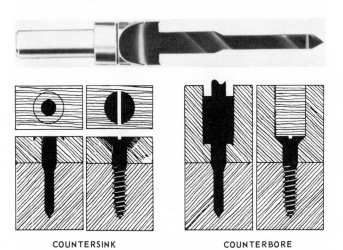

COUNTERSINK   COUNTERBORE

Fig. 8-21. Special bit for screw holes.
(Stanley Tools)

the pilot hole, shank hole, and either score the surface for countersinking or counterbore the work for recessing the screw head. Fig. 8-22

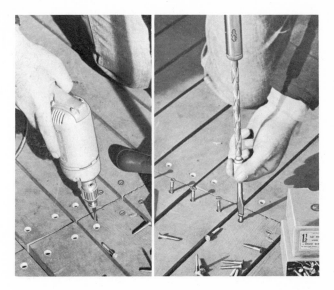

Fig. 8-22. Left. Drilling countersunk holes with special bit. Right. Setting screws with a spiral ratchet screwdriver.

shows a similar type of bit designed for drilling and countersinking being used in an electric drill. Drill bits of this kind are designed to match given sizes of screws. Bits are available for the commonly used screw sizes.

Special Fasteners

Fig. 8-23 shows a number of metal fasteners especially designed for woodwork. The hanger bolt has wood screw threads on one end and machine threads on the other. Lag screws and carriage bolts are often used for rough construction or for concealed work in cabinetmaking. Stove bolts are used frequently in metal work and are sometimes useful in joining certain parts in woodwork.

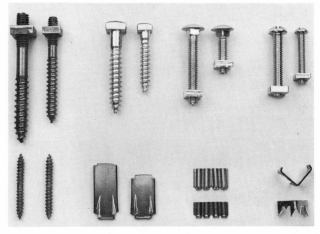

Fig. 8-23. Special fasteners. Top row. Hanger bolts, lag screws, carriage bolts, stove bolts. Bottom row. Dowel screws, splines, corrugated fasteners, chevrons.

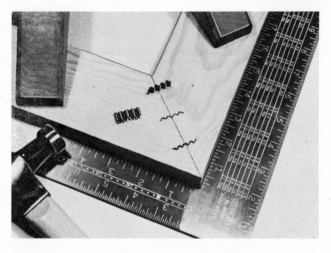

Fig. 8-24. *Using corrugated fasteners to hold miter joint.*

Corrugated fasteners are used for rough work and can be quickly applied. They drive and hold best when set at an angle with the wood grain. For an installation like the one in Fig. 8-24, they should penetrate the wood about one-half of its thickness. Hold or clamp the parts in position and then drive the fastener into one side and then the other. The ones set in the opposite side should be staggered so they are not aligned with the ones on the face side. Corrugated fasteners are available in sizes of 1/4, to 3/4 in. They are packed in units of 100.

Steel splines can be driven into soft wood along the grain but it is better to cut a saw kerf first. Clamp the stock together so you can cut into the edges or ends of both pieces at the same time. Use a backsaw or dovetail saw and cut to a depth equal to one-half of the spline width. Clamp or hold the pieces together and drive in the spline as shown in .Fig. 8-25. The spline length should be about equal to the thickness of the stock. They are available in several sizes

Fig. 8-25. *Fastening a butt joint with steel splines.*

and are sold in lots of 100. Chevrons work in about the same way as splines but are designed especially for miter joints.

Dowel screws have wood screw threads on each end. If you set them in two pieces of the same kind of wood they will penetrate each piece an equal distance if you drill the holes exactly the same. To set only one end clamp the other end between two hard wood blocks. Do not use pliers or you will damage the threads.

Metal plates and angles, Fig. 8-26, can be used in many ways to assemble parts and re-inforce wood joints. They are attached with screws and since they are unattractive they should be used in cabinetwork only where they can be concealed.

Fig. 8-26. *Left. Flat corner plate. Center. Bent corner iron. Right. T-plate.*

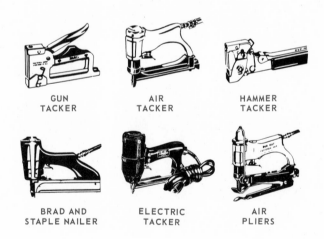

Fig. 8-27. *Tackers, staplers and nailers.*

Production Equipment

Today the building trades and industrial plants use automatic fastening equipment and machines that save a tremendous amount of hand labor. This results in better control in the quality of their products. The equipment is available in a wide range from hand operated staplers to large multi-unit power drivers.

Fig. 8-27 shows examples of hand-powered, and air and electric powered portable equipment. Such equipment is used extensively in cabinet shops, furniture factories, sash and millwork plants, toy factories, and many other industries

Fig. 8-31. *Using a staple nailer to attach a plywood panel onto a corner cabinet. Drives staples 5/8 to 2 in. long. Air-operated at 50 - 100 psi.*

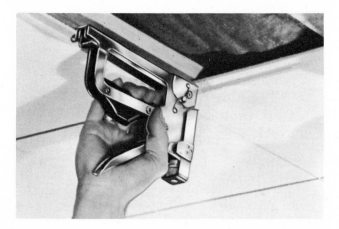

Fig. 8-28. *Hand-powered gun tacker being used to staple ceiling tile to wood furring strips.*

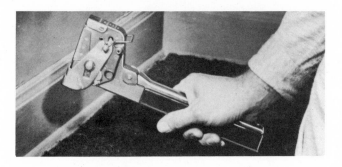

Fig. 8-29. *Hammer tacker being used to install a carpet pad. It is used like a hammer and drives a staple on each stroke. Uses staples 3/8 to 9/16 in. long. (Fastener Corp.)*

Fig. 8-32. *Electrically operated tacker. Drives staples up to 9/16 in. long.*

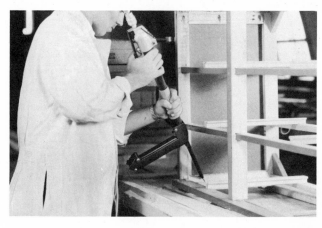

Fig. 8-33. *Nailing drawer slides in place with a long nose staple nailer. Air operated. (Fastener Corp.)*

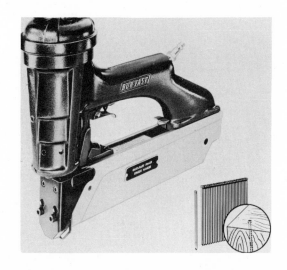

Fig. 8-30. *An air driven finish nailer. Can be used for face nailing operations on exposed surfaces of cabinets and trim. Drives a nail (see inset) up to 2 in. long. Air pressure – 80 psi.*

that work with wood and wood products. Pneumatic (air) powered tackers and nailers are popular because the power mechanism can be built of light weight materials and thus makes a unit that is easily handled. Nearly all the portable tools can be operated with one hand which frees the other hand to hold and position the material. See Figs. 8-28 to 8-34.

Fig. 8-34. A portable, pneumatic nailer that drives round headed nails, 6d through 9d. It is 4 to 5 times faster than driving the same nails by hand.

Fig. 8-36. Nailing machine attaching molding to a furniture panel. Screw-nails are driven from the bottom side at rates up to 60 per minute. Operated by electricity and compressed air from 60-125 psi. (Auto-Nailer Co.)

Fig. 8-35. Automatic nailing machine. Adjustable to drive nails of 13 to 17 gauge up to 2 3/4 in. long. Parts are clamped together and nails driven from above. Electrically powered. Nailing rate up to 145 per minute.

Fig. 8-37. A heavy-duty nailing machine for mass production of housing sub-components. A box sill is being nailed. Pressure is applied to the top and sides while nail is driven from below. Drives nails of 8-10 gauge and up to 5 in. long.

Fig. 8-38. A gang of air driven nailers being used to attach 1/2 in. plywood sheathing to a house wall section.

Building housing sub-components on a production line. Air driven portable nailers are being used.

Automatic nailing machines are adaptable to light or heavy work. They press the wood members together and hold them while the nails are driven. Many of the newer machines make their own nails from coils of special threaded wire. The threads run in a spiral around the wire so it will provide greater holding power like the threaded nails shown previously in this Unit. At a touch of the foot control, wire is fed into the machine and a nail is made and driven instantly. Adjustments can be made for different nail lengths, and also to provide for setting and clinching. Figs. 8-35 to 38 show several models and sizes of nailing machines in operation.

Test Your Knowledge

1. The two types of nail hammers are the curved claw and the _____ claw.
2. The two sizes of hammers recommended for work in the school shop are the 10 oz. and the _____ oz.
3. The only difference between the box nail and the casing nail is the shape of the head. True or False?
4. The difference in length between a 6d nail and an 8d nail is _____ inch.
5. Threaded or _____ nails will have three or four times as much holding power as that of a smooth nail.
6. When selecting nails for a job, always select the largest size so you will not need to use so many. True or False?
7. When driving a nail in hard wood it will help to drill a small pilot hole, or apply _____ or _____ to the point.
8. The sizes of nail sets vary by sixty-fourths with the largest size being about 1/8 in. True or False?
9. A common wood screw, made of mild steel with a flat head is abbreviated with the letters _____.
10. The next larger gauge number of a No. 8 screw would be a No. _____.
11. When drilling holes for screws the shank hole must be made larger than the pilot hole. True or False?

12. The flat headed screw should be countersunk so that the head is well below the surface of the wood. True or False?
13. Large screws can be set with a screwdriver bit mounted in a _____.
14. A bolt with wood screw threads on one end and machine screw threads on the other is called a _____ bolt.
15. Corrugated fasteners will drive into end grain easier than into side grain. True or False?

Outside Assignments

1. Make a visual aid by mounting nails, screws, and other metal fasteners on a framed panel. Try to include some threaded or coated nails. You might want to use epoxy glue for mounting these metal parts. Include a carefully lettered or typewritten label with each item.
2. Write to a manufacturer of a nailing machine and request a descriptive folder. Study the folder and prepare a paper describing the operation of the machine and list the kinds of work it will do. You can secure addresses from your local lumber dealer.
3. Design one or several practical joints that are held together with a hanger bolt. Try to keep the metal fastener concealed as much as possible. Rapid assembly and disassembly could be a feature of the joint. Prepare carefully made orthographic or pictorial drawings of your design.

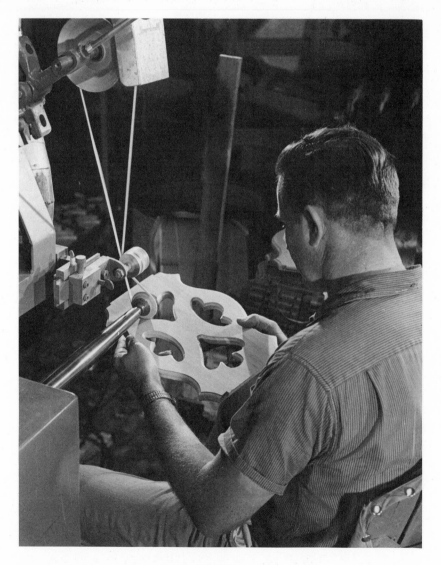

Using a spool sander to smooth intricate contours. A special garnet cloth belt rides on flat surfaces of idler pulleys, then flexes to match shape of drive pulley (called the spool). Top idler pulley is counterbalanced to provide correct belt tension.
(Norton Co.)

8-12

Unit 9
SANDING AND
PREPARING FOR FINISH

Sanding is the process where wood fibers are cut with an abrasive (a hard material that cuts and wears away a softer material). This smooths the wood surface and prepares it for finishing coats.

Sanding operations are usually not performed until all edge tool work has been completed. However, there are exceptions. For example: when cutting out small intricate parts it may be better to sand the surface of the blank first. There will be times when a coarse sanding operation can be used to shape and form the parts. Such operations are usually performed with power sanders. You should not however, try to substitute a sanding operation for those that can best be performed with planes, chisels, and other tools. Individual parts, especially their inside surfaces, are always sanded before the final assembly. A final touch up sanding is then given to all exposed surfaces just before the finish is applied.

Coated Abrasives (Sandpaper)

Since sandpaper is not made of sand, industry has adopted and uses the term "coated abrasive." This is a more descriptive term that can be generally used for various kinds of abrasive material that is applied to paper or cloth, and then made into sheets, discs, drums, belts, and other forms. There are four principal kinds of abrasive material used for woodwork; flint and garnet which are natural (mined or quarried) materials; and aluminum oxide and silicon carbide which are artificial (manufactured) materials. See Fig. 9-1.

FLINT is actually quartz (silicon dioxide) which is found in natural deposits. Flint which is one of the oldest abrasives used for woodwork, has been largely replaced by newer and better materials. It is, however still used for maintenance work and such operations as removing paint and varnish. GARNET is reddish brown in color and is the same natural mineral as the semiprecious jewel. It is the most widely used natural abrasive material. It is an excellent abrasive, especially for hand sanding.

FLINT

ALUMINUM OXIDE

GARNET

SILICON CARBIDE

Fig. 9-1. Shapes and cutting points of the four principal kinds of abrasive grains used in woodwork, enlarged.

Manufactured abrasives are formed in electric furnaces at temperatures of over 4000 degrees. ALUMINUM OXIDE, made of bauxite, coke and iron filings, is a brown material that appears more tan in color in the finer grades. It is hard and tough, and although it is more expensive than natural abrasives, it will cut faster and wear longer. SILICON CARBIDE, made of silica (sand) and cokes, is blue-black in color and the sharpest and hardest of the four abrasives. It is almost as hard as a diamond. On the Mohs' scale it has a rating of 9.5 while a diamond is rated at 10. Silicon carbide is used extensively in production work. In the school shop it is the abrasive usually found on wet-or-dry papers that are designed for sanding finishes.

Abrasive materials are crushed and then sifted through accurately woven silk screens as shown in Fig. 9-2. The mesh of the screens are numbered according to the openings per linear inch and this number is used to designate the grit size or grade of the abrasive. For example: a medium grade of abrasive is No. 80. This is sifted through a screen that has 80 openings per inch along one side and which actually has a total of 6400 openings

Fig. 9-2. Batteries of vibrating silk cloth screens, sift and separate abrasive grains into various sizes.

per square inch. Screens are used to sift grades from 12 to 220. Finer grades (240 - 600) are segregated by special processes called hydraulic sedimentation and air flotation.

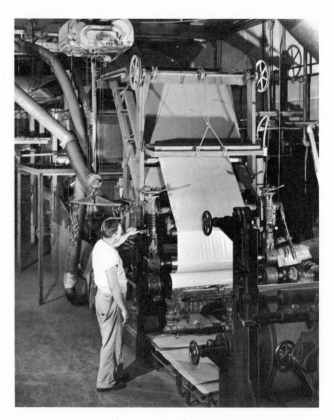

Fig. 9-3. Front end of a machine for making coated abrasives, consisting of in-feed roll rack, rotary two-color printer, adhesive roll coater, abrasive grain dispenser, sizing machine or sizer, drying chambers, and traveling racks.

The abrasive grains are glued to "backings" which includes such materials as paper, cloth, paper-cloth combinations, and fiber. Paper weights are designated by the letters A, C, D, and E. The lightest weight is A and is used for the finer grades of finishing papers. E is the heaviest and is used for belts, discs, and drums on sanding machines. Cloth weights include J or Jeans cloth which is light and flexible, and used to make belts for such operations as sanding molding. X weight, called Drills cloth, is used for flat sanding belts on large production machines.

The abrasive particles are glued to the backing in a huge "making machine" such as shown in Fig. 9-3. This will take backing material up to 50 in. wide and has a production capacity of 30,000 yards per day. The backing material is first printed with the trademark, grade size, weight of paper, and other markings. An accurate coating of glue is then applied with rollers and the backing moves into chambers where the abrasive is deposited, either by gravity or an electrostatic process. The coated abrasive is then allowed to pre-dry as it travels in long festoons. It is then given a second or sizing coat of glue and the final drying takes place. Study the drawing, Fig. 9-4.

The electrostatic coating process (also called electro-coating) is shown in Fig. 9-5. The abrasive grains are carried between two electrodes which create an electrical field of 50,000 volts. The electrical charge drives the grains upward into the glue where they are embedded vertically to form the abrasive surface.

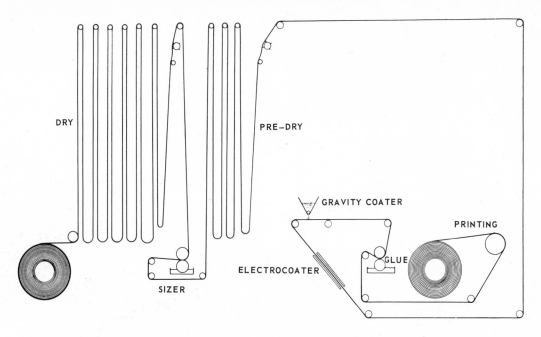

Fig. 9-4. Diagram showing the operation performed in machine shown in Fig. 9-3.

Abrasives are applied to the backing to form either a closed coat or an open coat. In CLOSED COATING the grains are packed closely together and cover the surface completely. This is used

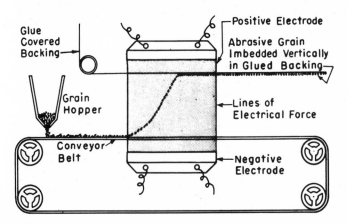

Fig. 9-5. A diagram of the electrostatic coating process.

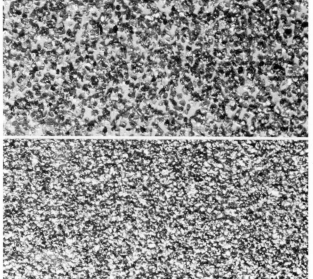

Fig. 9-6. Above. Open coating. Below. Closed Coating.

for heavy sanding operations, especially on power machines. OPEN COATING leaves spaces between the grains so that only about 70 percent of the surface is covered. This helps keep the abrasive from "loading-up" especially on soft materials. The spaces let most of the cuttings drop free from the backing. See Fig. 9-6.

After the coated abrasives have cured they are flexed. In this process a tightly drawn sheet of the material is passed over a metal edge to break the stiffness of the glue bond and make it more flexible. Large sheets are then cut into standard forms that are listed under five classifications: sheets, rolls, belts, discs, and specialities. See

Fig. 9-7. Specialities include such fabricated forms as cones, sleeves, strips, slotted discs, cartridge rolls and bands.

Abrasive Grades and Selection

The grade of an abrasive depends on the size of the abrasive grains or particles. The older method of grading is referred to as the 0 or number system. A newer system, already mentioned, indicates the number of openings per linear inch of the silk mesh through which the abrasive grains are screened. Current listings of abrasive paper grades usually include both the

Fig. 9-7. Some forms of coated abrasives used for woodwork.
(Norton Co.)

aught number and the mesh number. A wide range of abrasive grades are available as shown in the table in Fig. 9-8. The coarse, very coarse, and extra coarse grades are seldom used in the school shop. They are used in heavy sanding operations on industrial machines. Notice that flint paper does not carry a grade number but is listed under five descriptive grade titles.

GRAIN TYPES	SILICON CARBIDE	ALUMINUM OXIDE	GARNET	FLINT
EXTRA COARSE	12 16 20	16 20 4 3½	16 20 4 3½	
VERY COARSE	24 30 36	24 30 36 3 2½ 2	24 30 36 3 2½ 2	Extra Coarse
COARSE	40 50	40 50 1½ 1	40 50 1½ 1	Coarse
MEDIUM	60 80 100	60 80 100 ½ 0 2/0	60 80 100 ½ 0 2/0	Medium
FINE	120 150 180	120 150 180 3/0 4/0 5/0	120 150 180 3/0 4/0 5/0	Fine
VERY FINE	220 240 280	220 240 280 6/0 7/0 8/0	220 240 280 6/0 7/0 8/0	Extra Fine
EXTRA FINE	320 360 400 500 600	320 400 9/0 10/0	320 400 9/0 10/0	

Fig. 9-8. Grade sizes for coated abrasives used in woodwork. The 0 number is listed directly below the mesh number of the kinds and grades where it is still used.

Abrasive papers are packaged in lots of 25, 50 and 100 sheets, called sleeves. Ten sleeves are called a unit. The standard sheet size is 9 in. by 11 in. Flint paper is sold in sheets 9 in. by 10 in.

The grade of abrasive paper you select will make considerable difference in the speed and quality of your work. A carefully planed surface can be sanded with a 4/0 paper and be nearly ready for finish. If light tool marks show on the surface it will probably be best to start with a number 2/0 and then finish with a 4/0. The exact grade of paper that you will need depends on the kind of wood, surface condition, and the type or quality of work you are doing. When changing from a coarse grade to a finer grade, do not move more than two 0 numbers. For example, it would take a great deal of sanding with a number 5/0 paper to remove the heavy scratches left by a number 1/0 paper. Coarse grades of paper are used for such operations as shaping edges or removing gouge marks.

Using Abrasive Paper

A full sheet of abrasive paper will usually be too large for your work and you will need to divide it into several smaller pieces. Lay the sheet, grain side down, on a flat surface and tear it along a steel bench rule, as shown in Fig. 9-9. When working with coarse grades or using a wooden straightedge it is best to scribe a line in the paper with a sharp scratch awl. Paper can also be folded and firmly creased, and then torn along the fold line.

Fig. 9-9. Tearing a sheet of abrasive paper into smaller pieces.

When sanding flat surfaces, the paper should be mounted or held on a sanding block. The paper will last longer, resist loading, and do better work if the block has a rubber or felt cushion. The rubber sanding block shown in Fig. 9-10 holds one-fourth of a standard sheet.

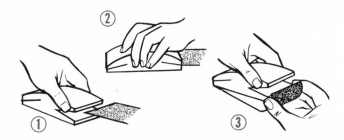

Fig. 9-10. Attaching abrasive paper to rubber sanding block. Be sure the paper is properly aligned before closing the jaws.

Before starting to sand a surface, remove pencil marks with a rubber eraser or a scraper. Keep your hands clean during sanding operations and when you handle the work after sanding. SANDING SHOULD BE DONE IN THE DIRECTION OF THE WOOD GRAIN. Abrasive paper will cut faster across the grain. If you have a heavy defect to remove, you may want to resort to this method, but remember you will need to do a great amount of sanding with the grain to remove the "cross grain" scratches.

It takes both pressure and motion to make abrasive paper cut. You can apply these best when the wood is held in a vise or clamped to a bench top. See Fig. 9-11. Protect sanded surfaces

Fig. 9-11. Sanding a surface.

and edges with smooth blocks of scrap wood. Use full strokes and move uniformly over the whole surface. Sand just enough to produce a smooth surface. Excessive sanding on some woods will undercut the soft grain between annular rings and produce a wavy surface. Thin veneers of hardwood plywood must be sanded lightly and carefully.

A sanding block should be used when sanding edges, chamfers and bevels. Try to keep the block from rocking so these surfaces will stay flat and not become rounded. End grain is hard to sand. It is usually best to sand it in only one direction, lifting the block on the return stroke. Fig. 9-12 shows a setup that prevents the end of a board from becoming rounded during a sanding operation. Cut out special blocks to fit concave curves

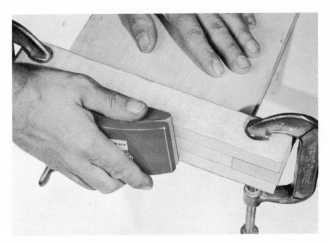

Fig. 9-12. A setup for sanding end of board when it must be kept straight and true.

and irregular shapes. Some shapes can be sanded with the paper wrapped around a dowel rod or a wood file. For small intricate parts, tear the paper into narrow strips and use it in this form or glue it (use rubber cement) to thin narrow strips of wood.

Complete the sanding operation by brushing off the sand dust and cleaning your workbench. Brush away the dust carefully so you do not fan it into the air and cause it to spread throughout the shop. A vacuum cleaner, Fig. 9-13, will be helpful in this cleanup and it also is very effective in removing dust from the surface, wood pores and joints of your work.

Sanding leaves tiny wood fibers only partially cut from the wood surface. A light application of moisture from a damp sponge will cause these fibers to swell and raise above the surface. After they dry they will feel like whiskers and can be removed with a few light strokes of fine paper. This operation is called "raising the grain" and is an important operation in high quality work.

Fig. 9-13. Cleaning sanded work with vacuum cleaner.

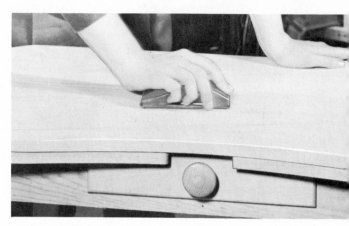

Fig. 9-15. Some surfaces can be sanded best after the article is assembled.

Fig. 9-14. Using moisture to raise the wood grain.

Fig. 9-16. Using sanding board to sand small pieces.

WOODY SAYS:

"Sanding is an important woodworking operation. Select the proper grade of abrasive paper for your work and sand just enough to smooth the surface. Excessive sanding may undercut soft spots in the wood grain and corners and edges may become rounded and uneven."

In Fig. 9-14 the grain is being raised only on the inside surfaces of a project. After assembly and final touchup sanding, the other surfaces will receive the same treatment.

Sanding Small Pieces

When wood parts are small it is often easier to clamp or hold the abrasive paper against a flat surface and move the wood over it. Fig. 9-16 shows such a procedure using a "sanding board." The board holds a full sheet of paper that is

Fig. 9-17. Using hand scraper.

attached with masking tape. A cleat along the underside is clamped in the vise to hold the board in position.

Using a Wood Scraper

Cross-grained, curly or wavy-grained wood is very difficult to plane and should be smoothed with a wood scraper. A scraper will not insure a perfectly flat surface so a plane should be used first if possible, taking very light cuts and planing across the grain if necessary. The scraper can then be used to smooth the surface before the sanding operation.

The HAND SCRAPER, Fig. 9-17, can be either pulled or pushed. It is held at an angle of about 75 deg., the angle will vary depending on the way the scraper was sharpened. Heavier cuts can be made when the scraper is pushed. Grip the scraper between the thumb and fingers on each end and then move the thumbs nearer the center and use them to apply the force.

To sharpen a scraper, first lay the scraper flat on the bench, then draw the burnisher (hardened steel rod) over each side. Place it in

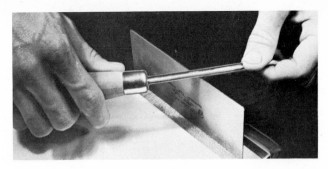

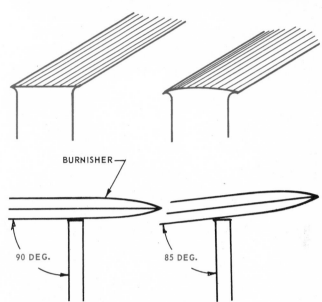

Fig. 9-19. Above. Using a burnisher to form cutting edges. Below. Drawings of edge and angles.

the vise and draw-file the edge square with the sides as shown in Fig. 9-18. The corners become very sharp and are somewhat dangerous so it is good practice to round them slightly. Hone the edge on an oilstone until it is smooth and sharp on each side. It can be laid flat on the stone for a few strokes to remove any wire edge that may have formed. With the scraper again held in a vise, run a burnisher along the edge. Hold the burnisher at an angle of 90 deg. with the sides for the first stroke and then gradually tilt it for the next three or four strokes until it reaches an angle of about 85 deg. Repeat this operation with the burnisher tilted toward the opposite side. See Fig. 9-19. Use a drop of oil on the burnisher and press it down firmly. This operation will form a slight hook on each corner of the edge that will cut a fine silky shaving. A scraper can be sharpened several times with the burnisher before it will need to be filed and honed.

The CABINET SCRAPER, Fig. 9-20, works like the hand scraper. It is easier to hold and is better to use if you have a large amount of heavy scraping to do. To adjust the cut, first turn the adjusting thumbscrew out and clear of contact with the blade. Set the scraper on a flat surface

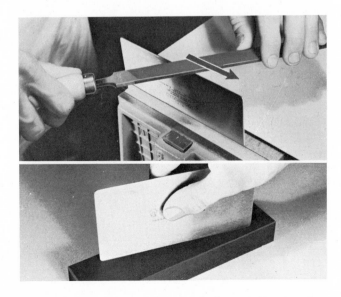

Fig. 9-18. Sharpening hand scraper. Above. Filing the edge. Below. Honing the edge.

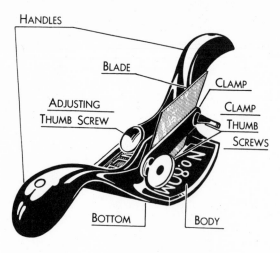

Fig. 9-20. Parts of a cabinet scraper.
(Stanley Tools)

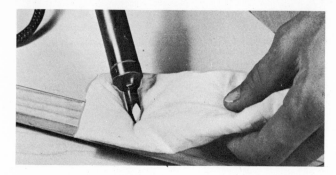

Fig. 9-22. Using a hot soldering iron and a damp cloth to
swell a dent.

and place the blade in position with it resting on the surface, and then tighten the clamp thumbscrews. Now by turning the adjusting thumbscrew you bend the blade slightly causing it to cut into the surface of the work. See Fig. 9-21.

Fig. 9-21. Using the cabinet scraper.

The blade of the cabinet scraper is sharpened by the same method as the hand scraper with the exception that the edge is usually filed to form a 45 deg. bevel.

Repairing Defects

Large defects in wood can be repaired by cutting out the area with a chisel and then carefully fitting in a piece of wood of similar grain and color. This kind of a repair takes considerable time but will hardly be noticed if skillfully done.

To repair a small dent in wood, place a drop of water in the depression. The water will soak into the wood fibers and swell them back to near their original position. When the dent is large, use a hot soldering iron and damp cloth, Fig. 9-22.

Too much steaming or wetting is undesirable, especially when working with interior plywood. Allow the surface to dry thoroughly before sanding.

Checks, cracks and holes can be filled with stick shellac, wood putty, or plastic wood. These materials will not take stain properly and you must select a color that will match the final finish. Stick shellac comes in various colors and can be melted and applied with an electrically heated knife. Colors can be intermixed to secure the proper shade. See Fig. 9-23. Wood putty is mixed

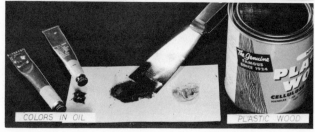

Fig. 9-23. Repairing a wood surface. Above. Melting stick shellac into the defect with a burn-in knife. Center. Wood putty is easy to mix and use. Below. Adding color to natural shade of plastic wood.

9-8

with water for use. It will take stain fairly well. However, it is usually better to color it with dry powders if the required shade is considerably different. On work that will be finished with paint or enamel, the color of the patch will not need to be considered. Plastic wood is available in several colors. A natural shade can be tinted with colors-in-oil. Place a bit of the color on a paper towel and then mix a small portion of plastic wood with it using a putty knife. Keep the can covered except when removing some material. If the plastic wood becomes too hard, it can be softened with lacquer thinner.

Plastic wood shrinks when it dries, so large patches should be filled above the level of the wood. Sand the patches smooth with the surface of the wood after they have hardened.

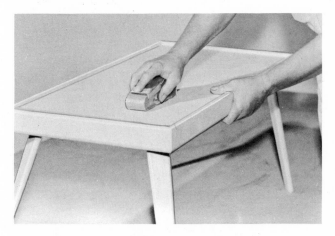

Fig. 9-24. Final sanding before finish is applied.
(Norton Co.)

The Final Touch

After your project is assembled and all defects have been repaired, give it a final light sanding with 4/0 to 6/0 paper. Use a block on large surfaces as shown in Fig. 9-24, and a small pad on edges, ends, and other areas, Fig. 9-25. Use the

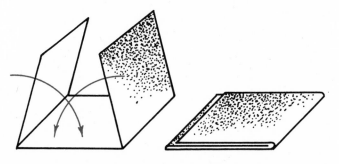

Fig. 9-25. A finger-tip pad for final touch-up sanding. Fold as shown. Use both sides and then interchange the flaps.

pad to soften all corners and arrises. With these very slightly rounded corners, there will be less danger of cutting through when rubbing down a coat of finish. Softened corners feel so much better "to the touch" and they also wear better. Be careful that the abrasive paper does not pick up wood splinters along a sharp edge of the work.

Inspect the wood surfaces carefully. You can do this with a close visual inspection and also by feeling them with your hand. Your finger tips are sensitive and can detect variations as fine as a few thousandths of an inch; so fine that they can hardly be seen.

Finally, give the project a grain raising operation if necessary and then dust it carefully. Use a brush or a vacuum cleaner to remove all dust and lint, and it is ready for the first coat of finish.

Test Your Knowledge

1. The abrasive material that has been used through the years for sanding wood is called _____ and is made from quartz.
2. Which one of the following abrasive materials is not used for wood sanding? (Garnet, aluminum oxide, emery, silicon carbide.)
3. The mesh of the screens used to sift abrasive grains are listed by the number of openings per square inch. True or False?
4. The weights of paper used for coated abrasive backings are designated by the letters A, C, D and _____.
5. The grains of abrasive are deposited on the backing either by gravity or an ____ process.
6. An open coated paper will have about 70 percent more abrasive on the surface than one that is close coated. True or False?
7. The next finer grade to a number 1/2 abrasive paper would be a number _____.
8. Standard packages of abrasive paper sheets are called _____.
9. A sanding block should be used when sanding edges, chamfers, and bevels. True or False?
10. To sharpen a wood scraper you need a file, oilstone, and _____.

Outside Assignment

1. Prepare a visual aid showing the various kinds and grades of abrasive paper and/or cloth. Attach small swatches of the material to a panel and label them carefully.
2. Develop several sample pieces of wood showing the results of improper sanding. Include a piece of fir that has been oversanded, a

piece with cross-grain scratches or rounded edges or corners. Include others that you feel are important.

3. Conduct an experiment to find the proper grades of abrasive paper to use in a given sanding operation. For example, count the number of strokes it takes to remove similar tool marks from two pieces of wood of a given size using different grades of paper. Determine the grades that should be used to bring the surface to the final required condition. Since various species of wood will have different sanding characteristics, use the same kind throughout your work. Prepare a paper describing the experiment and the results.

Using portable power sander to polish a lacquer finish.
Operation requires nylon fabric belt and special abrasive.

Unit 10
WOOD FINISHING

The application and treatment of the wood finish is an important step in making your project. The beauty and satisfaction that result from the best in design, materials and workmanship can be minimized or enhanced in the finishing room.

To do a good job of wood finishing, you must know the properties of the wood, the characteristics of the finish and the correct methods of application.

When you are proceeding with the construction of a major project it is a good idea to try out some of the finishing operations you will use on your project, by experimenting on scrap stock.

Finishing Room

Most school shops have a separate enclosed area for the application of finishes. This should be well lighted, properly heated, and special attention should be given to ventilation and cleanliness. The air should be free of dust and have a humidity range of 25 to 40 percent. The room temperature should be 70 degrees or above.

Materials and supplies should be carefully organized. There should be space for bulk storage and easily accessible space for small working quantities as shown in Fig. 10-1. Arrange containers in an orderly manner and in such a way that the labels can be read without turning them around. All containers should have neat and accurate labels.

Working surfaces (tables or bench tops) should be of metal or composition material that will not be harmed by the finishes. Walls, ceilings and floors should be of materials that can be easily cleaned.

Safety

Most finishing materials are combustible. Many are volatile (vaporize rapidly) so only a spark is needed to cause a fire or an explosion. Every precaution should be made to eliminate or control these hazards. Keep volatile materials in closed metal containers. For working supplies of such materials safety cans such as shown in Fig.

Fig. 10-1. Finishing materials in working quantities.

Fig. 10-2. Safety containers for volatile thinners. Spring keeps spout closed when not in use.

10-2 are desirable. Store rags soiled with finishing materials in closed metal containers or dispose of them at once. Open flames or any equipment that might cause sparks should not be allowed in the area. An approved type of fire extinguisher should be available and its operation should be made clear to everyone. The extinguisher should be inspected periodically.

Always be sure there is adequate ventilation and keep solvent vapors at a minimum not only because of the fire hazard but also the health hazard that is involved. Inhalation (breathing) of concentrated vapors may be injurious. Prolonged contact of some materials with the skin is harmful so wash your hands often and prevent direct contact as much as possible. Wear rubber gloves for bleaching operations.

Maintenance of Equipment and Materials

Wood finishing requires extra attention to maintenance and housekeeping responsibilities. You might leave lumber racks and tools in disorder and be able to correct them the next day but in the finishing room, paint filled brushes, open containers and spilled materials must be cared

Fig. 10-3. Be sure to wipe out lip before closing container.

for at once or loss and damage will result. Below is a list of general directions that you should follow as you perform your finishing operations.

1. Clean up your materials and return them to their proper place as soon as you have finished your work.
2. Close containers by first wiping out the lip and then sealing the lid tightly. Wipe off the outside. See Fig. 10-3. Open containers by prying carefully all the way around the lid.
3. Keep storage shelves in order with materials in their proper places and labels turned to the front.
4. Clean brushes carefully and return them to their place of storage.
5. Clean any working surfaces that you have used.
6. Rags that contain finishing materials should be discarded by taking them directly to the school incinerator or storing them in a metal container.
7. Store your project in an approved location.
8. Use care while working around other students' projects. Do not touch wet surfaces or "spatter" them with a finish you are using.
9. Do not use the finishing area for sanding, rubbing or polishing a finish.
10. The finishing room is designed for the mixing, application, and drying of finishes. Its use should be restricted to these activities.

Preparing Work

Exposed surfaces to be finished must be smooth and free of dust, dirt, glue, and grease. Bottoms, backs and inside surfaces are usually given at least a sealer coat and should not show unnecessary pencil marks, dirt, or serious blemishes.

Usually it is best to disassemble large pieces as much as possible. For example, removing the back panel of a bookcase will make it easier to brush or spray the shelves as well as the panel. Hardware that has been prefitted should be removed. For some objects you may want to prepare a special hanger or pallet that will support the work during the application and/or drying of the finishing coats.

Brushes

There are many grades, kinds, and sizes of brushes. A few of the more common brushes are shown in Fig. 10-4. The skilled craftsman takes

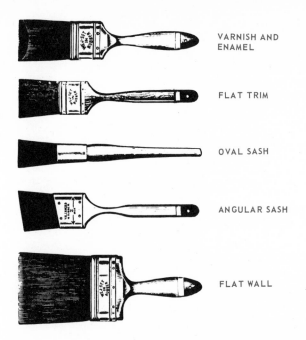

VARNISH AND ENAMEL

FLAT TRIM

OVAL SASH

ANGULAR SASH

FLAT WALL

Fig. 10-4. Five kinds of brushes.

pride in having quality tools for the forming and shaping of wood and also gives careful attention to the selection of quality brushes for finishing operations.

Fig. 10-5 shows the parts of a brush. The bristle used in brushes is obtained from animals, particularly Chinese hogs which grow long hair, and from man-made synthetic bristle. Hog bristles are oval in cross section, and have natural tapered and flagged (split) ends. These flagged ends provide paint holding ability through capillary attraction. Nylon, a man-made product, is also used extensively for brushes. It is made into

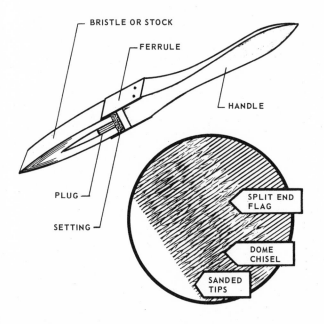

BRISTLE OR STOCK

FERRULE

HANDLE

PLUG

SETTING

SPLIT END FLAG

DOME CHISEL

SANDED TIPS

Fig. 10-5. Parts of a brush. Inset shows the tip of a quality brush.

filaments that are soft, fine, tapered, and have flagged ends that are similar to hog bristles. Nylon stock will wear longer than true bristles, and is especially well suited for water base materials. Other materials used for brushes include: horse hair, ox hair, fitch hair and tampico (cactus) fibers.

A quality brush will have a smooth taper from the ferrule to the tip, formed by varying lengths of bristle. Inside the brush is a plug made of wood, metal, fiber or plastic that forms a reservoir to hold the paint. It must be properly proportioned. Low-quality brushes are often made with an oversize plug to make the brush appear thicker. The setting holds the bristle or stock together in the ferrule. Rubber settings have been used extensively, however, today they are rapidly being replaced with epoxy resin settings that are tough, durable, and resistant to solvents and thinners.

The size of brushes are determined by their width, thickness, and length of the exposed bristle. The thickness is sometimes specified as single (X), double (XX), or triple (XXX).

Fig. 10-6. Dip a brush into finishing material one-third to one-half of its bristle length.

Using and Cleaning Brushes

A new bristle brush should have any loose bristles removed and then be soaked in linseed oil for a short time. Soaking is not required for nylon brushes. When using a brush, dip it into the paint or material only about one-third to one-half of the bristle length and then pull it lightly over the edge of the container or a large strike wire to remove excess material on the outside as shown in Fig. 10-6. Select the correct size and kind of brush for the work. Usually it is best to use the smallest size that will still do the work satisfactorily. Avoid using the brush edgewise or jabbing it into corners, cracks, or holes. Do not allow the brush to stand on its bristles either in the finishing material or in a thinner.

Brushes that are used from day to day may be kept suspended in a thinner (never water) or in some cases the finish being used. The rubber brush holders shown in some of the illustrations work well for shellac, lacquer and certain synthetic finishes. They are not satisfactory for finishes with an oil base. It is best to thoroughly clean a brush after it has been used. See Fig. 10-7.

Fig. 10-7. Materials for cleaning a brush.

To clean a brush, first remove as much of the material as possible by pulling it over the edge of the container and then wiping it with a rag or paper towel. Wash the brush thoroughly in the correct thinner and again wipe it off as much as possible. Do not clean a nylon brush in paint and varnish remover, or materials containing acetone or lacquer thinner. Now wash the brush in a commercial brush cleaner or a detergent and rinse well in clear water. Carefully strip out the excess water, straighten the bristles or stock and wrap in a porous paper towel. After it is dry the brush can be left in this wrapping or placed in its original jacket for storage.

Staining

Staining is the first step to consider in the finishing schedule. It will emphasize or de-emphasize the grain and will add color to the wood surface. Most stains used on exterior woodwork have a preservative feature. Staining is not essential in obtaining a finished surface. Many woods have the most beauty when finished natural using clear finish.

Stains are generally classified in three groups. They are water, oil, and spirit (alcohol or acetone base). Spirit stains dry and set up rapidly. Their use is generally limited to spray application. Industry uses a stain similar to spirit stain called non-grain-raising (N.G.R.). It is fast drying like spirit stain but has better clarity and fade resistance. There are two general types of oil stain; penetrating and pigmented. See Fig. 10-8. Pene-

Fig. 10-8. Penetrating and pigmented oil stains.

trating stains are brushed on and the excess is wiped off. A cloth pad can be used for the application. The stain should dry 24 hours. Then it should be sealed with a thin coat of shellac. The shellac seal is especially important on dark stains such as mahogany or walnut to prevent the stain color from "bleeding" into the finished coats. Lighter tones can be produced by thinning with mineral spirits, also by wiping dark stain immediately after application. Soft porous woods are usually given a wash coat of shellac (7 parts alcohol - one part shellac) before applying a penetrating stain. End grain may be coated with mineral spirits or thinned linseed oil before applying the stain, to prevent excessive penetration. Fig. 10-9 shows the application of an oil stain. See also, Figs. 10-10 and 10-11.

Pigmented stains are applied in about the same manner as penetrating stains. For heavy "toning" effects, allow these stains to dry without wiping. They dry in about twelve hours, and usually do not require a shellac sealer. Carefully study the manufacturer's directions and instructions on the label. Try out the stain on a scrap of wood before applying it to your project. You can see the final appearance better if you coat the sample with sealer. It is difficult to change the effect obtained with an oil stain after it is applied, so

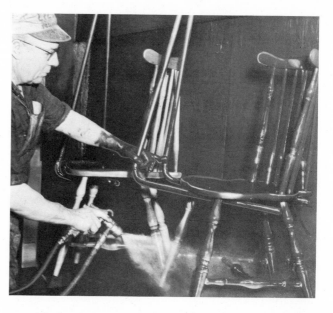

Fig. 10-9. A-Applying oil stain. B-Wiping stain after it has set for a few minutes. Always try out a stain on waste stock before applying it to your project.

Fig. 10-10. Spraying stain on Early American chairs in furniture factory. The chairs are supported by a carrier attached to an overhead conveyor line. (Heywood-Wakefield Co.)

it should be right the first time. Use turpentine or a turpentine substitute (mineral spirits) for a thinner.

Water stains are made by mixing dry powders and water. They come in a variety of colors and shades. The grain of the wood should always be raised before using this type of stain, by moistening with water. Water stain penetrates deeply and has little tendency to fade. Additional coats can be

Fig. 10-11. Spraying and wiping toning stain on production line in a furniture factory. (Mersman Bros. Corp.)

Fig. 10-12. Using water stain to darken sap streak in walnut. To make stain a small amount of dry powder is mixed in warm water.

Fig. 10-13. Mixing a commercial wood bleach. Note that the worker is wearing rubber gloves.
(Sherwin-Williams Co.)

applied to darken the wood. If the work is too dark, it can be lightened, using a sponge and hot water. Fig. 10-12 shows water stain being used to color a sap streak. After it dries the entire surface should be given a light coat of stain. Reduce the strength of the stain on end grain or apply a wash coat of shellac to prevent excessive penetration. Allow water stain to dry at least 12 hours before completing the finishing schedule.

Ready prepared water base stains are also available. These may be applied with a brush, roller, or cloth pad. They are then wiped in about the same way as described for pigmented oil stains. They dry rapidly, so on large projects individual sections should be completed before proceeding to others. Ready prepared water base stains do not raise the grain as much as regular water stain and do not penetrate very deep. They should not be sanded until after a sealer coat has been applied. They work best on wood that does not require a paste filler.

WOODY SAYS:

"The characteristics and methods of application for a finishing material may vary somewhat from one brand to another. Read and follow the manufacturer's recommendations printed on the label of the container or in their instruction booklets."

Bleaching

Wood bleaching is the process of removing some of the natural color from the wood. If a light tone is required it is usually best to select a light colored wood, however, there may be some situations where it is necessary to lighten a dark wood or change the stained color of an article being refinished.

Bleaches commonly used by students are commercially prepared and consist of two solutions. The solutions are mixed together in a glass or

porcelain container and the mixture is applied to the bare wood with a rubber sponge or cotton rag. WEAR RUBBER GLOVES throughout the operation as shown in Fig. 10-13. Since woods will vary in the way they respond to bleaching, it is essential that test strips be made on inconspicuous places or on sample stock.

When the bleach has surface-dried, sponge lightly with clear water to remove any residue. Allow the surface to dry for at least 12 hours and then sand lightly and proceed with the finishing schedule.

Paste Filler

Walnut, oak, ash, mahogany and butternut are some of the common hardwoods that have large open pores and are referred to as open-grain woods. See Fig. 10-14. For a smooth surface finish these pores need to be filled with a paste filler.

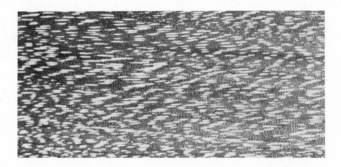

Fig. 10-14. Surface of walnut shows large pores that require filler.

Paste filler contains silex (powdered quartz), linseed oil, turpentine and driers. It can be purchased in a natural shade (light buff) and in several colors. Natural paste filler can be colored by adding colors ground in oil. See Fig. 10-15. For a walnut shade use Vandyke brown and burnt umber. For mahogany use Vandyke brown and Venetian red. Filler can also be colored with oil stains. Stir the material thoroughly and thin with mineral spirits or naphtha to a thin creamy consistency. Use a thin mix for woods with small pores and a heavier mix for those with large pores.

Fig. 10-15. Materials for coloring paste filler.

Fig. 10-16. Applying wash coat of shellac.

Fig. 10-17. Above. Applying paste filler. Center. Wiping off. Below. Closeup view.

Prepare the wood surface for filler by applying a wash coat of shellac or lacquer as shown in Fig. 10-16. A wash coat of lacquer can be prepared by reducing sanding sealer, one part with five parts of lacquer thinner. After the wash coat is thoroughly dry, sand it with a 6/0 paper. Always work with the grain. This thin coating will seal in a previously applied stain coat and make the surface smooth and somewhat harder so that it will take the filler better and the excess filler will be easier to remove. This also prevents staining action by the filler.

Apply the filler with a stiff brush and thoroughly coat the surface by first brushing with the grain, Fig. 10-17, and then across the grain. On a small surface you can simply pour out a small amount of filler and spread it with your finger tips or the palm of your hand. In a short time (10-20 min.) the filler will lose its wet or shiny appearance and the excess should then be wiped off. Use a coarse rag or piece of burlap and WIPE ACROSS THE GRAIN. Use the palm of your hand to smooth the surface and

pack the paste into the wood pores. The filler should be in the pores of the wood and not on the surface. Finish by wiping with the grain, using very light pressure. Use a rag wrapped around a small stick to remove excess filler from corners and small openings.

Once the filler has hardened it is difficult to remove. You should apply it only to a section or area that can be conveniently wiped before it becomes too hard. A cloth lightly saturated with mineral spirits may be used to remove filler that has partially hardened. Inspect the surface carefully, Fig. 10-18. If the pores are not properly filled repeat the operation after one hour. After the filled surface has dried overnight it can be sanded lightly with fine paper. Industry uses fast drying fillers that harden in 10 - 15 minutes.

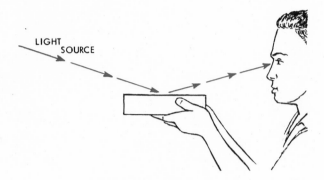

LIGHT SOURCE

Fig. 10-18. How to inspect a finish.

Sealers

The purpose of using a sealer coat is to "tie down" the stain and filler already applied and prevent absorption of the finished coat into the wood. When working with a close grained wood that is not stained, the sealer will be the first coat of finishing material applied. It will seal the porosity of the wood and act as a foundation for surface coats. A sealer coat should be applied to all surfaces of your project even though they are underneath or otherwise hidden and are surfaces that may not receive additional finish. The purpose is to seal the wood surfaces from moisture and dirt. In Fig. 10-19, the bottom of a chair seat is being

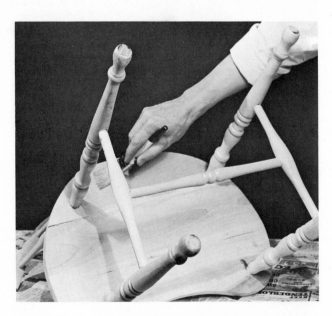

Fig. 10-19. Sealing the underside of a chair seat to protect it from dirt and moisture. (Sherwin-Williams Co.)

sealed to exclude moisture that can cause dimensional change and possible warpage.

Shellac is used extensively as a sealer. It is a gum produced by the lac bug of Southeast Asia. The refined gum flakes are dissolved in alcohol; the average store product being a 4 lb. cut (4 lbs. of shellac per gallon of alcohol). Shellac dries dust free in about 15 minutes and can be rubbed or recoated in about 2 hours. Only fresh shellac should be used. Mixtures over six months old tend to deteriorate and do not dry properly. When using shellac for a sealer coat, the 4 lb. cut should be reduced with an equal amount of alcohol. Coats of shellac are usually smoothed with steel wool because they will load dry papers.

Lacquer base sealer (called sanding sealer) is designed for spray application but can be brushed on smaller projects. It will dry so you can handle your project in about 10 minutes, and can be sanded with a 6/0 dry paper in about 30 minutes. It cuts off as a powder, does not load the paper, and provides a smooth surface on which to apply finish coats.

Additional coats of shellac or sanding sealer may be used for final coats for small projects where a tough finish is not required. Shellac is not waterproof and will water spot. Sanding sealer is soft and does not resist wear for which reason it is not well suited for use as finish coats.

In addition to shellac and lacquer, there are many oil-base sealers available that can be applied by brushing or spraying. These sealers provide an excellent sealer for the wood and have good sanding qualities. They usually require overnight drying.

Shading and Glazing

With surface filled, sealed, and ready for final coats, shading or glazing may be undertaken. The shading operation is usually performed by spraying a dye tinted lacquer (shading lacquer) over the surface to add a light tone or shade of color and make it more uniform, or provide some special effect or variation. Similar results can be secured by adding the required color tint to a commercial glazing liquid, brushing it on and then wiping it off with a rag or clean brush. Most glazes have an oil base and require several hours to dry.

Special effects can be secured by applying tinted or shaded glaze to carvings or moldings and then wiping the glaze from the high spots and leaving it in the recesses. This procedure is sometimes used in restoring and refinishing furniture to give it a so-called antique effect.

Applying Topcoats

After the wood has been stained, filled and sealed, you are ready to apply the final surface finishes. Many new products are available in the area of synthetic varnishes and brushing lacquers. Synthetics are finishing materials using man-made resins. Most of the fast drying varnishes and enamels you buy today are synthetic. These are sold under many trade names. With a few exceptions, lacquer topcoats should never be applied over an oil base sealer, however most synthetics may be applied over a lacquer base sealer. Lacquer is a product containing nitro-cellulose which dries and hardens largely through evaporation. In using such finishes, always study the manufacturer's recommendations on the label. Some synthetic varnishes require a special sealer and thinner.

When applying lacquer and synthetic varnish, as in applying all finishes, the SURFACES OF YOUR PROJECT MUST BE CLEAN. Brush carefully and then wipe with a tack cloth (cloth treated so it will pick up lint and dust). Commercially prepared tack cloths are available at reasonable cost. See Fig. 10-20.

Fig. 10-21. Brushing finish coat.

Fig. 10-22. Good lighting is important. Keep the work between you and a major source of light.

Fig. 10-20. Wiping surface lightly with a tack cloth before applying final coat.

Thin the finish if necessary, so it will flow easily. Dip the brush in the material about one-third of the bristle length and then rub the brush against the inside edge of the container to remove the excess material. In applying finishing material to your project, move the brush over the surface with just enough pressure to cause the bristles to bend a little, as shown in Fig. 10-21. Use fairly long strokes working in the direction of the grain of the wood. Work rather quickly, complet-

ing one section at a time. On some finishes which are slower drying you can brush first across the grain and then finish with the grain. When using fast drying finishes, move the loaded brush from the dry surface into the wet surface. Do not go back over the work after it has been coated. Keep the surface being coated between you and a major light source so you will have a good view of the work and will not miss any spots. See Fig. 10-22.

Usually it is best to coat "hard-to-get-at" surfaces first. Brush edges and ends before the faces; bottoms before the tops. On some jobs you may find it best to coat the bottom surfaces, allow them to dry, then turn the project over and do the sides and top. See Fig. 10-23. You can make a tripod on which to rest the work by driving nails

Fig. 10-23. Coating bottom surfaces first.

Fig. 10-24. Work supported on small nails driven into underside.

Fig. 10-25. Above. Materials for cutting down a finish. Below. Cutting a finished surface with wet-or-dry paper held on a felt pad. Oil is being used as a lubricant.

all the way through a thin piece of wood. Fig. 10-24, shows a project with small nails driven into the underside to support it during the application and drying of finishing coats. Some pieces may be coated all over, then hung by a string or wire to dry.

On most projects, you should apply at least two coats of varnish or lacquer. The first coat should be cut down dry with 3/0 steel wool or 6/0 finishing paper. Clean the surface carefully and apply a second coat.

Rubber brush holders and mason jars save a lot of brush cleaning when these finishes are used a great deal. They are not "foolproof," however, and will require complete cleaning from time to time. Each time you finish using the material, you should wipe off the jar and bring the level of the finish to a midpoint on the bristles of the brush.

Sanding and Rubbing

Cutting down finished surfaces with abrasive paper, steel wool, or a powdered abrasive is an important part of producing a good finish. If brush marks, dust specks, and other imperfections are not removed, they will form a part of the finish and become even more noticeable as the next coat is applied. Always be sure the finish is dry and hard. Overnight curing at room temperature with normal humidity is usually sufficient for most synthetics.

First coats should be rubbed with dry finishing paper (6/0 - 8/0) or fine steel wool. At this stage the finish is quite thin and water or other lubricants could easily get under the surface. Use a small piece of abrasive paper and fold it twice into equal sections. This makes a good pad with the grain side of one flap interlocking with the paper side of the other flap. Attach the paper to a sanding block when working with large flat surfaces. Always clean the surface carefully after rubbing, especially when steel wool is used.

When cutting the second coat, or any additional coats, use a wet-or-dry silicon carbide paper with water or rubbing oil. The paper will cut rapidly with water and a little slower and finer with oil. See Fig. 10-25. Work carefully so you smooth the surface but do not cut through. A 400 or 500 grade paper will remove imperfections and leave a dull sheen to the surface. A brighter sheen can be obtained by rubbing with pumice stone and oil, or rottenstone and oil, as shown in Fig. 10-26. A commercially prepared rubbing compound is recommended for polishing the final coat of hard lacquer and synthetic finishes. See Fig. 10-27. FINISHES SHOULD ALWAYS BE RUBBED IN THE DIRECTION OF THE WOOD GRAIN.

Finishes are available that dry to a soft, rubbed-effect luster without final rubbing or polishing. These however, do not usually have the fine appearance of a carefully hand rubbed finish.

Penetrating Finishes

Special penetrating finishes are available which are referred to as "rub-on" and "close to the wood" finishes. These penetrate into the wood surface and bring out the beauty of the grain. They also provide a finish that protects the wood and is resistant to water, alcohol, heat, and abrasion. There are a number of kinds available with such brand names as Dura-seal, Sealacell, Minwax, and Watco. Application procedure varies some-

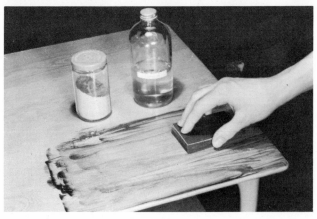

Fig. 10-26. Above. Materials for polishing a finish. Below. Rubbing a final coat with rottenstone and oil. Felt pads that have been used for a coarse abrasive should not be used for a fine abrasive.

Fig. 10-27. Commercial rubbing compound.

Fig. 10-28. Materials for a penetrating finish.

what for which reason you should study and follow the manufacturer's directions. See Fig. 10-28.

For satisfactory results the surfaces must be carefully prepared. Final sanding should be done with a 6/0 or finer paper. The finish is usually applied with a soft cloth pad and allowed to penetrate for 10 to 30 minutes. Additional finish is applied as needed. Small parts can be dipped. After the finish has penetrated into the wood, the excess is removed with a clean dry cloth. Allow the finish to dry thoroughly (usually overnight) and polish with fine abrasive paper or steel wool. Additional coats can be applied in the same manner. After the final coat is rubbed down, paste wax may be applied as shown in Fig. 10-29.

Fig. 10-29. Applying coat of paste wax over penetrating finish.

A penetrating finish may be used on either closed or open grain wood. When applied to open grain wood, it will produce an open pore, close to the wood finish, such as used on Danish Modern furniture. It can also be applied over stain and filler coats before applying paste filler. Finishes of this type are available in colors where stained effects are desired.

For projects such as cutting boards and wooden utensils boiled linseed oil can be used to produce a satisfactory finish. Since the oil tends to darken the wood, it is most effective on walnut, mahogany and cherry. First coats are sometimes reduced with mineral spirits to get better penetration. Linseed oil dries and hardens slowly and should not be recoated for 48 hours. It provides a tough and durable finish.

WOODY SAYS:

"Most finishes are combustible, so keep them away from heat, sparks and open flames. Keep the room well ventilated. Do not leave finishing materials on your hands too long. Avoid breathing vapors. Keep containers closed when not in use. Oily rags should be kept in approved metal containers."

Paint and Enamel

If you build your project of a softwood or one that does not have an attractive grain pattern, you may want to finish it with paint or enamel. Paint is a general term used to identify opaque finishes. Paint is a mixture of oils, emulsions, driers, and pigments. Enamels consist of natural or synthetic varnishes with pigments added.

Surfaces need not be as carefully prepared for opaque finishes as for clear finishes; however, they should be smooth and clean. Small checks, cracks, and nail holes can be filled with water putty, preferably after the undercoater or primer has been applied. Before painting, knots or sap streaks (often present in wood such as pine) should be sealed with a coat of shellac.

Enamel finishing materials are shown in Fig. 10-30. Brush on a coat of undercoater. This should be tinted to near the same color as the enamel. The undercoater will seal the wood pores and form a foundation for the finish coats. After it is dry, sand lightly, wipe off the surface carefully, and apply a coat of enamel. If it is necessary to apply a second coat of enamel, the first coat should be cut lightly with a fine abrasive paper. The final coat should not be rubbed. If a soft sheen is desired, a semi-gloss enamel or paint should be selected.

Oil base paints are prepared and applied in about the same way as enamel. Use turpentine or mineral spirits for thinning these materials and also for cleaning brushes. Always mix paint and enamels thoroughly before using.

Fig. 10-30. Materials for an enamel finish.

Color selection is an important consideration when working with paints and enamels. You should study reference materials to learn more about the principles that apply. Here are a few of the basic terms and definitions with which you should be familiar:

HUE: A particular name of a color, like red or orange.

PRIMARY COLORS: Red, blue, yellow.

SECONDARY COLORS: Violet, green, orange.

INTERMEDIARY COLORS: Red-violet, blue-violet, blue-green, yellow-orange, red-orange.

RELATED COLORS: Hues side by side on the color wheel. See Fig. 10-31.

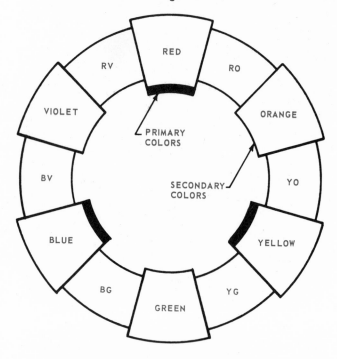

Fig. 10-31. Color wheel.

COMPLEMENTARY COLORS: Hues opposite each other on the color wheel.

VALUE: The lightness or darkness of a color.

TINT: Color nearer white in value. Pure color with white added.

SHADE: Color nearer black in value. Pure color with black added.

Fig. 10-32. Using masking tape to separate colors.
(Norton Co.)

When working with several colors or intricate patterns and designs, masking tape will often help secure a professional looking job. See Fig. 10-32. Masking takes a little more time at the start but usually results in an overall time saving. Apply the tape carefully and avoid stretching as much as possible. Remove it as soon as the finish has set by pulling it from the work at about a 90 deg. angle. Masking (pressure-sensitive) tape is perishable and should not be stored for long periods of time.

Latex emulsion paints are a satisfactory finish for wall shelves, picture frames and other projects that are not subjected to hard use. These paints are easy to apply, dry quickly, require no primer, and water is used for a thinner. They are available in a wide range of colors and can be applied with a spray gun, brush, or roller. See Fig. 10-33.

Fig. 10-33. Latex emulsion paint.

When painting large surfaces a roller can often be used to good advantage. See Fig. 10-34. A brush with nylon bristles is recommended for water base finishes. Brushes with regular bristles will absorb moisture and will become "soggy" and lose their rigidity and snap. Brushes and rollers should be cleaned in soap and water immediately after use. Brushes or equipment used in the application of some exterior latex paints must be cleaned in a commercial brush cleaner. Spatters and drops of latex emulsion paint are easily wiped up with a

damp rag immediately after they are spilled but are difficult to remove after they have set for 15 minutes or more. Application of latex exterior paint is shown in Fig. 10-35.

Fig. 10-34. Using roller to apply latex wall paint.
(Sherwin-Williams Co.)

Fig. 10-35. Exterior latex (water-base) paint being applied to exterior surface. This paint has high resistance to blistering and peeling. (Sherwin-Williams Co.)

Finishing Schedules

It is good practice to develop a finishing schedule for major projects and include it in your plan of procedure. This will make it easy for your instructor to check your ideas and make suggestions. It will also help you plan your work. You may want to experiment with several of the operations in the schedule in order to check the materials or improve the procedures. Considerable experimenting and trial-and-error work is usually done by furniture manufacturers to arrive at the most desirable tone, shade, or final finish before they go into full production. Listed below are several schedules that may serve as a guide as you prepare one of your own.

SCHEDULE FOR NATURAL FINISH ON WALNUT:
1. Apply water stain. Allow to dry for 12 hours.
2. Shellac wash coat (7-1). Dry 30 minutes and sand with 5/0 dry paper. Clean surface.
3. Fill with walnut paste filler. Dry 24 hours. Sand lightly.
4. Apply sanding sealer. Dry 1 hour and sand with 5/0 dry paper. Clean surface.
5. Apply synthetic varnish. Dry overnight and sand with 6/0 dry paper.
6. Apply second coat of synthetic varnish. Dry overnight. Sand with No. 400 wet-or-dry paper and water.
7. Rub to satin finish with pumice stone and oil.

SCHEDULE FOR LIGHT, CLOSE GRAINED WOOD:
1. Apply a brown pigmented oil stain. Allow to set for 10 minutes and wipe lightly. Dry 12 hours.
2. Spray sanding sealer. Dry 30 minutes and sand with 5/0 dry paper. Clean surface.
3. Spray clear gloss lacquer. Dry 2 hours. Sand lightly with 5/0 dry paper to remove any imperfections. Clean surface.
4. Spray semi-gloss coat of clear lacquer.

Polyurethane, Epoxy and Polyester Resin

Manufacturers of finishing materials conduct extensive programs of research that result in the improvement of existing materials and the development of new materials. One of the newer finishing materials is polyurethane. It is clear, fast drying and is highly resistant to wear and abrasion. It also has high resistance to chemicals, alcohol and grease.

Polyurethane can be applied over most sealers and fillers; however, it is usually best to apply it directly to clean dry wood, Fig. 10-36. First

Fig. 10-36. Applying a clear polyurethane finish.

coats can be thinned with a special thinner or mineral spirits. Allow overnight drying and sand between coats. Some manufacturers recommend that additional coats be applied within a 48 hour period.

Epoxy resin finish can be applied to wood, metal, fiberglass and nearly any type of surface. It too has high resistance to moisture, acids, abrasion and weathering. Industry uses epoxy resin coatings on foundry patterns, printed electrical circuits, bows and arrows, fiberglass products and many other products that require an unusually tough finish.

Epoxy resin is a two-part product. The two containers are sometimes fastened together as in Fig. 10-37. Shake the containers and then pour

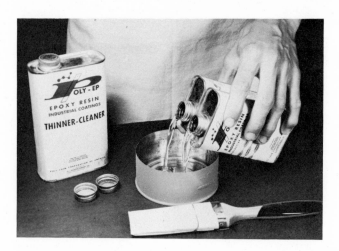

Fig. 10-37. Mixing epoxy resin. The two cans are permanently attached.

equal amounts into a mixing pot. Stir for several minutes and then let the mixture set for 30 minutes before applying. The first coat on new wood should be reduced with a special thinner that must also be used for cleaning brushes and equipment. It will be dry to the touch in about one hour, and can be recoated in about 4 hours. Pot life (length of time mixed portion in pot should be used) is 24 hours but it can be kept longer if refrigerated. Manufacturers provide specific instruction for their product which should be followed closely.

COMPRESSORS are classified as being piston or diaphragm type. The piston type requires a reserve pressure tank. Portable compressors are usually of the diaphragm type. These can deliver

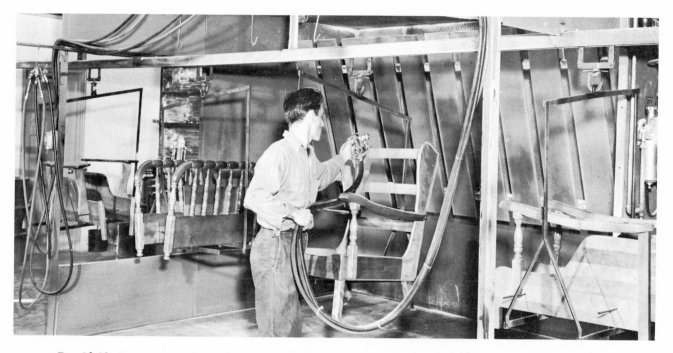

Fig. 10-38. Spraying in industry. Furniture parts are carried through the spray booth by an overhead conveyor. (DeVilbiss Co.)

Polyester resin films are clear and hard and form a surface that is quite comparable to that of a plastic laminate material. The liquid resin must be mixed with a catalyst (substance which by its presence produces reaction between other substances). It is then applied in a heavy coat to form a film (4 to 10 mils). The strength and hardness of a polyester finish is not secured in films as thin as conventional finishes. Since work with this resin must be carefully controlled its application is largely limited to industrial production, where it is used extensively for the finish on desk and table tops.

Spray Equipment

Modern production woodworking plants employ a wide range of spray equipment in their finishing departments. Many of the new fast-drying finishes are designed especially for spray application. See Fig. 10-38.

Conventional spraying equipment, consisting of a compressor, transformer, hose, hand guns and an approved spray booth is usually included in the school shop layout. If the shop equipment at your school includes spray equipment, you will want to become experienced in its use.

a relative large volume of air at a lower pressure. Fig. 10-39 shows a small diaphragm compressor that will provide 2.5 cubic feet of air per minute (CFM) at 25 pounds per square inch (psi) of pressure. Many different types are available.

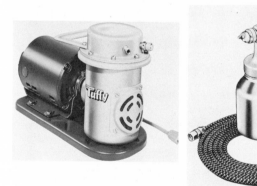

Fig. 10-39. A small diaphragm compressor, hose, and spray gun.

An AIR TRANSFORMER is shown in Fig. 10-40. It is a device that filters out oil, dust and moisture, and regulates the air pressure. AIR HOSE carries the compressed air from the transformer to the gun. It is reinforced with fabric embedded in the rubber or on the outside surface. The minimum size of hose needed to operate a single gun is 1/4 in. ID. Too long a length of small hose will result in excessive pressure drop.

SPRAY BOOTHS are compartments or enclosures designed to confine and exhaust or filter overspray and fumes created by the spraying

Spray guns may have either an internal mix or external mix spraying head. See Fig. 10-43. The external mix gun is used to apply fast drying materials and is easier to clean. It also provides greater control of the spray pattern. The internal mix gun is used for slow drying materials and is the best type to use when air pressures are limited.

Fig. 10-40. Compressed air equipment. The transformer consists of: A-Condenser. B-Filter. C-Air regulator. D-Pressure gauges. E-Outlet valves. F-Drain.

PISTON TYPE COMPRESSOR

DIAPHRAGM TYPE COMPRESSOR

TRANSFORMER

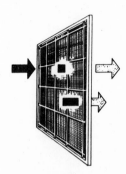

WATER WASH BOOTH. Literally washes paint pigments out of the exhaust air. Most efficient for removal of paint pigments from exhaust air regardless of paint viscosity or drying speed. Most acceptable to all fire, health and building codes. Use where production is continuous.

FILTER BOOTH. Traps overspray particles in filter elements. Suitable for production work with slow drying or light viscosity materials, and intermittent or light production with all types of materials. Regularly scheduled filter replacement keeps booth at top efficiency.

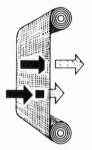
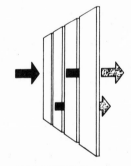

DISPO BOOTH. Similar in overspray removal to the filter booth. Filter element is a cloth curtain, placed on rollers. As the cloth becomes saturated with pigment, new cloth is gradually rolled into place, either manually or automatically. Cloth rolls easily replaced.

BAFFLE BOOTH. Use where exhaust air to the outside does not have to be free of paint particles. Suitable for intermittent production with quick drying materials. Baffles assure an even air flow distribution through the spray booth work area.

Fig. 10-41. Four types of spray booths. (Binks Mfg. Co.)

operation. They are essential for the safe indoor operation of spray equipment. The type is determined by the method used to trap or dissipate the overspray. Fig. 10-41 shows some standard types. The dry baffle type where the exhaust air goes directly to the outside is the one commonly used in school shops.

The SPRAY GUN shown in Fig. 10-42, uses compressed air to atomize the material and spread it on the surface of the work in a controlled pattern. Spray guns may have either an attached container (as shown in Fig. 10-42), or a separate container. They also may be classified as a bleeder type or nonbleeder type. In the nonbleeder gun the trigger controls both air and material flow. In the bleeder gun, air passes through the gun continuously and prevents pressure build-up in the lines. It is the type that is used with small diaphragm compressors that do not have a pressure tank.

Guns may vary in the way the material is fed. In the suction feed gun, the stream of compressed air passing over the fluid tip creates a vacuum allowing atmospheric pressure to force the material from the cup. In the pressure feed gun, air pressure enters the cup and the material is forced to the fluid tip. This is the type of gun used in production work where the material is brought to the gun through a hose connected to a pressurized supply tank. Fig. 10-44 shows a cross section of a nonbleeder, external mix, suction feed type of spray gun. Study the various parts so you will know their relationship and how they work.

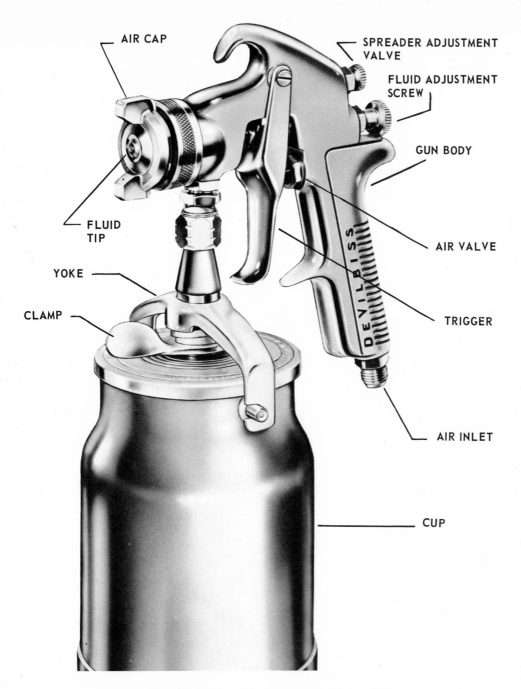

AIR CAP

SPREADER ADJUSTMENT VALVE

FLUID ADJUSTMENT SCREW

GUN BODY

FLUID TIP

AIR VALVE

YOKE

TRIGGER

CLAMP

AIR INLET

CUP

Fig. 10-42. Parts of a spray gun with attached cup.

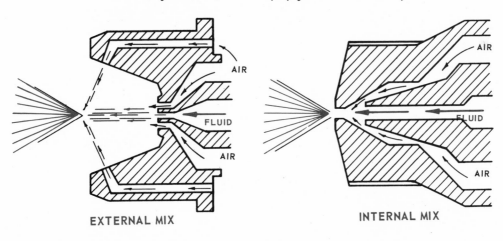

AIR

FLUID

AIR

EXTERNAL MIX

AIR

FLUID

AIR

INTERNAL MIX

Fig. 10-43. Types of spray heads. The spray head (nozzle) consists of an air cap and a fluid tip.

Adjusting the Gun

Most finishing materials will need to be reduced for spraying. Standard lacquers are reduced about 25 percent. The material should be thoroughly mixed and strained into the cup. Attach the cup to the gun and adjust the air pressure to about 25 lbs.

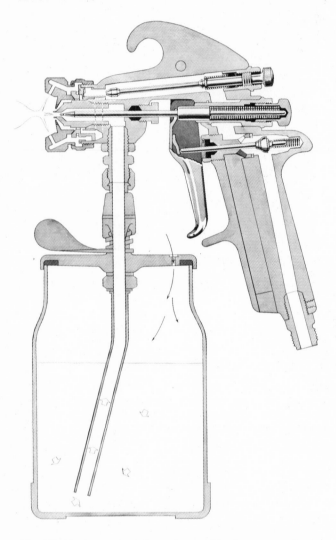

Fig. 10-44. A section view of a nonbleeder, external mix, suction feed type of spray gun.
(DeVilbiss Co.)

Open the fluid adjustment screw and check the pattern by triggering the gun while it is held stationary and aimed at a test surface. The shape of the spray pattern can be changed by turning the spreader adjustment valve. With the adjustment closed you will secure a perfectly round shape and then as it is opened, air flows through the wings of the air cap and forms an elliptical pattern. See Fig. 10-45. Spray patterns for internal mix gun heads are varied by using different shaped nozzles.

After you have selected a desirable pattern for your work, you will need to adjust the material or fluid flow. Large patterns will require lots of material and the fluid adjustment screw will need to be nearly wide open. You may also need to readjust the air pressure at the transformer. Always select a size of spray pattern that will fit your work. Using a large pattern on a small surface will result in excessive overspray and loss of material. Too much air pressure will cause overatomization and waste material.

WOODY SAYS:

"To reduce overspray and obtain maximum efficiency always spray with the lowest possible air pressure."

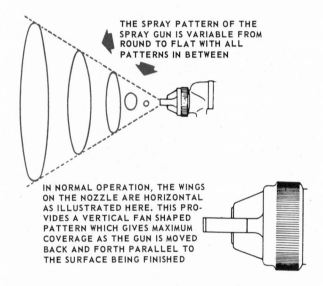

THE SPRAY PATTERN OF THE SPRAY GUN IS VARIABLE FROM ROUND TO FLAT WITH ALL PATTERNS IN BETWEEN

IN NORMAL OPERATION, THE WINGS ON THE NOZZLE ARE HORIZONTAL AS ILLUSTRATED HERE. THIS PROVIDES A VERTICAL FAN SHAPED PATTERN WHICH GIVES MAXIMUM COVERAGE AS THE GUN IS MOVED BACK AND FORTH PARALLEL TO THE SURFACE BEING FINISHED

Fig. 10-45. Spray patterns of the external mix gun.

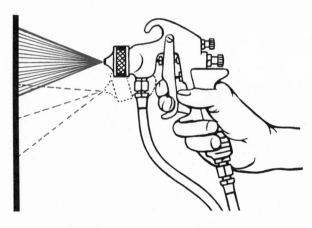

Fig. 10-46. Hold the gun perpendicular to the surface. Tilting (dotted lines) will result in an uneven pattern.

WOOD FINISHING

Using the Gun

Practice using the spray gun by coating a test panel. The gun should be held perpendicular to the surface and moved in even strokes parallel to it as shown in Figs. 10-46 and 47. The stroke should be started before the trigger is pulled and released before the stroke is finished.

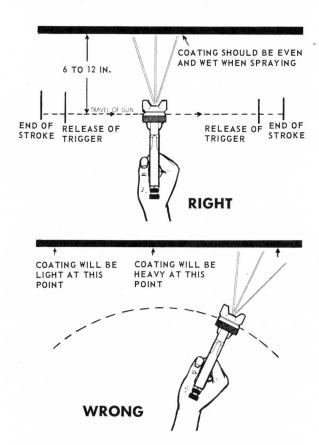

Fig. 10-47. Stroking procedure.

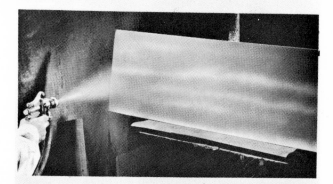

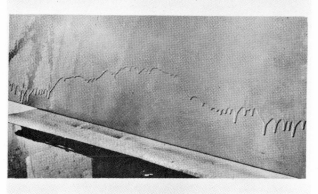

Fig. 10-48. Top. Gun held too far away. Bottom. Gun held too close and stroked too slowly. (E. I. DuPont DeNemours Co.)

Fig. 10-49. Work set on a turntable in the spray booth. The wings of the air cap are in a vertical position to form a horizontal pattern as the gun is stroked up and down with the grain.

The weight of the coat will vary with the speed of the stroke and the distance between the gun and the surface. Try to lay down an even, wet coat. If the gun is held too far away the coat will be light and you may secure a surface as shown in Fig. 10-48. If the gun is held too close and moved too slowly you will build too heavy a coat and it will sag. LAP EACH STROKE HALF WAY over the preceding stroke to obtain a uniform finish.

To set up your project work for spraying, disassemble it and handle it in about the same way as for a finish with a brush. If possible, the project should be supported on a turntable as shown in Fig. 10-49. This will make it easier to move the work as you proceed from one surface to the next. Keep the surface being coated between you and a major light source so you can best see the coat being applied. It is easier to spray a

horizontal surface than a vertical one so try and arrange your work so that most of it can be coated in the horizontal position.

Spray hard-to-reach surfaces and edges first. Fig. 10-50 shows the edges being sprayed. The face of the panel is then filled in. When spraying a level surface, always work from the near to the far side so the movement of the air toward the

Fig. 10-50. Spray edges first and then top surface.

booth will pull the overspray away from the wet surface. To minimize overspray, edges should be sprayed with the gun set at a small pattern. A fuller pattern can be used, if the gun is held close and stroked rapidly.

You will need to study your work and determine the best procedure to follow. Fig. 10-51 shows a suggested sequence of strokes for rectangular pieces.

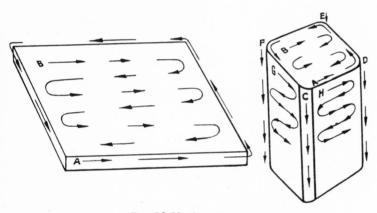

Fig. 10-51. Spraying sequence.

Faulty Operation

Unsatisfactory work may be caused by defective equipment or poor operational technique. Study the manufacturer's manual for directions concerning a particular style or type of gun. Problems which may be encountered include:

FAULTY PATTERNS; usually caused by dirty or clogged air caps or fluid tips. Remove and clean in correct thinner. Too much pressure used with a thin material can cause trouble.

RUNS AND SAGS; excessive material in pattern, material too thin, gun held close to surface, and/or motion too slow.

ORANGE PEEL; material does not flow together smoothly because it is too heavy and dry when it reaches the surface. Hold gun closer and thin material.

BLUSHING; a cloudy appearance in the film due to moisture. Caused by high humidity and thinners that evaporate too rapidly.

SPITTING GUN; air entering the material line through the packing around the needle valve (oil and tighten). Loose connections between the siphon cup and gun. Vent hole in the cup may be plugged.

Fig. 10-52. Spray gun with extra cups for different material.

Gun Cleaning and Care

A spray gun is easy to maintain and clean, if you have extra cups for materials as shown in Fig. 10-52. When you have finished with the gun, release it from the cup and loosen the air cap. Hold a cloth over the cap, pull the trigger and force material back into the cup as shown in Fig. 10-53. Attach a cup that is about half filled with thinner; shake and trigger the gun several

Fig. 10-53. Forcing material from the gun back into the cup.
(DeVilbiss Co.)

Fig. 10-54. Oiling the air valve. Also oil the fluid needle packing gland and the trigger bearing screw. See Arrows.

Fig. 10-56. Using an aerosol spray can for touch-up work. (Sprayon Products Inc.)

times while it is held in the spray booth. Wipe off the outside of the gun and disconnect the air hose. The air cap should be removed and placed in thinner, especially if it is an internal mix type, and the fluid tip should be wiped clean. Guns that will be stored for a period of time should be disassembled and completely cleaned and dried. Do not soak the entire gun in thinner as it will dissolve the lubricant in the valve packings.

Proper lubrication is important. The fluid needle packing gland should be oiled often. Also place a drop of oil on the air valve stem and the trigger bearing screw. See Fig. 10-54. When cleaning clogged holes in the cap or fluid tip always use a wooden match stick or toothpick. Do not use wire, nails or metal tools. See Fig. 10-55.

mechanical refrigerators. This gas in liquid form is loaded in the spray can along with the material. It creates pressures of about 40 psi at 70 degrees. When the valve of the can is pushed the solution is released and forms a spray as it is emitted from a tiny orifice (opening).

In a typical aerosol can, the material is mixed by shaking the can and then swirling the metal ball (located in the container) around the bottom. Hold the valve 10 to 12 inches from the surface as shown in Fig. 10-56. After use, wipe the valve, invert the can and release the valve to allow a small amount of clear gas to clean the orifice.

Cans of gas propellant are available for use with a small spray gun as shown in Fig. 10-57.

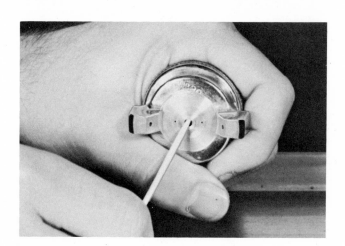

Fig. 10-55. Cleaning the air cap.

Aerosol Spraying

Many finishing materials are available in aerosol cans. These are especially handy for small jobs.

The blast that atomizes the material is not air, but Freon gas, which is the same gas used in

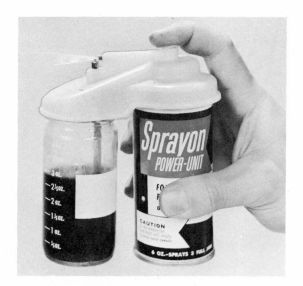

Fig. 10-57. Small self-powered spray unit.

This self-powered unit can be loaded with materials such as used by a regular gun. The materials should be thinned and the spray unit handled in about the same way as a regular spray gun. A unit of this type will work satisfactory on many small articles. See Figs. 10-58 and 59.

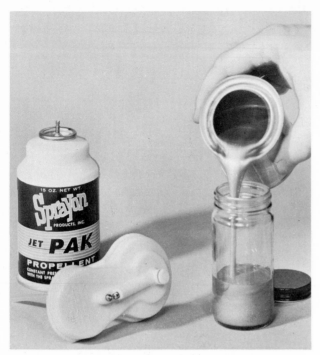

Fig. 10-58. Filling the material cup.

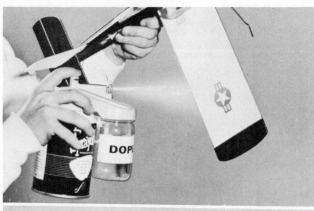

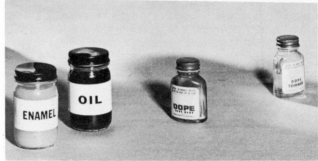

Fig. 10-59. Using the self-powered spray unit.

WOODY SAYS:

"Aerosol cans should not be exposed to temperature over 120 deg. F. Do not place them where they will be exposed to sunlight shining through glass. Never puncture or incinerate an aerosol can."

Industrial Spraying

Guns with cups are seldom used in production work. Pressure fed guns are supplied with material through hose lines and pipes that are connected to pressurized tanks or special pumps. The spray operator can work continuously without interruption. See Fig. 10-60.

Fig. 10-60. Spraying the final coat of lacquer on a production line.
(Mersman Bros. Corp.)

Fig. 10-61. Automatic rotary spraying machine. An electrical device turns on the guns when a surface to be coated is passing underneath. (Binks Mfg. Co.)

Production setups often employ automatic gun heads that are pneumatically or electrically operated. These guns are mounted on carriers that move back and forth or up and down as the work moves along a conveyor line or around a revolving table. Fig. 10-61, shows a rotary spray machine where the spray guns are mounted on arms and are automatically turned on when work passes underneath. The conveyor carries the work at speeds of about 100 ft. per minute.

A spindle spraying setup is shown in Fig. 10-62. The work is placed on conveyorized spindles, sometimes called a chain-on-edge machine. As the spindles pass in front of the spray guns, they are automatically rotated and the guns are triggered to provide a uniform coat on all sides of the work.

In AIRLESS SPRAYING the material is atomized by high (hydraulic) pressure rather than compressed air. Fig. 10-63 compares the equipment arrangement of airless spraying with that of conventional spraying. In the airless spraying

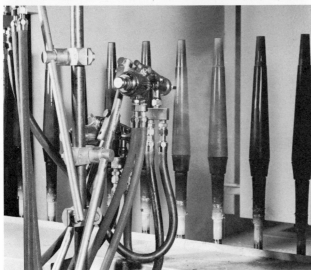

Fig. 10-62. Above. Automatic spraying of turned legs, stain coat. Legs move into an infrared drying oven. Below. Close-up showing a spraying station equipped with three automatic guns. Only two are being used for the legs in process. Legs rotate as they pass by the guns.

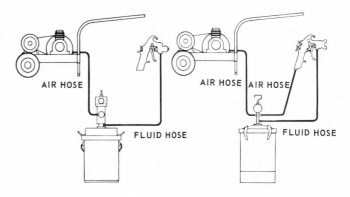

Fig. 10-63. Left. Airless spraying. Right. Spraying in conventional manner.

Fig. 10-64. Airless spray gun. Spray tip is made of tungsten carbide.

method, a special pump delivers paint to the spray gun under fluid pressures as high as 3000 psi. Atomization occurs as the material is forced through the small orifice of the gun nozzle. The valve seat, needle, and tip are made of tungsten carbide to resist the excessive wear caused by the material passing through the nozzle at such high pressure. See Figs. 10-64 and 65. Heavy coats can be applied without fogging or overspray.

The HOT-SPRAYING of materials, either by conventional or airless methods is often employed in production work. By heating the material, the viscosity of a high solids product can be reduced without the addition of extra solvent. This results in a reduction of the number of coats; the finish has less tendency to sag and such problems as blushing (finish taking on grayish cast while drying) are eliminated. In this process the material is heated to a temperature of 160 to 200 deg. F. Gun cups are available that have thermostatically controlled heating units.

ELECTROSTATIC SPRAYING is used extensively in the metalworking industry. It cannot be used successfully in wood finishing without first applying a conductive material to the wood surface. In the electrostatic process the material receives a negative charge from a special spray gun, or a revolving disc that throws the material into the air by centrifugal force. The negatively charged particles of material are attracted to the product which has received a positive charge. Even coats can be applied and there is little overspray or loss of material. See Fig. 10-66.

Fig. 10-65. Pump and material tank for airless spraying.

Fig. 10-67. A double roller coater with variable speeds of 40 to 120 fpm.

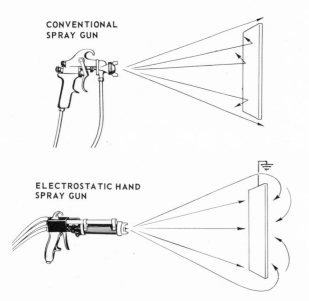

Fig. 10-66. Electrostatic spraying. (Ashdee Corp.)

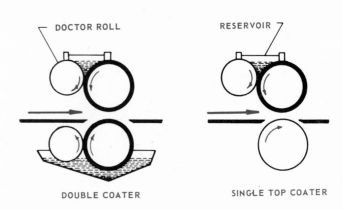

Fig. 10-68. Roll arrangements in roller coating machines.

Roller Coating

In roller coating the work is passed between synthetic rubber rollers which carry a film of the finishing material. The rollers revolve in a reservoir of the material and then against a chromium plated doctor roll that accurately controls the film thickness. Roller coaters can be used to apply nearly any type of finishing material to plywood, hardboard, particle board, metal sheets and other flat work. See Figs. 10-67 to 10-70.

Curtain Coating

Curtain coating is a high speed production process where the work is passed through a falling, continuous stream (curtain) of the finishing material. The curtain is formed by flowing the finishing material over a weir or dam. It then drops from the skirt of the weir by gravity either onto the work or into a gutter which returns the material to a reservoir to be recirculated. The thickness of the film varies with the rate of flow

and the speed at which the work moves. Accurate films of from 1 to 25 mils can be applied with a machine such as shown in Fig. 10-71.

Fig. 10-72 shows a diagramatic view of a pressure curtain coater. The three main com-

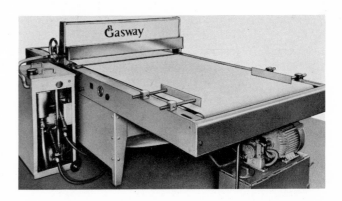

Fig. 10-71. Curtain coating machine. Conveyor belt moves at speeds from 50 to 450 fpm. (Gasway Corp.)

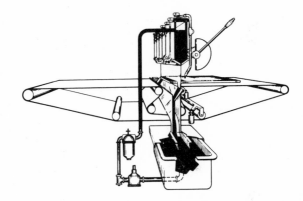

Fig. 10-72. Operation of a pressure curtain coater. (George Koch Sons, Inc.)

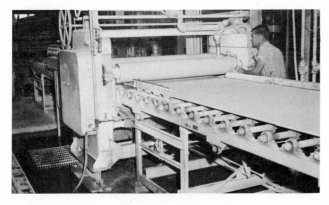

Fig. 10-69. Infeed view of a single top side roller coater applying paint to insulating boards. (Black Bros. Co.)

Fig. 10-70. Plywood panel feeding into a double roller coater. The visible rolls provide movement into the first unit which dusts and cleans the panel before the coating of finish is applied in the second unit. (Union Tool Corp.)

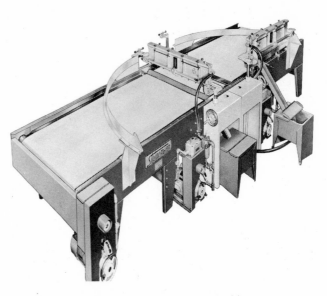

Fig. 10-73. A double-head pressure curtain coater. (George Koch Sons, Inc.)

ponents consist of the curtain forming head, the conveyor belt and the material circulating and filtering system. The orifice for the head is composed of a stationary knife and a movable knife that can be accurately adjusted to provide the required curtain thickness. Application speeds may run as high as 800 fpm. At this rate of application, it is often necessary to heat the surface of the wood to reduce the dry time. Intense electric radiant heat can raise the surface temperature of a wood panel to 200 deg. in as little as 10 seconds. The panel is then passed through the curtain coater and the finish dries in two or three minutes. Fig. 10-73 shows a double-head pressure curtain coater; Fig. 10-74 shows an installation view of curtain coating machines.

Fig. 10-74. Curtain coaters applying finish to kitchen cabinet components. After coating, the work moves into a forced air flashoff tunnel and then into an infrared oven.

Flow Coating and Dipping

In the flow coating method, the work is carried by an overhead conveyor, or placed in a chamber where a bank of low pressure nozzles eject streams of the finishing material. The excess drains off into catch basins and is recirculated through the system. In dipping the product is completely immersed into a tank. The viscosity of the finishing material must be carefully controlled to prevent lower surfaces and edges from holding an excessive film. The position of the parts, and dripping and drying procedures must be correct to prevent tears, curtains, and sags.

Flow coating and dipping are used extensively by metalworking industries but are not well adapted to wood products, except to apply stains or penetrating sealers.

Tumbling

This method is often used to finish knobs, buttons, golf tees, beads and other small wooden objects. The parts are placed in a drum or barrel with a small amount of lacquer, enamel or wax. The barrel is then revolved at a speed of about 25 rpm causing the parts to continually fall and tumble over each other. Additional finishing material is placed in the barrel as required. As they dry, the parts polish each other to a smooth, satiny finish.

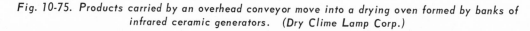

Fig. 10-75. Products carried by an overhead conveyor move into a drying oven formed by banks of infrared ceramic generators. (Dry Clime Lamp Corp.)

Fig. 10-76. Large pieces of furniture moving into a radiant heated oven on a floor-based conveyor.

Force Drying

Finishing materials dry, harden, and cure by one or a combination of evaporation, oxidation, and polymerization (mixing of compounds causes them to have different properties). All of these actions take place more rapidly at elevated temperatures.

In high volume production work it is important to dry the finish as rapidly as possible. Wet parts can be loaded on conveyors and placed in huge ovens that are heated by various methods. Today, modern woodworking plants use open-end ovens that cover a moving conveyor line. See Figs. 10-75 and 76. Radiant heat is used since hot air would escape from the ends of the oven too rapidly. Infrared rays are most efficient since they penetrate into the finishing films. These rays can be provided by banks of conventional infrared light bulbs or by special ceramic generators. Temperatures are carefully controlled and seldom exceed 180 deg.

Wet surfaces cannot be exposed to high temperatures immediately or they will bubble and blister. They are usually given a "flash-off" period to allow excess thinners and solvents to evaporate. This may be done at room temperature or in an enclosure where warm air is circulated and exhausted.

Conveyor Lines

Production finishing systems require some type of conveyor line to move the product from one station or stage of the process to the next. They may consist of an overhead monorail or floor-based equipment. Usually they are powered. Sometimes the product is pushed along by hand over free moving balls or rollers. Powered floor-based equipment consists of a slowly moving chain that carries pallets (bases for the product) along two parallel rails on which skate wheels are mounted. See Figs. 10-77 and 78. The pallets can be spread wide apart for some application or rubbing operation, or brought together (close-packed) for a drying stage.

Fig. 10-77. Tables rest on pallets which are carried along powered conveyor line. (Mersman Bros. Corp.)

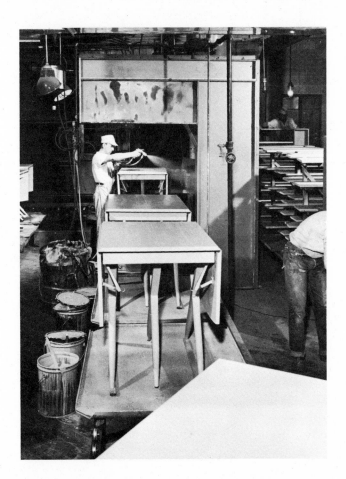

Fig. 10-78. Dining tables carried on a powered conveyor. Pallets ride over wheels mounted on parallel rails.

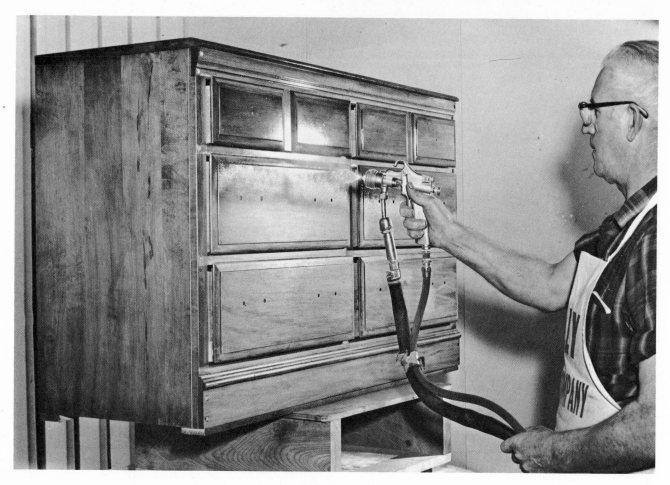

Industry photo. Skilled craftsman spraying final coat on fine piece of furniture.
(Heywood - Wakefield Co.)

Fig. 10-79. Closed loop conveyor line. Only the section through the drying oven is powered. Cabinets
make two complete circuits in the finishing process.
(Northway Products Co.)

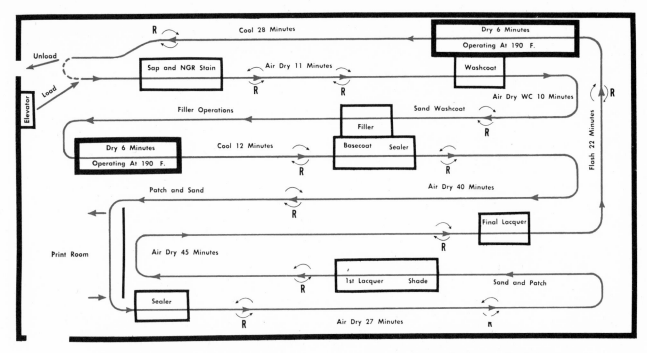

Fig. 10-80. Layout of a finishing system in a larger furniture plant. Cabinets are loaded on conveyor line from elevator in upper left corner. Points marked R indicate rotation of cabinets from width to breadth or vice versa to take up less space on line. Conveyor moves at 6.11 fpm.

In small plants a closed loop system, see Fig. 10-79, may be used where the product is moved around the same conveyor line several times before the finish is complete. Large plants employ a complete single conveyor line where the product is completely finished when it reaches the end. Fig. 10-80 shows a layout of such a system in a large factory where 480 TV and stereo cabinets are finished in an eight hour period (one per minute). Study the sequence and see how many of the operations you have learned about, from your work in the school shop.

Test Your Knowledge

1. A volatile finishing material is one that _____ rapidly.
2. A true brush bristle is oval in cross section, is tapered and has _____ ends.
3. Low quality brushes usually have a very small plug. True or False?
4. Industry uses a N.G.R. stain which is the abbreviation for _____ _____ _____.
5. Spirit stains dry so rapidly that they are usually applied with a spray gun. True or False?
6. Which of the following kinds of wood do not ordinarily require a paste filler? (Ash, hickory, butternut, cherry, mahogany.)

7. Paste wood filler can be thinned with turpentine, mineral spirits or _____.
8. A sealer should be applied to only those surfaces of your project that will receive additional coats of finish. True or False?
9. Shading and glazing operations should be done just before the sealer coat. True or False?
10. Just before applying topcoats of finish the surface should be brushed and then lightly wiped with a _____.
11. The first topcoat of finish should be rubbed with 6/0 - 8/0 _____ finishing paper.
12. Finishes should be rubbed in the same direction as the wood grain. True or False?
13. Final sanding of a surface to receive a penetrating finish should be done with a _____ or finer grade of paper.
14. The liquid part of paint is called the _____.
15. The sealer coat for enamel is called undercoater and for paint it is called _____.
16. Epoxy resin finishes can be applied to nearly any kind of material. True or False?
17. A device that filters the compressed air and regulates the pressure for spray finishing is called an air_____.
18. An external mix type of spraying head can be used with either a pressure feed or a suction feed. True or False?
19. If the coat you are spraying is too heavy and sags are forming, the best thing to do is hold the gun farther away from the surface. True or False?

Outside Assignments

1. Prepare a sample finishing board using stain and paste filler. As you apply each coat, mask out a part of the previously applied finish so that when it is completed you can see each stage of the schedule. Apply appropriate labels.

2. Develop a list of at least 15 manufacturers of paint and other wood finishing products. Include complete company name and address. Write these firms for their latest literature.

3. Prepare a chart listing basic kinds of finishing material along the sides and across the top include such headings as; purpose and use, drying time, thinners, how applied, and special directions.

4. Prepare sample panels finished with shellac, lacquer, varnish, penetrating and other finishes. Conduct controlled tests of these surfaces by submitting them to abrasion, scratches, dents, heat and such common household materials as detergents, fruit acids, cooking oil and grease. Prepare a paper describing the tests and listing results and conclusions.

5. Study reference materials concerning finishing by tumbling. Design and build a small tumbling machine. Experiment with various types of finishing materials. Use small parts that are either purchased or produced in the shop. Prepare a paper describing the operation of your tumbling machine and give directions for its use.

POWER EQUIPMENT SAFETY RULES

Modern power woodworking machines can save lots of time. Learning how to use them safely will be an important part of your experience in the shop. Whether or not you are permitted to use power equipment will depend on your maturity and ability, and the policies established by your instructor.

Although a beginning student will usually do most of his work with hand tools, there will be certain basic machine operations that will save time and may be appropriate if performed under close supervision.

Before operating any power tool or machine you must become thoroughly familiar with the way it works and the correct procedures to follow in its use. As you learn to use a machine the correct way, you will also be learning to use it the safe way.

Study the following chapters carefully and give close attention to the demonstrations and directions given by your instructor. Know and understand the following general safety rules that apply to power machine operation. You must also learn the specific safety rules that apply to each machine.

1. Always be sure you have the instructor's approval to operate a machine. He knows you and the machine, and can best make the decision as to whether you have "what it takes" to operate it safely.

2. Wear appropriate clothing. Remove coats or jackets; tuck in your tie and roll up loose sleeves. Wear a shop apron and tie it snugly.

3. You must be wide awake and alert. Never operate a machine when you are over-tired or ill.

4. Think through the operation before performing it. Know what you are going to do, and what the machine will do.

5. Make all the necessary adjustments before turning on the machine. Some adjustments on certain machines will require the instructor's approval.

6. Never remove or adjust a safety guard without the instructor's permission.

7. Use approved push sticks, push blocks, feather-boards, and other safety devices. Some operations may require the use of a special jig or fixture.

8. Keep the machine tables and working surfaces clear of tools, stock, and project materials. Also keep the floor free of scraps and excessive litter.

9. Allow the machine to reach its full operating speed before starting to feed the work.

10. Feed the work carefully and only as fast as the machine will cut it easily.

11. Maintain the MARGIN OF SAFETY specified for the machine. This is the minimum distance your hands should ever come to the cutting tool while it is in operation.

12. If a machine is dull, out of adjustment, or in some way not working properly, shut off the power immediately and inform the instructor.

13. You are the one to control the operation. Start and stop the machine yourself. If someone is helping you, be sure they understand this and know what they are expected to do and how to do it.

14. Do not allow your attention to be distracted while operating a machine. Also, be certain that you do not distract the attention of other machine operators.

15. Stay clear of machines being operated by other students. See that other students are "out of the way" when you are operating a machine.

16. When you have completed an operation on a machine, shut off the power and wait until it stops before leaving the machine or setting up another cut. Never leave a machine running and unattended.

17. Machines should not be used for trivial operations, especially on small pieces of stock. Do not play with machines.

18. Do not "crowd around" or wait in line to use a machine. Ask the present operator to inform you at your work station when he has finished. Common standards of courtesy may slow you down a little but they will make the shop a more pleasant and safer place to work.

Unit 11

PLANING MACHINES

The jointer and planer (also called a surfacer) are power planing machines that smooth the surfaces of lumber, and form faces and edges that are straight and true. The jointer is the most versatile of the two machines and is a direct counterpart of the hand plane. It will plane surfaces, edges, bevels, chamfers, and tapers. The planer is a single purpose machine that planes the stock to a uniform thickness. See Fig. 11-1.

Planing Sequence

The sequence of operations for planing and squaring stock on power machines is about the same as for hand tools. Select the best face and plane it on the jointer. The jointer table works like the hand plane bed or bottom which guides the cutting edge, planing off the high places until a flat, true surface is formed. The planer will only partially straighten a surface. Its bed is relatively small and if the stock has cup or bow, the pressure of the rollers tend to flatten it during the planing operation and the stock then springs back into a warped form as it leaves the machine. The planer will remove a small amount of warp after a number of passes through the machine. This, however, may result in the stock becoming too thin.

Select and plane the best edge with the planed surface held against the fence of the jointer. If the grain is running in the wrong direction, this operation can be delayed until the second face has been planed.

Now move to the planer and plane the second face parallel to the first face and bring the stock to the required thickness. If a planer is not available this operation can be performed on the jointer, however, the thickness cannot be as accurately controlled. With the stock straight and true on two faces and one edge, you are ready to rip it to the required width on the table saw. See Fig. 11-2.

When the stock is straight and there are no serious defects, the procedure is simple. If the stock is warped, it will be necessary to rough cut large pieces into smaller ones before planing and surfacing to finished size, if full thickness is required. See Fig. 11-3. Rough cuts to length can be made with a handsaw, radial arm saw, or band saw. Ripping cuts in rough stock can be made with the handsaw or band saw. Do not use the table saw for ripping or crosscutting until at least one surface and one edge are straight and true.

Give careful attention to rough cutting of your stock. Cut it into smaller pieces only to the extent necessary to maintain the required thickness. Many small pieces will require extra handling and may be under the required size for safe machine operation.

Fig. 11-1. Left. An 8 in. jointer. The bed is 48 in. long and it is driven by a 1 1/2 hp motor. Right. An 18 in. surfacer. Variable feed from 15 - 40 fpm. Can be equipped with a 3 or 5 hp motor.

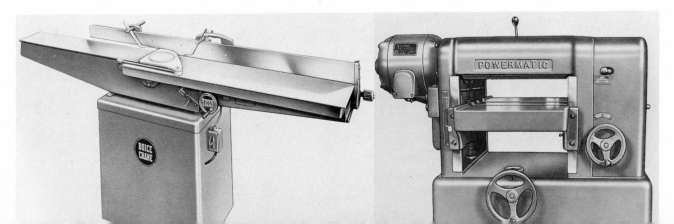

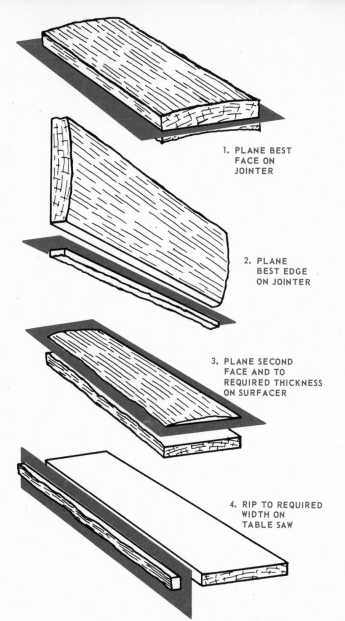

1. PLANE BEST FACE ON JOINTER

2. PLANE BEST EDGE ON JOINTER

3. PLANE SECOND FACE AND TO REQUIRED THICKNESS ON SURFACER

4. RIP TO REQUIRED WIDTH ON TABLE SAW

Fig. 11-2. Sequence for planing stock on power machines. (To make the drawings clear an excessive amount of stock is shown being removed. In actual practice this is only a small amount.)

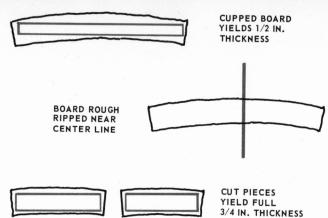

CUPPED BOARD YIELDS 1/2 IN. THICKNESS

BOARD ROUGH RIPPED NEAR CENTER LINE

CUT PIECES YIELD FULL 3/4 IN. THICKNESS

Fig. 11-3. Rough-cut cupped lumber to maintain thickness. This also applies to lumber that is bowed.

Boards that are too wide for the jointer can be rough ripped into narrower widths. They may be rough planed with a hand plane to secure one flat face and then both surfaces can be finished on the planer. Be certain to turn the flat face down as the stock is fed into the machine for the first cut.

Jointer

Parts and Adjustments

Principal parts of a jointer are shown in Fig. 11-4. The cutterhead (not shown in the photo) holds three knives and revolves at a speed of about 4500 rpm. The size of the jointer is determined by the length of these knives. This also determines the maximum width of stock the jointer will handle.

The three main parts that can be adjusted are the infeed table, the outfeed table and the fence. The outfeed table must be level with the knife edges at their highest point of rotation. This is a critical adjustment. If the table is too high the

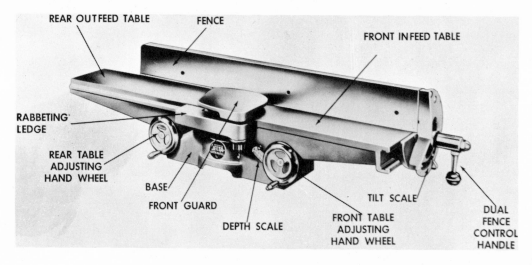

Fig. 11-4. Parts of a jointer.

stock will be gradually raised out of the cut and a slight taper will be formed. If it is too low the tail end of the stock will drop as it leaves the infeed table and cause a "bite" in the surface or edge. Check with your instructor before making any changes in the setting of the outfeed table.

The fence guides the stock over the table and knives. When jointing an edge or squaring stock, it should be perpendicular to the table surface. The fence can be tilted to other angles when cutting chamfers or bevels.

To make a cut on the jointer, the infeed table is set below the level of the knives and outfeed table as shown in Fig. 11-5. Most jointers have a scale that indicates this distance, which is referred to as the "depth of cut."

Safety Rules for the Jointer

(These are in addition to general safety rules for operating power-driven machines.)
1. Be sure you have the instructor's approval to operate the machine.
2. Before turning on the machine, make adjustments for depth of cut and position of fence.
3. Do not adjust the outfeed table or remove the guard without your instructor's approval.
4. The maximum cut for jointing an edge is 1/8 in. and for a flat surface, 1/16 in.
5. Stock must be at least 12 in. long. Stock to be surfaced must be at least 3/8 in. thick unless a special feather board is used.
6. Feed the work so the knives will cut "with the grain." Use only new stock that is free of knots, splits and checks.
7. Keep your hands away from the cutterhead even though the guard is in position. MAINTAIN AT LEAST 4 IN. MARGIN OF SAFETY.
8. Use a push block when planing a flat surface. Do not apply pressure directly over the knives with your hand.
9. Do not plane end grain unless the board is at least 12 in. wide.
10. The jointer knives must be sharp. Dull knives will vibrate the stock and may cause a kickback.

WOODY SAYS:

"The jointer is one of the most dangerous machines in the wood shop. Follow the above safety rules carefully and also the general safety rules listed on page 10-30."

Planing an Edge

This operation is also called jointing an edge. Examine your stock and determine the direction of the grain. Turn it so it will feed properly. Be certain that the fence is square and tight, and that the guard is in position and properly adjusted. Set the infeed table for the correct depth of cut and turn on the machine.

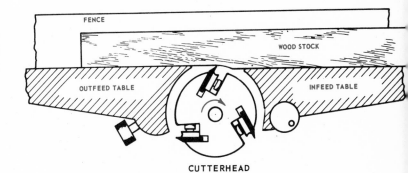

Fig. 11-5. How the jointer works. Note the direction of the wood grain.

Place the stock on the infeed table and press it lightly against the fence. Stand close to the machine so you can work in a natural position without bending over or reaching out too far. Move the stock into and through the cut as shown in Fig. 11-6. Step your hands alternately to new

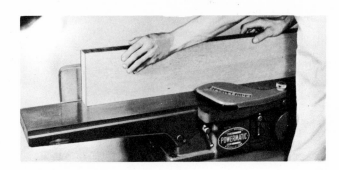

Fig. 11-6. Planing the edge of a large piece.

positions on the stock, feeding with first one hand and then the other so the cut will be continuous and smooth. The rate of feed will vary with the kind and size of wood and the depth of cut. It should seldom be slower than 10 fpm.

When planing narrow stock follow the procedure shown in Fig. 11-7. Start the cut keeping your left hand well back of the cutterhead. When a foot or more of the stock has passed over the knives, "step" the left hand across the knives and press the stock against the fence and outfeed table as you continue to move it forward. Feed

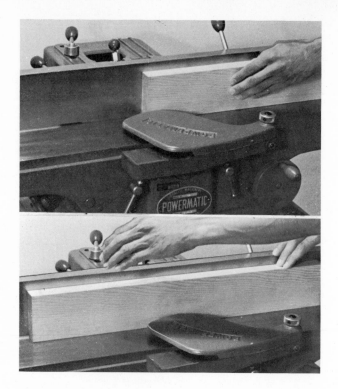

Fig. 11-7. Planing narrow stock. Above. Starting the cut.
Below. Stepping the left hand across the knives.

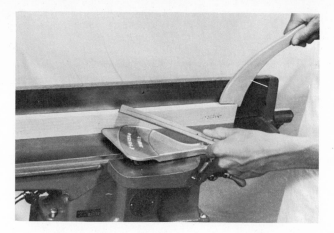

Fig. 11-8. Using push stick on a small piece.

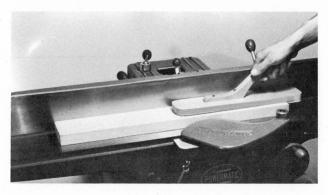

Fig. 11-9. Using a pusher block for a surface cut.

the stock as previously described with the left
hand over the outfeed table and the right hand
over the infeed table. Neither hand needs to pass
over the knives and violate the 4 IN. MARGIN
OF SAFETY. Finish the cut with the left hand,
or step the right hand over the knives and finish
the cut with both hands.

Narrow pieces of stock that are close to the
12 in. minimum length should be handled with
a push stick as shown in Fig. 11-8.

Planing a Surface

Turn your stock so you will be feeding the
grain of the wood in the right direction. If there
is some warp in the board, turn the concave
(dished in) surface down so the stock will not
rock on the table. Set the depth of cut at about
1/16 in., check the fence and guard, and turn on
the machine.

Place the stock on the infeed table and move
it into the knives. The left hand should be kept
well back of the knives and then "stepped" over
them to hold the stock down on the outfeed table.
Finish the cut by placing a "pusher block" on the
end of the board as shown in Fig. 11-9. Boards
with twist or "wind" create an extra problem.
Apply pressure on the low points and try to keep
the board from rocking during the cut.

Thin, narrow strips can be surfaced with considerable safety by using the setup shown in
Fig. 11-10. Here a feather board is clamped to

the fence so that it applies firm pressure to the
stock as it passes over the knives. Feed the stock
in about half way, then move around to the outfeed table and pull it through. The stock should
be at least 2 ft. long.

Planing End Grain

End grain or plywood can be planed without
splitting off the edge by following the procedure
shown in Fig. 11-11. First make a cut in about
one inch and then reverse the piece and finish
the cut. The board should be at least 12 in. wide.
The cut should be light and the feed slow, however, too slow a feed will dull the knives excessively and may burn the wood.

Bevels and Chamfers

To cut bevels and chamfers the fence is set
at an angle with the table. Machines will vary
in the way this adjustment is made. The fence
can be set either away from the table or toward
the table as shown in Fig. 11-12. When possible
the fence should be tilted toward the table as it is
usually easier to hold the stock in position. A
series of cuts will be required to complete the
work.

Planing a Taper

Lay out the taper on the work and mark a line at the point where it starts. Place the part on the infeed table with the mark about 1/2 in. beyond the high point of the knives. Clamp a stop block onto the table so it just touches the end to be tapered. Lower the infeed table an amount equal to the taper or some even proportion of it.

Start the machine, set the end of the piece against the stop, pull the guard open and carefully lower the piece onto the outfeed table and knives as shown in Fig. 11-13. Using a pusher block or push stick, move the part forward, keeping the tapered end firmly on the infeed table as shown. In the example, the depth of cut was set at one-half the total taper required and the part was passed over the jointer twice. Duplicate parts do not need to be laid out when cut with the same setting.

The cutterhead will dig in a little at the start of the taper. This is the reason for setting up the cut to start slightly back of the exact point. After the taper is cut, this can be smoothed with one light pass over the jointer set for a standard cut, or by using a hand plane. If the piece to be tapered is longer than the infeed table, mark the mid-point and plane the tapered end (as previously described) to one-half the amount required. With the part resting on this surface, take regular jointer cuts until the total taper is formed.

Planing a Rabbet

To plane a rabbet, first set the fence to provide the correct width by measuring the exact distance from the end of the knives to the fence. Lower the infeed table to provide the required depth, then feed the stock as shown in Fig. 11-14. When cutting a large rabbet in hard wood it is usually best to set the infeed table to only part of the required depth and form the rabbet in several passes over the machine. You will need to lower the table after each pass until the required depth is attained.

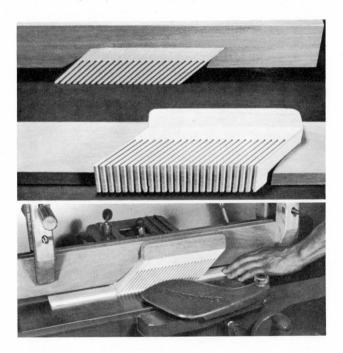

Fig. 11-10. Above. Feather boards for the jointer. Below. Surfacing a thin piece of stock.

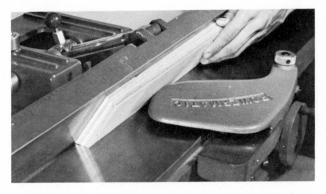

Fig. 11-12. Planing a bevel. Final cut is being made.

Fig. 11-11. Planing end grain. The guard has been pulled away to show the cut.

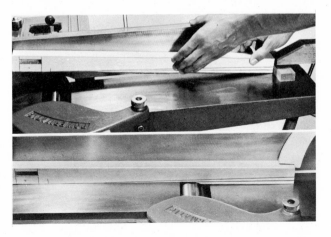

Fig. 11-13. Planing a taper. Above. Lowering work onto knives. Below. First cut half finished. Note: The guard has been held open to show the cut.

Special Setups

Various fixtures can be designed and built to perform specialized operations on the jointer. Fig. 11-15, shows a carrier being used to machine a small surface on a tripod lamp leg. The same carrier can be used to hold other small parts. Usually such setups are justified only when many pieces are being produced on a mass production basis. Always have your instructor check any special setup before you operate them.

For your regular project work, where you will be planing only a few pieces, making special set-ups to handle small parts on the jointer will usually not justify the time required and you should do the work by hand. If you plan your work carefully you will be able to machine most of your stock while it is in large pieces.

Sharpening Jointer Knives

Jointer knives must be kept keen and sharp to do good work. Dull knives will vibrate the stock, cause "kickbacks" and increase the hazards of operation.

If there are no serious nicks in the edges, the knives can be honed a number of times before grinding is required. To hone the knives the following procedure can be used:

1. Disconnect the electrical power by pulling the plug or turning off the main switch and locking the panel.
2. Remove the fence, lower the infeed table, and clean the cutterhead.
3. Lower the outfeed table until a straightedge resting on it aligns with the knife bevel with about 5 deg. of clearance. See Fig. 11-16.
4. A gauge block can be made so that the infeed table can be adjusted to this setting. The other knives are then easily set in the same position.
5. Drive a wooden wedge between the cutterhead and frame to lock it in position.
6. Wrap a piece of paper around one end of a silicon carbide oilstone, saturate it with oil, and hone the knife edge as shown in Fig. 11-17. Stop as soon as a slight wire edge starts to form.
7. Repeat the operation on the other two knives. Try to hone each knife the same amount.
8. Use a fine slip stone and lightly stroke the front of the knife to remove the wire edge. Keep the stone aligned with the surface of the knife.
9. Clean the machine and readjust the table,

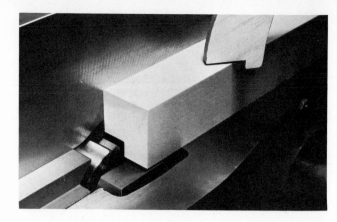

Fig. 11-14. Cutting a rabbet. Work carefully. Guard cannot be used.

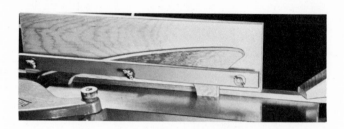

Fig. 11-15. Special carrier for an odd-shaped part.

Fig. 11-16. Setting cutterhead to hone knives. Outfeed table is lowered slightly.

fence, and guard. Inspect all settings carefully, connect the power and make several trial cuts.

The knives may be jointed lightly before the honing operation, by holding an oilstone on the table and just touching the high point of the rotating edge. The cutterhead should be turned by hand unless the machine is equipped with a special jointing attachment.

WOODY SAYS:

"Be careful when honing jointer knives. They become razor sharp and you can receive a serious cut if your fingers should slide along one of them."

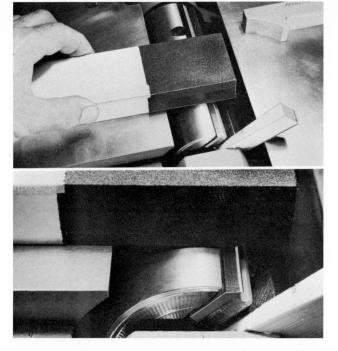

Fig. 11-17. Above. Honing knives with a fine oilstone. Below. Close-up view.

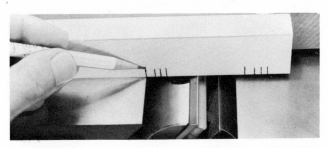

Fig. 11-18. Checking the height of the knives with a wooden straightedge. The cutterhead is turned by hand and each knife should move the straightedge on equal amount. Note that the No. 3 knife is too high.

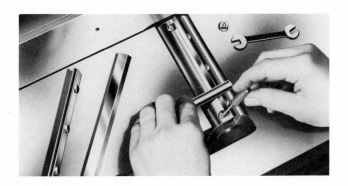

Fig. 11-19. Setting jointer knives. The height of the knife is being adjusted by turning a screw lifter.
(Boice-Crane Co.)

After the knives have been honed a number of times they will require grinding. This is a "tricky" job unless you have specialized grinders that will insure an accurate bevel (30 - 35 deg. included angle) with the edge straight. The knives

must also be balanced. Usually it is best to remove the knives from the machine and send them to a saw shop where they can be ground by an expert. On some machines it is easy to remove the entire cutterhead for grinding and adjustment.

There are a number of procedures that can be followed when setting jointer knives. A typical procedure that will work for most machines includes the following steps:

1. Disconnect electrical power, remove fence and lower infeed table. Clean all parts and apply a light film of oil.

2. Place a knife and gib in position and tighten the gib screws just enough to hold them in place.

3. Adjust the position of the knife so that the heel extends above the cutterhead about 1/16 in. Shift the horizontal position of the knife so that the end extends about 1/32 in. beyond the edge of the outfeed table.

4. Adjust the outfeed table to align with the high point of the knife.

5. Place a bar magnet on the outfeed table and over the knife. Loosen the knife and allow the magnet to hold it in position. Roll the cutterhead so the edge of the knife is above the center line (high point of the knife rotation). Tighten the gib screws. Perform this operation on each end of the knife.

6. Repeat these operations for the other two knives.

7. Check the height of each knife with a straightedge as shown in Fig. 11-18. Lower the outfeed table slightly and with the straightedge in position, roll the cutterhead so the knives will move the straightedge about 1/8 in. Make a mark at the edge of the table for each knife movement. The distance between these marks should be equal. Readjust any knife that is high or low.

8. Check the height at both ends of each knife.

9. Tighten each gib screw securely, going over the entire cutterhead several times.

10. Adjust the outfeed table and replace the fence and guard. Turn on the machine and make several trial cuts.

Jointer designs will vary with different makes and models. Study the manufacturer's instruction manual for details concerning a given machine. Some cutter heads are equipped with screw lifters that simplify knife setting. See Fig. 11-19. Manufacturers provide various devices for checking and adjusting the jointer knives such as the gauge, Fig. 11-20.

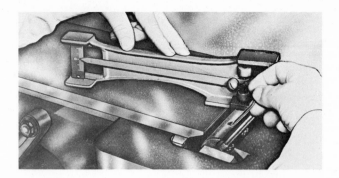

Fig. 11-20. *Checking the height of the knife with a special gauge. (Powermatic, Inc.)*

Some jointers, especially larger machines, can be equipped with a knife grinding attachment as shown in Fig. 11-21. Here the knives are precision ground without removing them from the cutterhead.

Fig. 11-21. *Motor driven knife grinding and jointing attachment. (Oliver Mach. Co.)*

Lubrication

Modern machines are often equipped with sealed bearings that seldom need attention. Check and follow the manufacturer's recommendation for lubrication schedules. All machines will require a few drops of oil on controls and adjustments at regular intervals. Clean and polish working surfaces with 600 wet-or-dry paper and oil when required. These surfaces can be kept smooth and clean by wiping them often with a light oil or furniture polish. Some craftsmen like to apply a coat of paste wax to protect the surface and reduce friction.

Power Planes

When the work to be planed is large and heavy, it is easier to move the tool than the work. The electric plane is powered equipment that can be used for jobs such as planing doors, beams, assembled work. It will perform heavy planing jobs with speed and accuracy.

Fig. 11-22 shows the parts of a standard model. The motor operates at a speed of 20,000

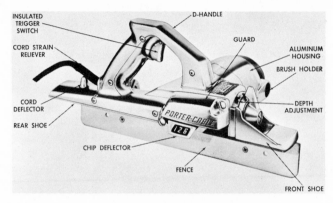

Fig. 11-22. *Parts of an electric plane. (Rockwell Mfg. Co.)*

rpm and drives a spiral cutter mounted on the motor shaft. The cutters are often carbide-tipped. The adjustments of the plane work like a jointer turned upside down. The depth of cut is controlled by raising or lowering the front shoe which corresponds to the infeed table of the jointer. The rear shoe, like the outfeed table, is kept level with the cutter. The fence of the plane is adjustable for planing bevels or can be removed for a surfacing operation as shown in Fig. 11-23.

Fig. 11-23. *Using an electric plane to surface a heavy beam. (Skill Corp.)*

Hold and operate the power plane in about the same manner as a hand plane. The work should be securely held in such a position that the operation can be easily performed. Start the cut with the front shoe resting firmly on the work and the cutterhead slightly behind the surface. Be sure the electric cord is clear and will not become fouled. With your hands gripping the toe or knob, and the handle, start the motor and move the plane forward with smooth even pressure on the work. When finishing the cut, apply extra pressure on the rear shoe. See Fig. 11-24.

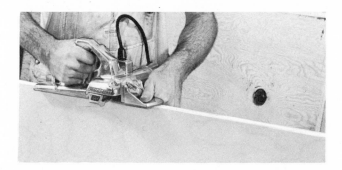

Fig. 11-24. Using an electric plane to trim the edge of a door.

WOODY SAYS:

"Portable power tools, even though they are small, can be just as dangerous as stationary woodworking machines when they are not properly used. You should be certain that you know how to operate the equipment and then follow the safety rules."

Safety Rules for Power Planes

(In addition to general safety rules on page 10-30.)

1. Study the manufacturer's instructions for detailed information on adjustments and operation.
2. Be certain that the machine is properly grounded.
3. Hold the standard power plane in both hands before you pull the trigger switch. Continue to hold it in both hands until the motor stops after releasing the switch.
4. Always be sure the work is securely clamped and held in the best position to perform the operation.
5. Do not attempt to operate the regular power plane designed for two hands, with one hand.
6. Disconnect the electric cord before making adjustments or changing cutters.

The power block plane, Fig. 11-25, is a small, light machine that can be used on small surfaces and edges. It has about the same features and adjustments as the regular power plane, but is

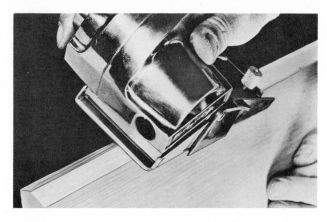

Fig. 11-25. Planing a chamfer with a power block plane.

designed to operate with one hand. When using this tool, the work should be securely held or clamped in place. The control surfaces are small and kickbacks can occur. Be sure the hand not holding the plane is kept well out of the way. The power block plane is a convenient tool for many cabinet making operations but its use should be limited to the experienced craftsman.

Planer

Parts and Adjustments

The planer is also known as a thickness planer or a surfacer. The size of a planer is determined by the maximum width of stock it will plane. See Fig. 11-26.

The surfacer or planer is a self-feeding machine. As the stock enters the machine the top surface is gripped by a corrugated feed roll that is powered and moves the stock forward. The stock next moves under the chip breaker and into the cutterhead. The chip breaker presses down on the stock in front of the cutterhead and prevents excessive chipping by the knives. The pressure bar is located behind the cutterhead and rides on the planed surface. It holds the stock firmly down on the bed and prevents it from vibrating and chattering. Behind the pressure bar is the outfeed roll which is powered and moves the stock out of the machine. See Fig. 11-27. Directly under the infeed and outfeed rolls are two rolls that are set slightly above the surface of the table and help carry the stock. They are usually free-turning on small machines, while on larger machines they are powered. The table and lower roll assembly is adjustable up and down for various thicknesses of stock.

The speed of the cutterhead usually ranges between 3000 and 3600 rpm. It may be directly driven or belt driven. The feeding mechanism

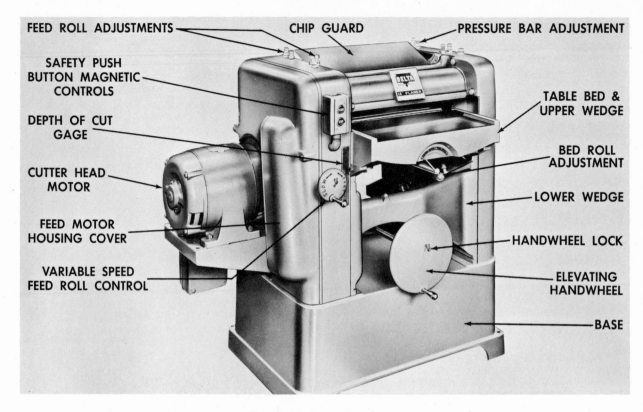

FEED ROLL ADJUSTMENTS — CHIP GUARD — PRESSURE BAR ADJUSTMENT

SAFETY PUSH BUTTON MAGNETIC CONTROLS

DEPTH OF CUT GAGE

CUTTER HEAD MOTOR

FEED MOTOR HOUSING COVER

VARIABLE SPEED FEED ROLL CONTROL

TABLE BED & UPPER WEDGE

BED ROLL ADJUSTMENT

LOWER WEDGE

HANDWHEEL LOCK

ELEVATING HANDWHEEL

BASE

Fig. 11-26. Parts of a planer.

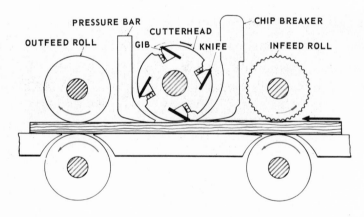

PRESSURE BAR
OUTFEED ROLL
GIB
CUTTERHEAD
KNIFE
CHIP BREAKER
INFEED ROLL

Fig. 11-27. How a planer operates.
(Forest Products Lab.)

may be powered by the cutterhead motor or by a separate motor, and can be adjusted to provide speeds of 10 to 50 fpm. See Fig. 11-28.

Planers produce a large amount of fine shavings and wood dust, and should not be operated without an adequate dust collection arrangement. Dust collectors are of two general types; a central system where ducts from a number of machines are connected to a single blower and filter, and unit collectors that are attached directly to one machine and contain the blower and filtering unit in a single cabinet. In operating a planer these safety rules should be observed:

Safety Rules for the Planer

1. Be sure you have the instructor's permission to operate the machine.
2. Adjust the machine to the correct thickness of cut before turning on the power.
3. Stock should be at least 12 in. long or several inches longer than the distance between the centers of the feed rolls.
4. Surface only new lumber that is free of loose knots and serious defects.
5. Plane with the grain or at a slight angle with the grain. Never attempt to plane cross grain.
6. Stand to one side of the work being fed through the machine.
7. Do not look into the throat of the planer while it is running.
8. Do not attempt to feed stock of different thicknesses, side by side through the machine, unless it is equipped with a sectional infeed roll.
9. Handle and hold the stock only in an area beyond the ends of the table.
10. If the machine is not working properly, shut off the power at once and inform the instructor.

You should observe also the general safety rules listed on page 10-30.

Operating the Planer

Adjust the height of the bed so that the thickness gauge reads about 1/16 in. less than the thickness of the stock. Examine the stock and determine the direction of the grain; also be sure that the bottom surface of the board is flat. See Fig. 11-28.

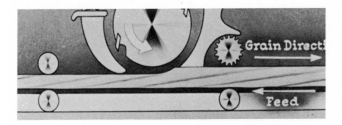

Fig. 11-28. Planer feed and grain direction.
(Jam Handy Organization)

Fig. 11-29. Feeding stock into the planer

Fig. 11-30. To prevent this, support long boards as they enter and leave the planer.

Fig. 11-31. Butt the ends of short pieces together. They also can be turned at a slight angle to provide a smoother feed.

Turn on the machine, lay the end of the stock on the table and feed it into the machine as shown in Fig. 11-29. Raise up on the other end until the stock has progressed beyond the pressure bar. Move to the rear of the machine and support long boards as they come from the machine. If not supported, they will tend to force up the pressure bar and a nick will be made in the end of the board as shown in Fig. 11-30.

Return the stock to the front of the machine without turning it over or changing its position. Check the thickness. If a second cut is necessary set the machine. See if the second cut should be made on the opposite side of the stock. If so, turn it END OVER END so the grain will be feeding correctly.

When surfacing a number of pieces to a given thickness run the thickest pieces first. As they are reduced to the thickness of the other pieces, run all of them through the machine at the same setting. The thickness of the cut will be determined by the width of the stock, the hardness of the wood and the finish desired. An average cut is about 1/16 in.

When surfacing several pieces of short stock, they should be fed as shown in Fig. 11-31. By butting the ends together the pieces will push each other out of the machine and they will be less likely to stick under the pressure bar.

Thin stock (under 3/8 in.) should be surfaced by placing it on top of a carrier board. This board must be straight and true and somewhat longer and wider than the stock. A strip of thin wood glued to the end of the carrier will help keep the stock in position during the planing operation.

Square parts, such as legs, can be planed to finished size by first squaring two adjacent faces on the jointer and then planing the two opposite faces at the same thickness setting.

Adjusting and Sharpening the Planer

Requirements and recommendations for planer maintenance will vary with different makes and models. Study the manufacturer's maintenance manual for detailed instructions.

The bed of the planer must be parallel with the cutterhead and move smoothly up and down. Adjustments involve the jack screws and gibs. The maintenance manual should be checked before any of these adjustments are made. The lower rolls carry the stock slightly above the surface of the bed. The height will vary with the kind and condition of the stock. Rough stock will require a high setting (.025 in.) while hard, smooth lumber can be planed at a low setting (.005 in.). For general purpose work a setting of .010 to .015 in. is usually satisfactory. When rolls are set too high, a snipe or bite will appear on the ends. If set too low, the stock will not feed through the machine easily.

The pressure bar is spring mounted and adjustable. The setting should provide enough pressure on the stock to prevent vibration. It should not be so great however, that it restricts the movement of the stock through the machine. This is one of the most important adjustments on the planer. Check the maintenance manual for directions.

Planer knives can be honed in somewhat the same manner as jointer knives. Some machines may have a frame that will support one end of the oilstone, or a metal clip can be attached, so that it will ride on the cutterhead as shown in Fig. 11-32. Some machines are equipped with a jointing attachment that can be used lightly before the honing operation.

Fig. 11-34. Grinding attachment on a 72 in. production planer. A diamond grit wheel is being used to grind carbide knives. (Buss Machine Works)

shown in Fig. 11-33, and 34. The device consists of a motor driven grinding unit that slides back and forth along a bar mounted on the machine. Since it is so important that all knives be exactly the same height, the attachment usually includes a jointing device. This consists of an abrasive stone that is held in a carrier against the knives while the machine is running. After jointing, the knives are ground. See Fig. 11-35.

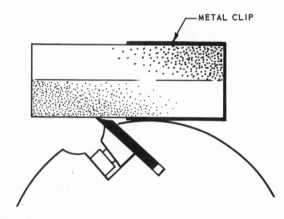

Fig. 11-32. Honing planer knives with an oilstone.

Knives can be ground by removing them from the machine and resetting them with a special gauge or dial indicator. Many modern machines are equipped with a knife grinding attachment as

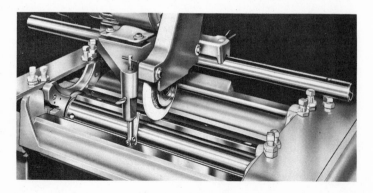

Fig. 11-33. Knife grinding attachment mounted on an 18 in. planer. (Rockwell Mfg. Co.)

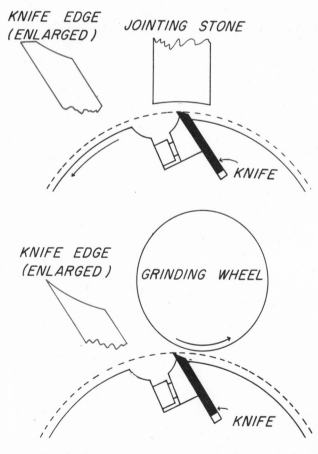

Fig. 11-35. Jointing and grinding planer knives.

The rolls, cutterhead, and bed must be kept clean and free of gum and pitch. Gum on the rolls tends to hold wood chips that indent the surface of the stock as it passes through. Use a cloth saturated with kerosene or mineral spirits to clean the machine parts. Heavy coatings of pitch or gum may require the use of a fine grade of steel wool.

Lubrication schedules will vary depending on the make or model. Check the manufacturer's recommendations and follow them carefully.

Industrial Planing Machines

To plane a flat surface on warped lumber, industry employs a machine called a facer, see Fig. 11-36. The machine resembles the regular jointer with the addition of a special feeding mechanism. This mechanism consists of a belt

Fig. 11-37. Heavy duty single surface planer. Available in widths up to 60 in. Bed adjustment is powered. Variable speeds from 20 to 120 fpm.

nism can be raised or lowered for various stock thicknesses. Machine widths will vary from 24 to 36 in. with feeding rates of 40 to 100 fpm.

Industrial surfacers and planing machines are manufactured in a wide range of sizes. Fig. 11-37 shows a heavy-duty machine that is available in a width of 60 in. Production machines are usually equipped with knives that are jointed and ground in the machine with diamond grinding wheels. They are manufactured with such precision that accuracies of .001 in. can be maintained in the surfacing operations. In addition to wood they are used to plane rubber or vinyl tile, hardboard, fiberboard, composition siding, and plastic laminated sheets. Double surface planers, with a cutter head above and below the bed or table are available and are often used in production work.

Fig. 11-36. 36 in. facer. The cutterhead has a diameter of 5 1/2 in. and is driven by a 15 hp motor at a speed of 4200 rpm. The overhead feed belt is driven by a 1 1/2 hp motor. (Newman Machine Co.)

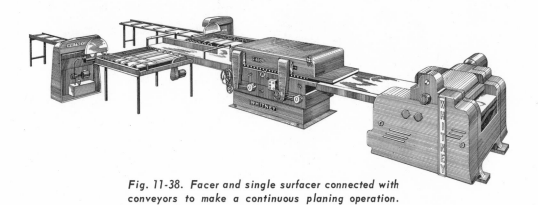

Fig. 11-38. Facer and single surfacer connected with conveyors to make a continuous planing operation.

or chain that is studded with spring loaded shoes or rubber toes. They feed and hold the lumber firmly but do not flatten it, as it moves over the cutterhead in about the same manner as you feed stock on a regular jointer. The feeding mecha-

Facers and planers are usually combined in a production planing operation as shown in Fig. 11-38. Power operated cut-off saws are used to cut the rough lumber to length and remove serious defects. A transverse conveyor carries it to the infeed conveyor of the facer where the bottom surface is planed flat and true. From the facer the stock moves into the planer and the top surface is planed to provide the required thickness.

The operations of the facer and single surfacer or planer are combined in a production machine called a "straitoplane," Fig. 11-39. Lumber is carried over a table and cutterhead in the same manner as the facer and then goes through a single surfacer located on the outfeed table.

Fig. 11-39. A combination jointing and surfacing machine. Cutterheads are 6 in. in diameter and directly driven by 15 hp motors. A 3 hp motor is used for the variable feed mechanism.

Fig. 11-40 shows rough cutting and planing machines in a woodworking plant. The ripsaw is used to cut boards that are too wide or have ex-

cessive cup. The transverse conveyor carries the ripped boards across to the infeed table of the planer. A swinging cut-off saw is used to trim the ends and remove serious defects.

Test Your Knowledge

1. The sequence of squaring operations is about the same whether you are working with hand tools or power tools. True or False?
2. The size of the jointer is determined by the length of the _____.
3. The three main parts that can be adjusted on the jointer are the infeed table, outfeed table, and the _____.
4. To control the depth of cut on the jointer, the outfeed table is moved up and down. True or False?
5. Even though the guard is in place and you are holding the stock, your hands should never come closer than _____ to the cutterhead while it is in operation.
6. Thin strips can be surfaced on the jointer if you use a _____.
7. To plane end grain on the jointer the board must be at least _____ in. wide.
8. When surfacing a warped board, the concave surface should be turned downward. True or False?
9. The metal blocks that hold the jointer knives in the cutterhead are called _____.

Fig. 11-40. In-plant view of a rough cutting and planing operation.
(Oliver Machinery Co.)

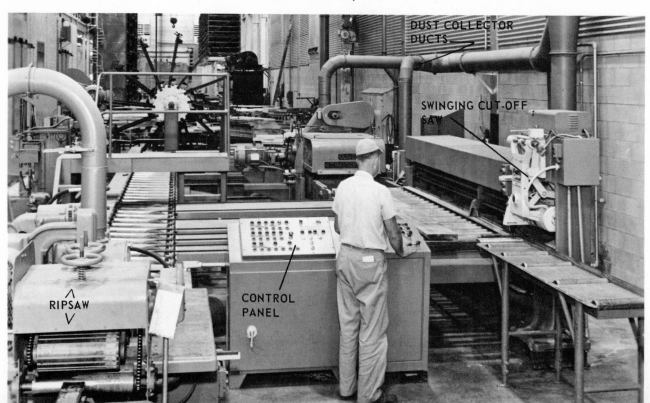

10. The depth of cut of the power plane is changed by raising or lowering the _____ _____.

11. The pressure bar of the planer rides on the stock and prevents excessive chipping by the knives. True or False?

12. The depth of cut of the planer is adjusted by turning the hand wheel that raises and lowers the machine bed. True or False?

13. Thin stock can be planed by placing it on a _____ board.

14. Before grinding planer knives mounted in the cutterhead they are usually _____.

15. An industrial planing machine that works like the jointer is called a _____.

16. If the cutterhead of a planer has 4 knives and turns at a speed of 3600 rpm, how many cuts will be made per linear inch of surface when the stock is fed at a rate of 30 fpm?

Outside Assignments

1. Select a small jointer that would be satisfactory for a home workshop. Prepare complete specifications including size, length of bed, speed, adjustment features, motor size and other items. Include a cost estimate.

2. Prepare complete specifications for a planer that would be appropriate for a school shop. Include size, cutterhead speed and diameter, cutterhead motor size, rates of feed, motor size for feed mechanism, floor space, net weight and other items. Secure information from supplier's and manufacturer's catalogs.

3. Prepare and present to the class a report on dust collection systems. Include both central systems and unit collectors. Use blackboard drawings to describe how cyclones work. Suggest ways to control dust in the home workshop either with home-made or purchased equipment. Write to manufacturers for descriptive literature. You can secure addresses from your local lumber dealer or woodworking magazines.

4. Prepare a written report on the historical development of woodworking machines. Include such early sources of power as hand, foot, water and steam, and such power transmission devices as line shafts, jack shafts and flat belts. Describe and compare babbit lined bearing boxes with modern antifriction (ball and roller) bearings. Compare the speed, safety and automatic control of modern machines with early developments.

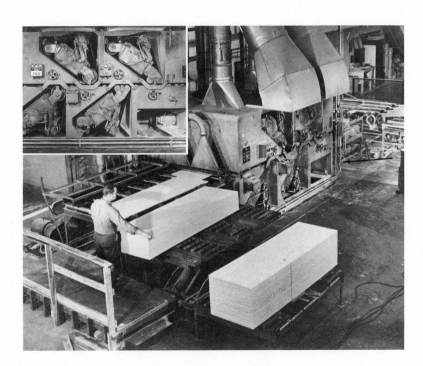

Using a modern wide belt sander to smooth particle board substrate (core or base stock) in the production of wood veneer and plastic laminate panels. Both sides are surfaced in a single pass through machine at speeds up to 120 fpm. Because machine will hold a thickness tolerance of plus or minus three thousandths (.003) of an inch, the operation is often called abrasive planing. (Norton Co.)

Fig. 12-1. Tilting arbor table saw.

Fig. 12-2. A 16 in. table saw with a tilting arbor and rolling table. The arbor is tilted and elevated by hydraulic power. Note the control panel.

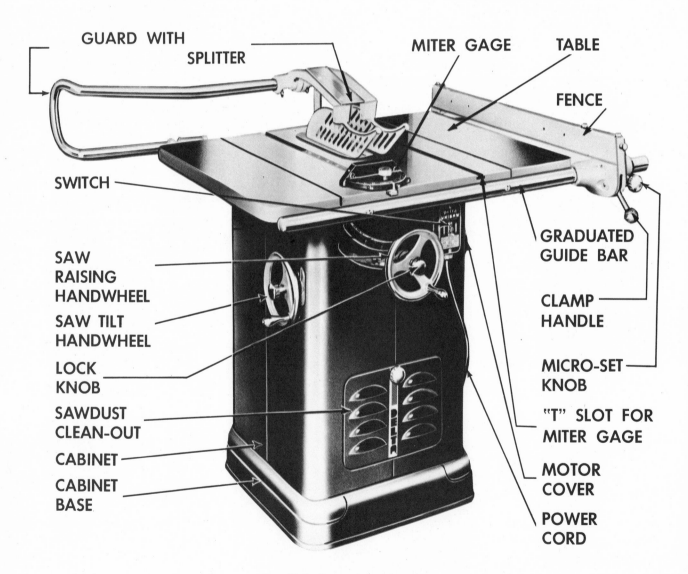

GUARD WITH SPLITTER

MITER GAGE

TABLE

FENCE

SWITCH

SAW RAISING HANDWHEEL

SAW TILT HANDWHEEL

LOCK KNOB

SAWDUST CLEAN-OUT

CABINET

CABINET BASE

GRADUATED GUIDE BAR

CLAMP HANDLE

MICRO-SET KNOB

"T" SLOT FOR MITER GAGE

MOTOR COVER

POWER CORD

Fig. 12-3. Parts of a table saw.
(Rockwell Mfg. Co.)

Unit 12

CIRCULAR SAWS

There are many kinds and sizes of saws that use a circular blade. In the school shop you will learn to use a table saw and may have experience with a radial arm saw and a portable electric saw. Industry uses circular saw blades on a wide range of specialized production machines, some of which are described later in this Unit.

Table Saw

The table saw is also called a circular saw or bench saw. Sometimes it is referred to as a variety saw, because of the many sawing operations it will perform. Fig. 12-1 shows a heavy-duty tilting arbor table saw. The arbor is the shaft on which the blade is mounted. It can be set to cut angles with the table remaining horizontal. Some smaller table saws have a fixed arbor and the table is tilted to make angular cuts. The tilting arbor saw is generally considered to be more accurate and easier to operate than the tilting table saw.

On some saws the section of table to the left of the blade is mounted on bearings and can be moved forward and backward. See Fig. 12-2. This permits accuracy and easy stock handling when crosscutting wide boards. The table can be locked in position for ripping cuts. Still another type of saw is called a universal saw. It has two saw arbors mounted on a large trunnion. By placing a crosscut blade on one and a rip blade on the other, a shift from ripping to crosscutting is easily made by simply turning a handwheel which brings the correct blade above the surface of the table.

The general size of a table saw is indicated by the diameter of the largest blade it will carry. The usual size range is from 8 in. to 16 in., however some heavy production table saws use a 20 in. blade.

Parts and Adjustments

Fig. 12-3 shows the main parts of a table saw. There are two handwheels located under the table;

one for tilting the arbor and one for raising and lowering the blade. The table has a throat insert plate that can be removed when mounting blades. It is replaced with a special insert when the dado is used. The fence is adjustable to various positions along the table, and is used to guide the stock when making ripping cuts. On some models the fence can be tilted at an angle. The miter gauge, also called a cut-off gauge, slides in grooves that are milled in the table, and is used for crosscutting.

An under-the-table view of a 10 in. tilting arbor saw is shown in Fig. 12-4. The arbor carries the saw blade which is mounted between

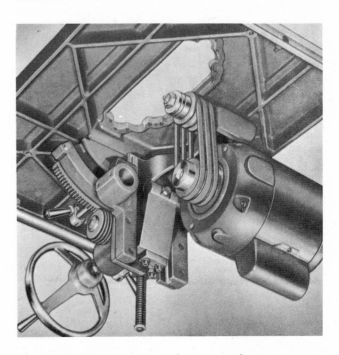

Fig. 12-4. Tilting and elevating mechanism.

a flange and a collar. The collar is held in place with a nut which may have left-handed threads. Procedures for aligning the table and blade as well as other adjustments will vary with different makes and models. Always check and follow the operator's manual provided by the manufacturer.

Guards

Saw guards are not foolproof and their use will not eliminate completely the hazards of table saw operation. They should however, be standard equipment on all machines and used for all operations.

A good guard covers the blade but does not completely hide it from view. It should include a splitter that prevents the saw kerf from closing behind the blade and also prevents stock from feeding back over the top of the blade. The guard should be equipped with an anti-kickback device that will prevent the blade from throwing the work back toward the operator. A good guard should be easy to use and keep in adjustment. Fig. 12-5 shows a guard that employs plastic shields and has a splitter and anti-kickback feature.

Saw Blades

To specify a circular saw blade you should list the kind, diameter, gauge, number of teeth, and arbor hole size. The common kinds of blades are the RIP, CROSSCUT, ROUGH CUT (RC) COMBINATION, STANDARD OR FLAT-GROUND COMBINATION AND HOLLOW GROUND COMBINATION. There are other kinds, designed for special work with such names as trimmer, edger, groover, inserted tooth groover, and concave groover.

The gauge (thickness) of a blade varies with its diameter. A large blade will require a greater thickness to support the rim and prevent it from vibrating. Heavy cuts in hard wood will require extra blade thickness. The gauge of the blade however, must be kept to a minimum; a thick blade will cut a wide kerf, waste stock and require more power. Saw manufacturers use the Birmingham and Stubbs gauge for indicating blade thickness.

The number of teeth will indicate their size and the coarseness of the cut. It will also determine the rate of feed. Fine tooth saws must be fed slowly because the gullets are too small to handle sawdust from heavy cuts. Large teeth can be fed rapidly but make a rough cut. The following table lists some appropriate gauges and number of teeth for average work in the school shop.

Arbor holes for 8 and 10 in. blades are usually 5/8 in. in diameter. Blades 12 in. and 14 in. in diameter usually have a 3/4 or 1 in. arbor hole.

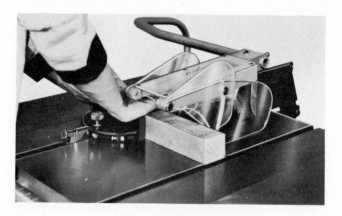

Fig. 12-5. Using a saw guard.
(Boice-Crane)

Fig. 12-6. Left. Rip saw blade. Right. Crosscut blade.

Rip and crosscut blades, Fig. 12-6, are for a single purpose. The rip blade teeth are filed straight across to form chisel shapes that do a fast and efficient job of cutting along the grain. The hook angle is at least 30 deg. Crosscut blades have teeth that are filed to a point and cut through the wood fibers easily when fed across the grain. The rip blade leaves a rough cut when used for cut-off work. The crosscut saw should be used only for cut-off or miter work. If it is used extensively for ripping it will heat and dull rapidly. This is especially true when it is used to cut end grain, such as cheek cuts of tenons.

Fig. 12-7 shows two types of combination blades. They cut well both with the grain and across the grain. Combination blades do not work as efficiently or stay sharp as long as the rip or

SIZE	GAUGE	DECIMAL EQUIVALENT	NO. TEETH RIP	NO. TEETH CROSSCUT	NO. TEETH R.C. COMB.	NO. SECTIONS STAN. COMB.
8 in.	18	.049	36-40	100-120	30-44	12-14
10 in.	16	.065	30-36	72-100	36-44	14-16
12 in.	14	.083	24-36	72-100	40-44	16-18
14 in.	13-12	.095-.109	24-36	60-100	44	18-20

Fig. 12-7. Left. Rough cut combination. Right. Standard flat-ground combination.

crosscut when applied to the latters specific operation, so are seldom used in production work. For example, in a production ripping operation the best blade to use would be a rip blade. Combination blades however, are suitable for use on a single arbor saw for general purpose work and save a great deal of blade changing time. The rough cut combination has teeth that look like rip teeth but with a smaller hook angle. The teeth are filed at an angle across the top to form a modified chisel shape. The standard flat ground combination has some crosscut teeth and some rip teeth. The rip teeth, called rakers, are filed straight across and are not set.

A hollow ground combination blade is shown in Fig. 12-8. The shape of the teeth is similar to those of the flat ground combination but are not set. The clearance for the blade is secured by grinding a gradual taper from the rim to the hub or collar area. The thickness is usually reduced about 3 gauges. For example, one manufacturer's 10 in. hollow ground blade has a rim gauge of 14 and tapers to a gauge of 17 at the edge of the saw collar. This kind of blade is often called a planer blade since the sides of the teeth actually

plane the wood resulting in a very smooth surface. Its use should be limited to high quality finish work on stock that is straight and true. Since the clearance is so slight, it will burn easily if there is binding of the kerf caused by warped or casehardened stock.

Various other kinds of saw blades are available. Fig. 12-9 shows a blade that is designed especially for fine cuts in hardwood plywood. Carbide tipped teeth are used extensively in production work because they will stay sharp at least 10 times longer than standard blades. They are not dulled by hardboard, plastic laminates, and other materials that have an abrasive effect on regular blades. A special hardened steel tooth

Fig. 12-9. Special blades. Left. Plywood. Right. Carbide tipped blade.

Fig. 12-10. Grinding the surface is one of the important steps in the manufacture of high quality saw blades. (Huther Bros. Saw Mfg. Co.)

Fig. 12-8. Hollow-ground combination.

blade is available that stays sharp longer than a conventional blade. It cannot be filed and is sharpened by grinding. Fig. 12-10 illustrates a step in the manufacturing of saw blades...grinding the surface.

Safety Rules for the Table Saw

(In addition to the general safety rules listed on page 10-30.

1. Be certain the blade is sharp and the right one for your work.
2. The saw is equipped with a guard and a splitter. Be sure to use them.
3. Set the blade so it extends about 1/4 in. above the stock to be cut.
4. Stand to one side of the operating blade and do not reach across it.
5. MAINTAIN A 4 IN. MARGIN OF SAFETY. (Do not let your hands come closer than 4 in. to the operating blade even though the guard is in position.)
6. Stock should be surfaced and at least one edge jointed before being cut on the saw.
7. The position of the stock must be controlled either by the fence or the miter gauge. NEVER CUT STOCK FREE HAND.
8. Use only new stock that is free of knots, splits and warp.
9. Stop the saw before making adjustments to the fence or blade.
10. Do not let small scrap cuttings accumulate around the saw blade. Use a push stick to move them away.
11. Resawing and other special set-ups must be inspected by the instructor before power is turned on.
12. The dado or any special blades should be removed from the saw after use.
13. Students helping to "tail-off" the saw should not push or pull on the stock but only support it. The operator must control the feed and direction of the cut.
14. As you complete your work, turn off the machine and remain until the blade has stopped. Clear the saw table and place waste cuttings in the scrap box.

Changing Saw Blade

Remove the table insert plate (also called a throat plate) and raise the arbor to its highest point. On universal saws the work can be done under the table, with the blade at its lowest point. Place a wrench on the arbor nut and turn it in the same direction that the saw turns when in oper-

ation. This will be left-handed on most machines. Hold the blade stationary with a piece of wood wedged between the teeth and the table or frame. Remove the nut, collar, and blade. Do not lay the blade on the table or a metal surface.

Before mounting another blade, check the arbor, flange, collar and nut. They must be clean and free of pitch, gum, and rust. Use a cloth lightly saturated with kerosene or mineral spirits to clean the saw parts. Rust should be removed with a piece of 600 wet-or-dry abrasive paper.

The arbor flange should have a small notch or punched hole on the outside edge that is turned up when the blade is mounted. Place the saw on the arbor with the teeth pointing in the correct direction and the trademark turned up. Replace the collar with the recessed side against the blade. Hold the blade with a piece of wood and tighten the nut by turning it in the opposite direction of blade rotation as shown in Fig. 12-11. Replace the table insert.

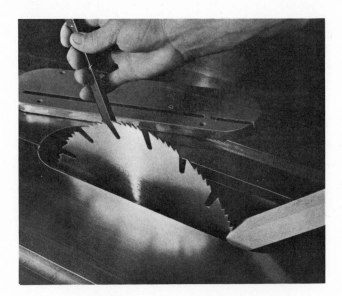

Fig. 12-11. Tightening saw arbor nut.

By always mounting the blade with the arbor in the same position and with the trademark up, the perimeter of the blade should run true. The clearance of the arbor hole will always be located in the same position and correction will be made if the arbor is slightly off center.

Ripping to Width

Stock to be ripped must have at least one flat face to rest on the table and one straight edge to run along the rip fence.

Raise the blade until it projects above the table a distance equal to the thickness of the stock

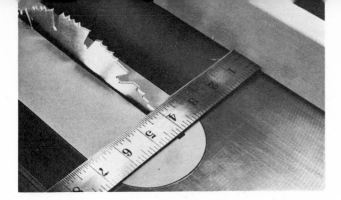

Fig. 12-12. Setting the fence.

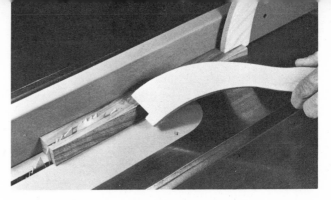

Fig. 12-14. Ripping small pieces. Guard cannot be used.

plus 1/4 in. Unlock the fence and move it along the guide bar to the required width. For an accurate setting check the measurement between the fence and the point of a tooth on the blade that is set toward the fence as shown in Fig. 12-12. Lock the fence in position, place the guard over the blade, and start the machine.

Place the stock flat on the table with the straight edge against the fence and move the stock into the blade. Continue a steady feed through the entire cut. Keep your hands at least 4 in. away from the blade even though it is covered by a guard. See Fig. 12-13. When the saw is operating, stand slightly to one side of the cutting line. When cutting long boards have someone support the stock as it leaves the table. Avoid reaching over the saw to "catch" short pieces. Have a helper take them or let them fall into a stock cart or to the floor.

Ripping Small Pieces and Strips

Narrow strips and short pieces can be ripped as shown in Fig. 12-14. Use a push stick in each hand. For this job the guard cannot be used, so special care must be taken when performing this operation.

Standard practice places the stock between the fence and the blade with the waste to the outside. Very thin strips however, will be fouled between the fence and blade so they are usually cut as shown in Fig. 12-15. The edges of the stock must

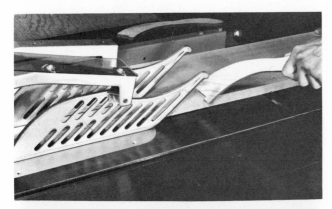

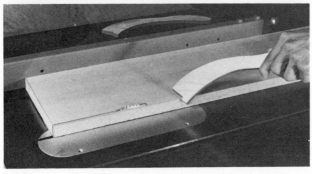

Fig. 12-13. Ripping stock to width. Above. Guard in position. Below. Guard and splitter removed to show operation.

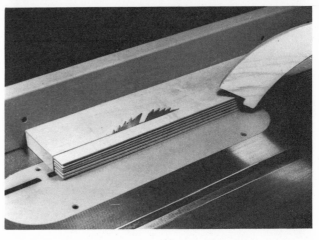

Fig. 12-15. Above. Ripping a single strip. Below. Ripping off thin strips after they were formed by edge cuts. Note: Push sticks being used. Most guards will interfere with these operations.

be parallel and the rip fence reset after each cut. Sometimes the edge is jointed and sanded before it is ripped, thus providing a finished strip for veneering or inlay. By another method, the thin strips are first formed by cuts made in the edge of the piece and then all of them are ripped off at once.

When cutting thin strips and veneers, the slit in the table insert may be too wide or the veneer may slip under the fence. An auxiliary table surface should be used. It can be made by setting the fence, lowering the blade below the table and then clamping a piece of 1/8 in. hardboard to the table. Turn on the saw and then elevate the blade so it cuts through the hardboard and to the height required.

WOODY SAYS:

"Always think through the operation before turning on the machine. Know what you are going to do and what the machine will do. If you have the slightest doubt about how it will work, check with your instructor first."

Resawing

Resawing is a ripping operation where the stock is cut on edge into two thinner pieces. If the width of the stock does not exceed the maximum height that the blade can be raised, the operation can be completed in one cut. For wider boards set the saw to cut a little above the center-line and make two cuts. Keep the same face of the stock against the fence for both cuts. Fig. 12-16 shows a resawing setup with the second cut just being started. A feather board increases the

Fig. 12-16. Making the second cut of a resawing operation.

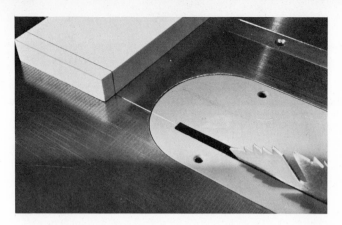

Fig. 12-17. Aligning stock with line scribed in saw table.

Fig. 12-18. Above. Squaring stock to a marked line. Below. Guard removed to show operation.

accuracy and safety of resawing operation. Wide boards can first be cut on the table saw and then the center section cut apart on the band saw.

A feather board may be made by ripping a series of saw kerfs about 1/8 in. apart in the end of a board cut off at an angle of about 30 deg. The strips that are formed are like a series of "springs" that apply a smooth, even pressure. For ripping operations the feather board should be set in a position so it will hold the stock against the fence, but will not close the saw kerf and pinch the saw.

Fig. 12-19. *Cutting small piece by clamping it to a larger one.*

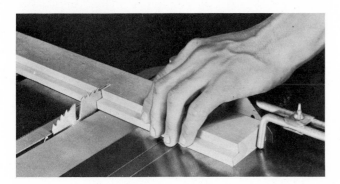

Fig. 12-20. *Cutting duplicate lengths using stop rod. Guard can be used for this operation.*

Beginning students should perform their first resawing operations by setting the saw slightly below the center of the work, leaving about 1/4 in. to hold the two pieces together after the second cut. The pieces can then be cut apart with a handsaw.

Since resawing operations require heavy ripping cuts always use a sharp rip blade.

Crosscutting to a Line

When you have only a few cuts to make, it is easiest to square lines across the surface of the stock and follow them in the crosscutting operation. Make a check mark on the side of the line where the saw kerf will be located. The guard tends to obscure the blade and it is often helpful when aligning the cut to use a line scribed in the table surface. Since most of your work will be located to the left, it should extend back from the left side of the blade as shown in Fig. 12-17. When using this line, allowances will need to be made for blades of different gauges or settings.

Set the height of the blade the same as for ripping (1/4 in. above the work). Move the fence

to one side and well out of the way. Place the miter gauge in the table slot and set it for a right angle (90 deg. mark on the protractor scale). Check the guard to see that it is in position and properly aligned.

Hold the stock against the miter gauge with your left hand. Align the cutting mark with the saw blade, or the scribed line, so that the saw kerf will be on the waste side of the line. Turn on the motor, grasp the knob of the gauge in your right hand, and move the stock through the cut as shown in Fig. 12-18.

Use a push stick to move waste cuttings away from the blade and make additional cuttings as required. When you complete your work, turn off the motor and wait for the blade to stop before leaving the machine. Clear the table, and pick up waste cuttings and place them in the scrap box.

Maintain the same margin of safety (4 in.) as for ripping. If you have small pieces to cut, you should do the work by hand or clamp the stock to another piece as shown in Fig. 12-19. The guard cannot be used for the setup shown so you should be especially careful.

Cutting Duplicate Parts to Length

When you have a number of pieces to cut that are 6 in. or longer in length, you can use a stop rod mounted in the miter gauge as shown in Fig. 12-20. The work is fed in from the right side to the stop and then moved through the saw. The

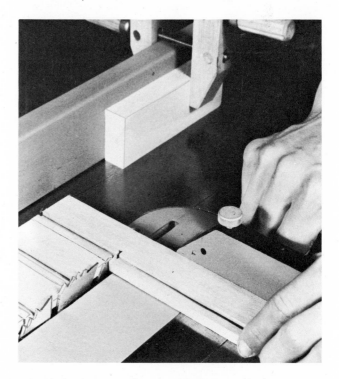

Fig. 12-21. *Using a clearance block to cut duplicate parts.*

guard will not interfere with this operation and should be used. Be certain that the metal stop rod is not in the line of the blade.

Pieces can be cut to the same length by attaching a clearance block to the fence as shown in Fig. 12-21. The block must be thick enough so the distance between the fence and the blade will be greater than the diagonal measurement of the pieces being cut. The end of the stock is squared, and the stock is then moved from the left along the miter gauge until it is against the clearance block. Hold the stock firmly to the miter gauge and make the cut. Repeat the operation for additional pieces. The clearance block should be located back of the saw blade a distance equal to the width of the stock.

Duplicate parts may be cut to length between the fence and blade if HELD FIRMLY AGAINST THE MITER GAUGE THROUGHOUT THE OPERATION. See Fig. 12-22. As the stock is cut off, you must continue to hold it against the miter gauge as you move it clear of the saw, either out to the rear of the table or back to the starting position. If the cut piece is left unsupported between the blade and fence it may turn in a diagonal position and be violently thrown back by the blade.

Cutting Plywood

Special attention must be given to crosscutting plywood because the pieces are usually wider and there is a tendency for fine hardwood veneers to splinter along the surface. Ripping usually creates no extra problems. Lines should be squared across the pieces and followed while making the cut as shown in Fig. 12-23. Sometimes it is better on wide pieces to reverse the position of the miter gauge and hold it against the front edge of the work. For a fine finish use a special plywood or hollow ground blade. The combination blade may work better if it is raised higher than 1/4 in. above the surface of the stock but always check with your instructor before doing this. Large pieces of plywood are difficult to handle on the table saw. For these cuts a handsaw, or a portable circular saw, or sabre saw, should be used.

Cutting Angles, Bevels, and Tapers

Angles are cut across the face of the stock by holding the stock against the miter gauge which is set at the required angle. There is a tendency for the stock to "creep" along the face of the gauge so it must be held firmly. This movement can also be prevented by gluing (use rubber cement)

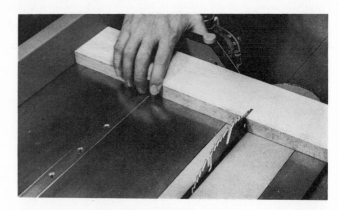

Fig. 12-22. Cutting duplicate parts between the fence and blade. Hold stock firmly to the miter gauge. Guard can be used.

Fig. 12-23. Cutting plywood with a special blade. Guard can be used.

Fig. 12-24. Cutting a compound angle using a miter gauge clamp.

a piece of abrasive paper to the face of the gauge. Some miter gauges can be equipped with a clamping attachment as shown in Fig. 12-24. Compound angles are formed by tilting the blade and setting the gauge at an angle.

Bevels and chamfers may be cut by tilting the blade and using the miter gauge to guide flat, rectangular stock. On some pieces, especially

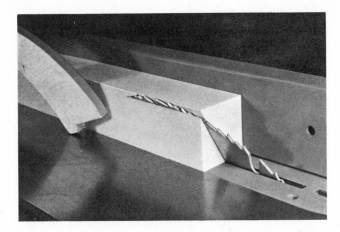

Fig. 12-25. Ripping a bevel. Fence is positioned on the left side of the blade.

Fig. 12-26. Cutting a taper with a special fixture. Splitter guard can be used.

Fig. 12-27. Cutting a rabbet. The second cut is being made.

long strips, it will be best to rip the bevel as shown in Fig. 12-25. The fence must be moved to the left of the saw blade, otherwise the stock may wedge between it and the blade and be kicked back. When you are performing any of these operations for the first time, always have your instructor check your setup before turning on the machine.

Cutting a taper on the table saw, using a special fixture is shown in Fig. 12-26. The stock is held at an angle while it is fed through the cut. The notches in the tail of the fixture can be cut on the band saw to provide the required taper After the notched block is cut away by many different setups, a new one can be glued on. When cutting a taper on two opposite edges, as shown, you will need to make two notches; one for the first cut and one for the second. Use a push stick to hold the stock in the fixture. A splitter guard will also help hold the work. It is usually best to move the work through the cut and have a helper remove it after it has cleared the back of the blade.

WOODY SAYS:

"Have your instructor check all special setups before performing the operation. He will let you know if the cut can be made safely."

Cutting Rabbets, Dados and Grooves

These joints can be cut rapidly and accurately with a dado head. When you have only a few joints to cut however, it may not justify the time required to mount the dado head and it will be best to use a single blade.

To cut a rabbet, first lay out the width and depth on the front end of the piece. Raise the blade to the correct height to cut the depth and set the fence to the width. Measure from the outside of the blade to the fence. Make the first cut with the stock held flat on the table and against the fence. The blade is now raised to equal the width and the fence adjusted so the cut will meet the one made for depth. Fig. 12-27 shows the second cut being made. Making the cuts in this sequence will prevent the waste strip from being trapped between the fence, blade, and work.

You can use the same procedure to form a rabbet on the end of wide stock. For stock that is narrow, use both the fence and miter gauge. Set the fence to provide the correct width and raise

Fig. 12-28. Cutting a dado with a series of cuts. Guard can be used.

Mounting a Dado Head

The dado head, Fig. 12-30, consists of two blades and a number of chippers. By assembling various combinations, widths of 1/4 in. to 13/16 by sixteenths can be obtained. A single blade will cut a width of 1/8 in. Diameters of 6, 8, and 10 in.

Fig. 12-30. Parts of a dado head. (Rockwell Mfg. Co.)

the blade to cut the depth. Hold the stock against the miter gauge and fence and make the first cut. Remove the waste with a series of cuts, moving the stock a little further away from the fence on each stroke but holding it securely against the miter gauge.

Fig. 12-28 shows a dado being cut with a single blade. Set the blade to the correct height and then make a series of cuts inside the layout lines. All of the waste can be removed with the blade, or a chisel may be used. If you are cutting several duplicate pieces, use the fence to make the outside cuts.

A groove can be formed by making a series of cuts with a single blade. See Fig. 12-29. The outside cut should be made first, as shown. Move the fence toward the blade a distance equal to the kerf width for each cut until the other side of the groove is reached. When cutting several duplicate parts, run each piece over the machine before changing the fence setting.

are the most common, however larger sizes are available. A special table insert must be used. See Fig. 12-31. You can make a wooden insert by shaping a piece the same size as the metal part. The dado can be mounted, lowered below the table and the insert set in place. With the dado running, raise it through the insert to cut the slot. Be sure the insert is held firmly in place while making the cut.

Fig. 12-31. Table inserts for dado heads.

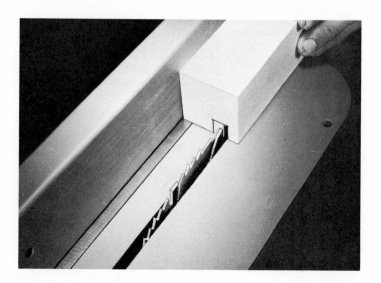

Fig. 12-29. Cutting a groove with a single blade.

Fig. 12-32. Mounting a dado head. Note position of swaged chipper (arrow).

The dado head is mounted on the arbor with the blades on the outside. The arrangement of the chippers is not critical except that the ones next to the blades must be set so their wide, swaged edges are located in the gullets as shown in Fig. 12-32. The cutting edges of the chippers overlap so it is possible to use paper washers between them to secure a slightly wider make-up.

Using a Dado Head

The dado head can be used to cut dados, grooves, lap joints, rabbets, and interlocking joints. The stock can be held and controlled with the fence or miter gauge, used separately or in combination.

To cut a groove, raise the dado head to the correct height and adjust the fence. Feed the stock through the machine as shown in Fig. 12-33.

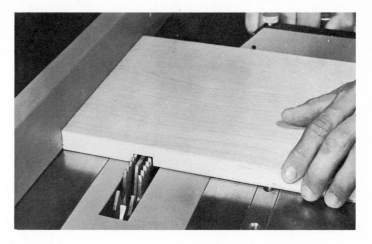

Fig. 12-34. Cutting a dado using both the fence and miter gauge.

a first cut that just scores the surface (about 1/16 in. deep) and then set to the required depth and take the final cut.

Rabbets can be quickly and accurately cut using the dado head as shown in Fig. 12-35. A wood pad is clamped or screwed to the fence and then set in the required position with the dado below the table. With the dado head running, raise it and allow it to cut into the wood pad to the required height. When doing this, always be certain that the dado will not strike the metal fence.

 WOODY SAYS:

"Remove the dado head and any special setup you have made as soon as you have finished your work. Clear the saw table and place waste cuttings in the scrap box."

Special Fixtures and Setups

The table saw is a versatile machine and many special setups and fixtures can be used to insure accuracy and safety in its use. Shop-built

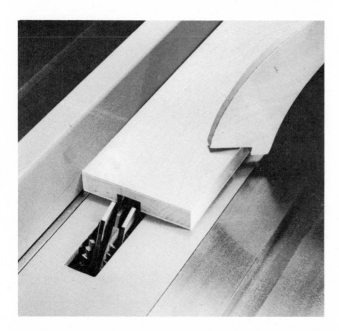

Fig. 12-33. Cutting a groove with the dado head.

Since you are removing a large amount of waste, feed the work slower than when using a regular saw blade. If the groove does not continue all the way along the piece, a stop can be preset on the fence.

When cutting dados, the stock is held against the miter gauge. On some work both the miter gauge and fence can be used. See Fig. 12-34. Extra care must be given to dado work to prevent splintering, especially when cutting plywood made of fine hardwood veneers. Always try a scrap piece first to check the work and see if the width and depth are correct. If there is a tendency for the wood to splinter, lower the dado head and take

Fig. 12-35. Cutting a rabbet with the dado head.

Fig. 12-36. Using a tenoning fixture.
(Rockwell Mfg. Co.)

Fig. 12-37. Above. Making cheek cuts on a tenon with a shop-
built fixture. Below. Opposite side being used to cut slots
for a feather in a miter joint.

fixtures should be carefully made and finished. A
coat of paste wax on sliding surfaces will usually
make them easier to operate.

Fig. 12-36 shows a commercial tenoner being
used to make cheek cuts. It slides in the table
slots and is adjustable. A similar shop-built
fixture is shown in Fig. 12-37. It rides on the
table and is guided by the fence. Either of these
devices can be used for various end grain cuts
which are hazardous to make without some special arrangement. The other side of the fixture
is used to cut slots for feathers in miter joints.
The frames were first glued together and then
the feather reinforcement was added.

Flat miter joints are easily and safely cut
with the fixture shown in Fig. 12-38. The auxiliary
table rides on the saw table and is guided by the
splines in the table slots. To assemble the fixture accurately, the splines were placed in the
slots, a bead of glue applied, and then the
auxiliary table was clamped in place.

Miter joints on the edge of stock, especially
plywood, are difficult to form. Fig. 12-39, shows
a setup that insures accurate work and will prevent splintered edges. A wood pad is attached to
the fence and then positioned so that the distance

Fig. 12-38. Cutting miter joints with a special fixture. Guard
can be used.

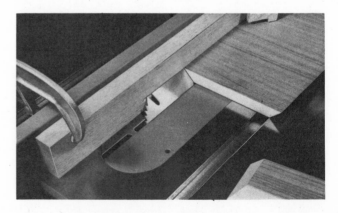

Fig. 12-39. Setup for cutting edge miters.

from the outside of the blade to the pad equals the thickness of the stock. The blade is lowered below the table and tilted to a 45 deg. angle. With the blade running, raise it through the table and allow it to cut into the pad to about the depth shown. DO NOT RUN IT INTO THE METAL FENCE. If the setup is correct, the blade will cut from the exact corner of the surface. The waste strip is trapped between the blade and fence and must be removed with care.

In Fig. 12-40 a box joint is being cut with the dado head and a fixture attached to the miter gauge. A square pin the exact size of the slot in the joint is used to position the cuts. After each slot is cut, it is slipped on the pin and the next one is cut. When making the setup, first mount the pin on the backboard and then attach the backboard to the miter gauge so the cut will be exactly in the correct position. A side and end of the box are usually clamped together and cut at the same time. They must be off-set an amount equal to the slot or pin width.

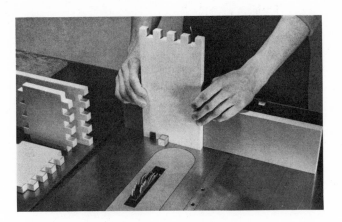

Fig. 12-40. Cutting box joints.

Cutting Sequence

Complicated joints and work on the table saw may require a series of cuts. The cuts must be carefully planned. Some cuts that can easily be made at first may be difficult or impossible to make at the end of the sequence. For example, the miter cut of the joint shown in Fig. 12-41, would be difficult to make after all the other cuts were complete.

Sharpening Circular Saw Blades

Sharp saw blades are a pleasure to use. They will produce fine, accurate work with speed and safety. Dull blades are dangerous to use because they resist the stock being fed into them and are more likely to cause kickbacks. They tend to heat and this causes pitch and gum to build on the blade which adds more friction and causes more heat to the point where the edge of the blade may snake (warp).

Blades should be kept bright and clean. Small amounts of pitch or rosin can be removed by wiping the blade with a cloth saturated with a special pitch and gum remover, kerosene, or mineral spirits. The gullets, see Fig. 12-42, should also be wiped clean. A good way to remove a heavy coating of pitch is to soak the blade in warm water. Wipe dry and oil lightly. Do not scrape the surface of the blade with a metal tool or use a coarse abrasive. Rust spots should be polished off with a 600 wet-or-dry paper and oil. Always clean the saw blade before sharpening it.

It takes considerable skill and some equipment to completely refit (sharpen) circular saw blades however, they can easily be filed a number of times before a complete sharpening job may be required. Many craftsmen file their saws three or four times, then send them to a saw shop for a complete machine sharpening operation as described later in this unit.

Basic kinds of saw blades were described in the section on the table saw. Each of these kinds are available in a wide variety of tooth sizes and shapes. Fig. 12-43 shows some of the types and sizes of crosscut teeth that are available. When sharpening, the original shape of the teeth should be maintained. Sometimes it is helpful to trace around a section of the teeth of a new blade and refer to this pattern during sharpening operations. Fig. 12-44 shows a profile of basic kinds of saw teeth with suggested filing angles.

Jointing

Jointing is the operation of "rounding" the blade so that all the teeth will be exactly the same height. It does not need to be performed each time before the saw is filed however, the tiny flats formed on the points of the teeth are a helpful guide to the inexperienced worker.

Be certain the blade is in the correct position by loosening the arbor nut and retightening with the flange mark and trademark up. Clamp an abrasive stone to the miter gauge and raise the blade until it just touches the stone. Turn on the machine and move the stone over the blade. See Fig. 12-45. Stop the saw and examine the blade. Tiny "flats" or "brights" should be visible on the points of the teeth. Rejoint if necessary. If the saw is in poor shape it may be impractical to strike the very short teeth. It may be better to

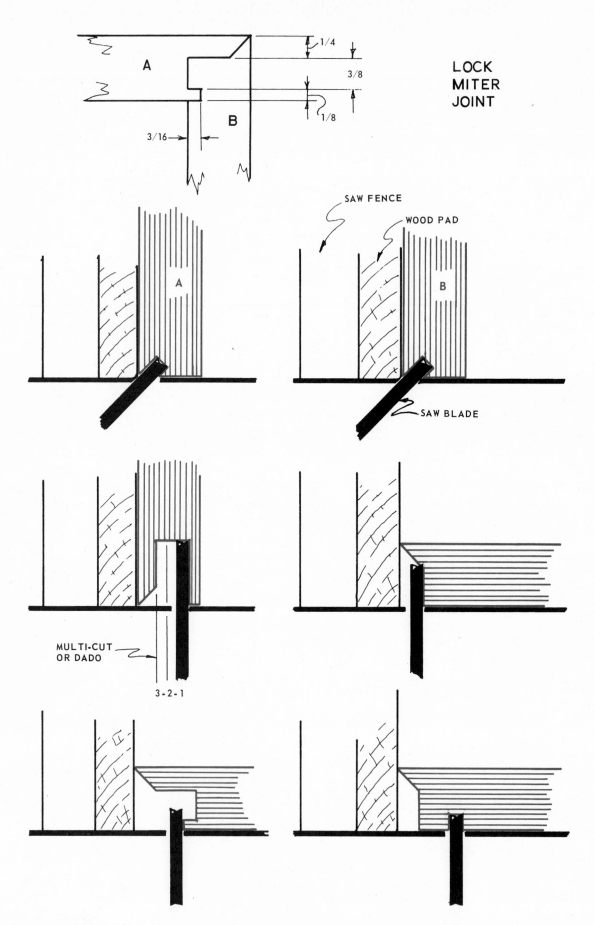

LOCK
MITER
JOINT

SAW FENCE

WOOD PAD

A

B

SAW BLADE

MULTI-CUT
OR DADO

3-2-1

Fig. 12-41. Sequence of cuts to make a locked miter joint.

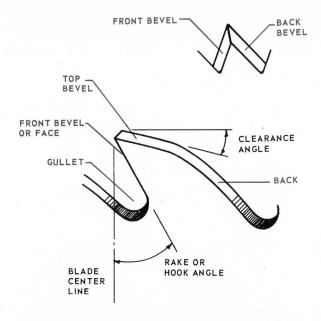

Fig. 12-42. Parts of a circular saw tooth.

allow these to remain short until the next time the saw is filed or completely reconditioned. The jointing should always be as light as possible so that during the filing operation, just a few strokes of the file will form a new point or edge.

Filing

Mount the saw in a filing clamp. Commercial clamps are available that will hold different blade sizes and adjust to various filing angles. A shop-built clamp like the one shown in Fig. 12-46 may also be used.

For rip and rough cut combination blades, select an 8 in. smooth, or dead smooth, mill file. Set the blade so the teeth are supported close to the saw clamp and file the top bevel of teeth that are set away from you. File rip teeth straight across. For combination teeth drop the file handle about 15 deg. Use light full strokes, form-

Fig. 12-43. Crosscut blades.

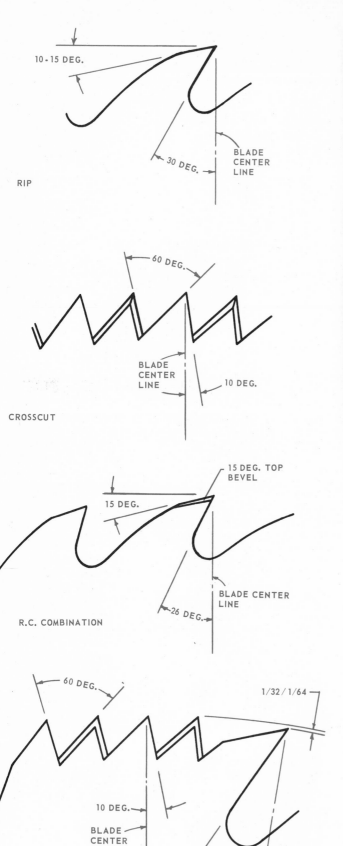

RIP

10 - 15 DEG.

30 DEG.

BLADE CENTER LINE

CROSSCUT

60 DEG.

BLADE CENTER LINE

10 DEG.

R.C. COMBINATION

15 DEG. TOP BEVEL

15 DEG.

BLADE CENTER LINE

26 DEG.

COMBINATION

60 DEG.

1/32 / 1/64

10 DEG.

BLADE CENTER LINE

30 DEG.

Fig. 12-44. Basic tooth forms and angles.

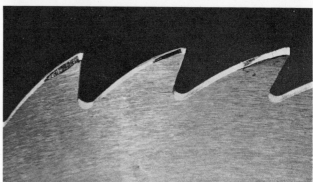

Fig. 12-45. Above. Jointing a blade. Wear goggles for this operation. Below. Jointed blade. Note flats. Jointing has been heavier than normal so it would show in photograph.

Fig. 12-46. Shop-built saw clamp. A strip of leather is glued along the top edge of the jaws which are hinged at the bottom.

ing a bevel with the required clearance. The file will cut smoother and easier if you use a diagonal stroke as shown in Fig. 12-47. Watch the jointed flat and stop just as soon as it disappears. Filing

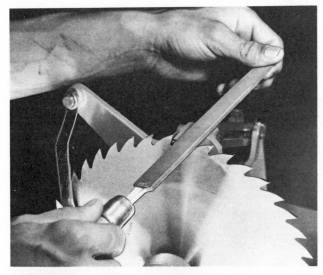

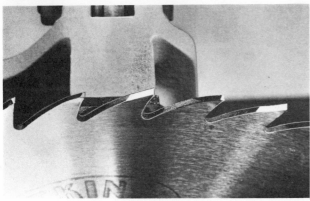

Fig. 12-47. Above. Filing a RC combination blade. Below. close-up view. Two teeth have been filed.

beyond this point will lower the tooth and it will not do its share of the cutting. After you have filed all the teeth set away from you, reverse the blade in the clamp and file the remaining teeth. The teeth of some combination blades have a front bevel that may be filed very lightly.

Crosscut teeth on small blades are usually shaped so they can be filed with a taper file. Position the file so it will cut the back bevel of one tooth and the front bevel of an adjacent tooth. The file will usually cut smoother if the handle is dropped slightly. Most of the filing is done on the back bevel so first file this bevel of all teeth set away from you. Stop filing as soon as about one-half of the jointed flat has been removed. Reverse the blade in the clamp to file the remaining bevels and remove the balance of the flats. Large blades may have a rounded gullet and you

should use a special crosscut saw file with a rounded edge. BE SURE TO MAINTAIN THE ORIGINAL TOOTH SHAPE WHILE FILING EACH BEVEL SEPARATELY.

The crosscut teeth of regular combination blades are filed in the same way as described above. The raker tooth is filed straight across and about 1/64 in. lower than the points of the cross cut teeth.

Setting Teeth

After a number of sharpenings the teeth will require additional set. The amount of set required will vary with the kind of work. Generally blades used on table saws are given 2 gauges of set on each side. Blades for portable saws are set 2 1/2 gauges on each side. Too much set is undesirable as it produces a rough cut, creates extra strain on the blade and requires extra power. A blade with 4 gauges of set (2 on each side) will make a kerf that is about 1 1/2 times the thickness of the blade. See Fig. 12-48.

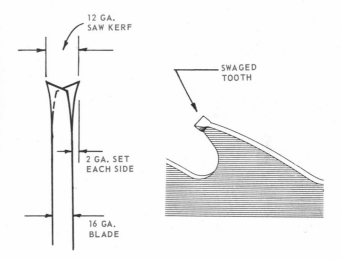

BLADE THICKNESS	SAW KERF; (2 GAUGES OF SET ON EACH SIDE)	INCREASE
18 ga. (.049)	14 ga. (.083)	.034
16 ga. (.065)	12 ga. (.109)	.044
14 ga. (.083)	10 ga. (.134)	.051
12 ga. (.109)	8 ga. (.165)	.056

Fig. 12-48. Gauges of set and saw kerf width.

Saws of 14 gauge and lighter can be set with a hand set as shown in Fig. 12-49. Follow the manufacturer's directions in adjusting the set. Only the top 1/8 to 5/32 in. of the tooth should be set. Observe the direction of the previous setting

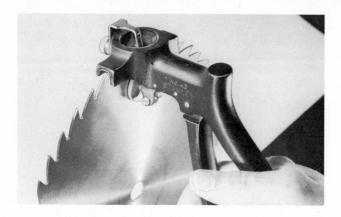

Fig. 12-49. Setting circular saw teeth with a hand set.

and follow the same pattern. You can check your work by sighting across the flat surface of the blade, toward a major light source. Never set the raker teeth of combination blades, or any of the teeth of hollow ground blades. Large, heavy gauge saws will require special setting equipment.

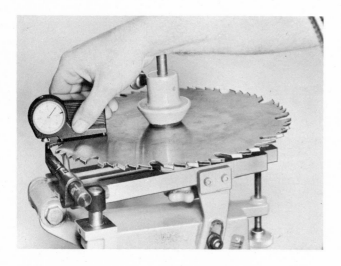

Fig. 12-50. Using a saw set gauge to check a flat ground combination blade.

Some saws have swaged teeth instead of set to provide clearance. In this process the ends of the teeth are made wider by upsetting or flattening them with a special tool.

Gumming

Gumming is the process of grinding and shaping the saw gullets (areas between teeth). The edge of a thin abrasive wheel is shaped to the required contour and the saw is held in a special fixture as shown in Fig. 12-51. The depth of the cut can be accurately controlled. When gumming a blade without special equipment, a reference circle

Fig. 12-51. Gumming a saw with a special grinder. Depth and shape can be accurately controlled. (Foley Mfg. Co.)

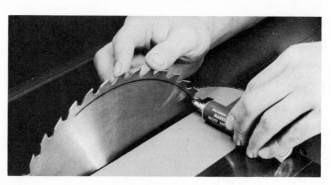

Fig. 12-52. Marking a reference circle for a gumming operation.

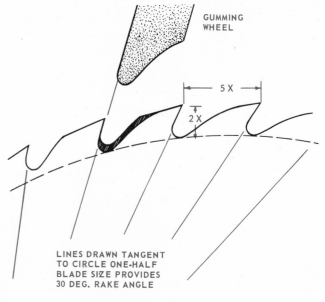

Fig. 12-53. Gumming layout for rip teeth.

should be made on the blade as shown in Fig. 12-52. Lines should be laid out from the front bevel or face of each tooth to serve as a guide during the grinding operation. The depth of the gullet should equal about two-fifths of the distance between the points of the teeth. See Fig. 12-53. The face of the tooth is ground only just enough to clean the surface so that correct spacing can be easily maintained. Heavy grinding will produce too much heat and burn the teeth. It is best to grind lightly, skip every other gullet, and go around the blade several times until the required depth is attained.

Dado Heads

To sharpen a dado head, the entire assembly should be mounted on the arbor and jointed. The blades are then filed in about the same way as a combination saw blade. See Fig. 12-54. A special file may be required. On some blades a smooth, square file will fit the teeth best. Chippers are filed straight across with a clearance angle of about 15 deg.

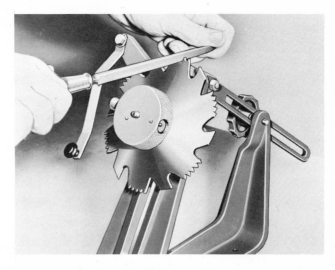

Fig. 12-54. Filing a dado blade held in a commercial saw clamp.

When the teeth of circular saw blades and dado heads become badly misshapen, they should be sent to a saw shop or factory where they can be completely refitted by experts, Fig. 12-55. Here precision machines and equipment will be used

Fig. 12-55. Skilled craftsmen straighten and tension blades in a modern saw factory.
(Huther Bros. Saw Mfg. Co.)

Fig. 12-56. Saw filing machine.

to grind, file, set, and tension the blade so that it will be like new. Fig. 12-56, shows a special filing machine being used to sharpen a circular saw.

Radial Arm Saw

Parts and Description

In this machine the motor and blade are carried by an overhead arm while the stock is held stationary on a table. The arm is attached to a vertical column at the back of the table and can be set at various angles. The depth of cut is controlled by raising or lowering the overhead arm. Fig. 12-57 shows the parts of a typical model.

The motor is mounted in a yoke so that it can be tilted for angle cuts. The yoke is suspended from the arm on a pivot which permits the motor

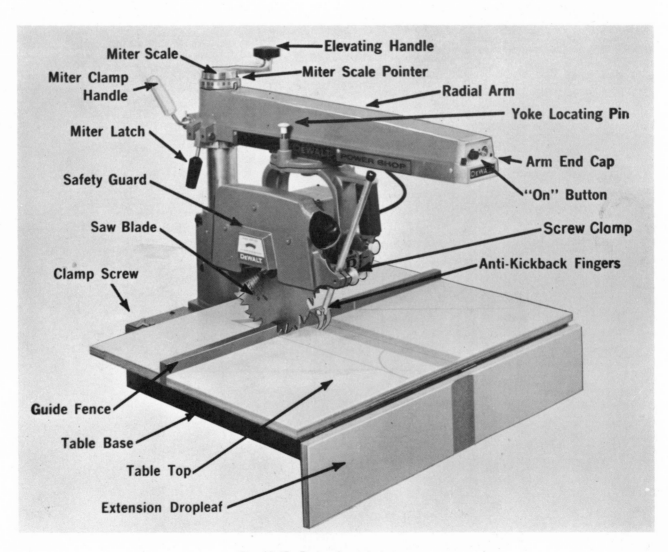

Fig. 12-57. Parts of a radial arm saw.
(Black and Decker Mfg. Co.)

12-20

to be rotated in a horizontal plane. Various adjustments make it possible to perform many sawing operations. The radial arm saw is used in woodworking shops and is valuable to the building trades. Where the pieces to be cut are large it is easy to hold the work stationary and move the saw blade.

When crosscutting, mitering, beveling, and dadoing, the work is held firmly on the table and the saw is pulled through the cut. For ripping and grooving the blade is turned parallel with the table and locked into position. Stock is then fed into the blade in somewhat the same manner as a table saw.

The radial arm saw uses the same kind of blades as a table saw, and its size is determined by the diameter of the largest blade it will carry. Blades are mounted by the same method as used for the table saw.

Safety Rules for the Radial Arm Saw

(In addition to the general safety rules on page 10-30.)

1. Stock must be held firmly on the table and against the fence for all crosscutting operations. The ends of long boards must be supported level with the table.

2. Before turning on the motor be certain that all clamps and locking devices are tight and the depth of cut is correct.

3. Keep the guard and anti-kickback device in position. Do not remove them without your instructor's permission.

4. Always return the saw to the rear of the table after completing a crosscut or miter cut. Never remove stock from the table until the saw has been returned.

5. MAINTAIN A 6 IN. MARGIN OF SAFETY. To do this you must keep your hands this distance away from the path of the saw blade.

6. Shut off the motor and wait for the blade to stop before making any adjustments.

7. Be sure the blade has stopped before you leave the machine.

8. The table should be kept clean and free of scrap pieces and excessive amounts of sawdust.

9. Secure approval from your instructor before making ripping cuts or other special setups. When ripping stock it must be flat and have one straight edge to move along the fence.

10. When ripping, always feed stock into the blade so that the bottom teeth are turning toward you. This will be the side opposite the anti-kickback fingers.

Fig. 12-58. Crosscutting with lower guard in position. Anti-kickback fingers are raised about 1/4 in. above the work.

Crosscutting

Use a crosscut or combination blade. Set the radial arm so it is perpendicular to the table fence and lock the motor in a horizontal position. Adjust the elevating handle until the blade is about 1/16 in. below the surface of the table. Be certain that the yoke locating pin is tight. Move the saw over the table and check to see that the guard rides easily over the table fence.

With the saw against the column, place your work on the table and align the cut. Hold the stock firmly against the table fence with your hand at least 6 in. away from the path of the saw blade. Turn on the motor, grasp the saw handle and pull the saw firmly and slowly through the cut as shown in Fig. 12-58. The saw may tend to "feed itself" and you must keep complete control over the rate of feed. When the cut is complete, return the saw to the rear of the table and shut off the motor.

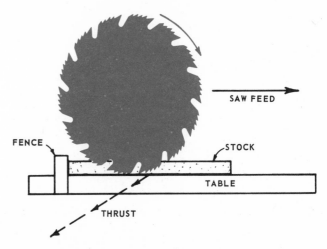

Fig. 12-59. Blade rotation and feed.

Fig. 12-60. Cutting a miter. Lower guard has been removed to show operation.

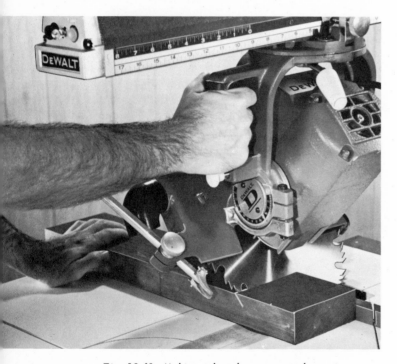

Fig. 12-61. Making a bevel cut across the grain.

Fig. 12-62. Cutting a compound miter. Lower guard cannot be used.

Duplicate parts can be cut to length by using stops clamped along the fence. Always make certain that the stock is against the fence before starting the cut. The saw can be operated either with the left or right hand, with the other hand holding the work. The long part of the work should always be on the side of the holding hand. Small pieces, where the hand cannot be kept at least 6 in. away from the cutting line, should be clamped to the table or cut with hand tools.

Miters, Bevels, and Compound Miters

The radial arm saw is ideal for making miter and bevel cuts. It is easy to handle on large pieces and precision cuts can be made.

To cut miters, swing the radial arm to the required angle and then follow the same procedure as for crosscutting. See Fig. 12-60. The lower guard can be used for cuts of this kind.

Bevel cuts across the grain are made with the radial arm at right angles to the table fence. Elevate the arm so the blade will clear the table and then tilt the motor to the required angle. Lower the arm until the blade will cut about 1/16 in. below the table surface and proceed as in regular crosscutting as shown in Fig. 12-61. The lower guard cannot be used for this operation when the bevel angle approaches 45 degrees.

Compound mitering combines the two previous operations. Tilt the motor to the required angle and then swing the radial arm into position. Be certain all clamps are securely locked. Make the cut as shown in Fig. 12-62.

WOODY SAYS:

"When crosscutting or making miter or bevel cuts, always return the saw unit to the rear of the table immediately after completing a cut."

Ripping Cuts

To set up for ripping cuts, release the yoke and turn the motor 90 deg. so the blade is parallel with the fence. Lock the yoke and move the saw along the radial arm to secure the correct measurement between the fence and the blade. Lock the saw unit in place and adjust its height so the blade will cut just under the surface of the table. Adjust the guard and set the anti-kickback fingers so they will ride on the top surface of the stock.

Study the diagram in Fig. 12-63, so you will be certain to feed the stock in the correct direc-

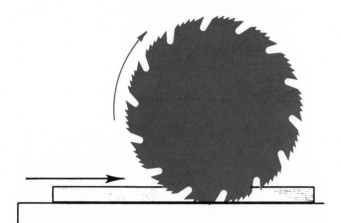

Fig. 12-63. Feed direction for ripping cuts. View from column side.

tion. Turn on the motor and feed the stock as shown in Fig. 12-64. Use push sticks and do not permit your hands to come closer than 6 in. to the operating blade.

Bevel ripping is shown in Fig. 12-65. To make the setup, first raise the radial arm and then tilt the motor unit to the required angle. Then lower it until the blade just touches the table and set it for the required width of cut. Be sure to adjust the guard and anti-kickback fingers for the thickness of your stock as shown. Use push sticks and push boards to finish the cut or have an assistant "tail" the stock from the other side.

Dados and Grooves

Mount a dado head on the saw arbor following about the same procedure as for the table saw. On some machines an Allen wrench is used to hold the arbor when tightening the nut. See Fig. 12-66. When a full width dado head is used, it may not be possible to use the outside collar because you must have the nut turned on the full depth of its threads. Replace the guard and check its clearance.

Set the radial arm and other adjustments as described for crosscutting. Lower the dado until it will cut the correct depth in your stock. Measure the distance for this setting and then make a trial cut in waste material that is the same thickness as your stock. Also check the width of the dado cut.

Fig. 12-64. Above. Making a ripping cut. Below. View at rear of blade showing position of splitter and anti-kickback fingers.

Fig. 12-65. Ripping a bevel.

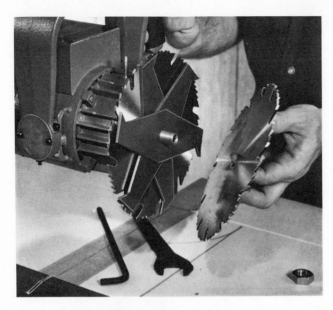

Fig. 12-66. Mounting a dado head.

Fig. 12-67. Cutting a dado. Lower guard can be used.

Fig. 12-68. Cutting a groove. Rear view.

Place the stock on the table with the layout lines turned up and the edge against the fence. Pull the dado head up to the edge of the fence and align the stock. Now push it back, turn on the motor and pull it slowly through the cut, Fig. 12-67. Always return the motor unit to the rear of the table immediately, and then remove the stock or set up additional cuts. Use stop blocks set along the fence to position duplicate parts.

WOODY SAYS:

"Unless you have had a great deal of experience on the radial arm saw, have your instructor check each special set-up before you perform the work."

To cut grooves, Figs. 12-68 and 69, the machine is set up in the same manner as for ripping and the same procedures and precautions are followed. Fig. 12-69 shows a safe procedure being used to cut a groove in the edge of stock with the motor unit turned in a vertical position. A rabbet cut can be made with the same setup by simply raising the saw unit.

Portable Circular Saw

The portable circular saw is used extensively by carpenters for framing and other rough construction work. It may be used in shops for cutting stock to rough size. Fig. 12-70 shows the parts of a standard model.

The size is determined by the diameter of the largest blade it will carry. Sizes range from a 4 1/2 in. blade powered with a 1/6 hp motor to a 12 in. blade which uses a 1 1/2 hp motor. A practical size is 7 in. which will cut to a depth of slightly over 2 in. and can be used for rough framing work. The depth of cut is adjusted by raising or lowering the position of the motor on the base. On most saws it is possible to tilt the base so that bevel cuts can be made. Some models have a ripping guide or fence.

Portable saws are usually guided along the cutting line "free-hand" and require extra clearance in the saw kerf. Blades are set at least 2 1/2 gauges on each side to provide this extra clearance.

Fig. 12-71 shows a cut being started with a portable saw. Note the direction of blade rotation and the movement of the saw. As the blade enters

Fig. 12-69. Cutting an edge groove. Note the special guard.

the cut the telescoping guard is pushed back by the stock. A spring returns the guard to closed position when the cut is complete.

Safety Rules for the Portable Circular Saw

(In addition to the safety rules listed on page 10-30.)

1. Stock must be well supported in such a way that the kerf will not close and bind the blade, during the cut or at the end of the cut.

2. Thin materials should be supported on benches. Small pieces should be clamped in a vise or onto a bench top or sawhorse.
3. Be careful not to cut into the bench, sawhorse or other supporting devices.
4. Adjust the depth of cut to the thickness of the stock, plus about 1/8 in.
5. Check the base and angle adjustment to be sure they are tight. Plug in the cord to a grounded outlet and be sure it will not become fouled in the work.
6. Always place the saw base on the stock with the blade clear before turning on the switch.
7. During the cut, stand to one side of the cutting line.
8. Large saws will have two handles. Keep both hands on them during the cutting operation. Small saws should also be guided with both hands when possible.
9. Always unplug the machine to change blades or make major adjustments.
10. Always use a sharp blade that has plenty of set.

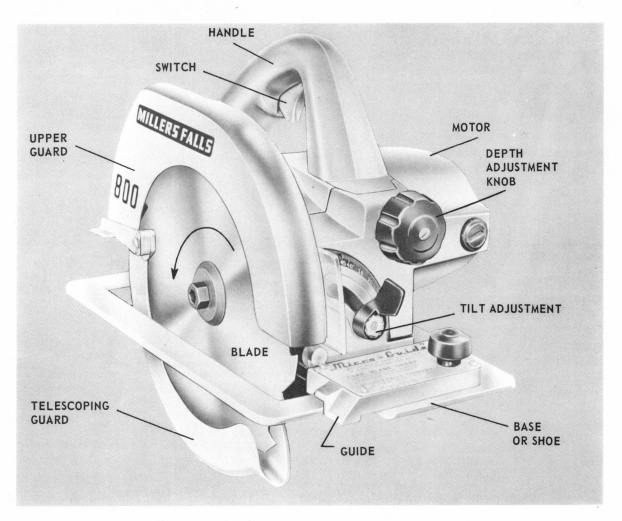

Fig. 12-70. Parts of a portable saw.

Fig. 12-71. Blade rotation and feed.
(Rockwell Mfg. Co.)

Using the Portable Circular Saw

When using a portable saw, make layout lines that can be easily followed, or clamp straight-edges to the surface of the work that will guide the saw. Some saws have a ripping fence and it should be used for ripping cuts.

Grasp the handle of the saw firmly in one hand with the forefinger ready to operate the trigger switch. The other hand should be placed on the stock, well away from the cutting line. Some saws will require both hands on the machine. Rest the base on the work and align the guide mark with the layout line. Turn on the switch, allow the motor to reach full speed and then feed it smoothly through the cut as shown in Fig. 12-72. Release the switch as soon as the cut is finished and continue to hold the saw until the blade stops.

Fig. 12-73. Using a portable saw in house construction.
(Millers Falls Co.)

The portable saw may be used to make cuts in assembled work. For example, flooring and roofing boards are often nailed into place and then the ends are trimmed. Fig. 12-73 shows a carpenter using a portable saw to cut an opening in composition sheathing after it was nailed to the studs. Sharpening a portable saw blade is shown in Fig. 12-74.

Industrial Machines

Circular saws, like those you have learned to use in the school shop, are also used in industry. Table saws and radial arm saws are among the basic power equipment found in smaller wood-

Fig. 12-72. Making a cut across the grain.

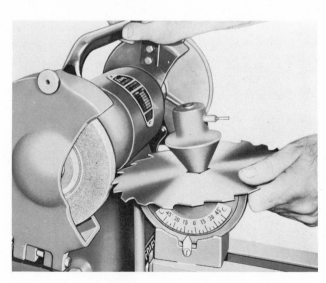

Fig. 12-74. Sharpening a portable saw blade.
(Foley Mfg. Co.)

working plants and cabinet shops. Patternmaking shops will also have about the same power wood-working machines as the school shop. Fig. 12-75 shows a table saw in operation in a custom kitchen cabinet shop. In large production plants the cutting principles of these basic machines are applied in the design of huge automatic machines that handle hundreds of board feet of lumber per hour.

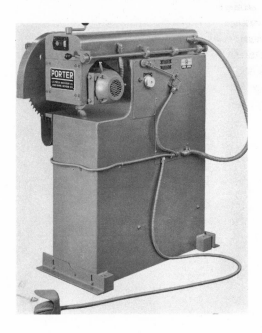

Fig. 12-75. Cutting plywood on a table saw in a commercial cabinet shop. (Tannewitz Works)

Fig. 12-76. Cut-off saw with hydraulic feed. Length and number of strokes adjustable (0-45 per min.). The 18 in. blade is driven by a 7 1/2 hp motor.

Cut-Off Saws

Industrial cut-off saws operate in about the same way as the radial arm saw, except that they have a power feed and cannot be adjusted for angle cuts. Fig. 12-76 shows a model where

the feed is operated by hydraulic power. A touch of the foot pedal moves the blade through the cut at a controlled speed and then returns it to the back position. The length of the stroke is adjustable for any length up to 36 in. The cut-off saw requires extension tables on both sides as shown in Fig. 12-77.

Fig. 12-77. Cut-off saw with extension table. Note stops for duplicate cutting along right hand side. (Ekstrom, Carlson Co.)

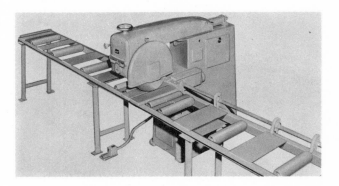

Fig. 12-78. Carbide tipped dado head.

Rough crosscutting is sometimes done with a swinging cut-off saw. It differs from the previously described saw in that the sawing head is mounted on an overhead swing arm which is pulled through the stock by hand.

Modern production machines require rugged, long lasting blades. Teeth with carbide tips are universally used which stay sharp many times longer than those on conventional type blades. Fig. 12-78 shows a carbide tipped dado head with blades that are hollow-ground. Carbide blades require precision sharpening equipment. See Fig. 12-79. The carbide tip is too hard to be ground with a conventional abrasive and a special diamond wheel is used.

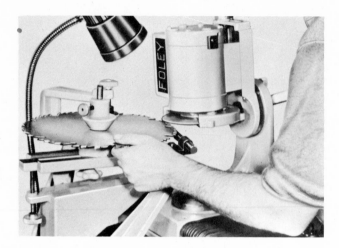

Fig. 12-79. Precision grinding a carbide tipped blade with diamond wheel.

Straight-Line Rip Saw

Machines of this type, Fig. 12-80, will rip boards very accurately. The motor and blade are located in the table and an endless chain on each side, feeds the stock in a straight line. Overhead is an assembly of rollers that apply pressure to the stock and hold it firmly on the table and feed chains.

Fig. 12-80. Straight-line rip saw. Variable feeds 60-180 fpm. Arbor is 2 in. dia. and driven by a 20 hp motor. Feed motor 2 hp. (Diehl Machines Inc.)

The straight-line rip saw, Fig. 12-81, is also designed with the blade and motor unit located above the table. The endless feed belt located in the table, makes a slight dip as it moves directly under the blade.

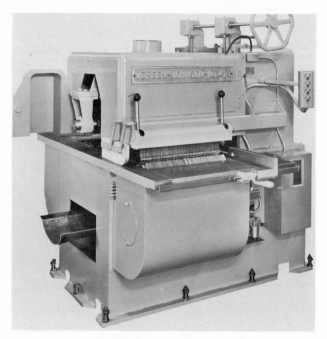

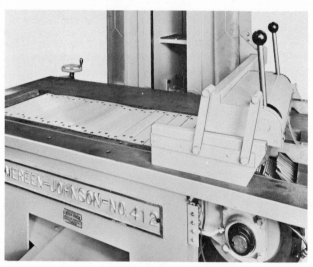

Fig. 12-81. Above. Straight line rip saw with arbor above table. Below. Sawing head removed to show slat bed feed. Note the dip under the arbor position to provide clearance for blade. Several blades can be mounted at one time.

Cut-off and rip saws are used in combination with facers and planers to rough mill and prepare stock for finished machine operations as shown in Fig. 12-82.

Gang Rip Saw

The gang rip saw operates about like the straight-line rip except that a number of blades are mounted on the saw arbor. To permit blades to operate at various positions across the table, rollers are used to feed the stock instead of a belt or chain. All of the rollers are powered and operate somewhat like those on a planer. This

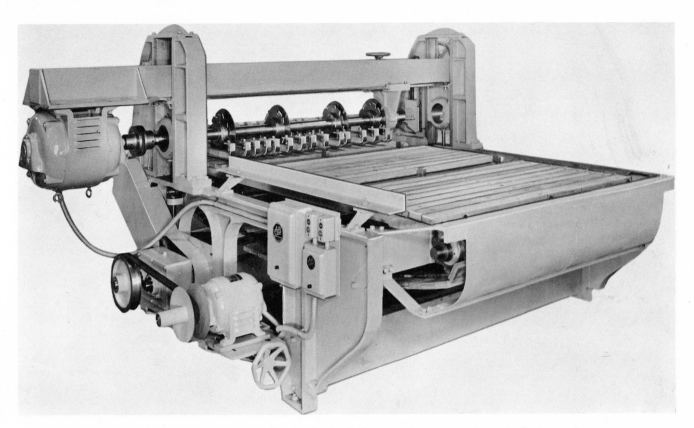

Multiple cutting and grooving machine with slat bed. View shows setup for multiple drawer front ripping and grooving. Blade and dado combination cuts part to size and forms joint.
(Mereen—Johnson Mach. Co.)

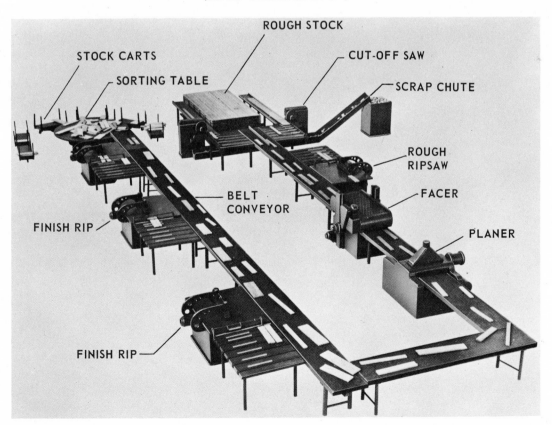

Fig. 12-82. Scale models used to plan a milling layout.
(Porter Mach. Co.)

machine, like the straight-line rip saw, will cut boards very accurately. Fig. 12-83 shows a heavy-duty model that can be equipped with a 150 hp arbor motor. As many as 10 cuts can be made at one time through hardwoods 3 in. thick.

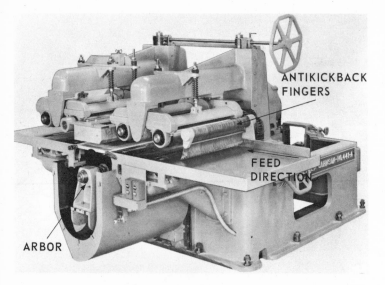

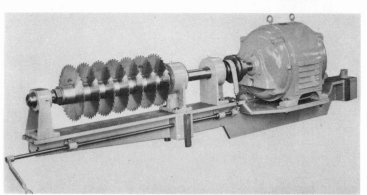

Fig. 12-83. Above. Gang rip saw. Arbor is located below the table. Note the anti-kickback fingers. Center. View showing arbor and feed motors. Note variable feed drive. Cover has been removed to show roller chain drive. Below. Motor, arbor and blade assembly. 10 blades can be mounted at one time. (Mereen - Johnson Mach. Co.)

Double-End Sawing Machines

These machines consist of feed chains that carry the work past sawing heads located on each side. The chain is often equipped with rubber pads that protect the surface of finished material. Rubber tired rollers hold the stock securely on the feed chains. The sawing heads can be set at various angles for beveling and other special work. See Fig. 12-84.

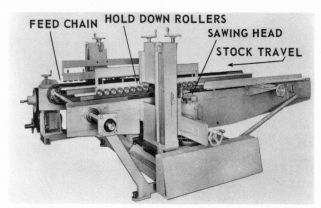

Fig. 12-84. Basic double-end sawing machine. Space between sawing heads is adjustable for various widths of material.

Two double-end machines are sometimes placed together with a special conveyor unit between, as shown in Fig. 12-85. This makes it possible to cut panels and doors to finished size in one operation. The work is fed into one machine where it is cut to width and then moves out on conveyor rolls where it is picked up by the second machine and cut to finished length. An in-plant view of such an arrangement is shown in Fig. 12-86.

Multiple Cutting and Grooving Equipment

Machines in this group usually have a long saw arbor that extends across either a conveyor chain or a slat bed as shown in Fig. 12-87. Small rubber tired or composition wheels hold the work firmly against the conveyor. Blades and dado heads can be set at various positions along the arbor to cut stock to size and form grooves and dados in cabinet and furniture parts.

A variation of the previously described machine is shown in Fig. 12-88. Here blades are mounted on swinging arms and are driven by belts from pulleys mounted on the main drive shaft. The blades can be positioned anywhere across the slat bed and raised out or dropped into the work by switches on the operator's console.

Fig. 12-85. Two double-end machines set up for a door and panel sizing operation. Note sanding attachment on first unit. On second unit the cut is across grain so a trim saw is used above and below to prevent splintering. (Mereen - Johnson Mach. Co.)

Fig. 12-86. Double-end sawing machines ripping and multiple crosscutting 5 ft. x 10 ft. flake-core board into smaller pieces of exact dimension.

Fig. 12-87. Multiple saw and groover. Will handle stock up to 96 in. wide and from 1/4 in. to 3 in. thick. Various arrangements of blades and dados can be made along the arbor. Feed rates from 15 to 45 fpm. (Mereen - Johnson Mach. Co.)

Fig. 12-88. Multiple cutup machine with a slat feed bed. Arms are raised and lowered by pneumatic power and controlled from the operator's console.
(Kohler - Joa Corp.)

Double-End Tenoners

This is a very versatile machine that can be set up to perform a wide variety of operations, Figs. 12-89 and 90. It combines features of double-end saws and multiple grooving equip-

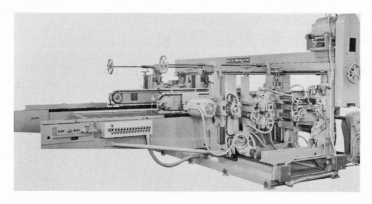

Fig. 12-89. Double-end tenoner.

ment. It is described in more detail in another section of this book. Fig. 12-90 shows a double-end tenoner being used to cut formed plywood drawer fronts to size. A scoring saw first makes a shallow cut just through the hardwood veneer and then a trimmer saw completes the cut. This procedure prevents any splintering of the edge.

Custom Built Machines

Modern production woodworking machines are becoming more and more specialized. Many

specially designed machines are required. Companies that build these machines maintain a staff to design modifications and special features required by their customers. Their basic models are flexible to allow for changes and revisions as well as improvement in design.

Test Your Knowledge

1. A table saw that has two arbors is called a _____ saw.
2. To completely specify a circular saw blade you should list the kind, size, gauge, number of teeth and _____ .
3. A 16 gauge blade is thicker than a 14 gauge. True or False?
4. The hook or rake angle of a rip blade is usually about _____ deg.
5. The regular combination blade has some crosscut teeth and some teeth shaped like a rip tooth but called _____ .
6. Stock must be surfaced and at least one edge must be jointed before it can be cut safely on the table saw. True or False?
7. To loosen an arbor nut, turn it in the same direction that the blade turns in operation. True or False?
8. When stock is ripped so that two thinner pieces are produced, the operation is called _____ .
9. Duplicate parts that are about 4 in. long should be cut to length by attaching a _____ _____ to the fence.
10. What is the name of the cut that is made when the miter gauge is set at an angle and the blade tilted?
11. When the two blades of the dado head are set up without chippers, they will cut a width exactly _____ .
12. The dado head can be used to cut rabbet joints. True or False?
13. The sharpening operation that makes all the teeth the same height is called _____ .
14. For general work saw blades are set _____ gauges on each side.
15. Gumming is the process of cleaning the saw blade before it is sharpened. True or False?
16. The radial arm saw uses the same kind of blades as a table saw. True or False?
17. When ripping stock on the radial saw, always feed into the blade so that the bottom teeth are turning toward you. True or False?
18. An industrial machine that will rip stock accurately enough for gluing is called a _____ rip saw.

*Fig. 12-90. Double-end tenoner cutting formed plywood drawer fronts to size.
(Mereen - Johnson Mach. Co.)*

Outside Assignments

1. Study manufacturer's catalogs and select a table saw that would be appropriate for a home workshop. Prepare complete specifications of the machine. Include the size of blade, arbor, table and motor. Also include adjustment features and accessories that would be desirable. Prepare a cost estimate.
2. Prepare double size profile drawings of a number of styles of rip teeth. Study reference books and manufacturer's bulletins for information.
3. Visit a home construction site and interview one of the carpenters. Secure information about the operations he performs with a portable circular saw and the kinds and size he prefers. Summarize the interview in a written paper or make an oral report to your class.
4. Design an interlocking joint that could be used to join drawer fronts and sides. Prepare a set of drawings like the ones in Fig. 12-41, showing the cutting sequence you would follow.
5. Design a gumming fixture that would attach to the tool grinder in your shop. Make use of slides or a swinging arm that would hold the blade in the correct position as each gullet was ground. Make appropriate drawings to record and present your ideas.

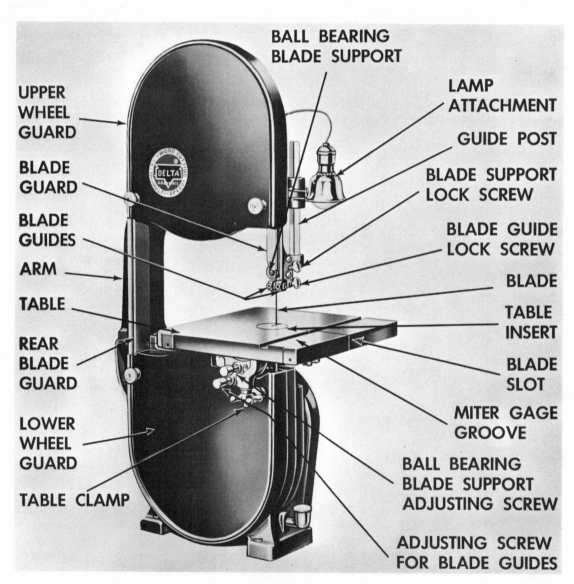

Fig. 13-1. Parts of a band saw.

Unit 13

BANDSAW, JIG SAW, AND SABER SAW

The band saw, jig saw, and saber saw are designed especially for cutting curved outlines; however, they also can be used for straight cuts where great accuracy is not required. They are somewhat more safe to use than circular saws because the cutting action is perpendicular to the surface of the stock and there is no possibility of kickback. Band saws are used for large curves in thick stock while jig saws will cut intricate

patterns and designs in thin material. The saber saw is especially helpful when cutting large sheets of plywood or hardboard where it is easier to move the tool than the work.

Band Saw

Size and Parts

The size of a band saw is determined by the diameter of its wheels. Band saws such as shown in Figs. 13-1 and 13-2, are designed principally for cutting curved work and are called narrow band saws. They range in size from 10 to 42 in. and carry blades under 1 1/2 in. in width. Fig. 13-1 shows the parts of a typical band saw. The wheels are fitted with rubber tires that cushion the blade and prevent it from slipping. The top wheel is adjustable up and down to permit some difference in blade length and to provide tension. It can also be tilted in or out so that the blade will run in the center of the wheel surface.

A blade guide assembly is located above and below the table. The assembly holds the blade in position and prevents it from being pushed off of the wheel during a sawing operation. The guide located above the table, Fig. 13-3, can be moved up and down to adjust for various thicknesses of stock. When properly adjusted, the guides do not touch the blade except when a piece of wood is being cut.

The cutting speed of a band saw is given in surface feet per minute (S.F.M.). It can be calculated if the wheel diameter (D) and rpm are known. Use the following formula:

$$S.F.M. = \frac{D \times 3.14 \times RPM}{12}$$

Blades

To specify a certain band saw blade you must list the width, length, gauge, and tooth style and spacing. The most commonly used widths are 1/4, 3/8, 1/2, and 3/4 inch. The length of the

Fig. 13-2. Modern 20 in. band saw. 1 hp motor. Wheel speed -- 900 rpm or 4500 S.F.P.
(Powermatic, Inc.)

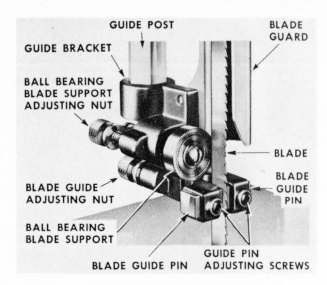

Fig. 13-3. *Parts of upper guide. Lower guide is similar.*

blade will be determined by the particular machine being used. To calculate the length of a blade, take twice the distance between the wheel centers (H) and add 3.14 times the diameter of the wheel. L = 2H + 2πR.

The thickness (gauge) of a blade must be correct for the wheel size. The continual flexing of the blade as it passes over the wheels causes metal fatigue and takes place rapidly when the blade is too thick for a given wheel diameter. Manufacturers recommend the following gauges:

Wheel Diameter	Recommended Thickness
10 - 20 inches	25 gauge
24 - 30 inches	22 gauge
36 - 40 inches	21 gauge
40 and over	20 gauge

Tooth size and spacing will be determined by the kind of work required. Coarse teeth will provide for faster cutting but will not cut very smooth.

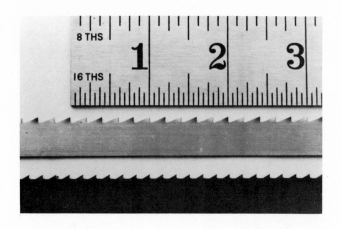

Fig. 13-4. *Above. Standard 1/2 in. blade. Below. Skip tooth blade. These teeth are hardened and will stay sharp longer.*

For general purpose work a 4, 5, or 6 point blade is generally used. Blades are specified by listing the numbers of points, or teeth per inch. Fig. 13-4 shows a close-up view of two general purpose blades.

Band saw blades are sold either in given lengths that are joined and ready for use or in rolls of 100 ft. or longer. When purchased in rolls the correct length is cut and the ends are welded together with a machine. See Fig. 13-5.

Fig. 13-5. *Band saw blade welder. Welds blades up to 1 in. wide and adjustable for various gauges.*
(Stryco Mfg. Co.)

Sharpening and Coiling

Band saw blades have many teeth and considerable time is required to set and file them by hand. Small shops often prefer to use skip tooth blades with hardened teeth which stay sharp longer than regular blades. They cannot be filed and are discarded when they become dull.

Regular blades are filed and set in about the same way as a hand rip saw. The shape and angle are shown in Fig. 13-6. A special band saw file

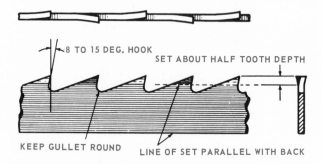

Fig. 13-6. *Shape and angle of band saw teeth.*
(Simonds Saw and Steel Co.)

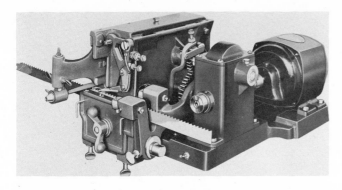

Fig. 13-7. Automatic filing and setting machine. Feed rate 65 teeth per minute. Adjustable to any narrow band saw blade. (Wardwell Mfg. Co.)

should be used. It has rounded edges that keep the bottom of the gullets round and minimizes checks and cracks in the blade. The same type of file that is used for hand filing, can be mounted in an automatic filing machine, Fig. 13-7.

Storing, shipping, and handling blades is easier if they are coiled. Fig. 13-8 shows a sequence of steps to follow.

A. With the teeth pointing away from you, grasp the blade in the palms of your hands and step on it with one foot. Your index fingers should point down along the back of the blade.

B. Using your index fingers, push the two lower sections away from you and permit the upper loop to swing toward you.

C. Continue the motion with the lower loops swinging toward each other and the upper loop swinging downward and underneath. Raise your foot so the blade can turn on edge.

D. Cross the loops and release the blade. It will fall together in three equal loops.

Long blades may be coiled into additional loops by enlarging one of the three loops and holding it as shown in Fig. 13-9. Repeat the above procedure and the blade will then be coiled in five loops.

Mounting Blades

It is important to install band saw blades carefully and keep them in adjustment if the full life of the blade is to be secured. The steps listed below should be followed:

1. Disconnect the electrical power and open the wheel guard doors. Pull the table alignment pin and remove the throat plate if necessary.

2. Loosen the upper and lower guide assemblies and push them back out of line with the wheels.

3. Uncoil the blade and place it on the wheels with the teeth to the front and pointing down over the table. If the teeth are in the wrong direction turn the blade inside out.

4. Raise the top wheel to apply tension. Most machines have a scale to show the correct

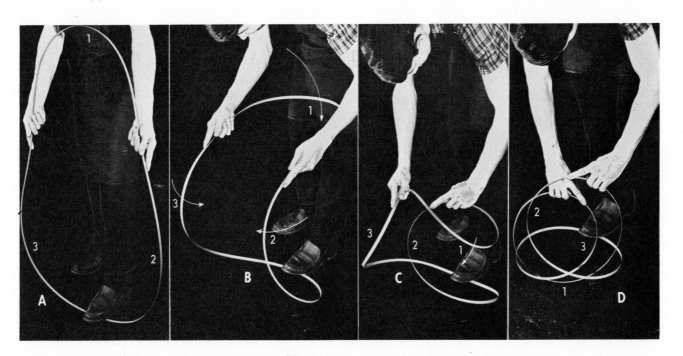

Fig. 13-8. Coiling a band saw blade. A-Starting position. B-Loops 2 and 3 pushed away and swinging toward the center. Loop 1 swings back and downward. C-Motion continued. Loop 1 swinging downward and underneath. D-Loop 2 and 3 overlapped and on top of loop 1. Release Blade.

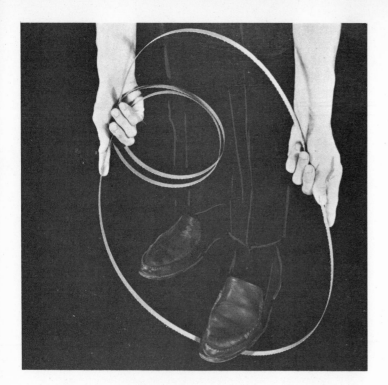

Fig. 13-9. Starting position when adding two more loops.

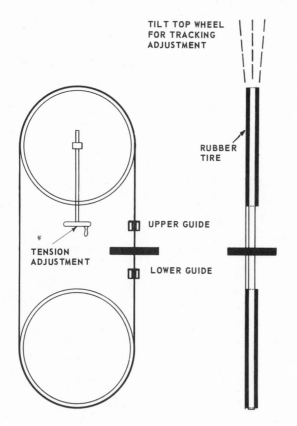

Fig. 13-10. Adjustments for mounting blade.

tension for various blade widths. See Fig. 13-10.

5. Roll the machine by hand and adjust the top wheel with the tilting mechanism until the blade tracks smoothly near the center of the tires.

6. Move the saw guides forward until the front edges of the jaws are even or slightly back of the tooth gullets. The blade should move evenly between them with about 1/64 in. clearance on each side. See Fig. 13-11. Lock the guide assemblies in position.

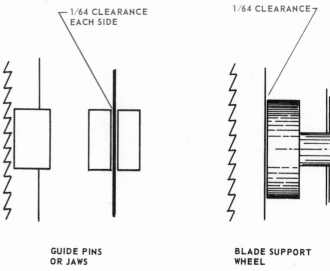

Fig. 13-11. Guide clearance.

7. Move the blade support wheel forward on each guide assembly until it is 1/64 in. away from the back edge of the blade. Lock them in place.

8. Again roll the machine by hand and check all adjustments and clearances. Have your instructor check the adjustments. Replace the throat plate and pin and close the wheel guard doors.

9. Connect the power, turn on the machine and you are ready to make a trial cut.

Maintenance

Keep the blade free of gum and pitch. It can be cleaned by wiping with a cloth saturated with a pitch and gum remover or mineral spirits. The band saw tires may gather an accumulation of sawdust and gum and should be cleaned occasionally with a stiff brush. As tires become grooved from blade wear they can be smoothed with coarse abrasive paper glued to a large block of wood. The lower wheel can be easily and safely dressed by removing the blade and running the wheel under operating power. The top wheel should be turned by hand. Driving the top wheel with a blade for this operation is extremely hazardous and should be undertaken only by a skilled operator.

Tire shape can be maintained longer if the blade tension is released when the saw is to stand idle for a considerable length of time.

Lubrication requirements will vary with different machines. Check the operator's manual furnished by the manufacturer for recommendations. This manual will also provide information concerning wheel alignment, tire replacement and other maintenance aspects. The occasional application of a coat of paste wax to the table will prevent rust and help keep the surface smooth and clean.

Safety Rules for the Band Saw

(In addition to the general safety rules on page 10-30.)

1. Wheel guard doors must be closed and the blade properly adjusted before turning on the machine.
2. Adjust the upper guide assembly so it is 1/4 in. above the work.
3. Allow the saw to reach full speed before starting to feed the work.
4. The stock must be held flat on the table.
5. Feed the saw only as fast as the teeth will remove the wood easily.
6. Maintain a 2 in. margin of safety. (This means that the hands should always be at least two inches away from the blade when the saw is running.)
7. Plan saw cuts to avoid backing out of curves, whenever possible.
8. Make turns carefully and do not cut radii so small that the blade is twisted.
9. Stop the machine before backing out of a long curved cut.
10. Round stock should not be cut unless mounted securely in a jig or hand screw.
11. If you hear a clicking noise, turn off the machine at once. This indicates a crack in the

Fig. 13-12. Ripping rough stock to remove some of the cup.

Fig. 13-13. Roughing-out parts before making finished cuts.

blade. If the blade breaks, shut off the power and move away from the machine until both wheels stop.

12. Turn off the machine as soon as you have finished your work. If the machine has a brake, apply it smoothly. Do not leave the machine until it has stopped running.

Roughing Cuts

Since there is no tendency for kickback, the band saw can be used to cut rough lumber to length and width. Pieces that are warped should be handled carefully. It is usually best to turn the concave side down so the stock will rest firmly on the table without rocking.

When making cuts in rough lumber, lay out cutting lines with chalk. Adjust the upper guide to about 1/4 in. above the thickest part of the stock. If you are right handed, make a ripping cut by standing to the left of the cutting line. Feed the work with the right hand and guide it with the left hand. Move the work through the cut at a smooth, even speed. The rate of feed will vary with the kind and thickness of the wood and the blade size and speed. See Fig. 13-12. For rough crosscutting, it is usually best to stand to the right of the sawing line, holding the stock in the right hand and feeding it with the left.

Fig. 13-13 shows roughing-out cuts being made after stock has been surfaced and finished cutting lines drawn. Holes have been bored to free the blade for sharp turns. Stay well away from the cutting lines so that there will be sufficient stock for the finished cuts.

Straight Finished Cuts

Some band saws are equipped with a fence and miter gauge. They are adjusted and used in the same general way as the table saw. Since their purpose is to guide the work accurately through the cut, the stock must be surfaced so it will be flat on the table and have a straight edge against the fence or gauge. The blade must be properly sharpened or it may tend to crawl or lead away from the line of cut. The table can be tilted for making angle cuts.

Cutting Curves

The basic purpose of the band saw is to cut curved work. The size of the curve (radius) that can be cut without straining or twisting the blade will be determined by the width of the blade and the amount of set in the teeth. A sharp blade with normal set will cut the following curves:

Blade Width	Minimum Circle
1/4 in.	2 in. dia.
3/8 in.	3 in. dia.
1/2 in.	4 in. dia.
3/4 in.	6 in. dia.

The curves will likely vary in size in a given piece of work. In Fig. 13-14, a finished cut is being made along a larger curve while a sharp point was passed by and will be cut later. Note the relieve cuts made before the main cut was started, to free the blade in the sharp curve.

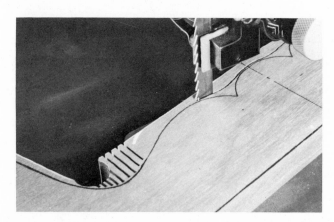

Fig. 13-14. Making a finished cut along large curves. Details will be cut after this cut is completed.

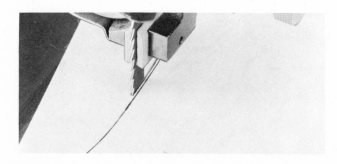

Fig. 13-15. Cutting on waste side of the line with a 1/16 in. allowance.

The teeth of a band saw blade are chisel shaped and do not leave a smooth surface. For many jobs, the kerf should be located in the waste stock and far enough away from the line to allow for smoothing. This allowance will vary with the coarseness of the blade but should seldom be less than 1/16 in., as shown in Fig. 13-15.

Feed the work straight into the blade and do not try to change the position of the cut by applying side pressure. Keep your eye on the line a little ahead of the blade so you can see how to adjust the position of the work to feed correctly.

Small curves can be cut with a wide blade by using one of the methods shown in Fig. 13-16.

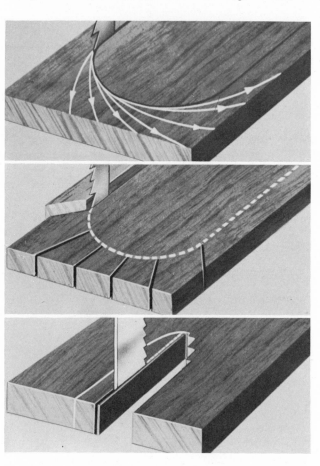

Fig. 13-16. Cutting sharp curves with a wide blade. Above. Tangent cuts. Center. Relief cuts. Below. Nibble cuts. (Jam handy Organization)

 **WOODY SAYS:**

"Applying side pressure, or cutting too small a radius will damage the saw blade. Burned marks on the cut surface of the work indicate that improper procedures were used."

Cutting Sequence

When working with complicated patterns, always study the sequence of cuts you will use. Often it is worthwhile to number the cuts on the work. Chalk marks along the finished line can be used to indicate the direction of the cut and the order in which it will be made. Fig. 13-17 suggests a sequence of cuts to be followed in cutting out the part shown. It will be necessary to back out of only two short straight cuts.

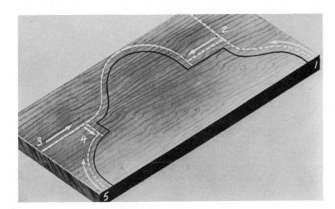

Fig. 13-17. Cutting sequence.
(Jam Handy Organization)

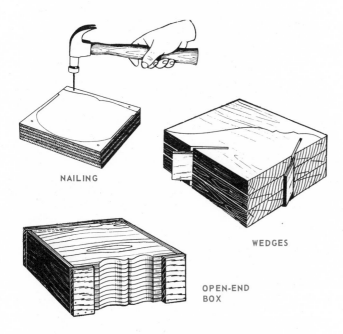

NAILING

WEDGES

OPEN-END BOX

Fig. 13-18. How stock can be held for multiple sawing.

Multiple Sawing

To save time in production work, duplicate parts can be stacked together and cut in a single operation. This is called multiple or pad sawing.

The layers can be held together by several methods, Fig. 13-18. If you use nails be certain that they are located well away from the cutting line.

Compound Sawing

This operation involves two sets of cuts, usually made at right angles to each other. In Fig. 13-19, the hull of a sail boat is formed by laying out the pattern on the top and sides and then making the two sets of cuts shown. After the first cut is made, the waste is spot glued back to support the stock during the final cuts. Nails can be

Fig. 13-19. Compound sawing.

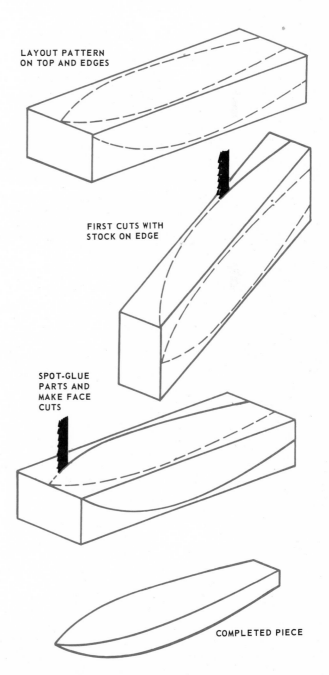

LAYOUT PATTERN ON TOP AND EDGES

FIRST CUTS WITH STOCK ON EDGE

SPOT-GLUE PARTS AND MAKE FACE CUTS

COMPLETED PIECE

13-7

used to rejoin the work if they are carefully placed. Compound sawing can be applied to more complicated shapes such as cabriole legs or carving blanks.

Resawing

Stock can be resawed on the band saw to produce two or more thinner pieces as shown in Fig. 13-20. A simple guide should be used to control the thickness and help hold the stock on edge. Use a sharp blade, at least 1/2 in. wide. Band saw blades are thinner than circular saw blades and thus reduce the amount of waste in a resawing operation. On wide boards however, it is often helpful to first make circular saw cuts in from each edge and then finish the operation on the band saw.

Fig. 13-21. Above. Resawing attachment. Below. Resawing attachment in operation.
(Northfield Foundry and Machine Co.)

Fig. 13-20. Resawing, using a simple guide clamped to the table.

Band saws can be equipped with a resawing fixture or attachment. See Fig. 13-21. This consists of a special fence and pressure rolls that guide and hold the work so that accurate cuts can be produced.

Special Setups

A wide range of special setups can be made on the band saw to produce duplicate parts in production work. One of these is pattern sawing where the work is mounted on a master pattern which moves along a stop or guide as the cut is made. Some setups are produced on an auxiliary

table that has slots or grooves. Pins on the underside of a carrier, move through these slots and control the direction and position of the cut. The work is held or clamped on the carrier.

Jig Saw

Sizes and Parts

The size of a jig saw (sometimes called a scroll saw) is determined by the distance from the over arm to the blade. The one shown in Fig. 13-22 is a 24 in. size. It is a standard model with four-step pulleys that provide different cutting speeds. Variable speeds are usually available that range from about 600 to 1800 C.S.M. (cutting strokes per minute). A pitman drive moves the lower chuck (not shown) up and down. The upper chuck is attached to a bar that moves inside the tension sleeve. The tension sleeve includes a spring that keeps the blade from buckling on the up stroke. It can be adjusted up or down for various blade lengths.

Selecting and Installing Blades

Blades vary in thickness, width, length, and number of teeth per inch. They are usually 5 in. long, however, 6 in. lengths are available. Fig. 13-23 lists some of the common sizes used for woodwork. Select the largest blade that will still provide the type of finish and width of cut required. It will be less likely to heat and break.

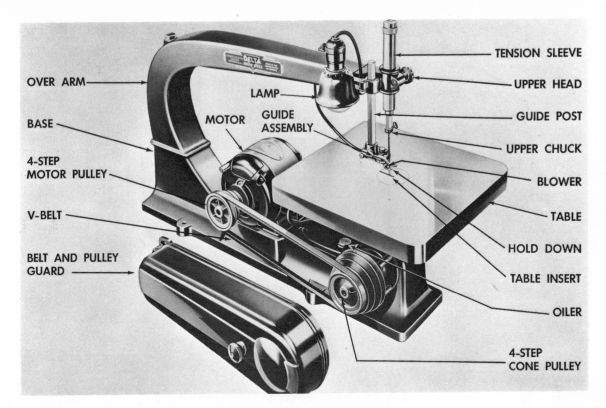

OVER ARM
BASE
4-STEP MOTOR PULLEY
V-BELT
BELT AND PULLEY GUARD

LAMP
MOTOR
GUIDE ASSEMBLY

TENSION SLEEVE
UPPER HEAD
GUIDE POST
UPPER CHUCK
BLOWER
TABLE
HOLD DOWN
TABLE INSERT
OILER
4-STEP CONE PULLEY

Fig. 13-22. Parts of the jig saw.

A good size for general work is .020 thick and .110 wide with 15 teeth per inch. For soft wood use a blade with larger teeth (10 per inch suggested) and for hard woods a blade with finer teeth.

To install a blade in a jig saw, remove the table insert and turn the saw by hand until the lower chuck is at its highest point. Loosen the thumbscrew of the lower chuck and see that the jaws are clean. Insert the blade about 1/2 in. with

the TEETH POINTING DOWNWARD. Hold the blade straight up-and-down and tighten the thumb-screw. See Fig. 13-24. Replace the table insert.

Loosen the thumbscrew on the upper chuck. Pull the chuck down over the blade and tighten the thumbscrew as shown. Do not use pliers or wrenches to tighten thumbscrews. Position the tension·sleeve so it is about 3/4 in. above the upper chuck when the blade is moved to its highest point. Roll the saw over a few turns by hand to see if the blade is clear and runs up and down in a straight line.

Adjust the guide assembly so the blade runs freely on its sides, and the blade support roller just touches the back of the blade. Tighten the guide assembly as shown in Fig. 13-25.

Jig saws of different makes will vary in exact requirements for adjustments and lubrication. Check the operator's manual for specific information.

Safety Rules for the Jig Saw

(In addition to the general rules on page 10-30.)

1. Be certain the blade is properly installed in a vertical position with the teeth pointing down.
2. Roll the machine over by hand to see if there is clearance for the blade and if the tension sleeve has been properly set.

THICKNESS	WIDTH	NUMBER OF TEETH	
.008	.035	20	
.010	.045	18	
.020	.085	15	
.020	.110	7	
.020	.110	15	
.020	.110	10	
.028	.187	10	

Fig. 13-23. Blade sizes.

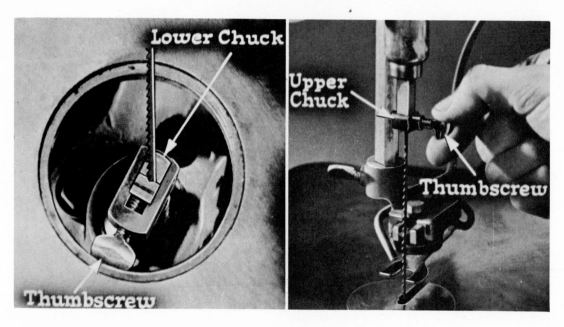

Fig. 13-24. *Left. Blade mounted in lower chuck. Right. Tightening blade in upper chuck.*
(Jam Handy Organization)

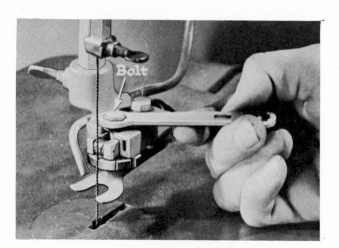

Fig. 13-25. *Adjusting the guide assembly.*
(Jam Handy Organization)

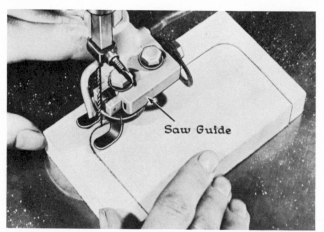

Fig. 13-26. *Making a simple cut.*
(Jam Handy Organization)

3. Check the belt guard to see that it is closed and tight.
4. Keep the holddown adjusted so the work will not be raised off the table.
5. When the saw is running, do not permit your fingers to get directly in line with the blade. Usually the work can be held on either side of the cutting line as shown in Fig. 13-26.

Cutting Procedures

Stock to be cut on the jig saw should be carefully prepared. Surfaces should be smooth and cutting lines laid out with a sharp pencil. Curves are usually cut as the last step in the fabrication sequence. For example, in Fig. 13-27, the ends

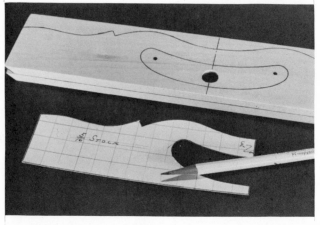

Fig. 13-27. *Work prepared for cutting on jig saw. Note that the mitered corners have already been cut.*

of a tray have been surfaced and squared to size and the miters for the corner joints have been cut and fitted.

Loosen the guide post and position the guide assembly so that the holddown springs will rest on the top of the work. The stock can be placed at the side of the blade to make this setting. Start the saw and feed the work forward into the blade. You will get the smoothest cut possible if you feed the work slowly. Keep the blade cutting just on the outside or waste side of the line. Give the blade plenty of time to cut its way clear as you go around corners.

Before cutting complicated designs, you should work out the "route" you will follow, as was suggested for operating the band saw. This will often eliminate the need to back out of long cuts, or make sharper turns than the blade permits. Note the procedure in Fig. 13-28, where the first cut was made all the way along the outline and then the details were cut. Drilling small holes in the waste stock at corners will often make the cutting easier.

Internal Cutting

When the work includes internal curves and designs, drill or bore holes in the waste area and thread the blade through these holes. To thread the blade, first remove it from the upper chuck and raise the holddown to its highest position. Roll the saw by hand so that the blade is at its lowest point and then thread the blade through the hole as shown in Fig. 13-29. Replace the blade in the upper chuck, adjust the holddown and make the cut. When there are many internal cuts to make, it is faster to use a saber sawing setup. A shorter blade is clamped in only the lower chuck as shown in Fig. 13-30. Since the blade will not be held taut by the upper chuck assembly, the blade must be heavy enough to resist the feed pressure.

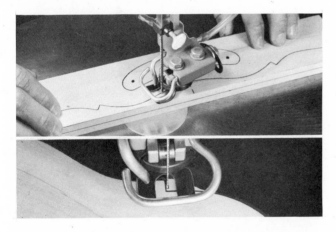

Fig. 13-28. Cutting procedure. Above. Cut along main outline and bypass details. Below. Cut details.

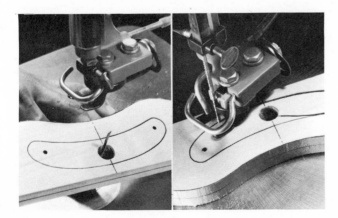

Fig. 13-29. Internal cutting. Left. Threading blade. Right. Making the cut.

Fig. 13-30. Blade setup for saber sawing. Note that the chuck has been turned 90 deg. and the blade fastened in the V jaws. (Rockwell Mfg. Co.)

WOODY SAYS:

"After changing blades or making any adjustments, always roll the jig saw several turns by hand to check the movement before turning on the motor."

Marquetry and Angle Sawing

Marquetry is a method of forming designs by sawing two or more kinds of wood that are fastened together in a pad and then interchanging the pieces as shown in Fig. 13-31. A very fine blade must be used. Designs usually include internal cuts and a very small drill should be used for the threading hole or, since the blade is fine, it may be satisfactory to cut through the outside

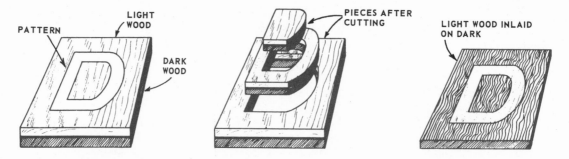

Fig. 13-31. Simple marquetry.

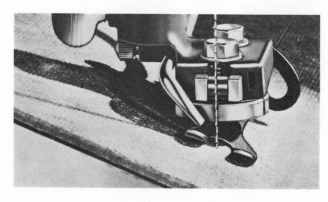

Fig. 13-32. Holddown spring adjusted for table tilt. (Rockwell Mfg. Co.)

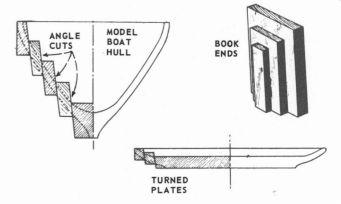

Fig. 13-33. Angle sawing ideas.

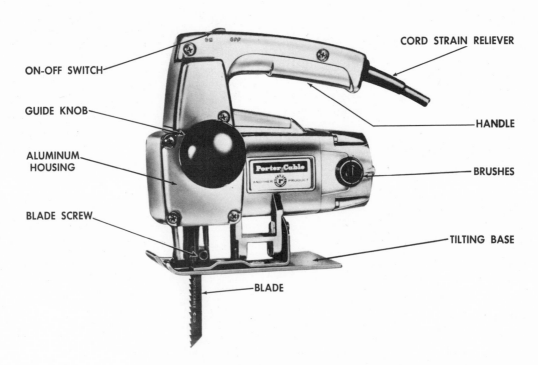

Fig. 13-34. Parts of a saber saw.

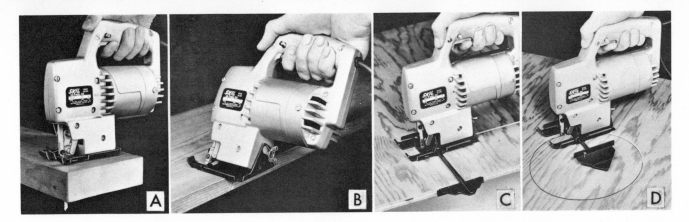

Fig. 13-35. Using a saber saw. A-Straight cutting. B-Angle cutting. C-Using a fence. D-Using a circle cutting guide.
(Skil Corp.)

areas to reach the internal cuts. Intricate inlay pictures, consisting of many kinds of veneer, can be made by this method.

Marquetry and inlay work is sometimes sawed with the table at a slight angle so when the pieces are assembled, the saw kerf will be closed, Fig. 13-32. When cutting at an angle the work must be kept on one side of the blade. The angle of tilt will vary with the width of the saw kerf.

Angle sawing can be applied to thick stock in such a way that the piece cut out will slip partially through the outside piece and fit tightly. It can be applied to such work as boat hulls, lamp bases, and other simple projects as shown in Fig. 13-33.

Saber Saws

Parts and Description

The saber saw, also called a bayonet saw, is a portable electric jig saw that can be used for a wide range of light work. It is used by carpenters, cabinetmakers, electricians and home craftsmen. A standard model and its basic parts are shown in Fig. 13-34. The stroke of the blade is about 1/2 in. and it operates at a speed of about 4000 strokes per minute.

Various blades are available for wood cutting with a range of 6 to 12 teeth per inch. For general purpose work a blade with 10 teeth per inch is satisfactory. Always select a blade that will have at least two teeth in contact with the edge being cut. Saws will vary in the way the blade is mounted in the chuck, so you should study the manufacturer's manual. Also follow the lubrication schedule as specified in this manual.

Safety Rules for Saber Saws

(In addition to those listed on page 10-30.)
1. Make certain the saw is properly grounded through the electrical cord.

2. Select the correct blade for your work and be sure it is properly mounted.
3. Disconnect the saw to change blades or make adjustments.
4. Place the base of the saw firmly on the stock before starting the cut.
5. Turn on the motor before the blade contacts the work.
6. Do not attempt to cut curves so sharp that the blade will be twisted. Follow procedures described for band saw operation.
7. Make certain the work is well supported and do not cut into sawhorses or other supports being used.

Using the Saber Saw

The saber saw can be used to make straight or bevel cuts as shown in Fig. 13-35. Curves are usually cut by guiding the saw along a layout line however, circular cuts may be made more accurately with a special guide or attachment.

The blade cuts on the up stroke so splintering will take place on the top side of the work. This must be considered when making finished cuts, especially in fine hardwood plywood. Always hold the base firmly against the surface of the material being cut.

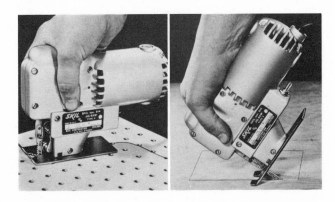

Fig. 13-36. Left. Cutting curves in thin material. Right. starting an internal cut.

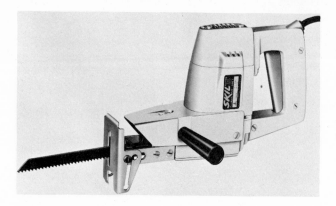

Fig. 13-37. Reciprocating saw.

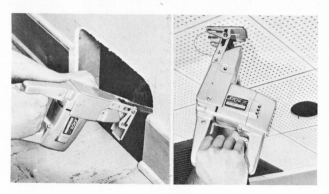

Fig. 13-38. Using the reciprocating saw. Left. Rough cut. Right. Finished cut.

Fig. 13-39. Sharpening a band mill blade that is 16 in. wide. The blade has teeth on both edges so the log can be cut on both the forward and return pass. (Weyerhaeuser Co.)

When cutting internal openings a starting hole can be drilled in the waste stock or the saw can be held on end so the blade will cut its own opening as shown in Fig. 13-36. This is called plunge cutting and must be undertaken with considerable care. Rest the toe of the base firmly on the work, turn on the motor, and then slowly lower the blade into the cut.

Another portable power tool is the reciprocating saw shown in Fig. 13-37. It is operated in about the same way as the saber saw. Fig. 13-38 shows several of the typical operations it will perform.

Industrial Machines

Band saws somewhat larger but otherwise similar to the ones you have operated in the school shop are used to form curved parts and

Fig. 13-40. Cutting tennis racket frames to finished thickness. The frame is mounted in a special carrier that moves across the table of a 42 in. band saw. (Wilson Sporting Goods Co.)

various other work in commercial cabinet shops, patternmaking shops, and furniture factories. See Fig. 13-40.

Fig. 13-41 shows the application of a 54 in. band saw in a resaw machine. The band saw wheels are 9 in. wide and carry a blade 27 ft.

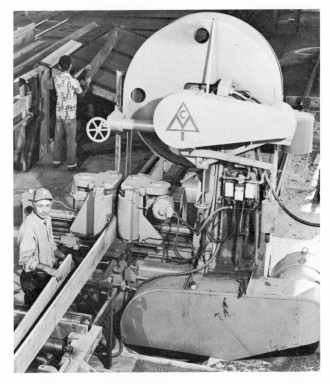

Fig. 13-41. Resawing lumber on a large vertical band resaw machine. A special generator places drag on the top wheel to add stiffness to the blade.
(Northeast Ohio Machine Builders Inc.)

long. Pneumatic power is used to control the rollers and guides which feed the work at variable speeds of 60 to 360 fpm. Power is furnished by a 75 hp motor. Stock from 1/2 in. to 24 in. in thickness may be handled.

Giant band saws are used to cut logs in lumber mills, Figs. 13-39 and 13-42. They are called band mills and include a carriage that moves the log through the cut. The carriage travels on steel tracks and is adjustable to various positions and rates of feed. These machines often use blades as wide as 16 in. and more than 60 ft. long.

Test Your Knowledge

1. The wheels of band saws are equipped with rubber tires to cushion the blade and prevent it from _____.
2. To specify a band saw blade you should list the gauge, length, style and spacing of teeth and the _____.

Fig. 13-42. A band saw with a blade 12 in. wide cuts a log over 6 ft. in diameter into lumber.
(Forest Products Laboratory)

3. If a 30 in. band saw requires a blade 17 ft. long, what is the distance between the centers of the wheels? Give your answer to the nearest inch.
4. What is the cutting speed (S.F.M.) of a 20 in. band saw if the wheels turn at a speed of 800 rpm? Give your answer to nearest 10 feet per minute.
5. A long band saw blade could be coiled into 3, _____ or _____ loops.
6. The upper guide assembly should be set about _____ in. above the work.
7. Multiple sawing is an operation where the work is first cut on one face and then turned 90 deg. and cut on the adjacent edge or face. True or False?
8. When adjusting the position of the tension sleeve of the jig saw, roll the saw so the blade will be at its lowest point. True or False?
9. The upper chuck is not used when performing saber sawing operations. True or False?
10. When several different kinds of wood are fastened together in a pad and the parts interchanged after cutting, the work is called _____.
11. To perform an angle sawing operation, the table of the jig saw is tilted. True or False?
12. The blade of the saber saw cuts on the _____ (up, down) stroke.

Outside Assignments

1. Calculate the cutting speed of the band saw in your shop. Also calculate the peripheral speed of the blade of the table saw. Compare

the two speeds. Convert them into miles per hour. Prepare a summary of your calculations and include the formulas used.

2. Prepare a list of five manufacturers that produce narrow band saws and jig saws. Include the company's full name and address.

3. If you had a choice of either adding a band saw or a jig saw to your home workshop

equipment, which would you select? Make a choice and then prepare a paper listing your reasons and considerations.

4. Develop design sketches for a circle cutting fixture that could be used on the band saw in your shop. Use an auxiliary table and make it adjustable for cutting circles from 6 in. to at least 12 in. in diameter.

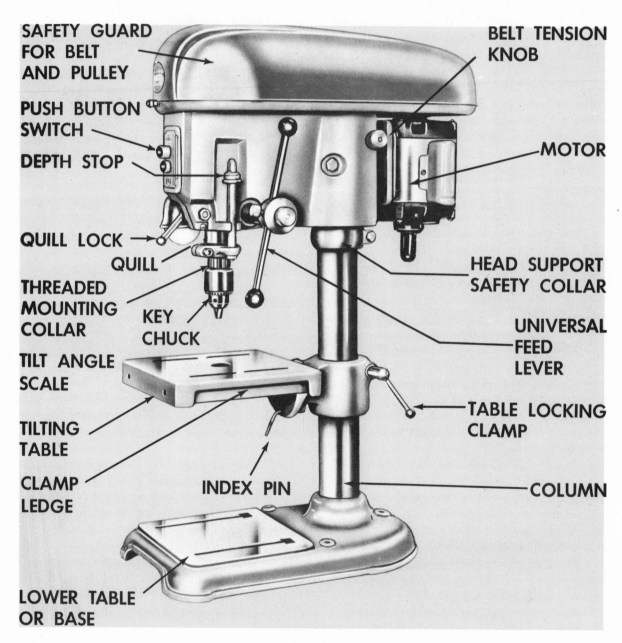

SAFETY GUARD FOR BELT AND PULLEY

PUSH BUTTON SWITCH

DEPTH STOP

QUILL LOCK

QUILL

THREADED MOUNTING COLLAR

KEY CHUCK

TILT ANGLE SCALE

TILTING TABLE

CLAMP LEDGE

INDEX PIN

LOWER TABLE OR BASE

BELT TENSION KNOB

MOTOR

HEAD SUPPORT SAFETY COLLAR

UNIVERSAL FEED LEVER

TABLE LOCKING CLAMP

COLUMN

Fig. 14-1. Parts of a drill press.
(Rockwell Mfg. Co.)

13-16

Unit 14
DRILL PRESS, MORTISER, AND TENONER

In wood fabrication, producing round holes and square and oblong mortises plays an important part. The drill press and mortiser are power machines used to produce them. Large school shops will usually have both a drill press and mortiser while smaller shops may have only a drill press and use an attachment for mortising operations. The tenoner is not a drilling or boring machine but since industry uses it to cut tenons that fit into mortises, it is included in this section.

Drill Press

Sizes, Parts and Adjustments

The drill press is such a versatile machine it is widely used in smaller woodworking shops, school shops, and home workshops. In addition to

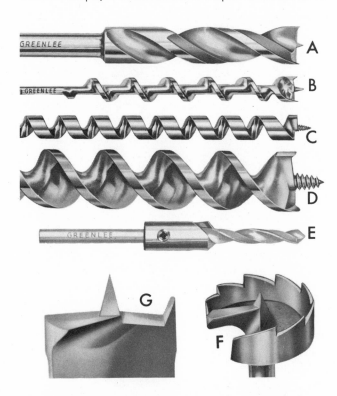

Fig. 14-2. Machine bits. A-Spur machine bit. B-Solid center bit. C-Single twist bit for portable drill. D-Double twist bit for portable drill. E-Adjustable countersink on drill. F-Multi-spur bit. G-Machine center bit.

regular drilling and boring operations, it can be equipped with attachments for mortising, routing, shaping and sanding. The drill press is available in either floor or bench models. Some have heads that adjust in or out from the support column and tilt at various angles. In production work, several drilling heads may be mounted on a single table.

Fig. 14-1 shows a bench model drill press. Its main parts consist of a base, column, table and head. The table is adjustable up and down on the column and can be tilted. The chuck is carried by a spindle that revolves inside a sleeve called a quill. The quill assembly can be moved up and down by a feed lever, and is spring loaded so it will return to its uppermost position. The length of the stroke is adjustable.

Drill press sizes are given as twice the distance from the column to the center of the spindle. Sizes range from 14 in. to 20 in. with a 15 in. size often used in the school shop. Spindle speeds are usually varied by shifting a belt on step pulleys however, variable speed drives are also available. For wood drilling and boring operations, speeds should range from 400 to about 1800 rpm.

Wood Boring Bits

Fig. 14-2 shows some common boring bits. You will recognize several that look like regular auger bits used in the brace. Power bits seldom have a feed screw because the feed is controlled by the machine. Those with feed screws are mainly designed for use in portable drills. Most power bits have a brad point, Fig. 14-3, that centers the bit in the work. The spur machine bit is the type most often used in the drill press. It is available in sizes from 1/4 in. to over 1 in. by thirty-seconds. Holes under 1/4 in. are drilled with a straight shank twist drill which is ground to a somewhat sharper point than those used for metalwork. An included angle of about 80 deg. is recommended.

Power bits must be kept clean and sharp to do good work. They should be carefully handled and stored, and wiped off occasionally with a cloth saturated with light oil. Power bits are sharpened with a file in about the same manner as described for regular auger bits in Unit 4, with the exception that cutters are usually filed on the bottom side. When sharpening bits always try to maintain the original angle and shape.

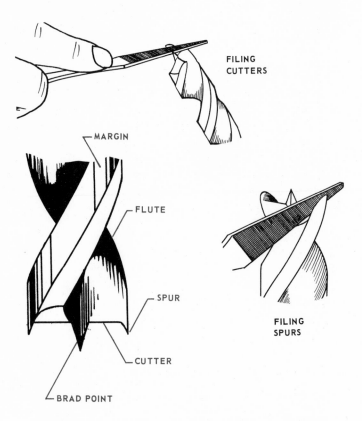

Fig. 14-3. Parts of a machine bit and sharpening operations.

Safety Rules for the Drill Press

(In addition to those listed on page 10-30.)

1. Check the speed setting to see that it is correct for your work. Holes over 1/2 in. should be bored at the lowest speed.
2. Use only an approved type of bit. Bits with feed screws or those that have excessive length should not be used.
3. Mount the bit securely to the full depth of the chuck and in the center. Remove the key immediately.
4. Position the table and adjust the feed stroke so there is no possibility of the bit striking the table.
5. The work should be placed on a wood pad when the holes will go all the way through.
6. Work that will be held by hand should be center punched.
7. Small or irregular shaped pieces must be clamped to the table or held in some special fixture.

8. Feed the bit smoothly into the work. When the hole is deep, withdraw it frequently to clear the shavings and cool the bit.
9. When using some special clamping setup, or a hole saw or fly cutter, have your instructor inspect it before turning on the power.
10. Always have your instructor check setups for routing and shaping.

Basic Procedures

The speed setting will vary with the kind of wood and the size and type of bit. Bits over 1/2 in. in diameter should be used at low speeds (400 to 800 rpm) especially when boring hard wood. If large bits are driven at high speeds they will heat and may be damaged.

Handle bits carefully. When inserting a bit in the chuck it is good practice to place a piece of wood on the table to protect the cutting edges and points if it should slip out of your hand or the chuck. See Fig. 14-4. Adjust the height of the table to provide about 1/2 in. of clearance above the work.

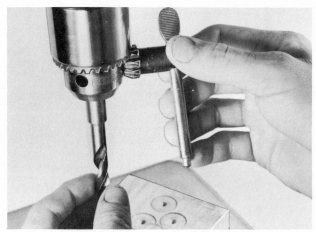

Fig. 14-4. Mount the bit to the full depth of the chuck. Always remove the key.

When boring only a few holes, each one should be laid out and the center punched. The part can then be held and guided by hand. If the hole goes all the way through, support it on a flat piece of scrap stock as shown in Fig. 14-5. This will not only protect the table but will also support the edges of the hole on the bottom side and prevent splintering.

Hold the stock firmly with one hand, turn on the motor and bring the bit down close to the surface with the feed lever. Align the point of the bit with the punched hole and then feed the bit into the work with a smooth, even pressure. When the

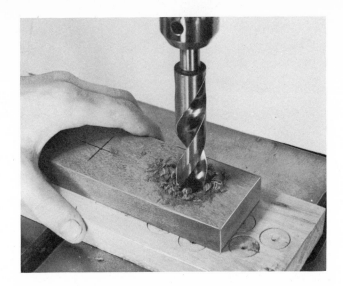

Fig. 14-5. Boring a 3/4 in. hole.

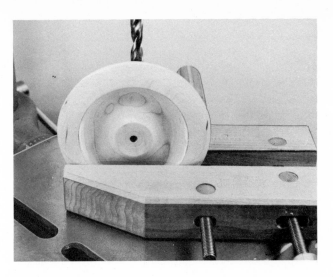

Fig. 14-7. Boring round stock clamped in a hand screw.

hole is through, raise the bit, clear away the cutting and place the work in position for the next hole, or if your work is complete, stop the machine, remove the bit and clear the table.

To bore a hole to a specified depth, use the depth stop. To make this setting, lower the bit along the edge of the work to the required depth, lock the quill in this position and then set the stop. Unlock the quill and bore the hole. It is good practice to use the stop even though the hole goes through, as it will control the depth of the bit in the wood pad and insure against it striking the table.

Stock that is round or has irregular shapes must be clamped to the table or held in special supports. See Figs. 14-6, and 14-7. In Fig. 14-6, the V-block is centered with the bit and then clamped in position to insure a hole through the center of the dowel. Metal vises are available that will rest on the table and hold irregular shaped pieces.

When drilling holes in the end or edges of stock it is often best to turn the table to a vertical position. The work can be supported on the lower table

and held in position by the regular table, or it can be clamped to the regular table as shown in Fig. 14-8. A straightedge can be clamped in a vertical position to serve as a fence. Holes through lamp stems or similar parts should be drilled in from each end. When drilling deep holes, raise the bit out of the work frequently to clear the cuttings and allow it to cool.

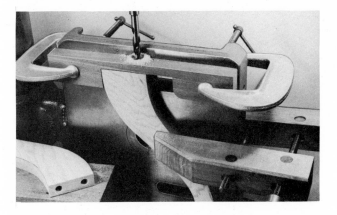

Fig. 14-8. Boring dowel holes in irregular shaped parts. Table is turned to a vertical position.

Boring Holes at an Angle

To tilt the table, loosen the nut and pull the pin located underneath. Use a sliding T-bevel to position the table at the required angle, Fig. 14-9. The miter gauge of the table saw can also be used. When the table is in the required position, tighten the nut.

The work should be clamped to the table or held against stops as shown in Fig. 14-10. The bit will not feed easily into a slanted surface and may tend to tear the wood. For best results, clamp scrap stock over the position of the hole and bore through it, and on into the work.

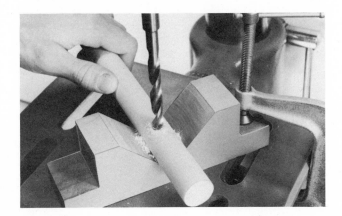

Fig. 14-6. Using a V-block to bore round stock.

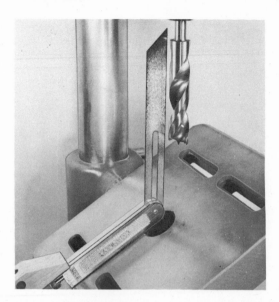

Fig. 14-9. Using a sliding T-bevel to set the table at an angle.

Fig. 14-11. Hole saw.

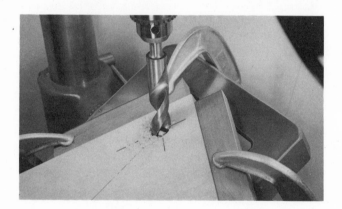

Fig. 14-10. Boring a hole at an angle.

Fig. 14-12. Cutting 1/8 in. hardboard with a hole saw.

When you have completed your angle boring, level the table, replace the index pin and tighten the nut.

Cutting Large Holes

Large holes in thin stock can be cut easily and quickly with a hole saw like the one shown in Fig. 14-11. Various size blade segments fit into grooves in the head and are held in place with a setscrew. The center drill must be set deep enough to be thoroughly imbedded in the work before the saw comes in contact with the surface. Fig. 14-12 shows the hole saw in operation. Use the lowest speed (about 400 rpm).

A fly cutter, Fig. 14-13, is sometimes used to cut a large hole. The cutter is mounted on a beam that is adjustable through the center hub. As with the hole saw, the center drill must be well imbedded in the stock before the cutter comes in contact with the surface. This tool is

Fig. 14-13. Cutting a large hole with the fly cutter. Always clamp the work securely to the table.

somewhat hazardous to use so take extra precautions. Always clamp the work securely to the table and operate the machine at its lowest speed. Have your instructor check the setup before turning on the power.

Boring Duplicate Parts

When a number of equal size pieces require the same boring operation, you will save time and produce more accurate work by building a fixture or making a special setup. A simple arrangement consists of an auxiliary table with a stationary fence. By clamping it in the correct position, a series of holes can be bored along a straight line. Stops can be set along the fence to locate the exact position of the hole as shown in Fig. 14-14. Instead of a stop, a previously bored hole can be used to space the next one. See Fig. 14-15.

Pins and stops of various sizes and shapes can be attached to the auxiliary table to position the work. See Fig. 14-16. Small parts may require some kind of a clamping device to hold them during the boring operation, Fig. 14-17. Fig. 14-18 shows a fixture that was used to bore holes at an angle in lamp bases for a mass production project. After the first hole was bored, it was aligned with the index point to position the second hole, and the second hole was then used to align the third.

Mortising Attachment

The mortising attachment for the drill press uses about the same kind of hollow chisel and bit as a regular mortising machine, Fig. 14-19. The length of the bit is usually shorter. The bit fits inside the hollow chisel and cuts a round hole while the square hollow chisel cuts out the corners as the assembly is forced through the

Fig. 14-16. A simple fixture being used to locate holes at the corners of a square piece.

Fig. 14-14. Boring duplicate parts. Above. Part held against the fence and a stop. Below. Spacer block used to locate second hole.

Fig. 14-17. Clamping device to hold small parts during a boring operation.

Fig. 14-15. Fixture for boring equally spaced holes. Taper the lower end of the dowel pin slightly so it can be easily slipped into the previously bored hole.

Fig. 14-18. Fixture for boring holes at an angle in a circular part.

Fig. 14-19. Hollow chisel and hollow chisel bit. (Greenlee Tool Co.)

wood. Hollow chisels and matching bits for drill press attachments are available in sizes from 1/4 in. to 3/4 in. by sixteenths.

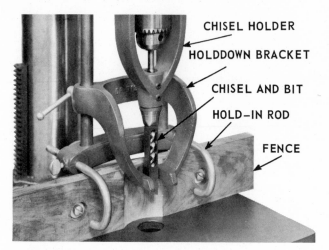

CHISEL HOLDER
HOLDDOWN BRACKET
CHISEL AND BIT
HOLD-IN ROD
FENCE

Fig. 14-20. Mortising attachment mounted on the drill press. (Rockwell Mfg. Co.)

Fig. 14-20 shows a standard attachment installed. To make the installation use the following procedure:

1. Remove the depth stop bracket from the quill and mount the chisel holder. Attach the depth stop.
2. Attach the fence and hold-down bracket to the table. It is best to include an auxiliary wood table larger than the drill press table.
3. Mount the hollow chisel into the holder as far as it will go.
4. Thread the matching bit into the chisel and tighten it in the chuck with the spurs of the bit extending 1/16 in. below the points of the chisel.
5. Have your instructor check the settings and clearances and then make trial cuts.

Cutting a Mortise

Adjust the fence to the correct position from the chisel and also align the sides of the chisel so they are parallel to the fence. See Fig. 14-21. Set the depth stop to the required setting. Adjust the hold-down so it will just touch the top of the

work without scarring or denting the surface. Stops can be clamped to the fence to control the position of the mortise. Check the settings by making a trial cut in extra stock of a size equal to that of the work.

Fig. 14-21. Set the chisel so the front face is parallel with the fence.

Align the chisel at one end of the mortise and make the cut, then move the work and make the cut at the other end as shown in Fig. 14-22. Stops can be used at either end of the table or fence to

Fig. 14-22. Cutting a mortise.

position these cuts. Now make cuts along the mortise according to the pattern shown in Fig. 14-23. Alternating strokes will equalize the side pressure on the bit; cutting four sides on the first pass and two on the second. This procedure is especially important when using chisels 1/2 in. and smaller since unequal pressure will cause the chisel to bend and rub on the rotating bit.

When mortises meet at a corner, like the one shown, it is best to cut the first mortise just deep enough to meet the line of the second mortise and then cut the second mortise to the full depth. This will prevent the internal corner from splitting off.

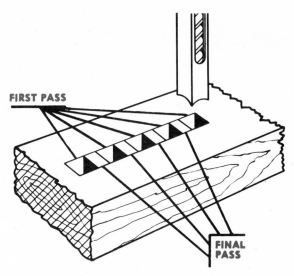

Fig. 14-23. Sequence of cuts for making a mortise. (Greenlee Tool Co.)

Sanding, Routing and Shaping

Fig. 14-24 shows an arrangement for drum sanding on the drill press. An auxiliary table with an open throat is used to support the work. As a section of the sanding drum becomes worn it can be raised or lowered to a new position.

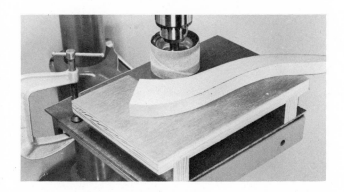

Fig. 14-24. Using an auxiliary table for a sanding operation.

Fig. 14-25. A routing operation on the drill press. (Rockwell Mfg. Co.)

If the drill press is equipped so that speeds of at least 3000 rpm can be secured, a satisfactory job of routing can be performed with it. The router bit must be mounted in a special adapter. Never attempt to mount and use a router bit in a regular key chuck. A fence or other type of guide should be used to control the work. Study and follow the directions for standard router operation. When the fence is behind the bit, the feed should be from left to right as shown in Fig. 14-25.

Light shaping operations can also be performed on the drill press. See Fig. 14-26. A fence

Fig. 14-26. Using a shaping attachment. (Rockwell Mfg. Co.)

and auxiliary table are needed, and a special adapter must be used to hold the shaper cutter. High speeds are essential for good work. Follow procedures described in the section on the shaper.

 **WOODY SAYS:**

"Routing and shaping setups on the drill press can be hazardous. Always have your instructor inspect and approve them before you turn on the power."

Portable Electric Drill

The portable electric drill is manufactured in a wide range of types and sizes. The general size is determined by the chuck capacity. Sizes of 1/4 in. to as large as 1 1/4 in. are available; however, 1/4, 3/8 and 1/2 in. are the most common. For general work in the school shop a

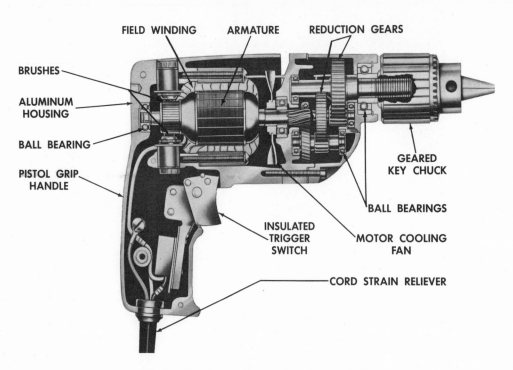

Fig. 14-27. Parts of a portable electric drill.
(Rockwell Mfg. Co.)

1/4 in. size is generally adequate. The speed is fixed for each drill, with small sizes running at high speeds and large drills at lower speeds. Drills of 1/4 in. capacity usually operate at speeds of 1000-2000 rpm. Fig. 14-27 shows the parts and gearing of a standard model. Fig. 14-28 illustrates a power bit set for a portable drill.

2. Stock to be drilled must be held in a stationary position so it cannot be moved during the operation.
3. Connect the drill to a properly grounded outlet.
4. Turn on the switch for a moment to see if the bit is properly centered and running true.
5. With the switch off, place the point of the bit in the punched layout hole.

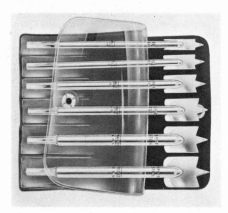

Fig. 14-28. Power bit set for a portable drill. 3/8-1 in.
(Stanley Tools)

Safety Rules and Directions

1. Select the correct drill or bit for your work and mount it securely to the full depth of the chuck.

Fig. 14-29. Using a portable electric drill.
(Stanley Tools)

6. Hold the drill firmly in one or both hands and at the correct drilling angle.

7. Turn on the switch and feed the drill into the work. The pressure required will vary with the size of the drill and the kind of wood. See Fig. 14-29.

8. During the operation, keep the drill aligned with the direction of the hole.

9. When drilling deep holes, especially with a twist drill, withdraw the drill several times to clear the cuttings.

10. Follow the same precautions and procedures as when drilling holes with a hand drill or the drill press.

11. Always remove the bit from the drill as soon as you have completed your work.

WOODY SAYS:

"Never operate a portable electric tool while standing on wet ground or any wet surface."

Cordless portable drills are handy to use for many jobs and eliminate the hazard of electrical shock. They are used for general maintenance work and are sometimes used on production work where electrical cords would interfere with the operation. Power is supplied by a small nickel-cadmium battery that can be recharged. A standard 1/4 in. model will drill over 200 - 1/4 in. holes through 3/4 in. stock before recharging is required. Fig. 14-30 shows a cordless drill and the charger unit.

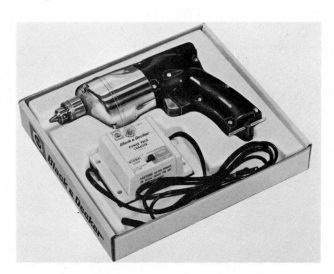

Fig. 14-30. Cordless drill and charger.

Fig. 14-31. Using a cordless drill to install cabinet hardware. (Black and Decker Mfg. Co.)

Using a portable drill is shown in Fig. 14-31. Many attachments are available for use with a portable drill. Most of them are satisfactory for light work. Fig. 14-32 shows a saber saw attachment mounted on a 1/4 in. drill.

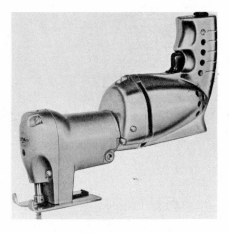

Fig. 14-32. Saber saw attachment for a portable drill. (Millers Falls Co.)

Industrial Boring Machines

Large industries use multiple spindle or gang boring machines. Some machines use horizontal spindles but most of them have vertical spindles as shown in the boring machine designed especially for chair seats, Fig. 14-33. Hydraulic or pneumatic power is used to lower the spindle assembly into the work or lift the table and work into fixed drilling heads. Machines can be set up with each individual stroke controlled by the operator or for automatic cycling at various rates.

Some gang borers have a main horizontal shaft that drives each spindle through a gear mechanism and universal joints. Others, like the seat boring machine, use flexible shafts. The spindles can be adjusted to various positions and angles. Air clamps are used to hold the work on the table.

Fig. 14-34. Boring machine with individual air motors that can be adjusted to various positions or angles. Air cylinders feed the units into the work. Operates with 75 psi air pressure. (Nash – Bell – Challoner)

Fig. 14-33. Chair seat and back boring machine. 15 spindles are equipped with needle bearings and driven by motors through flexible shafts. Strokes are hydraulically activated at a rate of 12 per minute.
(Nash – Bell – Challoner)

Fig. 14-34 shows a boring machine that can be set up for a great variety of work. Each boring head is self-contained and adjustable. The spindles are driven by air motors and can be placed in a vertical or horizontal position, or even located under the table. The model shown is also equipped with a trim saw unit. Figs. 14-35 and 14-36 show production boring machines in operation.

Mortisers

The hollow chisel mortiser, Figs. 14-37, and 38, is a type of mortiser widely used today because it is compact, adaptable to light work, and can be utilized in multiple head assemblies. Fig. 14-37 shows a standard model that is equipped with a power feed stroke mechanism.

Fig. 14-35. Gang borer in operation. The spindle carriage moves up and down over the stationary table. Stroke can be adjusted from 1 to 12 in. spindle speed is 1950 rpm. (Greenlee Bros. and Co.)

The mortiser table can be raised or lowered and tilted to various angles. It is moved horizontally by a rack and pinion attached to a handwheel. This movement can be adjusted with stops to provide a mortise of a specified length. The motor head is lowered into the work, either by foot power or a separate motor. When fitted with regular bits, the mortiser can be used for standard boring operations.

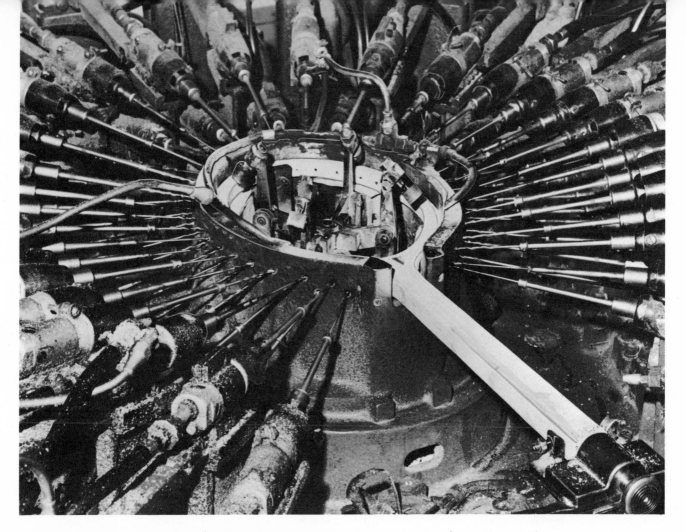

Fig. 14-36. A specialized machine used to bore 64 holes in a tennis racket frame at a single stroke. Individual air motors are used to drive each bit. (Wilson Sporting Goods Co.)

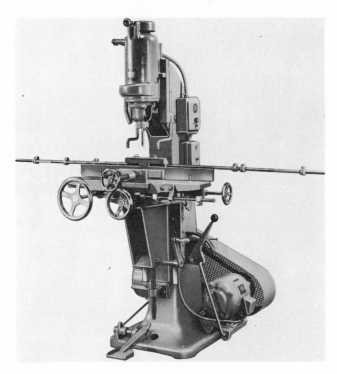

Fig. 14-37. Hollow chisel mortiser. The head motor size is 5 hp and the feed motor used to stroke the head up and down is 1 hp. (Oliver Mach. Co.)

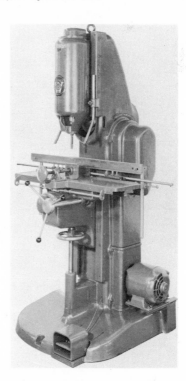

Fig. 14-38. Hollow chisel mortiser with adjustable powered stroke from 2 - 4 in. Strokes can be varied from 15 to 45 per minute. (Whitney and Sons)

14-11

The mortiser uses the same type of hollow chisels and bits as were described in the section on the drill press. Fig. 14-39 shows how a chisel and bit are mounted. The chisel bushing is set with a 1/32 in. spacer until the bit is mounted. After the bit setscrew is tightened, the spacer is removed and the chisel bushing is moved up and set to provide the required clearance.

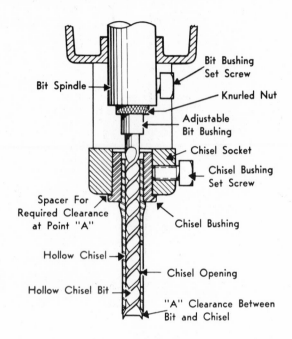

Fig. 14-39. Hollow chisel and bit. Parts and mounting.
(Greenlee Bros. and Co.)

The regular mortiser is easier to use and more accurate than the drill press attachment. The table can be set up so that duplicate parts are clamped in place and the mortise cut by stroking the machine and turning the handwheel which moves the table to various cutting positions between the stops.

A multiple head mortiser is shown in Fig. 14-40. As many as eleven heads can be attached to the beam. Pneumatic power is used to raise the table and work into the chisels. Each hollow chisel head is powered with a 1 1/2 hp motor.

Tenoners

Tenoners are production woodworking machines that are used to cut plain tenons or tenons with shaped shoulders like those found in panel doors or window sash. Besides these basic operations, they can be set up to cut various corner joints for cabinets, cases, and chests. With a dado attachment, grooves and dados can be cut in various locations in the surface of the work. Tenoners may be either single-end or double-end.

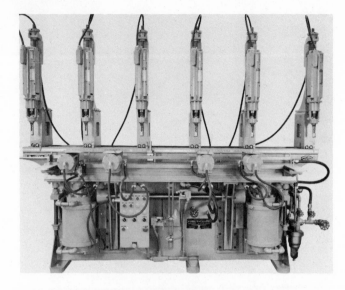

Fig. 14-40. A multiple head mortiser. Two 10 in. air cylinders raise the table up and down at rates from 0 to 30 strokes per minute. The length of the stroke can be varied up to a maximum of 8 in. Air cylinders clamp the work in position. (Nash — Bell — Challoner)

Single-End Tenoners

The standard design of a single-end tenoner consists of two tenoning heads, two coping heads, a cut-off saw and a movable table, Fig. 14-41.

Fig. 14-41. Single-end tenoner.
(Oliver Mach. Co.)

In operation, the stock is clamped or held to the table and moved forward through the tenoning heads which make the cheek and shoulder cuts. It then passes by the coping heads which are mounted on vertical arbors and form contours on the shoulders if it is necessary for them to fit over molded edges. Finally the stock moves by the cut-off saw where the tenon is cut to length.

The cutting heads are powered by individual motors and can be adjusted to various vertical and horizontal positions. The coping heads may be tilted to secure angle cuts. Work can be moved through the machine at an angle by adjusting the table fence.

Double-End Tenoner

The double-end tenoner, as the name indicates, consists of two cutter assemblies. They are both mounted on a heavy base and one can be moved

Fig. 14-43. Modern double-end tenoner. Assembly in foreground can be moved to various positions on the base to adjust for different widths of work. View shows infeed end. Adjustments are powered. (Kohler – Joa Corp.)

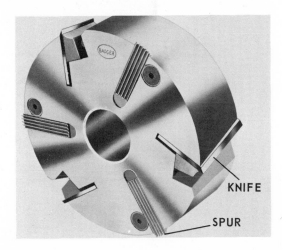

Fig. 14-42. Standard tenon head. Knives are set at an angle to make a smooth shearing cut. Spur cuts through cross-grain fibers. (Wisconsin Knife Works)

along the base to provide settings for various lengths or widths of work. Two feed chains carry the work through the machine at speeds of from 15 to 60 fpm. A pressure beam, with a rubber padded chain, rides on top of the work and holds it down on the feed chain. See Figs. 14-42 and 43.

In Fig. 14-44, the pressure beam has been swung away from the cutting heads to show their arrangement. In this particular machine, the work first moves by the cut-off saw and then scoring saws, before it reaches the tenoning and coping heads. The scoring saws rotate so they will cut

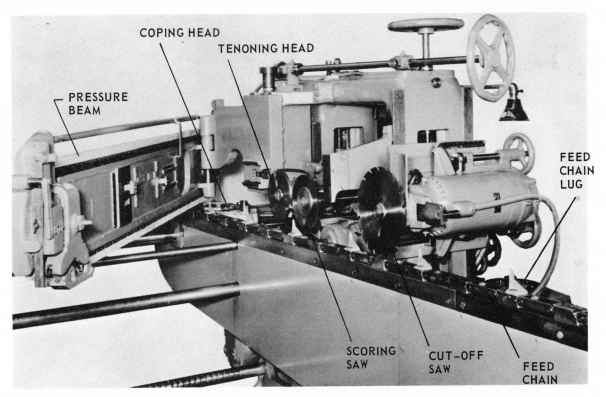

Fig. 14-44. Cutting units on one side of a standard double-end tenoner. Pressure beam is swung out to show assembly. (Greenlee Bros. and Co.)

14-13

Fig. 14-45. Double-end tenoner in operation.
(Greenlee Bros. and Co.)

into the surface (climb sawing) and thus have no tendency to splinter the work. Fig. 14-45 shows a double-end tenoner in operation.

The drawing and close-up view in Fig. 14-46, shows how the bottom check rail of a window sash is cut with the coping heads. The milled-to-pat-

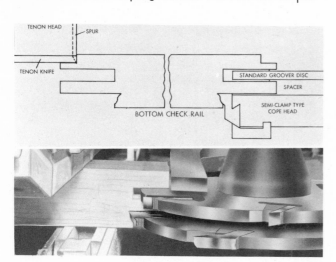

Fig. 14-46. Above. How the tenon head and coping head form the joint for a window sash rail. Below. Close-up view of coping head making the cut. (Wisconsin Knife Works)

tern cutters are clamped into the coping head in about the same manner as the dado head shown in Fig. 14-47.

The versatility of cutter head design is coupled with the double-end tenoner to form the lock-miter joint shown in Fig. 14-48. This joint is used to make all kinds of case goods; cedar chests, chests of drawers, boxes and other items that require tight, strong corners. It requires pre-

Fig. 14-47. Dado head used on a double-end tenoner.
(Wisconsin Knife Works)

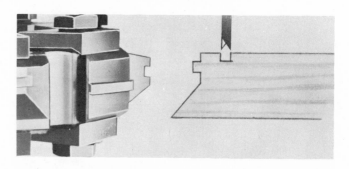

Fig. 14-48. Coping head equipped with special milled-to-pattern cutters form miter lock joints.
(Wisconsin Knife Works)

cision machining with tolerances held to close limits and is a good example of one of the many kinds of work the machine can perform.

Setting up and maintaining the double-end tenoner for work of this nature requires a craftsman who knows the characteristics of different woods and how joints are designed and proportioned. He must also be an expert in the care and operation of woodworking machines. Its a highly satisfying experience to see fine, precision work moving off of a machine like this and knowing that you were responsible for the setup. How would you like such a job?

Test Your Knowledge

1. The spindle of the drill press revolves inside a sleeve that is called a _____ .
2. A 15 in. drill press will have measurement of _____ in. from the center of the spindle to the column.
3. The spur machine bit has a _____ _____ instead of a feed screw.
4. Stock that will have holes bored through its thickness should be placed on a _____ _____ during the operation.
5. Stock that will be held by hand does not need to be center punched. True or False?
6. Work may be supported on the lower table of a bench drill and held in position by the regular table. True or False?
7. Large holes in thin stock can be cut with a fly cutter or_____ _____ .
8. When installing a mortising chisel and bit on the drill press, the hollow chisel is first mounted in the key chuck. True or False?
9. The depth stop on the drill press is not used when cutting a mortise. True or False?
10. By setting stops on the table or fence, the position and _____ of the mortise can be controlled.
11. When using the portable drill the bit should be set in the punched hole before the motor is turned on. True or False?
12. Industrial boring machines use either hydraulic or _____ power to feed the boring tools into the work.
13. The hollow chisel mortiser can be used for regular boring operations. True or False?
14. As work is moved through the single-end tenoner, it is first cut by the tenoning heads and then by the _____ _____ .

Outside Assignments

1. Prepare a selected list of drill press attachments that would be practical for the home workshop. Include a complete description and estimated cost of each one.
2. Visit the local office of your electric light and power company and secure information concerning the need and method of grounding power machines and portable electric tools. Prepare a paper summarizing the information or make an oral report to the class.
3. Select or design a project such as a cribbage board that requires many holes. Prepare design sketches of a fixture that could be mounted on the drill press to drill or bore the holes with precision and speed.

Chucking and boring machine set up for chair legs for boring rung holes, trimming bottom end and forming tenon on top end. Latter operation is called chucking (see page 5-9). (Goodspeed Machine Co.)

Special cutterhead mounted on a double-end tenoner and used to form finger-joints on the ends of short pieces of stock. The pieces are then glued together to produce useable lengths. (Wisconsin Knife Works)

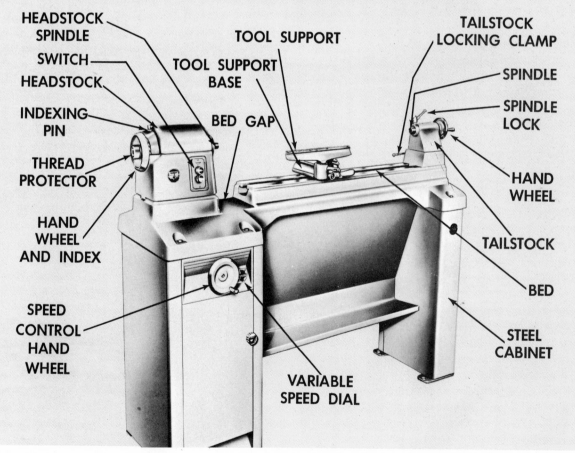

HEADSTOCK SPINDLE

SWITCH

HEADSTOCK

INDEXING PIN

THREAD PROTECTOR

HAND WHEEL AND INDEX

SPEED CONTROL HAND WHEEL

TOOL SUPPORT

TOOL SUPPORT BASE

BED GAP

VARIABLE SPEED DIAL

TAILSTOCK LOCKING CLAMP

SPINDLE

SPINDLE LOCK

HAND WHEEL

TAILSTOCK

BED

STEEL CABINET

Fig. 15-1. Above. A 12 in. wood turning lathe. (Oliver Machinery Co.) Fig. 15-2. Below. Major parts of the lathe. (Rockwell Mfg. Co.)

14-16

Unit 15
LATHE

The operating principle of the lathe is different than that of other power woodworking machines. In standard wood lathe operation the wood is mounted in the machine and rotated while the cutting edge is held stationary and controlled by the worker. It requires considerable skill to hold the cutting tool in the correct position and also control the feed and direction of the cut.

The standard hand turning wood lathe, Fig. 15-1, may have a variable speed motor or a belt drive that provides speeds ranging from about 600 to 3600 rpm. The size of the lathe is called the SWING and is determined by the largest diameter of work that can be turned or twice the distance from the bed to the center of the spindle. Several sizes of lathes are available, however, a 12 in. swing is the most commonly used. More complete specifications for the lathe would also include the length of the bed and the horsepower of the motor. Standard lathe beds are usually 36, 48 or 60 in. in length.

Parts of Lathe

The basic parts of the lathe are shown in Fig. 15-2. It is advisable to study and learn the name of the lathe parts so you will be able to clearly understand the operating directions that follow.

The HEADSTOCK is rigidly fixed to the left end of the lathe bed and carries a spindle that is threaded on both ends. The threads on the inside end are right-hand and those on the outside end are left-hand. They are used to attach the faceplates on which stock is mounted when turning projects such as disks and bowls. The spindle is hollow with the inside end tapered internally to carry the shank of the spur or live center.

The hollow spindle permits the use of a KNOCKOUT BAR to remove the spur center or other taper shank tools.

The TAILSTOCK is movable and can be locked in any position along the bed. It also has a spindle that is hollow and holds the cup center, (also

called a dead center). This spindle can be moved in and out of the tailstock by turning the handwheel. The cup center is removed by turning the handwheel counterclockwise until the spindle is completely retracted (withdrawn) into the tailstock.

The TOOL REST (also called a tool support) clamps to the bed and can be adjusted up and down, at any position along the bed, Fig. 15-3. Tool rests are available in several different lengths. The top edge must be straight and smooth so that the lathe tools can be easily moved. To remove nicks and true this edge use a mill file in about the same way as when sharpening a hand scraper.

Fig. 15-3. Tool rest — also called a tool support.
(Jam Handy)

Turning Tools

A set of turning tools (also called turning chisels) usually includes about six different shapes. Each shape or kind of tool is available in several sizes (widths), Fig. 15-4. The GOUGE, which is a round-nose, hollow tool is used for roughing out and making cove cuts. The SKEW is a double-ground, flat tool used to smooth cylinders and cut shoulders and beads. The PARTING TOOL is a double-ground tool used for cutting-off work and for making sizing cuts. The SPEAR POINT (also called a diamond point), ROUND NOSE and SQUARE NOSE are all single bevel tools used wherever their shape best fits the contour of the work.

Sharpening Lathe Tools

In wood turning it is important to keep your turning tools sharp. In sharpening, follow about the same procedures you used for sharpening plane blades and chisels. Gouges and round nose tools are difficult to sharpen so you should ask your instructor to help with these. Study the angles

Fig. 15-4. Wood turning tools. This set includes three sizes of gouges and skews. (Oliver Machinery Co.)

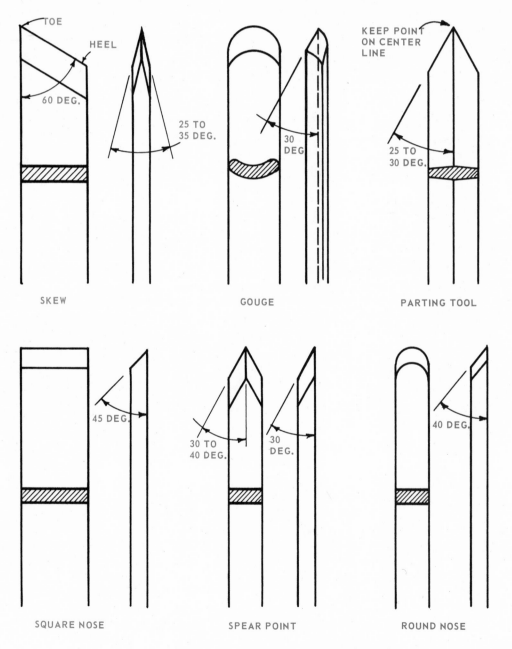

Fig. 15-5. Grinding angles for turning tools.

and bevels shown in Fig. 15-5, and try to maintain about the same shape when grinding your tools.

Most wood turners prefer to grind the skew with a flat bevel. To do this the grinding is done on the side of the abrasive wheel as shown in Fig. 15-6. If the wheel is true, each bevel can be ground to a perfect plane. Continue to grind until a fine wire edge appears and then hone on an oilstone. When honing the skew keep the ground bevel in contact with the surface of the stone.

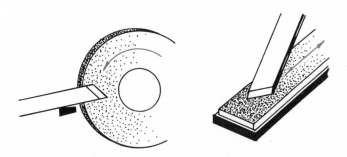

Fig. 15-6. Grinding and honing a skew.

The gouge should be ground on the side of the abrasive wheel with a rolling motion, Fig. 15-7. Be sure the bevel extends completely around to the sides. Remove the wire edge on the oilstone. Keep the bevel in contact with the stone, moving it back and forth and at the same time rolling it from side to side. Remove the wire edge from the inside surface with a slipstone as shown in Fig. 15-7.

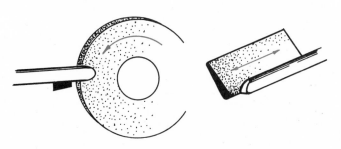

Fig. 15-7. Grinding and honing a gouge.

The parting tool and the square nose tool should be ground on the edge of the grinding wheel. This will form a slightly hollow-ground bevel that is desirable for these tools.

Using the side of the grinding wheel is considered good practice only when the cut is very light. It is more difficult to dress and reface the side than the edge. Heavy grinding and reshaping operations of any of the lathe tools should be done on the regular grinding edge.

Turning Speeds

You will need to develop good judgment and exercise great care in selecting the proper turning speeds. The most important factor is the diameter of the work. Consideration must also be given to the kind of wood and the type of cut. Check with your instructor if you have any doubt about the speed you have selected.

WOODY SAYS:

"Be sure to keep the tool from "burning" while it is being ground, by frequently dipping it in water. Lathe tools are made from steel that is heat treated and the temper may be damaged by excess heat."

Always rough out work at a low speed (600-1000 rpm). After the work is round and true you can increase the speed. Stock that is 6 in. in diameter and larger should be turned at speeds under 1000 rpm. Diameters of 4 in. should not exceed speeds of 1500 rpm. Speeds over 2000 rpm should be limited to work 2 in. and under in diameter.

It will be very hazardous for you to exceed these recommendations, especially when turning thin walled bowls and disks as they may break and fly apart because of centrifugal force (the force tending to make rotating bodies move away from the center of rotation).

Slower speeds are quite satisfactory and the tools will stay sharp longer. This is especially true if you are doing most of the work by the scraping method which wears away the tool edge rapidly. Sanding at high speeds causes the abrasive paper to heat and glaze and also results in excessive dust being thrown into the air.

High speed may be helpful when applying a French polish finish. Heat generated by the friction aids in setting up and hardening the finishing material.

Drawings for Turned Objects

Turned objects often have many curves, beads and coves that are hard to specify in a working drawing. Fig. 15-8, shows two methods commonly used. A half section has the advantage of showing both the inside and outside contour. Note the method of specifying diameters. In the second

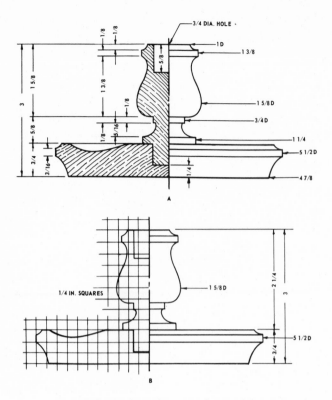

Fig. 15-8. Working drawings for wood turning.

drawing a grid (squares) has been drawn over the contour so that an accurate full-size template or pattern can be developed even though detailed dimensions are not included.

WOODY SAYS:

"Before starting to work on the lathe, you should study carefully the following rules and also review the general rules for power machine operation on page 10-30."

Safety Rules for the Lathe

1. Before starting the machine; be sure that spindle work has the cup center properly imbedded, tailstock and tool rest are securely clamped, and there is proper clearance for the rotating stock.
2. Before starting the machine for faceplate work, check to see that the faceplate is tight against the spindle shoulder and the tool support has proper clearance.
3. Wear goggles or a face shield to protect your eyes, especially when roughing out work.

4. Select turning speed carefully. Large diameters must be turned at the lowest speed. Always use the lowest speed to rough out work.
5. Wood with knots and splits should not be turned. Glued-up stock should cure at least 24 hours.
6. Keep the tool rest close to the work.
7. Remove the tool rest for sanding and polishing operations.
8. Use a scraping cut for all faceplate work.
9. Remove both the spur and cup centers when they are not in use.
10. When you stop the lathe to check your work also check and lubricate the cup center.
11. Keep the lathe tools sharp, hold them firmly and in the proper position.
12. Keep your sleeves rolled up and other loose clothing away from the moving parts of the lathe and work.

Spindle Turning

When the wood stock is mounted between the lathe centers, Fig. 15-9, the general operation is called spindle turning. This type of turning is used to produce table and chair legs, lamp stems, ball bats and other long round objects.

Fig. 15-9. Spur center and cup center.

Mounting Stock

Select stock that is sound and free of splits and knots. The stock should be approximately square. Square the ends, allowing an extra inch of length so the piece can be trimmed after the turning is complete.

Locate the center of each end by drawing diagonal lines across the corners. If you are using hard wood, drill a hole about the size of the pin in the spur center on one end. Also use a hand-saw or band saw to make saw kerfs about 1/8 in. deep, Fig. 15-10. The roughing out cuts will be easier to make if you plane off the corners of stock that is over 3 in. square.

Hold the stock vertically with the dead center end resting on the lathe bed or other solid support. Drive the spur center into the hole and saw kerfs so that it is embedded about 1/4 in.

Insert the spur center, with the work attached, into the spindle of the headstock. Slide the tailstock into position so that the point of the cup center contacts the center of the work. Lock the tailstock to the lathe bed and turn the handwheel so that it forces the cup center into the wood.

the chips are thrown to the right. Study Fig. 15-12. Make additional cuts until the stock is round. Stop the lathe and move the tool rest to a new position if the work is longer than the rest.

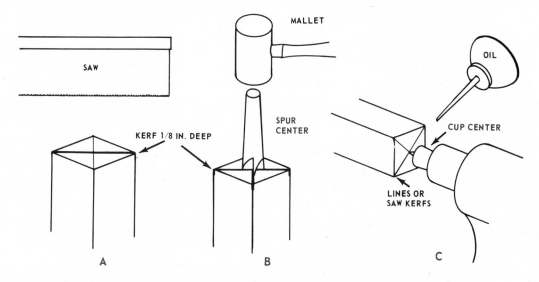

Fig. 15-10. Procedure for mounting stock between centers.

With the lathe set on the lowest speed, turn on the power for just a moment and force the cup center deeper into the work. A beginner should turn the lathe by hand instead of using the power. This will form a "bearing" in the wood, the depth of which should be about 1/8 in.

Back out the cup center and lubricate with oil or wax and move it back into position. Leave a slight clearance so that the lathe turns easily and then LOCK THE TAILSTOCK SPINDLE CLAMP. As you progress with the turning, check the cup center from time to time to be sure it has sufficient lubrication and is not overheating.

Turning a Cylinder

Adjust the tool rest so that it is about 1/8 in. above the centerline and clears the work by about 1/4 in. Rotate the lathe by hand to check this clearance. LOCK THE TOOL REST in this position.

Be sure the lathe is set at the lowest speed and then turn on the power. Select a large gouge and hold it firmly on the tool rest. First, make a series of individual cuts along the work as shown in Fig. 15-11. These cuts will prevent long splinters from developing when a full pass is made.

You are now ready to make a cut the full length of the stock or as long as the tool rest will permit. Move the tool from left to right, holding it well up on the work so the ground bevel rides on the cut being made. Also roll the gouge so that

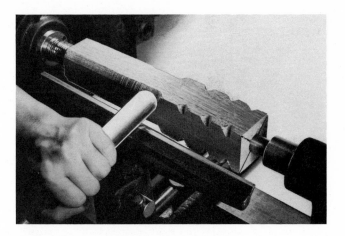

Fig. 15-11. First full roughing cut.

Fig. 15-12. Final roughing cut.

Fig. 15-13. Finishing a cylinder with the skew in a scraping position.

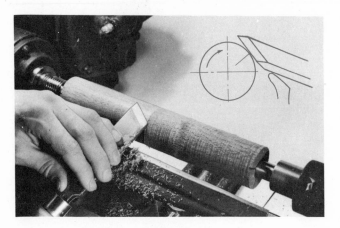

Fig. 15-14. Finishing a cylinder with the skew making a shearing cut.

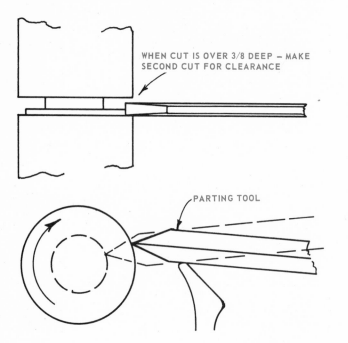

WHEN CUT IS OVER 3/8 DEEP — MAKE
SECOND CUT FOR CLEARANCE

PARTING TOOL

Fig. 15-15. Using the parting tool to make sizing cuts.

For a right-handed person, the right hand should grip the tool handle near the end. The left hand guides the tool along the rest and may be placed on top of the tool with the palm down or underneath with the palm up. Beginners usually like the "palm-down" position, especially for roughing out stock as it provides a more positive grasp on the tool.

The cylinder can now be finished with a skew. Adjust the tool rest parallel with the work. The amount the speed can be increased depends on the diameter of the work. The skew can be used either to make a shearing cut, or a scraping cut. The beginner may prefer to use the scraping cut as shown in Fig. 15-13, since it is easier and requires less practice. When making a scraping cut the tool is held in a level position with the tool edge contacting the work even or slightly above the horizontal center line. The tool rest will need to be slightly below the center line.

Experienced wood turners use the skew to make shearing cuts because of the speed and quality of work that can be produced. For this type of cut, place a large skew slightly above the work and about 2 in. from the driven end. Slowly pull the tool back until the cutting edge touches the cylinder half way between the heel and toe. Roll the tool slightly until the edge starts to cut and then move the tool along the work just as you did with the gouge. Study Fig. 15-14. Reverse the position of the tool and cut toward the headstock from where the first cut was started. When cutting properly, the GROUND BEVEL OF THE SKEW RIDES ON THE WORK, therefore it is important that the tool be carefully sharpened with a perfectly flat bevel.

Lay Out and Turning to Size

With the lathe stopped, you can lay out various lengths and positions on the work and check diameters with an outside caliper. If the stock is a light colored wood and you make heavy layout lines, you will be able to see them when the lathe is running.

If the tool rest is placed close to the work, a rule can be placed upon it and layouts can be marked with the work rotating at a slow speed. When doing this use considerable care.

The parting tool should be used to cut the positions and diameters into the work. It is a scraping type tool and is easy to use. A good cutting action is secured if it contacts the work above the horizontal center as shown in Fig. 15-15. Work is often turned to size by holding the tool in one hand and the calipers in the other as shown in

Fig. 15-21. When parting tool cuts are deep, A CLEARANCE CUT MUST BE MADE about every 3/8 in. of depth to free the tool and prevent the point from overheating and burning. It is usually best to leave the sizing cut about 1/16 to 1/8 in. larger so that a finishing cut can be made after the contour is complete.

Tapers and Shoulders

Lay out the length of a taper and then with the parting tool, turn to the required diameter at each end. Use the gouge to rough out to within about 1/8 in. of the finished size. Scraping tools can be used to finish the taper or a shearing cut can be made with the skew. Always cut from the larger part toward the smaller part.

A shoulder can be cut with the parting tool and then a light cut (about 1/32 in.) can be made with the skew as shown in Fig. 15-16. This will leave a smooth surface that will require very little sanding.

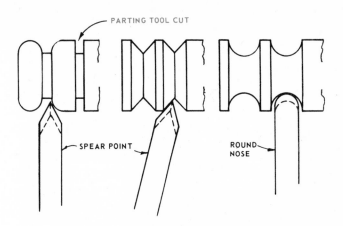

Fig. 15-17. Scraping beads, vees and coves.

First lay out the positions of each bead and make a vertical cut with the toe of the skew, Fig. 15-18. Now place the skew high on the work

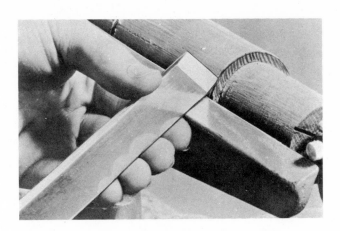

Fig. 15-16. Finishing a shoulder cut with the toe of the skew.

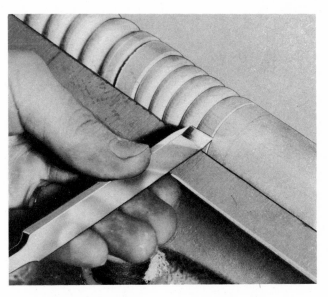

Fig. 15-18. First cut for forming a bead.
(Rockwell Mfg. Co.—Power Tool Div.)

Beads and V-Grooves

Beads and V-grooves can be scraped or cut. The easiest way is to scrape them, using the spear point tool. It is usually best to separate beads with parting tool cuts as shown in Fig. 15-17. Scraping is slower and the work will require considerable sanding but there is less danger of spoiling the work.

Cutting bead and V-cuts with the skew is the most difficult of the turning operations. When carefully done it will produce work that is so smooth that very little sanding is necessary. The beginner should expect to spend many hours of practice on sample pieces before he attempts to produce finished work for his project.

with the heel starting the cut as shown in Fig. 15-19. Rotate the tool from a horizontal to a vertical position, pulling it slightly toward you so that the heel will continue to cut. The entire cut is made with the heel of the skew. Keep the ground bevel riding on the work. Repeat the operation several times to secure the required depth. The other half of the bead is now formed following the same procedure but reversing the tool and movements.

V-cuts are formed in the same general way except that the skew is rocked straight into the work and not rotated. These cuts can also be cut using the toe of the tool in about the same manner used in finishing a shoulder cut.

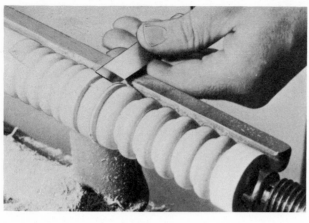

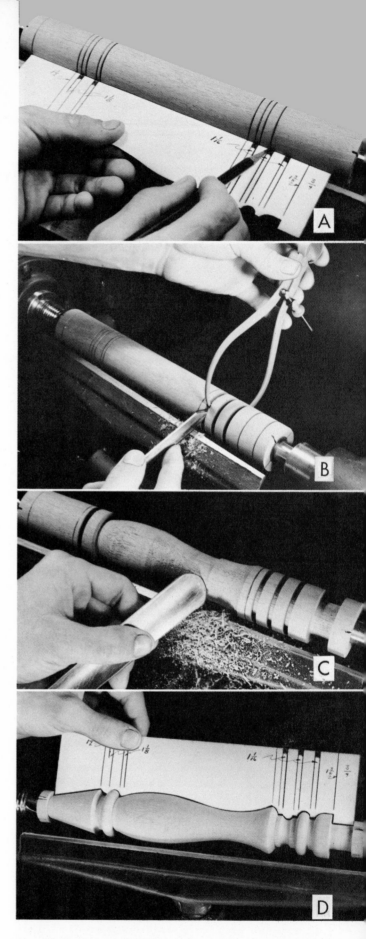

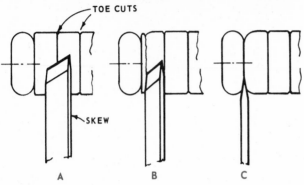

TOE CUTS

SKEW

A   B   C

Fig. 15-19. Second cut for forming a bead.

Coves

Coves can be scraped with the round nose tool. Set the tool rest so the cutting edge will touch the work on a horizontal center line or slightly above, Fig. 15-17.

The gouge is used to cut a cove. First, lay out the position of the cove and then rough out the shape by feeding the tool straight into the work. Start the finishing cut by holding the gouge on edge and in a horizontal position as shown in Fig. 15-20. Move the tool into the cut and at the same time

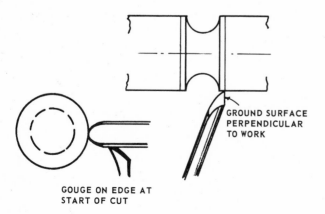

GROUND SURFACE
PERPENDICULAR
TO WORK

GOUGE ON EDGE AT
START OF CUT

Fig. 15-20. Cutting a cove with the gouge.

Fig. 15-21. Turning duplicate parts. A-Laying out the work. B-Sizing cuts with the parting tool and calipers. C-Roughing out the contour with the gouge. D-Checking with a template.

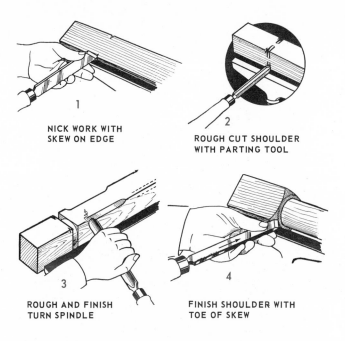

NICK WORK WITH
SKEW ON EDGE

2

ROUGH CUT SHOULDER
WITH PARTING TOOL

3

ROUGH AND FINISH
TURN SPINDLE

4

FINISH SHOULDER WITH
TOE OF SKEW

Fig. 15-22. Procedure for turning work with a square section.

roll it and lower the handle. KEEP THE GROUND SURFACE OF THE TOOL IN CONTACT WITH THE CONTOUR being cut. Continue to the bottom of the cove and then cut the other half, coming in from the other side.

Turning Duplicate Parts

When two or more pieces of the same size and shape are required, it is best to make a template. After the work is turned to a smooth cylinder the template can be used to lay out the position of the diameters as shown in Fig. 15-21. The parting tool and calipers are used to cut down to the various sizes and the contour is roughed out. Finished cuts are then made and the work carefully checked with the template as it nears completion.

Turning duplicate parts of a complicated design requires careful work. Remember that A GIVEN DEPTH OF CUT ACTUALLY REDUCES THE SIZE OF THE TURNING BY DOUBLE THAT AMOUNT. This means that to reduce the diameter 1/8 in. the depth of the cut must be only 1/16 in.

Partial Turned Sections

Sometimes a part of the turned piece includes a square section. For example, a turned table leg usually has a square section at the top where the rails join.

When such a piece is required, it must be squared to finished size and surfaced before

turning. Be very careful to accurately center the piece in the lathe so that the square will meet the turned rounds evenly on all sides.

Fig. 15-22, shows the procedure to follow. Making the layout and first cut with the skew will prevent splinters from breaking off when the parting tool is used. The final cut on the square can be made with either the skew or spear point.

Parts with Holes

Lamp stems and other parts that require a center hole can be drilled after the turning is complete. If the stem is long it may be easier to drill the hole first, then plug the ends and drill out the plug after the turning is complete.

Deep holes are hard to drill or bore, especially in end grain. It may be best at times to rip the turning blank apart, cut grooves, glue it together again and plug the holes. See Fig. 15-23. This is an especially practical solution when it is necessary to glue up two pieces of stock to secure the required thickness.

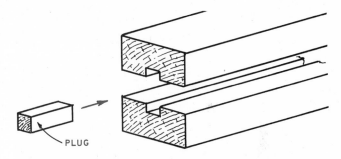

PLUG

Fig. 15-23. Cut grooves, glue up and plug ends of long pieces that require holes.

The blanks for the salt and pepper set shown in Fig. 15-24, were first bored on the drill press and then plugs were turned on the lathe to fit these holes. The hole in the midsection of the blank is smaller so that there are shoulders to keep the plugs from going all the way through. The plugs are inserted, and the blank turned. They are easily removed and can be used for turning additional pieces.

A long, thin turning will chatter and vibrate, unless it is supported with a steady rest. Such pieces may be turned in several sections and then assembled. Because of the tendency for slim pieces to vibrate, the SMALL DIAMETERS SHOULD BE TURNED LAST. It is also best to position the work in the lathe so that the SMALL-EST DIAMETERS ARE NEAREST THE TAIL-STOCK.

Sanding Lathe Work

Turnings can be sanded while they are rotating in the lathe. Work that has been scraped will require heavy sanding and you may need to start with a 1/0 or 2/0 grade. Follow this with 4/0 and then a final touch with a 5/0 or 6/0 grade. Work that has been produced with a shearing cut will require very little sanding.

small coves and fine details. A strip of paper held over a dowel or other wood forms may be helpful for sanding fine details.

Since you are actually sanding across the grain of the wood with the lathe turning, you should use a very fine grade of paper to finish the work. When the contour will permit, you will secure the smoothest surface by stopping the lathe and hand sanding in the direction of the grain.

Fig. 15-24. Turning parts with large holes. Left. Blank, plugs, template and finished turning. Right. Completed salt and pepper set.

A strip of abrasive paper held by the ends and at an angle with the work as shown in Fig. 15-25, produces good results. Use narrow strips for

Fig. 15-25. Sanding spindle work. Above. Using a strip of sandpaper. Below. Sanding a cove with the paper formed over a dowel.

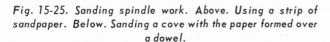

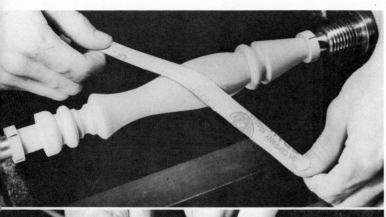

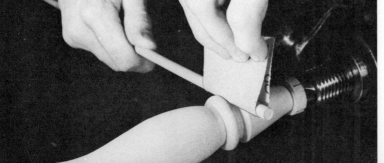

 WOODY SAYS:

"Do not over sand your work for this may "wash-out" details and spoil its appearance. Be sure to remove the tool rest when sanding."

Faceplate Turning

Mounting Work on Faceplates

When screw holes will not detract from the finished turning, the stock can be fastened directly to the faceplate. Usually, however, it is better to glue the work to a backing block.

Saw out the diameter of both the backing block and the stock for the finished turning. Check the surfaces to see that they are flat and will fit together smoothly. Spread glue on the surface of each piece, place a sheet of paper in the joint and clamp them together. Be sure that they are carefully centered with each other. Allow the glue to

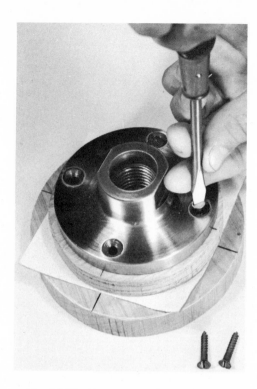

Fig. 15-26. Mounting work on a faceplate.

harden overnight and then mount the work on a faceplate as shown in Fig. 15-26.

After the turning is finished, use a large wood chisel to split the glue line. Keep the faceplate mounted on the lathe and work carefully all the way around the joint with the bevel turned toward the backing block.

Faceplate Turning

All faceplate turning should be done by the scraping method with the tool rest holding the cutting edge of the tool on or slightly above a horizontal line through the center of the work. The spear point, round nose or square nose are good tools to use. The gouge should not be used on faceplate work.

Screw the faceplate onto the lathe spindle until it is tight against the shoulder, before turning on the power. Then, set the lathe on the lowest speed and true the outside edge with a shoulder cut, using the spear point as shown in Fig. 15-27. Position the tool rest along the face of the disk and make a smoothing shoulder cut, once again using the spear point. Start at the outside edge and move the tool toward the center as shown in Fig. 15-27 (C). Diameters for the turning can be laid out with a rule and pencil with the lathe running, Fig. 15-28, but be sure that the surface is smooth and that you use extra care while performing the operation.

Contours of the work can be formed by using various combinations of the turning tools. Scraping cuts will dull the tools rather rapidly so you will need to hone them often and regrind the bevel now and then.

Applying Finishes

Turned pieces that are a part of a larger assembly of cabinetwork are usually removed from the lathe and finished after final assembly.

Fig. 15-27. Roughing out faceplate work. A-Making a shoulder cut with the spear point. B-Close-up view. Arrow shows direction of cut. C-Smoothing the face with a spear point.

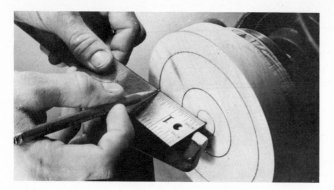

Fig. 15-28. Laying out diameters with the lathe turning at a low speed.

Fig. 15-30. Using the tailstock to rough out faceplate work.

Small bowls, trays and miniature turnings however, can be finished easily and quickly while the work is spinning in the lathe. A shellac and linseed oil finish (French polish) is commonly used. REMOVE THE TOOL REST BEFORE PERFORMING FINISHING OPERATIONS.

A ball of cotton folded inside a piece of cotton cloth makes a good pad. Saturate the pad with thin shellac and a little oil and apply it to the work while it is turning at a slow speed. After the work is coated, increase the speed and pressure to smooth and harden the finish, Fig. 15-29. You will not be able to build a very heavy (thick) finish without considerable practice. Overnight curing and hardening of a first coat before applying a second coat will make it easier for the beginner to secure a satisfactory finish by this method.

LINSEED OIL   SHELLAC

Fig. 15-29. Applying a French polish.

Open-grained woods can be filled in the usual way but the work cannot be spun until the filler has completely hardened because the centrifugal force will throw it out of the wood pores. Other finishes can also be applied to turned parts and rubbed down while they are turning on the lathe.

Using the Tailstock

When roughing out work that is mounted on a faceplate it is often advisable to use the tailstock and cup center to provide additional support, as shown in Fig. 15-30. This can continue to be used as long as it does not interfere with the work. When you discontinue using the tailstock, move it well out of the way and remove the cup center. ALWAYS REMOVE THE CENTERS FROM THE LATHE WHEN THEY ARE NOT IN USE.

Drilling and Boring Holes

A drill chuck, fitted with a tapered shank can be mounted in the tailstock and used for drilling and boring as shown in Fig. 15-31. The center should be marked and started with the spear point if you are using a large drill bit. With the lathe running at a slow speed you can advance the bit into the cut by turning the tailstock handwheel.

Fig. 15-31. Drilling a hole in stock in lathe.

Before making this setup, check the position of the tailstock by inserting both centers and bringing them together. The points of the spur center and cup center must align. If adjustment is necessary, secure help from your instructor.

Assembling Work in the Lathe

Fig. 15-32, shows a procedure that you can follow when making a candlestick or similar article. First turn the stem between centers and then turn the base which is mounted on a faceplate. The hole for the stem can be turned with the round nose tool. Use considerable care so you will get a good fit. The parts can be assembled with the glue using the tailstock to apply pressure and align the stem. After the glue has set up, further turning and finishing can be done.

Turned Chucks

After you have had success with standard faceplate turning, you may want to try more advanced procedures that include the use of turned chucks to mount and carry the work. Fig. 15-33, shows a sequence of operations used to produce a small box with a fitted lid.

First, turn the inside of the lid, sand and then cut it off with the parting tool. After cutting off the lid, turn the inside of the main body (note the

position of the tool support) and carefully form the rabbet so that you can press the lid tightly in place. Smooth the top of the lid and do further turning on the outside of the box if necessary. All of the outside surfaces can be sanded at this time.

Remove the lid and sand the rabbet so that there will be a little clearance. Also sand the inside of the box. Now cut off the main body of the box, again using the parting tool. Turn a rabbet (called a SPINDLE CHUCK) on the stock remaining on the faceplate. Reverse the box, press it on the chuck and smooth and sand the bottom.

Securing the "press fit" between the chuck and the work is the most critical part of the procedure. Measure and turn carefully, providing excessive taper until the part starts to slip in

Fig. 15-32. Assembling work in the lathe. Left. Turning the stem. Center. Turning the base.
Right. Parts glued and assembled.

Fig. 15-33. Chucking and turning a small box. A-Cutting off the lid with the parting tool. B-Using a round nose to turn the inside. C-Top has been pressed in place and is being finished. D-Cutting off the main body of the box. E-Mounting box on a spindle chuck to finish the bottom. F-Completed box.

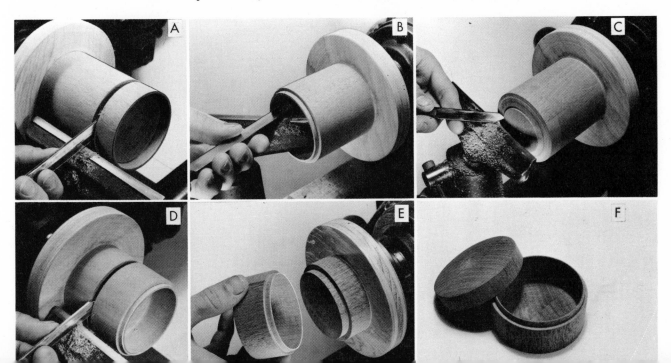

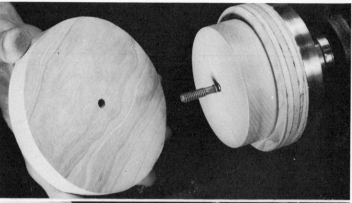

Fig. 15-34. Above. Mounting a drilled blank on a hanger bolt. Below. Turning the contour with a square nose tool.

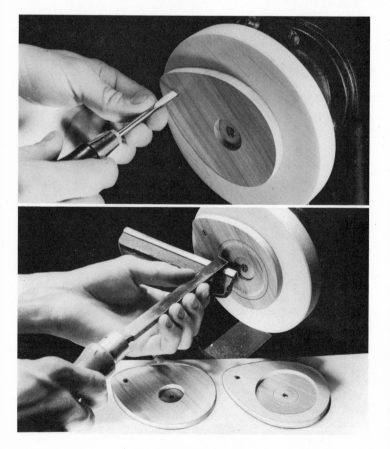

Fig. 15-35. Above. Mounting a blank with screws. Below. Turning the recess.

place; then, reduce the taper gradually until you can press the part tightly against the shoulder. A beginner should plan his layout with enough extra stock so that if he turns the first chuck too small he will have sufficient stock to make another one. A strip of fine sandpaper can be used to "shim-up" a loose fit. When the work is fitted to an inside turning or chuck, the mounting is called a RE-CESSED CHUCK.

Using Metal Fasteners to Mount Work

The design of some turned objects will permit the use of screws or other metal fasteners in faceplate mounting. In Fig. 15-34, a hanger bolt has been carefully set in the base stock mounted on a faceplate. Drilled blanks are then fastened in place with a washer and nut and the required contour is turned. The piece could be reversed for finishing the opposite side. The part being produced in Fig. 15-34, is the base for a small dresser lamp.

Fig. 15-35, shows wood screws being used to mount a blank which is being made into a glass coaster. The blank has been prebored on the drill press and the lathe is being used to enlarge the recess for the glass. The smaller outside hole will be enlarged to fit a stacking post. Always turn off center work at the lowest speed. Be sure the screws are flush or below the surface of the work.

A dowel screw (threaded on both ends) has been carefully set in the base stock and is being used to mount small blanks that can be turned into drawer and door pulls, Fig. 15-36. A disk of sandpaper glued to the surface of the chuck will help keep the blank from slipping.

Fig. 15-36. A screw chuck for turning small knobs.

Drill Chucks, Drive Chucks and Mandrels

A drill chuck, mounted on a tapered shank can be placed in the headstock and used to turn small parts. In Fig. 15-37, a 3/8 in. dowel has been glued into a 1 in. dowel and then chucked for the turning as shown. The parts being produced (feet for a dresser lamp) were needed for a mass production project so a special formed tool was ground to shape from a section of an 8 in. mill file. The metal in file stock will hold an edge quite well but it is very brittle and tools made from it should be used only on small diameters.

A drive chuck provides a good way to mount small blanks for miniature turnings. In Fig. 15-38, above, a 13/16 in. hardwood square is being driven into a 1 in. hole about 1 1/4 in. deep. The chuck is made by mounting a piece of hardwood on the faceplate, turning it true and then boring the hole with the round nose tool or a bit mounted in the tailstock. Remove the faceplate from the lathe and drill a smaller hole through the chuck so the knock-out rod can be used to drive out the blank when the turning is finished.

You will need small tools to make the miniature turnings shown in Fig. 15-38, below. They can be formed from discarded saw files. Grind and hone them in the same way you would the regular lathe tools.

Some small parts can be turned on a "mandrel," Fig. 15-39. The square stock, driven into the drive chuck, has been turned to a slight taper so that a thread spool can be pressed on tightly. If the mandrel becomes compressed and the spools slip after working several pieces, moisten it with water to swell it to its original size. Most spools are made from white birch, which is an excellent turning wood.

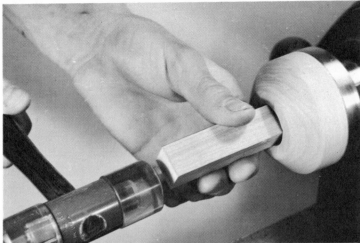

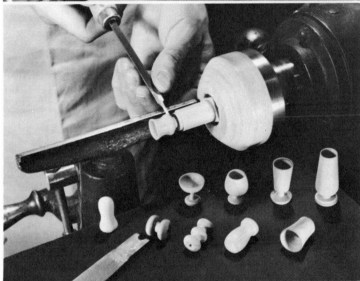

Fig. 15-38. A drive chuck. Above Driving a 13/16 in. square into a 1 in. hole. Below. Turning miniatures using a tool ground from a saw file.

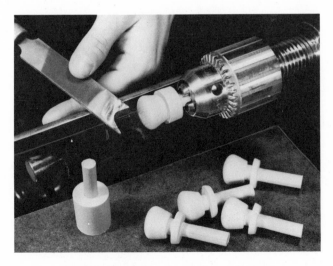

Fig. 15-37. Work mounted in a drill chuck.

Fig. 15-39. A mandrel for mounting and turning parts from thread spools.

Industrial Machines

Patternmaker's Lathe

The lathe, Fig. 15-40, is similar to the type you have learned to use in the school shop except it is usually larger and equipped with a carriage instead of a tool rest. The carriage is about like that found on a metalworking lathe. It is not powered, however, and is moved along the bed with a handwheel. There is a cross feed that is also hand operated and carries special tool bits. This arrangement permits the patternmaker to form with great accuracy the wooden parts that will be used to produce the molds for metal castings.

Automatic Lathes

Large furniture and cabinet factories use automatic turning lathes like the one shown in Figs. 15-41 and 42, to produce turned parts with speed and accuracy.

Fig. 15-40. A lathe designed for patternmaking.

The wood blanks are placed in a hopper and are automatically centered between a headstock and a tailstock about like you have used, except

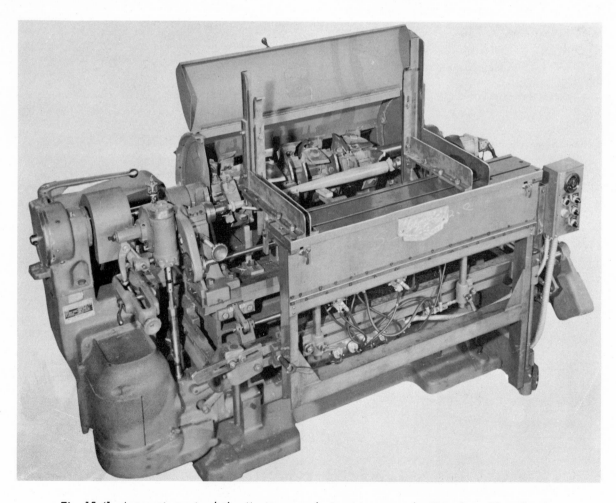

Fig. 15-41. Automatic turning lathe. Maximum stock size 4 in. square by 42 in. long. The arbor that carries the cutterhead assembly, turns at a speed of 2700 rpm and is powered by a 15 hp motor.

15-16

Fig. 15-42. Above. Hopper-feed swung outward to show mechanism. Turning blanks are stacked in the upper channels of the hopper and feed automatically into the lathe. Tail stock and carriage are operated by pneumatic power. Fig. 15-43. Below. Close-up view of cutterhead assembly producing a baseball bat. (Mattison Machine Works)

that the tailstock also carries a spur center and is power driven. The blank is then rotated at a speed of about 25 rpm. Behind this spindle is an arbor that carries cutterheads that can be made up in many shapes and sizes. This cutterhead assembly revolves at a high speed (2700-3600 rpm). In operation, the carriage with the slowly revolving blank of stock is moved backward and into the cutterheads which form the desired shape in just a few seconds. The carriage is moved forward and the finished turning is released and drops out of the machine. Another blank is placed between the centers and the operation is repeated. Average production is about 2400 turnings in an 8 hour day.

The cutterhead assembly consists of a great many knives that overlap each other in such a way that a smooth even surface is formed. The knives

are also ground and set at an angle so that a shearing cut is produced. Fig. 15-43, shows a cutterhead assembly being used to turn a baseball bat. It takes a lot of skill and know-how to set up, adjust, and maintain a modern automatic wood lathe.

Veneer Lathe

A veneer lathe is a giant machine used to cut veneer by the rotary method. The log is soaked for many hours, often in hot water so that the wood fibers are pliable. It is then hoisted into place between the lathe centers. As the log revolves a knife is fed slowly into its surface and a thin layer of wood is removed. After the log becomes a perfect cylinder, a continuous ribbon of veneer is peeled off. The thickness can be

Fig. 15-44.

MOTOR AND
VARIABLE
SPEED DRIVE

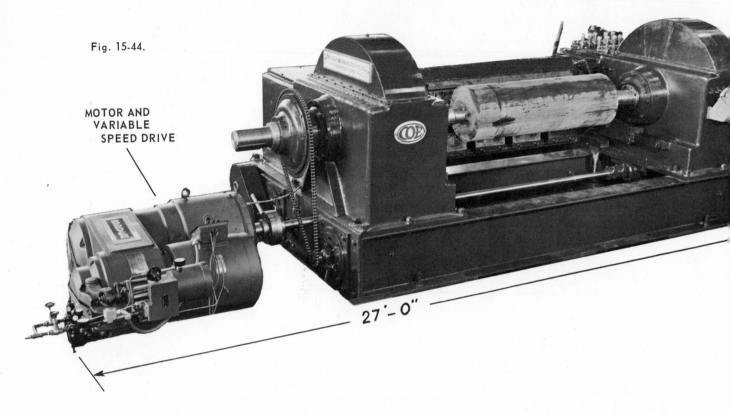

27'-0"

Fig. 15-44. Modern Veneer Lathe.
(Coe Mfg. Co.)

accurately controlled and veneers of 1/36 in. to 1/4 in. can be produced. Fig. 15-44, shows a modern veneer lathe that has variable speeds, automatic controls and a swing of 60 in. Its over-all length is 27 ft. and it weighs 26,000 lbs.

Test Your Knowledge

1. The size of a lathe is called the swing and is twice the distance from the lathe bed to the _____.
2. What is the chief purpose of the knock-out bar?
3. How is the cup center removed from the tail-stock?
4. Define the term, centrifugal force.
5. Why should the spur center and cup center be removed from the lathe when not in use?
6. When the stock is mounted between the lathe centers the turning operation is classified as _____ turning.
7. The cup center will overheat if it is too tight and is not _____.
8. When the skew is used to make a shearing cut the _____ rides on the surface that is being cut.
9. Sizing cuts on spindle work should be made with the _____ tool.

10. What depth of cut would you make if you wanted to reduce the diameter of a cylinder 1/16 in.?
11. In spindle turning it is usually best to position the work so that the largest diameters are nearest to the _____ (headstock, tailstock) of the lathe.
12. Why should power never be used to run the faceplate onto the lathe spindle?
13. Scraping tools that are used for faceplate turning include the round nose, square nose, and _____ _____.
14. Why is the tailstock sometimes used when roughing out faceplate work?
15. When mounting stock on a faceplate with screws why is it important that they be set flush or below the surface?
16. What size of hole would you bore in a drive chuck if you wanted to mount 5/8 in. squares?

Outside Assignments

1. Study the catalog of a supplier or manufacturer and develop a complete set of specifications for a wood lathe.
2. Prepare a list of the basic equipment you would need for wood turning in a home work-shop and secure a cost estimate.
3. Prepare a block chart showing the surface

feed per minute for various diameters and lathe speeds. List diameters of 1 to 12 in. across the top and speeds of 500 to 3000 rpm down the left side. Use the formula:

$$SFM = \frac{RPM \times \pi D}{12}$$

Convert some of the higher speeds into miles per hour.

4. Describe with sketches and notes how you would develop a lathe setup to produce 100 wheels that were 1/4 in. thick, 1 1/2 in. in diameter and that had a 1/16 in. center hole.
5. Describe with sketches and notes how you would turn and completely finish on the lathe, a napkin ring or ladies bracelet using spindle and recessed chucks.

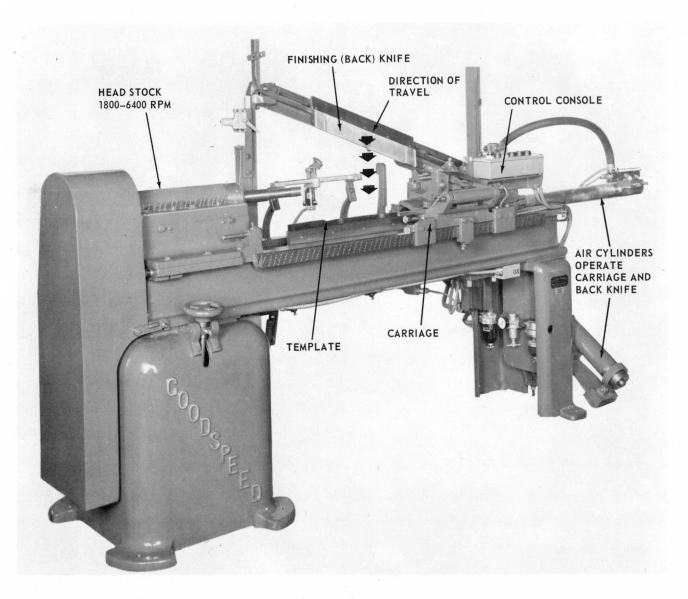

Automatic back knife lathe. Especially designed to turn diameters under 3 in. After stock is automatically mounted between centers, it is roughed out with a gouge or V-knife held in the carriage. The carriage moves along a template which results in a rough contour being produced on the work. The finished contour and surface is obtained as the back knife (ground to the required shape) moves downward past the turning with a smooth, shearing cut.

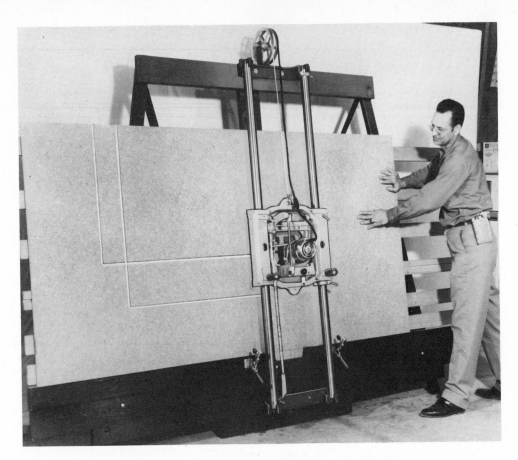

Panel router cuts dados, grooves and rabbets in plywood, particle board and plastic laminate panels. For horizontal cuts, router carriage is locked in place and panel is fed through as shown. For vertical cuts, panel is held stationary and carriage moves up or down along tubular ways.
(Herrmann & Safranek)

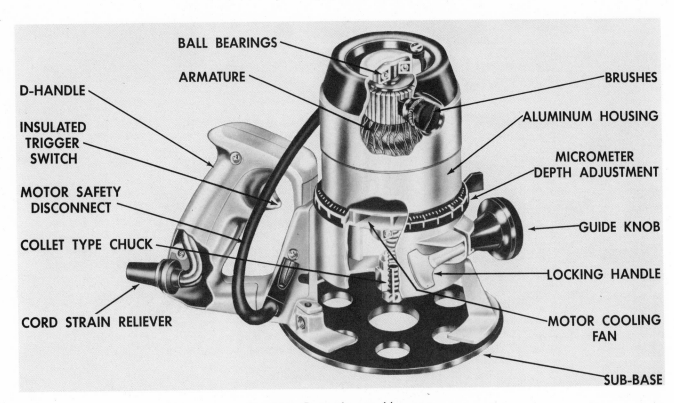

BALL BEARINGS

ARMATURE

BRUSHES

D-HANDLE

ALUMINUM HOUSING

INSULATED TRIGGER SWITCH

MICROMETER DEPTH ADJUSTMENT

MOTOR SAFETY DISCONNECT

GUIDE KNOB

COLLET TYPE CHUCK

LOCKING HANDLE

CORD STRAIN RELIEVER

MOTOR COOLING FAN

SUB-BASE

Fig. 16-1. Parts of a portable router.
(Rockwell Mfg. Co.)

Unit 16

ROUTER, SHAPER
AND MOULDER

Routers, shapers and moulders are designed to cut irregular shapes, and form various contours on edges and surfaces. The shapes may be decorative in nature or form the joints for construction and assembly. Cutters travel at high speeds, producing smooth surfaces that require little if any sanding. The router and shaper are manufactured in sizes that are practical for the school shop. The moulder, like the double-end tenoner, is a heavy production machine and is usually found only in large woodworking plants and factories.

Portable Router

Parts and Description

The portable router Fig 16-1, consists of a motor unit carried by an adjustable base. A collet type chuck is attached to the motor shaft and holds various cutting tools. The size of routers is given in terms of horsepower rating and range from 1/4 hp to as large as 2 1/2 hp on large heavy-duty machines. The motors turn at speeds of 20,000 rpm or higher.

Router Bits

Some of the most commonly used bits and cutters are shown in Fig. 16-2. The straight router bit has cutting edges on the end and sides and is used for slotting, grooving, inlay-work and background routing. A veining bit is similar to the straight bit except that it has a rounded end. The rabbeting bit is used for joinery work and usually has a pilot tip that controls the depth of cut.

A wide range of contour cutters for both convex and concave surfaces are available for light shaping operations. Nearly all of them have a pilot tip that guides the bit either along straight edges or curves. Consult a manufacturer's catalog for a complete description.

Sharpening a router bit is fairly simple if you use a holding fixture such as shown in Fig. 16-3. This holds the bit in alignment while being ground

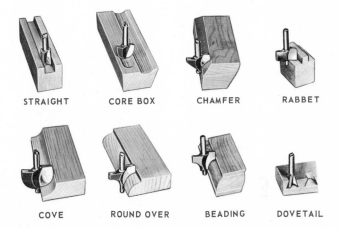

STRAIGHT   CORE BOX   CHAMFER   RABBET

COVE   ROUND OVER   BEADING   DOVETAIL

Fig. 16-2. Common router bits and the cuts they produce. (Stanley Tools)

on a small abrasive wheel mounted in the chuck of the router. The router must be firmly supported in an upside-down position. The bit can be

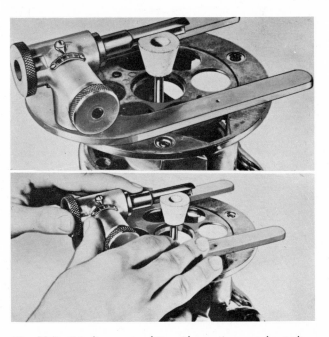

Fig. 16-3. Grinding router bits. Above. A special grinding wheel is mounted in router and a grinding fixture holds the bit. Below. Fixture slides on base and holds bit in perfect alignment. (Rockwell Mfg. Co.)

Fig. 16-4. Installing a router bit. Electric cord is unplugged. (Stanley Tools)

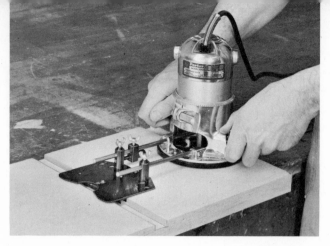

Fig. 16-5. Using a guide to cut a dado. (Rockwell Mfg. Co.)

held for free-hand grinding but it requires lots of skill. Router bits can be honed lightly with a small slipstone or oilstone. Always hone or grind the face of the cutter. Never try to sharpen the bevel side.

Safety Rules for the Portable Router

(In addition to the safety rules on page 10-30.)

1. The bit must be securely mounted in the chuck to a depth of at least 1/2 in. and the base must be tight.
2. As with all portable tools, be certain that the motor is properly grounded.
3. Wear eye protection when using the router.
4. Be certain the work is securely clamped and that it will remain stationary during the routing operation.
5. Place the router base on the work or template with the bit clear of the wood before turning on the power. Hold it firmly when turning on the motor to overcome starting torque.
6. Hold the router in both hands and feed it smoothly through the cut in the correct direction.
7. When the cut is complete, turn off the motor and do not lift the machine from the work until the motor has stopped.
8. Always unplug the motor when mounting bits or making major adjustments.

Mounting Bits and Adjusting the Base

Select the correct bit for your work. Be sure the bit is sharp. The motor should be disconnected and the router base removed. Insert the bit at least 1/2 in. or to the full depth of the chuck, lock the motor shaft and tighten the chuck using an approved type of wrench, Fig. 16-4.

Insert the motor unit into the base and lightly tighten the clamp. Measure and adjust for the correct depth of cut and then lock the base secure-

ly. Some routers have a special depth adjusting ring. When so equipped, the base is first set even with the bit and the adjustment ring is moved away from the base a distance equal to the depth. Resetting the base against the ring will then provide the required cut.

Using the Router

The router motor revolves in a clockwise direction (when viewed from above) and therefore should be fed from left to right when making a cut along an edge facing you. When cutting around the outside of oblong or circular pieces, always move the machine in a counterclockwise direction.

The rate of feed will vary with the hardness of the wood and size of cut. Routers have an induction motor which will slow down somewhat under load. Excessive loss of speed indicates too heavy a cut. When the work is heavy, it is best to reduce the depth of the cut and maintain a good rate of feed. The depth of cut can then be increased and a second pass made over the work.

Fig. 16-6. Left. Series of router cuts needed to form a dado. Right. Cutting a groove. (Stanley Tools)

Feeding router bits at a very slow rate causes them to heat and burn the wood as well as causing damage to the cutter. This is most likely to happen when making cuts on end grain.

For plain routing cuts the machine is sometimes guided along a layout line freehand. However, this is difficult to do and better work will usually be produced if some type of guide is used. Fig. 16-5 shows a standard guide attachment being used to cut a dado. The attachment includes a vernier-type adjustment that is helpful when making precision setting. In addition to dado cuts, it can be used for rabbets, grooves, and certain circular shapes. See Fig. 16-6. In Fig. 16-7, a shop-built guide is being used for a dado cut. The guide simply serves as a straightedge along which the router base can slide.

Fig. 16-7. Cutting a dado with a shop-built guide.

The router can be guided by a template (also spelled templet). A guide tip is attached to the router base with the bit extending through its center. This tip guides the router along a template which is usually made of plywood or hardboard. The contour of the template must be larger for inside cuts and smaller for outside cuts by an amount equal to the distance from the outside of the guide tip to the cutting edge of the bit. Fig. 16-8 shows a template ready for use.

Fig. 16-8. A template for routing.

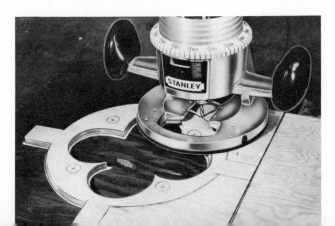

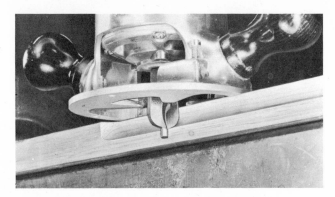

Fig. 16-9. Shaping an edge with the router. The pilot tip controls the depth of cut.   (Stanley Tools)

Shaping Edges

Most of the bits used for shaping an edge have a pilot tip that guides the router. See Fig. 16-9. Edges must be perfectly formed since any imperfections will be followed by the tip. The design of the shaped edge must allow 1/8 in. of surface on which the tip can ride. Feed the bit smoothly in the correct direction and with just enough side pressure to hold the pilot tip against the edge.

 WOODY SAYS:

"Always set the router base firmly on the work with the bit clear of the cut before turning on the motor."

If too much pressure is used, the friction between the tip and the wood will cause it to burn. The tip should always be kept smooth and bright; an accumulation of pitch or gum will cause it to burn, even though light pressure is applied.

Strips of small molding, Fig. 16-10, can be produced by first shaping the corner of a larger piece of stock and then ripping it off on the table saw.

Fig. 16-10. A procedure for making small moldings.

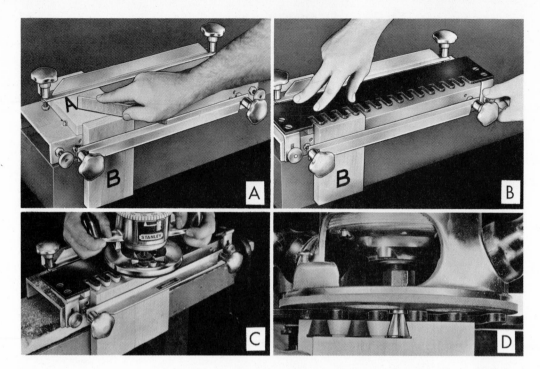

Fig. 16-11. Cutting a dovetail joint. A-Clamping stock in the fixture. B-Installing the template. C-Making the cut. D-Close-up view. (Stanley Tools)

Cutting Dovetail Joints

Dovetail joints can be accurately cut by using a special dovetailing attachment, dovetail bit, and a template guide tip. The following procedure should be followed when cutting a joint for a drawer side and front:

1. Clamp the dovetail attachment securely to the bench.
2. Fasten the template guide tip to the base of the router. Install the dovetail bit in the router (this must be done with the motor unit mounted on the base).
3. Adjust the depth of cut. A 9/16 dovetail bit is set to a depth of 19/32.
4. Clamp the stock in the attachment as shown in Fig. 16-11. Part A is the front of the drawer with the inside surface turned up. Part B is the drawer side with the inside surface turned out. Each of the parts must be carefully aligned and located against the pins.
5. Place the template in position as shown and tighten the clamp knobs.
6. Hold the router on the template with the bit clear of the work. Turn on the motor and carefully guide it in and out and around the ends of the fingers. When the cut is complete, turn off the motor and wait for it to stop before removing the router from the template. NEVER RAISE THE ROUTER OFF OF THE WORK WHILE THE MOTOR IS RUNNING.

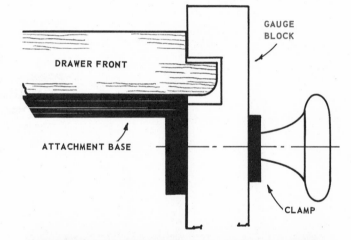

Fig. 16-12. Cutting dovetails in a rabbeted drawer front. Above. Using a gauge block to align the drawer front. Below. Completed joint.

7. Remove the parts and check the fit. If the fit is too loose, extend the bit slightly and if too tight retract it. The depth of the fit can be adjusted by moving the template in or out.

8. Make trial cuts in extra pieces that are the same size as your work, until a satisfactory fit is obtained and then cut the joints for your project. The joint for the right front drawer corner is made on the left end of the attachment and the left front corner is made on the right end.

When cutting dovetails in a rabbeted drawer front, Fig. 16-12, the drawer front and sides are cut separately. Mount the drawer front in the attachment, using a gauge block as shown, and then remove the gauge and cut the joint. Use a block the same thickness as the drawer front to set up the drawer side and leave it in place during the cutting.

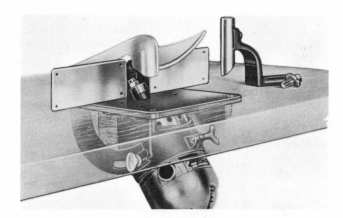

Fig. 16-13. Bench shaper attachment.
(Stanley Tools)

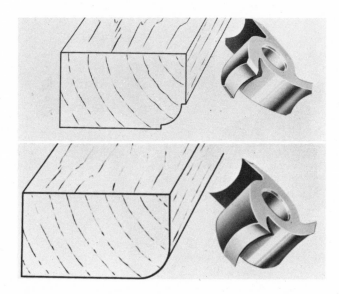

Fig. 16-14. Small shaper cutters with a 5/16 in. hole.

Fig. 16-15. Making a cut with the bench shaper attachment.
(Stanley Tools)

Fig. 16-16. Using a circular guide to control the depth of cut.
(Millers Falls)

Bench Shaper Attachment

The motor unit of the portable router can be mounted in a table plate and used as a small bench shaper, Fig. 16-13. The collet chuck is replaced with a small arbor or spindle (usually 5/16 in. dia.) that will carry shaper cutters as shown in Fig. 16-14.

One of the features of this shaper setup is that the motor unit can be tilted, Fig. 16-15, providing a greater variety of cuts with a given set of cutters. See also Fig. 16-16. When setting up and operating a bench shaper like this one, follow the same procedures and safety regulations as presented on page 16-8.

Using Routers in Trades and Industry

The building trades make extensive use of portable routers for such jobs as routing out stair stringers for risers and treads. It is also a valuable tool for cutting the gain for hinges in doors and jams. See Fig. 16-17.

In millwork and furniture factories, heavy-duty routers are used for a wide range of work. Since the bit travels at such a high speed, it can be used to cut out various irregular shapes faster than a band saw and also produces a smoother edge. Templates and fixtures are used to guide the machine through the cut. See Fig. 16-18. On large, heavy work, the router may be supported on swinging arms as shown in Fig. 16-19.

Fig. 16-17. Using a special template to cut the gain for passage door hinges. The template is also used on the door jam. (Rockwell Mfg. Co.)

Fig. 16-18. Using a heavy-duty router to cut Plexiglas windshields for motor boats. (Stanley Power Tools)

Fig. 16-19. Using a radial arm router to cut an opening in an outside door. Router head has a 5 hp motor. (Ekstrom, Carlson and Co.)

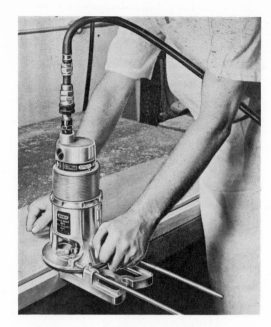

Fig. 16-20. Using an air router. Air motor operates at 9000 rpm, uses 24 cfm at 90 psi. (Stanley Power Tools)

Routers are often powered with air motors, Fig. 16-20, that have less weight per horsepower than electric motors. These are excellent for production work, Fig. 16-21, since they will provide for continuous operation at high speeds and under heavy loads without overheating. Because of their compact design, multiple units can be utilized in production setups as shown.

Fig. 16-21. Ganged air-router motors operate without overheating. (Stanley Power Tools)

Factories use a pin-type router, Fig. 16-22, for routing and profiling flat sheets of wood, plywood, and composition material. The work is usually mounted on a carrier or fixture that has a groove or channel cut on the bottom side. This channel rides over the table pin and guides the fixture throughout the required cut. The table pin is located directly below the router bit.

Shaper

Description and Parts

The shaper can be used to perform many operations. Basically it is designed to cut molding and form various decorative shapes on the edges of work. It can also be used to cut rabbet joints, tongue and groove joints, window sash joints, and many others. It consists of a vertical spindle that projects through a horizontal table. Work is moved over the table and the edge is fed into cutters mounted on the spindle. The depth of cut and position of the work is controlled by either the fence or by collars mounted on the spindle and pins set in the table. Various fixtures and special guides can also be used. Fig. 16-23 shows some of the important parts.

The spindle on small shapers is usually driven by a belt at speeds of 5,000 to 10,000 rpm. It can be moved up and down to provide various positions

Fig. 16-22. Production router. Overall height 68 in. Head unit is operated up and down by hydraulic power. 5 hp motor operates at 10,000 or 20,000 rpm.
(Porter Mach. Co.)

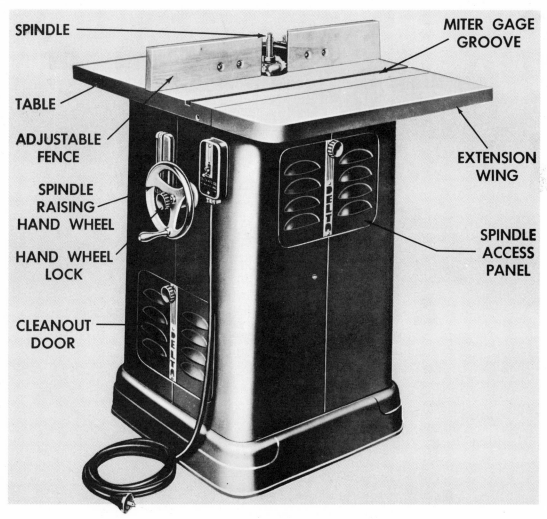

Fig. 16-23. A shaper and some of its parts.
(Rockwell Mfg. Co.)

for the cutter. The motor has a reversing switch so the spindle can be revolved in either direction, thus extending the variety of setups that can be made.

Shaper Cutters

There are two general types of shaper cutters; the assembled cutterhead and the solid wing cutter. The assembled cutter (also called an open-face cutter) is used on larger machines for production work. One type consists of flat knives with beveled edges that are ground to the required shape and then clamped between two collars. Extreme care must be used so the cutters will project an equal amount and be securely locked in place.

Fig. 16-24. Solid wing shaper cutters and shaper collars. The collars are used to space the cutters and also control the depth of cut. (Rockwell Mfg. Co.)

Solid cutters, Fig. 16-24, are recommended for work in the school shop because they are safer to use. A wide range of patterns are available with the most common size designed to fit on a 1/2 in. spindle. See Fig. 16-25.

Shaper cutters will stay sharp for a considerable length of time if they are kept clean and carefully handled and used. The solid wing cutters are sharpened by honing the face while it is held flat on an oilstone. See Fig. 16-26. If the edge is very dull it may be necessary to grind the face lightly. Use a fine grinding wheel and hold the front face of the cutter against the side of the wheel. Try to grind each wing the same amount. Do not attempt to grind or hone the beveled side of the edge.

Safety Rules for the Shaper

(In addition to the general rules on page 10-30.)
1. Be sure to get the instructor's permission before starting to set up and use the machine.
2. When possible, mount the cutter so that most of the cutting will be performed on the lower part of the edge. Any unused part of the cutter should be below the table.
3. An approved lock washer must be located directly under the spindle nut and the nut must be set tight.
4. Use the fence for all straight line shaping cuts and be certain it is properly adjusted and securely locked in place.
5. Use guards, feather boards, and hold-down devices whenever possible.

BEAD　　FLUTE　　90 DEG. FLUTE　　3-FLUTE　　3-BEAD

NOSING　　QUARTER ROUND　　OGEE　　COVE AND BEAD

QUARTER ROUND AND COVE　　BEAD AND COVE　　QUARTER ROUND AND BEAD　　LIPPED DOOR

GLUE JOINT　　DRAWER JOINT　　GROOVE　　TONGUE

Fig. 16-25. Standard cutter shapes.

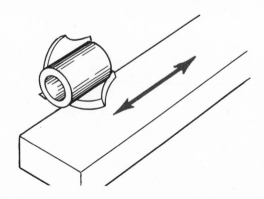

Fig. 16-26. Honing a shaper cutter.

6. Maintain a 4 in. margin of safety when using the fence or miter gauge and a 6 in. margin when using depth collars. If the part is too small to allow this margin, design and build a special holder or push board.

7. Cut only new stock that is straight and true and free of splits, checks, and knots.

8. Roll the spindle over by hand to check clearance of complicated settings. Snap the switch on and off quickly to check rotation of the cutter. Be certain the direction of feed is correct.

9. Have your instructor inspect the setup and inform him of the direction and order of feed you plan to use.

10. Make a trial cut on an extra piece of stock that is the same thickness as your project work.

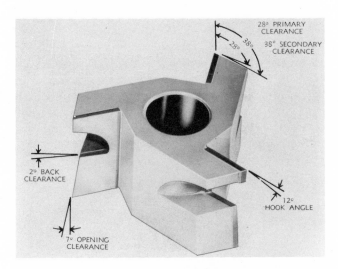

Fig. 16-27. Carbide-tipped lip door cutter. It will stay sharp much longer than a regular cutter.

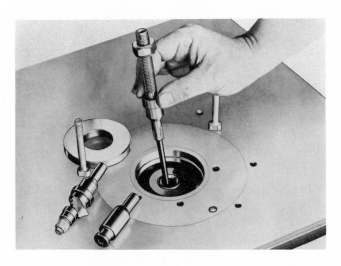

Fig. 16-28. Installing a spindle. Check operator's manual for detailed directions covering model being used. (Rockwell Mfg. Co.)

Installing Spindles and Cutters

Some shapers have interchangeable spindles. The most common sizes are 5/16, 1/2, and 3/4 in. When installing a spindle, be certain it is clean and fits smoothly into the slots and keyways. A light film of oil should be applied to mating surfaces. Makes and models will vary in the way that the spindle is clamped and secured. The operator's manual should be studied for detailed directions. Also refer to the manual for other adjustments and oiling schedules. See Figs. 16-27 and 28.

To install a cutter, remove the table insert and raise the spindle to its highest point. Be certain the spindle, cutters, collars, and nut are clean and free of pitch and gum, Fig. 16-29. Mount

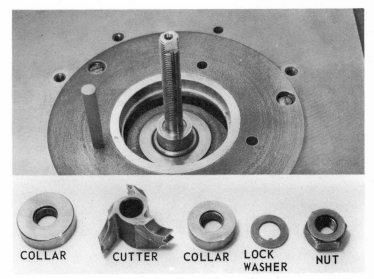

Fig. 16-29. Cutter setup ready to be installed from left to right.

the correct arrangement of collars and cutters on the spindle. Place the lock washer on the spindle and then turn on the nut and tighten it securely with an approved type wrench. ALWAYS PLACE THE LOCK WASHER DIRECTLY UNDER THE NUT. Replace the table insert if it can be used; check the clearance and adjust the cutter to the required height.

When installing spindles and cutters or making major adjustments on the shaper the power should be disconnected.

Shaping with the Fence

All straight cuts should be guided along the fence as shown in Fig. 16-30. Mount the fence on the table and check the alignment of the two sides with a straightedge. When only a part of the edge

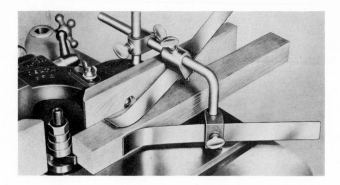

Fig. 16-30. Using the fence to guide straight cuts.
(Rockwell Mfg. Co.)

is cut the two sections are kept even and the part of the edge that is not cut continues in contact with the fence throughout the cut.

When the shaping cut removes all of the edge, the infeed section must be set back an amount equal to the depth of the cut. The work is first guided by the infeed fence and then after the edge is cut it should align and be guided by the outfeed section in the same way that the jointer tables operate. See Fig. 16-31.

WHEN ONLY PART OF THE EDGE IS SHAPED OUTFEED FENCE IS ALIGNED WITH INFEED FENCE

WHEN ALL OF EDGE IS SHAPED OUTFEED FENCE IS MOVED FORWARD TO SUPPORT THE WORK

Fig. 16-31. Fence adjustment. Note cutter rotation and direction of feed.

Adjust the fence to provide the correct depth of cut and lock it securely in position. Roll the cutterhead by hand to be certain it clears the fence. Adjust all guards and holddowns to insure safety in the operation.

Work that is guided only by the fence should be at least 10 in. long to provide satisfactory control. To shape the end of parts that are less than 10 in. wide, use a miter gauge or guide block as shown in Fig. 16-32.

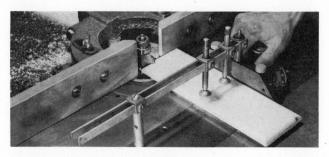

Fig. 16-32. Using a miter gauge to shape the end of a drawer front.

The shaper can be used to cut many types of joints. Fig. 16-33 shows a pair of cutters set up to form a stub tenon on a rail. Note that a supporting piece of stock is held against the back edge to prevent splintering the part at the end of the cut.

Fig. 16-33. Cutting a stub tenon using the fence and miter gauge.

Shaping with Depth Collars

Parts with curves and irregular shapes are held against table pins or special forms and the depth of cut is controlled by a collar, Fig. 16-34. The collar must be clean and bright, and the contact surface should be at least 3/16 in. wide.

When possible, mount the cutter so that the lower part of the work will be shaped and the depth collar will be located on top. A table pin is used to position the work, especially at the start of the cut. It should be located to the right of a cutter that is turning counterclockwise and left of one turning clockwise.

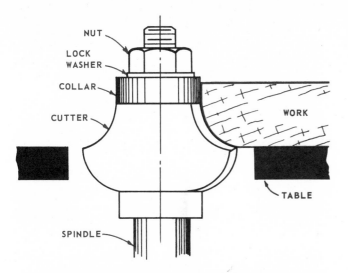

Fig. 16-34. The collar controls the depth of cut.

Fig. 16-35. Shaping a curved edge. Work is positioned against the starting pin. The collar controls depth of cut.

Fig. 16-35 shows a depth collar shaping operation. The cut should be started on the side grain and then carried into the end grain. Start the cut by placing the work securely against the table pin and then swing it slowly into the cut and at the same time move it forward in the direction of the feed. After the cut is started the use of the table pin is not critical, however, it is often helpful in turning corners.

Hold the work firmly against the depth collar but avoid too much pressure as it may cause

WOODY SAYS:

"Always maintain a full 6 in. margin of safety and use the ring guard when shaping irregular pieces. Never hold the work along the edge that has just passed by the cutter as a sudden kickback could throw your hand into the cutter."

burning of the work and collar. Heavy cuts should be handled by making a first cut at about one-half the depth and then making a second pass around the work at a full setting.

Pattern Shaping

An irregular shaped part can be cut to the exact outline and the edge shaped by using a pattern. The part should be cut to rough size on the band saw or jigsaw and then mounted on the pattern

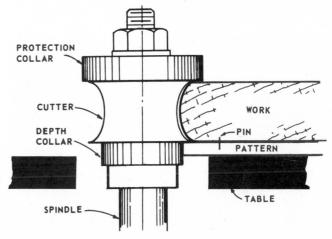

Fig. 16-36. Shaping with a pattern. 3/16 in. or 1/4 in. hardboard makes good pattern stock.

and held in place with clamps or pins. The pattern is designed to ride against the depth collar and guide the work through the cut. See Fig. 16-36. Note the large collar mounted on top to help guard the cutter. Follow the same feeding procedure as for regular work with depth collars. Fig. 16-37 shows a pattern shaping setup where the pattern rides against a special table insert. One side is shaped and then the work is turned over in the holder to shape the other side.

Fig. 16-37. Pattern shaping. Work is mounted in a holder and the depth of cut is controlled by a special table insert. (Rockwell Mfg. Co.)

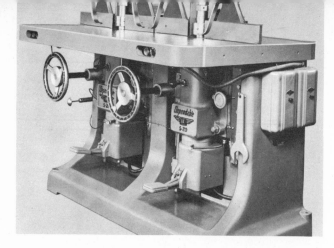

Fig. 16-38. *Double spindle shaper. Spindles are 1 1/4 in. in diameter and directly driven at speeds of 7200 rpm by 5 hp motors. (Dependable Mach. Co.)*

is often more appropriate. The spindles can be rotated in opposite directions, making it easy to follow the grain of the wood by alternating the work from one to the other when shaping irregular work. In Fig. 16-39, a double spindle shaper is being used to shape chair seats in a furniture factory.

The contour profiler, Figs. 16-40 and 41, is a high production machine. It consists of a table that moves back and forth and carries the work and a pattern by a high speed cutterhead. The cutterhead travels in or out as a roller guide follows the contour of the pattern. The work is held to the table with pneumatic or hydraulic

Fig. 16-39. *Shaping the edge of chair seats on a double spindle shaper. (Heywood-Wakefield Co.)*

Various fixtures can be made and set up on the table of the shaper to guide special work. For example, a simple V-shaped guide with a clearance hole for the cutter could be used for circular parts. Auxiliary tables can be used to carry the work through the cut in about the same way as those described for the table saw.

Industrial Machines

Single spindle shapers like the one described in the previous section are often used in industry, however, for heavy production a DOUBLE SPINDLE SHAPER like the one shown in Fig. 16-38

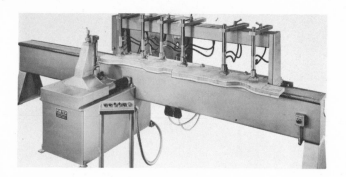

Fig. 16-40. *Contour profiler. Spindle is belt driven at a speed of 8500 rpm. Feed speeds variable from 0 to 60 fpm. Table is returned to starting position at 120 fpm. (Porter Mach. Co.)*

Fig. 16-41. Close-up view of contour profiler in operation.

clamps. Some models have a cutterhead assembly on both sides which increases the production rate in the machining of some parts.

In operation, the work (sometimes several layers) is stacked on the table, automatically clamped and then fed through the cut. At the end of the feed stroke, the cutterhead retracts, and the table returns rapidly to the starting position to be unloaded and reloaded by the operator. Fig. 16-42 shows some of the parts that can be produced.

Cutterhead rotation is in the feed direction to take advantage of the climb-cut principle. This causes the edge of the cutter knife to "lay down" the grain structure of the wood and produces an extremely smooth finish. Such feeding technique is not possible with regular hand-fed shapers.

Another automatic production shaper is the ROTARY PROFILER shown in Fig. 16-43. It consists of a revolving table that carries the work by a cutterhead. Templates or forms are fastened

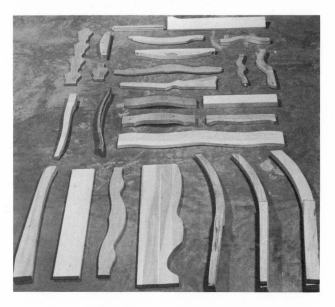

Fig. 16-42. Samples of parts produced on a contour profiler. (Ekstrom, Carlson and Co.)

Fig. 16-43. Rotary profiler. Cutterhead motor 20 hp – 7200 rpm. Table capacity is a 60 in. diameter with adjustable speed of 0 to 10 rpm. (Onsrud Machine Works)

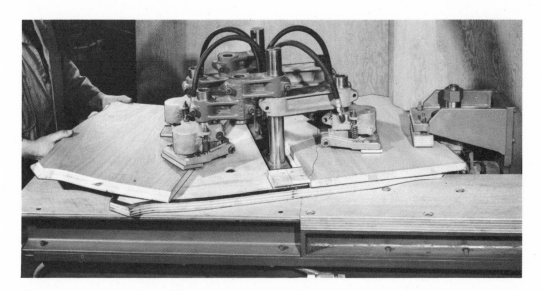

Fig. 16-44. The rotary profiler setup for two-station shaping. The air clamps automatically release the work as they turn to the operator's side. (Onsrud Machine Works)

Fig. 16-45. Rotary profiler with four station setup. Each station shapes a different side of the leg being formed. (Onsrud Machine Works)

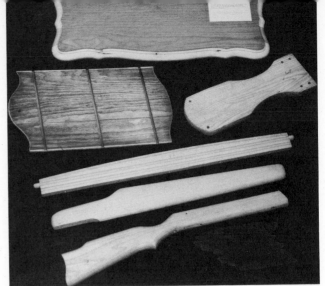

Fig. 16-46. Parts produced on a rotary profiler. (Onsrud Machine Works)

to the table and the work is then held in place by clamps operated by compressed air. The cutterhead operates in about the same manner as the one on the contour profiler. A roller, in contact with the pattern, moves the cutterhead in and out as the work is carried by. Compressed air is used to keep the roller against the template. The machine is especially safe to use since the operator works on the side opposite to the cutterhead location. See Figs. 16-44 and 45. The speed of the table rotation is automatically controlled with a special cam that speeds up or slows down the movement for various parts of the work piece. Fig. 16-46 shows samples of work produced on a rotary profiler.

Fig. 16-47. Dual table shaper. The cutterhead is mounted on the center overarm which swings to first one and then the other revolving table. (Onsrud Machine Works)

Fig. 16-48. Modern electric moulder. Top and bottom-head motors are 10 hp while side-head motors are 5 hp. Feed is variable from 20 to 150 fpm. Weight 10,000 lbs. (Diehl Machines, Inc.)

16-14

A DUAL TABLE SHAPER, shown in Fig. 16-47, permits continuous production of round, square, and rectangular parts up to 28 in. in diameter and 3 in. thick. The operator unloads and loads

cutter. It then moves by cutterheads on either side and finally passes over one located in the table. See Fig. 16-49. The cutterheads shown in the machine are all equipped with straight knives; how-

Fig. 16-49. View of moulder cutterheads. Dust hoods have been removed.
(Mattison Machine Works)

one table while work on the other table is being shaped. During the shaping cycle, work is held in place on the revolving table by an air clamp. The cutterhead and the pattern follower are mounted on an overarm which pivots between the two tables. The follower is held against the pattern by air pressure. Contact of the follower with the pattern, guides the cutter which produces a shaped part that is a duplicate of the pattern. At the end of each cutting cycle, the operator touches a foot switch that initiates a cutting cycle on the second table.

Moulder

This machine produces moldings for furniture and interior trim. In a single pass through the machine, four cutterheads form completely such items as window sash stock, door casings, baseboard, base shoe, tongue and groove flooring, and numerous other items.

Fig. 16-48 shows a modern moulding machine that will handle stock up to 4 in. thick and 8 in. wide. The bed or table of the moulder is made of highly finished hardened steel plates. The feed mechanism consists of an endless chain in one section of the table with overhead rollers. Roll pressure is usually provided by pneumatic power.

In operation, the stock first enters the feed mechanism and then passes under an overhead

Fig. 16-50. A six knife, side-clamp head for use on any spindle. Note the milled-to-pattern knives that are easily sharpened by grinding a single bevel.
(Mattison Machine Works)

ever, when set up to produce molded shapes, cutterheads like the one in Fig. 16-50 are used.

The cutterheads are mounted on a tapered spindle as shown in Fig. 16-51; each is powered by an individual motor. The motors for the top and bottom heads usually have a greater horsepower than the side-heads and are equipped with a chipbreaker that works in the same way as those

Fig. 16-51. Heads are mounted on tapered spindles that insure perfect alignment with no clearance requirement. View shows bottom spindle. (Yates-American Mach. Co.)

Fig. 16-52. Moulder in operation. Work is stacked in a hopper and automatically feeds into the machine. (Mattison Machine Works)

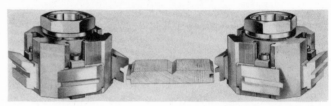

Fig. 16-53. Side-heads set up to produce tongue and groove edges. (Mattison Machine Works)

on thickness planers. The side-heads can be tilted in or out to increase the range of cuts.

Moulders are equipped with motors that operate at 3600 rpm on standard 60 cycle current. By adding a frequency changer that will convert the current to 120 cycles the motors will produce 7200 rpm. See Figs. 16-52 and 16-53.

Test Your Knowledge

1. The bits of a portable router are held in a _____ type of chuck.
2. Router sizes are designated by the size of the _____.
3. The router bit must be mounted in the chuck to a depth of at least one-half inch. True or False?
4. When cutting the outside edge of a circular piece, always feed the router in a _____ (clockwise, counterclockwise) direction.
5. When guiding the router with a template it is necessary to attach a _____ _____ to the base.
6. If a dovetail joint fits too tight, extend the router bit slightly so it will make a deeper cut. True or False?
7. The shaft of a regular shaper, on which the cutter is mounted is called a _____.

8. Solid wing cutters can be sharpened by honing the _____ (face, bevel).
9. When installing shaper cutters a _____ ____ should be located directly under the nut.
10. The two sections of the shaper fence should be perfectly aligned when the cut removes all of the edge being shaped. True or False?
11. When feeding stock from left to right, the cutter should rotate_____ (clockwise, counterclockwise).
12. A production shaper that consists of a long table which carries the work by a cutterhead and then returns to the starting position is called a _____ _____.

Outside Assignments

1. Select a make and model of shaper that would be satisfactory for a school shop. Prepare a complete list of specifications. Include a listing of shaper cutters you would recommend.
2. Prepare a visual aid by forming a milled-to-pattern knife out of wood. Demonstrate to the class how it is sharpened by sanding the bevel on a disk sander.
3. Visit a construction site or a local lumber yard and secure small samples or waste-cuttings of molding. Mount them on a panel with accurate and descriptive labels.

Unit 17

SANDING MACHINES

There are a great many kinds and sizes of sanding machines, ranging from small portable tools to giant multi-belt machines that weigh many tons. Small stationary disk, belt, and drum sanders as well as various portable machines are available and practical for use in the school shop. Power sanders cut the wood rapidly and create a great amount of dust. They should not be operated without proper and adequate connections to a central dust collection system or unit collectors.

Disk Sanders

Disk sanders, although not used extensively in production work, are a valuable tool in the pattern shop, small cabinet shop and school shop. The stationary machine consists of a metal disk that carries the coated abrasive, and a table to support the work. See Fig. 17-1. The table can be tilted at an angle and usually has a slot in which

various guides can be used. The chief purpose of the stationary disk sander is to form and shape parts while the portable disk sander, Fig. 17-2, is used mainly to prepare surfaces for finishing coats.

Fig. 17-2. Using a portable disk sander. (Norton Co.)

Selecting and Mounting Disks

Various grades of sanding disks are available, ranging from a No. 2/0 (100) to as coarse as No. 2 1/2 (30). For average work a No. 1 (50) is satisfactory. Paperbacked sanding disks are used on stationary sanders, while portable sanders, with a flexible disk, require a cloth backing.

On sanders with a metal disk, the paper is held in place by a special nondrying adhesive. The old disk is peeled off and, if the surface of the disk is clean, the coating of adhesive can be reused. With the disk turning under power, run a stick of wood from the center to the outside edge to spread the adhesive evenly. Apply a coat of adhesive to the disk as shown in Fig. 17-3. Spread it thoroughly over the entire surface and then carefully mount the disk in position on the machine and press it firmly in place. Be certain the edge of the abra-

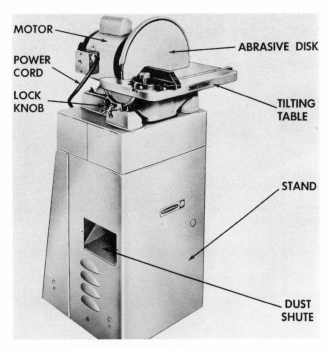

MOTOR

POWER CORD

LOCK KNOB

ABRASIVE DISK

TILTING TABLE

STAND

DUST SHUTE

Fig. 17-1. Parts of a stationary disk sander. The size is determined by the diameter of the disk.

Fig. 17-3. *Applying adhesive to a sanding disk.*

Fig. 17-5. *Sanding a miter joint.*

sive disk is accurately aligned with the edge of the metal disk. On some machines it is best to remove the table for this operation.

Using Disk Sander

The disk sander is used mainly for edge sanding. Hold the work firmly on the table and move it lightly against the disk. Use only the half of the disk that revolves downward past the table. Move the work along this surface and do not hold it at one place or excessive heat will be generated, causing the abrasive to load with gum and pitch. This will shorten the life of the abrasive and also cause burn marks on your work.

Pieces of irregular shapes are usually guided freehand. For accurate work on straight edges, use a miter gauge in the table slot as shown in Fig. 17-4. Other types of guides and auxiliary tables can be used for special work.

Fig. 17-6. *Using a fixture to form disks of a specified size. The disk is held in place by a sharp pin in the dovetail slide.*

to the surface of the disk. The pattern, which is slightly smaller than the finished part, rides along the metal strip and carries the work in about the same way as pattern shaping, Fig. 17-7.

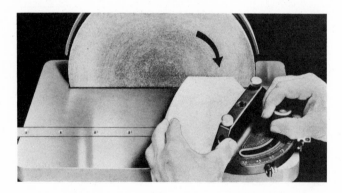

Fig. 17-4. *Forming the edge of an irregular shaped part.*

Fig. 17-5 shows miter joint sanding. Fig. 17-6 shows a special fixture for sanding wooden disks. If a large number are needed, it would be better to have the auxiliary table slide in the machine table slot so that various areas of the surface of the abrasive disk can be used. A pattern sanding setup can be made by attaching a metal strip that extends above the edge of an auxiliary table, next

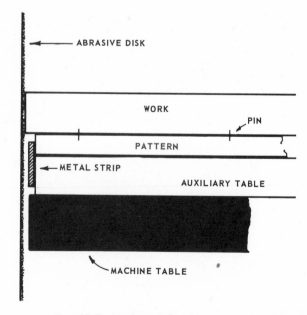

Fig. 17-7. *Sanding with a pattern.*

Belt Sanders

Fig. 17-8, shows a belt sander of the type often used in the school shop. The belt runs over two drums or pulleys and rides on a platen. One drum is powered. The other can be adjusted so the belt will track in the center of the platen. The sander can be positioned vertically as shown, or used in a horizontal position. Cloth belts are used. Grit sizes may range from No. 3/0 (120) to as coarse as No. 3 (24).

To replace a belt, remove the end and side guard, retract the tension spring and remove the belt. Select the belt to be used. Note the travel direction arrow printed on the inside surface, mount the belt so the travel arrow points in the correct direction, and adjust the tension. Roll the machine by hand to check the tracking of the belt. Replace the guards, turn on the machine and readjust the tracking if necessary. The tracking should be watched carefully for the first few minutes of operation.

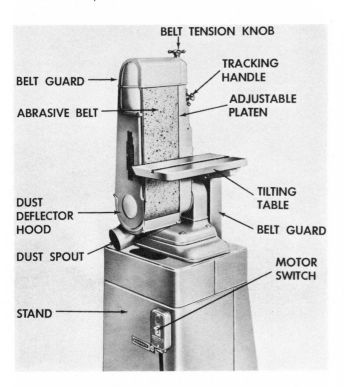

Fig. 17-8. Small stationary belt sander. Belt is 6 in. wide and 48 in. long. (Rockwell Mfg. Co.)

Flat surfaces can be sanded by holding the work as shown in Fig. 17-9. Thin strips should be held against the belt with a wood pad. See Fig. 17-10. When sanding long strips it is usually necessary to remove the end guard.

To sand small surfaces straight and true, use the table and miter gauge. A straightedge can be

Fig. 17-9. Sanding a flat surface. Belt travel is toward the table which serves as a stop.

Fig. 17-10. Sanding thin stock.

Fig. 17-11. Producing a square surface with the aid of the sander table and a straightedge.

Fig. 17-12. Using a shop-built fence.

clamped to the table as shown in Fig. 17-11. Curved edges are accurately sanded by using a shop-built fence, Fig. 17-12. Inside or concave

17-3

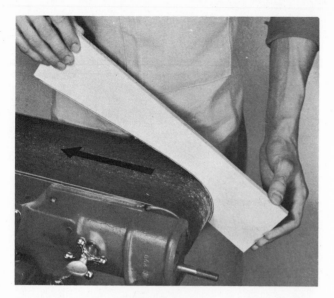

Fig. 17-13. *Using the idler drum to smooth an inside curve. Always replace the belt guard after this operation.*

curves may be sanded on the idler pulley or drum. The guard is removed and the work is held as shown in Fig. 17-13.

A combination belt and disk sander is shown in Fig. 17-14. The crank adjusts the tilt of the disk table.

Safety Rules for Sanding Machines

(In addition to those listed on page 10-30.)

1. Be certain the belt or disk is correctly mounted. The belt must track in the center of the drums and platen. Do not operate the disk sander if the abrasive paper is loose.
2. Check the guards and table adjustments to see that they are in the correct position and securely locked in place.
3. Use the table, fence and other guides to control the position of the work, whenever possible.
4. Small, also irregular-shaped pieces should be held in a hand clamp or some special jig or fixture.

Fig. 17-14. *A combination belt and disk sander. (Oliver Machinery Co.)*

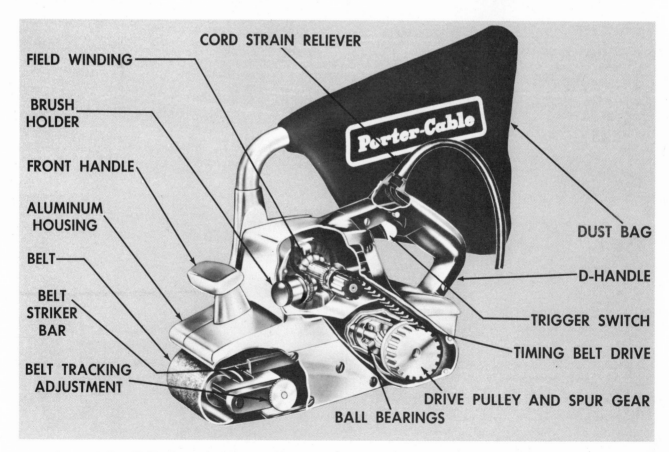

Fig. 17-15. *Parts of a 3 in. portable belt sander. Some machines have a worm-gear drive.*

Fig. 17-16. *Adjusting tracking of the belt.*

5. When sanding the end grain of narrow pieces on the belt sander, always support the work against the table.
6. Sand only on the side of the disk sander that is moving down toward the table. Move the work along this surface so it will not burn.
7. Always use a pad or push block when sanding thin pieces on the belt sander.

covered and powered. Fig. 17-15, shows a standard model equipped with a dust collector.

The size of portable belt sanders is determined by the width of the belt, and usually ranges from 2 to 4 in. The length of belts vary with different types and makes. Belts are made of cloth and coated with various grades of aluminum oxide. For average work in the school shop a No. 1/2 (60) or No. 1 (50) grade is most often used.

To install or replace a belt on a portable sander:

1. Unplug the electrical cord, clean off the excess dust and lay the machine on its left side.
2. Retract the idler (forward) pulley. Different makes and models will vary in design so check the operator's manual for detailed directions.

Fig. 17-17. *Using belt sander. The cord runs over the operator's shoulder to keep it out of the way.*

8. Do not use power sanders to form and shape parts where the operations could be better performed on other machines.
9. Sand only clean new wood. Do not sand work that has excess glue or finish on the surface. These materials will load and foul the abrasive.

Portable Belt Sanders

The portable belt sander is designed to sand flat surfaces. It consists of two pulleys that carry the belt over a shoe. The rear pulley is rubber

3. Place the correct size of belt on the pulleys with the arrow (printed on the inside) pointing in the direction of travel.
4. Release the idler pulley so that correct tension is applied to the belt.
5. Support the sander on the heel of its base, turn on the switch and turn the tracking adjustment so the belt travels in the center of the pulleys. See Fig. 17-16. This adjustment may need to be corrected during the sanding operation. Never allow the belt to ride against the body of the sander.

Using Portable Belt Sander

Stock to be sanded should be firmly supported and held in position. The stock can be clamped in a vise or held by a stop mounted at the rear end of the work.

Be certain the switch is in the off position before plugging in the electric cord. Like all portable power tools, the sander should be properly grounded. Turn on the switch and check the travel of the belt to see if it is tracking properly.

Hold the sander over the work, then lower it carefully and evenly onto the surface. Move the sander forward and backward over the surface. At the end of each stroke, shift it sideways about one-half the width of the belt. See Fig. 17-17. Continue over the entire surface, holding the sander perfectly level and sanding each area the same amount. Do not press down on the sander since its weight is sufficient to provide the proper pressure for the cutting action. If it is allowed

Fig. 17-18. Belt sander being used on construction job by carpenter.

Fig. 17-19. Preparing a boat for finish.

to rock back on the rear pulley, the work will also be damaged. When you complete the work, raise the machine from the surface and then stop the motor.

The portable belt sander can save sanding time, but requires lots of skill to operate it properly. See Figs. 17-18 and 19.

WOODY SAYS:

"Applying excessive pressure to the belt sander will cause the motor to heat and the belt to load and foul. Always lift the sander off of the work before starting or stopping the motor."

Portable sanders are built with compact mechanisms that usually require special lubricants and extra attention to oiling schedules. Study and follow the manufacturer's recommendations as given in the operator's manual. Always clean the sander and empty the dust bag before putting the sander away.

Portable Finishing Sanders

Finishing sanders are used for final sanding where only a small amount of material needs to be removed. They are also used for cutting down and rubbing finishing coats. There are two general types; orbital and oscillating. In the orbital type, Fig. 17-20, the pad moves in a circular path about (3/16 or 1/4 in.) while the pad of the oscillating sander moves back and forth in a straight line. The orbital type cuts faster and is used for general work. The oscillating type is best for fine work, especially for rubbing down finishes.

Standard abrasive papers are attached to the sander pad with a clamp at the front and back edge. Many have pads that are sized so one-third of a standard 9 x 11 in. sheet can be used. Grades and types of abrasive papers are selected with about the same considerations as for hand sanding. Be certain the paper is stretched tightly over the surface of the pad.

Start the sander while it is off the work, then move it back and forth with the grain in the same manner as the belt sander. See Fig. 17-21. It can be guided by either one or both hands; however, extra pressure beyond the weight of the sander should not be applied. Excessive pressure will slow down the motor, causing it to heat, and reduce the efficiency of the machine.

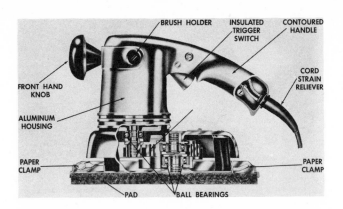

Fig. 17-20. Parts of a finishing sander.
(Rockwell Mfg. Co.)

Fig. 17-21. Using a finish sander.

Fig. 17-22. An air sander with straight-line action. 3000 oscillations per minute. Uses 10 CFM at 65 psi.
(Sundstrand Machine Tool)

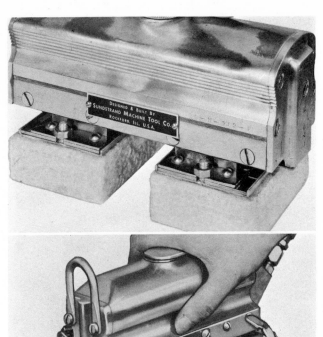

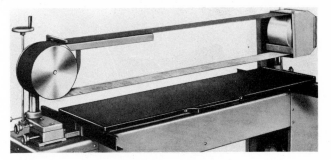

Fig. 17-24. Above. Sundstrand double-pad air sander with 3/4 in. stroke. Fig. 17-25. Below. Norton heavy-duty, double-pad sanding and rubbing machine.

When you have finished your work with the sander, clean it thoroughly before putting it away. Study the operator's manual for instructions on lubrication and adjustments.

Finishing sanders are often operated with compressed air, Fig. 17-22. The small oscillating air driven mechanism is light in weight and has no tendency to heat. Fig. 17-24 shows a double pad

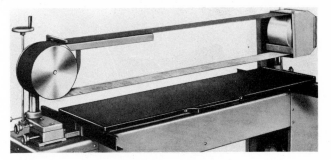

Fig. 17-26. Hand stroke belt sander with 9 in. drums. Belt is 6 in. wide, table 18 x 60 in.
(Boice - Crane)

machine that is designed specifically for padding and rubbing paste filler. A heavy-duty, air-driven, rubbing and polishing machine is shown in Fig. 17-25.

Hand Stroke Belt Sander

This type sander, Fig. 17-26, consists of a long belt that travels around two drums. A table, mounted on rollers, is located under the belt and can be moved in and out. The space between the belt and table can be adjusted. On some machines this is accomplished by raising or lowering the drums; however, most production equipment has a table that is moved up and down.

The work is placed on the table and the space between it and the belt is adjusted to about 1 in. A stop on the table prevents the work from sliding.

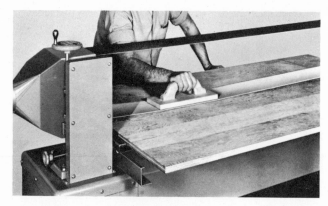

Fig. 17-27. Using the hand stroke belt sander. Belt speed 3000 sfm.

The moving belt is then pressed down against the surface of the stock with a block as shown in Fig. 17-27. The block is moved along the entire length of the work and then the table is pulled in or out to another position for the next stroke. A heavy-duty belt sander is shown in Fig. 17-28.

Fig. 17-28. Heavy-duty belt sander. Table 32 by 96 in. travels 33 in. in or out. (Oliver Machinery Co.)

Some hand stroke belt sanders are designed so the abrasive surface of the belt is turned inward and rides on the surface of the drums. Fig. 17-29. The belt return is located under the table and there is less interference with the sanding operation. Fig. 17-29 shows this type of sander being used to finish-sand a matched veneer table top. It is also used to sand drawer fronts, countertops, and on a great variety of flat panel stock.

Fig. 17-29. Finish sanding with a hand stroke belt sander. Belt is a 4/0 (150) aluminum oxide abrasive on an E weight paperbacking. (Norton Co.)

The belt sander is often equipped with a flexible belt (Jeans cloth) and used to finish-sand contours, molded edges, and other irregular surfaces. Handblocks made specifically to match a given contour are used to press the belt against the work as shown in Fig. 17-30.

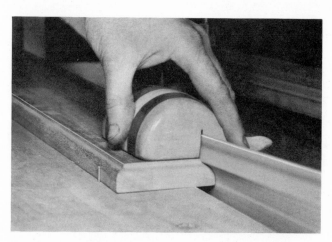

Fig. 17-30. Using a flexible belt and a contoured handblock to sand a shaped edge.

Brush-Backed Sanding Wheels

The brush-backed sanding wheel consists of a number of brushes located around the periphery of a wheel that stores strips of coated abrasive. These strips extend a short distance beyond the tips of the brushes. As the wheel revolves, the brushes press the abrasive against the work. This type sander is designed for smoothing and polishing various contours. Wheel faces range from 2 to 6 in. although they may be used in multiples for wider parts. Wheel speeds usually range from 600 to 1800 rpm. See Fig. 17-31.

Fig. 17-31. Using a brush-backed sanding wheel.

Radial FLAP WHEELS are similar to the brush-back wheel. See Fig. 17-32. They do not, however, use any back-up device but are composed of many flaps of abrasive strips, closely packed together. The usual production wheel

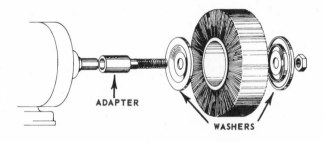

Fig. 17-32. Mounting for a radial flap wheel.
(Merit Products Inc.)

makeup consists of 800 to 1000 flaps of garnet or aluminum oxide abrasive on J-weight cloth. Grades of No. 1/2 (60) through 4/0 (150) are used for average to fine work. Speeds should seldom exceed 3000 sfpm.

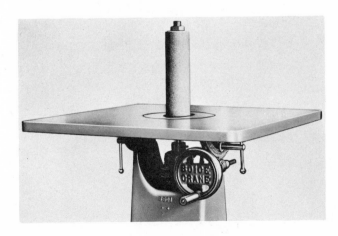

Fig. 17-33. Spindle sander. The spindle revolves at 2200 rpm and oscillates up and down with a 7/8 in. stroke.

Spindle Sanders

This type machine, Fig. 17-33, has a vertical spindle that projects through a horizontal table. The spindle revolves and also oscillates up and down, thus producing a smooth finish. The table can be tilted for angle work. This sander is used for a wide range of work and is especially valuable in patternmaking. See Fig. 17-34.

Fig. 17-34. Oscillating spindle sander in use.

Pneumatic Sanding Drums

Figs. 17-35 and 36, show a sanding machine that uses rubber sanding drums which are inflated with compressed air. This provides a cushion that will conform to an irregular surface and produces a smooth even finish. Abrasive

Fig. 17-35. Pneumatic drum sander. This can be equipped with drums from 2 to 26 in. in diameter.
(Ekstrom, Carlson and Co.)

Fig. 17-36. Using drum sander to finish formed plywood chair seats.

Fig. 17-37. *A pneumatic drum and backstand unit carries a belt for finish sanding operation on chair back.*

The pneumatic drum is sometimes used with a backstand unit to carry a sanding belt, Fig. 17-37. Belts wear better than drums because the flexing tends to remove the sand dust and the abrasive particles have a longer time to cool between contacts with the work.

Edge Belt Sanders

The edge belt sander, Fig. 17-38, uses a belt carried in a vertical position. The drums and platen oscillate up and down (about 1/2 in.) at a rate of 130 cycles per minute. The side and end tables adjust up and down and can be tilted. Straight edges and bevels are sanded on the side of the machine, while curved edges can be worked against the idler pulley or drum. To reduce friction, the platen is often covered with graphite-coated canvas.

Automatic Stroke Sanders

The automatic stroke sander is similar to the hand stroke sander with the addition of a pressure block that is accurately carried back and forth over the work. The stroking mechanism is

cloth in the form of sleeves, is slipped over the drum before it is inflated. The amount of air pressure can be varied for different types of work.

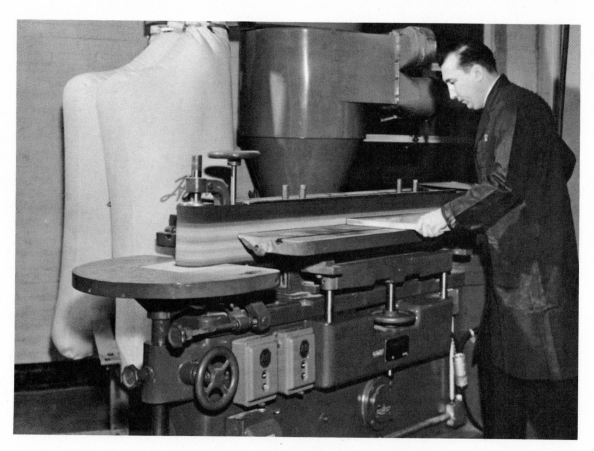

Fig. 17-38. *Edge belt sander. Note the dust collection cyclone and filter bags in the background.*
(Norton Co.)

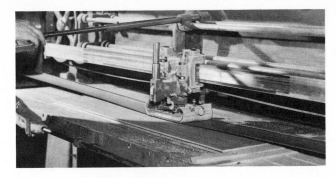

Fig. 17-39. Automatic stroke sander in operation.

powered by a separate motor and can be adjusted to various rates in a range from 45 to 140 fpm. The pressure on the work and the length and position of the stroke can also be regulated. See Fig. 17-39.

The automatic stroke sander shown in Fig. 17-40 has a conveyorized table that carries the work slowly through the machine as the belt is stroked against the surface.

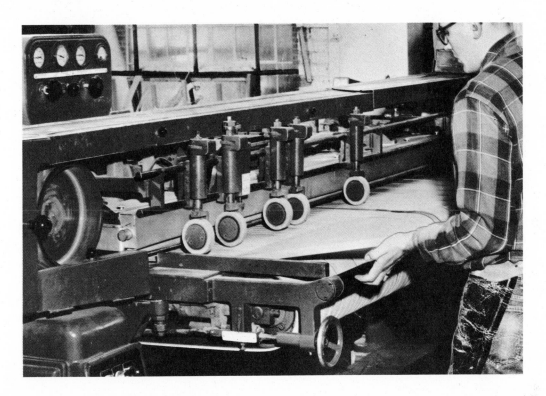

Fig. 17-40. Feed-through automatic stroke sander. Work is placed on the conveyorized table and carried under the belt. (Mersman Bros.)

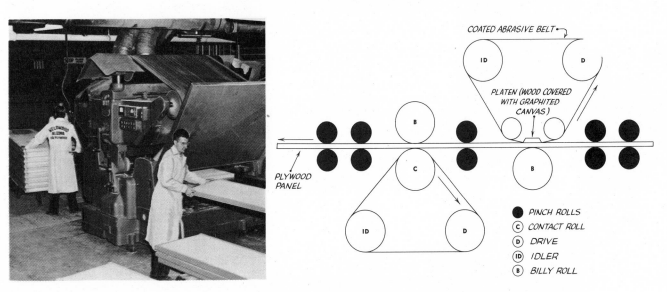

Fig. 17-41. Left. Sander with belts 20 ft. long. Motors that drive the belts and feeding mechanism total 150 hp. (Mattison Machine Works)   Fig. 17-42. Right. Diagram shows how plywood panel proceeds through wide belt sander. (Norton Co.)

Wide-Belt Sanders

Fig. 17-41 shows a giant, wide-belt machine being used to sand core stock for flush doors. These high production machines usually sand both the top and bottom surfaces at feed-through rates of from 20 to 150 fpm. The plywood industry has largely replaced the older multi-drum sanders with this type of equipment. Some have belts as wide as 72 in. that travel at speeds of 5000 sfpm. The diagram in Fig. 17-42, shows how a plywood panel proceeds through a machine as it produces a fine finish and also controls the thickness of the stock to a few thousandths of an inch.

A high production three-stage belt sander, Fig. 17-43, combines fast stock removal with a high quality finish. A traveling bed carries the work under the first two belts which brings the stock to the selected thickness. The last belt removes only a slight amount of material and produces the final high quality finish required by the furniture and cabinetmaking industries.

Test Your Knowledge

1. Stationary disk sanders have a _____ that supports the work.
2. When using the stationary disk sander, the work should contact only the half of the disk that is moving _____ .
3. To track the belt on a sander, the (idler drum, powered drum) is adjusted.
4. The size of a portable belt sander is determined by the length of the belt. True or False?
5. The portable belt sander is placed on the work piece before the motor is turned on. True or False?
6. The two general types of finishing sanders are the _____ and oscillating.
7. You should use the same grades of abrasive paper for a finishing sander as for hand sanding. True or False?
8. The hand stroke belt sander is adjusted so that the belt runs about _____ above the work.
9. On the edge belt sander, the drums and _____ oscillate up and down.
10. The stroking mechanism of automatic stroke sanders can be operated at rates as high as 1000 fpm. True or False?

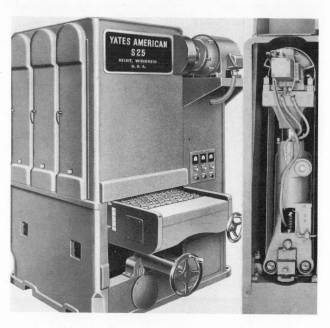

Fig. 17-43. Left. Three stage belt sander handles work up to 24 in. wide and 6 in. thick. Feed rate adjustable from 20 to 60 fpm. Right. Covers removed to show belt carrying unit driven by a 25 hp motor. Sanding belts are 25 in. wide by 103 in. long and travel at a speed of 4700 fpm. (Yates-American)

Outside Assignments

1. Select a power sander that would be practical for a home workshop. List the factors you considered in making your choice. Prepare complete specifications for the machine and include cost figures.
2. Design a mounting or holder that would convert a portable belt sander into an edge sander. Try to include some of the features of the industrial machine described in this Unit. Prepare working drawing sketches of your design.
3. Design a small (2 in. or less in dia.) flap wheel that could be mounted in the chuck of the drill press. Develop a practical method of attaching the cloth or paper flaps to the hub. Prepare the necessary design sketches to present your ideas clearly.
4. Develop working drawing sketches of a fixture that could be mounted on a stationary belt sander to finish long, thin, narrow strips. Use feather-boards to apply pressure and some type of fence to guide the work. Include special guards to protect the worker.

Unit 18

FURNITURE AND CABINETWORK

Furniture is a term applied to movable articles such as chairs, tables, desks, and beds used to furnish rooms in homes and commercial or public buildings. Cabinetwork, although similar in nature, is a term usually applied to cases, cabinets, counters, and other interior woodwork that is fixed in place and is non-movable after it is installed. Some pieces of furniture are called cabinets (TV, stereo, and storage) and this results in some confusion in the terminology.

Although methods of construction are often the same, cabinetwork in general does not require the high level of perfection in design, accuracy, and finish that is found in most furniture.

Today, nearly all of our furniture is produced in large factories. This is also largely true of cabinetwork, however, some is still made in smaller cabinet shops and by carpenters working on the construction site.

Types of Construction

FRAME construction consists of several similar pieces, that are usually fastened together at their ends. Examples would include picture frames, bulletin boards, trays, mirror frames and component parts of some furniture and cabinetwork.

LEG AND RAIL is the type of construction used for tables, chairs, benches and stools. The basic parts (legs, rails, stretchers, braces) are nearly always made of solid stock and joined together with various joints. Mortise and tenon joints have been used for quality work through the years, but today, with so much improvement in adhesives, dowel joints are considered to be as strong, especially when reinforced with glue blocks or special metal fasteners.

BOX or CHEST and CASE. Boxes or chests consist of sides, ends, and a top and bottom. Various joints are used in the corners while the bottom and top can be attached flush, or set in

rabbets or grooves. If the structure is turned on its side it would be called case construction with the bottom becoming the back and the sides becoming the top and bottom. Shelves could be installed and doors mounted on the front. This is the type of construction used for bookcases, cabinets and built-ins. Because the surfaces are large and wide, plywood or other manufactured panels are used.

CARCASS construction is similar to case construction with more internal details. It usually includes drawers as well as doors. Instead of solid panels, framed panels are often used. It is the type of construction used in knee-hole desks, dressers and buffets.

FRAME WITH COVER. This type of construction is used mainly in cabinetwork for such items as wardrobes, closets, and other built-in units. It consists of frames of various design that are then covered with thin plywood or hardboard to provide a finished surface.

Standard Sizes

In the design and construction of furniture and cabinetwork, careful attention must be given to certain standard sizes that have been established from a study of the human anatomy. These dimensions will apply equally well to any style of furniture. Some sizes are critical while others may vary. For example, the height of a dining table or home desk should be 29 to 29 1/2 in., while the width and depth of the desk top may vary considerable depending on its purpose and use. Another important requirement for dining tables and desks is ample knee space. The distance from the seat of the chair to the underside of the top or rails must be at least 7 in. Leg room for knee-hole desks should seldom be less than 24 in. wide.

Fig. 18-1, shows a number of standard furniture items along with overall sizes. The height dimensions are usually the most important and

Fig. 18-1

LAMP TABLE: Above. Overall size; 28 long, 24 wide by 20 in. high. Solid stock can be used throughout. If the top is made of solid stock, provision must be made for expansion and contraction across the grain. In fabrication, the joints for the legs and rails should first be made and fitted and then the contours can be cut and the corners rounded.

DROP LEAF DINING TABLE: Below. With the leaves down, the size is 42 x 26 by 29 in. high. Leaves are 10 in. wide. Mortise and tenon joints should be used for the legs and rails. The top is made of lumber core plywood with a rule joint at the hinge line. Leaves can be supported with a wooden slide, running through the rails. (Heywood - Wakefield)

Fig. 18-1 Continued

CORNER TABLE: Below, left. 30 by 30 by 21 in. high. The three legs under the spacers can be turned in one piece including the spacer. Form the tenons in the lathe and then cut the spacer and leg apart. A dowel screw could be used to reassemble them into the top.

END TABLE: Below, center. 28 long, 18 wide by 20 in. high. Top and shelf could be made of plywood or solid stock. Shelf attachment can be made with a wood screw and screweye combination shown elsewhere in this unit.

COFFEE TABLE: Below, right. 48 long, 20 wide by 14 in. high. Top can be either solid wood or plywood with a matching laminated plastic surface. Turned legs could be attached with either a round tenon or a patented metal bracket.

Fig. 18-1 Continued

DOUBLE DRESSER WITH HANGING MIRROR: Left. Overall; 56 wide, 19 deep, by 30 in. high. Upper drawers are fitted with trays to hold accessories. Lower drawers have movable partitions. Top and sides of lumber core plywood. Drawer fronts are solid stock. Top could be a plastic laminate to match night table. Mirror is plate glass, 24 x 36, in a frame that tapers in depth from top to bottom.

CHINA HUTCH ON BUFFET: Right. China hutch is 47 in. wide, 12 deep and 38 in. high. It is equipped with sliding plate glass doors above the two small drawers. Shelves are adjustable. Buffet is 48 wide, 18 deep and 30 in. high. Top is surfaced with matching laminated plastic. Fitted with three drawers and a large compartment with adjustable shelves.

DESK AND CHAIR: Left. Desk is 50 wide, 20 deep and 29 1/2 in. high. Top can be made of plywood or solid stock. If made of solid wood, it must be secured to the rails with flexible attachments to allow for expansion and contraction across its width. Drawer section rests on the stretcher and is fastened to front rail. Chair, overall; 18 wide, 21 deep and 31 in. high. Seat can be made of 3/8 plywood and padded with polyurethane foam. It should be attached to the rails with screws so that it can be easily removed to replace the covering material.

ARM CHAIR: Right. Overall; 29 wide, 30 deep, by 29 high. Solid wood frame. Seat frame fitted with rubber webbing. Polyurethane seat and back cushion. Details of construction shown in another section of this unit.

should receive the most considerations. The following list includes additional items not included in the figure:

	HEIGHT	WIDTH	DEPTH
Card Tables	28	30	30
Typewriter Tables	26	Vary	Vary
Ping Pong Tables	30	60	180
Bookcases	Vary	Vary	10
Kitchen Base Cabinets	34-36	Vary	25
Kitchen Wall Cabinets	18 (above base)	Vary	12
Work Bench	34	48 min.	22-24

Standard dimensions should be applied accurately to the design of chairs. See Fig. 18-2. The height and depth of the seat are critical measurements. The angle of the seat and back are also important if maximum comfort is to be attained.

proper atmospheric environment. Interior wood products in service will dry out during the heating season and absorb moisture during the high humidities of summer months, causing a dimensional change across the grain of plus or minus 1/8 in. for each 12 in. of width. The hydroscopic nature of wood makes this a tremendous force that can result in joint failure and the destruction of an assembly.

Waterproof finishes on the surface will slow down the expansion and contraction action somewhat but it cannot be prevented entirely. In the design and construction of your project, you should give careful attention to this problem, especially when the width of solid stock parts is considerable.

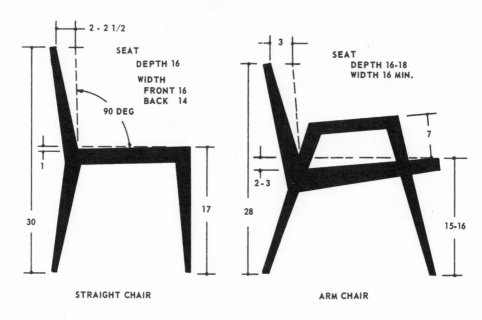

Fig. 18-2. Standard sizes for chair construction.

Using Solid Stock

Today, commercially produced furniture and cabinetwork includes a great amount of plywood, especially when wide surfaces are required. Using plywood saves production time because large panels are available and surfaces are already sanded. The greatest advantage however, is that it provides a strong, stable material that is free from excessive swelling and shrinking. Beautiful grain patterns are available in veneer covered plywood that may be used in place of the more expensive solid stock.

Solid wood, even though properly dried, is stable only in one direction -- along the grain. Across the grain, expansion and contraction can be controlled only by keeping the wood in the

Fig. 18-3 shows a night table built largely of solid stock. It is 20 wide, 15 deep and 25 in. high. There is no problem of stability with the legs and rails that form the base, however, the top, shelf, bottom, and sides are all made of solid stock, and the direction of the grain must run as shown by the arrows. This way these members can all expand and contract together. A frame or plywood panel cannot be used for the bottom unless some flexible coupling is used to join it to the sides. The dimensions of the back will not change since it is bounded by edges running along the grain. Here a plywood panel must be used. The base will be stable in size and should be attached to the solid bottom of the main section with devices that will permit movement.

Fig. 18-3. Grain direction in solid wood construction.

Framed Panels

For large areas in case and carcass construction, framed panels are often used. See Fig. 18-4. Such construction is also used for

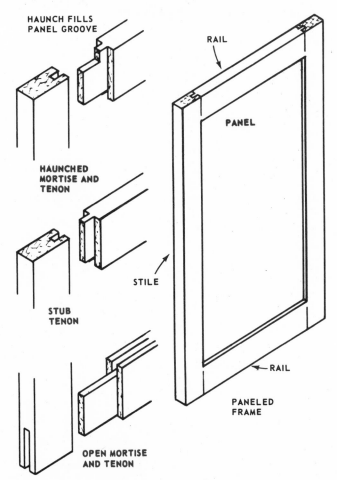

HAUNCH FILLS
PANEL GROOVE

HAUNCHED
MORTISE AND
TENON

STUB
TENON

OPEN MORTISE
AND TENON

RAIL

PANEL

STILE

RAIL

PANELED
FRAME

Fig. 18-4. Joints used to construct a framed panel.

doors (called panel doors) and provides a stable assembly. The vertical members are called stiles and the horizontal members are called rails. The unit can be divided into several sections by using additional rails. The corner joints may be doweled but a stub tenon or haunched mortise and tenon is more often used. A groove is cut around the inside of the frame to carry the panel. When framing glass doors, a rabbet and stop is used instead of the groove so that the glass can be replaced if broken.

Panel construction is a common form used in carcass assemblies and makes extensive use of the framed panel, Fig. 18-5. Corner posts or

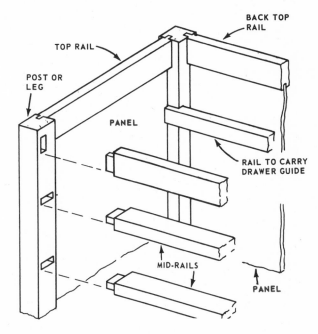

BACK TOP
RAIL

TOP RAIL

POST OR
LEG

PANEL

RAIL TO CARRY
DRAWER GUIDE

MID-RAILS

PANEL

Fig. 18-5. Framed panels in carcass construction.

legs replace the stiles and can carry rails and/or panels on several faces. Rails are attached to the posts to frame openings for drawers or doors. It provides a strong, sturdy method of construction that is often used in quality furniture.

When the design requires flush panels, the corner posts are rabbeted to carry the panel and the rails are set behind the panel.

Making a Master Layout

When working with complicated structures involving shelves, doors, and drawers it is good practice to make a full size layout. This can be made on a piece of plywood or cardboard as shown in Fig. 18-6.

Follow the dimensions of your working drawing carefully. Sectional views will usually be most helpful. Draw each member full size and

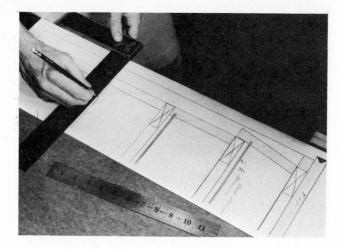

Fig. 18-6. Making a full-size layout.

Constructing Web Frames

In case and carcass construction, internal framing components are often required. They are called web frames or usually just frames. Plywood panels could be used but this would waste material and might add excessive weight to the structure. Fig. 18-7 shows how a standard web frame fits into simple case construction. An alternate method is shown in Fig. 18-8.

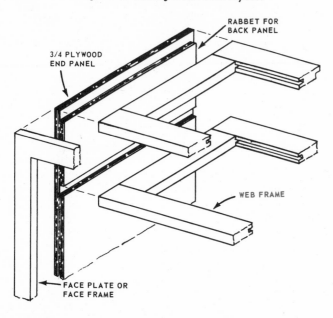

Fig. 18-7. Using web frames in case construction. Terminology as specified by Architectural Woodworking Institute.

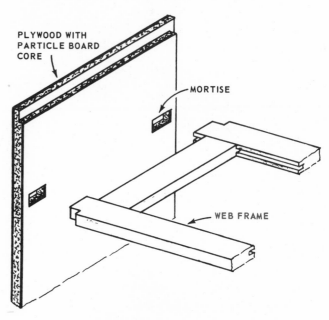

Fig. 18-8. Alternate method of joining web frame to side. This may be used when a full groove across the panel would weaken it.

show various clearances that may be required. This master layout will be especially valuable when cutting side or end panels to size and locating joints. It can also be referred to for exact sizes and locations of drawer parts and many other detailed dimensions that are not included in the working drawing.

Fig. 18-9 shows the joints being cut for a frame assembled with stub tenons. The required stock is cut to thickness and width and then cut to length with each part about 1/8 in. longer and wider than required. The groove for the tenon is cut all the way across the front and back since it will be used to carry a center drawer guide in this particular assembly. Normally the groove could be cut in from each end just far enough for

Fig. 18-9. Left. Cutting grooves in the front and back pieces. Push sticks are used in each hand to finish the cut. Right. Cutting the stub tenon using a dado head and fence pad.

Fig. 18-10. Gluing web frames.

Fig. 18-12. Above. Cutting dado joints in side or end panels. Below. Cutting a single shoulder tongue on the side of the frame, using a dado head.

the tenon. The frames are then glued together, Fig. 18-10. Check carefully to see that they are square and lie in a perfect plane. After the glue has cured, the surfaces can be sanded lightly.

In Fig. 18-11 the frames are being trimmed to exact size, following the same procedure you would use in squaring a solid panel. In some structures it may be necessary to separate the area by installing a hardboard or plywood panel in the frame. This is often done in chests of drawers and is referred to as dustproof construction. The separation would also be important in banks of locked drawers since access to the drawer below could otherwise be gained by simply removing the drawer above.

Fig. 18-11. Trimming web frame to size. Saw guard removed to show saw.

Assembling Panels and Web Frames

If the side or end panels are of plywood, the frames can be set in dados and glued. The dados should be laid out and cut first, as shown in Fig. 18-12. It is best to make the depth of the groove somewhat less than half the thickness of

plywood. The edge of the frame is now cut to size to match the dado, using a setup as shown. The dado could be cut to match the full thickness of the frame, however, it will be easier to secure an accurate fit by the method shown and the joint will be slightly stronger.

In Fig. 18-13, a trial assembly is being made of a drawer section for a kneehole desk. When

Fig. 18-13. Making a trial assembly of web frames and a side panel.

constructing a unit like this that has many parts, it is best to glue the frames into one side panel with the other side panel clamped in place dry. After the glued side of the assembly has set up the other panel is removed and the glue applied.

When the drawer sections are complete, they are joined together with the center section, Fig. 18-14, and the top, legs, and rear panels are attached. This general procedure and method of construction can be applied to cabinets, chests, and similar products. Side panels of solid stock could be used in these structures if the grain runs parallel to the frames.

of the simplest is to apply a thin veneer which can be purchased or produced in the shop. Any regular contact bond cement can be used. Porous woods should be double-coated.

Fig. 18-14. Basic assembly of a kneehole desk. The bottom brace strips are removed after back panels and the top are attached.

Finishing Plywood Edges

When using plywood in the construction of furniture and cabinetwork, any exposed edges will need to be covered. This will include the edges of tops, case fronts, and may also include the edges of doors, shelves, and drawer fronts. In furniture factories, plywood is often fabricated with a banding core of solid stock that matches the veneer.

There are a number of ways to cover the edges of either veneer core or solid core plywood. One

Cut the veneer strips to size. It is usually best for the strip to be 1/16 to 1/32 in. wider than the edge of the plywood. A pair of sharp scissors or shears can be used to cut ends and miters. Apply the glue or cement, Fig. 18-15, allow it to dry, and then carefully place the strips in position. Press or roll them firmly. Water based glues such as polyvinyl and urea resin do not work well because they tend to curl the veneer and the strips must be clamped.

Sometimes it is better to use solid wood strips for the banding and edge finish. See Fig. 18-16. Larger strips can be glued in place and then shaped later. The V-strip provides an attractive appearance and is especially valuable for veneer core doors where butt hinges will be used since screws do not hold well in the edges. The solid strip may be applied so that it forms a wider width for an apron around a table top. Where solid edge banding meets at a corner, it should be mitered and carefully fitted. Use regular glue and clamps.

The banding strip could be cut from the plywood and a miter joint used. This makes it easy to secure a perfect match. With some woods, it

Fig. 18-15. Veneering plywood edges. Left. Applying contact cement. Right. Placing veneer strips in position.

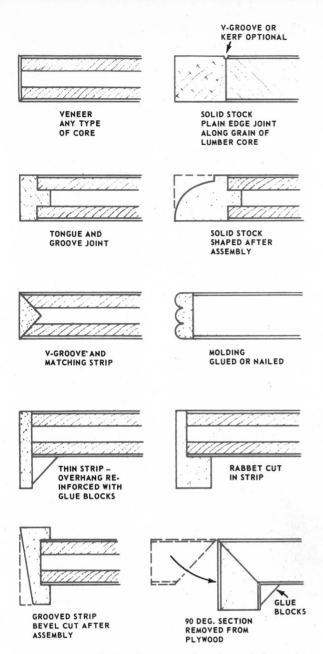

VENEER
ANY TYPE
OF CORE

V-GROOVE OR
KERF OPTIONAL

SOLID STOCK
PLAIN EDGE JOINT
ALONG GRAIN OF
LUMBER CORE

TONGUE AND
GROOVE JOINT

SOLID STOCK
SHAPED AFTER
ASSEMBLY

V-GROOVE AND
MATCHING STRIP

MOLDING
GLUED OR NAILED

THIN STRIP –
OVERHANG RE-
INFORCED WITH
GLUE BLOCKS

RABBET CUT
IN STRIP

GROOVED STRIP
BEVEL CUT AFTER
ASSEMBLY

90 DEG. SECTION
REMOVED FROM
PLYWOOD

GLUE
BLOCKS

Fig. 18-16. Methods of trimming the edges of plywood.

is possible to make a 90 deg. V-cut just to the face veneer and then moisten and bend the edge into position.

Drawers

There are two general types of drawers; lip and flush. They usually fit into framed openings of the structure, however, sometimes they are carried by special supports attached to the underside of a top or frame. Flush drawers, Fig. 18-17, are used in most furniture and must be carefully fitted. Lip drawers have a rabbet along the top and sides of the front which covers the clearance and permits greater freedom in the fit. They are used mainly in built-in cabinetwork.

Sizes and designs in drawer construction vary widely. Fig. 18-18 shows standard construction

Fig. 18-17. Flush type drawers. Note the carefully matched grain patterns.   (Drexel Furniture Co.)

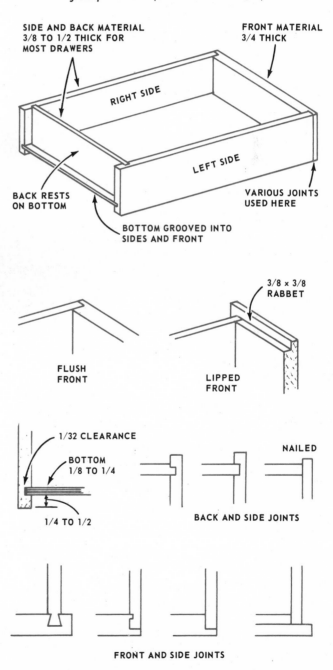

Fig. 18-18. Standard drawer construction.

with several types of joints that are commonly used. The joint between the drawer front and the drawer side receives the greatest strain and should be carefully designed and fitted. In the highest quality of work, each corner is dovetailed and the bottom grooved into the back as well as the front and sides. Also the top edge of the drawer sides is rounded as shown in Fig. 18-19. Drawers that are to be fitted very accurately may be constructed with the sides set about 1/16 to 1/8 in. deeper into the fronts so that a slight lug is formed. This lug is then trimmed to form a good fit.

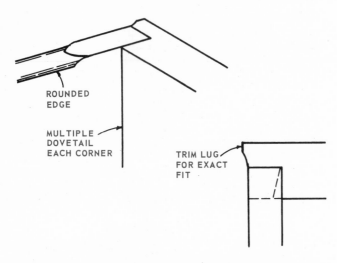

ROUNDED EDGE

MULTIPLE DOVETAIL EACH CORNER

TRIM LUG FOR EXACT FIT

Fig. 18-19. Premium grade (highest) drawer details as established by the Architectural Woodworking Institute. Bottom is grooved into front, sides and back. Sides and back must be of hardwood.

Drawers are usually not constructed until after the case or cabinet in which they will fit has been assembled. The following procedure should be considered in building drawers for either furniture or cabinetwork.

1. Select the material for the fronts. Grain patterns should match or blend with each other. Solid stock or plywood may be used.
2. Cut the drawer fronts to the size of the opening (if flush type) allowing a 1/16 in. clearance on each side and on the top. This clearance will vary depending on the depth of the drawer and the kind of material. Deep drawers with solid fronts will require greater vertical clearance. For lip drawers, add the depth of the rabbets to the dimensions.
3. Select and prepare the stock for the sides and back. A less expensive medium hard wood can be used. Plywood is usually not satisfactory for these parts. Surface the

Fig. 18-20. Cutting lock joint in drawer front. Left. Cutting groove. Right. Trimming tongue to length.

stock to thickness, rip it to finished width and then cut it to the required length with allowance for the joints. The surfaces should be rough sanded either before or after cutting to length.

4. Select the material for the bottom. Hardboard or plywood should be used. The bottoms can be trimmed to final size after the joints for the other drawer members are cut.
5. Cut the groove for the bottom in the front and sides.
6. Cut the joints in the drawer fronts that will hold the drawer sides. Fig. 18-20 shows a sequence for cutting a locked joint. For lip drawers, cut the rabbet first and then the required joint.
7. Cut the matching joint in the drawer sides. BE CERTAIN TO CUT A LEFT AND RIGHT SIDE FOR EACH DRAWER.
8. Cut the required joints for the drawer sides and backs. See Fig. 18-21.

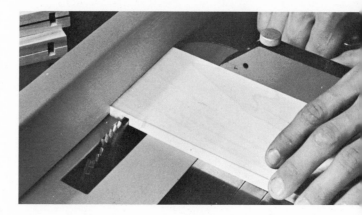

Fig. 18-21. Cutting dado in sides to hold drawer backs.

9. Trim the bottom to the correct size and make a trial assembly as shown in Fig. 18-22. Make any adjustments in the fit that may be required. The parts should fit smoothly and not be so tight that they will be difficult to assemble after the glue is applied.

Fig. 18-22. Above. Trial assembly. Below. Parts ready to be glued.

10. Disassemble and sand all parts. The top edge of the sides are often rounded between points about 1 in. from each end.
11. Make the final assembly. A number of procedures can be used. One method is to first glue the bottom into the front and then glue one of the front corners as shown in Fig. 18-23. Be sure the bottom is centered.

Fig. 18-23. Gluing drawer. Left. Bottom in place and glue being applied to a front corner. Right. Placing the second side in position -- final operation.

The side grooves are usually not glued. Turn the drawer on its side and glue the back into the assembled side. Finally glue on the remaining side as shown. Clamps or a few nails can be used to hold the joints together until the glue hardens.

12. Carefully check the drawer for squareness and then drive one or two nails through the bottom into the back. If the bottom was carefully squared you should have little trouble with the operation. Wipe off the excess glue.

After the glue has cured, make a selective fit of each drawer to a particular opening. Install and adjust drawer guides. Place an identifying number and/or letter on the underside of the bottom so it will be easy to return the drawer to its proper opening after sanding and finishing operations. The inside surfaces of quality drawers should always be sealed and waxed.

Drawer Guides

Three common type drawer guides are: corner guides, center guides, and side guides. The corner guide is often formed in the structure by the side panel and frame, however, it may be necessary to add a spacer strip as shown in Fig. 18-24.

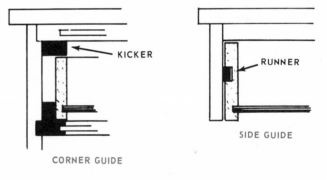

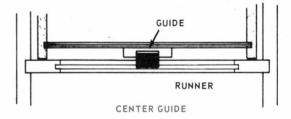

Fig. 18-24. Types of drawer guides.

The center drawer guide consists of a strip or runner fastened between the front and back rails. A guide which is attached to the underside and back of the drawer, rides on this runner. The runner is attached to the frame or rails with screws and can be adjusted so that the clearance on each side is equal and the face of the drawer aligns with the front of the structure.

In drawer openings where there is no lower frame, a side guide may be the most practical to use. Grooves are cut in the drawer side before it is assembled and matching strips are fastened to the structure. This type of guide would be a good one to use for a drawer located directly under the top of a coffee table or occasional table.

The drawer carrier arrangement may require a "kicker" or some other device to keep the drawer from tilting downward when it is pulled open. Wooden drawer guides should be carefully fitted and the parts given a sealer coat of finish. If the sealer on the moving parts is sanded lightly and then waxed, the drawer will work almost as smooth as if it had been installed with some of the various patented nylon rollers or slides.

Fig. 18-25 shows a commercial back bearing for a center slide and how it is installed. For large drawers, or those that will carry con-

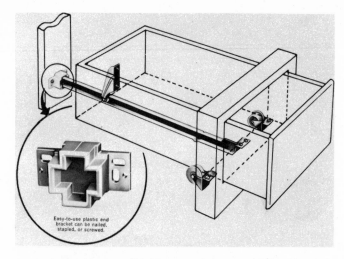

Fig. 18-26. Three roller drawer slide assembly. Flanged plastic rollers provide smooth, quiet operation. (Amerock Corp.)

Fig. 18-27 presents several methods of installing adjustable supports. Lay out the arrangement carefully so that the shelves will be perfectly level. Usually it is best to do the cutting or drilling before the structure is assembled. This is essential when using one of the patented shelf standards where slotted strips are set in grooves cut in the sides or back.

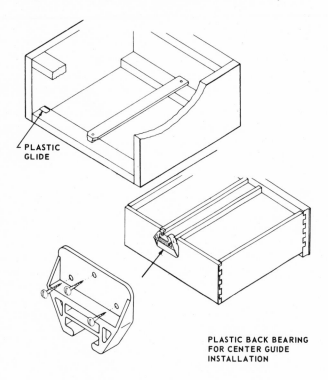

Fig. 18-25. A patented guide installation. (Ronthor Reiss Corp.)

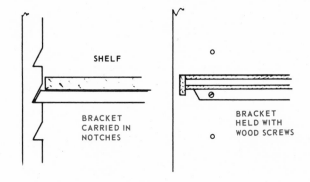

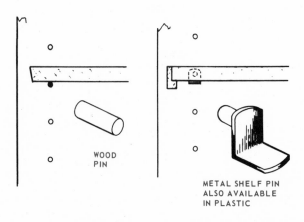

Fig. 18-27. Shelf supports.

siderable weight, a commercial, 3-roller drawer slide like the one shown in Fig. 18-26 might be used. It is available in several sizes and supports a weight up to 50 lbs.

Shelves

In some work, it may be necessary to fit and glue the shelves into dados cut in the sides of the structure to provide additional strength. When possible however, it is better to make them adjustable, up and down, so that they can be used for various purposes.

Standard shelving that is 3/4 in. thick should never be carried on supports that are spaced more than 42 in. apart. This applies especially to shelves that will carry books and other heavy loads.

Swinging Doors

There are two general classifications of doors; swinging and sliding. Doors may be made of plywood, panel and frame, or a frame covered with thin plywood as shown in Fig. 18-28. Solid stock

Fig. 18-28. Shop-built hollow-core door. Frame is 5/8 in. thick and covered with 1/8 in. plywood "skins." Completed door at left.

is seldom used, unless the door is very small, because it will very likely warp and excessive clearances must be provided across the grain to prevent it from sticking during humid weather. Regardless of the material used, doors should be finished with the same sequence of finishing coats on both the inside and outside surface.

Swinging doors may be hung flush with the opening, overlay the opening, or be inset part way like the lipped drawer front, Fig. 18-29. The flush door is usually installed with butt hinges, however, surface hinges, knife hinges or various

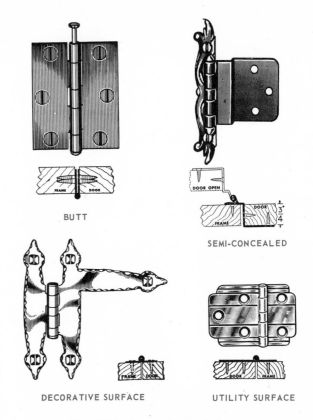

BUTT

SEMI-CONCEALED

DECORATIVE SURFACE

UTILITY SURFACE

Fig. 18-30. Hinges for flush doors. (Amerock Corp.)

patented invisible hinges can be used. See Fig. 18-30. Select a hinge that will be appropriate for the size of the door. The size of a hinge is determined by its length and width when open. On large doors three hinges should be used.

After the door is carefully fitted to the opening with about 1/32 in. clearance on each edge, it should be held in position with small wedges and the position of the hinges marked on the door and frame. Remove the door from the opening and lay out the position of the hinge leaf on the edge of the door and the frame. Also mark the depth and then cut the gain, as shown in Fig. 18-31.

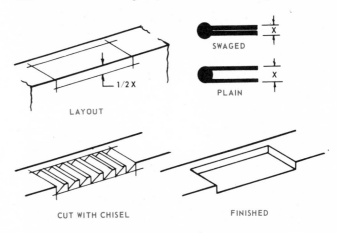

LAYOUT

SWAGED

PLAIN

CUT WITH CHISEL

FINISHED

Fig. 18-31. Gain for a butt hinge.

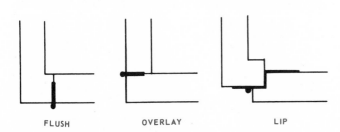

FLUSH

OVERLAY

LIP

Fig. 18-29. Types of swinging doors.

The total gain required for the hinge can be cut entirely in the door, however for fine work it is best to gain equally into each member. On large doors it is practical to use the portable router for this operation.

Install the hinges on the door and then mount the door in the opening. Use only one screw in each hinge leaf. Make any necessary adjustments in the fit and then set the remaining screws. It may be necessary to plane a slight bevel on the edge of the door opposite the hinges.

Stops are set on the door frame so that the door will be held flush with the surface of the opening when closed. They may be placed all around the opening or just on the lock or catch side. On small doors, the catches used to hold them closed may also serve as stops, Fig. 18-32.

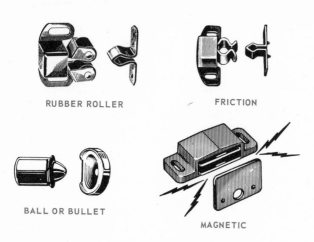

RUBBER ROLLER   FRICTION

BALL OR BULLET

MAGNETIC

Fig. 18-32. Door catches.

Flush doors on fine furniture and cabinetwork are sometimes installed with concealed hinges. The one shown in Fig. 18-33, is simply set in carefully aligned holes. After the hinge is in-

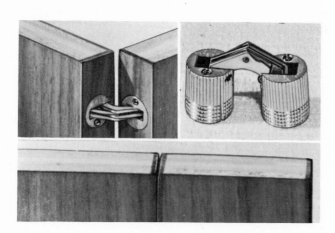

Fig. 18-33. Fully concealed invisible hinge for flush doors.
(Selby Furniture Hardware)

serted, a setscrew is turned to create a wedge effect that fastens it securely in place. It can be mounted successfully in particle board, plywood, or solids.

Overlay doors provide an attractive installation in some contemporary styles of furniture. Butt hinges can be used, however, the one shown in Fig. 18-34, is especially designed for this type of door and is somewhat easier to install.

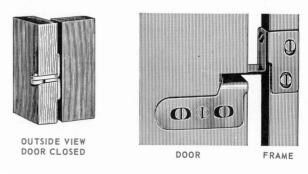

OUTSIDE VIEW
DOOR CLOSED

DOOR   FRAME

Fig. 18-34. Hinge for overlay door.
(Amerock Corp.)

Lip doors are easier to cut and fit than flush doors because the clearance is covered. They are used for kitchen cabinets and other built-in cabinetwork. The door is cut to the size of the open-

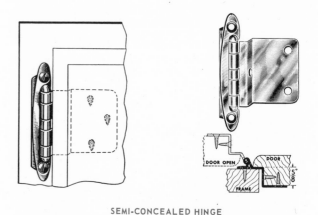

SEMI-CONCEALED HINGE

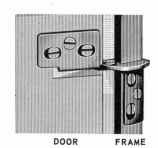

DOOR   FRAME

CONCEALED HINGE

Fig. 18-35. Hinges for lip doors.

ing plus the width of the lip on each edge. Clearance of about 1/16 in. is provided on each edge with additional allowance for the hinge. Fig. 18-35 shows several types of hinges that are used on lip doors.

WOODY SAYS:

"Hinges and other hardware items should be installed and fitted and then removed before finishing coats are applied."

Sliding Doors

Sliding doors are often used in furniture and cabinetmaking where the swing of regular doors would be awkward or cause interference. They are adaptable to various styles and structural designs. See Fig. 18-36.

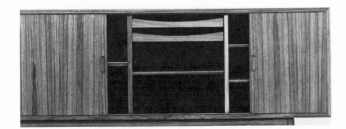

Fig. 18-36. Cabinet fitted with sliding doors.
(George Tanier Inc.)

A sliding door arrangement can be constructed as shown in Fig. 18-37. Grooves are cut in the top and bottom of the case (before assembly) and the doors are rabbeted so that the edge formed will match the groove with about 1/16 in. of clearance. Cut the top rabbet and groove deep enough that the door can be inserted or removed by simply raising it into the extra space. The doors will slide smoothly if the grooves are carefully cut, sanded, sealed and waxed. Excessive finish should be avoided. Sliding glass doors are heavy and a special plastic or roller track should be used. Follow the manufacturer's recommendations for installation.

A wide range of sliding door track and rollers are available. Fig. 18-38 shows a self-lubricating plastic track that is easy to install and provides smooth operation for case and cabinet doors. Overhead track and rollers are used for large wardrobe doors and passage doors.

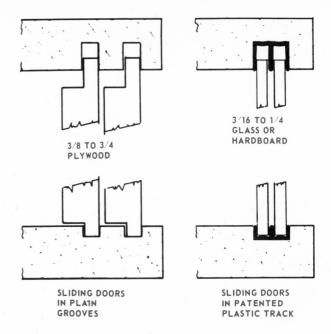

Fig. 18-37. Sliding door details.

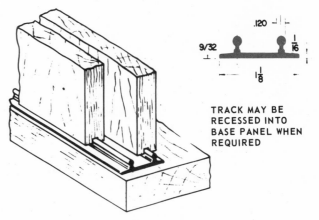

Fig. 18-38. Plastic door track installation.
(Ronthor Reiss Corp.)

Fig. 18-39 shows the installation of a tambour (flexible) door. Strips of wood with grooves in the ends are glued to a heavy cloth backing and ride

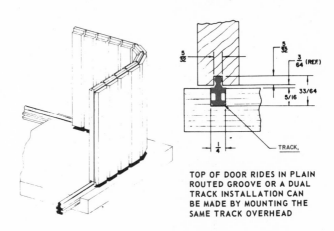

Fig. 18-39. Tambour sliding door detail using plastic track.

18-15

Fig. 18-40. Left. Beautiful furniture top with a matched grain pattern. Right. Skilled craftsman matches veneer and assembles it with a special taping machine.
(Drexel Furniture Co.)

on a plastic track. The track is set in a routed groove and may be curved as shown. Installations of this type are a bit "tricky" and you should experiment with a small section of door and track before cutting and preparing the finished assembly.

Tops

The top is the most important surface of chests, tables, and cabinets. It should be smooth and attractive and have a high resistance to abrasion and wear. Fig. 18-40 shows a skillfully matched grain pattern on a plywood table top with a banded edge of solid wood.

Tops can be made of plywood or solid stock. See Fig. 18-41. Plywood offers the advantage of stability and warp resistance but requires band-

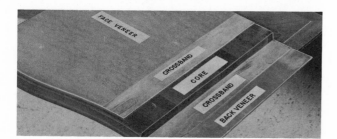

Fig. 18-41. Plywood fabricated especially for tops. The edge of the lumber core matches the face veneer.

ing or other edge treatment. Solid tops should never be banded across the end grain and special care must be given to the edge joints and grain match. In the school shop, table and desk tops of solid stock are usually glued and prepared after the base structure is complete so they can be attached immediately and thus reduce the possibility of warpage.

When the design permits, the top should be attached as a separate component of the structure. This is usually possible in the construction of tables, desks, and some cabinets. Fig. 18-42 shows several methods that can be used. Solids should always be attached in such a way that expansion and contraction across the grain can take place.

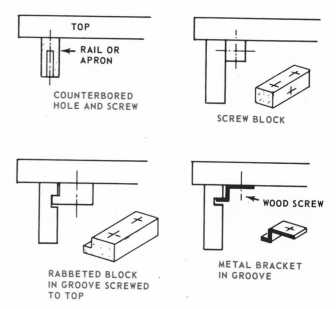

Fig. 18-42. Methods of attaching tops.

Tables are often designed with drop leaves so that space can be conserved when they are not in full use. The patented hinge, Fig. 18-43, improves the appearance when the leaf is down, since it eliminates the unsightly gap that would be formed by a conventional hinge. A rule joint, Fig. 18-44 is also used for this purpose and can be formed with special shaper cutters.

18-16

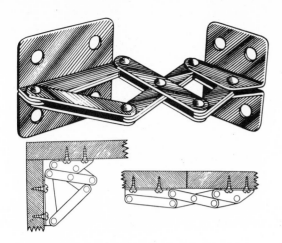

Fig. 18-43. Patented drop leaf table hinge.
(Selby Furniture Hardware)

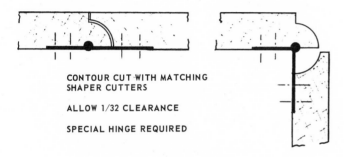

CONTOUR CUT WITH MATCHING
SHAPER CUTTERS

ALLOW 1/32 CLEARANCE

SPECIAL HINGE REQUIRED

Fig. 18-44. Rule joint detail.

Tops may swing up to give access to the inside of the structure. Examples would be found in such articles as chests or record players. Special hinges and self-balancing supports are available and should be used for the installation. See Fig. 18-45.

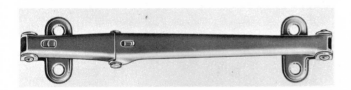

Fig. 18-45. Drop leaf support.
(Stanley Tools)

Legs

There are many and varied ways to form and attach legs. In some structures the corner posts are extended to serve as legs; in others the legs are attached as individual units or secured to a separate frame or base.

When the furniture is large or when it will carry considerable weight, it is best to attach the legs to a frame, using well designed mortise

and tenon or dowel joints, Fig. 18-46. If the legs are long, extra bracing may be required. This assembly is then attached to the main structure. One of the advantages of subassemblies like these is that they can be built and finished as separate units. They also make handling, storing and shipping easier.

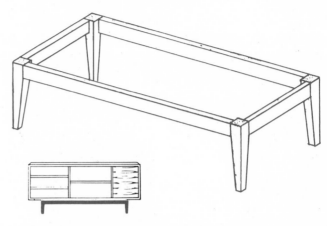

Fig. 18-46. Leg and rail base assembly constructed as a separate unit.

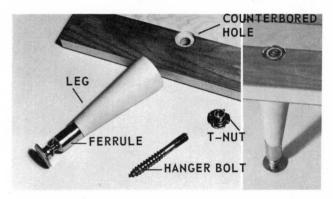

Fig. 18-47. Hanger bolt and T-nut provides a flush mounting. Left. Parts. Right. Assembled.

Fig. 18-48. Splayed leg attached with a hanger bolt.

Many leg attachment devices are available. Fig. 18-47 shows the use of a hanger bolt and T-nut which provides adequate strength and a trim appearance. Splayed legs often present special problems. In Fig. 18-48, a hanger bolt is used to attach a leg to a rail which is set at an angle. The leg is also set at an angle on the face of the rail, forming the required compound angle.

A unique method of attaching a shelf and leg, using a screw and screw eye in combination, is shown in Fig. 18-49. A commonly used bracket

Fig. 18-50. Corner bracket and hanger bolt. Rails are fastened to top.

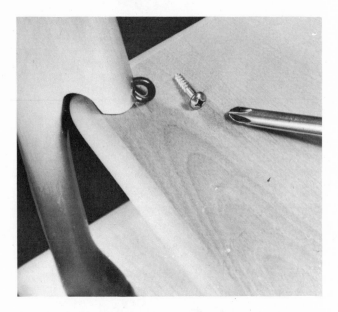

Fig. 18-49. Leg attached to a shelf with a screw eye and screw. View from underside.

and hanger bolt, Fig. 18-50, makes a strong joint. The rails are secured to the top and the leg can be quickly assembled or disassembled. Fig. 18-51 shows a leg of a traditional style table attached with screws and glue blocks.

Fig. 18-51. Table leg attached with screws and glue blocks. (Drexel Furniture Co.)

Hardware and Metal Trim

In addition to hinges, catches and leg attachments, there is a wide range of other metal items used in furniture and cabinetwork. Much of it is exposed to view so it should be carefully selected. You should give consideration to the size, style, material and finish. Fig. 18-52 shows several styles and designs in quality knobs and pulls for drawers and doors.

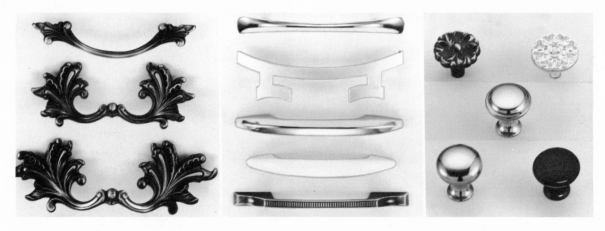

Fig. 18-52. Drawer and door hardware. Pulls with 3 in. centers, knobs. (Amerock Corp.)

Pulls and other metal trim should be fitted before the work is finished. In Fig. 18–53, a drawer knob which was prefitted, is being removed before the finishing operations.

Fig. 18-53. *Removing the drawer pull before finishing operations.* (Sherwin-Williams Co.)

Fig. 18-54. *Using a jig to drill holes for drawer pulls.*

You should give careful attention to the location of pulls, knobs and other surface hardware. Drawer pulls, for example, look best when they are placed slightly above the center line. Be certain they are centered horizontally and are perfectly level. If you have very many to install, you can save time by making and using a drilling jig similar to the one shown in Fig. 18-54.

Furniture Assemblies

From your experience in woodworking you will gain insight and understanding of furniture and cabinet construction which you can apply to the selection of commercially built units. Even though limitations in time, material, and equipment, may prevent you from constructing sizeable or complicated pieces, you should study diagrams of them as given in this unit, and learn how they are assembled. For example, see Fig. 18-55 on chairs.

Fig. 18-55. *Chair construction. 1-Steam bent solid shaped arm. 2-Back frame double-dowel joint. All joints glued with resin adhesives. 3-Side frame rail and double-dowel joint. Reinforcing lock screws and glue. 4-Front rail double-dowel joint. Reinforcing lock screws and glue. 5-Front leg wedged through tenon and flushed. Wedge is driven into tenon across grain to insure tight fit and prevent splitting. 6-Five rubber straps fitted with formed steel locking hardware provides ideal platform comfort. 7-Seat frame double-dowel construction. Entire frame is fastened to side frames and front rail. 8-Back frame securely fastened to rear leg and side frame rail with six heavy wire screws. 9-2 1/2 in. polyurethane foam back cushion filler. 10-4 in. polyurethane foam seat cushion filler. 11-Double welt box back zipper cushion. 12-Double welt box seat zipper cushion.* (Heywood-Wakefield Co.)

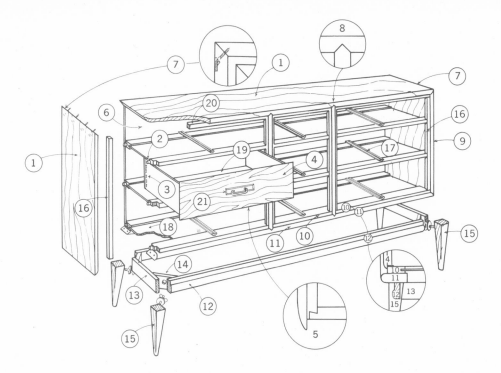

Fig. 18-56. Double dresser. 1-All exposed parts are solid hardwood, selected and matched for color. 2-Mortised and tenoned frame rail interior construction allows for normal expansion and contraction of the solid wood. 3-Drawers are custom-fitted and made with dovetail joints. 4-All drawer fronts are of one piece solid wood which eliminates unattractive joints. 5-Drawer fronts are fully lipped on four sides. 6-Hardboard backs are fitted flush into rabbeted top and ends. 7-Mitered top and end construction provides attractive appearance. Glue and screw lock construction assures a fixed joint and permits normal expansion and contraction. 8-Double-miter construction of vertical pilasters adds to the appearance. 9-Half-round front edges on all ends, tops and bottom rails. 10-Bottom interior frame rail tenoned to ends. 11-Bottom front rail mitered to ends and screwed to rail above. 12-Shaped front base rail adds design detail and prevents case from sagging. 13-Side base rails joined to front and rear base rails provide perfect supporting corner for leg. 14-Corner blocks glued and screwed to base frame. 15-Legs tapered from square at top to round at bottom and fitted to case with heavy hanger bolt construction, through the corner block. 16-End interior vertical frame rail for extra strength. 17-Combination wood and steel center drawer guides provide smooth drawer action. 18-Hardwood dust partitions throughout. 19-Drawer interiors finished and waxed. 20-Top interior horizontal frame rail for extra rigidity. 21-Custom hardware, a combination of soft and crisp forms, done in solid brass and finished in a soft, light satin sheen.

Although plywood is used in most furniture today, especially to form large surfaces, some fine furniture is built entirely of solid stock. The exterior of the attractive double-dresser shown in Fig. 18-56, is made of solid cherry. Study the construction details and note the provision made for expansion and contraction of the solid end panels and top.

provide more economical use of floor space than most furniture and if carefully planned, result in greater efficiency and convenience.

Modern built-in cabinetwork in the home includes kitchen cabinets, storage drawers and shelves, wardrobes, room dividers, and bathroom lavatory cabinets. Kitchens of today are made very attractive and convenient with such

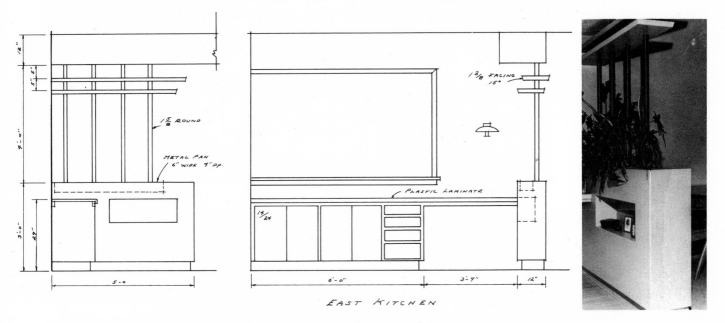

Fig. 18-57. Room divider and desk detail and photo of finished on-the-job built cabinetwork.

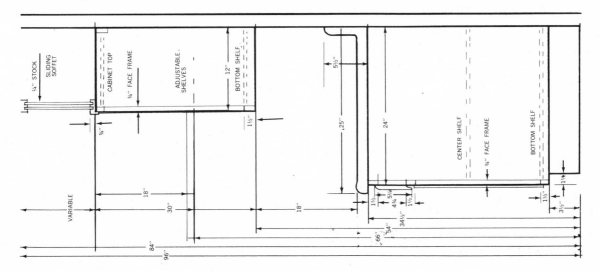

Fig. 18-58. Standard sizes for kitchen cabinets.
(Red Wing Wood Products)

Built-In Cabinetwork

The use of built-in cabinets and storage units is one of the most important developments in modern architecture and interior design. They

built-in appliances and equipment as wall ovens, surface cooking units, refrigerators, dishwashers and sinks. Storage units are designed with attention to the items that will be stored; space is carefully allocated and drawers, shelves, and other

base cabinet
36'' wide
24'' deep
34½'' high

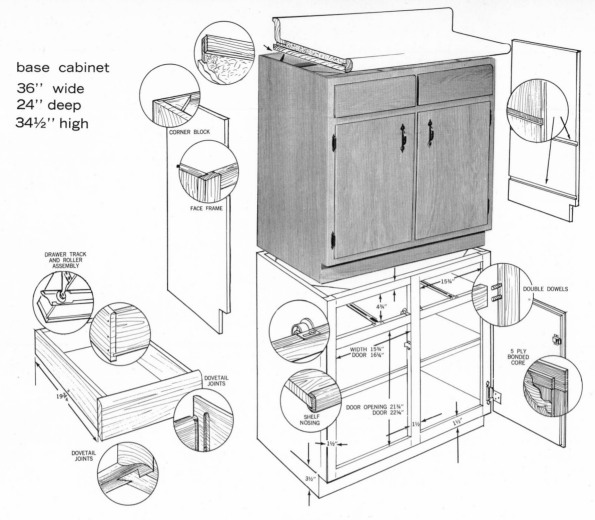

CORNER BLOCK

FACE FRAME

DRAWER TRACK
AND ROLLER
ASSEMBLY

DOVETAIL
JOINTS

19¾"

DOVETAIL
JOINTS

15¾"

DOUBLE DOWELS

4¾"

WIDTH 15¾"
DOOR 16¼"

SHELF
NOSING

DOOR OPENING 21¾"
DOOR 22¼"

5 PLY
BONDED
CORE

1½"

1½"

1½"

3½"

Fig. 18-59. Construction details of factory built kitchen base cabinet.
(Red Wing Wood Products)

Fig. 18-59A. Details on factory built wall cabinet.

Fig. 18-60. Modern factory built kitchen cabinets.
(Kitchen Kompact Inc.)

wall cabinet 36'' wide 12'' deep

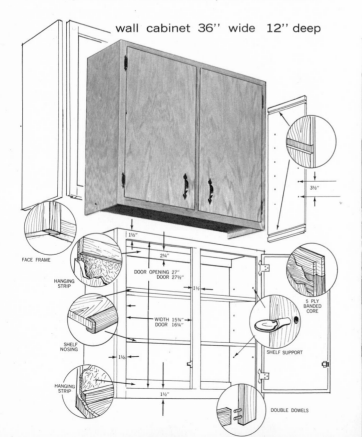

FACE FRAME

HANGING
STRIP

SHELF
NOSING

HANGING
STRIP

1½"

2¼"

DOOR OPENING 27"
DOOR 27½"

WIDTH 15¾"
DOOR 16¼"

1½"

1½"

1½"

3½"

5 PLY
BANDED
CORE

SHELF SUPPORT

DOUBLE DOWELS

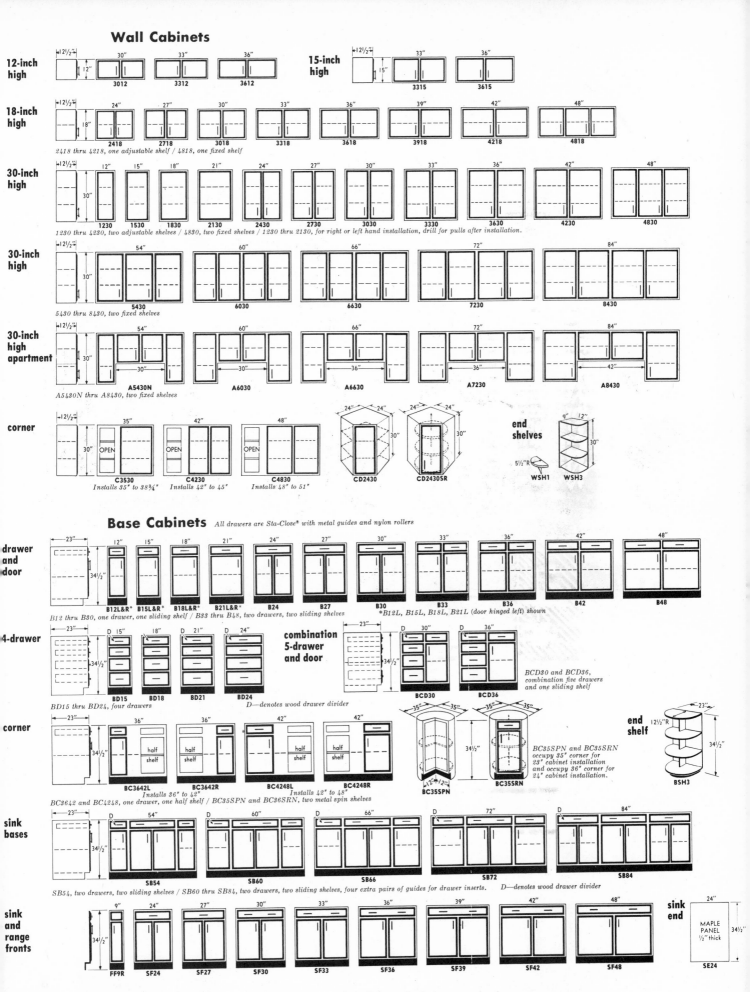

Fig. 18-61. Dimensions of standard base and wall units built by one manufacturer.
(I-XL Furniture Co.)

elements are proportioned to satisfy a specific purpose.

Built-in units may be constructed "on the job" or produced in millwork plants and factories. Mass produced factory units are available in a moderate prices. Mass produced parts are assembled with precision, using jigs and fixtures. Some factory-built cabinetwork is finished on the job; however in-plant finishes are usually superior and can be provided in various types and shades

On-the-job built cabinetwork in a family room featuring built-in T-V, stereo, and storage space.
Striped paldao hardwood plywood used on all exterior surfaces.
(American Forest Products)

wide range of sizes that can be adapted to various interior arrangements. Some are installed in basic framework that is built into walls and partitions of the building.

The architect's plan will show overall sizes and arrangements of built-in units. Drawings are carefully scaled and eliminates the need for extensive dimensioning of views. They serve as a guide to the cabinetmaker or are followed in the selection of factory-built components. Joinery details and the structure of cabinets built on the job are designed by the cabinetmaker, who must work within the requirements of the written specifications.

Factory-built cabinets are usually of high quality. Modern production machines can produce high quality work with unvarying accuracy and at

to match individual requirements. See Figs. 18-57, 58, 59, and 60.

Manufacturers offer a wide range of standard units, especially in the area of kitchen cabinets, Fig. 18-61. Usually they are also able to provide custom units to fill some specific requirement.

Test Your Knowledge

1. The standard height of a dining table is _____.

2. The greatest advantage of using plywood instead of solid stock is its strength and _____.

3. Expansion and contraction across the grain of solid stock can be eliminated by applying a waterproof finish. True or False?

4. In a framed panel the horizontal members are called rails and the vertical members are called _____.

5. Web frames can be trimmed to exact size after they are glued together. True or False?

6. The best adhesive to use for veneering the edge of plywood is _____.

7. Lip drawers are easier to fit than flush drawers. True or False?

8. The three common types of drawer guides are corner, center and _____.

9. If the guides do not prevent the drawer from tilting downward when it is open, you should install a _____.

10. Flush doors are usually installed with _____ hinges.

11. The joint in a drop leaf table top that is formed with shaper cutters is called a _____.

12. Hinges and hardware should not be fitted until all of the finishing operations are complete. True or False?

Outside Assignments

1. Study the construction of the kitchen cabinets in your home and then prepare a scaled sectional drawing of a typical base cabinet and include details of the joints used.

2. Prepare a check list of items to observe and examine when evaluating the quality of materials and construction in commercially built furniture.

3. Study an architectural standards manual and then prepare a drawing of a wardrobe unit. Include recommended sizes, heights, and space allotments for common clothing items.

Modern double end machine that automatically performs sawing, boring, chucking, gluing and dowel driving operations. In this view, furniture rails are being cut to exact length and holes for dowels are then precisely bored. Just the right amount of glue is inserted in the holes before the dowels are driven into place. Note the overhead dowel hoppers. Production rates up to 750 pieces per hour can be attained. Machine can be set up for miters and compound angles as well as the square ends on the work shown in the view. (Nash—Bell—Challoner)

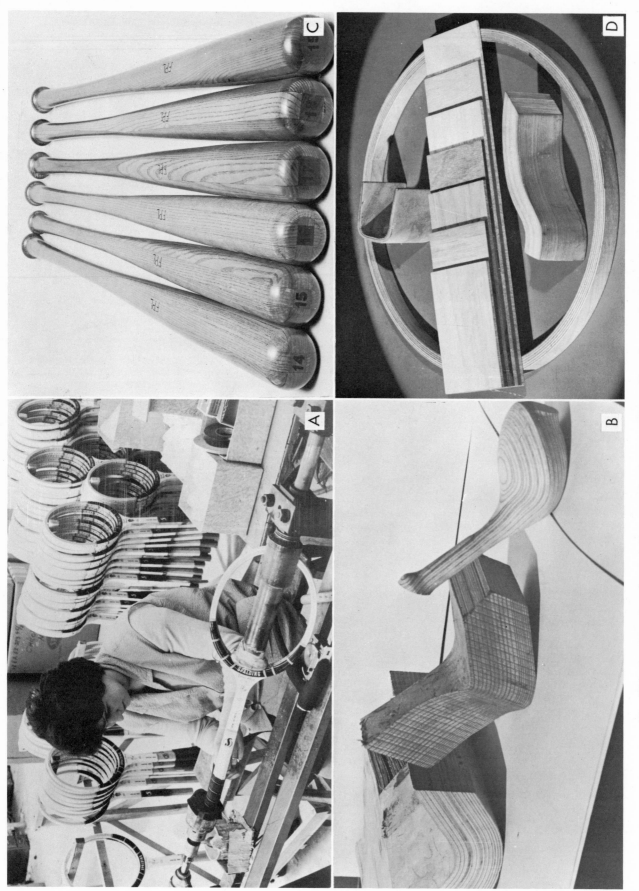

Fig. 19-1. Laminated products. A-Tennis racket frames are formed from layers of ash, beech or maple. (A. G. Spalding Co.) B-Golf club heads are made by laminating many layers of maple veneer. (Wilson Sporting Goods Co.) C-Laminated baseball bat made of a hickory core and ash faces. D-Laminated wood parts. Center piece shows plywood construction. (Forest Products Lab.)

Unit 19
LAMINATING AND BENDING WOOD

Curved wood parts can be formed by cutting the stock to the required shape or by bending. Cutting the curve with machines like the band saw, is often wasteful of material and the part is seldom as strong as a bent piece. Wood can be bent either by plasticizing (softening) it with steam or hot water, or by laminating and then clamping it in a form for drying and curing. Saw kerfs are sometimes cut on the concave side but parts produced by this method have very little strength.

Wood laminating is the process of forming parts (usually bent) by attaching two or more layers of wood together with the grain of each ply running in the same direction. Plywood is also composed of layers of wood but with the grain direction running at right angles in each successive layer. Laminated wood is used for curved parts of furniture, baseball bats, tennis rackets, golf clubs, boats, structural beams and many other products. See Fig. 19-1.

Selecting and Cutting Stock

Both hardwoods and softwoods can be laminated and bent; however, hardwoods have somewhat better bending characteristics. Hardwood species commonly used in industry for either solid or laminated bending include ash, birch, elm, hickory, maple, oak, sweet gum and walnut. Laminated structural members are made from such softwood species as Douglas fir, southern yellow pine, white cedar and redwood. More important than the kind of wood, is the quality and grain structure of a given specimen. Straight-grained stock that is free of knots, splits, checks and other defects should be selected.

When a strip of wood is bent, the inside surface is made shorter (compressed) while the outside surface is stretched. The thicker the stock, the greater this difference will need to be. Wood fibers are difficult to stretch, but fairly easy to compress, therefore the greatest change usually

occurs on the inside surface of the bend. Wood will bend across the grain or along the grain. Across-the-grain bends are seldom used in laminated parts and apply mainly to curved or formed plywood.

In the school shop, veneers are often used to produce laminated parts. Veneer is defined as a thin wood sheet, 1/8 in. or less in thickness. Wood over 1/8 in. thick is simply referred to as stock and is produced by resawing operations. Standard hardwood veneer thickness is 1/28 in. however, common thicknesses include 1/32, 1/20, and 1/16. In general, to save time and material, you should use layers of the thickest dimension that will still bend easily to the minimum radius of the part being produced. When the radius of bend is too sharp for the layer thickness, it may be necessary to moisten the surface and preform the wood before making the final assembly.

Laminating layers can be cut to rough size on the band saw or jigsaw. If 1/16 in. or thinner veneers are used, the cutting can be done with a pair of heavy scissors or snips as shown in Fig. 19-2. Cross-grain cuts are easily made; cuts along the grain will tend to split the veneer. The splitting can be minimized by dampening the surface. After the plies are cut to size they should be arranged carefully with the best surfaces on the outside.

Applying Glue

Urea resin glue fills the requirements for most laminating work done in the school shop. It has a sufficiently long assembly time, is strong, and stains the wood only slightly. Casein glue can also be used. It is less expensive, works best on oily woods but has a staining characteristic that may be undesirable.

Glue can be applied by various methods. Fig. 19-3 shows urea resin being applied rapidly with a roller. As the layers are coated, they are stacked in the proper position. When the entire stack or

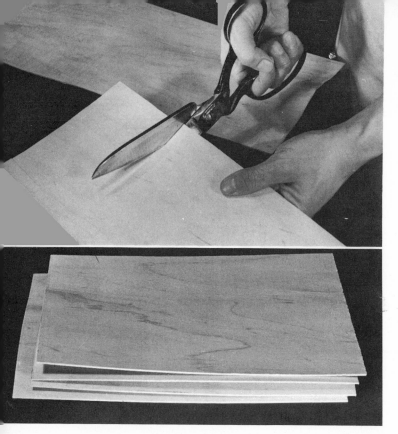

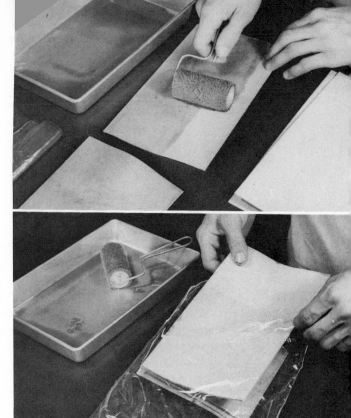

Fig. 19-2. Above. Cutting veneer to rough size. Veneer that is too dry (less than 6 percent M.C.) will splinter and break excessively. Below. Assemble the rough cut layers with the best surfaces to the outside.

Fig. 19-3. Above. Applying urea resin glue with a roller. Below. Placing the stack in a plastic bag.

laminate is coated, it is placed in a plastic (polyethylene film) bag or covered with wax paper to prevent the excess glue or "squeeze-out" from touching the form.

An industry photo, Fig. 19-4, shows strips for a tennis racket being fed into a glue spreading machine.

Clamping Forms and Devices

Fig. 19-5 shows the laminate placed in a form and pressure being applied with a shop-built press. A wide variety of forms and clamping devices can be designed and used. Some are fitted with machine bolts that are used to apply the

Fig. 19-4. Ash strips for a tennis racket frame being fed into a glue spreading machine.
(Wilson Sporting Goods Co.)

pressure. The forms must be accurately shaped so pressure will be evenly distributed. Male-female types must be concentric when spaced for the given laminate. Alignment pins may be necessary to insure that the two parts come together correctly.

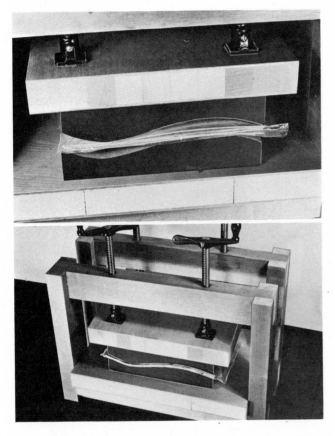

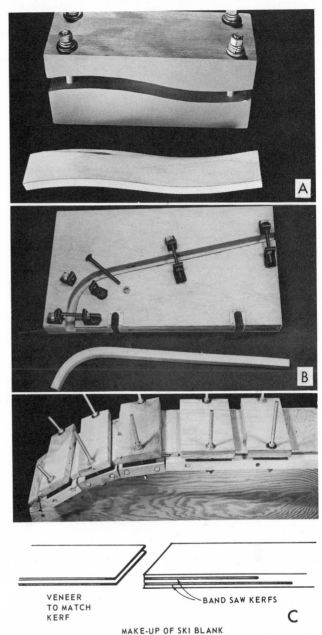

Fig. 19-5. Above. Laminate placed in the form. Below. Pressure applied in a shop-built press.

Surfaces of the form should be smooth and the curves should be free-flowing (faired). Sometimes it may be helpful to use a rubber pad between the form and the laminate or line the surface with light sheet metal. Wood forms should be finished with a coat of sealer and paste wax so that they can be easily cleaned and maintained. See Figs. 19-6 and 19-7.

VENEER
TO MATCH
KERF

BAND SAW KERFS

C

MAKE-UP OF SKI BLANK

Fig. 19-6. Clamping forms. A-Machine bolts are used to apply pressure and align the two parts of the form. Laminate consists of 7 layers of 1/16 in. veneer. B-Table leg. Six 1/8 in. laminations. C-Water ski. Two saw kerfs cut into the end of solid stock and then filled with veneer. Stagger the depth of the cuts and use a resorcinol glue.

Curing

Allow the laminate to remain in the form until the glue has thoroughly set and is almost completely cured. At room temperature, this will require about 24 hours for urea resin glue. If higher temperatures are applied this time can be greatly reduced. For example, urea resin will attain more than 90 percent of its total strength within one hour at a temperature of 140 deg.

The glue will have raised the moisture content of the wood and it is usually best to lay the part aside for several days before performing final shaping and finishing operations.

Cutting to Size and Finishing

The edges of the laminate can be trimmed and shaped with various hand tools. Or the band saw, jigsaw, or sabre saw can be used if certain pre-

Fig. 19-7. Forming a tennis racket in a high frequency press. Bonding and curing takes place in less than a minute.

cautions are observed. Special jigs and fixtures may be required to properly support the work.

Surfaces can be smoothed with scrapers, files, and abrasive paper, and finishing coats applied in the same manner as other wood products, Fig. 19-8.

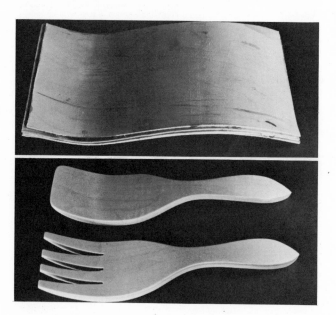

Fig. 19-8. Above. Salad set cured laminate. Below. Pieces cut out and ready for finish.

 WOODY SAYS:

"When trimming the rough edges of a laminate, you should wear goggles or safety glasses to protect your eyes from flying particles of hardened glue and wood chips."

Molded Plywood

Extensive use is made of molded plywood in furniture construction, especially for chairs and commercial seating. It is laid-up like regular plywood with the grain turned at right angles in alternate layers and then pressed in special dies that form the required curved surfaces. Fig. 19-9 shows a production setup for producing molded plywood that will be used for table aprons and chair backs. (For additional information on high

Fig. 19-9. Forming plywood in a high frequency press. Above. Placing the stack. Below. Opening the press after bonding is complete. (Drexel Furniture Co.)

Fig. 19-10. Chair seat and back made of molded plywood. (Herman Miller Inc.)

frequency presses, see page 7-13.) The surfaces can be formed in a single-curved surface or a double-curved surface like the seat and back of the chair in Fig. 19-10.

Single-curved molded plywood can be produced in the school shop with wooden forms and standard clamps. Fig. 19-11 shows a simple pressing arrangement to form a plywood seat for a TV stool from layers of 1/8 in. plywood. See also, Fig. 19-12.

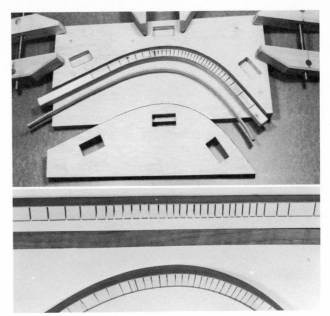

Fig. 19-13. Above. Forming press. Note sponge rubber pad. Below. Kerfed part, veneer strip and finished piece.

Bending with Kerfs

Thick stock can be bent easier if a series of saw kerfs is cut on the concave side. This reduces the size of the surface by removing some of the stock rather than compressing it. However, the part produced in this manner is weak and should be used only in assemblies where it can be securely attached to other supporting members. For example, such a part might be used to form the trim apron of a table top where the top itself or other members would provide the structural strength required. Another disadvantage results from the fact that the saw kerfs may telegraph (show through) on the outside surface. This can usually be avoided if the kerfs are not too deep and if the part is given a coarse sanding after the forming operation.

The depth, and spacing of the saw kerfs will vary with the kind of material and the radius of bend. You will need to experiment with a number of sample pieces to determine the best solution for your work. Fig. 19-13 shows a press used to form a part made from a piece of lumber core plywood. In this particular piece, a strip of veneer was glued to the inside surface. In some work the kerfed part could be attached directly to the structure with glue blocks set along the inside surface to hold it in place.

Bending Solid Stock

Curved parts can be formed from solid stock by plasticizing the wood with moisture and heat and then bending and clamping it in the required

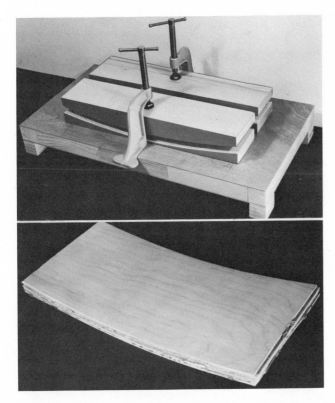

Fig. 19-11. Above. Plywood forming press. Below. Curved plywood made from 5 layers of 1/8 in. plywood. Individual layers of veneer could be used.

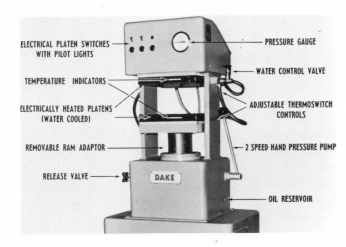

Fig. 19-12. Small hydraulic press for laboratories and school shops. (Dake Corp.)

19-5

shape until it cools and dries. This process is used extensively in industry, Fig. 19-14, but is not easily adaptable to work in the school shop, except for small parts.

Fig. 19-14. Bending solid wood furniture parts in special metal clamps. (Heywood-Wakefield Co.)

Stock for solid bending should be selected with about the same consideration as for laminated work. Air-dried stock with a moisture content of 12 to 20 percent will work best. Machine the stock to size, providing allowances for shrinkage and finishing. The ends should be seal-coated to prevent excessive absorption of moisture during the steaming process and to minimize end checking during the drying and fixing process. For severe bends, cut the stock so that the annual rings are perpendicular to the plane of the bend.

The length of time required for steaming or boiling the wood varies with the kind of wood, initial moisture content (M.C.), thickness of the stock, and the degree of curvature required. In general, most wood will need to be steamed, or boiled for about one hour for each inch of thickness. Plasticizing with steam, at or near atmospheric pressure, until the M.C. of the wood reaches 20 to 25 percent, will normally produce satisfactory results.

There are two broad classes of bends; those made with end pressure, and those without end pressure (free bends). Free bending is feasible only for slight curvatures. Bending with end pressure causes the wood fibers to be properly compressed on the inside of the bend and reduces tensile failures on the outside surfaces. Also there is less tendency of "spring-back" after the work is removed from the clamps. End pressure is usually applied with a metal strap (use galvanized iron or stainless steel) that is equipped with end fittings. This strap is applied to the convex side

of the stock. As the bend is made, it absorbs the tensile stress, and the wood cells are subjected only to compression forces.

The work must be held in the clamps until it has cooled and dried or "set." On heavy work this may take several days, even in special heated drying rooms. In production work, bent parts are removed from the bending apparatus soon after they have cooled and are then placed in special retaining clamps to hold them in position until the set is complete. The amount of time or drying necessary to set a bend varies with different kinds of wood and types of work.

Structural Laminates

The wood laminating process is applied to a wide range of structural members that are used in large buildings where it is necessary to have clear space unobstructed by supports. Laminated construction allows the architect a wide latitude in creating forms adapted to and expressive of the function and purpose of the structure and greatly extends the use of wood -- the most abundant, beautiful, and economical building material available. Fig. 19-15 shows parabolic arches, formed by the laminating process and incorporated into a dignified, functional design.

Fig. 19-15. Gracefully soaring parabolic arches of laminated wood used in church construction.

In addition to the flexibility in design, wood beam construction also provides a high fire resistance factor. Wood beams do not transmit heat like unprotected metal beams which lose their strength and quickly collapse under extremely high temperatures. Exposure of a wood beam to flame results in a very slow loss in its strength. It is weakened only in proportion to its slow reduction in cross section due to charring.

Fig. 19-16. After fire scene shows wood beam supporting twisted steel I beams. (Forest Products Lab.)

This takes place slowly and thus provides precious time in an emergency that may save life and material. See Fig. 19-16.

Laminated beams and arches must be carefully designed so that they will provide the strength required. Fig. 19-17 shows a sample arch being submitted to an extensive series of tests.

Fig. 19-17. Scientific testing of a laminated arch design. (Forest Products Lab.)

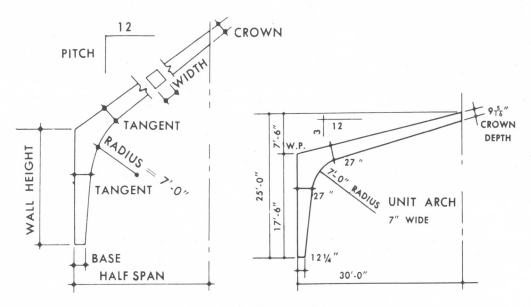

Fig. 19-18. Parts of a laminated V arch.
(Unit Structures Inc.)

Data gathered from these tests will be compiled and used in future design problems. The parts and general design of a typical V arch are shown in Fig. 19-18.

Most laminated structural members are made of softwoods. They are manufactured in industrial plants specializing in such production and then shipped, prefinished and ready for erection, to the building site.

The accompanying photographs, Figs. 19-19 to 19-24, show in-plant views of the fabrication of beams and arches. Lumber is carefully selected

and machined to size. To secure the required length, pieces must be end-jointed. Since end grain is hard to joint, a special hooked-scarf joint is used. In large laminates, a number of these joints may be required in each ply. They are always staggered so they do not align in adjacent layers.

Waterproof adhesives are applied and the layers are then clamped to forms. Because of the size of the units it is seldom practical to utilize heat in the curing process. After the beam or arch has cured, the edges and faces are ma-

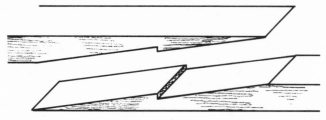

SPACE NOT LESS THAN 24 TIMES
LAMINATION THICKNESS

Fig. 19-19. Above. Assembling lamination for straight beam
11 x 36 in. by 65 ft. long. Note the form on the right used
for curved beams and arches. (Rilco Laminated Products)
Below. Drawing which shows hooked-scarf joint used to join
the end of laminations.

Fig. 19-20. Using an air operated "nut-runner" to tighten
the clamps. Note two laminations are in position with the
clamp screw running between them.

Fig. 19-21. Shaping, drilling and sanding laminated arches with heavy-duty portable power tools.
(Weyerhaeuser Co.)

Fig. 19-22. Prefinished arches are wrapped in waterproof covering for shipment to building site. (Rilco Laminated Products)

Fig. 19-23. Laminated arches provide unobstructed interior in a school field house. Arches like these with a cross section of 7 x 36 in. can carry a span of more than 150 ft. (Georgia-Pacific Corp.)

Fig. 19-24. Unit dome of laminated members used in the construction of a sports arena. (Forest Products Lab.)

chined to size. Today, many of the beams and arches are finished in the factory to specifications that will match the interior of the completed building. Prefinished units are carefully wrapped and handled so they will arrive at the construction site, free of damage.

Test Your Knowledge

1. When a piece of wood is bent, the outside surface is stretched and the inside surface is _____.
2. Veneer is generally defined as thin sheets of wood under _____ in. in thickness.
3. Polyvinyl glue is not satisfactory for laminating work because of its short assembly time. True or False?
4. A curved male-female type of form must be designed and used for a given laminate thickness. True or False?
5. The spacing and depth of kerfs for bending solid stock will vary with the kind of wood and _____ of the bend.
6. When steaming and bending wood, kiln dried stock works better than air dried. True or False?
7. The length of time required for steaming wood for bending will vary with the kind of wood, initial M.C., radius of curve and _____ .
8. Wood beam construction provides flexibility in design and a high _____ _____ factor.

Outside Assignments

1. Prepare a proposal for experimental work in laminating, using thin hardboard core stock and veneer or plastic laminates for the surface layers. Suggest articles or projects for which this type of laminate would be appropriate.
2. Develop a design for a heated laminating form that could be used in the school shop.

Consider the use of a heating pad or the heating element of a discarded electric iron.
3. Secure descriptive folders from a company that manufactures laminated beams, arches and trusses. Your local lumber dealer may be able to furnish addresses. Prepare a written report describing the various types, uses, design data, and finish. Also include information concerning appropriate roof decking materials, and methods of application.

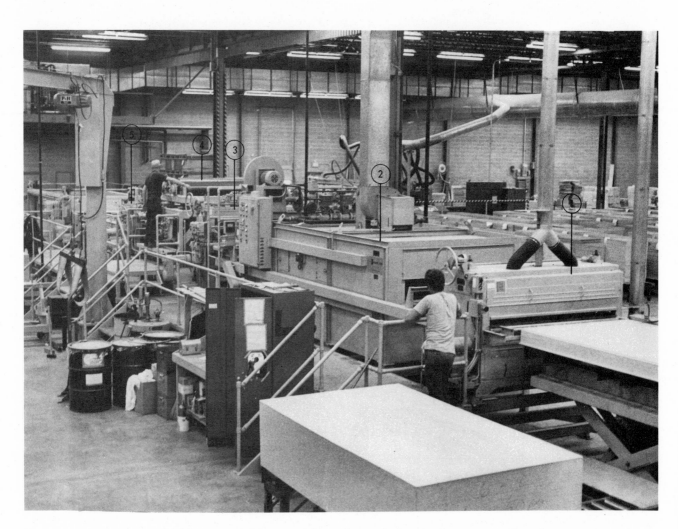

Laminating vinyl film to top and bottom surface of particle board substrate in a plant that manufactures kitchen cabinets. Panels move through machine at speeds up to 70 fpm. Basic components of machine are: 1—Panel cleaner. 2—Infrared heating oven. 3—Adhesive applicator. 4—Vinyl unwind and rotary press laminator. 5—Automatic cutoff. The vinyl film being applied is printed with simulated wood-grain patterns.   (Black Bros.)

Unit 20

UPHOLSTERY AND
PLASTIC LAMINATES

Upholstery and plastic laminates consist of different materials and unrelated processes, but since they are both applied to wooden structures to form finished surfaces, they are grouped together in this Unit. A short section describing the application of ceramic tile is also included.

Upholstery

New and improved materials have simplified upholstery methods and procedures. Sinuous (sagless) springs, rubber webbing, and latex and plastic foam, eliminate such time consuming operations as installing webbing, sewing and tying springs and packing hair. There is still however, much more to upholstery than can be presented in this short section so you will need to study some of the reference books before undertaking a major job.

Jute webbing is a stout, closely woven strip, 3 to 4 in. wide. It is used to form the base for coil springs and stuffing materials. Steel webbing is available in several types, with a 3/4 in. width being the most common. It is perforated for nails and may be corrugated with small loops through which coil springs can be attached. Plastic and rubber webbing are used in modern furniture to support cushions or to form the finished seating surface.

Burlap is a coarse fabric made from jute or hemp fibers. A 40 in. width is commonly available in various weights (ounces per sq. yard). The 10 oz. weight is satisfactory for covering springs or webbing, or for forming rolled edges. Denim is a strong, twilled cotton fabric which has excellent wearing qualities. It can be used for a seat surface that will be covered with cushions or sewed to the finish fabric for "pull strips."

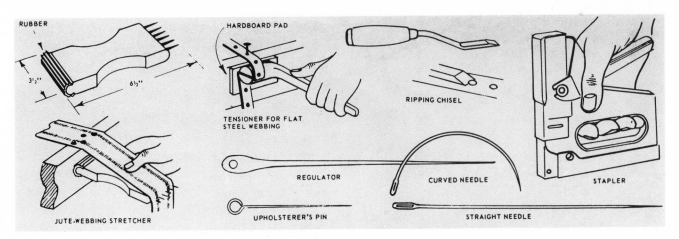

Fig. 20-1. Special tools for upholstery.

Tools and Materials

Some of the basic tools, in addition to those usually available in the school shop, are shown in Fig. 20-1. You will also need an upholsterer's hammer, Fig. 20-2, and a pair of heavy-duty shears. A flexible steel tape is often helpful when measuring irregular surfaces or curved contours.

Muslin is also made of cotton and is used to cover stuffing materials. The unbleached type is satisfactory. Cambric, a light cotton cloth, is made dust proof by sizing or glazing. It is used to enclose the underside of upholstered furniture to give it a finished appearance.

Coil springs are used for seats, backs, and cushions. They are available in various sizes and

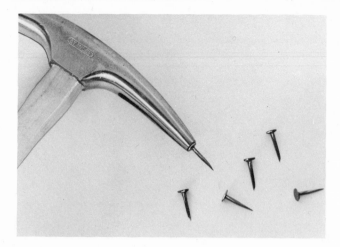

Fig. 20-2. Magnetic upholsterer's hammer. Tacks are picked up as shown and set in position with a short, accurate stroke. The hammer face is then used to finish the driving.

degrees of stiffness. Sinuous springs are available in continuous rolls or precut lengths. They do not require webbing or other bases and are attached to the top side of the rails with special clips.

Padding or stuffing materials cover the springs to form soft, smooth contours. Rubberized hair and Spanish moss are often used. Latex foam (also called foam rubber) and plastic foam are used extensively in modern furniture. These newer materials are waterproof, durable, and come in a wide range of thicknesses and degrees of softness. A layer of cotton batting is often used between the stuffing material and the final cover. This is available in rolls 27 in. wide and in thicknesses of 3/4 and 1 in. Cotton batting is usually torn, instead of cutting with shears, since this forms a tapered edge.

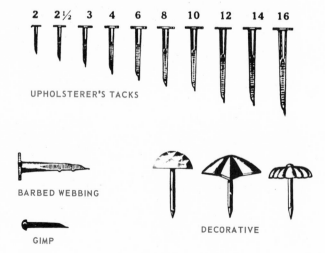

Fig. 20-3. Upholsterer's tacks.
(Upholsters Supply Co.)

Regular upholsterer's tacks are blued and range in size from No. 1 (3/16 in.) to No. 16 (13/16 in.), Figs. 20-3. Webbing tacks have barbs to give them greater holding power. Fancy or decorative tacks are available in a wide range of designs and are used mainly for antiques and novelty items.

Frames

Wood for the construction of frames that will be upholstered should take and hold tacks well. Select a soft-textured hardwood that will provide sufficient strength and use sturdy joints that are reinforced with screws, dowels, and glue blocks. After the frame is assembled, round sharp edges and corners where they will contact the upholstery materials. See Fig. 20-4.

Seat frames, or other frames that will carry springs are usually made of five-quarter stock. Exposed surfaces should be finished before the final cover is applied. Sometimes it is practical to prefinish wood trim strips and attach them after the covering is complete.

Detachable Seats and Back

Chairs, like those shown in Fig. 20-5, are easy to upholster. The seats and backs are held in place with screws and can be easily attached or removed. The padding material is supported on webbing attached to a frame or placed directly on a plywood base.

For an open base frame, first attach webbing to the top side and then cover it with a layer of burlap. It is best to include an edge roll when using loose-fill stuffing materials. The thickness of the padding is usually about 1 in. A layer of cotton batting can be applied over the stuffing materials and all of the padding is then held in place with a muslin cover. Nailing or tacking can be done on the underneath side, Fig. 20-6. Follow the procedure shown later in this Unit for attaching the finish fabric.

Tight Spring Construction

Fig. 20-7 shows a cutaway view of typical construction using coil springs and foam padding. Sinuous springs could be substituted for the webbing and coil springs or an extra thick layer of foam padding could be supported on webbing attached to the top edge of the chair rails as shown.

Webbing is used to provide a resilient foundation or base to hold springs or padding. Strips

Fig. 20-4. Assemblying a furniture frame that will be upholstered.
(Fastener Corp.)

DETACHABLE SLIP
SEAT & BACK

Fig. 20-5. Chairs with slip seats.

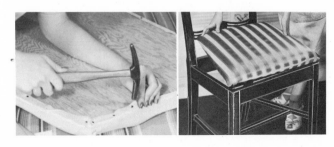

Fig. 20-6. Left. Tacking muslin cover in place. Right. Replacing slip seat. (Natural Rubber Bureau)

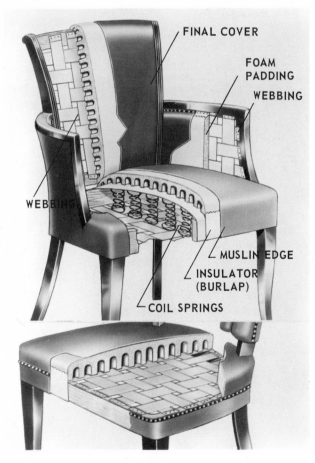

FINAL COVER

FOAM
PADDING

WEBBING

WEBBING

MUSLIN EDGE

INSULATOR
(BURLAP)

COIL SPRINGS

Fig. 20-7. Above. Tight spring construction. Below. Rubberized webbing and latex foam padding.
(U. S. Rubber Co.)

are spaced at least 1/2 in. apart and applied in various ways as shown in Fig. 20-8. To determine the correct tension for rubber webbing, make a mark on the strip that is 10 percent shorter than

Measure the inside distance between the rails and then cut the spring so it is about 1/2 in. longer. Hold the spring down flat on the work bench when measuring this length. When the

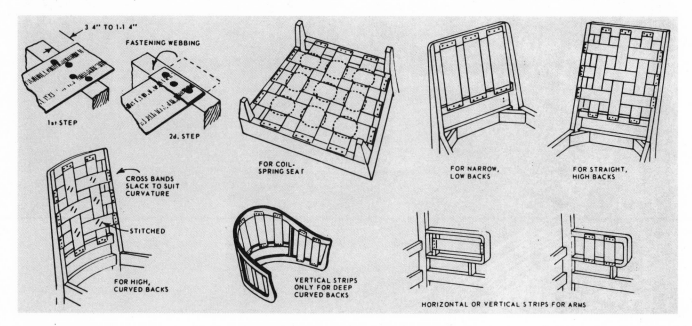

Fig. 20-8. How to apply and use webbing.

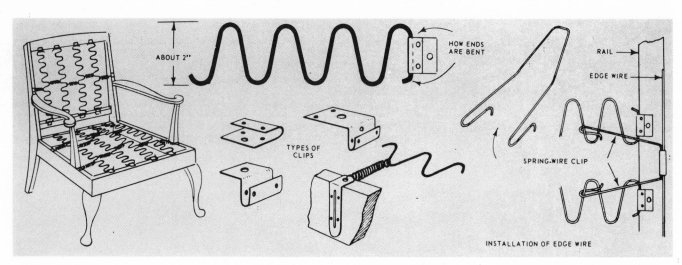

Fig. 20-9. Sinuous (sagless) springs.

the span, and then pull the webbing until this mark is aligned with the inside edge of the frame. When applying either jute webbing or rubber webbing, always try to secure equal tension in each strip.

Sinuous springs are easy to install and eliminate the webbing and twine tying required when using coil springs. Use a No. 9 gauge for chair seats and a No. 11 gauge for backs and such lighter work as foot stools. The springs should run up and down on backs and from the front to the back on seats. See Figs. 20-9 and 20-10.

Fig. 20-10. Sinuous spring clips and helical springs.
(No-Sag Spring Co.)

spring is attached, it should have a crown of about 1 1/4 in. to 2 in. Each 1/2 in. increase or decrease in the spring length will change the crown height by about 1/4 in. Bend the ends of the spring as shown.

WOODY SAYS:

"Use care when holding sinuous springs straight for measuring and when cutting and installing. The tempered steel could snap back and cause an injury."

Fig. 20-11. Installing sinuous springs.
(No-Sag Spring Co.)

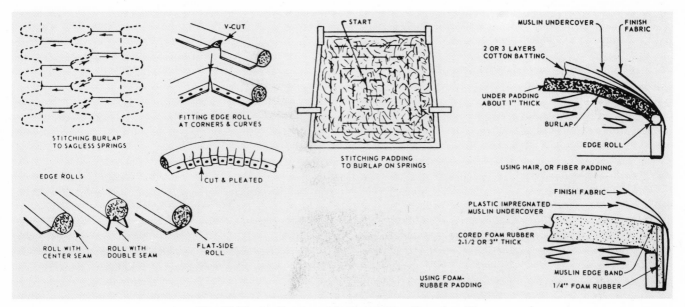

Fig. 20-12. Application of burlap, edge rolls and padding.

The springs are fastened to the frame with clips and spaced about 4 in. on center. Fasten the clip with one nail so it projects over the inside edge of the frame 1/8 in. The other nails are driven after the spring is in place. Alternate the position of every other sinuous spring so the helical springs can be installed in a straight line as shown in Fig. 20-11. The number of helical springs required is not critical. They should be attached with the opening turned inward so they will not snag or tear the padding. The helicals on the outside edge can be attached to the frame with nails or special clips.

Padding

The spring or webbing base is covered with a layer of burlap to protect and hold the padding. When using latex or plastic foam it is usually best to include an "insulator" of cotton felt, canvas, or sisal to bridge the springs and further protect the stuffing.

Edge rolls, Fig. 20-12, are fastened to the edge of the frame to prevent loose stuffing materials from working thin. Commercially produced rolls are available in various sizes or you can make your own by wrapping a roll of stuffing material in a strip of burlap or muslin.

Padding, also called stuffing, is available in loose or pad form. It is placed in position and usually stitched to the burlap spring cover. Pads are 1 to 1 1/2 in. thick and made of curled hair or rubberized fiber. Layers of cotton batting are placed over the stuffing material and held in position with a muslin cover.

Latex or plastic foam is easy to apply and since it is so resilient it is often used without a spring foundation. These materials are available in various types, shapes and densities. See Fig. 20-13. Prepare a pattern of the shape to be covered and add 1/2 in. on each edge. The pattern is then laid out on the foam with a wax pencil or

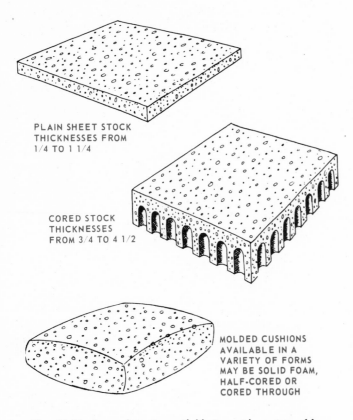

PLAIN SHEET STOCK THICKNESSES FROM 1/4 TO 1 1/4

CORED STOCK THICKNESSES FROM 3/4 TO 4 1/2

MOLDED CUSHIONS AVAILABLE IN A VARIETY OF FORMS MAY BE SOLID FOAM, HALF-CORED OR CORED THROUGH

Fig. 20-13. Latex foam is available in a wide variety of forms and sizes. Grades of compression include soft, medium, firm, and extra firm.

Fig. 20-14. Above. Laying out pattern on foam material. Add 1/4 to 1/2 in. Below. Cutting with large scissors. (Natural Rubber Bureau)

Fig. 20-15. To form a tapered edge, cut a bevel on the underside. (Natural Rubber Bureau)

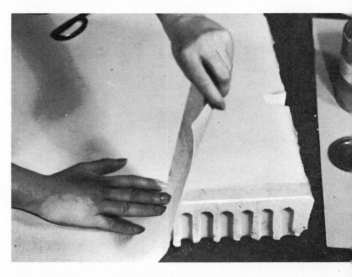

Fig. 20-16. Using rubber cement to attach a tacking strip. Use a strip about 1 in. wide to reinforce the edge of cutouts for arm and back supports.

ball-point pen as shown in Fig. 20-14. Thickness of 2 in. or less can be cut with scissors, Fig. 20-15. Thick slabs can be cut with a band saw.

The foam pad is held in position with muslin strips. The strips are cemented to the foam and then tacked to the frame. Brush the muslin and the latex foam with a liberal coat of rubber cement. Let this coat become dry and then apply a second coat. When the second coat becomes tacky, press the strips firmly in place, Fig. 20-16. Allow this assembly to dry for about 1 hr. before tacking it to the frame. Pieces of latex foam can be joined together with rubber cement in the same manner as used to apply the muslin.

When mounting latex or plastic foam directly to a plywood base, you should drill 3/8 in. holes spaced about 3 in. apart to permit free passage of air through the material. It is usually best to cover foam padding with a muslin cover, especially when the finish fabric is plastic, leather, or a loosely woven or stretchy material. See Fig. 20-17.

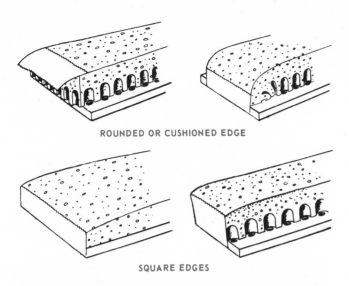

ROUNDED OR CUSHIONED EDGE

SQUARE EDGES

Fig. 20-17. How edges are formed. Strip is either tacked or stapled to frame or base.

which it will be used. Most fabrics are available in 54 in. widths. You should develop patterns of the pieces needed and then arrange them carefully on the material to secure economical cuts. Be certain to align the pattern of the back with the seat and when possible, run the warp threads up and down and from front to back to secure the greatest wear.

The cover is first placed in position and carefully aligned and then the center of each side is tacked as shown in Fig. 20-18. Start from the center and tack toward the corners. Do not pull the cover too tight as this will make a hard surface and place unnecessary strain on the fabric. On most work, the edge should be turned under as it is tacked. Pull the cover into position and then drive the tack or staple half way between the last fastener and the spot where you are pulling the

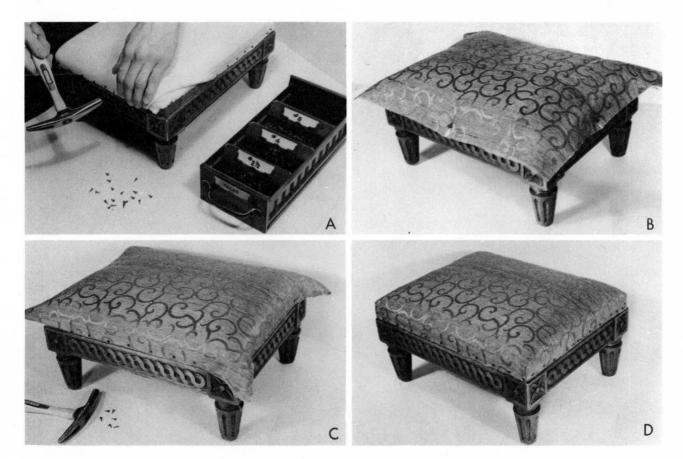

Fig. 20-18. A-Tacking the muslin cover. B-Finish cover in position and temporarily tack in the center of each side. C-Sides tacked to within about 2 in. of corners. D-Corners folded under, trimmed and tacked.

Final Cover

There are many kinds of fabrics and plastic materials suitable for the finished cover. Select a color, texture, and pattern that will be appropriate for the design and the decor of the room in

cloth. Fasten the material to within about 2 in. of the corners and then fold the corners under and tack and/or sew, Fig. 20-19.

To cover the staples or tacks, a decorative cloth or plastic banding called gimp is used. It is about 1/2 in. wide and is attached with glue or

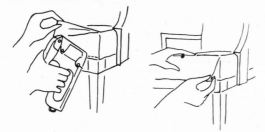

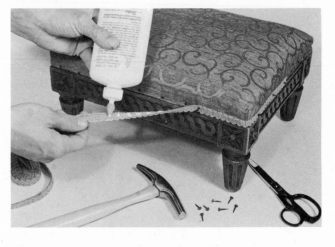

Fig. 20-19. How to form a corner. Left. Pull the material around the corner, lift up the excess, and staple. Then pull the remaining cloth straight down and trim it to size. Right. Fold the remaining edge underneath and tack or staple it in place. It may be necessary to sew the vertical slit shut. Use thread that matches the fabric and will not show.
(Natural Rubber Bureau).

small headed gimp tacks. When gluing gimp, use temporary tacking to hold it in place until the glue sets. See Fig. 20-20.

Fig. 20-20. Covering the tacked edge with gimp. Apply droplets of glue to the gimp and use temporary tacking to hold it in place until dry.

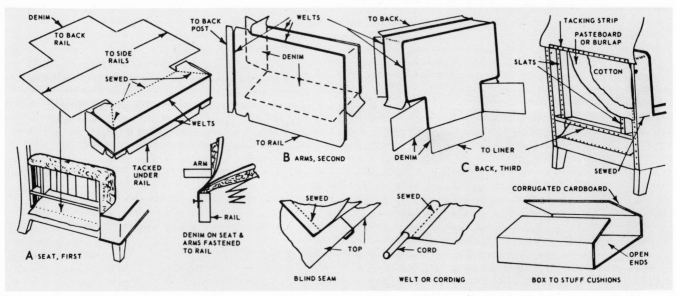

Fig. 20-21. Steps and details for attaching finish cover. Denim strips, sewed to the finish fabric serve as pull and tacking strips and reduces the amount of fabric required.

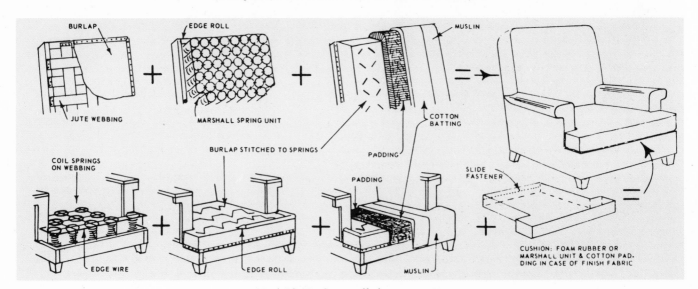

Fig. 20-22. Overstuffed construction.

Fig. 20-21 shows some details and procedures used to cover major pieces of upholstered furniture. It is unlikely that you will undertake an upholstery project of this size and it is included mainly for your study so you can gain some understanding of how such work is done. Fig. 20-22 shows how overstuffed chairs are constructed. See also Figs. 20-23 and 20-24.

Plastic Laminates

Plastic laminates of the high-pressure type provide a hard, smooth, sheet of synthetic material that is highly resistant to wear and scratching. They are unharmed by boiling water, alcohol, oil, grease, and ordinary household chemicals. Because of these characteristics, they are widely used as a surface material for tops of furniture

Fig. 20-23. Using an air driven stapler to attach a muslin cover to the seat of a restaurant booth.
(Fastener Corp.)

Fig. 20-24. View of the upholstery department in a furniture factory.
(Drexel Furniture Co.)

and cabinetwork. Plastic laminates are also used for wainscotting and wall paneling in the home and are especially practical in commercial and institutional buildings where surfaces may be subjected to a great amount of wear.

High pressure plastic laminates are available in thicknesses from 1/10 to 1/32 in. A 1/16 in. thickness is most commonly used. See Fig. 20-25. It consists of seven layers of paper, similar to that used in common paper bags, (Kraft paper) impregnated with phenol-formaldehyde

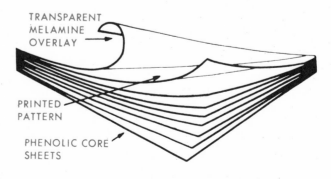

TRANSPARENT
MELAMINE
OVERLAY

PRINTED
PATTERN

PHENOLIC CORE
SHEETS

Fig. 20-25. Construction of a plastic laminate.

Fig. 20-26. *Processing paper to be used as the layers in a plastic laminate. (Formica Corp.)*

Layout and Cutting

Plan your work carefully so that the position of the pattern will be correct and there will be a minimum amount of waste. Plastic laminates are available in standard widths of 24, 30, 36, 48, and 60 in. Standard lengths include 5, 6, and 8 ft. however, lengths of 10 and 12 ft. are also available. A soft lead pencil can be used to make layout lines. When working with dark colors, place a strip of masking tape in the layout area and then draw the line on the tape.

Plastic laminates can be cut to rough size with a handsaw, table saw, portable saw or portable router, Fig. 20-27. Use fine-toothed blades

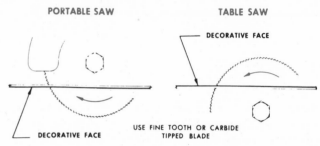

Fig. 20-27. *Cutting plastic laminate with circular saws.*

resin. On top of these is placed a pattern sheet which is made in various colors, designs, and wood grains. A transparent sheet, impregnated with melamine resin, is placed over the pattern sheet and the entire build-up is then bonded in huge presses at temperatures of over 350 deg. A polished stainless steel plate is used next to the top lamination which imparts a perfectly smooth surface to the laminate. See Fig. 20-26.

Although the laminate is very hard, it does not possess great strength and is serviceable only when bonded to plywood, particle board or hardboard. This base or core material must be smooth and dimensionally stable. Hardwood plywood (usually 3/4 in. thick) makes a satisfactory base; however, some plywoods, especially fir, have a coarse grain texture which may telegraph (show through). Particle board which is less expensive than plywood, provides a smooth surface and adequate strength, and is therefore used extensively.

When the core or base is free to move and is not supported by other parts of the structure, the laminated surface may warp. This can be counteracted by bonding a backing sheet of the laminate to the second face. It will minimize moisture penetration or loss and provide a balanced unit with identical materials on either side of the core. For a premium grade (highest) of cabinetwork, Architectural Woodwork Institute standards specify that a backing sheet be used on any unsupported area exceeding 4 square feet. Backing sheets are like the regular laminate without the decorative finish and are usually thinner. A standard thickness for use opposite a .060 in. (1/16) face laminate is .020 in.

and support the material close to the cut. Regular woodworking tools will grow dull rapidly so it is best to use carbide tipped tools whenever a large amount of laminate is to be cut. Laminates 1/32 in. thick, which are used on vertical surfaces, can be cut with tin snips.

It is best to make the roughing cuts 1/8 in. to 1/4 in. oversize and then trim the edges after

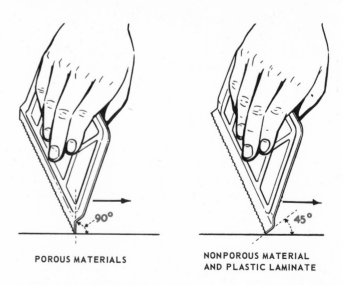

Fig. 20-28. *Using a spreader to apply contact cement.*

the laminate has been mounted. Handle large sheets carefully because they can be easily cracked or broken. Also be careful not to scratch the decorative side.

WOODY SAYS:

"Always wear adequate eye protection when cutting a plastic laminate with power equipment. The cuttings are hard and sharp and fly from the machine at high speed."

Applying Adhesives

Although various types of adhesive can be used, contact cement is preferred because no sustained pressure is required. This is applied with a spreader, roller, or brush to both surfaces to be joined. In production work contact cement is often sprayed.

On large horizontal surfaces it is easiest to use a spreader, Fig. 20-28. For soft plywoods, particle board or other porus surfaces the spreader is held with the serrated edge perpendicular to the surface. On hard nonporous surfaces and the plastic laminate, hold the edge at a 45 deg. angle as shown. A single coat should be sufficient.

An animal hair or fiber brush may be used to apply the adhesive to small surfaces or those in a vertical position. Apply one coat, let it dry thoroughly and then apply a second. All of the surface should be completely covered with a glossy film. Dull spots, after drying, indicate that the application was too thin and another coat should be applied.

Stir the adhesive thoroughly before using and follow the manufacturer's recommendation. Usually, brushes and applicators must be cleaned in a special solvent.

WOODY SAYS:

"Regular contact cement is extremely flammable. Keep it away from heat, sparks and open flame. Be sure there is adequate ventilation and avoid breathing the vapor. Keep the container closed when not in use."

Fig. 20-29. Using a rotary press to bond plastic laminate to a passage door. Pressure is applied by pneumatic cylinders. (Black Bros. Co.)

Drying and Bonding

Let both surfaces dry for at least 15 minutes or longer. You can test the dryness by pressing a piece of paper lightly against the coated surface. If no adhesive sticks to the paper, it is ready to be bonded. This bond can be made any time within an hour (time varies with different manufacturers). If the assembly cannot be made within this time, the adhesive can be reactivated by applying a thin coat of adhesive to each surface.

Bring the two surfaces together in the exact position required because they cannot be shifted once contact is made. When joining large surfaces, place a sheet of heavy wrapping paper (called a slip-sheet) over the base surface and then slide the laminate into position. Withdraw the paper slightly so one edge can be bonded and then remove the entire sheet and apply pressure. Some manufacturers recommend the use of dowel rods or a backing sheet instead of the paper separator.

Total bond is secured by the application of momentary pressure. Industry uses pinch rollers or rotary presses like the one shown in Fig. 20-29. Hand rolling provides satisfactory results if the roller is small (3 in. or less in length), Fig. 20-30. Long rollers apply less pressure per

Fig. 20-30. Applying pressure to the laminate with a hand roller. Press down hard with both hands.

square inch. Work from the center to the outside edges and be certain to roll every square inch of surface. In corners and areas that are hard to roll, hold a block of soft wood on the surface and tap it with a rubber mallet.

Trimming and Finishing

Trimming and smoothing the edges is one of the most important steps in the application of a plastic laminate. A block plane or file can be used; however, an electric router equipped with a carbide tipped bit will produce precision work at a much faster rate. When using a router some device must be used to control the depth of cut. An adjustable patented guide can be used or you can clamp or screw a wood guide block to the router base as shown in Fig. 20-31. Make the adjustment carefully so the bit will cut even with the surface with about 1/64 in. clearance.

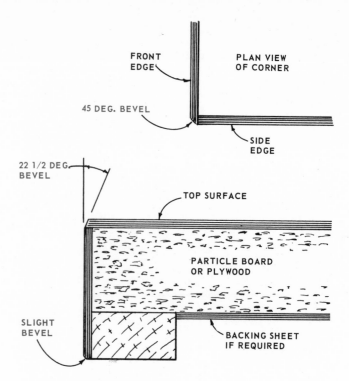

Fig. 20-32. Bevels for plastic laminate corners are important in the production of quality work.

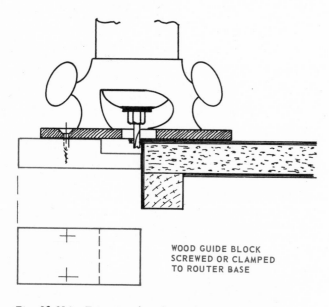

WOOD GUIDE BLOCK
SCREWED OR CLAMPED
TO ROUTER BASE

Fig. 20-31A. Trimming the edge with router; using shop-made guide block.

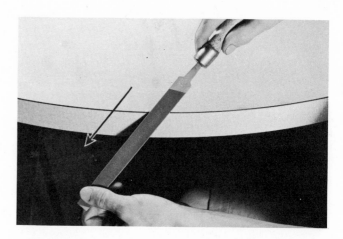

Fig. 20-33. Filing a corner bevel.

Fig. 20-31. Trimming the edge with router; using adjustable patented guide.

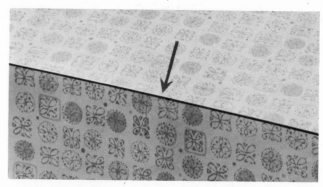

Fig. 20-34. Finished corner. Note the skillfully made match of the laminate pattern. (Formica Corp.)

The corners of a plastic laminate application should be beveled, Figs. 20-32 and 20-33. This will make them smooth to touch and they will also wear better. The angle can be formed with a smooth mill file as shown. Stroke the file downward and be careful not to damage the surface of the edge trim strip. Some routers can be equipped with an adjustable base or a special bit that will make this cut. Final smoothing and a slight rounding of the bevel should be done with a 400 wet-or-dry abrasive paper. Fig. 20-34 shows a finished corner on a cabinet top. See also Figs. 20-35 and 20-36.

Fig. 20-35. Heat resistance factors make plastic laminates an ideal surface material for counters with built-in cooking units. (Formica Corp.)

Fig. 20-36. Prefabricated wall panels made by bonding 1/32 plastic laminate to 3/8 in. particle board. Table tops are covered with a standard 1/16 in. laminate. (Formica Corp.)

When working with plastic laminates be especially careful that files, edge tools or abrasive papers do not scratch or otherwise damage the finished surfaces.

Ceramic Tile

Ceramic tiles are used to finish walls in bathrooms, kitchens and other areas where an attractive and impervious surface is required. Small pieces are set in patterns and called mosaics. The same materials and procedures of application can be applied to table tops, plaques, small boxes and novelty items.

Ceramic tiles are made from clay, flint, and feldspar. They are formed by a method called "dry-pressing," in steel dies, and are then baked and glazed. They are available in a wide range of sizes. Miniature tiles are carefully spaced and attached to a nylon net backing that makes them easy to handle and apply. They usually come in units one foot square.

The exposed wood parts of the structure should be finished before the tile setting operations. Apply a coat of sealer to the surface where tiles will be set. Make a "dry" layout of the tile arrangement and pattern, Fig. 20-37. If the tiles

Fig. 20-37. Above. Making a "dry" arrangement of the tiles. Below. Breaking tiles with a nippers. Note the net backing.

are mounted on a net backing, it can be easily cut with scissors. To cut a tile, scribe a line on the glazed surface with a file and break along this line. Miniature tiles can be broken with a pair of nippers as shown. Remove the tiles from the surface, keeping them in the proper arrangement.

The tiles are set in a special mastic or adhesive that is applied with a spreader as shown in Fig. 20-38. Hold the spreader firmly against the surface, allowing only that which comes

Fig. 20-38. Applying adhesive.

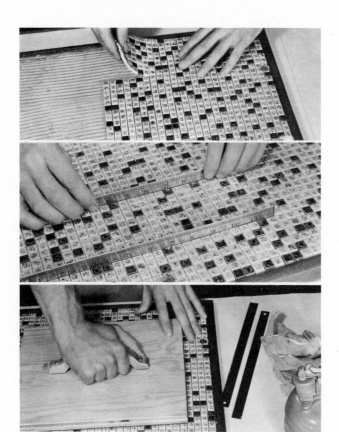

Fig. 20-39. Above. Laying the tiles lightly into the adhesive. Center. Aligning the tile with steel rules. Below. Pressing tile into the adhesive bed.

through the notches to remain. Mastics are slow drying so you do not need to hurry. Tools and equipment can be cleaned with mineral spirits. A putty knife can be used to apply the mastic to small areas.

Fig. 20-40. Above. Spreading the grouting cement. Below. Packing and smoothing.

Set the tiles lightly in place and check the arrangement carefully, Fig. 20-39. Use strips of cardboard or metal to align the spacing between the tiles. When they are all in the correct position, press them down firmly with a flat board as shown. The adhesive should ooze up not more than half way between the tiles. Clean off any excess adhesive and allow the work to set-up for several days. Check the manufacturer's recommendations.

The space between the tiles is filled with grouting cement, it comes in a powder form and is mixed with water to a creamy consistency. Spread it thoroughly over the work as shown in Fig. 20-40. Be certain the space between the tiles is well filled. Wipe off the excess with a squeegee or damp sponge. Allow the grout to set

Fig. 20-41. Finished table.

up for about 15 minutes and then use your finger tips and a cloth to pack, smooth, and level the joints even with the edges of the tile. The grout should be permitted to harden for several days before the article is placed in service. A silicone sealer may be applied to waterproof the grouted joints. The finished table is shown in Fig. 20-41.

Test Your Knowledge

1. Burlap is specified by its weight in ounces per_____.
2. A light cotton material that has a heavy sizing coat and is used to enclose the underside of upholstered work is called _____ .
3. Sinuous springs can be mounted on a webbing base about like coil springs. True or False?
4. It is considered good practice to place loose fill padding directly on a webbing base. True or False?
5. Each 1/2 in. increase or decrease in the length of a sinuous spring will change the crown height about_____ in.
6. If the position of every other sinuous spring is reversed, the_____ springs can be installed in a straight line.
7. Edge rolls prevent loose fill stuffing materials from working away from edges. True or False?
8. Cotton batting is usually held in place with a _____cover.
9. Latex foam with equally spaced holes in the underside is called_____ stock.

10. Finish covers are first carefully positioned and then temporarily tacked at the corners. True or False?
11. A standard thickness of plastic laminate used on table and counter tops is_____in.
12. There is a tendency for the grain of regular fir plywood to telegraph through a plastic laminate. True or False?
13. To prevent a laminated surface from warping, a _____ is bonded on the opposite face.
14. A nylon brush can be used to apply regular contact cement if a bristle brush is not available. True or False?

Outside Assignments

1. Prepare a detailed step-by-step procedure to follow when replacing the cover and padding materials of a chair with a slip seat.
2. Secure small samples of the various types of latex foam, polyurethane foam, and some of the newer synthetic padding materials such as Dacron batting. Mount them on a display board with descriptive labels listing their properties, application methods and costs.
3. Plastic laminates can be bent and formed at elevated temperatures. Experiment with sample pieces using an electric iron or infrared heat lamp. Prepare a written report or make an oral report to the class, listing and describing your findings. Design a small project that would utilize a curved plastic laminate surface.

Using portable router to make cutout in plastic laminate counter top.
Hardboard template is clamped in proper position and guides cut.
(Black and Decker)

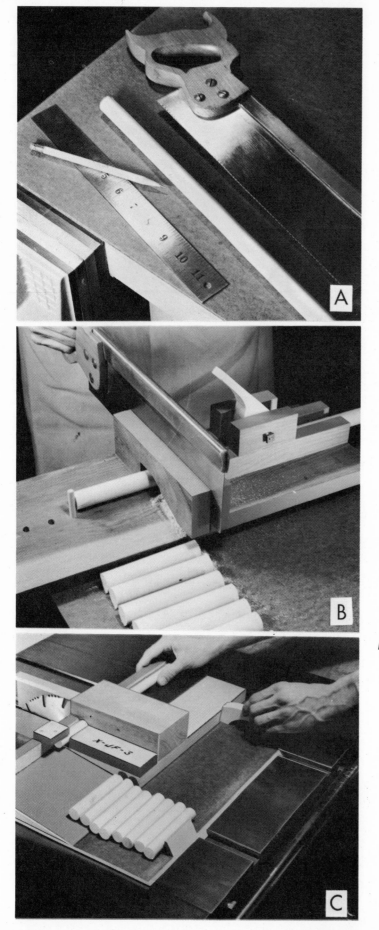

Fig. 21-1. Cutting dowels to specified length.
A-Standard hand tools produce 2 per minute.
B-Hand sawing jig produces 5 per minute.
C-Table saw fixture. Rate of production, 15 per minute.

Unit 21

MASS PRODUCTION

Science and invention, coupled with industrial know-how have made America a great nation. We have developed systems of mass production that provide our people with a tremendous range of products that make their lives easier and more enjoyable. Items that were considered luxuries just a generation ago, now have become common and are available to everyone.

Although wood products are seldom produced at the high volume reached by such metal products as automobiles and refrigerators, the same general procedures, methods, and considerations must be applied to the manufacturing process.

All manufacturing plants, whether they are large or small, build a few custom products, or mass produce items for wide distribution, include such departments and divisions as; business and finance, product selection, design and engineering, production, inspection, storing, packaging and shipping. In the mass production plant there are certain additional elements that receive special attention:

1. PRODUCT SIMPLIFICATION. Designing or redesigning the product so that it is easy to produce and still includes attractive and functional features.

2. STANDARDIZATION OF PARTS. Given parts will all be the same. They are interchangeable in an assembly. Worn, or damaged parts can be easily replaced after the product is placed in service.

3. SPECIAL MACHINES AND TOOLS. This includes jigs and fixtures, and special set-ups that can be applied to standard equipment so it will perform a given operation with speed and accuracy.

4. ORGANIZATION OF MACHINES, MATERIALS AND WORKERS. Careful analysis of the work so that jobs can be broken down into simple operations and arranged in proper sequence. Controlled movement of materials and assemblies from one station to the next. Synchronization of all operations, so that the right things are at the right place at the right time. Assignment and coordination of workers and jobs.

Already you may have experienced in a small way the efficiency that can grow out of mass production. Possibly you have constructed a pair of matching end tables or similar project and found that you were able to produce them in less than double the time necessary to produce one.

Production time for each item can be further reduced as larger quantities are produced, especially if the work is carefully organized and attention is given to the development of special devices. For example, Fig. 21-1, compares several methods of cutting a dowel to a specified length. The hand sawing jig greatly improves the accuracy and quality of the work which is very important in producing parts that are interchangeable. The sawing fixture mounted on the table saw provides the same accuracy plus a higher production rate. In its operation, the dowel is fed through the holder to the stop and the fixture is then moved forward to make the cut. When the dowel is cut off it drops slightly, clears the stop and is pushed onto the ramp where it rolls back out of the way of the next piece.

You may want to design and produce a small item on a mass production basis working by yourself. If you carefully planned and organized the work, built a pilot model, and constructed a special jig or fixture for several of the key operations, you would gain considerable experience even though you actually produced only a relatively small number of units.

It is likely, however, that your instructor may want to develop a mass production project involving a group of students or even the entire class. This will provide an experience more closely related to modern industry that includes the careful control of material flow, production schedules, and the coordination of the efforts of many people.

Selecting and Designing

The selection and design of your individual projects have been determined largely by your personal interests and desires. When selecting an article to be mass produced in large numbers and widely distributed it will be especially important that you consider its function and appear-

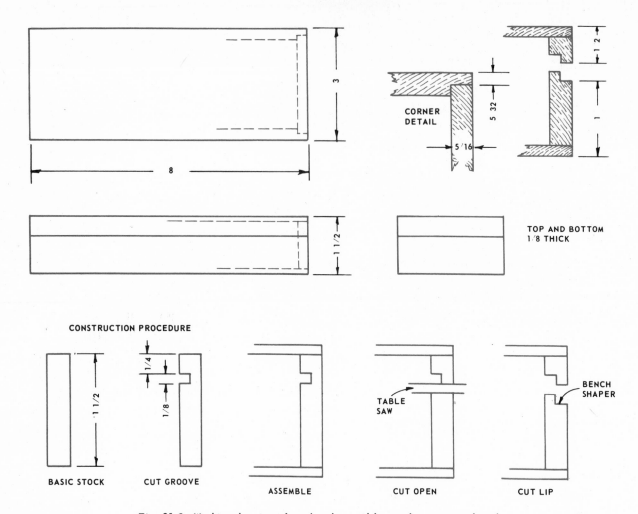

Fig. 21-2. Working drawing of card and pencil box to be mass produced.

ance and whether others will want to buy and own it. Business and industry gives great consideration to this matter and refers to it as MARKET RESEARCH. Manufacturers try to develop products that have a high level of consumer appeal. They give little attention to the personal whims of the designer or engineer.

After an article has been tentatively selected for mass production, study it carefully to determine if it can be adapted to mass production methods and efficiently built in the shop with standard tools and machines. By designing and constructing special setups, this equipment can often be adapted to mass production requirements.

Parts that cannot be efficiently produced in the shop might be purchased from some outside source. Industry quite often does this. For example, some factories specialize in turned parts while others produce only formed plywood units which they then sell to companies that manufacture the finished items of furniture, cabinetwork, and other wood products.

Try to visualize the article in production so you can judge if there can be easy movement of

materials through the shop, with storage space for subassemblies and finished products. Large pieces may create many extra problems in this respect so it is usually best to select small articles which actually become advanced woodworking problems when planned and produced on a mass production basis.

After your sketches and ideas become stabilized, prepare a working drawing of the article. In addition to the usual details of construction, include the number that will likely be produced along with suggestions on special procedures and setups that might be used to produce it in the most efficient way. See Fig. 21-2.

Pilot Models and Production Ideas

As soon as the working drawings are stabilized, you should build a sample unit or pilot model. This will provide a check on the design and may reveal certain improvements that can be made. As the various operations are performed they should be studied carefully to determine what special jigs or fixtures can be developed for the mass production setup. Fig. 21-3 shows the construction of a pilot model. Changes and improvements may be so extensive that several models may need to be built before a satisfactory solution is found. The original working drawing should, of course, be corrected and revised accordingly.

Fig. 21-3. Building a pilot model.

should be drawn full size. An example of such a sketch is shown in Fig. 21-4. The only "key" or exact dimensions are the size of the box. The sizes of the various parts of the jig are usually not critical and can be determined by the good judgment of the builder.

Operational Analysis

During the construction of the pilot model, a great deal will have been learned about the operations and procedures best suited for the production. Now you should make a break down of all of the parts and subassemblies and under each one list the detailed operations in the order they will be performed. Working from this analysis, prepare an operations flow chart like the one shown in Fig. 21-5.

The symbols used in the sample chart are similar to those recommended by the A.S.M.E. (American Society of Mechanical Engineers). It shows the sequence and order of operations, assembly points and inspection points. Rectangles connecting to the operations indicate the construction of special jigs and fixtures. Numbering

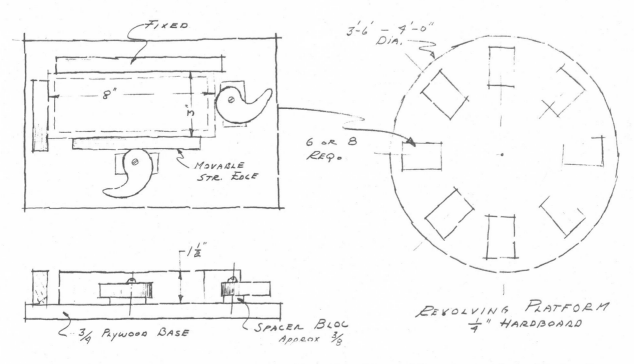

Fig. 21-4. Sketch of a gluing jig for card and pencil box. The only critical dimensions are those of the box. Sometimes colored lines are used to define the outline of the work from the jig or fixture.

As you think of ways to mass produce the article, record your ideas in sketch form. These can be very simple drawings or diagrams. Instead of including dimensions, try to make the drawing to an approximate scale. Small details

the operations makes it easier to assign workers and keep records. When the chart is complete it should be posted in the shop for easy reference by all students assigned to the project. See Fig. 21-6.

The experience you have had in making PLANS OF PROCEDURE for your regular project work will be helpful as you prepare an operational analysis and a flow chart for mass production work.

There are three requirements. The jig or fixture must provide a way to make the part or perform the operation rapidly, it must be safe to operate, and it must also produce work that is accurate within the limits specified. The inter-

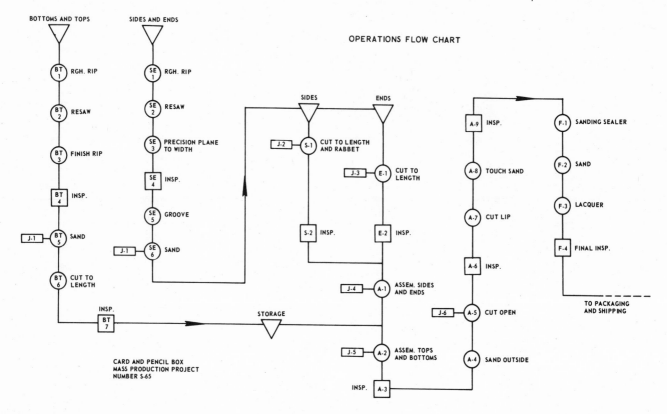

Fig. 21-5. Operations flow chart.

Tooling-Up for Production

Designing and constructing special tools, set-ups, jigs and fixtures is one of the most important steps in developing a mass production project. It compares with the work of the tool designer in industry, who is a highly skilled mechanic and knows basic mathematics, drawing, and manufacturing methods. He must be able to analyze operations and then develop various tools, machines and devices so these operations can be performed quickly, safely, and accurately.

The construction of the pilot model probably provided some ideas of what special tooling might be used. Now you will need to refine these ideas, develop the setups and try them out. These devices are called jigs and fixtures. A JIG is generally defined as a device that is attached to the work and guides the tool. A FIXTURE is somewhat similar except that it is usually mounted on or attached to the machine or tool and holds and/or guides the work as the operation is performed.

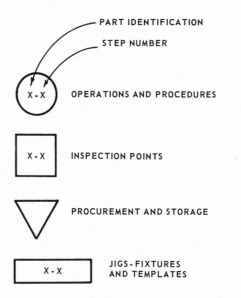

Fig. 21-6. Flow chart symbols.

changeability of parts is an essential element in mass production and depends on this accuracy. Note the jig construction in Fig. 21-7. You will

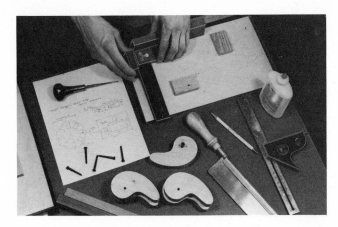

Fig. 21-7. Building a jig.

always need to maintain a higher degree of accuracy in the jig and fixture building than will be required in the work that it performs. If the tolerance permitted in the fabrication of the part is 1/16 in. then you will usually need to construct the jig or fixture to within 1/32 in. of the size requirements. This is no doubt a higher level of accuracy than you have had to maintain in your regular project construction, where you worked with individual pieces and could easily adjust each part to secure the desired fit.

WOODY SAYS:

"When designing and building fixtures for power machines, be sure to include some type of guard arrangement. Guards should protect the operator but not completely hide the cutting tool from view."

The size of the production run (number of articles to be produced) will determine how extensive and complicated the jigs and fixtures should be. Production runs of 10 to 50 units will not justify the intricate tooling-up that would be required for runs of 100 to 1000. In industry the tooling-up process might include the purchase of additional equipment, specialized machinery, and require extra space and other facilities. All of this would be expensive and would not become a profitable operation until many thousands of units had been produced and sold.

In the school shop, since we are more interested in educational experiences than profitable operation, it is justifiable to develop far more extensive jigs and fixtures than the size of the run

might indicate. They should be designed as small, separate units that can be quickly attached and set up for use on benches and machines and then easily removed and stored at the end of the working period.

Equipment Layout and Production Lines

The selection and arrangement of equipment in industrial plants is so important that a special plant layout department is often included in the total organization. Members of this group are continually searching for new and better ways to refine and improve the flow of materials and the use of machines and equipment. They plan the arrangement of work stations and layout production lines where the product is assembled as it is carried along on continuous or intermittent moving conveyors. It requires a tremendous amount of careful planning to organize all of the tools, machines, supplies, materials and workers in such a way that the product will be produced with speed and efficiency.

Fig. 21-8. Mechanized conveyor carries kitchen wall cabinets along assembly line in a modern woodworking plant. (Kitchen Kompact Inc.)

Woodworking plants generally do not make extensive use of moving production lines, except in the final assembly and finishing departments. See Fig. 21-8. Duplicate parts are usually stacked on stock trucks or carts and moved from one area or work station (places where operations are performed) to another. Fig. 21-9 shows a typical work station with parts stacked on either side of the operator. See also Fig. 21-10.

The average school shop is not designed for mass production work and it would be impractical to make extensive rearrangements for any particular product. It is worthwhile, however, to make

Fig. 21-9. Assembly of front frame, sides and back of a kitchen base cabinet starts here and then doors, drawers, trim and other fittings are added as it travels along the conveyor shown in background.

Fig. 21-11. Window parts being formed on a moulder. (Andersen Corp.)

Fig. 21-10. A typical work station in a modern plant. Hardware is being attached to window jambs. (Andersen Corp.)

operation. It is especially important to check the time required at each station. If the time seems too long and it appears that a bottleneck (delay) may be created, one of the following adjustments should be made:

1. Refine the procedure or method.
2. Improve the operator's performance.
3. Break the operation down into two or more steps.
4. Duplicate the setup and add more operators (workers).
5. "Stock pile" or "bank" materials in overtime work sessions.

Handling and Storing Materials

The transportation or flow of material and parts from one machine or work station to another requires special equipment. Woodworking industries use pallets, lift trucks, stock carts,

a drawing of the equipment layout, as it exists, assign work stations and draw coded lines indicating the flow of material. This assignment of stations and space will be helpful even though there may be overlapping of routes and other interference that would not be permitted in a regular industrial operation.

After the work stations have been established and the flow of materials and parts have been determined, it will be a good idea to try out each

Fig. 21-12. Parts and subassemblies in storage. (Kitchen Kompact Inc.)

roller conveyors, belt conveyors and palletized conveyors. Fig. 21-11, shows a typical mill room operation where the work pieces are neatly stacked on pallets and then moved by lift trucks to the next station or to a storage area. When machines are setup to produce a specific part or certain subassemblies are being fabricated, many more units are produced than can be immediately used in the final assembly section. They are stockpiled and stored as shown in Fig. 21-12.

In the school shop the movement of material, parts and assemblies is limited to stock carts, tote trays and stock boxes. A stock cart, Fig. 21-13, can be used not only to transport material from one station to another but can also serve as a storage unit. At the beginning of the work period

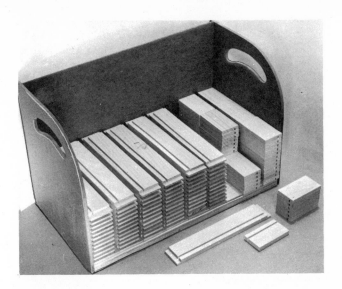

Fig. 21-14. A tote tray can be used for organizing, transporting and storing small parts. If the parts are carefully stacked (as shown) it is easy to count and check them.

Fig. 21-13. A stock cart that is adaptable to production work in the school shop.

it can be quickly moved from the storage area to the work station and returned at the end of the session. Tote trays and boxes can be used in about the same way for small parts, Fig. 21-14.

Inspection Points

In the operations flow chart, you have probably noted the squares that are used to mark inspection points. They usually follow those operations where high accuracy and quality of work is especially important if the parts are to fit properly with other units or assemblies. You can readily see that it would be poor practice to just wait and see if the parts fitted properly at another station along

the production line. By that time many defective pieces might have been produced, resulting in a great deal of wasted time and materials.

Inspection points will vary greatly as to the methods and procedures used. At some points, a visual check may be all that is needed with parts stacked together so that imperfect ones can be quickly spotted. Other points may require that each part, or every tenth part, or a certain percentage of parts be accurately checked with a rule or gauge or some special measuring device or instrument. Industrial operations often require the assignment of an entire department or group of experts to this area of work which is referred to as QUALITY CONTROL.

The final inspection is a very important one in the area of furniture and cabinetwork. Not only must the unit be square and true with drawers, doors and other working parts fitting smoothly and with the proper clearance, but the finish must also be carefully inspected. Fig. 21-15, shows final inspection in a furniture factory. If

Fig. 21-15. Final inspection point in a large furniture factory. (Drexel Furniture Co.)

Fig. 21-16. Using a carrier board to plane stock to finished thickness.

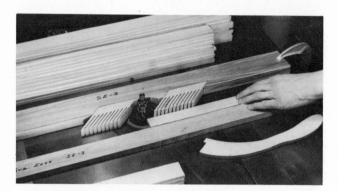

Fig. 21-17. Precision planing stock to width on the shaper. Ring guard has been removed for this photo.

Fig. 21-18. Portable belt sander, held in a cradle to sand thin side strips.

Fig. 21-19. Fixture for cutting box ends to exact length. Regular saw guard is used for this operation.

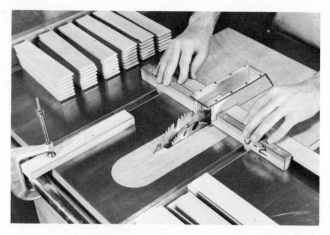

Fig. 21-20. Sides are cut to length and rabbeted in a single operation. A section of a dado head is mounted on each side of the saw blade. Note plastic covered guard.

Fig. 21-21. Mass producing parts for a window frame on a double-end tenoner. Parts are cut to length and jointed on each end in a single pass through the machine.
(Andersen Corp.)

a company wants to maintain a reputation of producing quality products, it will be necessary to carefully inspect each unit before it is packaged and shipped.

Operating the Production Line

If the planning and preparation has been carefully done it will be enjoyable and exciting to actually get the article into production. A high level of perfection in timing and movement of work, however, should not be expected. Even in industrial plants, where personnel is highly trained and experts handle the work, it may require many weeks or months to perfect the production lines and remove all the bugs (problems).

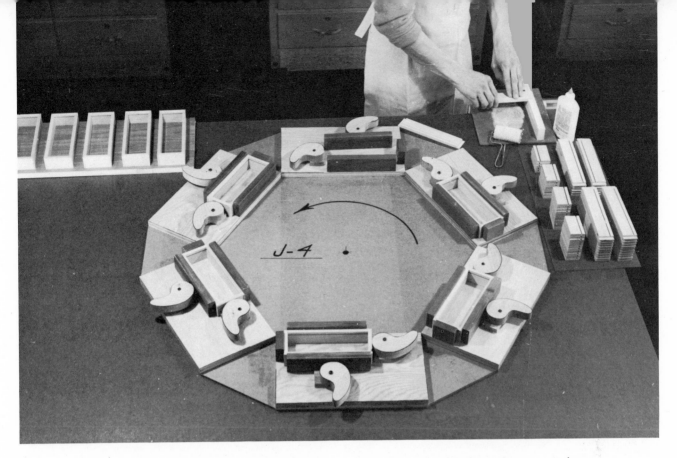

Fig. 21-22. *Gluing setup for assembly of sides and ends. The polyvinyl glue makes an initial set in the time required for the subassembly to travel around the turntable.*

Fig. 21-22A. *Rabbet joints are pressed against the applicator bar after glue has been spread on bar with roller.*

Photographs, Figs. 21-16 to 21-28, show a mass production project carried out in a school shop.

Workers can be assigned to the various work stations, using the coded numbers on the operations flow chart or other systems can be devised. Everyone should have an opportunity to practice their operations before the production run. Some workers may need special training and extra practice. When the run is of short duration a given student may have several assignments, first at the beginning of the line and later at the end.

Fig. 21-23. *A modern air press for assembling chair under structure to seats. One of many mass production operations in a furniture factory.* (Heywood-Wakefield Co.)

Parts that include time consuming operations and are likely to cause problems during the production run should be fabricated ahead of time. Also, all the basic stock should be selected and rough milled.

It will be quite a challenge to coordinate all the stations and keep the flow of work moving. Bottlenecks will very likely develop because of errors in planning, malfunctions in equipment, or inability of the workers. Sometimes the problems

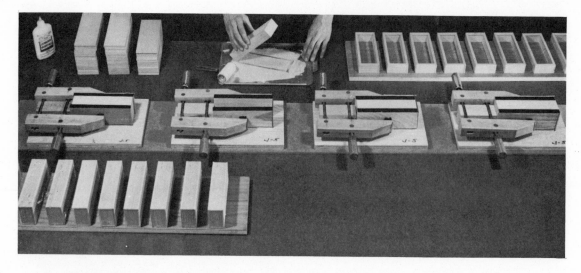

Fig. 21-24. Gluing tops and bottoms to the side and end assemblies. The clamping units are mounted on a carrier that is waxed on the underside and slides easily back and forth in front of the operator.

Fig. 21-25. Sanding outside surfaces on a stationary belt sander.

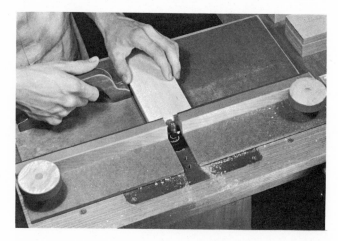

Fig. 21-27. Cutting a rabbet on the lower section to receive the lipped top. A small bench shaper is being used.

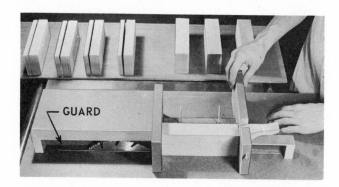

Fig. 21-26. Cutting the box open. Cut is made half way on one side and then the box is turned over to cut the other side.

may be so severe that production will need to be closed down for the day. While supervisors or foremen make adjustments and repairs, the balance of the workers can return to their regular individual project work.

Records and Evaluation

At the end of the production run it will be especially valuable to review the total operation. Records should include such items as number of parts produced, total time required, percentage

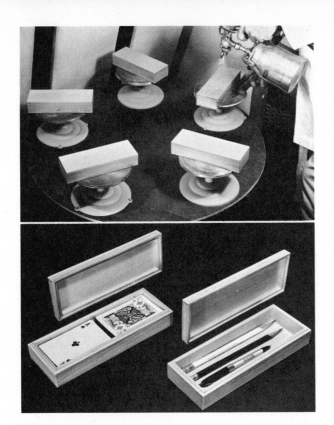

Fig. 21-28. Above. Spraying a final coat of lacquer on outside surfaces. Small turntables are mounted on the larger revolving table. Below. Finished boxes.

of waste or number of parts rejected, parts reclaimed or reworked and total material and supplies used.

These records should be studied and evaluated along with a review of some of the problems and bottlenecks. Improved practices and organization will probably be evident and these should be discussed. Highlighted also, should be some of the operations or special jigs and fixtures that performed especially well. Those that did not meet expectations should also be pointed out, along with reasons for their failure.

Products

From the very start of a mass production project, some plan must be formulated concerning the use to be made of the articles that will be produced. For short runs, the students involved in the work may want to divide the articles among themselves. On larger production runs it may be necessary to organize and establish a business committee to handle the distribution and sales as well as control the money and pay for materials used.

A production finishing operation in a large furniture factory that specializes in tables. (Mersman Bros. Corp.)

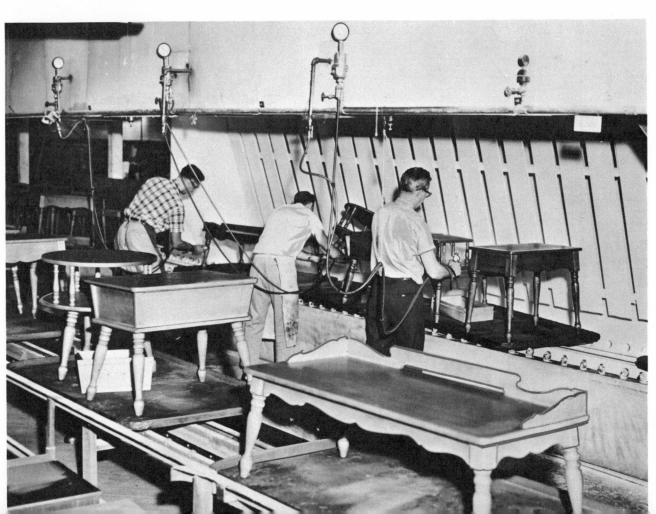

Even though the emphasis in the school shop is directed toward the production aspects of a mass-produced article, some attention can well be given to a study of such business and financial factors as capital outlay, raw material costs, labor costs, overhead and other expenses. Organization and control of all these along with an efficient sales and distribution plan will be essential if the entire operation is to be profitable. In our modern industrial plants, the smooth running and efficient production line will help insure a profit only if it is a part of a sound and well administered business structure.

Test Your Knowledge

1. Designing or redesigning a product so that it can be efficiently produced on a mass production basis is called _____ _____ .
2. Producing large projects on a mass production basis in the school shop results in extra problems in material handling and _____ .
3. An experimental or sample unit of a product that will be mass produced is usually called a _____ _____ .
4. An operational analysis should be prepared before drawing a flow chart. True or False?
5. On an operations flow chart, the square symbol is used to indicate an _____ _____ .
6. A device that attaches to the work piece and guides the tool while the operation is being performed is called a _____ .
7. Woodworking factories use moving conveyor lines in nearly all areas of their operations. True or False?
8. Platforms or bases on which parts or materials are stacked are called _____ .
9. When loading a tote tray or stock box the parts should be carefully stacked so they can be easily inspected and _____ .
10. Points along the production line where there is interference with the smooth flow of material and parts, are commonly referred to as _____ .

Outside Assignments

1. Select or design a small article that can be mass produced in the school shop. Make an operational analysis and then prepare a flow chart.

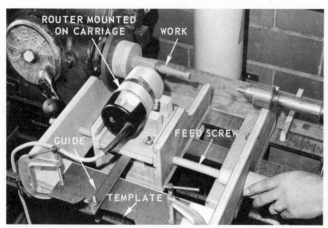
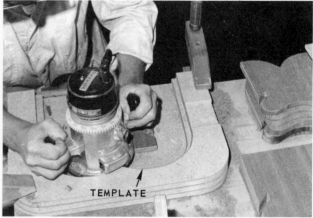

Shop built jigs and fixtures used in mass production projects. *Top Left.* Fixture mounted on lathe bed supports portable router. Spring (not visible) holds guide against template as carriage is fed along the cut from right to left. *Top Right.* Blanking-out top contour of book holder end-piece. Router cut is guided as edge of base moves along template. *Bottom Left.* Four place assembly and gluing jig. By the time the fourth compartment is filled, the first unit can be removed. *Bottom Right.* Fixture on disk sander accurately smooths one side and both circular ends in a single operation. Carrier is guided by pins located on underside.

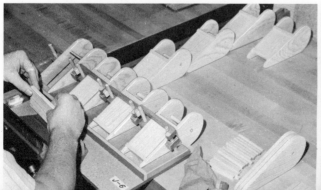
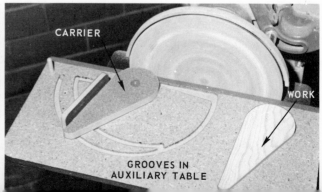

2. Prepare sketches of a jig or fixture that could be used for some "key" operation in a mass production project. Include a written explanation of how it works and some of its features.

3. Design a gauge that could be used to check the thickness or width of mass produced parts to determine if they are within acceptable limits. Such a device is commonly called a "go and no-go" gauge. It has two gaps spaced so an acceptable part will slip by the first gap but not the second.

4. Study the history of the development of mass production. Use such resources as the Encyclopedia Americana. Learn of the contributions made by James Watt, Eli Whitney and Henry Ford. Prepare a written paper or make an oral report to your class.

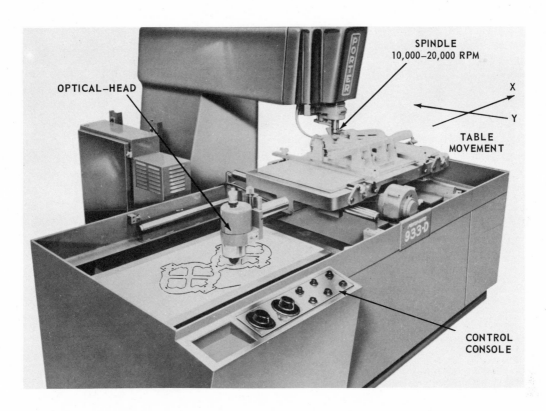

OPTICAL-HEAD

SPINDLE
10,000–20,000 RPM

X

Y

TABLE
MOVEMENT

933-D

CONTROL
CONSOLE

Above. Automatic Optical-Head Router. The electronic optical scanner follows black line drawings with a tolerance of plus or minus .005 in. This directional data is transmitted to the router table for X and Y movement. An additional signal is provided by code marks on the drawing to raise and lower the spindle for automatic hole-to-hole indexing. Feed speeds can be varied from 0 to 160 ipm. Below. Close-up view of spindle and work. Note the design of the table fixture with air clamps located at the back.

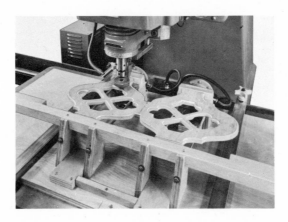

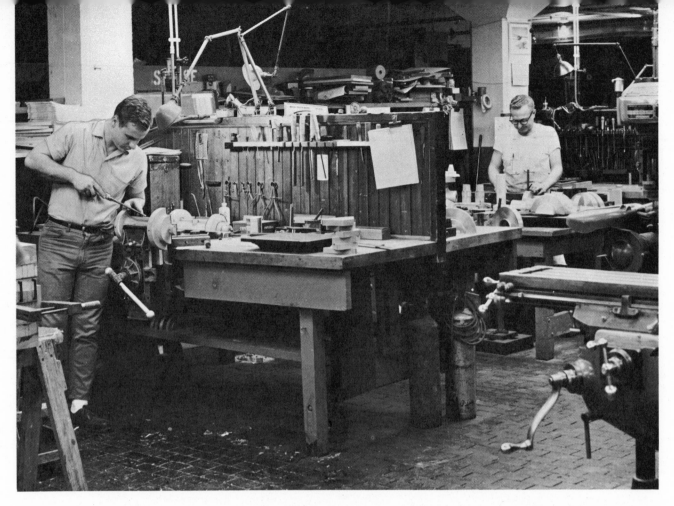

Fig. 22-1. Patternmakers at work in an industrial plant. Note the special patternmaker's vise used to hold the pattern.

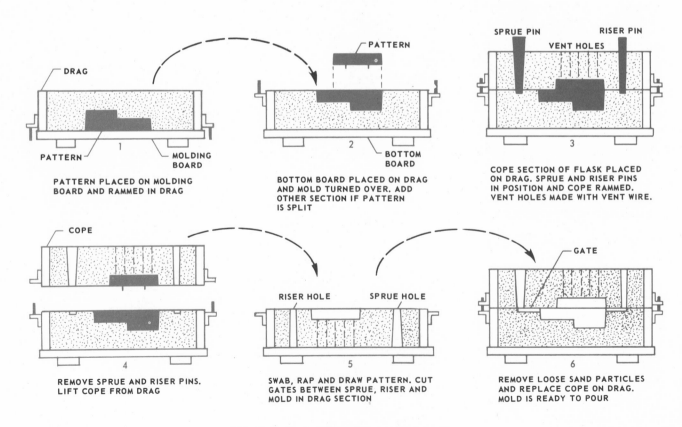

1 — PATTERN PLACED ON MOLDING BOARD AND RAMMED IN DRAG

DRAG
PATTERN
MOLDING BOARD

2 — BOTTOM BOARD PLACED ON DRAG AND MOLD TURNED OVER. ADD OTHER SECTION IF PATTERN IS SPLIT

PATTERN
BOTTOM BOARD

3 — COPE SECTION OF FLASK PLACED ON DRAG. SPRUE AND RISER PINS IN POSITION AND COPE RAMMED. VENT HOLES MADE WITH VENT WIRE.

SPRUE PIN
RISER PIN
VENT HOLES

4 — REMOVE SPRUE AND RISER PINS. LIFT COPE FROM DRAG

COPE

5 — SWAB, RAP AND DRAW PATTERN. CUT GATES BETWEEN SPRUE, RISER AND MOLD IN DRAG SECTION

RISER HOLE
SPRUE HOLE

6 — REMOVE LOOSE SAND PARTICLES AND REPLACE COPE ON DRAG. MOLD IS READY TO POUR

GATE

Fig. 22-2. Steps followed in making a mold.

Unit 22

PATTERNMAKING

Patternmaking is the building and construction of models and forms (patterns) that are used in the foundry to make metal castings. Production work and automatic molding machines require metal patterns, however wood is nearly always used to make the original or master patterns from which these metal patterns are produced. See Fig. 22-1.

The knowledge and skills that you have gained in woodwork can be applied to this important area of work. Some of the first patterns that you are likely to make of decorative articles (probably wall plaques, candlesticks, trays, etc.) will not require great attention to size, however as you progress to advanced projects involving patterns of machine parts, you will need to work to exact dimensions. Patternmaking requires the highest level of accuracy of any of the woodworking trades.

The Molding Process

A patternmaker must be skillful, and have a broad knowledge of woodworking tools and materials. He must also understand foundry methods and procedures. Fig. 22-2 shows a sequence of basic steps that are followed in making a sand mold using a simple pattern.

The mold is made in a FLASK which is either a wood or metal frame. It consists of two sections that are aligned with pins and sockets. The lower section contains the pins and is called the DRAG. The upper section is called the COPE. The separation between the two is called the PARTING. Complicated patterns may require additional sections (CHEEK FLASKS) between the cope and drag.

After placing the pattern on the molding board, it is dusted with a PARTING COMPOUND so that it will be easy to DRAW (remove) from the mold. Parting compound is also dusted over the drag before the cope is rammed so the two sections will not stick together.

The SPRUE PIN is used to make a hole in the cope through which the metal is poured into the mold. The RISER PIN forms a hole for the metal to rise into when the mold is full. It permits air to escape from the mold and may absorb some of the shrinkage when the metal cools. The vent holes also allow air, steam, and gases to escape as the metal is poured.

The sprue and riser pins are removed from the cope and then the cope is carefully lifted from the drag. Sand along the edges of the pattern is swabbed (moistened) to make it firm. The pattern is rapped lightly to loosen it in the mold and then carefully drawn. Gates (channels) are made in the drag so the metal can flow from the sprue hole into the mold cavity and from the cavity to the riser. Cores, if required, are placed in the mold and loose sand particles are blown away. The cope is then returned to its position on the drag.

Shrinkage, Finish and Draft

When metal changes from a liquid to a solid state it contracts or shrinks. The pattern therefore must be made oversize by an amount equal to this shrinkage. The amount of SHRINKAGE ALLOWANCE varies with the kind of metal or alloy, the size of the casting, and the shape of the casting. Although there are standard shrinkage allowances, application may vary depending on the nature of the work.

STANDARD SHRINKAGE PER FOOT

SMALL CASTINGS		LARGE CASTINGS	
Cast Iron	1/8 in.	Cast Iron	1/10 in.
Brass	3/16 in.	Brass	1/8 in.
Aluminum	3/16 to 1/4 in.	Aluminum	5/32 to 3/16 in.
Cast Steel	1/4 in.	Cast Steel	1/8 in.

The patternmaker uses a special shrink rule, Fig. 22-3, that is made slightly longer than a standard rule to compensate for the metal shrinkage. Shrink rules are available in a range of sizes to provide various allowances. In working with a shrink rule select one that corresponds to

Fig. 22-3. A shrink rule (above) compared with a standard rule (below). This 9/32 size provides double shrinkage allowance when building a master pattern from which an aluminum alloy pattern will be made for the production of a cast iron part.

the requirement of the casting for which the pattern is being made, then use it in the same way as a regular rule.

Castings for machine parts, especially those that will fit into assemblies, are machined to form smooth and accurate surfaces. Machining operations require extra metal in the casting and this FINISH ALLOWANCE must be added to the pattern. Finished surfaces of a part are designated on the working drawing by a V symbol on the edge view. The kind and quality of the machine operations is often specified with numbers and notes.

The amount of finish allowance depends on the size and quality of the casting, the kind of metal and the method of machining. General finish allowances may vary from 1/16 in. on small

brass castings to as much as 1/2 in. on large cast iron parts. Small aluminum castings, as produced in the school shop, usually require about 1/8 in. finish allowance. Top surfaces of castings require greater finish allowances than bottom surfaces because slag and impurities will normally rise to the top of the mold.

DRAFT is the slant or taper formed on the vertical surfaces of the pattern so that it can be easily drawn from the mold, Fig. 22-4. Normal draft allowance is approximately one degree or 1/8 in. per foot, however, additional amounts may be required when the surface is large or the wood grain runs in a horizontal direction. Additional draft must also be provided on the internal surfaces of recesses and pockets, especially if they are located in a position where the sand of the cope is lifted out when the mold is separated to remove the pattern.

Materials and Tools

Woods generally used for patternmaking are white pine, sugar pine, and mahogany. These are durable, stable, and have good working qualities. Patterns that will be subjected to hard usage or require extensive lathe work are often made of cherry wood. It is best to use plywood or laminated stock for large pieces that might warp if made of solid material.

Standard woodworking hand tools and machines are satisfactory for patternmaking. A spindle sander and disk sander are especially valuable for shaping parts and applying draft to inside and outside curves. Additional hand tools and supplies include shrink rules, fillet irons, brass dowels, rapping plates, metal letters and figures, and fillet material. See Fig. 22-5.

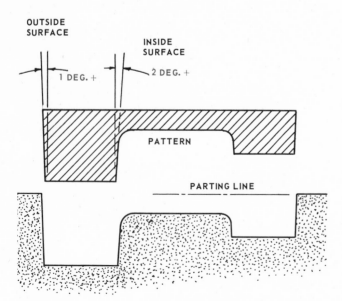

Fig. 22-4. Draft on the vertical surfaces of a pattern permits easy removal from the mold.

Fig. 22-5. Pattern letters and figures are used for identification purposes. Some have spurs or pins that are driven into the wood. Those with a plain back are cemented in place.

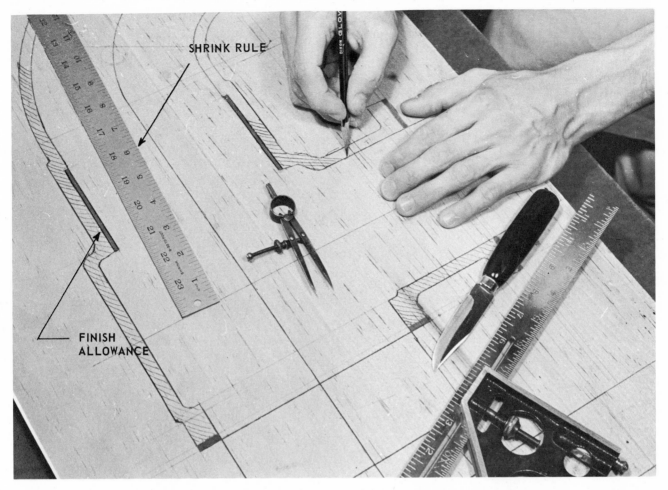

Fig. 22-6. Making a full-size drawing of the pattern on a layout board.

Layouts

Some patterns can be produced by simply following the dimensions given on the working drawing. When the part is complicated and includes finish allowances and coring, it is best to make a full-size layout on cardboard or a wood layout board. This layout is then referred to for shapes and sizes during the construction of the pattern.

The patternmaker uses a soft pine layout board as shown in Fig. 22-6. Dimensions are laid out with a shrink rule and lines cut into the wood surface with a knife and dividers. These lines are often traced with a sharp pencil to make them more readable, (see Unit 3, Fig. 3-20). The edges of the board should be straight and true so squares can be used to lay out lines in the same manner that a T-square is used on a drawing board. Sectional views are usually most valuable. Symmetrical parts may require only a half view. Details, such as spotfacing, milled slots or drilled holes are not included in the layout.

A standard procedure to follow when making a pattern layout is shown in Fig. 22-7. It may include all or part of the following steps:

1. Determine the position of the pattern in the mold and select the parting line. Consider what coring will be required.
2. Lay out the exact shape and size of the part using a shrink rule.
3. Add finish allowances. Colored lines will help define these additions.
4. Add draft.
5. Lay out cored areas not already shown and add core prints.
6. Draw curves not included in the layout that may be needed for templates or checking the work.

Constructing the Pattern

Study the work carefully and determine the easiest and best procedure to follow. Most patterns are build by assembling separate pieces rather than shaping them from solid stock. Segment and stave construction is used for large

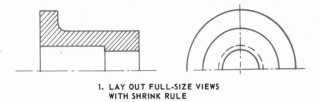

1. LAY OUT FULL-SIZE VIEWS
WITH SHRINK RULE

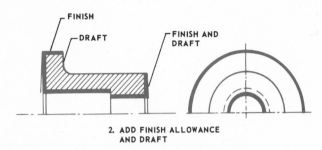

FINISH
DRAFT
FINISH AND
DRAFT

2. ADD FINISH ALLOWANCE
AND DRAFT

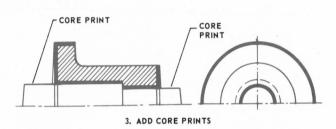

CORE PRINT
CORE
PRINT

3. ADD CORE PRINTS

Fig. 22-7. Procedure for making a pattern layout.

patterns that have circular or curved contours.

Start with the main parts and then add ribs, webs, bosses and other details. Run the grain in the direction of the greatest length to minimize dimensional change in the pattern. When possible, form the draft on the parts by planing, sawing, or sanding before they are assembled. Check the parts by placing them directly on the layout board. Finish sand exposed surfaces before assembly, being careful to maintain true surfaces and accurate sizes.

Draw fine lines on the parts to show assembly points and glue them together. Check the work with squares and rules, Fig. 22-8. Some parts may need to be clamped or held with brads but most of them can be simply set carefully in place and not handled until the glue has hardened. See also Fig. 22-9.

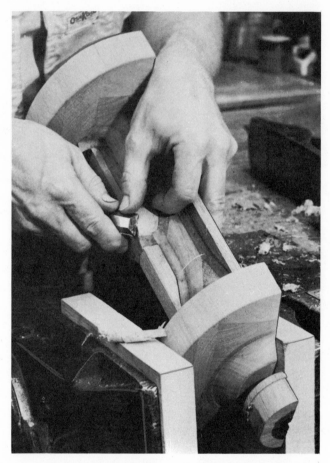

Fig. 22-9. Final work on pattern in an industrial plant. A patternmaker must be highly skilled in the use of hand tools.
(Fisher Controls Co.)

Fig. 22-8. Assembling a pattern with glue.

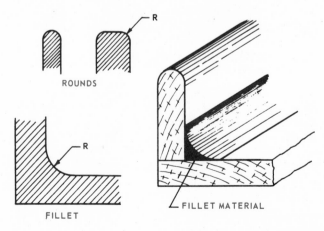

R

ROUNDS

R

FILLET

FILLET MATERIAL

Fig. 22-10. Fillets and rounds. Specified by the radius size.

FILLETS and ROUNDS add to the strength and appearance of a casting, Fig. 22-10. Fillets also eliminate sharp corners in the mold that would tend to "wash-off" when the metal is poured. Most rounded corners and edges are formed on parts before assembly while fillets must be added after assembly. Wax fillet stock is available and is pressed into the corners and shaped with a hot fillet iron. Leather fillets, Fig. 22-11, are more durable than wax fillets and are available in various sizes. They are glued in place and smoothed with a cold fillet iron.

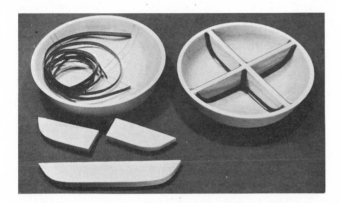

Fig. 22-11. Leather fillets applied to a one-piece pattern for a small-parts tray. Since the cope sand will extend down inside the pattern, the separating ribs must have considerable draft.

Many pattern shops use a fine grade of acetone base plastic wood for fillets. The material is formed into a roll of the required size, placed in the corner and shaped with a regular fillet iron, Fig. 22-12. The fillet iron is dipped into lacquer

Fig. 22-12. Using a special plastic wood for fillet material and smoothing with a fillet iron dipped in lacquer thinner.

thinner to keep the material from sticking to it and to help form a smooth fillet. Brushing a coat of lacquer thinner into the corner before applying

the plastic wood may cause it to adhere better. After the fillet has hardened, it is sanded with fine abrasive paper.

When turning patterns on the lathe, fillets can be easily formed along with the required shape.

After the pattern is assembled, fillets installed, and a final check made of sizes, draft and other allowances it should be lightly sanded and finished. Shellac was formerly used as a finishing material, but today brushing lacquers are extensively used because they are more durable and dry rapidly. A sealer coat should be applied and sanded, and then a final coat applied and rubbed smooth so the pattern can be easily withdrawn from the mold.

Color coding of the various parts and surfaces is good practice. In the past, black was generally used to denote unfinished surfaces and the faces of core boxes. A new code recommends black for core prints and core areas while unfinished surfaces are given a clear coating. Red is always used to identify machined surfaces.

Fig. 22-13. Above. Preparation of stock for a split pattern. Center. Turning sequence. Below. Finished pattern and core box.

Split Patterns

Some patterns will need to be made in two parts with one section located in the drag and the other in the cope. The dividing line or split is located at the parting line of the mold.

Cylindrical patterns that are turned on the lathe, usually are designed in this way. Fig. 22-13 shows a sequence of steps to follow when constructing and turning a split pattern. The two sections are squared to size and wood or brass dowel pins are installed on the mating surfaces. The dowels must be tapered and carefully fitted so the parts will be held in proper alignment. Provide just enough clearance so easy separation can be made.

The two parts are then fastened together. Either corrugated fasteners or screws may be used. Glue may also be used in just the area of the waste stock. Center the piece carefully, so the parting line will be along the center of turning. After turning the main body to rough size, a recess is cut to receive the blocks that will form the flange. These blocks are first cut to size and then clamped together for boring of the center hole. Next they are glued in place and after the glue has set the turning is completed. Be sure the parting lines are properly aligned.

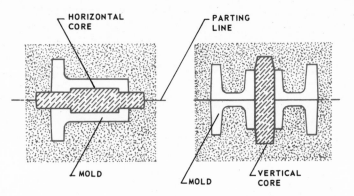

Fig. 22-15. Cores are used to form the interior of castings.

satisfactory and require no baking. Simple cylindrical cores are available in various diameters and are used for production. The patternmaker designs his work to take advantage of stock sizes whenever possible.

Core prints are the projections added to patterns which make the impressions in the mold that will seat and carry the core. The length and diameter of the core print depends on the size and weight of the core. The length of horizontal core prints for cores over 1 in. in diameter is usually equal to the diameter of the core. Core prints under 1 in. in diameter are maintained at a length of from 3/4 to 1 in. Horizontal cores are sometimes supported at only one end, Fig. 22-16,

Fig. 22-14. One half of a split pattern made of metal for production work. The flanges of the master wood pattern were turned as separate units and then attached to the main body. (Fisher Controls Co.)

Fig. 22-16. Cores in position in the drag. Note that these particular cores are supported on only one end. (Fisher Controls Co.)

Cores and Core Prints

Recesses, large holes, cavities and interiors of castings are formed with cores, Fig. 22-15. Dry sand mixed with a special binder is formed in core boxes and then baked in an oven. Wire is often used to reinforce cores that are large and complicated. Cores made from a mixture of sand, water glass, and carbon dioxide gas, are very

and it is then necessary to make the core print quite large to provide balance. See also Figs. 22-17 and 22-18.

Vertical cores can be set in impressions made by core prints located in the drag. When these are anchored in both parts of the mold, the top or cope end of the core print and core are tapered 10-15 degrees so that the core can be easily

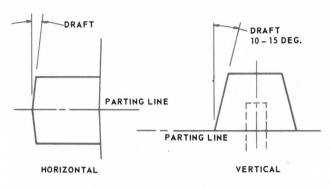

Fig. 22-17. *Proportion and draft for cylindrical or rectangular core prints. The length of a vertical core print is seldom over 1 in. even though the cross section is large.*

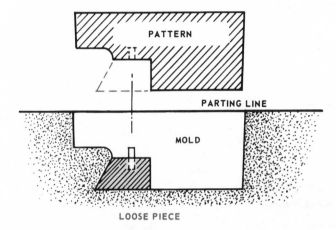

Fig. 22-18. *A pattern with a loose piece. The main section of the pattern is drawn from the mold and then the loose piece is removed separately. Loose pieces can be held in place with pins, dowels, or dovetailed slots.*

aligned with the impression when the mold is closed. Vertical core prints, located in the cope are often loose so they can be removed while the drag section is being rammed.

Core Boxes

Fig. 22-19 shows a simple cylindrical core box and the finished core. The box is rammed with the sand mixture and "dumped" to form a

Fig. 22-19. *Core box and dry sand core.*

half core. After identical halves are baked they are bonded together with a flour paste to form the completed core. A complete core is formed in a single ramming by using a split core box, Fig. 22-20.

Fig. 22-20. *Gear blank pattern and core box. The split core box is made by first setting the dowels and then clamping the pieces together to drill the hole.*

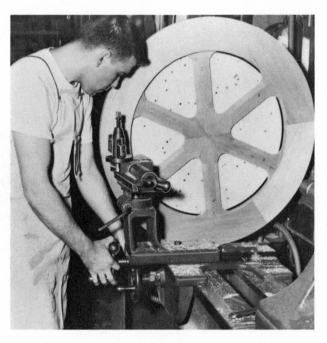

Turning a pattern for a large gear wheel blank on a pattern-makers' lathe. Note the segment construction of the rim (6 pieces) that provides greater stability and reduces cross-grain which is hard to work and finish.
(Manning Pattern Co.)

Plain cylindrical core boxes can be roughed out on the table saw as shown in Fig. 22-21. A diagonal fence guides the stock over the saw blade. The angle can be determined by raising the blade to the required depth and then setting the fence or guide strip at an angle that will provide twice this distance between the front and back edge of the blade. The cut is made by lowering the blade to about 1/8 in. above the table and making a pass over the machine. Additional passes are then made, raising the blade about

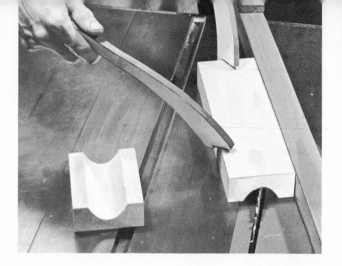

Fig. 22-21. *Roughing out a core box on the table saw. Always set the guide strip so the thrust of the blade will be toward it. Be sure to have your instructor check the setup before turning on the machine.*

1/8 in. each time. This method forms an eliptical shape which must then be sanded to a half circle with a round form. An inside ground gouge of the correct size can also be used.

Cylindrical core boxes that include several diameters are made in layers, Fig. 22-22. The stock for each layer is first cut to finished out-

Fig. 22-22. *A split core box that forms a core with several different diameters. Note the brass dowel pins.*

side dimensions. The required half-circles are then cut in each piece, after which the assembly is made. This same procedure can be applied to core boxes with internal shapes that are rectangular.

Match Plates

For production work in industry, patterns are mounted on metal plates, Fig. 22-23, which fit over the flask pins. They are called match plates because the two parts of a split pattern are mounted on each side in alignment so the impressions in the cope and drag "match" after the pattern is drawn and the mold is closed.

Fig. 22-23. *A wood pattern mounted on a match plate. (Fisher Controls Co.)*

Fig. 22-24. *Match plate for casting an anvil paperweight as shown at bottom of photo.*

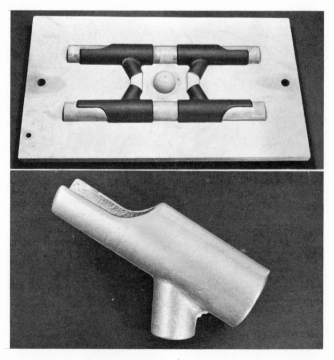

Fig. 22-25. *Above. Multiple unit match plate for fishing rod holders. Below. Sample casting.*

Rough castings as they come from the mold.
(Fisher Controls Co.)

Fig. 22-26. Left. Master pattern of a flanged housing for a thrust bearing. Right. Metal match plate ready for the foundry.

In the school shop, the plate can be made of plywood. Fig. 22-24 shows a match plate for casting an anvil paperweight. To align the halves of the pattern, first drill two holes all the way through the pattern and then use one of the halves to guide the bit for drilling the plate. Be sure to keep the bit perpendicular to the parting line. Insert dowel into the holes to align and hold the pattern. Gates, runners, and impressions for sprue and riser pins are included on the plate.

For production work, multiple or gang patterns can be mounted on a single plate, Fig. 22-25. One-piece patterns can also be mounted on plates and usually saves time in molding; especially if gates, runners and sprue recesses are included.

Fig. 22-26 shows a multiple pattern match plate used for high volume production in industry. The master pattern is made of wood and used to form the sand mold in the conventional way. The cope and drag are then separated by an appropriate amount, the edges are enclosed and the mold poured. Gates and risers are included in the casting process. The master pattern must be built with double-shrink allowances; shrinkage for the metal pattern (usually an aluminum alloy) and shrinkage of the final casting.

Test Your Knowledge

1. A standard flask consists of two parts called the drag and _____.
2. The hot metal is poured into the mold through an opening called the _____ hole.
3. When molten metal cools and changes to a solid it expands slightly. True or False?
4. Small aluminum castings usually require about _____ in. finish allowance.
5. External surfaces should include a greater amount of draft than internal surfaces. True or False?
6. The best kinds of wood for pattern making are white pine, sugar pine and _____.
7. The size of the parts for a pattern can be checked by placing them on the layout board. True or False?
8. The rounded area formed on an inside corner of a pattern is called a _____.
9. The projections on a pattern that form the recesses for cores are called _____.
10. The internal surfaces of a complicated core box should be formed on parts or layers and then glued together. True or False?

Outside Assignments

1. Prepare a list of patternmaking and foundry terms. Include a clear and concise definition of each.
2. Select a working drawing of a cast machine part from an advanced drafting book. Make a full-size drawing, following the procedure suggested for pattern layouts. Include finish allowances, draft, coring and core prints. Prepare a written description of the procedure you would follow in the construction of the pattern and core boxes.

On-site erection of a manufactured home. After floor panels are assembled on foundation, kitchen-bathroom module (arrow) is set in place. This factory built unit is completely fitted with plumbing lines and fixtures. Walls and partitions are then assembled (as shown) and roof panels installed.
(Wausau Homes Inc.)

Fig. 23-1. Carpenters erecting concrete forms for a modern highway overpass.
(Georgia-Pacific Corp.)

Unit 23

CARPENTRY

Carpentry is a broad classification within the trades and industries concerned with the building of wooden structures. It involves the construction of industrial, commercial, and residential buildings and includes such work as the erection of concrete forms for bridges and superhighway overpasses. See Fig. 23-1.

A carpenter must have a good understanding of wood and construction methods, and be able to lay sills and joists, erect studs and rafters, and apply sheathing, siding, and shingles. He should be competent at setting door jams, hanging doors, applying wood trim, building stairs, and constructing cabinets. Because so many different skills are required, carpenters often specialize in either the area of rough construction or finish work.

In the limited space of this Unit it will be possible to present only basic and typical practices and procedures. Since nine out of ten American homes are of wood frame construction, the material presented will deal largely with this important area of work. See Fig. 23-2.

Plans

As in all areas of woodworking, it is essential for the carpenter to have adequate plans (working drawings) to follow throughout the construction project. Architectural drawings consist of

Fig. 23-2. Nine out of ten homes in the United States are of wood frame construction. Lumber and wood products are durable, easily fabricated and permit great versatility in design.

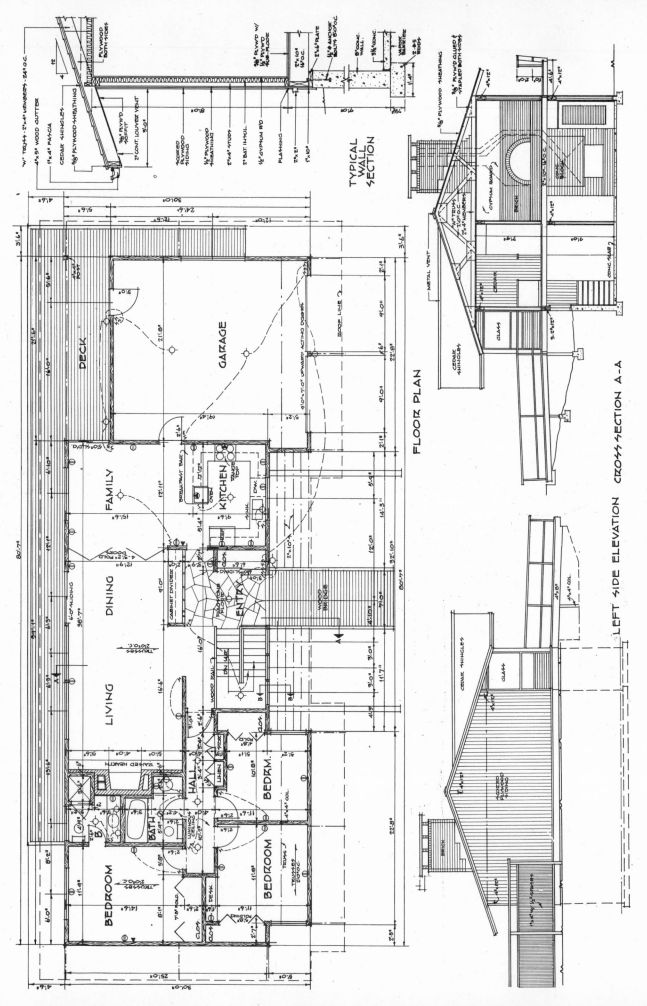

TYPICAL WALL SECTION

FLOOR PLAN

LEFT SIDE ELEVATION   CROSS SECTION A-A

Fig. 23-3. Part of a set of plans for a house. Architectural views have more flexibility in their arrangement than those in regular orthographic projection.

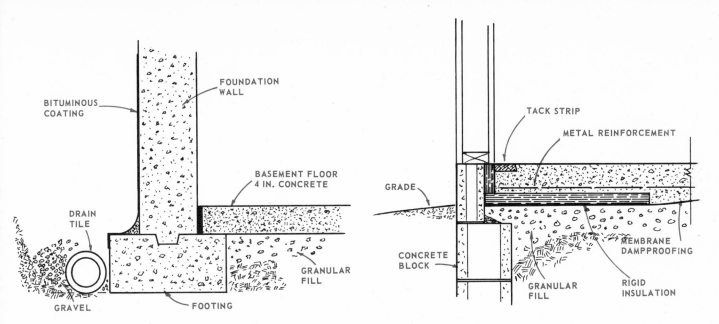

Fig. 23-4. Left. Foundation section. Fig. 23-5. Right. Concrete slab floor construction.

plans, sectional top views, elevations (front, side and rear views) and various details of construction. See Fig. 23-3. The plans should be drawn to meet all building codes in your area. A complete set of plans will include the following:

1. Site layout or plot plan.
2. Foundation plans.
3. Floor plans.
4. Front, right, left and rear elevations.
5. Sectional views.
6. Detail drawings.
7. Written specifications.

The floor plan will provide most of the dimensions needed; including overall size, location of walls, windows, doors, stairs and electrical and plumbing fixtures. The elevations show heights, roof angles, exterior materials and may include window and door sizes. Sections and detail views will provide sizes of structural materials and show methods of construction. Written specifications are needed to describe the kind and quality of materials, standards of application, and kind and quality of heating, plumbing and electrical equipment. Complete and accurate plans and specifications are of great value not only to the carpenter but also to the estimator, contractor and owner.

Because of the size of the structure, plans must be drawn to an accurate scale. A scale of 1/4" = 1' - 0" is generally used for plans and elevations of homes, while large institutional buildings are usually drawn to a 1/8 in. scale. Detail and sectional views need to be drawn larger so sizes and other information can be included. Architectural plans will show sizes in feet and inches. For example; standard ceiling height is given as 8' - 0" rather than 96 in., while the width of a standard door is 2' - 6", instead of

30 in. In carpentry work, you will soon become experienced with this method which is much more practical when working with large sizes typical of structural work. When you add or subtract these dimensions proceed as follows:

	6' - 8"			7' - 16"	
Addition	4' - 6"		Subtract	6' - 4"	
	2' - 4"			4' - 10"	
	12' - 18" or 13' - 6"			3' - 6"	

Footings and Foundations

Adequate and properly installed foundations are essential to all types of wood structures. See Fig. 23-4. Footings should extend far enough below the exterior grade to be free of frost action. They are nearly always made of concrete, however treated timber piling is sometimes used when certain unsatisfactory soil conditions exist and for temporary structures. The thickness (vertical dimension) of the footing is generally equal to the thickness of the foundation wall while the projection on each side is equal to one-half the wall thickness.

The foundation wall may be made of poured concrete or masonry units (brick, tile, concrete block). When masonry units are used, a 1/2 in. coat of cement mortar is generally applied to the exterior, and then coated with asphalt. Most plans call for drain tile to be laid along the footings and connected to a drainage system. Concrete blocks (8 x 8 x 16) are used in many areas for foundation walls in one-story construction.

Many homes today are built on a concrete slab floor. Although this is often done to conserve building costs, such a floor can be satisfactory if properly constructed with adequate insulation and a vapor barrier. Fig. 23-5 shows a detail section of a foundation wall and concrete floor that will be warm and dry. Wood, resilient tile, or carpet can be used for the finished floor.

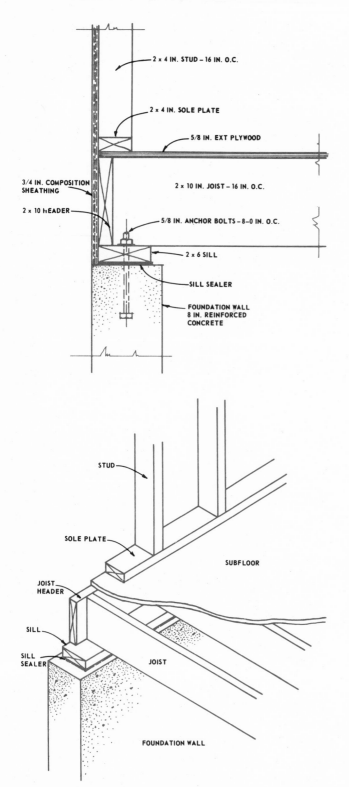

Fig. 23-6. Above. Detail from the architectural plans showing first floor framing at the foundation wall. Below. Pictorial view. This type of construction is called platform or western framing.

Floor Framing

Floor framing members consist of sills, girders and joists. The architectural plans will usually include a detailed drawing showing their size and how they fit together. See Fig. 23-6.

Sills are made of 2 in. lumber and secured to the foundation wall with bolts. An insulation and bedding strip called a sill sealer is used as shown. The bolts should be set at least 6 in. deep in poured concrete walls and 15 in. deep in masonry unit walls.

Girders (also called beams), resting on the foundation walls and posts or columns, support the floor frame between the foundation walls. See Fig. 23-7. They may consist of solid timbers,

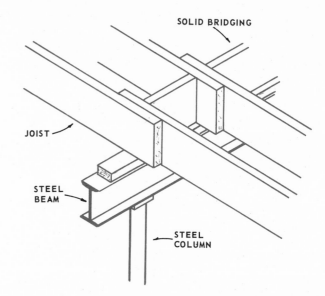

Fig. 23-7. Floor joists supported by a steel beam and column.

built-up members or steel I-beams. Sometimes a load-bearing partition can replace the beam. Today, bearing posts are frequently made of steel with a threaded section so the height can be adjusted.

Joists are the framing members that span the area between the supporting walls and girders. In residential construction they are usually 2 x 10 lumber spaced 16 in. O.C. (on center) and will carry a span up to about 16 feet. Lay out the position of the joist on the sill as shown in Fig. 23-8. Make a mark that will locate one side of the joist and then place an X on the side of the line where it will rest. Toenail the header in position and then set in the joists (crown up) and nail them securely.

Where a partition runs parallel to the joists, it is necessary to double the joists so the extra load will be adequately supported. If the partition

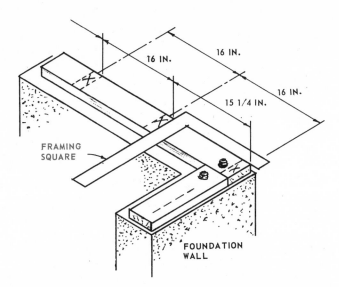

Fig. 23-8. *Laying out the position of floor joists on the sill.*

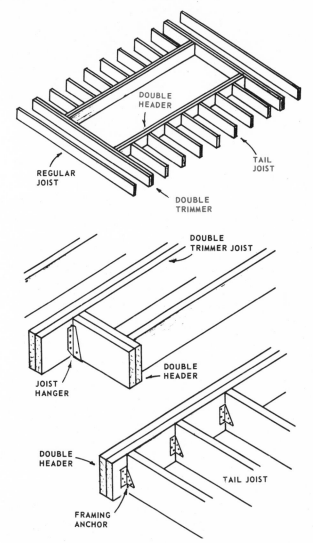

Fig. 23-10. *Above. Rough opening in a floor frame. Below. Close-up view of headers, trimmers. Openings for chimneys, fireplaces, should provide 2 in. clearance on all sides.*

will carry plumbing lines or heating ducts the joists are spaced on either side so that easy entry can be made, Fig. 23-9. Bridging is placed between the joists to keep them straight and transfer loads from one to the other. Diagonal wood or metal strips are placed in position as shown. Sometimes solid wood blocks are used. Bridging is nailed only at the top end when the joists are laid. The bottom ends are not nailed until the building is complete.

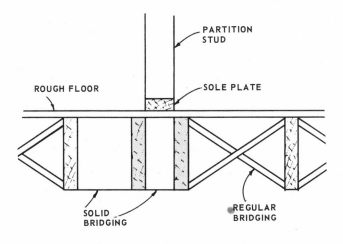

Fig. 23-9. *Double joists under partitions provide access for plumbing and heating when necessary.*

Joists must also be doubled around openings in the floor frame for stairways, chimneys, and fireplaces when the span of the header exceeds 4' - 0". These joists are called trimmers and support the headers which carry the tail joists. See Fig. 23-10. Metal anchors or hangers provide a secure and easy way to join the joist and headers.

When the floor frame is complete, the rough floor is laid, Fig. 23-11. In modern construction plywood is commonly used. It should be at least

Fig. 23-11. *Laying the rough floor. Note that the shiplap is run at an angle to the joists.*
(Weyerhaeuser Co.)

23-5

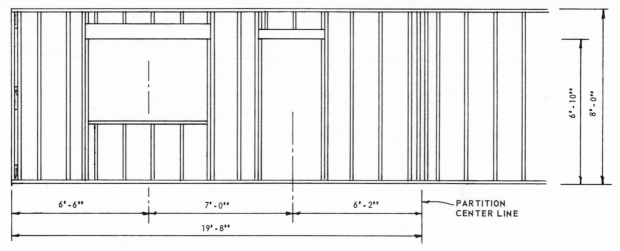

Fig. 23-12. Typical wall frame. The 8' - 0" height is extended sufficiently by the double plate to allow for floor and ceiling surface materials.

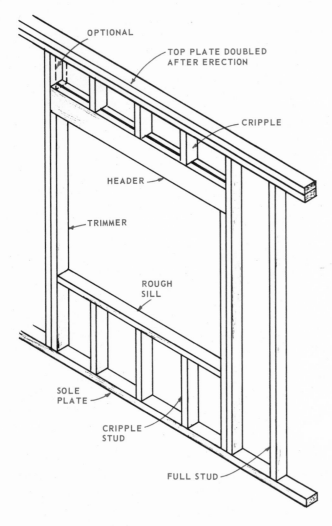

Fig. 23-13. Typical rough opening and framing members.

5/8 in. thick, with the long dimension of the sheet running across the joists and the joints broken (alternated) in successive courses.

Exterior Wall Framing

Standard wall framing members includes sole plates, top plates, studs and headers (also called lintels). Studs and plates are made from 2 x 4 lumber while headers usually require heavier material. In one-story construction, studs are sometimes placed 24 in. O.C., however 16 in. spacing is more commonly used. Fig. 23-12 shows a typical wall frame with a rough opening for a window and door. Also note the extra studs used at the corner and where a partition joins the outside wall.

Headers carry the weight of the ceiling and roof across door and window openings, Fig. 23-13. These are formed by two members nailed together with 1/2" plywood spacers so their thickness will be equal to that of the frame. For one-story construction 2 x 4 stock will span openings up to 4' - 0", 2 x 6 stock up to 6' - 0", 2 x 8 stock up to 8' - 0" and 2 x 10 stock up to 10' - 0". Sometimes 2 x 12 headers are used over all openings, regardless of their span, because it saves time in framing.

Wall frames are cut and assembled or partially assembled on the rough floor deck and then placed upright in position, Fig. 23-14. To lay out a wall section, first place the sole plate and top plate together and mark the regular stud spacing as shown in Fig. 23-15. Next determine the center lines for door and window openings and lay out the opening width. Mark for a trimmer stud (T) outside of these points. Outside of the trimmer stud, mark for a full length stud (X). Mark all of the original layout positions between the trimmer studs for cripple studs (C).

The position of rough openings are shown on the architectural plan. The size of the opening

Fig. 23-14. Wall frames are assembled on the floor and then raised into position.
(National Forest Products Assoc.)

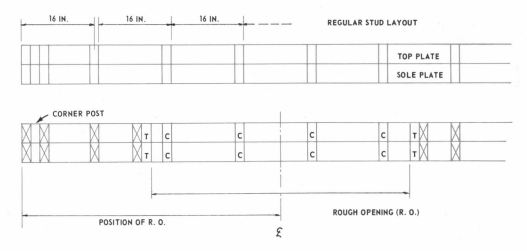

Fig. 23-15. Rough opening layout on sole and top plates.

may also be included in the plans or given in a separate door and window schedule. Rough opening sizes and/or special framing requirements are readily available from the manufacturer of the door or window unit.

After the plates are laid out, the headers are cut to length and assembled. All of the studs, trimmers and cripples are cut to length and then placed in position on the floor and the frame is

nailed together. The sections must be kept small enough so they can be easily raised into position. Sometimes the rough sill and lower cripples in a window opening are installed after the wall frame has been raised.

The wall section is carefully positioned and nailed to the floor. It is then accurately plumbed (made vertical) and temporarily braced until the entire wall frame is complete and sheathed. After the wall sections and partitions are in place a second or cap plate is nailed to the top plate with overlapping corners.

The exterior wall covering is called sheathing. It is nailed directly to the studs and forms a flat base on which the finish siding is applied. A wide

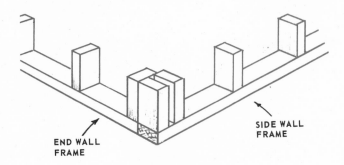

Fig. 23-16. Corner construction.

Fig. 23-17. Applying plywood sheathing to the wall frame. (American Plywood Assoc.)

variety of materials are used including plain boards, shiplap, gypsum board, composition board, and plywood. Today composition board and plywood are used extensively. See Figs. 23-17 and 23-18.

Partitions

Partitions may be either bearing or nonbearing. Bearing partitions carry part of the ceiling load and may also support the roof. Nonbearing partitions simply enclose space and provide a framework for the finish surfaces.

The center lines of the partitions are established from a study of the plans and then marked

Fig. 23-18. The sheathing may be applied to the wall section before it is raised into position. (National Forest Products Assoc.)

Fig. 23-19. Raising a main bearing partition. Note that a section of the double plate has been used to splice the top plate.

on the floor with a chalk line. Plates are laid out, studs and headers are cut and the partition is assembled and erected in the same way as outside walls, Fig. 23-19. Nonbearing partitions do not require headers. Openings can be framed with 2 x 4 lumber.

Erect long partitions first, then cross partitions, and finally short partitions that form closets, wardrobes, and alcoves. Fig. 23-20 shows two methods of joining partitions at corners and intersections. The top of nonbearing

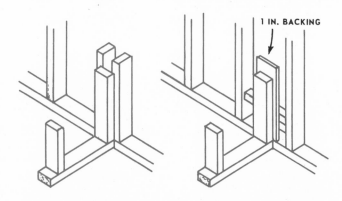

Fig. 23-20. Methods of joining partitions and walls. The backing provides a nailer for attaching the wall surface material.

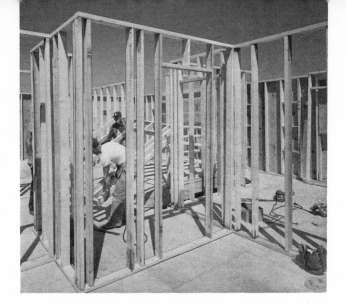

Fig. 23-21. Nonbearing partitions.

partitions, running parallel with the ceiling joists, are secured with blocking and a backing or nailer in about the same manner as shown in the right-hand view. Fig. 23-21, shows nonbearing partitions in place. The sole plate of door openings is cut out after the partition is erected.

Ceiling Frame

The ceiling frame consists of joists arranged somewhat like floor joists. Where they carry only the ceiling finish and do not support a second floor or the roof, 2 x 6 members placed 16 in. O.C. are generally used. These will carry spans up to about 14 ft. Ceiling joists usually run across the narrow dimension of the structure,

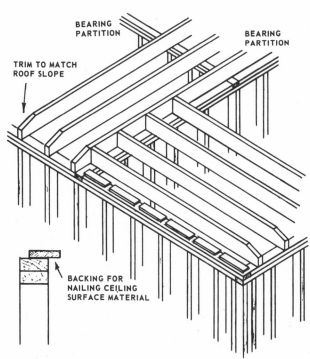

Fig. 23-22. Ceiling frame.

however some may be placed to run in one direction and others at right angles as shown in Fig. 23-22. By running joists in different directions, the length of the span can often be reduced.

Roof Frame

When the ceiling frame is complete and the outside walls sheathed, the roof frame is constructed. Fig. 23-23, shows some of the general types of roofs used in residential construction.

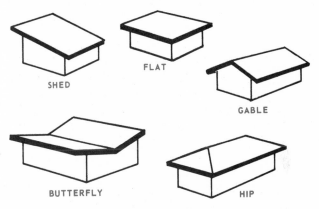

Fig. 23-23. Types of roofs.

The gable roof is used extensively and is easy to frame. It consists of common rafters and a ridge board. The slope or pitch of the roof may be given as a fraction formed by the rise over the span, however, when working with modern low-pitched roofs it is more practical to quote the rise and run (example: 4 to 12).

A common rafter can be laid out with the step-off method or its length can be secured from the rafter table on a framing square. When using the step-off method the framing square is laid on the stock with unit rise on the tongue and the unit run on the blade. The figures must be aligned with the edge to secure accuracy by this method. See Figs. 23-24 and 23-25. The carpenter sometimes attaches metal clips to the square so the alignment can be easier maintained.

Start at the top of the rafter, hold the square in position and draw the ridge line. Also mark the length of the odd unit (8 in. used in the example). Now shift the square along the stock until the tongue is aligned with the 8 in. mark; draw a line along the tongue and mark the 12 in. point on the blade for a full unit. Move the square to the 12 in. point and repeat the marking procedure. Continue until the required number of full units are laid out. Form the bird's-mouth by drawing a horizontal line (seat cut) to meet

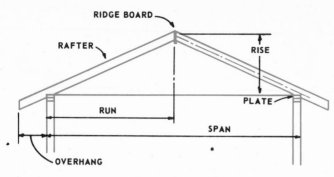

Fig. 23-24. Parts of a simple roof frame.

the building line so the surface will be about equal to the width of the plate. The size of the bird's-mouth may vary depending on the design of the overhang.

The overhang is laid out as shown in Fig. 23-26. Start with the plumb cut of the bird's-mouth and lay out full units first and then any odd unit. Always keep the unit rise and run carefully aligned with the edge of the rafter. The tail cut

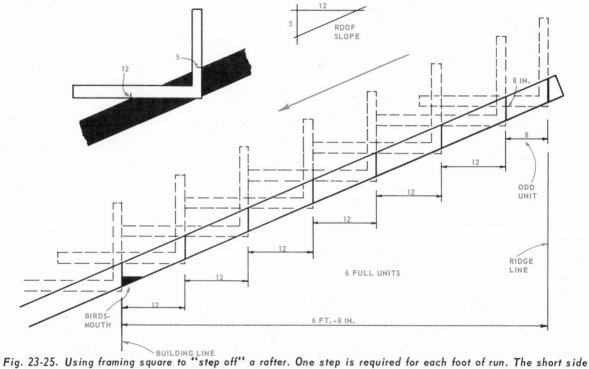

Fig. 23-25. Using framing square to "step off" a rafter. One step is required for each foot of run. The short side is held at 5 and the blade or long side at 12. The blade is always held at 12 regardless of the pitch. For 1/4 pitch you would hold the tongue at 6, 7/24 pitch at 7, etc.

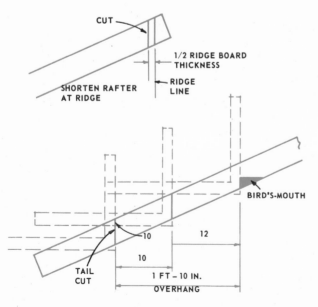

may be plumb, square, or a combination of a plumb and level cut. The rafter is shortened at the ridge, a horizontal distance equal to half the thickness of the ridge board. Make the cuts that you have laid out and label the rafter as a pattern. It can be used to mark the other common rafters needed in a given roof section. See Fig. 23-27.

Fig. 23-26. Laying out the overhang and shortening the rafter at the ridge.

Fig. 23-27. Installing common rafters. (Weyerhaeuser Co.)

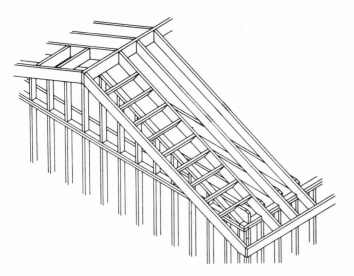

Fig. 23-27A. Framing for an overhanging gable end.

You can calculate the length of a common rafter using the tables of the framing square, Fig. 23-28. Under the full scale number that corresponds with the unit rise (example; 5) secure the number in the first line. This is the

line length of the rafter in inches for one foot of run. To find the length of the rafter from building line to ridge, multiply the units of run by the figure from the table as shown below:

Run = 6' - 8" = 6 2/3 units   Table No. = 13
Rafter Length = 6 2/3 x 13 = 86 2/3" =
    7' - 2 2/3"

Hip roofs or intersecting gable roofs may consist of some or all of the following rafters; common, hip, valley, jack and cripple. Fig. 23-35 shows a standard hip roof framing plan. When working with complicated roof framing it is often helpful to draw a carefully scaled plan like this one.

First cut and frame the common rafters and ridge boards. The ridge of a hip roof is cut to a length equal to the length of the building minus twice the run and plus the ridge board thickness. It should intersect with the common rafters as shown. See Figs. 23-29 and 23-30.

A hip or valley rafter extends from the plate to the ridge like a common rafter but at a 45 deg. angle; therefore the diagonal of a 12 in.

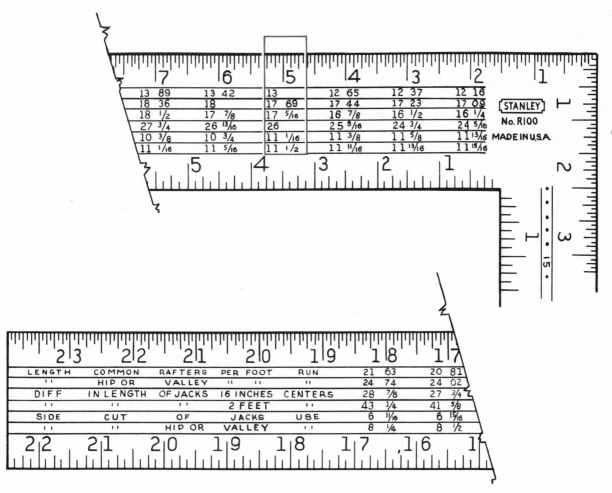

Fig. 23-28. Rafter tables on the framing square.

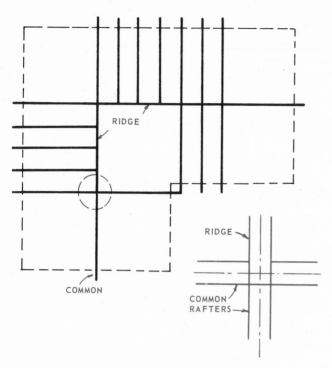

Fig. 23-29. *Install the common rafters and ridge boards as a first step in framing a hip roof.*

Fig. 23-30. *Common rafters being placed on a house that will require a complicated roof frame.*

square is used for the unit run. This is 16.97 in. or approximately 17 in. These rafters are laid out by the step-off method like the common rafter, except that the 17 in. mark is used on the blade of the square instead of the 12 in. The odd unit is also determined by the diagonal of a square as shown in the example in Fig. 23-31.

The length of hip and valley rafters can be determined from rafter tables. Secure the number from the second line. Using the same example as before, the calculations would be as follows:

Run = 6' - 8" = 6 2/3 units   Table No. = 17.69
Hip or Valley Length = 17.69 x 6 2/3 = 117.93
   = 9' - 9 15/16" = 9' - 10"

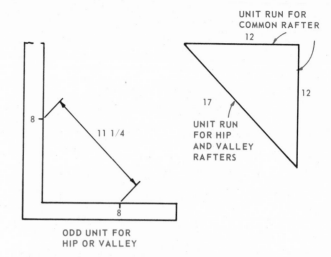

Fig. 23-31. *Unit run for a hip or a valley rafter.*

Hip and valley rafters must be shortened at the ridge by a horizontal distance equal to one-half of the 45 deg. thickness of the ridge, Fig. 23-32. The cheek cuts are then laid out using the figures from the sixth line of the rafter table (example 11 1/2). All the figures on the table are based on or related to 12 so place 12 on the blade and 11 1/2 on the tongue along the edge of the rafter as shown and draw the angle for each cut. Now draw plumb lines, using 17 on the blade and 5 on the tongue. The tail cuts at the end of the rafter are laid out using the same angle.

The top corners of a hip rafter will extend slightly above the plane of the roof. They could be planed off, however, it is easier to make the

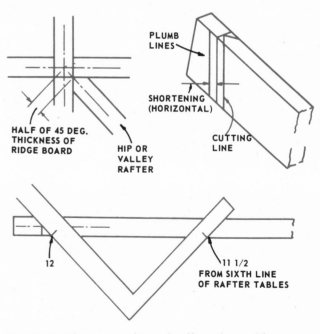

Fig. 23-32. *Shortening a hip and valley rafter and laying out cheek cuts.*

seat cut slightly deeper. The plumb cut of the bird's-mouth of valley rafters must be moved toward the tail by a distance equal to the 45 deg. thickness of the rafter. Hip and valley rafters are then added to the roof frame as shown in Fig. 23-33.

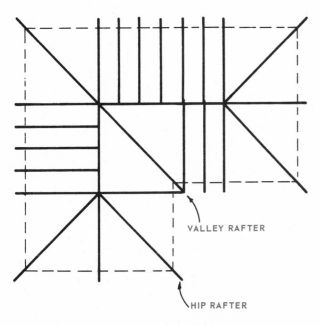

Fig. 23-33. Hip and valley rafters in place.

Hip jack rafters have the same tail or overhang as the common rafter. The length from the bird's-mouth to the hip rafter varies. The difference in length of adjacent rafters can be secured from the third or fourth line of the rafter table. For the example previously used, 26 in. is listed for rafters located 24 in. on centers.

For the first jack rafter down from the ridge, lay out the line length of the common rafter and subtract the common difference. Now shorten the length by one-half the 45 deg. thickness of the hip, Fig. 23-34. Square this line across the top edge and draw the cheek cut using the number from the fifth line of the table. Move down the rafter the common difference and mark the cutting line for the next jack. Continue until they are all laid out and then use this rafter for a pattern. Valley jacks will have a cheek cut at the lower end and a plumb cut at the ridge like a common rafter. Assemble the jacks in the roof frame as shown in Fig. 23-35.

Cripple jacks are rafters that run between hip and valley rafters. Their layout and cutting is somewhat complicated and beyond the scope of this book. Study a carpentry textbook for information about their use and other special roof framing problems.

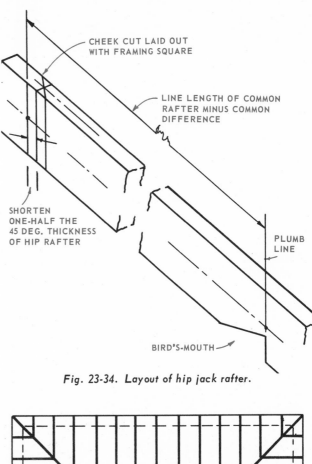

Fig. 23-34. Layout of hip jack rafter.

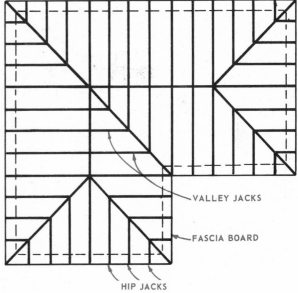

Fig. 23-35. Hip and valley jack rafters in place.

Roof Trusses and Flat Roofs

In modern construction, roof trusses are often used to form the roof frame. They are supported by the outside walls of the building and carry the load of the ceiling as well as the roof. In this type construction inside partitions can be a non-bearing type which generally permits greater flexibility.

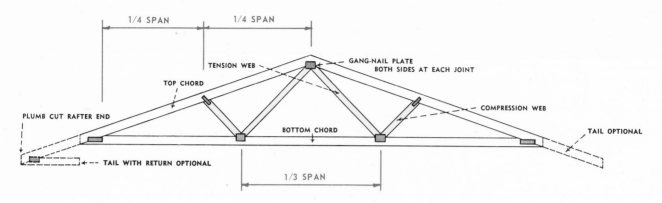

Fig. 23-36. W roof truss.

There are several different designs of trusses. The W truss, Fig. 23-36, is commonly used for residential construction. The connection of the various members is important. Plywood gussets, nailed and glued, or split rings, provide secure joints. Special gang nail plates are used for prefabricated trusses. See Figs. 23-37 and 23-38.

Today, flat roofs are often used in home construction. They provide the long, low appearance

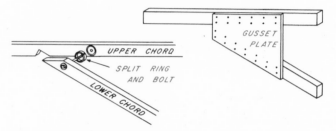

Fig. 23-37. Fastening methods used for trusses.

Fig. 23-38. Using a special jig to assemble trusses in a manufacturing plant. Gang nail plates are being used for connectors. (National Forest Products Assoc.)

sought for in contemporary designs. Fig. 23-39, shows a standard framing pattern where the ceiling joists are also the roof joists. Since the combined load of the roof and ceiling are carried by these members, they should be 2 x 10's or 2 x 12's. Check the building code in your particular area.

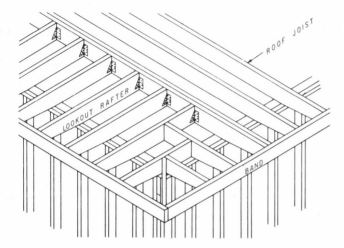

Fig. 23-39. Framing for flat roof.

Roof Sheathing and Finish

Sheathing materials for the roof include plywood, shiplap or plain boards. Plywood must be at least 3/8 in. thick when rafters are spaced 16 in. O.C. or 1/2 in. thick for 24 in. spacing. Prefabricated panels, Fig. 23-40, provide adequate strength and are easy to apply.

Fig. 23-40. Sheathing a hip roof frame using panels formed with solid boards bonded together with heavy kraft paper. Panels shown are 2 ft. wide and 16 ft. long. (Western Wood Products Assoc.)

A wide range of roofing materials are available. Sloping roofs are usually finished with shingles made from such materials as wood, asphalt, asbestos, or metal with a baked enamel finish. Roofing tile are made from clay or cement-asbestos. Flat or very low pitched roofs must be covered with a built-up roof that consists of layers of asphalt saturated paper, mopped together with hot pitch and then surfaced with gravel, crushed stone or marble chips.

Wood shingles, Fig. 23-41, are usually made from western red cedar. The first course is doubled and extends over the fascia about 1 in. The shingles should be spaced at least 1/8" apart to allow for expansion. Courses are laid with an exposure of 3 to 5 inches depending on the quality of the roof and climatic conditions.

Fig. 23-41. Laying wood shingles. The roof sheathing has been covered with felt roofing paper. Note the metal flashing in the valley.

Asphalt shingles are made by impregnating a heavy felt base with asphalt and covering the surface with mineral granules. The most common type is a triple-tab shingle which is actually three shingles in one. Asphalt shingles are made in weights of 45 to 325 lbs. per square (100 square feet). Because the shingles are uniform in size, they must be laid even and true to provide an attractive appearance.

Roof finish is often complicated by intersections, chimneys or other projections. Thin sheet metal called "flashing" is installed in such a way as to carry the water out to the surface of the shingles or form waterways to the edge of the roof. Flashing is also used over windows, doors, and other openings where water may penetrate.

Fig. 23-42. Installing casement window unit in rough opening. (Andersen Corp.)

Windows and Outside Doors

When the framing is complete and the sheathing and roof has been applied the next step is to install windows and exterior door frames.

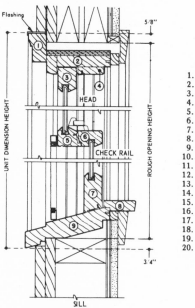

Parts Identification
1. Head Casing
2. Head Jamb
3. Upper Sash Top Rail
4. Head Stop
5. Upper Sash Check Rail
6. Lower Sash Check Rail
7. Lower Sash Bottom Rail
8. Stool
9. Sill
10. Side Casing
11. R.H. Side Jamb
12. R.H. Lower Sash Side Stile
13. L.H. Lower Sash Side Stile
14. R.H. Combination Side Stile
15. L.H. Combination Side Stile
16. Exterior Mullion Casing
17. L.H. Side Jamb
18. R.H. Upper Sash Side Stile
19. L.H. Upper Sash Side Stile
20. Side Casing

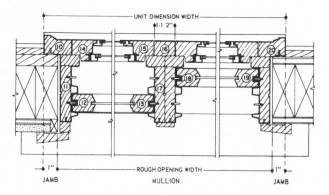

Fig. 23-43. Parts of a double hung window. The sash slide up and down. (Rock Island Millwork Co.)

Windows of various types and sizes are built and assembled in factories and are shipped to the construction site complete and ready to install in the rough openings, Fig. 23-42. They are placed in position, leveled on the rough sill and then secured to the wall according to specifications furnished by the manufacturer. Outside

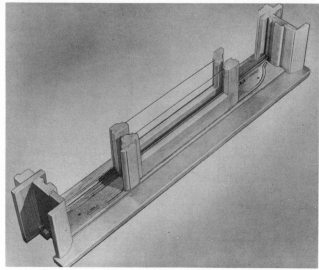

Fig. 23-44. Cut-a-way view of a modern sliding window unit. (Andersen Corp.)

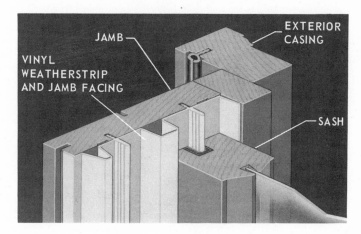

Fig. 23-45. Jamb section of a double hung window with special plastic channels.

casing is usually furnished with the window and may need to be cut to finished length before it is attached. Members consist of head casing (top) and side casing.

Double hung windows, Fig. 23-43 are commonly used; however many others are available. The casement window is often used too. It consists of a sash that is hinged on the side and swings outward. Awning windows are hinged across the top and also swing outward. Hopper

TABLE OF SIZES

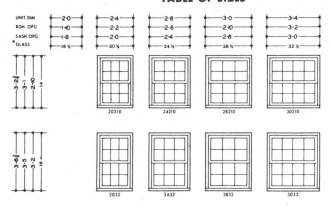

HOW TO FIGURE MULTIPLE OPENINGS

1-5/16" MULLIONS

ROUGH OPENING WIDTHS — add sum of single sash openings plus 1-5/16" for each mullion. Add 2" to this figure for overall rough opening width.

UNIT DIMENSION WIDTHS — add sum of single sash openings plus 1-5/16" for each mullion. Add 4" to this figure for overall unit dimension width.

4" SUPPORT MULLIONS

ROUGH OPENING WIDTHS — add sum of single sash openings plus 4" for each mullion. Add 2" to this figure for overall rough opening width.

UNIT DIMENSION WIDTHS — add sum of single unit dimension widths.

Fig. 23-46. Partial listing of double hung window sizes.

windows are similar in design to the awning type except that the hinge is at the bottom and the sash swings inward. Various types of sliding windows are also available. See Fig. 23-44. Today, in modern air conditioned homes, fixed window units are used extensively. These and various ventilating units are combined with window walls and picture windows.

Ventilating window sash are made weathertight with metal strips or operate in special

Fig. 23-47. Assembling window frames in special nailing machines.

metal or plastic channels, Fig. 23-45. Many units have self-contained storm sashes and patented screens that roll up or are easily detached from the inside. Many standard sizes of windows are available. A partial list is included in Fig. 23-46.

Outside door frames may be furnished assembled or knocked-down. The rough floor is cut away to provide space for the sill. Standard residential doors are 6' - 8" high. Outside doors are usually 2' - 8" or 3' - 0" wide. After the frame is set, the combination storm and screen door is hung so that it can be locked and provide security for the interior of the house.

Exterior Finish

After windows and door frames are set and cased, exterior finish consisting of cornice work, siding and trim can be completed.

The cornice, also called an eave, is formed by the roof overhang and provides a finished connection between the wall and edge of the roof. Diagrams of several closed or "boxed" cornice designs are shown in Fig. 23-48. An open cornice is sometimes used, exposing the rafters and underside of the roof sheathing. Wide overhangs

STANDARD HORIZONTAL SOFFIT - SLOPING ROOF

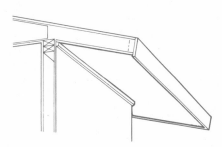

STANDARD SLOPING SOFFIT AND ROOF

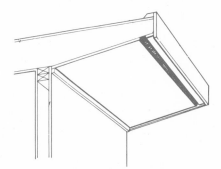

FLAT ROOF WITH SLOPING SOFFIT - NOTE VENT STRIP

Fig. 23-48. Cornice designs.

are used extensively in contemporary design because they provide shade for large window areas and also protect the building walls.

Fig. 23-49, shows the design and parts of a standard boxed cornice. The fascia board is usually set before the finished roof is laid. A ledger strip is nailed to the wall and carries the lookouts which are attached to each rafter. A nailing strip is sometimes attached to the back of the fascia. The ledger, lookouts, and nailing strip provide a frame to which the plancier or soffit material is applied. This surface material may be plywood, hardboard, solid stock or plaster.

A very wide range of exterior wall finishing materials are available. A partial list would include standard bevel siding, shake and shingle siding, composition boards, plywood, hardboard, and boards and battens. Fig. 23-50, shows the application of several common types.

To apply conventional bevel siding, Fig. 23-51, the carpenter first lays out a story pole (vertical division of space) so that the lap between each course can be adjusted to provide even exposures

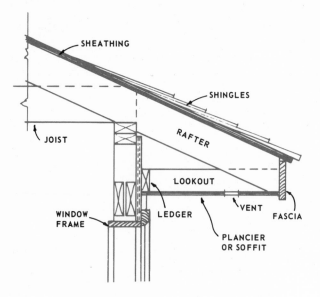

Fig. 23-49. Cornice construction and parts.

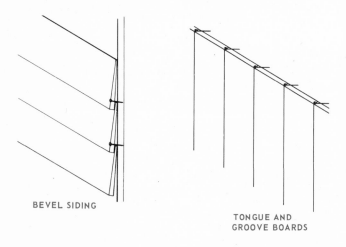

BEVEL SIDING

TONGUE AND GROOVE BOARDS

Fig. 23-51. Applying bevel siding. (Weyerhaeuser Co.)

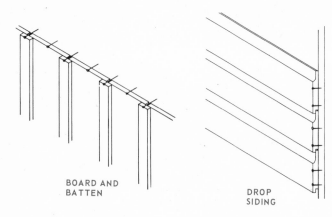

BOARD AND BATTEN

DROP SIDING

Fig. 23-50. Four types of wood siding.

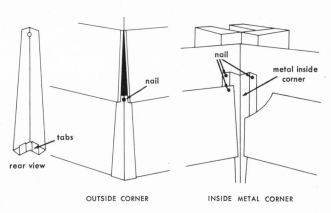

OUTSIDE CORNER

INSIDE METAL CORNER

Fig. 23-52. Using metal corners. (Masonite Corp.)

from the bottom to the cornice or trim (frieze) board. Sometimes adjustments can be made so the siding edge will align with window trim. A furring strip is placed under the bottom edge of the first course so it will have the same slope as the others. Rustproof nails should be used for exterior finish work. At corners, the siding can be mitered or cornerboards can be used. Metal corners like those shown in Fig. 23-52 provide a trim appearance. See also Fig. 23-53.

Fig. 23-53. Applying strips over exterior plywood to form a board and batten effect. (National Forest Products Assoc.)

*Fig. 23-54. Installing electrical wiring.
(Black and Decker Corp.)*

To protect exterior wood trim, a primer coat of paint or finish should be applied as soon as possible after it is installed.

Heating, Plumbing and Electrical

While carpenters complete the exterior finish of the house, other tradesmen are busy on the inside. Ductwork is installed in the floor, ceiling and walls, for heating and air conditioning. The electrician strings rough wiring, Fig. 23-54, (or runs conduit) through the framework, and sets the metal boxes for convenience outlets, switches, and lighting outlets. At this time he also installs the housings for recessed fixtures.

The plumber installs the drains and vent stacks and also the pipes that will carry the water service. In the installation of the heating and plumbing "rough-in," the tradesman must often cut through the structural framework. The carpenter should check over this work and revise or reinforce framing members wherever necessary. Fig. 23-55 shows an interior view of a house with the rough-in of heating, plumbing, and electrical ready for insulation and wall finish.

Insulation

Buildings that will be heated or air conditioned must be insulated. Thermal insulation is located in the outside walls, ceilings and sometimes in the floors. Various grades and thicknesses are available in such forms as batt, blanket, loose fill and rigid. Reflective insulation is often used and consists of thin metal sheets, usually aluminum, cemented to a paper or fabric backing.

In modern construction, fiber glass, made from tiny filaments of glass is used extensively for blankets and batts. Styrofoam (expanded polystyrene) provides a rigid form of insulation for concrete floors, masonry walls and roof decks.

In addition to thermal insulation, it is essential that a vapor barrier be included to prevent the flow of moisture from the warm interior to the cold exterior of the building. This vapor barrier must be placed on the warm side of the wall or insulation material. Plastic (polyethyl-

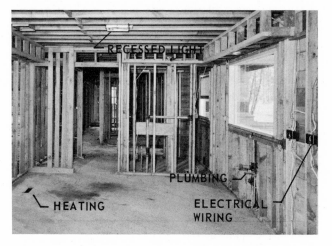

*Fig. 23-55. Interior view of house with electrical, plumbing and heating rough-in complete.
(Western Wood Products Assoc.)*

Fig. 23-56. Dry wall construction.
(Forest Products Laboratory)

Interior Wall and Ceiling Finish

Interior surfaces may be plastered, or finished with gypsum, wood, or composition panels. For a plastered surface, a base of gypsum boards (3/8 x 16 x 48) or metal lath is nailed to the wall frame. Inside and outside corners are reinforced with metal strips and reinforcement is also placed near the corner of openings where expansion and contraction of the frame might cause the plaster to crack. Grounds (wood strips that serve as guides and thickness gauges for the plaster) are set around the openings. In residential work two coats of plaster (rough and finish) are usually applied. The final coat can be troweled smooth or given a sand or textured surface.

Dry wall construction, Fig. 23-56, is used extensively in home construction. Materials and methods have been perfected which allow the expert in this field to apply a smooth unbroken surface. Large sheets of paper-faced gypsum panels are attached to the wall frame and the joints are then taped and sanded. Some appli-

ene) films are widely used for this purpose. Copper and aluminum foil provides an effective vapor barrier and may also serve as a reflective insulator.

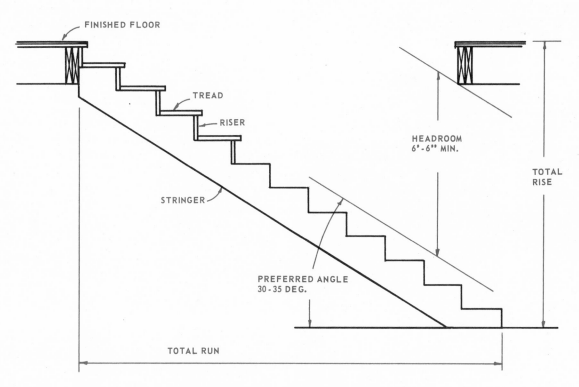

Fig. 23-57. Parts of a stairwell section.

In modern homes considerable attention is given to sound control. Various insulation materials are placed around plumbing lines and installed in partitions and floors to reduce the transmission of unwanted noise.

cations are made by first nailing on a base and then gluing the finished panels in place.

Plywood or hardboard panels with plain, textured, or grooved surfaces are used extensively. These are applied over gypsum board surfaces or attached to furring strips. Today, most of these materials are prefinished and require no further treatment after they are installed. A wide variety of ceiling tile are made from materials that absorb sound and provide an attractive appearance. They have edges with interlocking joints and are quickly and easily applied with a stapler.

Stairs

Stairs lead from one floor level to another through a stairwell opening which should be framed during the rough construction. The carpenter builds a rough stairs that can be used during the construction and then replaces it with finished stairs after the wall surfaces are applied. Main stairs are often prefabricated in a factory and then assembled and installed by the carpenter.

The main parts of a stair consist of treads, risers and stringers, Fig. 23-57. See also Fig. 23-58. The width of the tread and height of the

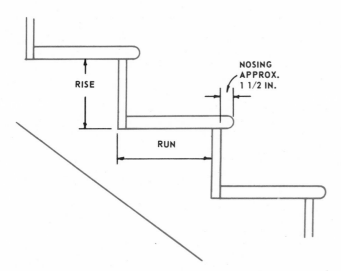

Fig. 23-58. Stair detail. The nosing provides toe space under the tread. Treads are usually made from 1 1/4 in. stock.

riser must be carefully proportioned. When the rise is low the width of the tread must be wide. As a general rule the rise plus tread should equal 17 to 18 in. Main stairs have a riser height of about 7 in. Basement stairs may have a somewhat larger riser but never over 8 in. It is very important that all of the risers are equal and all of the tread are equal in a given stair run. The minimum width of a stairs is 36 in.

To calculate the number and size of risers and treads, first divide the total rise by 7. For example, if the total rise is 7' - 10" or 94" this would be 13.43. Since there must be a whole number of risers, select the one closest to this

figure (13.43) and divide it into the total rise; 94" ÷ 13 = 7.23" or 7 1/4". In a stair run, the number of treads will always be one less than the number of risers. A 10" tread would be satisfactory for the example and would give a total run of 12 x 10" = 120 or 10' - 0". The stairs in the example will have 13 risers 7 1/4" high, 12 tread 10" wide and a run of 10' - 0".

The stringer is laid out with the framing square in about the same way as a rafter. The layout from the bottom tread to the floor must be reduced by an amount equal to the tread thickness. The simplest type of stringer is formed by attaching cleats on which the treads rest or cutting grooves into which the tread will fit. Riser panels may be eliminated, forming an open stairs which is often used in basements or to secure a special effect in contemporary construction. A stringer may be formed by cutting out the treads and risers in one piece and then attaching it to another piece as shown in Fig. 23-59.

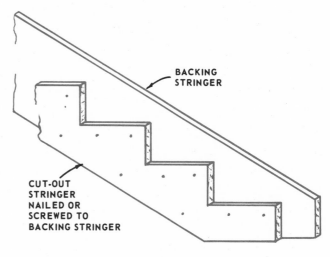

Fig. 23-59. Semihoused stringer construction.

A popular type of stair construction uses a stringer with tapered grooves into which the treads and risers fit. Wedges are driven into the grooves under the tread and behind the risers, Fig. 23-60. The treads and risers are joined together with rabbets and grooves and/or glue blocks, producing a stair that is strong and will not readily develop squeaks. An electric router and template are used in cutting the stringer.

Floors

Materials for finished floors include hardwood, linoleum, various kinds of tile and carpet. Standard hardwood flooring is 25/32 in. thick and 2 1/4 in. wide. It has tongue and groove edges and ends and is available in several species and grades. The sub-floor is covered with a 15 lb. asphalt saturated felt and the flooring is blind-nailed in place with a 1/2 in. space on each side wall to allow for expansion. The floor is sanded and finished after the other inside trim is complete.

When the finished floor will be linoleum, tile, or carpet an underlayment of plywood or hard-board is nailed and/or screwed to the sub-floor.

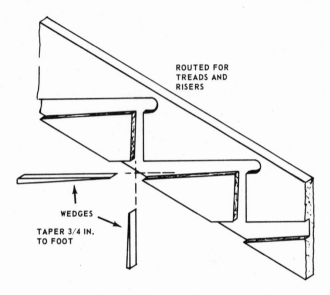

Fig. 23-60. Housed stringer.

Interior Doors

Interior doors, like outside doors are 6'-8" high. The most common width is 2'-6", however, bathroom and closet doors are often 2'-4" or 2'-2". They are hung in a frame consisting of side jambs and a head jamb which is usually 5 1/4 in. wide for plastered walls. The door frame is placed in the rough opening, carefully plumbed and squared using wooden shingles for wedges, and then nailed to the studs. Casing is nailed to the jambs and wall to further secure the frame and to trim (cover) the rough opening, Fig. 23-61.

The door is planed to fit the door frame with sufficient clearance for operation and with a slight bevel on the lock edge. After the door is fitted, gains are cut for the hinges and the hinges and lock are then installed. Stops (strips) are then set in place on each jamb. Set the stop on the lock jamb first, then the head stop, and finally the stop on the hinge jamb with about 1/32 in. clearance.

Today, many manufacturers supply prehung door units. The door unit with hardware and casing is completely assembled and fitted. The jamb is split with an interlocking joint so the entire unit can be installed in the rough opening in a short time.

Window Trim and Baseboard

Standard window trim consists of a stool, apron, and side and head casing, Fig. 23-62. The stool is set first. It must be notched on the ends to fit between the window jambs and also extend

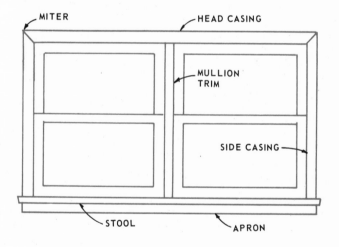

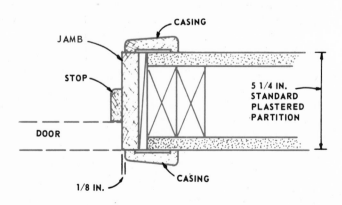

Fig. 23-61. Section through interior door jamb.

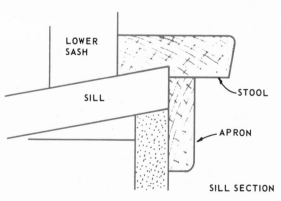

Fig. 23-62. Interior window trim.

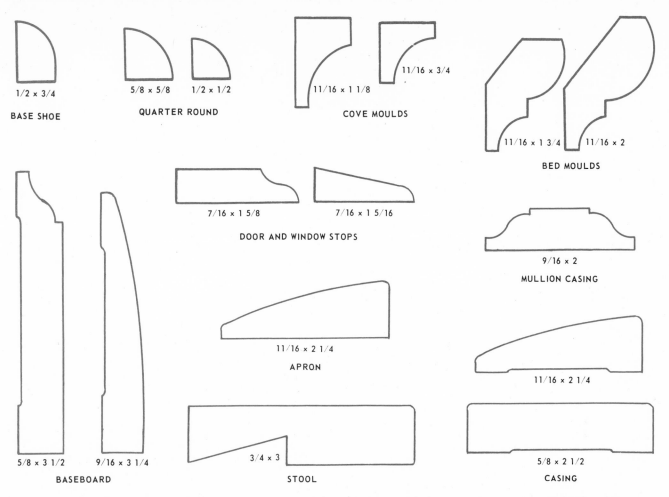

1/2 x 3/4
BASE SHOE

5/8 x 5/8   1/2 x 1/2
QUARTER ROUND

11/16 x 1 1/8   11/16 x 3/4
COVE MOULDS

11/16 x 1 3/4   11/16 x 2
BED MOULDS

7/16 x 1 5/8   7/16 x 1 5/16
DOOR AND WINDOW STOPS

9/16 x 2
MULLION CASING

11/16 x 2 1/4
APRON

11/16 x 2 1/4

5/8 x 3 1/2   9/16 x 3 1/4
BASEBOARD

3/4 x 3
STOOL

5/8 x 2 1/2
CASING

Fig. 23-63. Some of the standard wood trim and mouldings used for inside finish work. Note that the back surface of casings and baseboards have a milled recess so the edges will fit tight against the wall and jamb even though the surface is slightly irregular.

beyond them. Side and head casing is applied next. The side casing is butted tight against the stool and joins the head casing with a miter joint. Like the door trim, the window casing is set back from the edge of the jamb about 1/8 in. The apron is cut and fitted last so its ends will align with the side casing.

After the door casings are installed, the baseboard is cut and attached. It is butted against the door casing. Outside corners are joined with a miter while inside corners are usually coped. When it is necessary to splice the base, use a miter and be certain the joint occurs at a stud. If base shoe is required it is usually cut and fitted at this time but not attached until the floor finish or floor covering has been applied. See Fig. 23-63.

Cabinet Work

In modern construction, most of the kitchen cabinets and other built-ins are made in factories and shipped to the job where they are installed by the carpenter, Fig. 23-64. Information about this area of work is included in Unit 18.

Fig. 23-64. Installing factory built kitchen cabinets. The cabinets are usually shipped in sections and the carpenter attaches them to the wall or floor and installs the top.

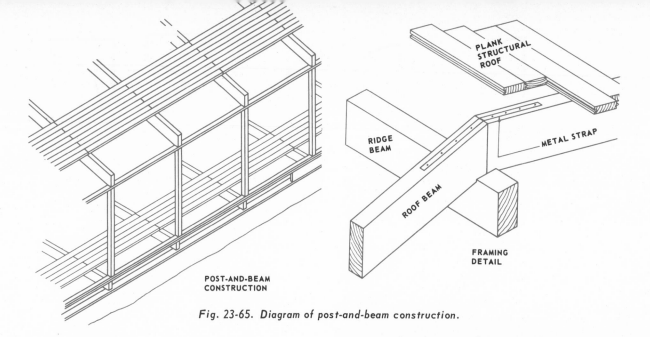

Fig. 23-65. Diagram of post-and-beam construction.

Post-and-Beam Construction

This type of construction was used for many years for large buildings and is referred to as "mill construction." Today, it is often applied to residential work since it permits flexibility in contemporary designs. Basically it consists of large framing members spaced further apart than the usual type of framing members. Plank subfloors or roofs, 2 to 4 in. thick, are supported on beams spaced up to 8 ft. on center. The beams are supported on posts or piers. Wall sections between the posts can be filled in with glass, masonry, or supplementary frames to which conventional surface materials may be applied. See Fig. 23-65.

Extensive use is made of this type of construction in the modern exposed ceiling. See Figs. 23-66, 23-67, and 23-68. The roof planks also

Fig. 23-66. Laying 1 1/8 in. plywood with tongue and groove edge joints on beams spaced 4' - 0" O.C. (American Plywood Assoc.)

Fig. 23-67. Laying 4 in. double tongue-and-groove planks on laminated beams.

serve as the ceiling surface, providing added height to living areas. Where they are carefully selected for appearance, no further ceiling treatment is needed except the application of stain and other finishing materials. In moderate climates no insulation is needed, however, in cold climates a rigid form of insulation is usually applied to the roof surface with mastic. A vapor barrier is frequently included between the wood planks and the insulation.

Since solid wood beams are expensive and often not available in the sizes required, many laminated beams are used. Beams are also constructed with a webbed frame and covered with plywood.

may consist of only precutting parts which are numbered, packaged, and shipped to the building site for assembly and erection. Most prefabricated or manufactured homes are built in panels. These wall panels may be completely constructed including windows, insulation, wiring, and interior and exterior finish. Although building with prefabricated panels reduces construction time on the job, a great deal of work still must be done on the site. This includes such items as foundation and masonry work; plumbing, heating, and electrical finish; decorating walls and ceilings; and the installation of cabinetwork, built-ins and equipment. See Figs. 23-69 to 23-74.

Fig. 23-68. Plank-and-beam ceiling used in dining area. (Western Wood Products Assoc.)

Many structures may utilize a combination of conventional and post-and-beam construction. The inclusion of a section of conventional studs and sheathing may, for example, add to the lateral stability of the completed frame. Where a plank-and-beam roof is supported by a stud wall, a post should be placed under the beam to carry the concentrated load.

Prefabrication

Prefabrication in building construction refers to the manufacturing of parts or "components" which are then shipped to the building site and assembled to form the structure. Prefabrication

Fig. 23-69. Prefabricated panels are built on assembly lines and then shipped to the site for erection. (National Forest Products Assoc.)

Originally prefabricated buildings were produced from the same set of components and were identical in appearance and function. Today, however, homes can be built using a wide variety of prefabricated units. The design can reflect the interest and desires of the owner and the materials can be adjusted to the requirements of the climate and environment of the area.

Fig. 23-70. Eight by eight foot frame moving along an assembly line.
(National Forest Products Assoc.)

Fig. 23-71. Placing insulation between the studs. Hydraulically operated mechanism is used to turn over panels.
(National Homes Corp.)

Fig. 23-72. Using a pneumatic nail driver to assemble a window unit in a 4 x 8 component wall panel.
(Andersen Corp.)

Fig. 23-73. A heavy-duty lift truck loads panels for delivery to building site.

Fig. 23-74. Prefabricated panels being erected on the building site.

Modular Design

This industrialization of home building was made possible through the coordination of manufacturers in producing standard size products and the planning procedure where modular or standard increments of 16, 24, and 48 inches, Fig. 23-75, are used to lay out foundations,

Shop or plant fabrication of components results in several advantages:
1. Accuracy and quality are easier to control.
2. Power equipment can be used for cutting and fastening.
3. Mass production techniques using conveyor lines and assembly jigs can be employed.

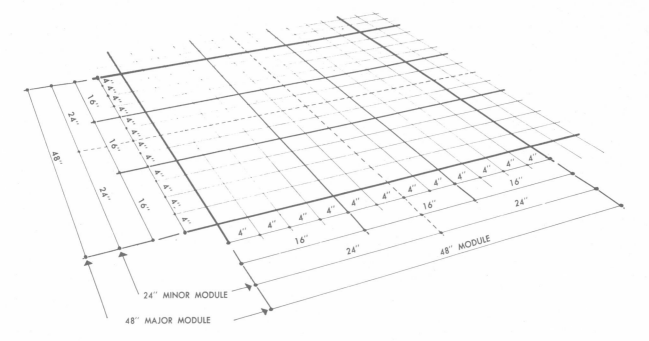

Fig. 23-75. Plans for modular houses, to be built with components or by conventional framing methods, are designed to exact size on a grid like the one above.

floors, walls, windows, doors and roofs, Modular design improves the efficiency and saves materials whether the house is framed by conventional methods, erected completely with shop-fabricated components or built using a combination of these methods.

4. Work is not interrupted by inclement weather conditions.
5. Large volume purchases results in reduced material costs.
6. Research and development is easier to carry out and apply to the operation.

Left. Model carpentry construction using a scale of 1 1/2" = 1' - 0". A brad pusher is being used to install a rafter. (Robert Burkgren) Right. Model constructed of modular sections. Trusses were assembled in a jig. (William Reams)

Test Your Knowledge

1. A wooden framework is used in the construction of _____ percent of the homes in the United States.
2. A foundation wall made of 8 in. concrete blocks will provide a basement ceiling height of 7' - 2" if _____ courses are used.
3. In standard floor framing the joists are supported between the foundation walls by a _____.
4. Tail joists formed by a rough opening in the floor frame are supported by trimmers. True or False?
5. The bottom member of a wall frame on which the studs rest is called a _____.
6. Nonbearing partitions should have about the same size of headers as the outside walls. True or False?
7. In a standard gable roof the run equals one-half of the _____.
8. When laying out a plumb cut on a common rafter, the framing square is positioned with the unit run on the blade and the unit _____ on the tongue.
9. When framing a hip roof the common rafters and _____ are assembled first.
10. To lay out a hip rafter, use _____ for the unit run instead of 12.
11. A rafter that runs from the plate and intersects a hip rafter is called a _____.
12. Wood shingles are laid with at least 1/8 in. space between them to allow for expansion. True or False?
13. A window with the sash hinged on the side is called a _____.
14. The framing member of a cornice that extends from the ledger to the rafter is called a _____.
15. The vapor barrier in an outside wall should always be located on the warm side. True or False?
16. The main parts of a stair consist of treads, risers, and _____.
17. The standard height of residential doors is _____.
18. Standard inside window trim includes head and side casing, a stool and _____.

Outside Assignments

1. Secure or prepare a chalk line and experiment with its operation. Demonstrate its use to the class and describe situations where it would be helpful to the carpenter.
2. When applying mouldings and trim, a coped joint is often used for inside corners. Secure information about this joint from reference books or visit with a carpenter. Prepare several sample joints.
3. From a study of reference books and other resources prepare a chart and/or drawings showing the recommended nail size and nailing pattern (number and spacing) for conventional house framing.
4. Prepare a check list for evaluating the quality of conventional home construction. Include such items as: Is the foundation wall waterproofed? Are floor joists the correct size for the span? Are window headers large enough? Is a vapor barrier included in the outside walls? Is the door and window trim carefully applied? Visit a home building job in your community and check the construction with your list. ALWAYS BE SURE TO OBTAIN PERMISSION FROM THE FOREMAN OR HEAD CARPENTER WHEN VISITING A BUILDING SITE.

Unit 24
BOAT BUILDING

You can apply the skills you have acquired in hand and machine woodwork to wooden boat construction. The procedure is somewhat similar to that used in any large structure where a framework is first assembled and is then covered with a surface material. The greatest difference is that instead of square joints and straight lines as in furniture, cabinets and carpentry, the construction is composed of many curved lines, and irregular shaped parts.

Before starting on a boatbuilding project, you should study reference books on boatbuilding that include additional information about construction, definitions of nautical terms, information about boat selection and handling, and state and national boating regulations.

A wide selection of boat plans is available from various companies. Some companies produce boat kits that provide all of the materials needed, in various stages of prefabrication.

framework consists of frames or ribs attached to a keel, stem, chines, battens and stringers. The chine is a frame member located where the side and bottom are joined. The covering for the hull is called planking. The part of the boat farthest forward is called the bow while the rear is called the stern. The gunnel or gunwale (pronounced gun'-l) is the section where the sides and deck meet.

Certain terms apply in a special way to boating; for example, any rope used is called a line, maps are called charts, the left side of the boat is the port and the right side the starboard.

Boat Plans

Boats should be designed by an expert who has had experience and understands the design problems involved. He first develops the shape and contour lines as shown in Fig. 24-2. Water lines

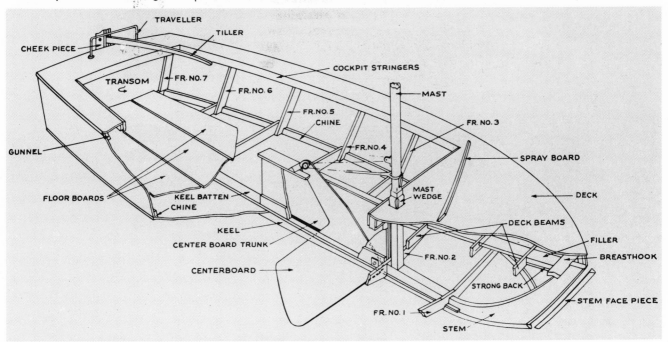

Fig. 24-1. Parts of a sailboat. The centerboard is lowered through the keel to prevent the boat from being shoved sideways by the wind.

Boat Parts

To follow and understand boat plans you must know some of the basic parts. See Fig. 24-1. The

(W.L.) represent horizontal planes through the hull and are plotted on the plan view as shown. These are used to lay out the various structural parts.

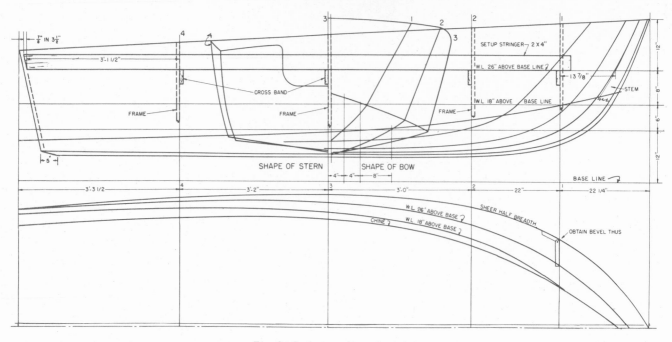

Fig. 24-2. Layout lines for a boat.

A complete set of boat plans will include a top view and a side elevation or profile view as shown in Fig. 24-3. At least one detailed section view, Fig. 24-4, showing the method of construction will be needed. Construction will require carefully scaled or dimensioned section-drawings

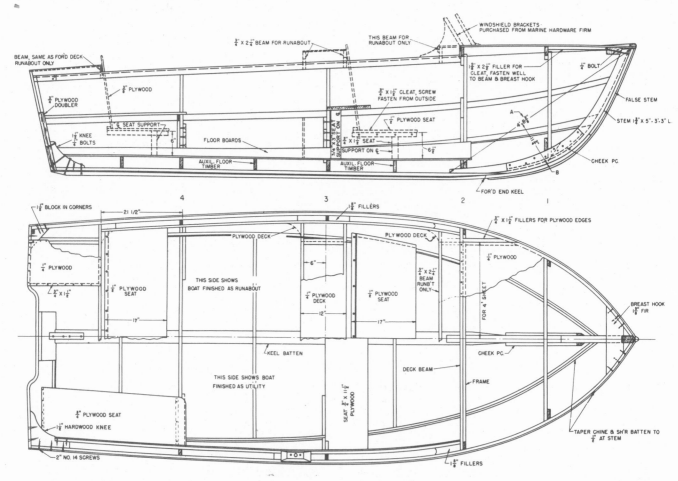

Fig. 24-3. Profile and plan view of a 13 foot outboard.

at each station point or frame. Other detail views, the quantity depending on the complications of the design, must also be included.

Materials

Hardwoods should be used for the boat frame members. Because of its strength, oak is most commonly used although ash and mahogany also have desirable characteristics. Marine or exterior types of fir or mahogany plywood are generally used for covering materials.

A regular exterior plywood can be used, however, marine plywood is preferable because no defects are permitted in the core layers and a given thickness has more plies. Three-eights

marine plywood is 5 ply and three-fourths is 7 ply. Both exterior and marine plywood are bonded with waterproof glue. Exterior plywood will carry a grade-trademark that reads EXT-DFPA, while the one on marine plywood will read MARINE-EXT-DFPA.

Screws, nails and other metal fasteners and fittings used must be of the type that resist rusting and corrosion. Brass, bronze or monel metal are recommended.

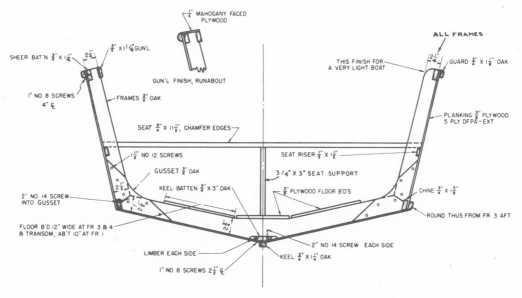

Fig. 24-4. Detailed section view.

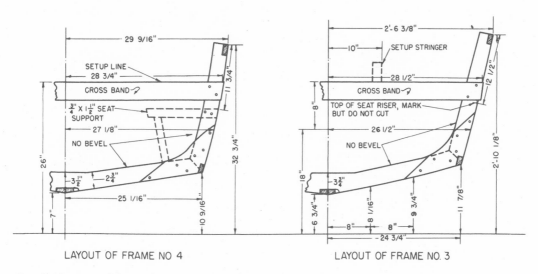

Fig. 24-5. Typical frame drawings included in a set of boat plans. Working from these views, full-size layouts are made. (American Plywood Association, Tacoma, Wash.)

Frames

After a careful study of the plans, make full-size layouts of the frames, Fig. 24-5. Use a large smooth surface with the edge serving as a base line. If you number each frame drawing to avoid confusion, you can superimpose all the drawings on the same set of reference lines. To draw curved lines, use a thin strip of wood as shown in Fig. 6-5, Unit 6.

Fig. 24-6. Assembly jig. Stringers are usually made of 2 x 4 stock.

apply waterproof glue and then drive the screws. Fasten a crossband to the frame, being careful to align the top edge of the band with the set-up line.

After all frames are assembled, cut the notches for the keel, chines, and sheer battens. Sometimes it is best to rough plane the required angle on the outside edges.

Assembly Jig

Nail blocks of wood to the stringers at each frame position. Fasten the stringers to saw-horses, Fig. 24-6. Be certain the stringers are parallel and that the blocks are in the correct position and directly across from each other.

The transom is usually mounted on the end of the stringers and then each frame is nailed in position. Check each for proper alignment before nailing the crossband to the stringer. Secure the stem in position with special bracing or attach it to the floor as shown in Fig. 24-7.

Fig. 24-7. Frames mounted on stringers and stem in position (seven frame boat).

Transfer the layout lines to the framing stock and cut it to shape. All frames are symmetrical so when you cut out a part for one side of a given frame you can turn it over and use it to lay out the other side.

Place the parts of the frame on the layout board with the gussets in place. Drill screw holes,

Battens, Chines and Stringers

Lay the keel batten in the frame notches and fit it to the stem. Check the fit and then drill holes, apply glue and screw it in place.

Fit and assemble chines, and sheer battens in a similar manner. Work from bow to transom,

Fig. 24-8. Framework complete for typical five frame boat.

screwing them to both sides of each frame before continuing to the next frame. Miter the forward ends of the battens to the stem and secure with glue and heavy screws. See Fig. 24-8, which shows a completed frame, and Fig. 24-9.

Fair (make smooth and even) the outside edges of the frame with a hand plane. The keel batten is beveled to conform with the frame bottoms. Fig. 24-10 shows the chine being planed. Bending a thin strip across frames and battens at various angles will show the exact bevels required.

Fig. 24-9. Steam bent oak ribs being used for a cabin cruiser in a boatbuilding plant. (Badger Boat Corp.)

Fig. 24-10. Planing the chine to conform with the frames. Note the strip being used to check the angle.

The edges of the frames will also require some fairing, especially where the curvature of the hull is great. Do not round off the edges but try to keep them flat so they will make good contact with the planking when it is applied.

Fig. 24-11. Left. Interior view of a large hull showing the keelson, stringers, ribs and planking. (Badger Boat Corp.)
Right. Cutting marine plywood into strips to form lapstrake planking. Two sheets are being cut at one time.
(Badger Boat Corp.)

Planking

The covering for the hull is called planking whether it consists of strips of solid wood or wide sheets of plywood. For rounded hulls that have a double-curved surface, strips of plywood are usually applied in an overlapping pattern somewhat like house siding. Fig. 24-11, shows strips of plywood being cut for this type of application. When the strips are placed edge to edge it is called CARVEL planking.

Flat, wide sheets of plywood are butted at the seam and must be carefully fitted. Study the plan and carefully lay out the pieces using a wood spline as shown in Fig. 24-12. A pattern can be

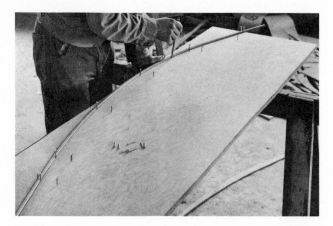

Fig. 24-12. Using a wood strip to lay out a smooth curve.

made by placing a large sheet of building paper directly on the hull framework. Cut out the pieces (an electric sabre saw is desirable) allowing

sufficient material for trimming and fitting. Clamp the piece in place to check the fit. For sharp bends, dampen the panel slightly and preform it. Allow the panel to dry thoroughly before gluing it in place.

Spread waterproof glue over the framework and clamp the planks in position. Drill screw holes and set the screws, Fig. 24-13. The size

Fig. 24-13. Above. Attaching sheet of plywood to side of hull framework. Below. Fitting bottom planking.

and spacing of the screws will vary with the size of the materials and design. Boat plans will include this information.

It is standard practice to countersink the screwheads below the surface of the plywood and then fill the depressions with a surfacing com-

WOODY SAYS:

"When using portable power tools in boatbuilding, be sure they are properly grounded."

pound. Laying a glue-soaked thread of candlewicking along the frame where planking joints occur will provide added insurance against leakage.

When the hull is planked, plane a flat surface along the ridge of the bottom for the outer keel. Fill the planking joint with special seam compound and attach the keel with screws.

Deck and Details

When the hull is complete, remove it from the assembly jig and turn it right side up, Fig. 24-14. It is best to leave some or all of the crossbands in place until the deck areas are framed. Brace the hull so it will remain securely upright while further work is being performed.

Fig. 24-14. When the planking is complete the hull is turned right-side up.

Fig. 24-15. Deck frame faired and ready for panels.

Cut and assemble the various deck and gunnel framing members. Band saw beams to shape and screw and glue them to the top of the frames. Add blocking and other reinforcement and then fair the frame and lay the plywood deck panels. See Figs. 24-15 and 24-16.

Fig. 24-16. Applying deck panels.

Fit and apply trim strips, seats, floor and details. Both metal and wood trim members are usually prefitted and then removed during the application of finishing coats. It may be desirable to apply a wood preservative and sealer to the inside of the hull before the floor boards are laid.

Finishing

Fill all cracks and screw holes with a special surfacing compound and then sand the surface smooth. A portable belt sander, Fig. 24-17, is helpful for this operation. Final sanding should be done by hand.

Follow standard wood finishing procedures as presented in Unit 10. Use finishing materials that are especially intended for marine work. Usually it is best to use sealers, primers and finish coats that are produced by the same manufacturer. This way you can be sure that each coat

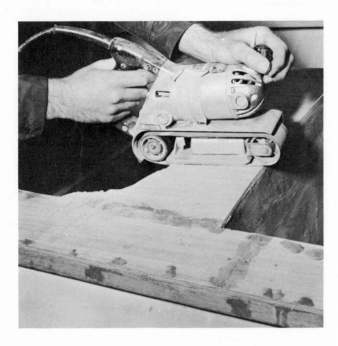

Fig. 24-17. Using portable belt sander to smooth filled holes. (Norton Co.)

will be compatible with the others. Some boat builders prefer to paint as they build; sealing, undercoating, and first-finish-coating the bottom before righting the hull and removing the jig.

Test Your Knowledge

1. The framing member located where the side and bottom planking are joined is called the _____.
2. One of the best hardwoods to use for a boat framework is _____.
3. A three-eights thickness of marine plywood has _____ plies.
4. Notches for the keel and chines are cut before the frame is attached to the stringer. True or False?
5. When the hull is covered with overlapping strips the construction is called _____ planking.
6. Resorcinol glue is waterproof and commonly used for boatbuilding. True or False?
7. The safest portable power tool to use for cutting out curves in plywood is the _____ .

Outside Assignments

1. Compile a list of the various types of small boat hulls. Include drawings and adequate written descriptions. You may also want to include methods of construction. Secure information from boatbuilding books and such resources as the Encyclopedia Britannica.
2. Prepare a written report on the legal obligations and regulations in connection with boat ownership. Include federal laws and also regulations that apply in your state. Present a summary of the report to your class.

Sheet of thin (and still flexible) particle board moves down conveyor from giant mat-forming machine. Inside machine, sawdust and fine chips are mixed with a urea resin binder and fed between stainless steel belts and heated rollers. Thicknesses of 1/8 in. to 1/4 in. can be produced. Automatic sawing machine in left foreground trims sheet to width, then cuts it into standard length panels. Thin panels produced are usually laminated into thicker pieces. (Georgia-Pacific)

Unit 25
WOOD TECHNOLOGY,
RELATED INFORMATION

The successful woodworker must know and understand the properties and characteristics of wood. In this Unit we will study this phase of wood technology and also learn something about forestry, lumbering and wood products. A section concerning occupational opportunites in woodworking and the home workshop is also included.

Structure and Growth

The basic structure of wood consists of long narrow tubes or cells (called fibers or tracheids) no larger around than a human hair. Their length varies from about 1/25 in. in hardwoods to approximately 1/8 in. in softwoods. Tiny strands of cellulose make up the walls of the cells which

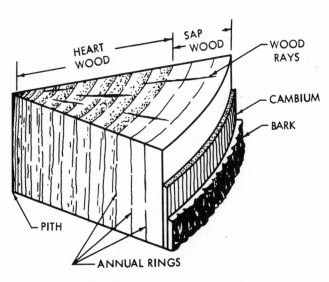

Fig. 25-1. Parts of a tree trunk.

are held together with a natural cement called lignin. This is a remarkable substance that is unaffected by water, common chemical solvents, or heat. It is this cellular structure that makes it possible to drive nails and screws into the wood. It also accounts for the lightweight, low heat transmission factors and sound absorption qualities.

The growing, working parts of a tree are the tips of the roots, the leaves, and a layer of cells just inside the bark called the cambium. Water is absorbed by the roots and travels through the sapwood to the leaves where it is combined with carbon dioxide from the air. Through the miracle of photosynthesis, sunlight changes these to food (carbohydrates) which is then carried back to the various parts of the tree.

New cells are formed in the cambium layer Fig. 25-1. The inside area of the layer (xylem) develops new wood cells while the outside area (phloem) develops cells that form the bark.

The growth in the cambium layer takes place in the spring and summer and forms separate layers each year. These layers are called annual rings, Fig. 25-2. In most woods the annual ring is composed of two layers; springwood and summerwood. In the spring, trees grow rapidly and the cells produced are large and thin walled. As the growth slows down during the summer

Fig. 25-2. Count the annular rings and you will know the age of the tree. Drought, disease, or insects can interrupt the growth and cause an extra or false ring to be formed.

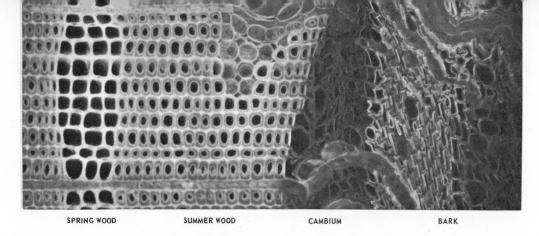

SPRING WOOD   SUMMER WOOD   CAMBIUM   BARK

Fig. 25-3. Section through an annual ring, magnified about 220X.
(Forest Products Lab.)

months the cells produced are smaller, thicker walled and appear darker in color. See Fig. 25-3.

The change from springwood to summerwood may be either abrupt or gradual depending on the kind of wood and growing condition. In such woods as maple, basswood and poplar there is little difference in the cells formed, while in oak, ash, and southern pine the difference is pronounced. These annual growth rings are largely responsible for the grain patterns that are seen in the surface of boards cut from a log. In tropical climates the growth of the tree is controlled more by wet or dry seasons than temperature changes. Generally the growth rings of woods grown in these areas are not as easily defined.

Sapwood contains living cells and may be several inches or more in thickness. Fast growing trees usually have a thicker layer. The heartwood of the tree is formed as the sapwood becomes inactive and usually turns darker in color because of the presence of gums and resins. In some woods such as hemlock, spruce and basswood there is little or no difference in the appearance. Sapwood is as strong and heavy as heartwood but not as durable when exposed to weather.

Wood Cells

The wood cells or fibers that make up the structural elements of the wood are of various sizes and shapes and are firmly grown together. The strength of the wood depends on the thickness and structure of the cell walls rather than the cell size. When magnified, a section of wood looks something like a honeycomb, Fig. 25-4.

Most of the cells run along the length of the wood; however, some run at right angles or radially to the center of the tree. These cell groups conduct sap across the grain and are called wood rays or medullary rays. In most kinds of wood they are small however, in oak and sycamore they are quite large and noticeable, especially when the wood is quarter-sawed.

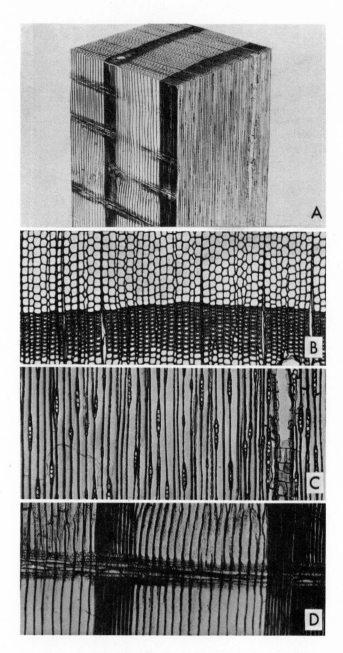

Fig. 25-4. A-Enlarged cube of southern pine, 1/4 in. square.
B-Cross section. C-Tangential section (cut at a right angle
to the radius). D-Radial section. Note the wood ray.
(Forest Products Lab.)

In addition to the regular cells and those in the wood rays, hardwoods contain some relatively large cells called vessels that provide main arteries in the movement of sap. Still other cells called Parenchyma, are found in both hard and softwoods, and function mainly for the storage of food.

These various cells, which differ in size, shape, and arrangement, along with deposits of resin and other coloring matter, all add together to provide interesting and attractive grain patterns and textures.

Moisture Content and Shrinkage

Before wood can be used commercially, a large part of the moisture (sap) must be removed. When a living tree is cut, more than half of its weight may be moisture. The heartwood of a "green" birch tree has a moisture content of about 75 percent. Most cabinet and furniture woods are dried to a moisture content of 7 to 10 percent.

The amount of moisture or moisture content (M.C.) in wood is expressed as a percent of the oven-dry weight. To determine the moisture content a sample is first weighed and then placed in an oven and dried at a temperature of about 212 to 220 deg. F. The drying is continued until it no longer loses weight. The sample is weighed again and this oven-dry weight is subtracted from the initial weight. The difference is then divided by the oven-dry weight, Fig. 25-5.

Moisture is contained in the cell cavities (free water) and in the cell walls (bound water). As the wood is dried, moisture first leaves the cell cavities. When the cells are empty but the cell walls are still full of moisture, the wood has reached a condition called the FIBER SATURATION POINT. This is about 30 percent for nearly all kinds of wood, Fig. 25-6.

The fiber saturation point is important because wood does not start to shrink until this point is reached. As the M.C. is reduced below 30 percent, moisture is removed from the cell walls and they become smaller in size. For a 1 percent moisture loss below the fiber saturation point, the wood will shrink about 1/30th in size. If dried to 15 percent M.C. the wood will have been reduced by about one-half the total shrinkage possible. A plain-sawed birch board that was 12 in. wide at 30 percent M.C. will measure only about 11 in. wide at 0 percent. In general hardwoods shrink more than softwoods. Fig. 25-7 shows the shrinkage in a 2 x 10 joist.

Wood shrinks most along the direction of the annual rings (tangentially) and about one-half as

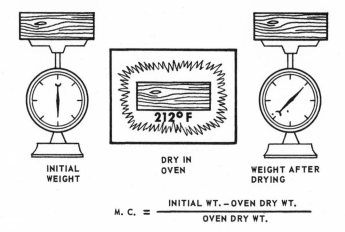

$$M.C. = \frac{INITIAL\ WT. - OVEN\ DRY\ WT.}{OVEN\ DRY\ WT.}$$

Fig. 25-5. How to determine moisture content.

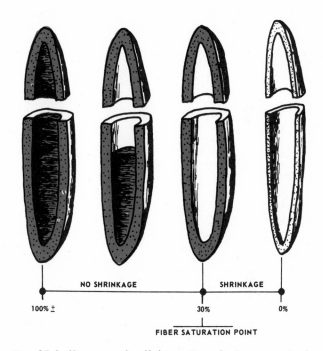

NO SHRINKAGE   SHRINKAGE

100% ±   30%   0%

FIBER SATURATION POINT

Fig. 25-6. How a wood cell dries. First the free water in the cell cavity is removed and then the cell wall dries.

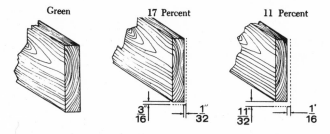

Green   17 Percent   11 Percent

$\frac{3}{16}$ $\frac{1}{32}$ $\frac{11}{32}$ $\frac{1}{16}$

Fig. 25-7. Dimensional change in a 2 x 10.

much across these rings. There is practically no shrinkage in the length. How this shrinkage affects lumber cut from a log is shown in Fig. 25-8. As moisture is added to wood, it swells in the same proportion that the shrinkage has taken place.

Drying Methods

Methods of drying or seasoning lumber vary with the use requirements. Today, because of the time saving and control factors, nearly all upper grades are kiln dried. Sometimes lumber is first air dried and then kiln dried.

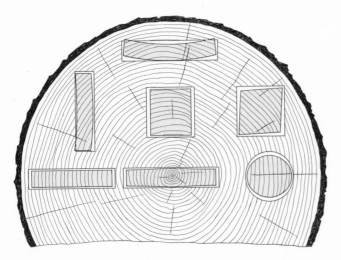

Fig. 25-8. *The shrinkage and distortion of flat, square and round pieces as affected by the direction of the annual rings.*

In air drying, the lumber is simply exposed to the outside air. It is carefully stacked with stickers (wood strips) between each layer so air can circulate through the pile. Boards are spaced well apart in the layers so air can also move vertically. Fig. 25-9 shows lumber air-drying in a sawmill yard.

Fig. 25-9. *Air drying lumber. Stacking method is called "flat piling."* (American Forest Products Industries)

The rate of air drying lumber can be partially controlled by varying the spacing between individual boards and the size of the pile. Because of the seasonal variations in climate and local weather condition, it is difficult to approximate the air-drying time for any particular species or thickness. Lumber that might become dry in 30 to 60 days during an active drying period may require more than 6 months under unfavorable conditions. The moisture content of thoroughly air-dried lumber, reduced during the spring, summer or early fall will be about 12 to 18 percent.

Lumber is kiln (often pronounced "kill") dried by placing it in an oven where the temperature and humidity are accurately controlled. The boards are stacked in about the same way as for air-drying, Fig. 25-10. When the green lumber

Fig. 25-10. *Hardwood lumber stacked on a truck and ready to enter a kiln. Note the "stickers" that separate the layers.* (Heywood-Wakefield Co.)

is first placed in the kiln, steam is used to keep the humidity high and the temperature is kept at a low level. Gradually, the temperature is raised and the humidity is reduced. Fans are used to keep the air in constant circulation over the surfaces of the wood. See Fig. 25-11.

A kiln schedule is a carefully complied set of temperatures, humidities and timings which are followed by the kiln operator. They will vary depending on the size (cross section) and kind of wood, and its initial moisture content. One inch lumber can usually be kiln dried to a level of 6 to 10 percent in about three or four days.

Improper drying, either air or kiln, can result in such seasoning defects as splits, checks, warpage, loosened knots, honeycomb, and internal stresses called case-hardening. Most of these are caused by drying the wood too rapidly. In case-hardening the surface layers dry, shrink and become fixed or set before the inside portion of the board. As the interior then dries below the fiber saturation point and starts to shrink it pulls on

the outside "shell," creating both compression and tension forces. When the board is cut these forces are released causing the kerf to close on (pinch) the saw blade or the stock to warp in various directions.

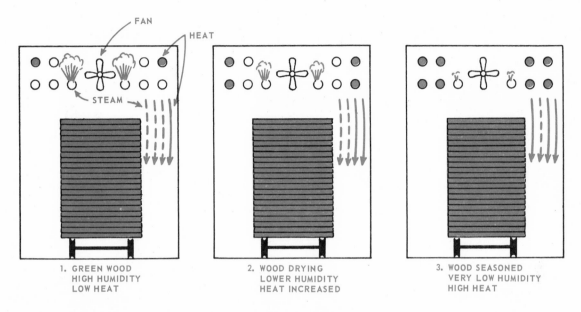

1. GREEN WOOD
   HIGH HUMIDITY
   LOW HEAT

2. WOOD DRYING
   LOWER HUMIDITY
   HEAT INCREASED

3. WOOD SEASONED
   VERY LOW HUMIDITY
   HIGH HEAT

Fig. 25-11. Kiln drying lumber.

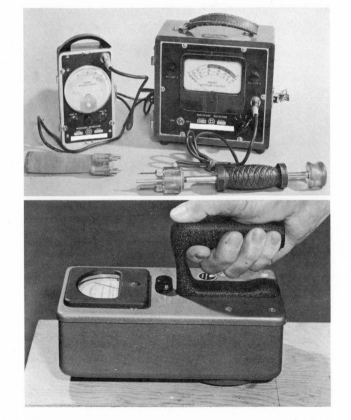

Fig. 25-12. Moisture meters. Above. Resistance type. Below. Radio-Frequency type.
(Forest Products Lab.)

Moisture Meters

The moisture content of wood can be determined by oven drying a sample as previously described or by using an electric moisture meter. Although the oven drying method is the most accurate, meters are often used because readings can be secured rapidly and conveniently. They are usually calibrated to cover a range from 7 to 25 percent with an accuracy of plus or minus 1 percent of the moisture content.

Two types of meters are shown in Fig. 25-12. One determines the moisture content by measuring the electrical resistance between two pin-type electrodes that are driven into the wood. The other types measures the capacity of a condenser in a high-frequency circuit in which the wood serves as the dielectric material of the condenser.

Equilibrium Moisture Content

A piece of wood will give off or take on moisture from the air around it until the moisture in the wood is balanced with that in the air. At this point the wood is said to be at equilibrium moisture content (E.M.C.). Since wood is exposed to daily and seasonal changes in the relative humidity of the air, it is continually making slight changes in its moisture content and therefore, changes in its dimensions. This is the reason doors and drawers often stick during humid weather but work freely the rest of the year.

Air can hold a certain amount of moisture at a certain temperature. Relative humidity expresses what percentage of this maximum is actually being held by the air. The chart which follows shows relative humidities required to permit wood to remain in equilibrium at various moisture contents when the temperature is 72 deg. F.

it to the required moisture content and the same atmospheric conditions should then be maintained throughout the manufacturing processes and until the finish is applied.

Wood Samples in Color

The color section, inserted between pages 2-12 and 2-13, shows both native and imported woods.

All of the samples shown are of woods that are commercially available. Some are scarce and

Moisture Content (EMC) Desired	5%	6%	7%	8%	9%	10%	11%	12%
Relative Humidity Required	24%	31%	37%	43%	49%	55%	60%	65%

Moisture changes in wood take place slowly under normal conditions. Paint and other finishes will slow this action still more, but will not entirely prevent it. Furniture and wood products should be fabricated from wood with a moisture content equal to the average it will attain in service. Fig. 25-13, shows the average E.M.C. for interior woodwork throughout the United States. Figures for framing and exterior woodwork vary considerably but usually are several percentage points above those for interior work.

For fine furniture and fixture work the wood should be kiln dried to an M.C. somewhat below that which service conditions demand. It should then be stored in an atmosphere that will bring

therefore quite expensive; while others are moderate in price and used extensively in fine furniture and cabinetwork. Fig. 25-14 shows a map of North America and the general localities in which various hardwoods grow.

Forests

Forest lands constitute one of our greatest natural resources. Total area, including Alaska and Hawaii, is about 775 million acres. Nearly one-third of the continental United States is either in forests or well suited by nature for their growth. Our forests provide the raw material for a wide range of wood-using industries. In addition

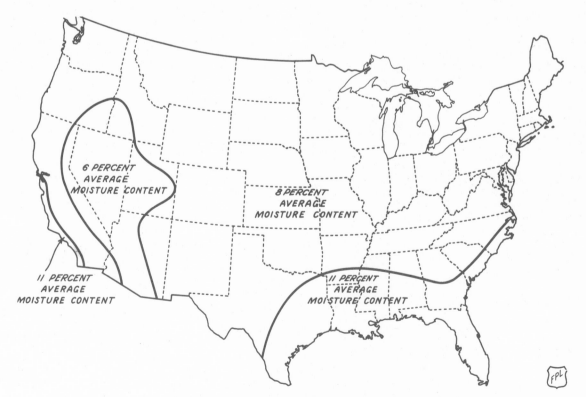

Fig. 25-13. Recommended M.C. averages for interior woodwork in various areas of the United States.

NORTH AMERICA

YEW

MAPLE (BIGLEAF)
MADRONE
MYRTLE   PINE (KNOTTY)
YEW
REDWOOD BURL
LAUREL
WALNUT (CLARO)

MADRONE

BIRCH
BASSWOOD   ASH   MAPLE   WHITE BIRCH
ASPEN   BEECH
(POPPLE)   BIRCH CHERRY   ASPEN
OAK HACKBERRY MAPLE   BIRCH
WALNUT   PEARWOOD   CHERRY
OAK ELM SYCAMORE
BUTTERNUT   BEECH MAPLE ASPEN
SYCAMORE   WALNUT   BEECH BIRCH
ASH   BUTTERNUT
OAK (WHITE) HACKBERRY CHERRY
PECAN   OAK (RED) HOLLY
CATALPA   TUPELO   OAK (WHITE)
GUM (RED) CEDAR (RED)
ELM   POPLAR

ASH
AMARANTH
OAK
CEDAR (SPANISH)   MAHOGANY
MAHOGANY   ROSEWOOD   (CUBAN)
KELOBRA (PAROTA)
CAPOMO (OJOCHE)   SATINWOOD
PRIMA VERA   LEMON WOOD
MAHOGANY   COCABOLO   SATINWOOD
CATIVO   JENISERO

KOA (HAWAII)

Fig. 25-14. Hardwoods of North America and where they grow.
(Fine Hardwoods-American Walnut Assoc.)

Fig. 25-15. More than 600 million acres of the United States
are best suited for forest lands.
(Forest Products Lab.)

Fig. 25-16. At left, Douglas fir; then hemlock, four Douglas
fir, two hemlock.

to this they help prevent excessive soil erosion, furnish ideal conditions for wildlife, and provide areas for outdoor recreation. See Figs. 25-15 and 25-16.

Today, our supply of trees is no longer dependent entirely on nature. Sound forest management practiced by forest industries and others under the American Tree Farm System insures

Fig. 25-17. Millions of seedlings being grown at a tree farm nursery. (Weyerhaeuser Co.)

Fig. 25-19. Felling (cutting) a tree with a power chain saw.

Fig. 25-18. A trained forester selects and marks a ponderosa pine for harvesting.

against the depletion of this important resource. Crops of trees are grown and harvested like other farm crops so our forests of today will also be our forests of tomorrow. Modern methods and equipment are used to plant tree seeds in nurseries, and then transplant them in the forests, Fig. 25-17. Airplanes are often used to apply spray for the control of insects and disease.

Lumbering

Trained foresters select and mark the trees that will be harvested, Fig. 25-18. In addition to good timber, they also choose trees that are susceptible to insects and disease. Some trees are chosen because when they are removed a nearby tree will grow more rapidly. Trees se-

Fig. 25-20. Transporting logs from the forests to the sawmill. Above. Skidding logs to a central loading point. Center. Hauling by rail. Below. Hauling by truck. Each load will provide enough lumber for a small house.

lected for harvest are cut down with power saws, Fig. 25-19. Limbs are removed and the trunk is then cut into suitable lengths. This process is called "bucking."

Fig. 25-21. A modern sawmill located in the West Coast area. Annual capacity, over 240 million board feet.

Fig. 25-22. Logs are sorted by size, species and general condition. (Weyerhaeuser Co.)

Fig. 25-23. Hardwood logs at a sawmill in Ohio.

Fig. 25-24. Logs are carried into the mill by the bull chain of a jack ladder.

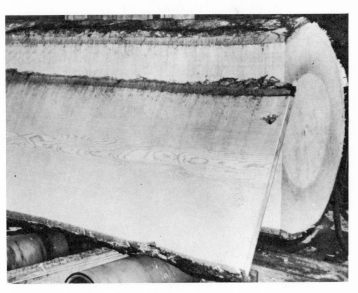

Fig. 25-25. Large logs are carried past a high speed band saw that produces slabs, timbers, or large pieces called "cants." (Georgia-Pacific)

The logs are skidded to a central point with crawler tractors, where they are loaded on trucks or railroad cars for the trip to the sawmill, Fig. 25-20. In a few areas logs are still floated down streams to the mill.

Sawmills are located close to the forests and logs seldom need to be transported more than 100 miles. Large mills, Fig. 25-21, are usually located on a river or lake so the logs can be stored in water until they are sawed. This prevents them from end-checking and insect damage. Also, it is easier to sort heavy logs by moving them around in the water, Fig. 25-22. Some hardwood logs do not float very well and they are usually stacked in the mill yard where they are sprayed with water to keep them from drying out, Fig. 25-23.

In large mills, logs are pulled up a jack ladder to the sawing deck where they are washed and the bark is sometimes removed, Fig. 25-24. Each log is then placed on the carriage of the headrig and moves through a giant band saw that cuts the log into boards and timbers, Fig. 25-25. Small hardwood logs are often cut with a circular saw that may have a blade 4 feet or more in diameter.

Fig. 25-26. Rough boards are cut to various lengths with multiple trimmer saws.

From the headrig the boards move to smaller edger and trimmer saws that cut them to proper widths and lengths. The rough boards are then sorted, graded and stacked either in the yard for air drying, or sent to huge ovens for kiln drying.

Fig. 25-28. Planing mill section of a large sawmill. (American Forest Products Industries)

Fig. 25-27. Green lumber moving into huge dry kilns. (Forest Products Lab.)

Large mills usually have a planing mill section where the dried lumber is surfaced and made into finished lumber, Fig. 25-28. After leaving the planers the lumber is again graded, trimmed to remove defects, sorted by length and grade, and then prepared for shipment.

Fig. 25-29. Modern mobile sawmill in operation. (Northeast Ohio Machine Builders)

Small mills are located throughout the country, especially where hardwood lumber is produced. In recent years, efficient mobile units like the one shown in Fig. 25-29 have been developed. These can be moved into the timber area so logs can be sawed near to the location where the trees were cut.

Plywood and Veneer

Top quality softwood logs are selected for plywood fabrication, Fig. 25-30. Because of the limited supply, a large part of the total production of some of the fine hardwoods is cut into veneer. This is used to face high grade plywood panels. Veneer, both softwood and hardwood, is also used to manufacture boxes, crates, food containers and other products that require thin pieces of wood. Such items as tongue depressors, mustard paddles, ice cream spoons and popsicle sticks are stamped from sheets of veneer.

Fig. 25-30. Selected "peeler" logs, cut from the lower portion of the tree, are used for plywood.
(American Plywood Association)

Fig. 25-31. Veneer being peeled from a Douglas fir log mounted in a giant lathe.
(Georgia-Pacific)

Prior to cutting the veneer, the logs are cleaned and the bark removed. Hardwood logs are heated in hot water vats or steam chambers to make the cutting easier and help insure smooth unbroken sheets.

Nearly all veneer, especially softwood, is cut by the rotary method. The log is mounted in a huge lathe and revolves against a razor-sharp knife that peels off a thin continuous ribbon of

Fig. 25-33. Enlarged view of rotary veneer cutting. A-Knife. B-Nose bar. C-Tight side of veneer. D-Loose side and cracks in the veneer.

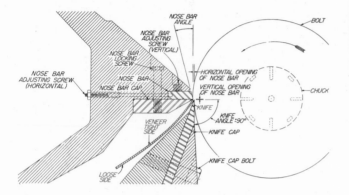

Fig. 25-32. Knife carriage of a veneer lathe. Angles and settings vary for different kinds and thicknesses of veneer. The nose bar is pressed tightly against the log.
(Forest Products Lab.)

wood. Fig. 25-32 shows a section drawing of the knife carriage of a veneer lathe. The angles and settings must be carefully controlled. Note that the thickness of the veneer is determined by the distance between the nose bar and the knife edge.

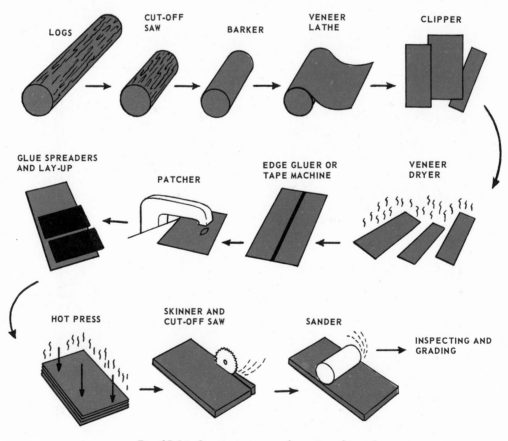

Fig. 25-34. Sequence in manufacturing plywood.
(Weyerhaeuser Co.)

As the veneer is cut, the wood fibers are compressed on one side and stretched on the other, forming what is called a tight side and a loose side, Fig. 25-33. The tight side should be used for the exposed face of plywood or veneer work.

Fig. 25-34 shows the steps in softwood plywood manufacturing. After the veneer is cut, giant knives, controlled by skilled operators, cut the veneer to proper width for full utilization. It then enters large ovens or dryers that operate at temperatures of about 350 deg. Travel time through a 100 foot dryer may vary from 6 to 20 minutes depending on the thickness of the veneer. When it emerges from the dryer, Fig. 25-35, the moisture content (M.C.) will have been reduced to about 4 percent.

Fig. 25-37. Veneer sheets are fed through a glue spreader and placed in the "lay-up."

Fig. 25-35. Sheets of veneer emerging from a modern dryer. (American Plywood Assoc.)

Fig. 25-38. Giant hydraulic press with heated platens and 20 openings (daylights). (American Plywood Assoc.)

(3, 5, 7,) and always the direction of the grain is placed at right angles to that of adjacent layers.

After the lay-up, panels go into powerful presses that exert pressure of more than 150 lbs.

Fig. 25-36. Grading table. Veneers are stacked in piles of uniform quality. (American Forest Products Industries)

Next the sheets are patched. Natural defects are cut out and replaced with solid wood, expertly glued into place. Next some of the sheets go through a glue spreader, Fig. 25-37, where an even coat of adhesive is applied to each side. These glue-covered pieces are stacked alternately with dry veneer to make up the plywood panel. Always there is an odd number of veneers

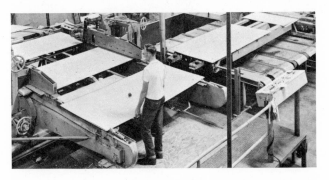

Fig. 25-39. Modern double-end machines trim the plywood panels to exact width and length.

per square inch. The platens (plates) of the press are heated to speed the setting of the glue. From the press, panels move through double-end machines, Fig. 25-39, that trim them to exact size. Wide belt sanders are used to sand the panel faces. Then comes inspection, the careful repair of blemishes, and final grading.

Hardwood plywood is manufactured in about the same way except that face veneers are more

For fine furniture and cabinetwork, the grain and figure patterns of hardwood veneers are matched in various ways to produce panels of interesting design. Sometimes they are assembled to form symmetrical patterns called "book matched" and "diamond matched." The figure pattern in the veneer is determined by the kind of wood, how the veneer is cut and the portion of the tree in which it is located, Fig. 25-42.

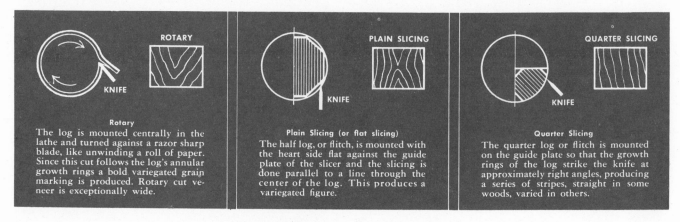

Rotary

The log is mounted centrally in the lathe and turned against a razor sharp blade, like unwinding a roll of paper. Since this cut follows the log's annular growth rings a bold variegated grain marking is produced. Rotary cut veneer is exceptionally wide.

Plain Slicing (or flat slicing)

The half log, or flitch, is mounted with the heart side flat against the guide plate of the slicer and the slicing is done parallel to a line through the center of the log. This produces a variegated figure.

Quarter Slicing

The quarter log or flitch is mounted on the guide plate so that the growth rings of the log strike the knife at approximately right angles, producing a series of stripes, straight in some woods, varied in others.

Fig. 25-40. Methods used to cut hardwood veneer.
(Fine Hardwoods-American Walnut Assoc.)

carefully matched, edge jointed, and glued. Quite often hardwood veneer is produced by slicing, Fig. 25-40. The flitch (log section) is moved downward against a knife edge, which cuts off sheets of the wood. Because the veneer is forced abruptly away from the flitch by the knife, fine checks or breaks may occur on the knife side. This corresponds to the loose side in rotary cutting and should be used for the glue side.

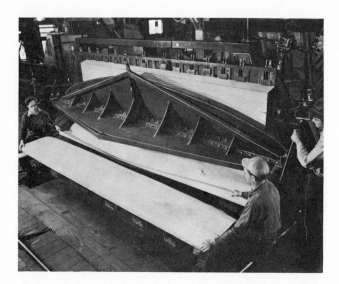

Fig. 25-41. Slicing veneer. The flitch moves up and down.
(American Forest Products Industries)

Hardboard

Hardboard is a manufactured product made by bonding together wood fibers. The wood is reduced to individual fibers and then reunited with lignin, the natural cohesive substance found in all wood. Other composition board products are made with synthetic binders. Various kinds of wood can be used to make hardboard. Residues (scrap and waste) from sawmills and plywood plants are used extensively. The wood is first chipped into thin pieces about 5/8 in. wide and 1 in. long, Fig. 25-44.

The chips are then reduced to individual fibers by either steam or special defibering machines. In the steam process the chips are placed in steam chests under tremendous pressure. When the pressure is relieved suddenly, the chips explode into tiny fiber bundles in about the same way some breakfast food cereals are formed.

After certain refining processes the fibers are mixed in a tank of water and then fed onto a moving screen to form a mat, Fig. 25-46. Another system is sometimes used where the fibers are blown into a large metal cone and settle down (into a mat) like snowflakes. The thick blanket travels through rollers that compress the interlocking fibers. This compressed mat is cut into rough panel sizes and placed in multiple presses where heat and pressure produce the thin, hard, dry

CROTCH

BURL

QUARTERED

ROTARY

STUMP WOOD

FLAT CUT

SECTIONS OF TREE FROM
WHICH VARIOUS TYPES OF
FIGURE PATTERNS ARE
OBTAINED. SOME SPECIES
PRODUCE SEVERAL
FIGURE TYPES.

Fig. 25-42. Types of cuts and sections of tree from which various figure patterns are obtained.
(Fine Hardwoods-American Walnut Assoc.)

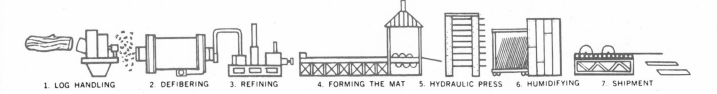

1. LOG HANDLING   2. DEFIBERING   3. REFINING   4. FORMING THE MAT   5. HYDRAULIC PRESS   6. HUMIDIFYING   7. SHIPMENT

Fig. 25-43. Processes used in manufacturing hardboard.

Fig. 25-44. Making wood chips for hardboard manufacture.
(Masonite Corp.)

Fig. 25-45. Wood chips are fed in big "guns" and placed
under tremendous pressure. When the pressure is released,
the chips explode and a burst of steam comes from the cyclones (2 shown).

Fig. 25-46. Checking the thickness of the "wet-lap" as it approaches rollers that squeeze out the water and compress the fibers.

Fig. 25-48. Hardboard is available in a wide variety of patterns and surface textures. (American Hardboard Assoc.)

sheets. After the panels are conditioned through a humidification process, they are trimmed to size. Fig. 25-47.

The manufacturing process may include certain additives and heat-treating which results in a product with increased stiffness, hardness and durability. This board is called tempered hard-

Fig. 25-49. Applying a prime coat to hardboard panels with a modern roller coater.

ment in wood technology where efforts in wood utilization are combined with modern adhesives and manufacturing equipment.

Special machines slice the wood flakes, Fig. 25-50, into the exact size required for the product being produced. The flakes are then mixed with a urea-formaldehyde resin adhesive. Boards that will be used in exterior applications are bonded with a phenolic resin.

Fig. 25-47. Cutting and trimming the hardboard into standard size panels. (Masonite Corp.)

board. Various surface textures and forms can be molded or cut into hardboard. See Fig. 25-48. Today, great quantities of hardboard are prefinished in prime-coats, colors, and wood-grained patterns.

Particle Board

Particle board is made by combining wood flakes and chips with resin binders and hot-pressing them into panels. This material, like hardboard, is a result of research and develop-

Fig. 25-50. Dry wood flakes for particle board are sifted as they move along a conveyor.
(National Particleboard Assoc.)

This mixture is then formed into sheets, either by an extrusion process or a mat-forming process similar to that used for hardboard. The sheets are cut to rough size and bonded in huge hot presses, Fig. 25-52. To complete the process, the edges are trimmed. The surface of particle board is sometimes filled and sanded or over-laid with various materials.

Fig. 25-51. Particle board mat after it has been pre-pressed by rollers and before it enters the hot press.

Fig. 25-52. A modern, giant hot press used in the manufacture of particle board.

Other Forest Products

In addition to lumber, poles, ties, veneer, plywood and various composition boards, many other items must be added to form a total list of products from our forests. For example; gums and resins harvested from living trees are used to make waxes, varnish, paint, driers, printing ink, rubber, insecticides, drugs, and chewing gum. Each year more than 15 million cords of pulp wood are used for paper and cardboard. Books, newspapers, magazines, packages for food, shipping boxes, and countless other paper based products must also be added to the list.

Through the magic of modern chemistry, wood cellulose is transformed into thousands of products such as lacquers, synthetic fibers for cloth, photographic film, plastics, linoleum, alcohol, and a component in the solid-fuels used in rockets.

Fig. 25-53. Particle board is used as a base for high-pressure plastic laminates. (National Particleboard Assoc.)

Development and Research

Although great progress has been made in the perfection of wood products and the full utilization of our forests, more new and spectacular developments will result from continuing programs of research. Many commercial lumber companies conduct such programs. A major institution devoted to scientific experimentation and testing of wood is the Forest Products Laboratory in Madison, Wisconsin. It is a division of the Forest Service of the United States Department of Agriculture, Fig. 25-54.

Fig. 25-54. Forest Products Laboratory, Madison, Wis.

The research conducted at the Forest Products Laboratory benefits producers, processors, distributors and consumers of all kinds of wood products and by-products. Accompanying photographs show a few of the many testing and research activities. Others include studies of wood structure and properties, grading, identification

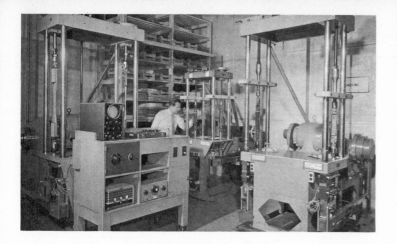

Fig. 25-55. Testing equipment being used to analyze sandwich panel construction.

Fig. 25-57. Scientific testing of the tensile strength of a fabricated panel. (Weyerhaeuser Co.)

and classification, mill equipment, utilization of residues, seasoning and kiln schedules, moisture control and dimensional stability, adhesives, plywood and hardboard fabrication, paints, finishes, wood preservatives, joints and fasteners, sandwich panel construction, and packaging.

Research studies are also conducted on wood pulp, paper, and chemical products. Special projects include the cutting and machining of wood with light (laser) and high-powered water jets, Figs. 25-58 and 25-59.

A recent development has been the chemical treatment of solid wood to improve its dimensional stability. The green wood is saturated with a solution of polyethylene glycol which penetrates into the fine structure of the cell walls. This provides a bulking action that restrains the walls from shrinking as the wood is dried. The treatment has been successfully applied to gun stocks, turned bowls, wood carvings and similar items.

Technical and scientific information about wood and wood products are available to industrial concerns, business men, farmers, teachers, and students.

Occupational Opportunities in Woodworking

Many occupational opportunities are available to persons who are interested and have ability in the area of woodwork. More than two million people are employed in processing, manufacturing, and distributing lumber and forest products. The United States produces one-third of the worlds lumber, over one-half of its plywood and nearly one-half of its paper and paperboard. Wood, always a desired material for furniture and interior finish for our homes, continues to grow in importance and popularity. Carpentry is, and will continue to be our largest single trade.

The carpenter and cabinetmaker work with many of the same tools, machines, and materials that you have become familiar with in the school shop. Other work that is closely related includes patternmaking, boatbuilding, and painting and finishing. Many of the illustrations in this book show in-plant and on-the-job scenes of these trades and occupations.

To enter these areas of work you should of course, complete your high school studies. Take

Fig. 25-56. Technicians testing a 2 x 10 floor joist to determine its bending strength. (Forest Products Lab.)

Fig. 25-58. Experimentation in the cutting of wood with a laser (light amplification by stimulated emission of radiation) beam.

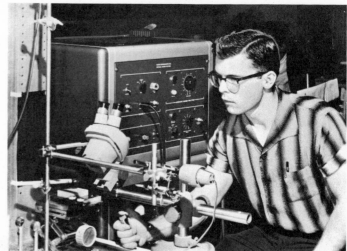

as many as possible of the woodworking courses offered, and other Industrial Arts courses, especially drawing. Students sometimes tend to minimize the importance of science, math, social studies and English. This is unfortunate because a top craftsman must have an appreciation and understanding of the social, economic, and scientific aspects of our world and be competent in reading, writing and speaking the English language.

Fig. 25-59. Cutting wood with a high-powered water jet. Pressures of 50,000 lbs. per square inch are used.

Industrial woodworking plants that make furniture, doors, windows and cabinetwork have some jobs that do not require a great amount of special training. However, the work of setting up machines, maintaining equipment, building jigs and fixtures, and directing the production schedule require skilled craftsmen who have had technical training. Manufacturers of modern woodworking machinery and equipment require personnel who have had experience in woodworking, not only for their production work but also for sales and service.

Further preparation for the woodworking trades and occupations may be secured in vocational-technical schools and/or apprenticeship training programs. Visit or write to these schools for information about their course offerings and secure information from forest product industries and trade associations. Visit with carpenters, cabinetmakers and the managers of any wood product industries that might be located in your community.

Many opportunities exist in the lumbering industry. Thousands of workers are needed to grow, harvest, process, distribute, and sell lumber and wood products. There are over 30,000 retail lumber yards in the nation. The people who work in these yards and also in hardware, paint, and furniture stores, should have a good understanding of wood and the basic processes used in its fabrication.

College degrees are generally required for those who work in forestry, forest product research and furniture and cabinet design. Private industry is a large employer of the technologist in these fields, and there are many career opportunities in the wood research and forest utilization programs of federal and state agencies. More than 40 of the nations colleges and universities have programs designed to provide training in this work. They offer such courses as Forestry, Wood Technology, Building Construction, Furniture Construction, and Wood Utilization.

If you have ability in woodwork and enjoy working with young people, the teaching profession can offer you a satisfying and rewarding career. Some 200 educational institutions throughout the country offer teacher education degrees in Industrial Arts and Technical subjects. Ask your instructor about opportunities in teaching as well as those in all the various areas of the woodworking field.

Detailed information about woodworking occupations is available in a bulletin entitled, JOB DESCRIPTIONS FOR THE LUMBER AND LUMBER PRODUCTS INDUSTRIES, which can be obtained from the U.S. Government Printing Office, Washington 25, D.C. Another bulletin, published by the National Forest Products Association, 1619 Massachusetts Ave., N.W., Washington, D.C., is entitled, OPPORTUNITIES UNLIMITED.

The Home Workshop

Woodworking is a popular spare-time activity. Many Americans have found that they can quickly shed the tensions that result from the rapid pace of our modern times as they become engrossed in some construction activity in their home workshop. Wood has always been a highly suitable material for this work because even the amateur with limited skills, can attain a fair degree of success with a relatively simple layout of tools and equipment.

When members of the family work together on hobby activities, closer relationships and common interests are developed. The home workshop can also be a valuable asset when it serves as a maintenance center for the home and its furnishings.

You can apply the experience you have gained in the school shop to the planning and equipping of a home workshop. It's very likely that your father

Fig. 25-60. Home workshop bench and tool panel. The bench top is made of two layers of 3/4 in.
plywood covered with hardboard. A hardwood facing strip is glued to the edge.
(Black and Decker Mfg. Co.)

or another member of your family may want to help you. A corner of the basement or garage may provide the space and you can make a start with a sturdy table or workbench and a tool panel. See Fig. 25-60. Either or both of these items might make a good project for you to build in an advanced woodworking course. If the bench is large, it will be best to construct it in sections and make the assembly at home. Thick maple bench tops, like those in the school shop, are expensive and hard to make. A satisfactory top can be constructed from one or two layers of 3/4 in. plywood, covered with 1/4 in. tempered hardboard. After the tool panel and bench are completed and equipped, you can use them to build racks and cabinets for materials and supplies.

It is well to start with a minimum list of hand tools and then add more as your activities grow. From a study of tool catalogs, prepare an initial list that includes sizes and descriptions, then ask your instructor to check it. You have worked with good quality tools in the school shop and should select a similar quality for your home shop. They will help you produce good work and if they are properly cared for, will last a long time.

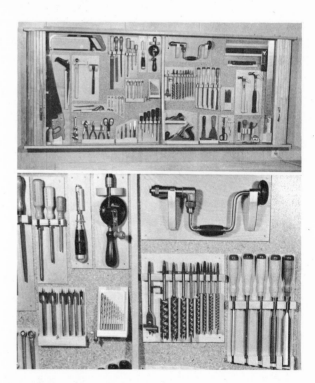

Fig. 25-61. Above. Well organized tool panel with custom-made tool holders and sliding doors, constructed by Bill Wagner. Below. Close-up view of tool holders.

Fig. 25-62. As a home workshop grows, power tools may be added. Note the portable tool panel that is stored in the base cabinet. (Black and Decker Mfg. Co.)

You may want to design and build holders like those shown in Fig. 25-61, for mounting the tools on your panel. Custom-built holders are usually more satisfactory than nails, screws, or metal clips. Attach the holder to a small sub-panel and then mount the unit on the main panel with small screws. This way it will be easy to replace the holder or change its position when making a revision of the tool layout.

As your home workshop develops, it is likely that you will include some power tools. Today, there is available, a wide selection of small, light equipment especially designed for the home shop. From your experience in the school shop you will be able to choose wisely the equipment which will best fit your needs. Here again it would be good practice to prepare a list with detailed specifications and then secure the advice of your instructor. As you add power equipment you must make sure that electrical outlets will not be overloaded and that proper grounding is provided.

WOODY SAYS:

"Small power woodworking machines present the same hazards in operation as the larger machines you have used in the school shop. Follow the safety rules and procedures you have learned. Your instructor will woot be around to help, and you will be on-your-own. Be careful and good luck."

Test Your Knowledge

1. The cellular structure of wood is held together with a natural cement called _____ .
2. New cells of wood and bark are formed in the _____ layer.
3. In some species of wood there is no difference in the appearance of sapwood and heartwood. True or False?
4. If a wood sample that weighed 56 grams was oven dried and then found to weigh 50 grams, the initial M.C. would have been ____ percent.
5. The fiber saturation point for nearly all kinds of wood is ____ percent M.C.
6. A plain sawed board will shrink less across its width than a board of same species that was quarter sawed. True or False?
7. When being dried, hardwoods usually shrink less than softwoods. True or False?
8. The strips of wood placed between the layers of lumber being dried are called _____ .
9. At the start of a kiln drying schedule the temperature is high while the humidity is maintained at a low level. True or False?
10. A seasoning defect that creates internal stresses in the lumber is called _____ .
11. In woodworking, the abbreviation E.M.C. stands for _____ .
12. A wood that is light yellow in color and used for making fine rulers and scales is called

_____ .
13. Cypress is a wood that is noted for its high resistance to decay. True or False?

14. The best known hardwood of the Hawaiian Islands is called _____.

15. More than one-half of the land area of the United States is best suited for growing timber. True or False?

16. Softwood veneer is usually cut by the _____ method.

17. As the veneer is cut, the wood fibers are compressed on one side. This side is called the _____.

18. When veneer is cut by moving the fitch downward against the knife edge the method is called _____.

19. Only hardwood chips are used in manufacturing hardboard. True or False?

20. A major institution in the United States, devoted to research and development of wood and wood products is _____.

Outside Assignments

1. Prepare a map of the United States and show the location of various softwood timber.

2. Secure a sample of wood from your school shop stock room and determine the moisture content by the oven drying method. If you weigh the sample at school and dry it out at home, be sure to wrap it tightly in metal foil or plastic film so it will not gain or lose moisture between the weighing and drying operations.

3. The tangential shrinkage of white oak from 30 to 0 percent M.C. is 9.0 percent; for ponderosa pine it is 6.3 percent. Secure percentages for other common woods in your shop and prepare a chart that shows these figures. Include a diagram that compares the actual measured shrinkage in a 12 in. width.

4. Conduct a study of the E.M.C. of wood in your school or home workshop. Prepare a chart that will show daily, weekly and monthly changes. A convenient way to secure M.C. readings is to prepare a wood sample (for pine about $3/8 \times 3 \times 10$), dry it completely in an oven and then reduce it in size until it weighs exactly 100 grams. As it gains moisture from the air you can make a direct reading of the M.C. For example, when it weighs 109 grams, the M.C. will be 9 percent.

A variety of light-duty power machines are available for home workshops. Observe same safety precautions in their operation as specified for larger equipment used in schools and industry. Even though regulations established by the Occupational Safety and Health Act (OSHA) cannot be enforced in home workshops, the good craftsman will understand underlying principles and apply them to his work.

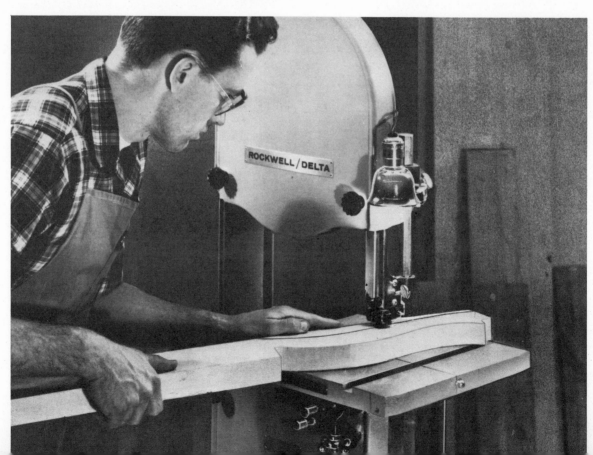

GLOSSARY OF TECHNICAL TERMS

Here are some words that apply to the various areas of woodwork, in addition to the ones used and defined in the instructional material.

ADHESIVE: A substance used to hold materials together by surface attachment. It is a general term that includes cements, glue, paste or mucilage.

ALKYD RESIN: A synthetic material which when combined with a drying oil, such as linseed oil or soybean oil, forms one of the most widely used vehicles for paints and enamels.

ALLIGATORING: A pattern of cracks in a finished surface caused by unequal expansion and contraction of separate coats.

ALUMINUM OXIDE: (AL_2O_3), an abrasive made by fusing Bauxite clay in an electric furnace. Used in the manufacture of grinding wheels, sharpening stones, and abrasive papers.

ANILINE DYES: Soluble colors made from coal tar derivatives and used for stain coats on wood

ANNUAL GROWTH RING: The growth ring of a tree, formed in a single year. Composed of springwood and summerwood.

ARBOR: A short shaft or spindle on which another rotating part is mounted.

ARRIS: An outside corner or edge formed by the meeting of two surfaces.

ATOMIZATION: The breaking up of paint into finely devided tiny droplets. Forming a fog or mist from a liquid. Usually accomplished in spray painting.

BARE-FACED TENON: A tenon shouldered on only one side.

BATTEN: A strip of wood placed across a wooden surface to cover joints or strengthen the assembly.

BLEACHING: Lightening the color of wood by applying a chemical solution.

BLEEDING: The movement of stain or dye from the wood into surface coats. For example, a white enamel applied over a mahogany oil stain will bleed (develop pink spots).

BLEMISH: Any defect, scar, or mark that tends to detract from the appearance of a surface.

BLUE STAIN: A stain caused by a fungus growth in unseasoned lumber. Often found in pine. It does not affect the strength of the wood.

BOILED LINSEED OIL: Linseed oil tnat has been combined with properly blended drying agents to shorten the drying time.

BURL: A swirl or twist in the grain of the wood, usually near a knot.

CALIPER: A tool for measuring the diameter of circular work.

CANT: A log with slabs cut off so that it is no longer round but flat on two or four sides; ready to be cut into boards. Also called a flitch.

CAPILLARY ACTION: The resultant of adhesion, cohesion and surface tension which causes liquids to rise in fine tubes or between closely spaced surfaces.

CATALYST: A substance which aids in bringing about a chemical action.

CAUL: Metal or wood forms or surfaces inserted between press platens to protect or shape a laminated assembly.

CENTRIFUGAL FORCE: The force tending to make rotating bodies move away from the center of rotation.

CHALKING: The decomposition of a paint film into a loose powder on the film surface. Mild chalking, accompanied by satisfactory color retention in tinted paint, is desirable.

CHECKS: Small splits running parallel to the wood grain, usually caused by improper seasoning.

CHUCK: A broad term meaning a device for holding a rotating tool or work piece during an operation.

CLEAT: A strip of wood fastened to another piece, usually to provide a holding or bracing effect.

CLINCH: Nails made to hold more securely by bending down the ends of the protruding points.

COLLAPSE: A seasoning defect resulting in the breakdown of wood cells, caused by too rapid or improper seasoning.

COLLAR BEAM: A horizontal member which serves to tie together and stiffen pairs of common rafters.

COMPATIBILITY: In wood finishing it refers to the ability of two or more materials to mix or "box" together and to form a homogeneous mixture.

COPE: The top half of a foundry flask. Also refers to the top half of the mold or pattern.

CORE: The center of a plywood panel. Plywood cores may be of either sawed lumber or veneer.

COUNTERBORING: To enlarge a hole through part of its length by boring.

COUNTERSINKING: To recess a hole conically for the head of a screw or bolt.

DADO: A groove cut across the grain of a board.

DAYLIGHTS: In woodworking it refers to the openings in a multiple press.

DECAY: Disintegration of wood substance due to the action of wood-destroying fungi.

DIMENSION LUMBER: Lumber from 2 in. to 5 in. thick.

DRAG: The bottom half of a foundry flask or mold.

DRIER: A catalyst added to a paint to speed up the curing or drying time.

DRIP CAP: A molding placed above an exterior door or window, causing water to drip beyond the outside of the frame.

DUTCHMAN: A piece fitted into the work to cover a defect or error.

EARTH PIGMENTS: Pigments mined from the earth such as ochre, umber, sienna and Vandyke brown.

ECCENTRIC: A circular part with the axis of rotation set off center. Used to convert a circular motion to a back-and-forth motion.

EMULSION: The suspension of very small particles of oil in water, or water in oil, by the aid of an emulsifying agent.

EMULSION PAINTS: Various types of oils, resin, varnish and lacquer are mixed or emulsified so they can be thinned with water. They dry quickly and are practically odorless.

EQUILIBRIUM MOISTURE CONTENT: The moisture content at which wood neither gains nor loses moisture when surrounded by air at a given relative humidity and temperature.

EVAPORATION: The change from liquid to a gas. When solvents leave a wet paint film, they do so by evaporation.

EXTENDER: A filler substance added to paint or glue to increase coverage, provide body, or impart other desirable qualities.

FAIR: (Lines and surfaces.) Without sudden change or angular deviation; smooth and flowing as in the "fair" surfaces of boats and airplanes.

FENCE: An adjustable metal bar or strip mounted on the table of a machine or tool to guide the work.

FIGURE: The pattern produced in a wood surface by the annual growth rings, wood rays, and knots.

FLASHING: Sheet metal or other materials used around openings in roof or wall surfaces to prevent the penetration of water.

FLATTING AGENT: An ingredient used in lacquers and varnishes to reduce the gloss or give a rubbed effect.

FLITCH: A portion of a log sawed on two or more sides and intended for remanufacture into lumber or sliced veneer. The term is also applied to the resulting sheets of veneer laid together in sequence of cutting.

FLOATING CONSTRUCTION: A method which permits wide panels in solid wood furniture to expand or contract without damage to the structure. For example, screws used in the assembly could be set in slotted holes.

FLOCK: Shredded cloth fibers. They are applied to a surface with a special adhesive to form a soft, felt-like finish.

FLOW: The property of a finishing material to spread or level to an even film.

FLUTING: Parallel grooves or furrows cut out of the surface of wood, usually to secure a decorative effect.

FURRING: Narrow strips of wood attached to a base surface or frame and upon which is then fastened other materials.

GLAZING: (1) Fitting window panes. (2) A filling of the pores of an abrasive stone with metal cuttings. (3) A finishing process where transparent or translucent coatings are applied over a painted surface to produce blended effects.

GLOSS: A type of finish that dries to a shiny or highly lustrous surface.

GLUE BLOCKS: Small blocks of wood, usually triangular in shape, that are glued along the inside corner of a joint to add strength.

GRAIN: The direction, size, arrangement, appearance, or quality of the fibers in wood.

GUSSET: A thin piece of metal or wood that forms a plate and is fastened to the surfaces of two or more structural members to secure or reinforce the joint.

HARDBOARD: A manufactured material made by forming wood fibers into sheets, using heat and pressure. The regrouped fibers are held together with the lignin in the wood.

HOLIDAYS: Areas of surface missed by a painter.

HOLLOW-CORE CONSTRUCTION: Sheet material such as plywood or hardboard (called skins) are bonded to a framed-core assembly consisting of strips or various other forms of spaced support. Used in flush door construction.

HOUSED JOINT: A joint formed by a recess that receives the entire end of the mating part. Similar to a mortise and tenon except that the tenon has no shoulders.

INLAY: A decoration where the design is set into the wood surface.

INSPECTION: The measuring and checking of work pieces and assemblies at various stages of fabrication to determine if they have been made according to specifications.

INTERCHANGEABILITY: This refers to mass produced parts that have been made to specific dimensions and tolerances so that any one of them would fit and work in a final assembly.

JIG: A device which holds the work and/or guides the tool while forming or assembling wood parts.

KEELSON: The inner part of a boat keel that is a part of the frame structure.

KERF: The slit or space made by the blade of any hand or power saw.

KILN: A heated chamber for drying lumber, veneer, and other wood products.

KNOT: Cross section of a branch or limb imbedded in the wood during the growth of the tree.

LAC: A natural resin secreted by insects that live on the sap of certain trees in oriental countries. The base for shellac.

LACQUER: A finishing material made of nitrocellulose which dries by evaporation of the solvents.

LAMINATE: To form a product by bonding together two or more layers of material. Each layer is called a lamination or ply.

LEDGER: A bearing strip attached to vertical framing (studs) on which horizontal members (joists) can be supported.

LEVELING: In finishing, refers to the formation of a smooth film on either a horizontal or vertical surface which is free of brush marks.

LINEAR: Pertaining to a line or consisting of lines. Linear measure refers to measurement along the length.

LINSEED OIL: A vegetable oil pressed from the seeds of the flax plant. Used extensively in the manufacture of oil base paints and finishes.

LINTEL: The horizontal supporting member spanning such openings as doors, windows and fireplaces. May be made of stone, wood, or metal.

MANDREL: A shaft or spindle on which an object may be mounted for rotation.

MARQUETRY: An ornamental surface built up of various wood veneers to form a pattern or picture. Usually cut on the jig saw.

MESH: Openings formed by crossing or weaving threads, strings or wire.

MILLWORK: Refers to materials made in woodworking plants. Includes doors, windows, stairways, moldings, and wood trim.

MINERAL SPIRITS: A petroleum solvent used as a substitute for turpentine.

MITER OR MITRE: The joining of two pieces at an evenly divided angle. A cut made at an angle, usually 45 deg.

MOLDING: (also moulding) Strips of wood, usually shaped for decorative effect, that are applied to surfaces, corners and edges of structures to provide a finished appearance.

MOSAIC: A surface decoration formed by small pieces of colored glass, stone, or tile, set in a ground of cement or mastic.

MULLION: The vertical separation between window units.

MUNTIN: The slender dividers between two or more panes of glass mounted in a single sash.

NAPHTHA: A volatile, inflammable liquid used as a solvent or thinner for paint and varnish.

NATURAL RESINS: Those resins used in finishes that are exuded from trees or secured from fossilized vegetable matter in the earth.

NOVACULITE (no-vak'yoo-lit): A hard, extremely fine grained siliceous rock, sedimentary in origin; it is used for whetstones.

ON CENTER (OC): The spacing of structural members from the center of one to the center of the next.

ORANGE PEEL: In finishing, a pebbled surface condition caused by rapid drying or improper application.

OXIDIZE: To unite with oxygen - a chemical reaction. Part of the drying process for some finishing materials.

PALLET: A portable platform on which materials are stacked for storage or transportation.

PARTICLE BOARD: A manufactured board composed of wood chips held together with an adhesive.

PARTITION: A wall that subdivides space within a structure.

PERIPHERAL SPEED: The speed of a point on the circumference of a revolving wheel or shaft. Usually given in feet per minute.

PHOTOSYNTHESIS: A process that takes place in the leaves of plants when they are exposed to light. Water and carbon dioxide are converted into carbohydrates.

PIGMENT: Finely ground powders that are insoluble and provide color and body to a finishing material.

PILASTER: A built-in projection in a straight masonry wall for reinforcement purposes.

PITCH POCKET: An opening extending parallel to the annual growth rings containing, or that has contained, liquid or solid resinous material.

PLUMB: Exactly vertical. Perpendicular to a level line.

PLAIN-SAWED: Lumber that is cut on a tangent to the annular growth rings.

PNEUMATIC: Pretaining to, or operated by air pressure.

POLYMERIZATION: A chemical action in which the molecules of a substance interlock with each other in a special way. Part of the drying process of certain finishing materials.

PUMICE: Porous volcanic lava that is crushed and graded and used for polishing finished surfaces.

QUARTER ROUND: A moulding with a cross section of one-fourth of a cylinder.

QUARTER-SAWED: Lumber that is cut at approximately a 90 deg. angle to the annular growth rings.

QUILL: The movable sleeve that carries the bearings and spindle of the drill press.

RABBET: A cut made in the edge of a board to form a joint with another piece.

RADIAL: Extending outward from a center or axis.

RAPPING PLATE: In patternmaking, a metal plate installed in the pattern to aid in rapping and drawing it from the mold.

RATCHET: A gear with triangular-shaped teeth that are engaged by a pawl, which imparts intermittent motion or locks it against backward movement.

REDUCE: To lower the viscosity of a paint by the addition of solvent or thinner.

RELATIVE HUMIDITY: The ratio of water vapor actually present in the air as related to the greatest amount of vapor the air can carry at a given temperature.

RESAWING: Ripping a board so the thickness is reduced or so that it is made into two thinner pieces.

RESPIRATOR: A shield for the nose and mouth that filters contaminated air.

RETARDER: A solvent added to a paint to reduce the evaporation rate.

ROTARY CUT: A method of cutting veneer where the entire log is centered in a huge lathe and turned against a broad knife.

ROTTENSTONE: A decomposed siliceous limestone used for polishing finished surfaces.

RPM (rpm): An abbreviation for revolutions per minute.

RUNS (finishing): Also called "sags" and "curtains." Irregularities in a surface finish usually caused by too heavy an application.

SABER SAWING: Cutting with a special blade mounted in only the lower chuck of the jig saw. Also applied to cutting with a portable saber saw.

SANDWICH CONSTRUCTION: Panels fabricated with high strength facing materials which are bonded to a low density core material or structure.

SCAFFOLD: A temporary framework for supporting workmen and materials during the erecting or repairing of a building.

SHAKE: A defect in wood running parallel to the grain. Caused by the separation of the spring and summer growth rings.

SHORING: An assembly of post and timbers used for bracing and support. Usually applied temporarily to units under construction.

SILICON CARBIDE (Si C): Produced by fusing silica (sand) and coke at high temperatures. Used as an abrasive and sold under such tradenames as Carborundum and Crystolon.

SILEX: Powdered quartz used as a base for paste filler.

SLEEPER: Wood strips placed in or on a concrete base to which sub-flooring or finished flooring is attached.

SLICED: A method of cutting veneer where a section of a log is thrust down along a knife edge that sheers off the veneer in sheets.

SOFFIT: The underside of a cornice, beam, arch or lowered section of a ceiling.

SOLIDS: Material remaining in a paint after the solvents have evaporated. Usually specified as a percentage of the initial weight.

SPLAT: A broad, flat upright section in the middle of a chair back.

SPLAYED: Applies to the leg of a chair or table that makes an angle outward in two directions from the top or seat.

SPLINE: A thin strip of wood inserted in matching grooves cut on the joining faces of a joint. Also, a flexible rod or rule used to draw curved lines.

STEAMED: This term when applied to walnut lumber, refers to a process where the green lumber is steamed in vats for the purpose of darkening the sapwood.

STICKERS: Strips of wood used to separate the layers in a pile of lumber so air can circulate around each board.

STORY POLE: A rod used for measuring and laying out door and window openings, siding or shingle courses, and stairways.

STRAIGHTEDGE: A straight strip of wood or metal used to lay out and check the accuracy of work.

STRETCHER: A horizontal structural member used to reinforce the legs of chairs, tables and desks.

TAPER: A gradual and uniform decrease in the size of a hole, cylinder, or rectangular part.

TEMPLATE: A pattern, guide, or model that is used to lay out work or check its accuracy.

THERMOPLASTIC: Resins that soften when subjected to high temperatures.

THERMOSETTING: Resins that can be cured with heat and after setting will not soften when heat is applied.

THINNERS: Volatile liquids that are used to regulate the consistency (thickness) of finishing materials.

TIMBERS: Construction lumber with a large cross section; 5 in. or more in both thickness and width.

TONGUE: A projecting bead cut on the edge of a board that fits into a groove on another piece.

TRACKING: Refers to the alignment of a blade as it runs on the band saw wheel.

TRIM: A general term that applies to the various wood strips and moldings used to finish door and window openings and corners where walls joint the ceiling and floor.

TUNG OIL: A drying oil obtained from the nut of the tung tree; also called Chinawood oil. Used in water-resistant varnishes and high gloss paints.

TURPENTINE: A volatile solvent used in wood finishes, which is made by distilling the gum obtained from the pine tree.

VARNISH: Composed of a gum or resin in a suitable carrying agent or vehicle, commonly linseed or tung oil. Solvent oils -- usually turpentine -- are added to make the varnish thin and fluid.

VARNISH STAIN: General-purpose interior varnish tinted with dye colors or pigments. Stains and varnishes in one coat. Seldom used on quality furniture except as quick refinish.

VEHICLE: The liquid part of a paint.

VENEER: A thin sheet of wood, either sliced, cut or sawed. Veneer may be referred to as a ply when assembled in a panel.

VESSELS: Wood cells of large diameter, that are set one above another to form continuous tubes. The openings of the vessels on the surface of the wood are referred to as pores.

WAINSCOT: Wood panels or other material applied to the lower part of an interior wall.

WANE: The presence of bark, or the lack of wood from any cause on the edge or corner of a piece of lumber.

WARP: Any variation from a true or plane surface. In lumber it may include bow, cup, crook, or wind (twist).

WATER STAIN: Colored dyes that are soluble in water.

WATER WHITE: Transparent like water. Used to describe a very clear lacquer or varnish.

WEB: A thin section of a pattern connecting two heavier sections to provide added strength in the metal casting.

Acknowledgments

Special credit is due the following companies and organizations for the valuable information, photographs, and illustrations they so willingly provided:

Adjustable Clamp Co., Chicago, Illinois.
American Forest Products Industries, Washington, D. C.
American Hardboard Assoc., Chicago, Illinois.
American Plywood Assoc., Tacoma, Washington.
Amerock Corp., Rockford, Illinois.
Amyx Manufacturing Co., West Plains, Mo.
Andersen Corp., Bayport, Minnesota.
Architectural Woodwork Institute, Nashville, Tenn.
Arvid Iraids, Cincinnati, Ohio.
Ashdee Corp., Evansville, Ind.
Auto-Nailer Co., Atlanta, Georgia.
Badger Boat Corp., Black Creek, Wisconsin.
Barnes Builders Supply, Cedar Falls, Iowa.
Baumritter Corp., New York, N.Y.
Binks Manufacturing Co., Chicago, Ill.
Black Bros. Co., Mendota, Ill.
Black and Decker Mfg. Co., Towson, Maryland.
Boice-Crane Co., Schiller Park, Ill.
Bowlathe Co., Westwood, Mass.
Brodhead-Garrett Co., Cleveland, Ohio.
Buss Machine Works, Holland, Mich.
Charles Bruning Co. Inc., Mount Prospect, Ill.
Carborundum Co., Niagara Falls, N.Y.
Coe Manufacturing Co., Painesville, Ohio.
Consoweld Corp., Wisconsin Rapids, Wisc.
Dake Corp., Grand Haven, Mich.
Dependable Machine Co. Inc., Greensboro, N. C.
DeVilbiss Co., Toledo, Ohio.
Diehl Machines, Inc., Wabash, Ind.
Dowl-it Co., Hastings, Mich.
Drexel Furniture Co., Drexel, North Carolina.
Dry Clime Lamp Corp., Greensburg, Ind.
E. I. DuPont DeNemours Co., Wilmington, Delaware.
T. C. Esser Co., Waterloo, Iowa.
Ekstrom, Carlson and Co., Rockford, Illinois.
Fastener Corp., Franklin Park, Illinois.
Fine Hardwoods-American Walnut Assoc., Chicago, Ill.
Fisher Controls Co., Marshalltown, Iowa.
Foley Manufacturing Co., Minneapolis, Minn.
Forest City Tool Co., Hickory, N. C.
Forest Products Laboratory, Madison, Wisconsin.
Formica Corp., Cincinnati, Ohio.
Gasway Corp., Chicago, Ill.
Georgia-Pacific Corp., Portland, Oregon.
Goodspeed Machine Co., Winchendon, Mass.
Greenlee Bros. and Co., Rockford, Ill.
Handy Manufacturing Co., Chicago, Ill.
Herrmann & Safranek, Atascadero, Calif.
Heywood-Wakefield Co., Gardner, Mass.
Huther Bros. Saw Mfg. Co., Rochester, N. Y.
Hyde Tools, Southbridge, Mass.
Independent Nail and Packing Co., Bridgewater, Mass.
Iowa State University, Dept. of Forestry, Ames, Iowa.
I-XL Furniture Co., Goshen, Ind.
Jam Handy Organization, Detroit, Michigan.
Kitchen Kompact, Inc., Jeffersonville, Ind.
George Koch Sons, Inc., Evansville, Ind.
Kohler-Joa Corp., Sheboygan Falls, Wisc.
J. M. Lancaster, Inc., Greensboro, N. C.
Lehigh Furniture Corp., New York, N. Y.
Lodge and Shipley Co., Cincinnati, Ohio.
Lufkin Rule Co., Saginaw, Mich.
Manning Pattern Co., Waterloo, Iowa.

Masonite Corp., Chicago, Ill.
Mattison Machine Works, Rockford, Illinois.
Mereen-Johnson Machine Co., Minneapolis, Minn.
Merit Products, Inc., Los Angeles, Calif.
Mersman Brothers Corp., Celina, Ohio.
Herman Miller, Inc., Zeeland, Mich.
Millers Falls Co., Greenfield, Mass.
Mueller's Furniture, Waterloo, Iowa.
Nash-Bell-Calloner Woodworking Machinery, Oshkosh, Wisc.
National Aeronautics and Space Admin., Houston, Texas.
National Forest Products Assoc., Wasnington, D. C.
National Homes Corp., Lafayette, Ind.
National Particleboard Assoc., Washington, D. C.
Natural Rubber Bureau, Washington, D. C.
Newman Machine Co., Inc., Greensboro, N. C.
Nichols Wire and Aluminum Co., Davenport, Iowa.
Nicholson File Co., Providence, R. I.
No-Sag Spring Co., Detroit, Mich.
Northeast Ohio Machine Builders Inc., Columbiana, Ohio.
Northfield Foundry and Machine Co., Northfield, Minn.
Northway Products Co., Rensselaer, Ind.
Northwestern Steel & Wire Co., Sterling, Ill.
Norton Co., Worcester, Mass.
Oliver Machinery Co., Grand Rapids, Mich.
Onsrud Machine Works, Inc., Niles, Ill.
Paxton Lumber Co., Des Moines, Iowa.
Perkins Glue, Lansdale, Penn.
Plastiglide Manufacturing Corp., Santa Monica, Calif.
C. O. Porter Machinery Co., Grand Rapids, Mich.
H. K. Porter Co., Inc., Pittsburgh, Pa.
Powermatic, Inc., McMinnville, Tenn.
Red Wing Wood Products, Inc., Red Wing, Minnesota.
Rilco Laminated Products, Inc., St. Paul, Minn.
Rock Island Millwork Co., Waterloo, Iowa.
Rockwell Manufacturing Co., Pittsburgh, Penn.
Ronthor Reiss Corp., New York, N. Y.
Selby Furniture Hardware Co., New York, N. Y.
Sherwin-Williams Co., Cleveland, Ohio.
Simonds Saw and Steel Co., Fitchburg, Mass.
Skil Corp., Chicago, Ill.
A. G. Spalding & Bros., Chicopee, Mass.
Sprayon Products Inc., Cleveland, Ohio.
Stanley Tools, New Britain, Conn.
Stryco Manufacturing Co., San Francisco, Calif.
George Tanier Inc., New York, N. Y.
Tannewitz Inc., Grand Rapids, Mich.
James L. Taylor Mfg. Co., Poughkeepsie, N.Y.
Thomasville Furniture Industries Inc., Thomasville, N. C.
Union Tool Corp., Warsaw, Ind.
Unit Structures, Peshtigo, Wisc.
United States Forest Service, Washington, D. C.
United States Plywood Corp., New York, N. Y.
United States Rubber Co., Mishawaka, Ind.
United States Steel, Pittsburgh, Penn.
Upholstery Supply Co., Milwaukee, Wisc.
Wagner Manufacturing Co., Cedar Falls, Iowa.
Wardwell Manufacturing Co., Cleveland, Ohio.
Washington Steel Products, Canton, Ohio.
Western Wood Products Assoc., Portland, Oregon.
Weyerhaeuser Co., Tacoma, Wash.
Baxter D. Whitney and Sons, Inc., Greensboro, N. C.
Wilson Sporting Goods Co., River Grove, Ill.
Wisconsin Knife Works, Beloit, Wisc.
Woodworking Machinery Manufacturer's Assoc., Phila., Penn.
Workrite Products Co., Burbank, Calif.
Yates-American Machine Co., Roscoe, Ill.

REFERENCES

Ansley, Arthur, MANUFACTURING METHODS AND PROCESSES, Chilton Co., Philadelphia, Pennsylvania.

Apple, James, PLANT LAYOUT AND MATERIAL HANDLING, The Ronald Press Co., New York, New York.

Bast, Herbert, ESSENTIALS OF MODERN UPHOLSTERY, Benziger Bruce & Glenco, Beverly Hills, California.

Capron, J. H., WOOD LAMINATING, McKnight Publishing Co., Bloomington, Illinois.

Cramlet, Ross C., WOOD TURNING VISUALIZED, Benziger Bruce & Glenco, Beverly Hills, California.

Cramlet, Ross C., WOODWORK VISUALIZED, Benziger Bruce & Glenco, Beverly Hills, California.

Crowther, Sam, THE SMALL BOAT GUIDE, Crown Publishers, Inc., New York, New York.

Cunningham, Beryl M. and Holthrop, Wm. F., WOODSHOP TOOL MAINTENANCE, Chas. A. Bennett Co., Peoria, Illinois.

Dal Fabbro, Mario, HOW TO BUILD MODERN FURNITURE, F. W. Dodge Corporation, New York, New York.

Douglass, J. H., WOODWORKING WITH MACHINES, McKnight Publishing Co., Bloomington, Illinois.

Durbahn, W. E., and Sundberg, E. W., FUNDAMENTALS OF CARPENTRY II, American Technical Society, Chicago, Illinois.

Feirer, John L. and Hutchings, Gilbert R. ADVANCED WOODWORK AND FURNITURE MAKING Chas. A. Bennett Co., Inc., Peoria, Illinois.

Feirer, John L., CABINETMAKING AND MILLWORK, Chas. A. Bennett Co., Inc., Peoria, Illinois.

Gerrish, Howard H., TECHNICAL DICTIONARY, Goodheart-Willcox Co., Inc., South Holland, Illinois.

Groneman, Chris H., GENERAL WOODWORKING, McGraw-Hill Book Co., New York, New York.

Groneman, Chris H. and Glazener, Everett R., TECHNICAL WOODWORKING, McGraw-Hill Book Co., New York, New York.

Hackett, Donald F., and Spielman, Patrick E., MODERN WOOD TECHNOLOGY, Benziger Bruce & Glenco, Beverly Hills, California.

Hammond, James J. and others, WOODWORKING TECHNOLOGY, McKnight Publishing Co., Bloomington, Illinois.

Haws, Robt. W., and Schaefer, Carl J., MANUFACTURING IN THE SCHOOL SHOP, American Technical Society, Chicago, Illinois.

Hjorth, H., and Holthrop, Wm. F., MODERN MACHINE WOODWORKING, Benziger Bruce & Glenco, Beverly Hills, California.

Hunt, DeWitt, SHOP TOOLS, CARE AND REPAIR, D. Van Nostrand Co., Princeton, New Jersey.

Kettering, Charles F., and Orth, Allen, AMERICAN BATTLE FOR ABUNDANCE -- A STORY OF MASS PRODUCTION, General Motors Company, Detroit, Michigan.

Klenke, William W., THE ART OF WOOD TURNING, Chas. A. Bennett Co., Peoria, Illinois.

Lindbeck, John R., DESIGN TEXTBOOK, McKnight Publishing Co., Bloomington, Illinois.

McDonnell, L. P., PORTABLE POWER TOOLS, Delmar Publishers, Albany, New York.

McGinnis, H., and Ruley, M. J., BASIC WOODWORK PROJECTS, McKnight Publishing Co., Bloomington, Illinois.

Merritt, Frederick, BUILDING CONSTRUCTION HANDBOOK, McGraw-Hill Book Co., New York, New York.

Miner, Harvey and Miller, John, EXPLORING PATTERNMAKING AND FOUNDRY, D. Van Nostrand, Princeton, New Jersey.

Moore, Franklin, PRODUCTION CONTROL, McGraw-Hill Book Co., New York, New York.

Olson, Delmar W., WOODS AND WOODWORKING, Prentice-Hall, Inc., Englewood Cliffs, New Jersey.

Panshin, A. J., and DeZeeuw, C., TEXTBOOK OF WOOD TECHNOLOGY, McGraw-Hill Book Co., New York, New York.

Romero, A. C., CONTEMPORARY DESIGNS FOR WOOD, Benziger Bruce & Glenco, Beverly Hills, California.

Roscoe, Edwin, ORGANIZATION FOR PRODUCTION, Richard D. Irwin, Inc., Homewood, Illinois.

Rusinoff, S. E., FOUNDRY PRACTICES, American Technical Society, Chicago, Illinois.

Scharff, Robert, BOATING HANDBOOK, McGraw-Hill Book Co., New York, New York.

Shea, J. G., COLONIAL FURNITURE MAKING FOR EVERYBODY, D. Van Nostrand Co., Princeton, New Jersey.

Smith, Ronald C., PRINCIPLES AND PRACTICES OF LIGHT CONSTRUCTION, Prentice-Hall, Englewood Cliffs, New Jersey.

Soderberg, George A., FINISHING TECHNOLOGY, McKnight Publishing Co., Bloomington, Illinois.

Tierney, Wm. F., MODERN UPHOLSTERY METHODS, McKnight Publishing Co., Bloomington, Illinois.

U.S. Department of Agriculture, Forest Products Laboratory, WOOD HANDBOOK NO. 72, U.S. Government Printing Office, Washington, D.C.

Wagner, Willis H., MODERN CARPENTRY, Goodheart-Willcox Co., Inc., South Holland, Illinois.

Wagner, Willis H., WOODWORKING, Goodheart-Willcox Co., Inc., South Holland, Illinois.

Zimmerman, Fred W., EXPLORING WOODWORKING, Goodheart-Willcox Co., Inc., South Holland, Illinois.

Zook, Wayne H., CONSTRUCTING AND MANUFACTURING WOOD PRODUCTS, McKnight Publishing Co., Bloomington, Illinois.

PERIODICALS

FURNITURE DESIGN AND MANUFACTURING, Graphic Arts Publishing Co., 7373 N. Lincoln Ave., Chicago, Illinois.

FURNITURE METHODS AND MATERIALS, 3095 Norbrook Drive, P. O. Box 16528, Memphis, Tennessee.

FURNITURE PRODUCTION, Production Publishing Co., 804 Church St., Nashville, Tennessee.

INDUSTRIAL WOODWORKING, Cleworth Publishing Co., One River Road, Cos Cob, Connecticut.

PROFESSIONAL BUILDER, 5 South Wabash Ave., Chicago, Illinois.

WOOD AND WOOD PRODUCTS, Vance Publishing Corp., 59 E. Monroe St., Chicago, Illinois

WOODWORKING & FURNITURE DIGEST, Hitchcock Publishing Co., Hitchock Bldg., Wheaton, Illinois.

USEFUL TABLES

Wood Screw Table

Length	Gauge Steel Screw	Brass Screw	Gauge No.	Decimal	Approx. Fract.	Drill Size A	B	C
1/4	0 to 4	0 to 4	0	.060	1/16	1/16		
3/8	0 to 8	0 to 6	1	.073	5/64	3/32		
1/2	1 to 10	1 to 8	2	.086	5/64	3/32	1/16	3/16
5/8	2 to 12	2 to 10	3	.099	3/32	1/8	1/16	1/4
3/4	2 to 14	2 to 12	4	.112	7/64	1/8	1/16	1/4
7/8	3 to 14	4 to 12	5	.125	1/8	1/8	3/32	1/4
1	3 to 16	4 to 14	6	.138	9/64	5/32	3/32	5/16
1 1/4	4 to 18	6 to 14	7	.151	5/32	5/32	1/8	5/16
1 1/2	4 to 20	6 to 14	8	.164	5/32	3/16	1/8	3/8
1 3/4	6 to 20	8 to 14	9	.177	11/64	3/16	1/8	3/8
2	6 to 20	8 to 18	10	.190	3/16	3/16	1/8	3/8
2 1/4	6 to 20	10 to 18	11	.203	13/64	7/32	5/32	7/16
2 1/2	8 to 20	10 to 18	12	.216	7/32	7/32	5/32	7/16
2 3/4	8 to 20	8 to 20	14	.242	15/64	1/4	3/16	1/2
3	8 to 24	12 to 18	16	.268	17/64	9/32	7/32	9/16
3 1/2	10 to 24	12 to 18	18	.294	19/64	5/16	1/4	5/8
4	12 to 24	12 to 24	20	.320	21/64	11/32	9/32	11/16
4 1/2	14 to 24	14 to 24	24	.372	3/8	3/8	5/16	3/4
5	14 to 24	14 to 24						

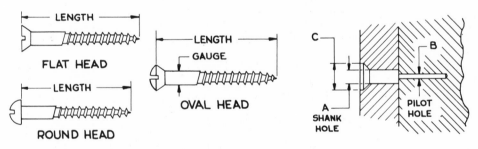

LENGTH

FLAT HEAD

LENGTH

ROUND HEAD

LENGTH
GAUGE

OVAL HEAD

C   B

A
SHANK
HOLE

PILOT
HOLE

Figuring Pulley Sizes and RPM

To Find:

RPM of Driven Pulley	Multiply diameter of driving pulley by its rpm and divide by diameter of driven pulley.
Diameter of Driven Pulley	Multiply diameter of driving pulley by its rpm and divide by rpm of driven pulley.
RPM of Driving Pulley	Multiply diameter of driven pulley by its rpm and divide by diameter of driving pulley.
Diameter of Driving Pulley	Multiply diameter of driven pulley by its rpm and divide by rpm of driving pulley.

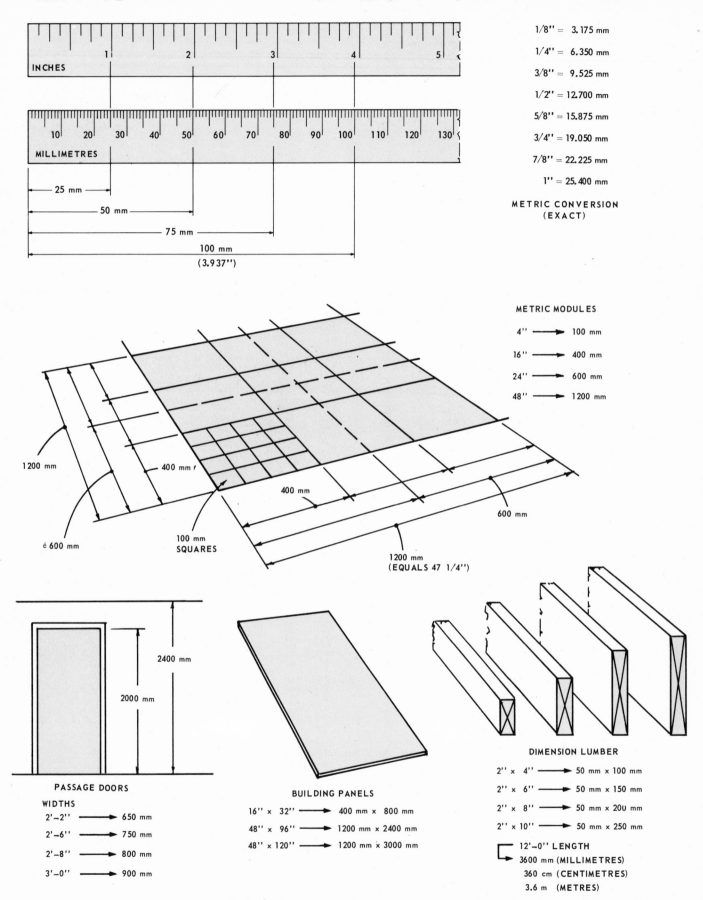

METRIC CONVERSION (EXACT)

1/8" = 3.175 mm
1/4" = 6.350 mm
3/8" = 9.525 mm
1/2" = 12.700 mm
5/8" = 15.875 mm
3/4" = 19.050 mm
7/8" = 22.225 mm
1" = 25.400 mm

METRIC MODULES

4" → 100 mm
16" → 400 mm
24" → 600 mm
48" → 1200 mm

PASSAGE DOORS

WIDTHS
2'–2" → 650 mm
2'–6" → 750 mm
2'–8" → 800 mm
3'–0" → 900 mm

BUILDING PANELS

16" x 32" → 400 mm x 800 mm
48" x 96" → 1200 mm x 2400 mm
48" x 120" → 1200 mm x 3000 mm

DIMENSION LUMBER

2" x 4" → 50 mm x 100 mm
2" x 6" → 50 mm x 150 mm
2" x 8" → 50 mm x 200 mm
2" x 10" → 50 mm x 250 mm

12'–0" LENGTH
3600 mm (MILLIMETRES)
360 cm (CENTIMETRES)
3.6 m (METRES)

Metric modules for carpentry. Basic unit of four inches is converted to 100 millimetres (3.937 inches) as proposed by the National Forest Products Association. Note that arrows are used to indicate conversions made on this basis.

26-10

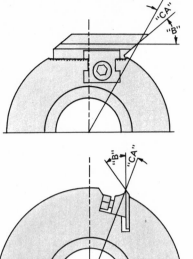

CUTTING ANGLES

These sketches illustrate the cutting angle and knife and bit bevel relation on a typical milled-to-pattern head and a round head.

FINISH AND RATES OF FEED

Knife Finish Ranges Generally Recommended according to wood species:

Kind of Wood	Knife Marks per Inch
Ash	11 to 14
Basswood	8 to 12
Beech	12 to 14
Birch (plain)	12 to 14
Birch (curly)	13 to 16
Cedar	8 to 12
Cherry	12 to 14
Cottonwood	8 to 12
Cypress	8 to 12
Elm (hard)	10 to 13
Elm (soft)	8 to 12
Fir	8 to 12
Gum	9 to 13
Hemlock	8 to 12
Hickory	12 to 15
Mahogany (plain)	12 to 14
Mahogany (figured)	14 to 16
Maple	12 to 14
Oak	12 to 14
Pine (yellow)	9 to 13
Pine (white)	9 to 13
Poplar	9 to 13
Redwood	8 to 12
Spruce	8 to 12
Sycamore	11 to 14
Walnut	12 to 14

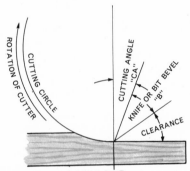

CUTTING ANGLES

	KILN DRIED 7% MOISTURE OR LESS		WET OR GREEN MORE THAN 7%	
	CA	B	CA	B
Ash	15°	35°	10°	35°
Basswood	10	30	20	30
Beech	10	35	15	35
Birch	10	35	15	35
Cedar	5	30	10	30
Cherry	10	35	15	35
Chestnut	5	35	10	35
Cottonwood	5	30	10	30
Cypress	5	30	10	30
Elm, Hard	0	40	5	40
Fir	10	35	15	35
Gum	20	35	25	35
Hemlock	15	35	20	35
Hickory	5	40	10	40
Mahogany	10	35	15	35
Maple	5	40	10	40
Oak	10	40	15	40
Oak Qtd.	10	40	15	40
Pine, Yellow	20	35	25	35
Pine, White	25	30	30	30
Pine, Ponderosa	25	30	30	30
Poplar	30	30	35	30
Redwood	5	30	15	30
Spruce	20	35	25	35
Sycamore	5	35	10	35
Walnut	5	35	10	35
Elm, Soft	5	40	10	40

RATES OF FEED

$$\frac{R.P.M. \times No.\ KNIVES}{FT.\ PER\ MIN. \times 12} = KNIFE\ MARKS\ PER\ INCH$$

R.P.M.	Knife Marks Per Inch	NUMBER OF KNIVES CUTTING				
		1	2	4	6	8
3600	10	30 Ft.	60 Ft.	120 Ft.	180 Ft.	240 Ft.
	12	25	50	100	150	200
	14	21	43	82	123	164
	16	18	37	73	112	146
	18	16.5	33.5	66.5	100	133.3
	20	15	30	60	90	120
4800	10	40	80	160	240	320
	12	33	66	133	200	266
	14	28	57	112	171	224
	16	25	50	100	150	200
	18	22.2	44	88	133	176
	20	20	40	80	120	160
6000	10	50	100	200	300	400
	12	41	83	166	250	332
	14	35	71	143	213	286
	16	31	62	125	185	250
	18	27	55	111	160	222
	20	25	50	100	150	200
7200	10	60	120	240	360	480
	12	50	100	200	300	400
	14	42	86	164	246	328
	16	36	74	146	224	292
	18	33	67	134	200	268
	20	30	60	120	180	240

(Wisconsin Knife Works Inc.)

INDEX